# Christ
# is
# Best

## A Devotional Study of Hebrews

*Tom Teply*

*Heb. 13:20-21*

### Thomas R. Teply, Ph.D.

Gold Beach, Oregon:  TigerClaw Enterprises
2005

CHRIST IS BEST is published by TigerClaw Enterprises, 94040 Doyle Point Road, Gold Beach, OR 97444-9533.

FIRST EDITION

*Library of Congress Cataloging-in-Publication Data*
Teply, Thomas Rogers
CHRIST IS BEST: A Devotional Study of Hebrews. 1st ed.
Includes biographical references and index of scripture passages.

1. Teply, Thomas R. 2. Bible Commentary. 3. Jesus Christ as prophesied in Hebrew Scriptures.
I. Title

ISBN: 0-9767830-0-2

Printed in the United States by
Morris Publishing • 3212 East Highway 30
Kearney, NE 68847
1-800-650-7888

# CONTENTS

# INTRODUCTION

## BENEFITS FROM STUDYING HEBREWS

"This is what I told you while I was still with you: Everything must be fulfilled that is written about me in the Law of Moses, the Prophets and the Psalms" (Lu. 24:44). This thought will be helpful as we begin our study of the book of Hebrews together. The main theme of Hebrews is the fact that Jesus Christ and his ministry are "better than" anything we find in the Old Testament by way of ministry from God to people. We will repeat that theme often as we go through our study.

Although this is a study of the New Testament book of Hebrews, our study will range afar through many books of the Bible, especially those of the Old Testament, since the object of Hebrews is to show the relationship between the old and the new ministries. There are more than one hundred quotations and allusions to Old Testament passages to be found in Hebrews;[1] we will discover a multitude of further links between Old Testament teachings and what we find in this New Testament book. Further, we will discover many connections between what the author of Hebrews wrote and the things we discover in many other New Testament books, especially in the gospels and the book of Acts, as well as in the thirteen books which Paul wrote, and other books. Therefore, one of the great benefits of this study will be to give us an overview of the teachings of the whole of the word of God; and we shall take care to relate each part to the whole. Because we will be studying many parts of the whole Bible, our study will be much larger than if we limited ourselves to a simple verse-by-verse exposition of Hebrews.

The study of the book of Hebrews should be of great help to a new Christian, or to someone who has little acquaintance with the Bible. The reason is because such a person need not read laboriously through the whole of the Bible in order to get a grasp of it all. After all, there is much in the Bible to cause a new reader to become discouraged: there is much duplication (as in the books of Kings and Chronicles); seemingly endless genealogies that occur in Genesis 5 and 10; ideas and doctrines that are incomprehensible to a person who has not yet found elaborations and explanations in other parts of scripture. This is said not to discourage anyone from reading through the whole Bible. Those who merely hunt and pick at the Bible are bound to miss vast amounts of teaching that God has for us all. This is true especially when we look for statements which we are sure will please us.

There ought to be great benefit to people who have been Christians for

---

[1] It is amazing that most of the quotations are virtually verbatim, especially since the author of Hebrews wrote in the Greek language, and the Old Testament was written in Hebrew. Some of the quotations, however, follow the Greek (Septuagint) version of the Old Testament which was in common use in apostolic times. We will note these quotations and allusions as we progress. Most English translations of the Old Testament have been made directly from the Hebrew and not from the Septuagint.

many years, and have studied God's word during that time. At the least, if you are such a person, you will be able to review, in short compass, what you have learned, and impress those teachings more firmly in your mind and spirit. You may also gain some new insights into the relationship between what is taught in the Old Testament and in the New.

## WHO IS THE AUTHOR OF HEBREWS?

My Professor of English Bible, Dr. Howard T. Kuist, reminded his class, "A great deal more heat than light has been shed on the authorship of the book of Hebrews." Truly much controversy has been generated over this single issue, which is lamentable. A brief discussion of this matter may help us to put this question and its possible answers in proper perspective at the beginning of our study. Surely the worst offender in this debate is the person who is positive he knows the name of the author.

It may be that your Bible is like many others, in that the title of this book is, "The Epistle of Paul the Apostle to the Hebrews." This is the title I find in the Scofield Reference Bible (the King James Version, or KJV) my parents gave me for Christmas in 1947. However, Scofield himself seems to reject Paul's authorship in an introductory statement for Hebrews. He wrote, "In Hebrews, James, First and Second Peter, and Jude we have a group of inspired writings differing in important respects from Paul's Epistles." Some other things he says in the statement reinforce that idea. It may be that Scofield himself did not believe that Paul wrote Hebrews, but to palliate those who did, he kept the title to avoid offending his purchasers. For centuries, many people have believed that Paul wrote Hebrews, and many still do.

There are several good reasons why people believe Paul wrote Hebrews. On the other hand, there is no positive evidence within the book, or anywhere else in scripture, that give real proof that Paul was the author.

Here, however, are arguments in favor of Paul's authorship. For one thing, there is a long tradition in the Church that Paul wrote the book. Every tradition must have some roots; but there are some plants that have been grafted onto roots of different plants. It seems that as far back as the third century, scholars in the Eastern portion of the Church generally thought Paul was the author, but those in what became the Roman Catholic church mostly denied his authorship.

Another reason why some people believe Paul wrote Hebrews is because they detect a number of "Paulinisms" here and there in the book. This argument could hold some weight if those Paulinisms were so peculiar as to have been totally neglected by any other author. On the other hand we see, for instance, many parallel passages throughout the four gospels that are identical from one to another, but it is quite certain that they were written by different authors (despite the "documentary hypothesis" applied to them by some scholars). We will note some of these Paulinisms as we continue our study.

2

A third reason why many people believe it was Paul who wrote Hebrews is because the trilogy we find in I Cor. 13:13 is repeated—not once but twice—in the book of Hebrews. The first instance of the trilogy is in Heb. 10, where verse 22 speaks of faith, verse 23 of hope (although the KJV wrongly translates the Greek word for "hope" as "faith" again), and verse 24 encourages disciples to love. Following this, we may recall that Heb. 11 is rightly called the great "faith" chapter of the whole Bible. Next, chapter 12 is filled with the essence of hope, although the term "hope" is found neither in the original Greek nor the English versions. But the first three verses are loaded with sentiments of hope:

> Therefore, since we are surrounded by such a great cloud of witnesses, let us throw off everything that hinders and the sin that so easily entangles, and let us run with perseverance the race marked out for us. Let us fix our eyes on Jesus, the author and perfecter of our faith, who for the joy set before him endured the cross, scorning its shame, and sat down at the right hand of the throne of God. Consider him who endured such opposition from sinful men, so that you will not grow weary and lose heart.

Finally, chapter 13 begins, "Keep on loving each other as brothers," and the theme continues in the chapter.

With regard to arguments of those who reject the Pauline authorship of Hebrews, one is that Paul does not identify himself in the opening words of the book. We read, for instance, that without exception the thirteen epistles attributed to Paul in the New Testament begin with the word "Paul." However, Hebrews begins, "In the past God spoke to our forefathers through the prophets at many times and in various ways, but in these last days he has spoken to us by his Son, whom he appointed heir of all things, and through whom he made the universe." In no other place in the book is the name Paul mentioned. One hint that might temper this argument is that at the end of the book, the author mentions "our brother Timothy." This, however, is a very fragile argument, especially in light of the fact that Paul usually called Timothy "my son."

Another argument used by some people is that in the book of Acts, Paul makes clear that God sent him as an apostle to the Gentiles, while his ministry to Jews was minimal at best. He told the crowd in the temple area (Acts 22:21): "Then the Lord said to me, 'Go, I will send you far away to the Gentiles.'" This does not conflict with what Paul said in his defense in Acts 26:19-20: "So then, King Agrippa, I was not disobedient to the vision from heaven. First to those in Damascus, then to those in Jerusalem and in all Judea, and to the Gentiles also, I preached that they should repent and turn to God and prove their repentance by their deeds." The apostle never shrank from preaching to Jews about Christ and his ministry, but it is clear that his principal mission was to the Gentiles. Paul expresses the sentiment in Gal. 1:15: "God, who set me apart from birth and called me by his grace, was pleased to reveal his Son in me so that I might preach him among the Gentiles...." Later (Gal. 2:7) Paul reaffirms this: "[The Jewish Christian leaders] saw that I had been given the task of preaching the gospel to the Gentiles, just as Peter had been given the task of preaching the gospel to the Jews." Of course this whole argument rests on the assumption that the book of Hebrews was written to Jewish Christians. It appears that one of the author's purposes was to wean the Jewish Christians from the Old Testament ministry; to stop worrying that the temple had been destroyed and the altar was gone so they could no longer make sacrifices, so they wondered how they could get to heaven. After all, the Old Testament had told them the only way to heaven was to take their sacrifices to the temple, give them to the priest, and have them offered on the altar for their sins. Having done that, they thought that on the Day of Atonement their sins would be washed away and they could go to heaven. But without the priest and his ministry, how could they hope to get to heaven? Incidentally, this remains a problem for faithful adherents of Judaism; the temple and altar are gone, and the priest no longer makes sacrifices for them. They need to discover that although the Levitical priesthood has ceased to exist, they (as well as Gentiles) now have the Great High Priest, even Jesus Christ, who makes the better sacrifice for them and makes the way to heaven for them.

Few people, then, would argue that Hebrews was written to Jewish people, although some, including myself, would agree that the doctrinal teachings found here are equally valid for Gentiles as well as for Jews. However, it is evident from the general trend of the book that it had to be written to people who were, first of all, well acquainted with the Old Testament (which was a general trait of Jews and not of Gentiles); and secondly, these people were in danger of returning to their Jewish legalistic and ritual roots. Therefore, the author continually emphasized his main theme that Jesus Christ and his ministry were "better than" anything to be found in the Old Testament practice.

Several people besides Paul have been proposed as authors of the book of Hebrews, such as Barnabas, Luke, Apollos, or Priscilla. My seminary professor, Dr. Kuist, summed it up best however, when he commented, "We may never know who was the human author of Hebrews, but there is no doubt that the real author was the Holy Spirit Himself!"

## THE KEY TO HEBREWS

Perhaps the best way to introduce this study of Hebrews is to point out, chapter by chapter, the particular people or elements that were written about in the Old Testament, over which Christ is superior. This may impress on our minds the key to understanding the book, the term "better than." Of course, we will elaborate on all these matters as we proceed.

The opening words of chapter 1 imply that Jesus is better than the Old Testament prophets: they were mere messengers, while Jesus was "a Son" (according to the Greek text). Surely we all recognize that a son is always more precious, valuable, important to a person than a mere messenger could ever be. Chapter 1 also points out that Jesus is better than angels. Angels were regarded highly by Jews of old, higher than any human could become. But Jesus was regarded much more highly than angels by His Father in heaven.

In chapter 2 the author quotes from Psalm 8 to show that although God caused His Son to become a man at a point in history, the Father exalted Him above both men and angels, the One who was "crowned with glory and honor because he suffered death..." (Heb. 2:9).

Jesus is compared with Moses in chapter 3:3, and was found to have "greater honor" than Moses, although Moses was deemed perhaps the greatest of men because he was chosen of God to be the conveyor of the law to the Jews. Other characters in the Old Testament who may have compared favorably with Moses were Abraham, the first Jew; and David, the great King, even though Solomon was more wealthy and wise than his father.

The rest of chapter 3 introduces the next famous person mentioned in chapter 4. Chapter 3 tells us of the rest which was made available to the people, expressed best in Ps. 95; and the rest was first provided to the Jews in the time of the great military leader Joshua, of whom we read in Heb. 4:8. Incidentally, the KJV translates Joshua's name as "Jesus" here, which has caused confusion to some who do not recognize that the Greek word for Joshua and Jesus is one and the same. Jesus is better than Joshua, because Jesus offers us an *eternal* rest, infinitely more desirable than an earthly one.

Turning from military/political leaders to religious ones, we read in chapter 5 the beginning of the most important part of Hebrews, which is the spiritual importance of the religious leaders and their ministries on behalf of the people. We are introduced here to Aaron, the first high priest of Israel, appointed to that tremendous position by God Himself. He was important in his own right, but he was exalted in the minds of the people in addition because he was Moses' brother. But Jesus was better than Aaron, even though Aaron was appointed by God, because Jesus' priesthood endures forever, while Aaron lost that position at his death. Also, Jesus' priesthood existed in a different line of priests: while Aaron was of the Levites, Jesus followed after the priesthood of Melchizedek.

Chapter 6 begins with a list of six rudimentary doctrines of Christ, based on Old Testament principles; then continues with an invitation to proceed to fuller, more important, indeed perfect doctrines that are expressed fully in the life and ministry of Jesus Christ. The idea is that Jesus Christ is the reality of what were in the Old Testament mere blueprints of the Savior and his works. For this reason the author tells us in verse 18 that we "take hold of the hope offered to us" which was merely promised to Abraham and his heirs, but has been revealed fully to us in Jesus Christ.

5

The theme of the high priesthood is picked up again in chapters 7 and 8. In 7:4 we read that even Abraham, the father of all Jews, gave his tithe to Aaron the Levitical priest (through his descendants), so that was exceedingly important. But we are reminded in verse 11 that Jesus' priesthood was even better than Aaron's, because Aaron's must have been flawed since it was superseded by that of Melchizedek. Further, in chapter 8, we read in verse 3 that the gifts and sacrifices our High Priest Jesus made were infinitely better than those which Aaron and his descendants made. After that, in verse 6, the author tells us that those better sacrifices were made through a better ministry, by means of a better covenant, and "it is founded on better promises." The theme of the "better covenant" is woven through the next two chapters as well.

A contrast is made in chapter 9 between the sanctuary (in the wilderness, verse 1) in which Aaron made his sacrifices, and the tabernacle (heaven itself, verse 11) in which Jesus offered Himself as the final, great sacrifice for the sins of the world. In the next verse, we read that it was the blood of goats and calves which were offered in the Levitical priesthood, but Jesus sacrificed His own blood in His sacrifice. And beyond that, in verses 16 to 18, we read of Jesus' better covenant, which in this treatment is called a "will" made between God and men. Since a will becomes effective only after the death of the testator, then Jesus' covenant-will is better than the old one because Jesus actually died to implement the will.

There is some difference of opinion of what the author is driving at in chapter 10, but we will study this more carefully when we get to it. Suffice it to say now that verse 9 tells us that Jesus' sacrifice set aside the old system because it was better. This argument reaches its climax in verse 26, where we see that Jesus' sacrifice is not only better than any past sacrifices, but it is also better than any *future* sacrifice that can possibly be made.

Let us summarize this brief introduction to the whole book by lumping together the last three chapters discussed above. Chapter 11 (especially verses 36 to 39) tells us of a better faith, chapter 12 of a better hope, and chapter 13 of a better love under Christ's ministry.

### ACKNOWLEDGMENT

I would be grossly remiss if I failed to name my lovely wife, Claire, as the one person who not only supported and encouraged me throughout the formation of this book, but also who read the manuscript many times. She made suggestions for improvement, and the book is superior because of it. The ultimate responsibility for every fault is solely mine.

# CHAPTER I
## JESUS IS BETTER THAN ANGELS.  HEB. 1:1 to 2:4.

For my own study and benefit, I struggled to make a translation of the book of Hebrews. I will share it from time to time in our study, in hopes that such an unscholarly translation will help us all grasp what the author originally intended us to know of Jesus and his ministry. Here is my translation of verses 1 to 4.

> Once upon a time, God, having spoken to our ancestors with many bits of information on many occasions by means of the prophets, in these last days has spoken to us by means of a Son, whom he established as the Heir of all things, and through whom he made the universe; who being the very radiance of his glory, and the precise representation of his full being [existence], and sustaining everything [that universe] by the word of his power, and having made cleansing for sins, he sat down at the right side of the Majesty in the high heaven, having been so much greater [better] than the angels, he has inherited a name that is so much better than theirs.

### Heb. 1:1.  In the past God spoke....

In order to get into the basic meaning of this opening paragraph, let us apply a grammatical device to help us find it. Before you read further, I invite you to find the "irreducible minimum" of that long sentence; that is, find the one noun that is the subject, and the verb (two words in this case) of the sentence: when you have done that, you will have an excellent knowledge of the contents of the whole sentence and its meaning.

I trust you have at least made a strong effort to do the exercise in the paragraph above. If you have completed the task, you should have found the irreducible minimum of the sentence to be "God has spoken." Everything else is related to that grand pronouncement, and is subordinate to it.

Now let us begin to relate each part of the sentence to this central statement. As we do, it will be well to say a few words about the statement itself. First of all, there is no more important person in all existence than the one true God. Therefore, whatever God does, or says, is of utmost importance to each part of creation, whether great or small, whether famous or unknown, whether useful or of no account. In this case, we are thinking about the fact that God "has spoken," more than about what He has done. It is imperative for us to acknowledge that God has spoken, lest anyone attempt to claim that we cannot, or need not, know anything about God if he has not revealed himself to us.

Not only is it important for us to accept the fact that God has spoken, but also we cannot escape the fact that "we have heard." This is found in the first verse of chapter 2. When we get to that part of our study, we will see the infinitely important ramifications of these statements together: "God has spoken," and "We have heard." Suffice it to say here that "we must cling to the things we have heard, so that we will not drift away" (my translation).

If God has spoken, then we may speak freely about "the word of God," which He has spoken and we have heard. Because of His speaking and our hearing, we have come to "the knowledge of the truth," as the author says in 10:26. The word of God, and our awareness of it and its truth, are absolutely foundational in our study of any detail about God, either who He is, or what He does, or what He wants us to do. We need not labor the point that a good foundation is essential to any building, whether constructed of material things or of thoughts. In the middle of the twentieth century, the General Electric Company built a huge new factory in which to make giant electric generators. The factory was well reinforced with thousands of tons of steel beams to keep it safe. One interesting item about the factory was that there was as much steel reinforcement below ground level in the foundation as there was above ground in the superstructure. That factory was built to stand for decades without moving an iota. On the other hand, I was involved in the construction of a public building, and discovered that one of the basement walls had been pushed in by the contractor. For years after that, I was deeply concerned that the part of the building above it would collapse from the faulty construction. Fortunately that has not yet happened, but it may yet some day fall in. So also with our thinking. We must have a sure foundation for our thoughts, or our whole system of thinking will be faulty, and any conclusions we may propose will be at best suspect. If our thinking about God is not based on what he has told us, we dare not claim that our thinking is valid.

In ancient times, that is, from the creation of the universe to the time of Nehemiah in 445 BC, or even of Malachi in 397, as expressed in the Old Testament, God spoke to "our ancestors." Let us never worry whether those ancestors had an opportunity to know God or salvation in Jesus Christ, because God spoke to all of them. He spoke "at many times and in various ways," or as I translated it, "with many bits of information on many occasions." God began to speak from the very beginning; He spoke in order to perform the act of creation. Each of the six days of creation is introduced, in Genesis 1, with the words, "And God said...." And Malachi, the last prophet, introduced his book of prophecy with these words, "An oracle: The word of the LORD to Israel through Malachi."

### ...to our forefathers....

Actually, the message was carried not only to the ancient Hebrews, but to the whole world. If any people did not hear God's message, it was not God's fault, but their own. The prophets were scattered through time and geographic space. In addition, many who heard the prophets directly carried the message to other people who may not have met any prophet. For instance, in the days at the end of the Exodus of Israel from Egypt, the people of Jericho knew all about what God had done for His people in delivering them from bondage and from the ravages of the forty-year trek through the desert. Rahab the Harlot reported this fact to the spies who preceded the downfall of the city (Josh. 2:9-11):

> I know that the LORD has given this land to you and that a great fear of you has fallen on us, so that all who live in this country are melting in fear because of you. We have heard how the LORD dried up the water of the Red Sea for you when you came out of Egypt....When we heard of it, our hearts sank and everyone's courage failed because of you, for the LORD your God is God in heaven above and on the earth below.

### ...through the prophets....

The instruments God used to communicate with the people of the world in those ancient times were the prophets he chose and even anointed[1] to receive his message and transmit it to everyone. The prophets may be thought of as rough equivalents of messengers, angels, and even apostles. The Hebrew word for "prophet" is נָבִיא, which means a spokesman, speaker, or prophet.[2] The Greek equivalent, προφήτης, is simply one who speaks forth, or one who solemnly speaks to people from God. The Hebrew word for "angel" is the same as our term "messenger," which is מַלְאָךְ; while the Greek word for both is ἄγγελος, a messenger, envoy, or angel. Our idea for an "apostle" has no counterpart in Hebrew, but in Greek it is ἀπόστολος, which is a delegate, messenger, one sent forth with orders.[3]

### ...at many times and in various ways....

God used to speak to people, not just once or twice, but often, and in ways different from the way He has spoken to us since the advent of Jesus into the world. God's speaking was not sporadic, nor merely occasional. He spoke sufficiently often to blanket the world with His message. The ways in which He spoke were both creative and varied, to say the least. Evidence for the times God spoke to people, and the distance to which His message was carried is found in Ps. 19:1-4:

> The heavens declare the glory of God;
>> the skies proclaim the work of his hands.
> Day after day they pour forth speech;
>> night after night they display knowledge.
> There is no speech or language

---

1 For instance, Samuel anointed Saul to be king, but Saul was also a prophet: the people who knew him "saw him prophesying with the prophets" (I Sam. 10:1 and 11). Also, Isaiah was anointed with a live coal placed by a seraph on his lips (Is. 6:6-7).

2 Francis Brown, S. R. Driver, and Charles A. Briggs, A HEBREW AND ENGLISH LEXICON OF THE OLD TESTAMENT. This will be henceforth indicated as "Brown, Driver, and Briggs." Pp. xix, 1126.

3 Joseph Henry Thayer, A GREEK-ENGLISH LEXICON OF THE NEW TESTAMENT. Pp. xix, 727.

where their voice is not heard.

Their voice goes out into all the earth,

their words to the ends of the world.

Here are a few additional ways God spoke to, and through, prophets of old. He spoke face to face with Moses (Ex. 33:11). He spoke to Isaiah out of the smoke and thunder and earthquake in the temple (Is. 6, the whole chapter). The Lord spoke to Elijah directly, but the chronicler at least implies that He could have spoken to him also in the wind, or an earthquake, or a fire, or even in a gentle whisper which the Hebrew calls a "voice of silence" (my translation), in I Kings 19:9-12.

God spoke not only in words, both spoken and written (remember the Ten Commandments on the tablets of stone, Ex. 31:18); but in other modes as well. The author of Hebrews tells us in 2:4 that God spoke in "signs, wonders and various miracles, and gifts of the Holy Spirit distributed according to his will."

### Heb. 1:2.   ...but in these last days....

The last days, according to the sentiment expressed here, began with the incarnation. When Jesus Christ came from heaven into the world, being born of the Virgin Mary, this was the single most important turning-point in all history. That this is acknowledged by virtually every civilized person in the world is attested by the calendar we all use to mark events in history. Because of some errors in calculation of time, we agree that according to our present calendar Jesus was born about 4 BC, instead of Zero BC/AD; likewise He died in 29 AD although He was thirty-three years old when He was crucified. To me it is an amazing fact that Christians and atheists, Mohammedans and animists, Communists and Taoists, and even most Jews, accept our calendar as indicating that an overwhelming event took place in the form of a Baby born in a manger in Bethlehem in the days of King Herod the Great.

These last days, or we might call them the end times, have continued from Jesus' birth to the present, and will proceed as long as the world exists in this form and inhabited by people. This is why it was perfectly feasible for Paul to hope that he would not see death until Christ's return, just as Simeon in the temple was promised that he would not "die before he had seen the Lord's Christ" (Lu. 2:26), except that Paul had not been given an actual promise. Paul hoped this wonderful possibility not only for himself, but he encouraged the people in one of his congregations (I Thess. 1:9-10), "...you turned to God from idols to serve the living and true God, and to wait for his Son from heaven, whom he raised from the dead—Jesus, who rescues us from the coming wrath." Later in the same letter (I Thess 4:17), Paul implies that he desires to be yet alive with many people in the church at Thessalonica when Jesus appears the second time on the earth, "After that, we who are still alive and are left will be caught up with them in the clouds to meet the Lord in the air. And so we will be with the Lord forever."

Paul is required, almost immediately, to temper such teaching with a warning that the Lord's coming was not to be expected in a moment, but certain events must occur before Jesus' arrival. That is why Paul needed to sit down quickly and dash off his second letter to the Christians in Thessalonica, where he wrote in 2:1-4:

> Concerning the coming of our Lord Jesus Christ and our being gathered to him, we ask you, brothers, not to become easily unsettled or alarmed by some prophecy, report or letter supposed to have come from us, saying that the day of the Lord has already come. Don't let anyone deceive you in any way, for that day will not come until the rebellion occurs and the man of lawlessness is revealed, the man doomed to destruction. He opposes and exalts himself over everything that is called God or is worshiped, and even sets himself up in God's temple, proclaiming himself to be God.

The Lord Jesus Himself gives the same kind of warning to His disciples just before He is crucified and taken from them (Matt. 24:4-8):

> Watch out that no one deceives you. For many will come in my name, claiming, "I am the Christ," and will deceive 'many. You will hear of wars and rumors of wars, but see to it that you are not alarmed. Such things must happen, but the end is still to come. Nation will rise against nation, and kingdom against kingdom. There will be famines and earthquakes in various places. All these are the beginning of birth pains.

In these instructions to His disciples, commonly called the Olivet Discourse, Jesus adds several other events that must take place before He returns or the world ends, including the so-called "Great Tribulation" (which some dispute as coming before Christ's return, but a careful reading of Jesus' own chronology in that chapter clears up the matter).

In sum, we can safely say that we are in the end times of the world, a period which began with Jesus' first Advent and will conclude with His second Advent. Although people dispute the correct interpretation of the various signs portending the termination of Earth, Jesus warned His disciples and us that all those things may have happened already, so that the way is paved for Jesus' return; therefore we must work, and watch, and be ready at any moment (see Matt. 24:42-43 and 25:13; Mk. 13:35-37; Lu. 19:13 and 21:36). The apostle Paul lived in the "last days." The author of Hebrews lived in the "last days." You and I live in the "last days." The rest of humanity will live in the "last days" until Jesus comes.

### ...he has spoken to us....

Again I must repeat my solemn warning: God has spoken; we have heard; therefore we are all without excuse. Jesus has not merely spoken; He has spoken *to us*. Because we are all living in "these last days," we are all included in the population that has heard. Since we have heard the message, we are left with no reason whatever to fail to live up to that message. Do not be confused by the idea that Jesus has been doing the speaking during the "last days;" Jesus is the Instrument of speaking, but it is God (the Father) who "has

11

spoken to us." Therefore, Jesus' fleshly absence from us does not prevent God's speaking. Paul heard Jesus speaking on the road to Damascus (Acts 9:5), long after Jesus had ascended to heaven. Not only that, but Jesus speaks to us through His messengers today, just as He did through his Old Testament messengers, and by other modes as well, including the heavens and all creation.

Paul gives us an inescapable proof that God has spoken to us, and to every soul that has ever walked the Earth, in Rom. 1:18-20:

> The wrath of God is being revealed from heaven against all the godlessness and wickedness of men who suppress the truth by their wickedness, since what may be known about God is plain to them, because God has made it plain to them. For since the creation of the world God's invisible qualities—his eternal power and divine nature—have been clearly seen, being understood from what has been made, so that men are without excuse.

### ...by his Son....

Most English translations follow the ordinary way to write these words, "he has spoken to us by his Son." This is not an erroneous rendering, but it would be better said as either "in a Son" or "by means of a Son." The important point I make here is that the Greek text has no definite article before the word "Son." The reason for making this an issue is certainly *not* to imply that God has many sons, any one of whom He could have chosen to be His Messenger. The reason to emphasize that it is "a Son" whom God chose is to make the infinitely great distinction between "a prophet," any prophet or other kind of messenger, and "a Son." Ordinarily, and certainly properly, one's son is esteemed and cherished far above any other person (with the exception of one's spouse) for the purpose of completing a job most acceptably.[4] You know your son better than anyone else, because you have lived with him all his life. You trust him more than anyone else, because you reared him yourself and know his character better than that of any other person. You depend on your son because he is part of you—he came from your own loins. Next in rank to a son would probably be a brother. This is why, for instance, Bobby Kennedy was probably the greatest Cabinet member in any United States President's list of helpers. All this is to say that God chose Jesus Christ, His only-begotten Son, to be the supreme Messenger to the world. No Old Testament prophet, no New Testament apostle, no latter-day ordained clergy could begin to compare in glory with God the Son. This is why it is so tremendously important that we heed the message the Son has conveyed to us.

Let us return to one more idea near the beginning of the previous paragraph, in order to obviate any confusion about how many Sons, or sons, are God's own children. God has three distinct kinds of descendants. All human

---

[4] The generic term "son" is used here to include a daughter as well as a son. In all my writing, I prefer to use the masculine, since that is still considered the most proper grammar. There is no intent to demean the feminine sex.

beings are God's children in the most basic sense, by virtue of the fact that He created us all. There is a second classification of children of God; they are those who have been adopted as children by faith in Jesus Christ as their Savior and Lord. The third category tells us that God is an ancestor. In these days of New Age thinking, it cannot be overemphasized that this last category has a population of exactly One. That One is Jesus Christ.

All the rest of the long Pauline-style sentence, from the middle of verse 2 to the end of verse 4 of chapter 1, is a tremendous doxology to Jesus, introducing the theme of the whole book of Hebrews, that Jesus is "better than" anyone and anything else in the universe. Try to keep this in mind as we examine each phrase of the doxology.

### ...whom he appointed....

The text tells us much more than that Jesus exists merely as the "heir of all things." The clause adds the extremely important detail as to how He became that Heir. Our study version says that God Himself made it happen: "...whom he appointed heir of all things." If God the Father decides to do something, there is none better to make the appointment: His own Person and Character lends its weight to the transaction. If a servant should appoint her master to wash the dishes, such a decision would be quite meaningless; if the master appoints her servant to be the dishwasher, that appointment makes the job as good as done.

I chose to exchange the English word "appointed" for the word "established" here. My term appears to me to be broader in its implications, in that an appointment is a single act whose results are not noted but left up in the air; while an establishment is something that is not only set forth in the first place, but it continues to have a logical continuation of effects relative to the initial "appointment."[5]

### ...heir of all things....

That Jesus is the Heir of God implies the prior relationship between a Father and His Son. We should add the idea of heirship to that of sonship, especially in Jewish circles, since the oldest son was supposed to be designated as the principal heir of a father's goods. (In the case of the Prodigal Son, the first-born was scheduled to receive two-thirds of his father's land and the Prodigal the rest. But the Prodigal evidently asked his father for his portion of personal property, not of the land.) Many places in the Old Testament speak of this concept; for evidence you may study again the story of how Jacob wrenched the birthright from his older brother Esau, in Gen. 25:24-34. Land was the principal item of inheritance in ancient times, and was to be passed

5  My authority for choosing the term "established" here is the THEOLOGICAL DICTIONARY OF THE NEW TESTAMENT, Vol. VIII, pp. 152-153, the discussion of the Greek term τίθημι. This ten-volume set is usually known as TDNT.

from father to sons through the generations. It appears that the oldest son was to receive twice as much land as any other son, while the other sons received lesser portions, but equal to each other. This is spelled out in Deut. 21:15-17, although this may be a special case, since it is talking about two sons of the same father but of different mothers. The older son is the child of the "hated" mother, while the younger is of the favored mother. The rule given was that the older son could not be stripped of his inheritance simply because his mother was disliked. Other rules of inheritance were that land was not to be transferred to a member of another tribe (Num. 36:5-9); if a man had no sons, there was a schedule of people in descending order who would receive the land (Num. 27:6-11, and see the story of Ruth in the book named for her); and Levites were not to own any land, but (Deut. 18:2) "the LORD is their inheritance."

Since Jesus is God's "heir of all things," it is amazing that we who are children of God (John 1:12 and Rom. 8:16) in a different category from him are also "heirs of God and co-heirs with Christ"! (Rom. 8:17). There is a catch to this, however. If we wish to be heirs of all the good and glorious things which Christ will receive, we must be willing also to partake with Him in all the hurtful things as well, for the same verse in Romans mentioned here adds that we are co-heirs only "if indeed we share in his sufferings in order that we may also share in his glory." Jesus predicted that this would be so, when He told His disciples, "If [the people of the world] persecuted me, they will persecute you also....In this world you will have trouble. But take heart! I have overcome the world" (John 15:20 and 16:33). The apostle Paul wrote of his willingness, even eagerness, to share in Christ's sufferings, knowing that was the only way he could also share in his resurrection (Phil. 3:10-11): "I want to know Christ and the power of his resurrection and the fellowship of sharing in his sufferings, becoming like him in his death, and so somehow, to attain to the resurrection from the dead." We dare not attempt to be like the lesbian who a few years ago broke up with her lover and sued her to get half ownership of the lover's house, but refused to sue for half the business because it was heavily mortgaged.

### ...and through whom he made the universe.

Jesus, who is God, is the Creator of everything that has been made. Too often we simply assume that Gen. 1:1 is talking about God the Father alone when it says, "In the beginning God created the heavens and the earth." (The Hebrew word for "God" here is the plural form אֱלֹהִים, which resonates of the Trinity.) It is right to assume that the Father was a participant in the creation, but it is wrong to believe that the Son and the Holy Spirit were not involved. Rather, the act of creation was the work of the Trinity.

We read in two places in the book of Job that the Spirit was also the Creator (Job 26:13, 33:4):

By his breath the skies became fair;

14

> his hand pierced the gliding serpent....
> The Spirit of God has made me;
> the breath of the Almighty gives me life.

We need to recognize that in Hebrew the term translated "breath" is the same word for "spirit," that is, רוּחַ. This is true at least in 26:13, but the word for "breath" in 33:4 is a different word, נְשָׁמָה. However, both these Hebrew words for "breath" are used together in Job 34:14, and it is obvious they are intended to be synonymous.

That the Son is co-Creator with the Father and the Spirit is evidenced by such New Testament verses as John 1:3, "Through [the Word] all things were made; without him nothing was made that has been made;" I Cor. 8:6, "...for us there is but one God, the Father, from whom all things came and for whom we live; and there is but one Lord, Jesus Christ, through whom all things came and through whom we live;" and Col. 1:15-16:

> He is the image of the invisible God, the firstborn over all creation. For by
> him all things were created: things in heaven and on earth, visible and in-
> visible, whether thrones or powers or rulers or authorities; all things were
> created by him and for him.

Some people want to believe that Jesus is not God, but is merely one of the created beings, by virtue of the phrase in verse 15, "the firstborn over all creation." That seems to say that Jesus was the first thing created. But the Greek word for "firstborn," πρωτότοκος, although often used in both the Old Testament Greek version (called the Septuagint, often abbreviated as the LXX), and the New Testament Greek to mean "the first child of a mother," more often refers to an exalted position or status. A. T. Robertson, in his discussion of Col. 1:15-16, says of the two words for Jesus, "image" and "firstborn," "Paul takes both words to help express the deity of Jesus Christ in his relation to the father as *eikon* (Image) and to the universe as *prototokos* (First-born)."[6] Paul uses the same term for Jesus just three verses later, where he calls Jesus the "firstborn from the dead." Gerhard Friedrich refers to Ps. 88:28 (our English version's Ps. 89:27), which says,

> I will also appoint him my firstborn,
> the most exalted of the kings of the earth.

Friedrich points out that the term "firstborn" here has nothing to do with being the first in a class.[7] Probably the best proof that Jesus was not a created first-born is found in the first verse of this argument, John 1:3, which states clearly that there are two categories of beings or things: first, the Creator; and secondly, everything that has been created. The verse states further that Jesus, the Word, occupies the first category, because "without him nothing was made that has been made."

\* \* \*

---

6 A. T. Robertson, WORD PICTURES IN THE NEW TESTAMENT, Vol. IV, p. 478.

7 Friedrich's complete exposition of the Greek πρωτότοκος follows the same argument. It is found in TDNT, Vol. VI, pages 871 to 881.

## Heb. 1:3.  The Son is the radiance of God's glory....

This phrase and the next may be the most difficult part of the whole book of Hebrews for the human mind to understand.  It is likely that the author wrestled often and long to capture the very best human words to describe what he wanted to say.  God is so infinitely far above us all in glory, and in His very being, that no combination of human words can begin to put into our minds an adequate picture of what our God looks like or is like.  Just as the author wrestled, so also let us wrestle with our Thesaurus to come, in English, as close to the Greek as we can.  The spread of two millennia between us makes the task more difficult.

The Greek word for "radiance" is ἀπαύγασμα, which is used only once in the New Testament.  This noun comes from the Greek verb ἀπαυγάζω, which in its intransitive use means *"to be bright, to shine forth."*[8]   Gerhard Kittel[9] claims that "Christ is the effulgence of the divine *doxa*, as sunshine is of the sun or light of light."  Thayer,[10] on the other hand, chooses to think of the noun as *"reflected brightness"* (his italics).

Perhaps we can understand the words "emission" and "reflection."  To think of Christ as being merely the "reflection" or "refulgence" of God's light means that He in no sense produces that light.  Much more glorious, however, is the light originating and shining from the Son, who is God Himself, than if He were merely one of the creatures reflecting a tiny part of God's light.

Here let us remember the story of Jesus' transfiguration in Matt. 17:2 and Mk. 9:2.  During the summer of 1978, my wife and daughter and I were privileged to travel to Israel.  One day we were standing on Mount Megiddo, looking northward over the vast Valley of Megiddo.  We saw in the distance two mountain peaks; a guide was telling a group that one of them was Mount Tavor, the Mount of Transfiguration.  The Greek word used for what happened to Jesus there is μεταμορφόω.  When we translate that word into the English "metamorphosis," we think of the extraordinary transformation of a lowly crawling caterpillar into a beautiful flying butterfly.  Jesus' glory shone so brightly that the disciples present were unable even to peek at Him.  We also remember that in Ps. 104:2, God "wraps himself in light as with a garment," but we are sure there is no other source for that light than God himself.  Paul saw a similar light when he saw Jesus on his trip to Damascus to persecute the Christians.  But all he could see of Jesus was "a light from heaven [that] flashed around him" (Acts 9:3).  This event occurred at midday, so Paul and those with him could easily compare the brightness of the sun with that of Jesus, and Jesus' light shone so brightly that the sun's rays were blotted out, and Paul was blinded from the brightness.  Jesus would be a blasphemer to

---

8  Thayer, his definition.

9  Gerhard Kittel, article, αὐγάζω, ἀπαύγασμα, TDNT, Vol. I, pages 507-8.

10  Thayer, *loc. sit.*, his definition.

say (John 8:12) "I am the light of the world" if He were not the very God who is light.

In great contrast, we mere humans have nothing like light with which to clothe ourselves. Our first parents attempted to clothe themselves with aprons of fig leaves, after they realized they were naked (Gen. 3:7). Their pitiful effort was totally insufficient to cover their sin of disobedience; so God needed to step in and clothe them with the skin of the lamb (Gen. 3:21). This is a tremendous picture from the days of our original forebears that Jesus would one day come into the world to be "the Lamb of God, who takes away the sin of the world" (John 1:29). Still, even the covering which God provides for us is as nothing compared to His covering of His own light.

This story is still not ended. We do have a light, which we can "let...shine before men, that they may see your good deeds and praise your Father in heaven" (Matt. 5:16). But even though Jesus says to His disciples that it is "your light," we know that our light is merely reflected from the Savior and not emitted from us. I like to think of the light which we let shine in the world as the kind of light which shines from a fluorescent bulb. The bulb contains a coating on its inner surface, but no light shines from it until an electric current is passed through it. The coating is energized, and then shines with light. We could not shine with "our" lights unless the Light of the world resides in us and gives us the power to shine for Him.

The brightness of Jesus is of such glory that we cannot begin to describe it in human terms. The author of Hebrews did his best, and we must accept his results. But some day, you who believe in Jesus Christ as your Savior and Lord are going to witness that brightness yourselves, because you will stand before God's throne of grace where Jesus will sit on the Father's right hand. You will be able to look upon Jesus and see His brightness. You will not be blinded by it then; your spiritual eyes will be able to accept the brightness. Then you will begin to see what John, Paul, and the author of Hebrews were trying to describe when they talked about the effulgence of the glory of Jesus Christ.

### ...and the exact representation of his being....

If you thought the study of the word "brightness" was difficult, we now approach a double difficulty, and it is even more controversial. Let us not faint, but press on to a greater understanding of what the author of Hebrews was driving at here.

The first difficult word, "exact representation," we must confront is the Greek χαρακτήρ, which when pronounced sounds like our "character." This begins to give us a sense of what it is about. Thayer gives us this definition of the Greek term: "1. prop. *the instrument used in engraving or carving....*2. *the mark* (figure or letters) *stamped upon that instrument ... the exact expression (the image) of any person* or *thing, marked likeness, precise* *reproduction in every respect* (cf. *facsimile*)." Wilckens' and Kelber's exposition of the term in the TDNT,[11] says substantially the same thing, at least with regard to the historic meaning of the term. Perhaps it will be easier to understand the meaning of the term as it is used here (it occurs no other place in the New Testament) if we think of seeing the reflection of something in a mirror. The mirror faithfully reproduces for the observer what is put before the mirror to reflect—with several demurrers. First, the reflection in a mirror is always the *reverse* of the image reflected; Jesus is not the reverse of God, but is identical to God. In fact, Satan worship involves reverse images, such as the upside down star. Secondly, the reflection is but a pale substitute for the real thing. A mirror never can gather all the light beams from the image reflected, but always loses some. But Christ is fully equal to God, because He *is* God, not a washed-out reflection. Thirdly, a mirror is always dusty and has imperfections however slight, so it never can produce a perfect reflection of the image. Jesus, however, has not the slightest flaw in His "exact representation" of God. In Hebrews (4:15) we shall see that Jesus was "yet without sin." Finally, it is not Christ, but we who reflect God's glory as He dwells in us by his Holy Spirit. I have already discussed Matt. 5:16, in which the light which shines from us is actually God's light shining through us to the world.

Another illustration that may help us understand the meaning of "exact representation" is the minting of coins. This is an appropriate picture of the meaning of the word. In the process of making a coin, a metal slug is placed in a powerful press which contains two dies, one for the obverse and the other for the reverse of the coin. Tremendous pressure is exerted on the slug; it is formed into the exact likeness of the dies. Every detail is perfectly reproduced. If there is the slightest flaw in the coin, it is discarded, and only the perfect ones are kept.

There are two errors in this picture, however, and both are fatal in the usage of the term here. For one thing, in minting a coin, the dies from which the coin is made are "negative" images, while the images on the coin are positive. Not so with Jesus as the "image" of God: both are positive; one is not the reverse of the other, but they are identical in every respect. The other fatal flaw in this picture is that neither the Father nor the Son is the original while the other is the "reproduction." Both are original. Both are equal in power and glory, as the Westminster Catechism says. Neither came before the other.

The second difficult word we must contend with is the the word translated "being," which comes from the Greek ὑπόστασις. Helmut Köster, in his article on the term in TDNT[12] gives the philosophical meaning of the term as "existence" or "reality." Köster's translator Bromiley has chosen the English word "essence" as the best translation in our present passage. It is not necessary to outline the controversy that has developed over the centuries

---

[11] Article by Ulrich Wilckens and Gerhard Kelber, TDNT, Vol. IX, pp. 418-423.

[12] TDNT, Vol. VIII, pp. 573-589.

about the proper meaning of this term.

Perhaps a better way for us to understand the meaning of ὑπόστασις is for us to agree with a suggestion made in Wilckens and Kelber's article, and accepted substantially by Köster, which is that there is a parallelism between the two phrases "radiance of God's glory" and "exact representation of his being."[13] Maybe the best way to understand all this is to say simply, "Jesus is God."

### ...sustaining all things by his powerful word.

The Greek slightly changes the word order of this phrase, so that it could read equally well as, "sustaining all things by the word of his power." In either case, it is God's word that is emphasized.

This idea parallels the fact that in the first place God created all things, also by the word of His power. We recall that during the six days of creation it was an almost effortless task for Him. Nine times over we read, "God said..." (Gen. 1:3, 6, 9, 11, 14, 20, 24, 26, 29), and all creation came into being. When we think of the years'-long diligent labor it takes thousands of people and machines to dream, design, fashion, and assemble just one Boeing 747 airplane, we may begin to comprehend what power God possesses to be able to begin with nothing and by a word to make billions of galaxies as well as infinitesimally small pieces of atoms, not to speak of living creatures so complicated that people still are discovering additional things about the secrets of how they subsist. We who accept the record of scripture acknowledge that it was God who made everything in the first place. We also willingly acknowledge that we could not in the slightest degree begin to create anything we observe, certainly not out of nothing; nor could we "invent" something that God has not already thought of.

After we agree that God creates, it is well for us also to agree that God sustains all that He has created. We must accept two facets of this truth. First, we must allow that God is actively involved in sustaining all He has made. He did not set everything off spinning, and then go away to hunt or sleep or do other things to forget His creation. God not only knows what is happening, He also decides what will happen. I realize that "predestination" is an evil term to some people, but since the Bible uses the very term four times (Rom. 8:28 and 29; Eph. 1:5 and 11), and other synonyms such as election, one cannot escape its truth without denying the truth of all of scripture.

The second thing we must accept about God's sustaining power over His universe is that it is not we who determine our own destinies. The first fault, and continuing greatest fault, of all humankind is that we want to do only what we want to do, and to have everything our way. One of my saintly seminary professors, Dr. Georges Barrois, used to tell us in class, "Adam said, 'I'm going to do as I damned please.' And he was!" Unfortunately for Eve as

---

13 Wilckens and Kelber's article, *op.cit.*

well and for every one of their descendants, the same holds true. I need not provide you with a treatise on predestination and free will. There are sufficient dissertations on the subject, and my addition would be unlikely to sway anyone. Simply let me repeat: the doctrine of God's decrees (which encompasses the doctrine of predestination) is inescapably taught in scripture. So get used to it.

It is Jesus who by His word does the sustaining. We may review John 1:1, 14, and 17, as well as I John 1:1-4, to remind us that our loving Savior is the Word. Therefore, the author of Hebrews is telling us that Jesus sustains all things by Himself. He is both Creator and Sustainer.

### After he had provided purification for sins....

One of the things we shall discuss later, especially in chapter 9, is that the purification Jesus provided for us is "better than" whatever purification was offered by the Old Testament sacrifices. As a matter of fact, Jesus' sacrifice for sin was the only means of purification and salvation to be offered to humans either in the past or in the future (as chapter 10 points out so clearly).

The Old Testament word for such purification is "atonement." In those days, and still today, atonement is just about the most important concept for Jews who remain faithful to their religion. Surely you have heard of the Jewish "Day of Atonement." The Hebrew word for atonement is כִּפֶּר. This noun comes from the verb כָּפַר, which principally means "to cover." This is a beautiful picture of what God does for a repentant sinner; He literally covers that person's sins with His own righteousness, so that God Himself never again looks on those sins. Let us flesh out that picture with a statement Isaiah made (Is. 61:10):

> I delight greatly in the LORD;
> > my soul rejoices in my God.
> For he has clothed me with garments of salvation
> > and arrayed me in a robe of righteousness,
> as a bridegroom adorns his head like a priest,
> > and as a bride adorns herself with her jewels.

You have never seen an oriental bride, nor will you. She is covered with her sheet-like garment, so that not even hands, feet, nor eyes are visible. When God looks upon a repentant sinner whose sins have been covered with His own "garments of salvation" and "robe of righteousness," not even God can see those sins. What a beautiful picture Isaiah has given us of Christ's purification from sins; how infinitely thankful we ought to be that He did it for us!

Purification of sins is what Jesus Christ came into the world to perform. Over a Christmas leave during my time at the U. S. Naval Academy, I went with my parents to their church, the Second Presbyterian Church in Lincoln, NE. During the Sunday school hour the Minister invited me to visit the classes in session. We entered the kitchen, where an adult class was meeting. As soon as we were seen, one class member called out, "Oh, Pastor, we are so glad you are here. We have been discussing a question for quite a while, and we don't know the answer. What was the purpose of the incarnation?" Apparently they were all aware of the significance of Christmas in defining the term "incarnation." As soon as I heard the question, Paul's word to his young friend in I Tim. 1:15 popped into my head: "Christ Jesus came into the world to save sinners...." The Pastor, after hardly a moment of hesitation, said, "That is a good question. Why don't you discuss it further among yourselves, and see if you can come up with a good answer?" Not wanting to interfere with the Pastor's influence in the congregation, I kept quiet. But from that day I have wondered whether the Pastor himself really knew the central purpose of the incarnation.

Surely other passages support the purpose of the incarnation. John gave us wonderful encouragement in I John 1:9, "If we confess our sins, he is faithful and just and will forgive us our sins and *purify* us from all unrighteousness." Paul wrote (in Tit. 3:5), "He saved us through the *washing* of rebirth and renewal by the Holy Spirit." And after Paul had made a long list of sins in I Cor. 6:9-10, he continued with this promise, "And that is what some of you were. But you were *washed*, you were *sanctified*, you were *justified* in the name of the Lord Jesus Christ and by the Spirit of our God" (emphasis added in all these passages). You may search for further references.

The books of Moses make many references to washings for purification of the people. Parts of the burnt offerings were to be washed (Lev. 1:9); if blood from the sin offering was splattered on a garment, it had to be washed off in a holy place (Lev. 6:27); if anyone touched the carcass of an unclean insect or animal, he was required to wash his clothes and he remained unclean until evening (Lev. 11:25 and 28); after a person had been cured of an infectious skin disease, or a sore with an itch, he had to wash his clothes after the priest had pronounced him clean (Lev. 13:6 and 34); a person who stayed in a house containing mildew needed to wash his clothes (Lev. 14:47); a man or woman who had a discharge from any part of his or her body was considered unclean, and had to wash; further, whoever touched an unclean person or part of his body had to wash himself and his clothes; and if such an unclean person touched a clay pot, the pot had to be broken and discarded (Lev. 15). Aaron was required to wash before dressing for the Day of Atonement, probably the most special day for the Israelites (Lev. 16). Anyone who ate anything found dead, or torn by wild animals, needed to wash both his clothes and himself in order to be cleansed (Lev. 17:15).

Not only the priests, also the Levites had to be cleansed (Num. 8:5-7): The LORD said to Moses, "Take the Levites from among the other Israelites and make them ceremonially clean. To purify them, do this: Sprinkle the water of cleansing on them; then have them shave their whole bodies and wash their clothes, and so purify themselves."
Numbers 19 describes how the priests were to concoct the "water of cleansing," which was to be used "for purification from sin" (verse 9). The

spoils of battle had to be cleansed either with fire if it could withstand that, or with the water of cleansing if it could not, in order to be purified (Num. 31:21-24), and the soldiers had to wash their clothes as well. Chapter 31 has to do with the war with evil Midian, but the same may have applied to battles with other peoples as well.

There was just one problem with all the Old Testament ritual washings and cleansings and purifications. None of them did a complete job of cleansing the people, no matter how sincere they were. Later on we shall see that the priestly sacrifices did not expiate sin (10:11): "Day after day every priest stands and performs his religious duties; again and again he offers the same sacrifices, which can never take away sins." The passage continues that it was Jesus' perfect sacrifice that perfected the believers.

Jesus was required to shed His blood as the way to purify us from sin. We shall see more of this in our discussion of Heb. 9:22. Some people shun the book of Hebrews, accusing it of being a "bloody book." Truly it is a bloody book—and for good reason. The whole Old Testament was built on the system of sacrifices of animals and birds on the altar in Jerusalem, as the only way to satisfy God's demand for justice against the ubiquitous sins of all the people. To complete the picture, the gospels in particular and the rest of the New Testament in general show that Christ is God Himself come in human form to pay for the sins of the people to justify God's forgiving them.

Let us gather together the several strands and weave them into the whole cloth. God made the universe and put mankind into it, all without flaw (Gen. 1:31): "God saw all that he had made, and it was very good." God then commanded Adam and Eve, "...you must not eat from the tree of the knowledge of good and evil, for when you eat of it you will surely die" (Gen. 2:17). They did eat, and they died that very day, spiritually. The same fate has overtaken us all, for David wrote in Ps. 14:3,

> All have turned aside,
>> they have together become corrupt;
> there is no one who does good,
>> not even one.

Paul reiterated what God had already said to all humanity through our first parents, "the wages of sin is death" (Rom. 6:23). Since God is a just God, He had bound Himself to punish all sin by death. However, He was willing to accept a substitute death to pay that punishment, and He did so through the death of His own Son Jesus Christ (Heb. 9:28): "...so Christ was sacrificed once to take away the sins of many people." Paul completed the picture best in Rom. 8:3-4. He wrote,

> What the law was powerless to do in that it was weakened by the sinful nature, God did by sending his own Son in the likeness of sinful man to be a sin offering. And so he condemned sin in sinful man, in order that the righteous requirements of the law might be fully met in us, who do not live according to the sinful nature but according to the Spirit.

If it were not for sin, every one of us humans would be perfect. Jesus would not be our Savior, because there would be no need for a Savior. We would all live in total innocence, in perfect harmony with all the expectations of God. We would not need to study the Bible in order to search how to get saved, or to discover what is right and wrong. It is not God's fault that Hebrews is a "bloody book." We have brought that curse upon ourselves. Let us never succumb to the wiles of those who would argue that we must rid ourselves of such a "vile" or "useless" book; by it we learn both why we are condemned and the one way to be freed from that condemnation.

### ...he sat down....

Even angels, who were made a little higher than we, and other heavenly beings, are required to stand before Almighty God. The prophet said in Zech. 6:5, "The angel answered me, 'These are the four spirits of heaven, going out from standing in the presence of the LORD of the whole world.'" John affirms this in Rev. 7:11, "All the angels were standing around the throne and around the elders and the four living creatures." But they did more. The verse continues, "They fell down on their faces before the throne and worshiped God...." If such spirit creatures must stand or prostrate themselves, then we mere human beings must also stand in awe and adoration of the Ruler of the Universe. John saw that this would be so in heaven, for he saw "a great multitude that no one could count, from every nation, tribe, people and language, standing before the throne and in front of the Lamb" (Rev. 7:9). If we do not stand before God, we will take a position of even greater humility. When John saw the vision of Christ, he reported (in Rev. 1:17), "I fell at his feet as though dead." When all beings in heaven saw Jesus take up the scroll to open it, "...the four living creatures and the twenty-four elders fell down before the Lamb" (Rev. 5:8). At other times the twenty-four elders were not required to stand or prostrate themselves, but Rev. 4:4 tells us, "Surrounding the throne were twenty-four other thrones, and seated on them were twenty-four elders. They were dressed in white and had crowns of gold on their heads." They may be the only creatures, other than Jesus, to whom is given the privilege of sitting in the presence of God.

### ...at the right hand....

Even the twenty-four elders are not given such an exalted place at which to sit near God as is our Savior, for it is said "he sat down *at the right hand* of the Majesty in heaven."

Foolish James and John, though they were in the inner circle of three favorite apostles of Jesus, may have thought that by this exalted status they should be privileged to sit next to Jesus in His glory. We read the story in Matt. 20:20-23 (its parallel is in Mark 10:35-40). The two brothers somehow inveigled their mother to ask this favor for them. She asked that one be given the right to sit at Jesus' right hand and the other at His left in the kingdom. Why I say the brothers must have initiated the request is because when Jesus heard it, he turned to the men and said to them, "You don't know what you are asking....Can you drink the cup I am going to drink?" When they answered (boastfully, and probably quite ignorantly) in the affirmative, Jesus did not actually refuse to fulfill their request, but rather pointed out that He did not have the authority to grant it. If Jesus was unable to give such permission, my strong presumption is that only the Father had such authority. No one else is greater than Jesus. Jesus acknowledged that His Father was greater, as He told His disciples in John 14:28, "...the Father is greater than I." Some of you will recall that Jesus also said in the same book (John 10:30), "I and the Father are one." There is no contradiction in these two statements, because in the first Jesus was acknowledging His filial submission to His Father; while in the second He was pointing out that both were members of the one triune God.

### ...of the Majesty....

As has been mentioned already, even the angels must give obeisance to God. Since angels are higher creatures than anything we apprehend with our five senses in the world, it stands to reason that everything in the world must exalt God because of His majesty. We like to compare ourselves with others, and try to find something in which we are superior to them, and sometimes we rightly discern. However, God is not merely superior to us; He is in a completely separate category from all His creation. He not only made us, He also reigns supreme over us. No one, not even Satan, is able to withstand God's will, nor can we. I confess to being more than a little queasy at the thought of some people who consider themselves so nearly equal to God that they feel free to call Him by familiar terms, or to say, as the title of a book suggests, "Are you running with me, Jesus?"—as if He had better shape up and catch up with us if He knows what is good for Him. Jesus is able to sit "at the right hand of the *Majesty* in heaven," solely because He is that Majesty on high. To me, one visible indication of how fully we recognize God's majesty is to observe what clothing people wear to church, God's house, to worship Him. When I was a boy, the very first suit I owned was given me, at age thirteen, by my uncle to wear at my brother's funeral. Before that, what I wore every Sunday to Sunday school and church was a shirt and tie, trousers, socks, the very best I had, clean and pressed; and the only pair of shoes I owned, polished for church. Some people have told me they don't want to make a "show" of fancy clothing at church, like the Pharisees did, so they wear grubbies, and not always clean, and surely not the best they own or wear on other occasions. One young fellow I confronted about his dress in church used the excuse of not wanting to show off. I asked him whether, if he ever got invited to the White House to dine with the President, he would wear his

Sunday grubbies to the banquet. He said, "Of course not; I'd wear the very best I had, and if that wasn't good enough, I'd go buy something better." If asked him if that were the case, whether he thought more highly of the President than of God. His response was that he didn't want to impress people with fancy clothes in church. All that brings me to one conclusion: if you fear dressing too nicely, so that you may offend people who might think you are a Pharisee, is it not true then that you are thinking about what people think of you instead of whether God is pleased with not only what you wear but what you think of His majesty?

The act of giving worship to God is the supreme form of acknowledging His majesty. Both the Old Testament word for worship, שָׁחָה, and its New Testament counterpart, προσκυνέω, mean in their milder sense, "to bow down," and in their most profound sense, "to prostrate oneself before." In biblical times, people often prostrated themselves in their act of worshiping God. Even in the presence of people such as kings, priests, and prophets, people showed their lowly estate by falling flat on the ground in humble recognition of their differing estates. Today, people almost never lie face down on the floor or ground to worship God. We may claim that we are prostrating ourselves *spiritually* or at least mentally to demonstrate our lowly position, but I sometimes wonder whether we really do recognize the majesty of God as the One who created and sustains all His creation.

### ...in heaven.

Jesus came to earth from heaven, and He went back to heaven fifty days after His resurrection. Heaven is His rightful home. After Jesus had fed the five thousand, they ran to the other side of the Sea of Galilee to find Him again, and He said to them (John 6:38), "I have come down from heaven not to do my will but to do the will of him who sent me." Jesus also agreed to the Father in John 17:11, "I am coming to you." And when He ascended from His disciples, the two angels told them (Acts 1:11): "This same Jesus, who has been taken from you into heaven, will come back in the same way you have seen him go into heaven." Also, when the Pharisees challenged Jesus, He spoke plainly to them of their different origins (John 8:23): "You are from below; I am from above. You are of this world; I am not of this world."

Jesus' eternal home is heaven. He existed there forever, and He will continue to be there through all eternity. He came to earth to provide a way for us to get to heaven, but that is only our adopted home, which we will inhabit after we leave life in this world. Because the Father has adopted us into His family (Rom. 8:23), we will be invited one day to live in His home: "...we wait eagerly for our adoption as [children], the redemption of our bodies."

Although Jesus' proper home is heaven, and He belongs there, yet He was willing to enter this sinful world in order to die for our sins. Psalm 8:4

tells us (in the KJV), "What is man, that thou art mindful of him? and the son of man, that thou visitest him?" It is likely that it was Jesus who "visited" Abraham on the plains of Mamre when He assured Abraham that he and Sarah would have a son. All this is recorded in Gen. 8. We are told that three "men" appeared to Abraham, but two of them were no doubt angels, as noted in Gen. 18:22 and 19:1, but the third was "the LORD," according to 18:13, 17, 20, and other verses in that chapter. "The LORD" must have been Jesus, in a pre-incarnate appearance, since John assures us in John 1:18 that no human has ever seen God. However, John must have been talking of the Father, since John himself leaned on Jesus' breast at the Last Supper; yet John wrote as strongly as any other biblical author that Jesus most certainly is God, as evidenced in the trilogy of verses John 1:1, 14, and 17, where he writes that God is the Word who became flesh and dwelt among us. Now, if Jesus was willing to come to earth to visit us, and further to die for our salvation, is it too much for Him to ask us to visit our neighbors to let them know the wonderful news of Jesus' dying for all those who believe in Him as Savior and Lord?

**Heb. 1:4. So he became as much superior to the angels....**

In this fourth verse, we begin to get into the very heart of what the book of Hebrews is all about. The author begins in no uncertain terms to tell us that Jesus' ministry is *better than* any ministry described in the Old Testament, and He is *better than* any person or group of people who administered or participated in that earlier ministry.

There may come confusion in the minds of some people because of the way the NIV translates the beginning of verse 4. We read, "So he became as much superior to the angels...." The implication of such a translation is that at one time in the past, Jesus was either inferior to, or at best merely equal to, the angels. But the Greek verb for "became," γίνομαι, has a sizable cluster of meanings as used in the New Testament. One definition is in fact "to become;" but it can also mean merely "to exist" without regard for either beginning or ending times. It is possible to assume, if necessary, that Jesus could not have been superior to them before angels were created, and then by their creation He immediately was better than they. Since Jesus existed eternally because He was not created, and since the angels were created by Jesus, and since Jesus never changed (Heb. 13:8), He was superior to them for as long as comparison could be made under those circumstances.

Why is it important to make a contrast between Jesus and angels? It is important for at least two excellent reasons. One reason is that angels were created as superior to humans or to any other creatures in the world. Secondly, the ancient Jews held the angels in exceedingly high esteem in their ritual and religion. Therefore, anyone considered higher than humans was greatly venerated by them.

The Jews regarded angels very highly for perhaps the main reason that angels were transmitters of the law to them. We know the Jews held the law in excessively high esteem. We read in all the gospels how Jesus debated with the Jews on the value of the law compared to other matters. For instance, in Matt. 23:23, Jesus criticized the Pharisees and other "teachers of the law" for emphasizing certain aspects of the law (such as tithing spices) while utterly neglecting more important aspects such as "justice, mercy and faithfulness." In fact, the whole of chapter 23 is Jesus' tirade against the teachers of the law and the Pharisees for their abuse and over-use of the law. Perhaps His greatest condemnation is in verse 13, "You shut the kingdom of heaven in men's faces. You yourselves do not enter, nor will you let those enter who are trying to." By their exaltation of the law, the Pharisees not only lost their own salvation; they prevented others from finding it.

Here is the biblical basis for the idea that the Jews believed the angels were the givers of the law to the people. In Deut. 33:2, in the KJV, we read, "The LORD came from Sinai, and rose up from Seir unto them; he shined forth from mount Paran, and he came with ten thousands of saints: from his right hand went a fiery law for them." The "ten thousands of saints" were supposedly God's angels. The verse is rather difficult to translate, and there is some dispute about it. The NIV translation mentions neither angels nor law, but follows a variant reading. The original Hebrew uses one of the words for "law" in the verse, but the last clause of the Septuagint is translated into English: "From his right hand there are angels with him" (my translation).

Further evidence that the Jews believed that angels mediated the law to them through Moses is found in several places in the New Testament. In Acts 7:53, Stephen defended himself before his accusers "who have received the law that was put into effect through angels but have not obeyed it." In addition, Paul says in Gal. 3:19, "The law was put into effect through angels by a mediator."

Virtually everyone would agree that angels are higher creatures than humans. One exception would be the Sadducees, who refused to believe in even the existence of angels. The apostle Paul, in his defense before the Sanhedrin, declared himself to be a dyed-in-the-wool Pharisee, as opposed to the Sadducees (both parties were represented in the Sanhedrin). Following that is an editorial comment by Luke in Acts 23:8: "The Sadducees say that there is no resurrection, and that there are neither angels nor spirits...." But angels are better than people, because they live in the spirit realm, which is much more sophisticated than the earthly realm; their ordinary place of abode is heaven; they are able to appear and disappear at will (see Gideon's encounter with one in Jud. 6:11 and 21); and they are used to defeat God's enemies, as when the angel of death smote Egypt's firstborn in the final plague in Moses' day. Most of Ex. 12 uses the words that it was the Lord Himself who smote the

27

firstborn, but in verse 23 we have an indication that God had an intermediary to do the actual work:

> When the LORD goes through the land to strike down the Egyptians, he will see the blood on the top and sides of the doorframe and will pass over that doorway, and he will not permit the destroyer to enter your houses and strike you down.

It is possible, therefore, that throughout the account of the Passover event we are to understand that it was the "angel of death" who destroyed the firstborn of Egypt and left the Israelites unscathed. John Calvin, in his commentary on the Pentateuch, said,[14] "The angel, whom God had delegated for afflicting Egypt, is here undoubtedly called 'the destroyer;' and, although He often executes His judgments by evil angels, it is to be gathered from other passages that this was one of the elect angels, who also was the minister of the people's deliverance under Christ as the Head." In that same vein, we read in Acts 1:18 that Judas bought the potter's field in which he was buried. But the gospels say it was the priests who bought the field. Even today we say "I did so-and-so," when it was actually someone else who did it. The Bible uses this thought process as well. For instance, in II Chron. 4:18 (KJV) we read, "...and Solomon made all these vessels..," when it was actually literally hundreds if not thousands of common laborers who did the actual work. And in Matt. 11:2-3 (KJV) we read that John the Baptist, who was then in prison, "sent two of his disciples, and said unto him...." In the Greek, the singular verb requires a singular (implied) subject. John didn't speak directly to Jesus, but he *did* speak, but only through his disciples.

It was for all these reasons, then, that the Jews held angels in most high esteem. Therefore, if Jesus is "better than" the angels, and if the author could convince the Jews that this is so, then they ought to be in great awe of Him because He is superior.

### ...as the Name he has inherited is superior to theirs.

The name (or names) Jesus inherited is superior to the names given to any of the angels. The name "Jesus" is the New Testament equivalent of the Old Testament "Joshua," and means "Savior;" the name "angel" is merely a "messenger." "Christ" is the "Messiah," the "Anointed One;" no angel was ever anointed (however, other special people in the Old Testament were anointed, such as Kings Saul and David, see I Sam. 16:13; Aaron the first High Priest and his successors, see Ex. 40:13; and strangely even Cyrus, Isaiah 45:1, was called God's "anointed," probably because he helped some Jews return to Jerusalem to rebuild the temple). Jesus was even given the name "God" as in Is. 7:14 (Immanuel) and 9:6 (the Mighty God), but such a name was never given to any angel. Although angels are probably referred to as sons of God in Gen. 6:2 and Job 1:6 (footnote), Jesus as the only true Son

---

[14] Calvin, John, CALVIN'S COMMENTARIES: 1 THE PENTATEUCH. This quotation from page 536.

28

of God is in a completely separate category of relationship to the Father. The author of Hebrews now presents a fuller explanation of these names of Jesus, and compares them with names given to angels.

### Heb. 1:5.    For to which of the angels did God ever say....

The author's question is obviously rhetorical; it is just as obviously certain what answer the author intended. We see immediately that whoever wrote the book of Hebrews fully intended to rely solely on his scriptures, the Old Testament, as the supreme authority for every argument he propounds. He introduces his letter with the concept: "God spoke." He peppers his book with no less than one hundred sixty-nine direct quotations from, and allusions to, passages in the Old Testament. His example is worthy of our emulation today. For what greater authority do we Christians have regarding who God is and what He does and what He requires us to do than the Bible? Certainly the earth, the heavens, and all that is in them are a testimony to God's being and work; but such testimony is subject to much controversy and varied interpretation. We do well to heed what we learn from the universe in which we live; but that is not the final word on God. Some people claim that the Holy Spirit is our source of all we must believe about God and His activities; but the knowledge of the Holy Spirit and His activities is highly subjective at best, as is evidenced by the varied ideas that rage about Him today. Still other people reject the Bible as their authority for what they believe about God and Jesus Christ, claiming that they can appeal to Him directly through prayer. Of course prayer is one of the very most important means of learning of God and His will, but how can one claim to know that what he has learned through prayer is more than the figment of his own imagination tinted heavily by his raging passions, without some objective standard by which to test his thoughts? From the beginning of its writing, the Bible has been, and continues to be, the only indelible rule to point us to the true knowledge of God the Trinity. It is true that the Bible must be interpreted correctly, but the Bible's best interpreter is itself.

Jesus used scripture to confute and defeat Satan at His temptation. All three synoptic gospels (Matt. 4:1-11; Mk. 1:13; Lu. 4:1-13) have a record, however brief, of the temptation. (Although John does not mention the event in his gospel, he lists the three classes of temptation from Satan in his first letter, I John 2:16, "...the cravings of sinful man, the lust of his eyes and the boasting of what he has and does..."). The first temptation, called "the lust of the flesh" in the KJV, was Satan's effort to get Jesus to change stones into bread because He was hungry after forty days of fasting. Jesus responded with scripture (Deut. 8:3, quoted in Lu. 4:4): "Man does not live on bread alone." The second temptation, the lust of the eyes, was to show Jesus all the kingdoms of the world; Satan offered them all to Jesus just as if he owned them and Jesus did not. Again, Jesus' response was from scripture, this time Deut. 6:13, quoted in Lu. 4:8: "It is written: 'Worship the Lord your God and serve him only.'" Satan decided in his final temptation (the "pride of life" of the KJV), to do what Jesus had already done twice—quote from scripture—and invite Jesus to throw Himself from the high pinnacle of the temple in Jerusalem, and as an inducement reminded Jesus of the promise in Ps. 91:11-12, quoted in Lu. 4:10-11:

> He will command his angels concerning you
> > to guard you carefully;
> they will lift you up in their hands,
> > so that you will not strike your foot against a stone.

Although Satan quoted the Psalm correctly, he certainly misused it as is evidenced in Jesus' scriptural reply (v. 12): "Jesus answered, 'It says: "Do not put the Lord your God to the test"'" (Deut. 6:16).

Although there was no written scripture in the days of Adam and Eve, still God had spoken directly to the couple, and doubtless both they and Satan recalled the words; still both Eve and Satan misquoted what God had said. Satan began the tragedy of errors by asking Eve (Gen. 3:1), "Did God really say, 'You must not eat from any tree in the garden'?" Of course that was not what God really said; rather He said (Gen. 2:16), "You are free to eat from any tree in the garden; but you must not eat from the tree of the knowledge of good and evil, for when you eat of it you will surely die." Satan sought to confuse Eve by misquoting what God had said. And he certainly did confuse her; for she added to what God had said in her reply (3:2-3), "We may eat fruit from the trees in the garden, but God did say, 'You must not eat fruit from the tree that is in the middle of the garden, and you must not touch it, or you will die.'" Satan knew he had Eve's attention when she added erroneously, "and you must not touch it." Then Satan compounded his scrambling of God's exact words by responding, "You will not surely die....For God knows that when you eat of it your eyes will be opened, and you will be like God, knowing good and evil." Satan was not only a liar; he was a deceiver. The first part of his response to Eve was an outright lie—whether God said it or not, and He did, it was still a lie: "You will not surely die." Satan was fully aware that "the wages of sin is death." How Satan knew to say the second part of his response to Eve we cannot know, because God never told Adam and Eve that if they ate the forbidden fruit they would become like gods with respect to knowing good and evil. Perhaps especially because it was a true statement, it was more attractive to Eve, so she fell into Satan's temptation, and with her fall she caused all humanity to fall with her, and with Adam whom she tempted.

Near the beginning of my ministry, a high school girl came to my office with one of her questions about life as a Christian. After I began to offer an answer, she interrupted with a tinge of irritation, "Mr. Teply, why do you always answer every question I ask you with some verse of scripture?" My response was in these general terms: I use scripture because it is the very best answer I can give you, since scripture is totally true, and is the best guide for anything we want to know about God or ourselves or what we ought to do. I might want to give you an answer from my heart or head, but that would be useless guidance, since I am fallible. But God's word will guide you without flaw, as long as you understand correctly what that word says.

### "You are my Son...."

Verse 5 contains two quotations from the Old Testament, both regarding the title "Son" which the Father gave to Jesus. The first is from Ps. 2:7:

> I will proclaim the decree of the LORD:
> He said to me, "You are my Son;
> today I have become your Father."

Part of the quotation from the Father to the Son not quoted in Heb. 1:5 continues in the next verse of the Psalm, which elaborates on the high estate in which the Father places His Son:

> "Ask of me,
> and I will make the nations your inheritance,
> the ends of the earth your possession.
> You will rule them with an iron scepter;
> you will dash them to pieces like pottery."

The author of Hebrews is attempting to make a large contrast between the Son and angels, as is evidenced by the opening words, "To which of the angels did God ever say...?" This is another rhetorical question, whose obvious answer the author expects, is twofold: 1. To no angel did the Father ever say such a thing; and 2. To Jesus the Father did in fact say it.

It may be questioned by some students of the Old Testament whether the Father never did call any angels His Sons. Appeal may be made to Gen. 6:2, where we read, "...the sons of God saw that the daughters of men were beautiful, and they married any of them they chose;" and two verses later we read something similar: "The Nephilim were on the earth in those days—and also afterward—when the sons of God went to the daughters of men and had children by them. They were the heroes of old, men of renown." It may be argued that "the sons of God" were simply angels, surely of a different category of creation from human beings. Since, however, the scripture does not actually call "the sons of God" angels, it is impossible to prove that they were intended to be called His sons. Further, in verse 4, quoted here, it appears that the Nephilim were the progeny of the "sons of God" and the "daughters of men;" the end of the verse calls them "men of renown." The "Nephilim"[15] were simply "giants,"[16] perhaps after the order of Goliath of Gath, so they may not have been angels at all. If that is the case, then the Father here did not call angels "sons."

---

[15] The word for "Nephilim" is found only here and in Num. 13:33.

[16] Brown, Driver and Briggs, page 658.

31

The second reference to "sons of God" may be more difficult to distance from angels. It is found in three places in Job: 1:6; 2:1; and 38:7. Unfortunately, the translators of the NIV have changed the term "sons of God" that is found in the Hebrew text to "angels." This change is an interpretation based on a totally unwarranted assumption, at least if there is any validity to the argument above related to Gen. 6:2 and 4. Beyond that argument, we see that Satan is likely although not assuredly one of the angels, though fallen, since he is never actually called an "angel" in scripture. Satan is, however, linked to fallen angels in Rev. 12:9, where we read of "Satan...and his angels with him;" and Jesus in Matt. 25:41 talks about the "eternal fire prepared for the devil and his angels." He is surely a spirit being, and dwells in the spirit realm (see Eph. 6:11-12 as one of several such references). At any rate, in the two instances in Job where the sons of God are mentioned along with Satan (1:6 and 2:1), the "sons of God" seem to be separated from "Satan," so that even if we should agree that Satan is a fallen angel, that does not necessarily mean that the "sons of God" are also angels.

Having questioned whether the "sons of God" mentioned in the Old Testament are actually angels, let us examine the matter from a different perspective. We have discussed this matter briefly under Heb. 1:2, "Spoken by a Son," but it is worth telling here as well. For the sake of argument, let us suppose that angels are in fact "sons of God." It is also true that people are also called "sons of God," or "children of God," in passages such as John 1:12-13 ("...to all who received him, to those who believed in his name, he gave the right to become children of God—children born not of natural descent, nor of human decision or a husband's will, but born of God;" in Lu. 20:36, where Jesus in His dispute with the Sadducees over the resurrection, says of people, "They are God's children, since they are children of the resurrection;" and in I John 3:1 ("How great is the love the Father has lavished on us, that we should be called children of God! And that is what we are!"). In line with that, Jesus was willing to call us "brothers." This idea is found in several places: Matt. 12:49 parallel to Mk. 3:34-35 ("Pointing to his disciples, [Jesus] said, 'Here are my mother and my brothers. For whoever does the will of my Father in heaven is my brother and sister and mother'"); Matt. 25:40 ("...whatever you did for one of the least of these brothers of mine, you did for me"); and Matt. 28:10 ("Go and tell my brothers to go to Galilee; there they will see me").

If, however, even human beings are called "children of God," then we must look at another aspect of whether God the Father ever called any angel His "Son." It is important to realize that human beings, when referred to as "children of God," are divided into two major overlapping categories. In the first place, all humans are called "children of God" by virtue of their having been created by God. Even the pagans claimed that. The apostle Paul in his sermon to the Athenians reminded them (Acts 17:28): "'For in [God] we live and move and have our being.' As some of your own poets have said, 'We are his offspring.'" However, in all the passages cited above which refer to humans as "children of God," we must note emphatically that only that part of the human population which is committed to Jesus Christ as Lord and Savior are called "children of God."

Years ago I heard a story which illustrates this difference. A young boy built a sailboat. He wanted to see whether it was "seaworthy," so he took it down to the river and set it afloat. It sailed merrily along, but the wind and current carried it away from him down the stream. He followed it for a long way, until he lost sight of it and could not follow it farther. Several months later, the boy happened by a shop where he saw his boat in the window. Gleefully he ran into the store and told the owner, "Sir, that's my boat in the window. I lost it in the river, and I want it back." The kindly owner replied, "I'm sorry, son, but I bought that boat from someone who brought it into the store. If you want it, you'll have to pay for it." The lad was very sad, but thought to himself, "I really want my boat back; so I'll work until I have enough money to pay for it." He ran errands and did odd jobs, saving all his earnings. Finally, he went back to the store and purchased the boat. Overjoyed that he had it back, he said as he left the store, "Little boat, I own you twice over now. I built you in the first place, and now I have bought you back. You are all mine!" In like manner, all people have been created by God, so we all are His children because of that. In addition, there are some people, not all, who have been saved by the blood of Christ who purchased us by His death on the cross. So we belong to God a second time by virtue of the price He paid for us on the cross, so we are "children of God" in a second and special sense, in a separate category from those who have turned away from God's salvation.

This is not the end of the story, however; the most important is yet to come. There is a third category of "Sonship" with respect to God, and that category contains but one Person, Jesus Christ. He is the only Son of God by virtue of the fact that He is God the Word (John 1:1), who became flesh and dwelt among us, full of grace and truth (John 1:14), and His name is Jesus Christ because grace and truth came by Him (John 1:17). There is no other person in that third category, not one human, not one angel, not even an archangel. In order to emphasize the fact that Jesus is in a unique sense God's Son, it may be noted that Jesus referred to the Father only as "My Father," or "your Father." He never called the Father "our Father," except when He was teaching the disciples to pray (Matt. 6:9 and Lu. 11:2), but He did not pray the prayer with them.

The uniqueness of Jesus Christ as the *only* Son of God may be illustrated by another story in Genesis. In the 22nd chapter, we read of God's command to Abraham to take Isaac to a mountaintop and there sacrifice him to God. In 22:2, God said to Abraham, "Take your son, your only son Isaac, whom you love, and go to the region of Moriah." But Isaac was not Abraham's only son, even at that time, for we read about the birth of Ishmael in chapter 16. (Later, after Sarah's death, Abraham had additional children, as recorded in Gen. 25:1-6, six sons of Abraham's wife Keturah, plus unnamed sons of Abraham's concubines. To them all Abraham gave gifts, but his entire inheritance was given to Isaac alone.) Ishmael, though the son of Hagar, was truly the issue of Abraham. Still, God recognized Isaac as the son of promise, and called him Abraham's only son. In like manner then Jesus is the only Son of God, although God may call humans His sons (children) in two different senses, and may even call angels His sons, still Jesus is in the supreme sense, the Son of God.

Whether, then, angels may be called "sons of God" in Genesis 6:2 and 4; or Job 1:6, 2:1, or 38:7; the question is moot, because they may in fact be "sons of God," but in an entirely different sense from God's addressing of His only begotten Son as "My Son." No creature can claim such a title, whether he be in the worldly or spiritual realm.

The Old Testament is not alone in calling Jesus "the Son of God." We read the same attribution in several places in the New Testament as well. When Jesus was baptized, the Voice came from heaven, "This is my Son, whom I love; with him I am well pleased" (Matt. 3:17; and its parallels in Mk. 1:9-11; Lu. 3:21-22). Virtually the same thing is said by the Father on the Mount of Transfiguration: "This is my Son, whom I love; with him I am well pleased. Listen to him!" (Matt. 17:5, and its parallels in Mk. 9:2-13; Lu. 9:28-36).

In discussing the question who may rightly be called "sons of God," it is sufficiently amazing that we should be called "children of God;" it is even more amazing that God Himself should call us "gods." When Jesus spoke with the Jews about His being, they wanted to stone Him "for blasphemy, because you, a mere man, claim to be God" (John 10:33). In response, Jesus said (verse 34), "Is it not written in your Law, 'I have said you are gods'?" This quotation is from Ps. 82:6. But how can we reconcile this quotation with the doctrine that all Christians hold, that there is but one God only and none other? Jesus explained it to the Jews, and His explanation supports the idea above regarding the three distinct categories of "children of God." Jesus said, "If he called them 'gods,' to whom the word of God came—and the Scripture cannot be broken—what about the one whom the Father set apart as his very own and sent into the world?" (John 10:35-36). So we are rightly called not only "children of God," but also "gods;" but there is still an impassable gulf between Jesus as "God" and "the Son of God" and everything else that exists.

### "...today I have become your Father."

Added to the statement in Ps. 2:7, "You are my Son," are the words, "today I have become your Father." The NIV translators no doubt used these words in an attempt to avoid ignorance on the part of the readers who might not understand the words, "This day have I begotten thee" (ASV), which more accurately reflect the original Hebrew. But the translators may have caused more confusion than lucidity by their attempted simplification. For some people will see a difference between begetting and becoming a father. Begetting requires action on the part of the father, while becoming a father implies a passive role, as when the child is finally born. At any rate, it may be asked, "When precisely did the Father beget the Son?" No assistance for an answer comes from either the Psalm or from the book of Hebrews. It may be viewed by some as the moment of conception of Jesus in Mary, of which we read in Matt. 1:18 and Lu. 1:28-35. In the latter passage we read that Jesus "will be called the Son of the Most High" (verse 32), and in verse 35 He "will be called the Son of God." The future tense in each case may lead some to think that Jesus was not "the Son of God" until He was born, but that is not the case. People who had contact with Him would not call Him by any name until they had actually met Him, although He was the eternal Son of God. John 17:5 should be adequate proof that Jesus was God's Son eternally: "And now, Father, glorify me in your presence with the glory I had with you before the world began." In addition, in explaining who Melchizedek was, the author of Hebrews (7:3) pointed out that "like the Son of God he remains a priest forever." The term "today" in this verse, then, may be understood in the sense of God's *eternal* "today." We from our vantage point in history, see only a fraction of time in the world. But God, looking down on all His creation, sees the end from the beginning; eternity is encompassed in His view.

**Or again,**
**"I will be his father,**
**and he will be my son"?**

We have already commented on the first of two Old Testament passages, Ps. 2:7, where God called Jesus "my Son," as pointed out by the author of Hebrews. The other is found in II Sam. 7:14, which is a very important chapter in the whole Bible. Here God promises to King David the establishment of none other than the Messianic kingdom, which will continue forever. God's promise follows on David's expressed intention to build a proper house for God, now that he has built his own cedar palace. God demurres, on the basis that David has been a "bloody" king, as David explains to his son Solomon (I Chron. 22:8): "But this word of the LORD came to me: 'You have shed much blood and have fought many wars. You are not to build a house for my Name, because you have shed much blood on the earth in my sight.'" In spite of God's prohibition for David to build the temple, God still makes a grandiose promise that not only will Solomon be David's successor on the throne, but that "Your house and your kingdom will endure forever before me;

your throne will be established forever" (II Sam. 7:16).  The quotation selected by the author of Hebrews goes much further than the mere earthly Davidic dynasty of which we read in the books of Kings and Chronicles (which dynasty failed in about 586 BC); it includes the kingdom of our Lord and Savior Jesus Christ, who was truly a descendant of David, and thus had the right to David's eternal throne.  No mere human could have fulfilled that prophecy of God; only "the Son" could do it.

The part of the statement in the quotation regarding God's Fatherhood of Jesus simply reinforces the filial position the Son held to the Father.

### Heb. 1:6.  And again, when God brings his firstborn into the world....

Here again the author of Hebrews raises in our minds the question of "when" the Firstborn came into the world.  This is similar to the question raised earlier when the author quoted Ps. 2:7, "today I have become your Father."  It may be profitable to return to that discussion in your reading before proceeding to the further discussion here.

What is the proper definition of the term "firstborn" as used of Jesus in this context?  The Greek word used here is πρωτότοκος, and it is acknowledged that the basic meaning of the term is "firstborn."

Since the idea of Jesus' being the "firstborn from the dead" has no relationship to a timeline, we need not be concerned about the fact that several people were revived before Jesus was resurrected.  Elijah raised the son of the widow of Zarephath (I Kings 17:17-23); Elisha raised the Shunammite's son (II Kings 4:18-37); Elisha's bones in the grave revived an Israelite man, perhaps a soldier (II Kings 13:20-21); Jesus Himself raised Jairus' daughter (probably Matt. 9:18-26; Mk. 5:22-43; Lu. 8:40-56); He also raised the widow of Nain's son (Lu. 7:11-15); and the most famous raising was Jesus' act in behalf of Lazarus (John 11:1-44).  Although there are several other accounts of the raising of people from the dead, all these occurred before Jesus Himself was raised.  However, there is a significant difference between Jesus' resurrection and the other raisings from the dead, because all the others died again, and their true bodily resurrection must wait until the end of the world.  One interesting borderline case is recorded in Matt. 27:51-53, where we learn that when Jesus had died, there was an earthquake and tombs were opened, and people came out and walked the streets of Jerusalem.  Several English versions imply that those people rose from the dead as soon as the tombs were opened.  However, it is possible to omit a period and a comma (there was no punctuation in the original manuscripts) and read that part of the account to say, "...the bodies of many holy people who had died were raised to life and came out of the tombs after Jesus' resurrection, and went into the holy city and appeared to many people."  It is not stated whether they died again and returned to their tombs; but if they did not die, then their resurrection occurred after Jesus' own resurrection, so He would still be, even in point of time, the "firstborn from the dead."

Related to the concept of Jesus as the "firstborn from the dead" is the idea, expressed in three places in the New Testament, of Jesus as the "Author" of God's best gifts to us. In Peter's second great sermon after Pentecost, he called Jesus the "Author of life" (Acts 3:15); the "Author of salvation" (Heb. 2:10); and the "Author and Perfecter of our faith" (Heb. 12:2). It is understood that an author precedes anything he may write, so Jesus must be the "Firstborn" of all His creation.

Having discussed the meaning of the term "firstborn," we now return to the discussion of "when" Jesus was brought into the world as the "firstborn." Since that term really has nothing to do with the matter of being the first in a group of several, nor does it have to do with a timeframe, we are not limited to think of Jesus' appearance upon earth simply as the point at which He was born of Mary. As a matter of fact, Jesus "came into the world" during Abraham's lifetime. We read the story in Gen. 18, when three "men" appeared to Abraham on the horizon one day while he was sitting in front of his tent. Verse 1 tells us that "the LORD" appeared to him. We may be certain it was not the Holy Spirit whom Abraham saw, since a human being cannot see a spirit, and we are sure it was not God the Father whom Abraham saw, since John tells us twice (John 1:18 and I John 4:12), "No one has ever seen God," but it was that same John who leaned on Jesus' breast at the Last Supper (John 13:25). In addition we must include the fact that John was sure that Jesus was God Himself (John 1:1, 14. 17). Therefore, it had to be God the Son whom Abraham saw that day. However, all this is part of the great mystery of the Trinity, because Jesus answered Philip's query about seeing the Father (John 14:9-10): "Anyone who has seen me has seen the Father....Don't you believe that I am in the Father, and that the Father is in me?" Incidentally, when the three personages appeared to Abraham, two were angels, because when Abraham finished pleading for Sodom and Gomorrah, Abraham returned home, and "The two angels arrived at Sodom in the evening..." (Gen. 19:1).

The very statement we have been discussing here, "when God brings his firstborn into the world," is a testimony to the fact that Jesus is "better than" all people and events recorded in the Old Testament; He is preeminent over not only all Old Testament matters, but is preeminent over all creation throughout all time. The author of Hebrews attests to this fact in even the most minute things he writes.

**...he says,**
## "Let all God's angels worship him."
These are words from God the Father about His Son Jesus. They are quoted from Deut. 32:43, but you will not find them in your translation of the Bible, since they do not occur in the original Hebrew text. However, some

ancient manuscripts of the LXX do allude to angels in this verse, while other manuscripts refer to "sons of God," perhaps meaning "angels" (which subject we discussed above). In addition, a footnote to Deut. 32:43 in the NIV states that copies of Deuteronomy in the Dead Sea Scrolls follow the LXX version.[17] Since the LXX was mostly used in the first century AD, the author of Hebrews was familiar with the words he quoted. A similar reference is in Ps. 97:7: "...worship him, all you gods!" Since the Bible makes clear in several places that there are no gods except our one and only living God, the reference in the Psalms most likely refers to angels.

Kleinknecht[18] gives us a probable reason why the LXX translators changed the words "sons of God" to "angels:" "...in order to avoid any suggestion of polytheism," since "The Haggada has gathered together a whole list of OT examples of human pretension," that is, people who claimed to be God, such as "Pharaoh (Ez. 29:9), Sennacherib (II K. 18:35), Nebuchadnezzar (Is. 14:14) and the prince of Tyre (Ez. 28:2)."

Whatever ancient manuscript we choose, it is obvious that the author of Hebrews wants us to understand that it was God the Father who was instructing all the angels to worship God the Son. Because the author included "all" angels, even the archangels Michael and Gabriel, and any others who exist, are required to fall before Jesus Christ in humble obeisance. Since the greater is worshiped by the lesser, the author intends us to understand that Jesus Christ is "better than" all the angels.

Here is the context in which this mandate from God to the angels comes. Moses is at the end of his life. He commands the Levites to put the book of the law (the Pentateuch, of which these words are a part), beside the ark in the Tabernacle (Deut. 31:24-26). Then in poetic form, Moses reminds the people of Israel of their continuing defection from God to idols; that God will wreak vengeance on them for it but will not utterly destroy them. Near the end of the poem, after God has stated what terrible things He will do to Israel in view of all peoples, Moses writes, "Let all God's angels worship him." At this point it is well to remember that it was Jesus—God the Son—who was with the children of Israel during their wandering in the wilderness. The apostle Paul reminds us of this in I Cor. 10:3-4: "They all ate the same spiritual food and drank the same spiritual drink; for they drank from the spiritual rock that accompanied them, and that rock was Christ." That is why Moses' disobedience in this instance was so heinous. When the people were in the Desert of Zin (the story is found in Num. 20:1-13), they murmured against Moses and God because they had no water to drink. God invited Moses to speak to the rock (verse 8) and God would cause water to gush forth to give drink to the people and their animals. Moses was obviously upset with the

---

[17]   Eduard Lohse, article υἱός, in TDNT, Vol. VIII, page 347, note 77, and Georg Bertram, article ὕψιστος, in the same volume, page 617, note 21, confirm this appearance in the Qumran MSS.

[18]   Hermann Kleinknecht, article, θεός, in TDNT, Vol. III.

people for their murmuring (verse 10), so instead of speaking to the rock, he struck it with his staff, not once but twice (verse 11). God in His mercy still allowed the water to flow to quench the people's thirst; but for Moses' disobedience God forbade him to lead the children of Israel into the Promised Land. He told Moses in verse 12, "Because you did not trust in me enough to honor me as holy in the sight of the Israelites, you will not bring this community into the land I give them." Moses' disobedience was not merely in striking the rock, but in striking his own Savior Jesus Christ, who Paul said was that Rock. Jesus Christ Himself alludes to the idea that either He, or the Holy Spirit, is also spiritual water in John 7:38-39: "'Whoever believes in me, as the Scripture has said, streams of living water will flow from within him.' By this he meant the Spirit, whom those who believed in him were later to receive." Again I say, Jesus Christ is "better than" angels.

### Heb. 1:7.  In speaking of the angels he says,
"He makes his angels winds,
his servants flames of fire."

The author of Hebrews now shifts gears; he has quoted three passages from the Old Testament that refer to Jesus Christ, and what the Father thinks of Him. Now the author quotes from a Psalm to show that angels are actually mighty creatures in God's sight. A side detail here is that if angels are so great, and angels are much greater than humans, then Jesus who is far superior to angels must be vastly superior to people. His prime purpose in adding this quotation, however, is to show that the Son must be astounding to be "better than" even the angels. So he quotes Ps. 104:4:

> He makes his angels winds,
> his servants flames of fire.

The NIV version of the verse from the Psalm reads quite differently from the way it is quoted in Hebrews. This is how the Psalm reads:

> He makes winds his messengers [the margin reads "angels"],
> flames of fire his servants.

It is difficult to understand why the translators of the verse in Psalms chose to change the order of the words. They make it seem as though God transformed winds into angels, and flames of fire into His servants. The order of words in the LXX of the Psalm is identical to the order of the Greek words in Hebrews 1:7, and both are compatible with the NIV translation in Hebrews. Although there may be some grammatical permission to reverse the order of the words, it is more likely that the Greek order is more fully compatible with the intent of the New Testament author. The main reason for this is that he introduces the quotation with the words, "In speaking of the angels, he says," intending that the emphasis be on angels rather than on the qualities God attributes to them.

It is important to note that the author relies on scripture as his only authority to prove his point. Throughout his letter he says virtually nothing without backing up each detail from a quotation from his Bible.

When we read, "He makes his angels winds," we need to know that the Greek word for "wind" here, in both the LXX and in Hebrews, is πνεῦμα, which in Greek can mean either "wind," or "breath," or "spirit." In talking with Nicodemus one night, you recall that Jesus said (John 3:8), "The wind blows wherever it pleases. You hear its sound, but you cannot tell where it comes from or where it is going. So it is with everyone born of the Spirit." The same Greek word is used for both "wind" and "Spirit" here. It would seem more sensible to use the translation "spirit" in the Psalm; the author is trying to build up the angels rather than debase them, so that he might show that Jesus Christ is even more exalted than angels could ever be in their highest estate.

The same is true of the second clause of the quotation. Please note that this verse in Psalms is in a grammatical form called synonymous parallelism; that is, the second line essentially repeats what the first line says, but uses different words. If that is so, then the "angels" of the first line are the same as the "servants" in the second. So both the Psalmist and the author of Hebrews intend us to understand that angels in their exalted state are spiritual beings (not mere humans like us), and are shining creatures like flames of fire. One group of creatures that may be considered a class of angels are those called "seraphim," and another called "cherubim." The cherubim held prominent place in Moses' tabernacle in the wilderness, as described in Exodus, because they overshadowed the Mercy Seat and protected the Ark of the Covenant. They were made of pure gold, which shone so brightly it was difficult to look upon them (although the people had no chance to see them). Likewise, there were cherubim of like glory and standing that graced the Holy of Holies in Solomon's temple (see I Kings 6 to 8, and II Chron. 3 to 5). Cherubim are mentioned often in Ezekiel, nearly always in connection with bright lights or flames. One other unique instance where real Cherubim are mentioned is in Gen. 3:24, when God set them to guard the tree of life from the hands of Adam and Eve; these Cherubim were armed with a flaming sword that turned in every direction.

Seraphim are mentioned only in Is. 6:2 and 6, in the account of Isaiah's commissioning by God to be His prophet. They were creatures chosen by God to cleanse Isaiah's lips with the fiery coal from off the altar. The Hebrew word for "saraph," שָׂרָף, comes from a verb root which means "to burn." So the seraphim were brightly burning creatures, manifold more radiant than mere humans could be.

Another use of the word "saraph" is the name of a fiery serpent, probably so called because of the burning effect of its poisonous bite. The word is used in this sense twice in Isaiah: as part of the condemnation of Philistia (14:29), and a similar condemnation of the "animals of the Negev" (30:6). You may recall the story found in Num. 21, when for the thirteenth time the children of Israel murmured against God and Moses in the wilderness, and God sent "fiery serpents" to bite and kill the people (verse 6); and Moses was commanded to make a "fiery serpent" of brass and hang it on a pole, so all who looked on it would not be killed by the real serpent (verse 8). Remember further that Jesus spoke of the brass serpent in John 3:14, and likened its benefit to His own infinitely greater benefit from His hanging on the cross. Fiery serpents were mentioned one more time in the Old Testament, in Deut. 8:15, where God reminded the people that as they had been tormented by the fiery creatures (translated as "venomous snakes" in the NIV) in the desert wanderings, the same thing, among other plagues, would face them if they turned from Him.

One detail of this discussion of the angels, whom God made spirits and flames of fire, is to show how much greater angels are than humans. Angels possess a light of their own, which is far more brilliant than the light that comes from people. Our light comes from Jesus, who says of Himself (John 8:12): "I am the light of the world. Whoever follows me will never walk in darkness, but will have the light of life." When we come to believe in Jesus as Savior and Lord, then we possess His light, but it is only His reflected light that shines from us. For instance, our moon's surface is made of glass beads in large part, so having no light of its own, it must reflect the light of the sun outward from itself. So its reflected light is far more pale that what the sun gives off. Likewise, we can never shine as brightly as Jesus does, although we may shine with great brilliance, as Daniel said of us (Dan. 12:3): "Those who are wise will shine like the brightness of the heavens, and those who lead many to righteousness, like the stars for ever and ever." One such person was John the Baptist, described by Jesus in this way in John 5:35, "John was a lamp that burned and gave light, and you chose for a time to enjoy his light."

Even our reflection is hampered by more than being just a reflection of Christ's light. We, as mirrors, become dusty and sooty with our sinfulness, so the light cannot return from our surface as clearly; some of our sins may be so heinous that it is like some of the silver loosening from the back of the mirror, so that part reflects no light at all. Without the presence of Jesus, we are lifeless and dark. But when Jesus enters our lives and energizes us, then we shine brightly, not of ourselves, but because Jesus has done it in us. Only then do the words of Jesus become meaningful (Matt. 5:16), "Let your light shine before men, that they may see your good deeds and praise your Father in heaven."

**Heb. 1:8.  But about the son, he says,**
**"Your  throne,  O  God,  will  last  for  ever  and ever...."**

Here the author returns to quotations about the Son who is "better

41

than" the angels. He began the series with three quotations that showed how greatly the Father exalted Jesus. Then he added but one quotation to show that the angels were also exalted by God, without comparing them to the Son. But now he returns with two lengthy quotations that show how Jesus is far above angels and everything else that exists.

The first quotation is from Ps. 45:6-7, which at its beginning is attributed to "the sons of Korah." Korah was a member of the priestly tribe, Levi, and we read in Num. 16 of his conspiracy together with two members of the tribe of Reuben (Jacob's firstborn), Dathan and Abiram, in their attempt to overthrow Korah's cousins, Moses and Aaron, from the leadership of the Israelites. For their efforts, the three rebels and their households and tents were buried by God in a rift in the ground that closed again over them. Another two hundred fifty rebel followers were also destroyed by God in fire. However, not all of Korah's children were with him when God's sentence was carried out, because we learn in Num. 26:11 that "the line of Korah, however, did not die out." Therefore, in King David's day there were "sons of Korah" who among other Levites ministered in God's house. Obviously, at least some "Korahites" were musicians for the sacred services, since Psalms 42/43, 44-49, 84, 85, 87, and 88 are all attributed to them.

At the beginning of Ps. 45 (our subject of study now), the authors are no doubt writing about either David or Solomon his son, or about both together, since God's promise of an eternal kingdom was made to them both (II Sam. 7:16 to David, and I Kings 9:5 to Solomon). Then, since God never called either David or Solomon "god," it is utterly certain that verse 6 of the Psalm begins a conversation between God the Father and God the Son. The Father says, "Your throne, O God, will last for ever and ever." It is important to emphasize that here God the Father calls God the Son "God," just as Jesus in the gospels often refers to His Father as "God." They are both "God," still they are one "God" (see John 10:30, where Jesus says, "I and the Father are one").

We should have no difficulty in acknowledging that the sons of Korah were fully aware that Jesus would come into the world one day as both God the Son and the Son of David. As Levites deeply involved in the worship and ceremonies of the house of God, they knew God's promise to Eve that her Descendant would bruise the head of Satan the serpent (Gen. 3:15), and neither David nor Solomon would have kept secret the fact that God had promised them an eternal Descendant (the same as Eve's) to sit on the throne forever. Some people might want to ask: if Jesus was David's Son, how could David call Him God, or Lord (Ps. 110:1)? In fact, Jesus put this question to the Pharisees (Matt. 22:41-46; Mk. 12:35-37; Lu. 20:41-44) after they and others tried to ensnare Him with their questions. Even those Pharisees were aware that the Messiah was to be a descendant of David; further, they remembered that David had called Him "Lord," and were startled, not by Jesus' question about the fact, but only about how it was possible for an ancestor to call one of his descendants "Lord."

God the Father mentions to the Son "your throne," which refers to Jesus' royal status. He was King of the Jews; further, He is called King of kings, and Lord of lords in Rev. 19:16 (the titles are reversed in Rev. 17:14). Paul also calls Jesus King of kings and Lord of lords in I Tim. 6:15. No mere angel was ever given the title "king," let alone King of kings, so Jesus is greater than them all.

The psalmists said Christ's throne would "last for ever and ever." The Hebrew phrase "for ever and ever," עוֹלָם וָעֶד, and its Greek translation in both the LXX (Ps. 44:7) and the New Testament quotation in Heb. 1:8 εἰς τὸν αἰῶνα τοῦ αἰῶνος, are the emphatic way to make explicit that eternity is intended. If the principal terms in either language are used alone, the meaning could be merely a very long period of time, such as an eon or age, or even during the existence of the created world.[19] For that reason alone, we are sure that the author of Hebrews means only Christ, not David or Solomon.

### "...and righteousness will be the scepter of your kingdom."

This statement reads in the Psalm, "A scepter of justice will be the scepter of your kingdom." In the Greek of this verse, both in the LXX and in Hebrews, the term for both "justice" and "righteousness," εὐθύτης, is close in meaning to the more common Greek word, δικαιοσύνη, except that the first word has more to do with a quality of being while the second leans toward the act of doing.[20] Otherwise, both terms mean either justice or righteousness in English. This can be demonstrated in the NIV of two verses in Rom. 3, verses 21 and 26, where the same Greek word and its cognates are used in both verses. Verse 21 is translated "But now a righteousness from God, apart from law, has been made known, to which the Law and the Prophets testify," while verse 26 reads, "...he did it to demonstrate his justice at the present time, so as to be just and the one who justifies the man who has faith in Jesus."

You may recall the beautiful picture of God's justice or righteousness which we find in Is. 61:10. See our discussion of it in Heb. 1:3.

Since some of the angels had fallen from God's will, the angelic realm can never be considered wholly righteous. Jesus, on the other hand, never sinned (see Heb. 4:15, I John 3:5, and several other passages, which will be discussed in connection with Heb. 2:10). Therefore, Jesus' kingdom rightly can be called righteous, but if angels had a kingdom, it would have no such right.

The "scepter" is a symbol of royal authority, like the mace, used in Roman and other lands. A crown is a symbol of position, a mace of power.

[19] This information comes from Brown, Driver and Briggs for the Hebrew terms, and Louw and Nida for the Greek.

[20] Louw and Nida, definitions of two terms.

Balaam predicted the Savior's use of a scepter in his oracle over Israel against Balak King of Moab in Num. 24:17:

> I see him, but not now;
>> I behold him, but not near.
> A star will come out of Jacob;
>> a scepter will rise out of Israel.

You may recall Handel used this verse in the MESSIAH. Also, when Jacob was blessing his twelve sons at the end of his life, he used the same terminology in the blessing of the tribal ancestor of Jesus (Gen. 49:10):

> The scepter will not depart from Judah,
>> nor the ruler's staff from between his feet,
> until he comes to whom it belongs
>> and the obedience of the nations is his.

We read of other instances in Old Testament times when the scepter was used as a symbol of power. When Esther was urged to approach her husband, King Xerxes, (he was known as Ahasuerus in the Hebrew Bible and in the KJV) she knew that unless the king extended the golden scepter to accept her presence, she could be slain. Read about this in Est. 4:11. Also, in Is. 14:5, Isaiah cries out against the king of Babylon:

> The LORD has broken the rod of the wicked,
>> the scepter of the rulers....

Of course, Balaam and the king of Babylon were wicked rulers, far different from Jesus Christ who was the utterly righteous King without rival or equal.

The hallmark of Jesus' eternal kingdom, of course, is righteousness; His kingdom therefore is in sharp contrast to every other kingdom that has ever existed. That is a contributing reason why the kingdom of our Savior is everlasting. Therefore we read in Prov. 14:34:

> Righteousness exalts a nation,
>> but sin is a disgrace to any people.

### Heb. 1:9.
### "You have loved righteousness and hated wickedness...."

This continuation of Ps. 45 is also a continuation of the theme of righteousness noted in the last sentence. Wickedness is the exact opposite of righteousness. We could think of a list of synonyms to help us grasp the full meaning of wickedness: sin, lawlessness, iniquity, evil, immorality, corruption, and the "flesh" as opposed to the "spirit" in Paul's writings. It would not be profitable to expound on a list of sins here (Paul urged his readers in Philippi, and us, in Phil. 4:8: "Finally, brothers, whatever is true, whatever is noble, whatever is right, whatever is pure, whatever is lovely, whatever is admirable—if anything is excellent or praiseworthy—think about such things"); but we may point out for further examination by those interested several lists found in the New Testament: Rom. 1:24-32; I Cor. 6:9-10; Gal.

5:19-21; Eph. 5:3-5; Col. 3:5-9; II Tim. 3:1-9; and scattered places in II Pet. 2. Today it is chic to defame such passages as "clobber verses," especially by those whose sins are listed in them. Such defamation of any part of God's word, however, does not detract from their intensity in God's sight; He will do all He has threatened to do to all those who fail to repent of their sins.

It is said of Jesus in this clause that He has "hated" wickedness. But are not we followers of Christ forbidden to hate? Even more grotesque to some is the idea that God the Father and more particularly God the Son should hate anyone. After all, does not the Bible say, "God so loved the world..."? How then can we accept the idea that God could hate even one person? You have no doubt heard people say, "I could not possibly believe in a God who would hate anyone!" It is possible that this line of reasoning may follow from a person who has an incomplete knowledge of all that scripture says about the character of God. It is less likely that some people would reject the thought that God could hate anyone when they know the Bible says it, but such people cannot accept the whole word of God as true in all its parts, else they would require themselves to believe that God hates not only evil as such, but also people who without thought of repentance commit evil.

Let us review at least a few passages to prove that the Bible does in fact say that God hates evil and evil people. At least one person is selected specifically as the object of God's hatred, in Mal. 1:2-3: "I have loved Jacob, but Esau have I hated...." In reading the context, however, we realize that God was not speaking of a single person, but of a nation fathered by that person. Continuing, God says (in verses 3-5):

> I have turned his mountains into a wasteland and left his inheritance to the desert jackals....They may build, but I will demolish. They will be called The Wicked Land, a people always under the wrath of the LORD.

Another instance of God the Son's hatred is in His words to Ephesus, recorded in Rev. 2:6: "You hate the practices of the Nicolaitans, which I also hate." This is not the only place where we read of God's offense at evil practices. There are numerous "imprecatory" Psalms, in which the Psalmist cries to God for redress against enemies. Psalm 97:10 urges, "Let those who love the LORD hate evil." Psalm 119 contains several such passages: verse 104, "I hate every wrong path;" verse 113, "I hate double-minded men;" verse 128, "I hate every wrong path;" and verse 163, "I hate and abhor falsehood." Proverbs 8:13 contains these words:

> To fear the LORD is to hate evil;
> I hate pride and arrogance,
> evil behavior and perverse speech.

Most of these passages, it is granted, speak of hating evil practices and not specifically hating the people who do those things. On the other hand, there are enough places in scripture that do include hating the evil people that we cannot escape that concept as well. We should also note that the verses mentioned not only say that God hates evil people and their evil deeds; they also say that we must follow God's example in hatred of both.

The scriptures show that hatred is reciprocal, as is noted by Michel:[21]

> As God hates evil and the righteous hate the ungodly, so on the other side there arises man's hate against God, the hatred of the ungodly for the righteous....One hates God by consciously transgressing His commandments, ignoring His will, and mocking and persecuting the righteous. Hatred against God is thus a sign of rejection and obduracy.

An example of such hatred of God by wicked people is found at the end of Ps. 74:

> Rise up, O God, and defend your cause;
>> remember how fools mock you all day long.
> Do not ignore the clamor of your adversaries,
>> the uproar of your enemies, which rises continually.

Some people like to make a distinction between God the Father and God the Son with respect to the treatment of evil people. One of my fellow Ministers told me that there are two different Gods portrayed in the Bible: there is the God of the Old Testament, who is a God of war, and of judgment, and of punishment, and even of hatred; then there is the God of our Lord Jesus Christ in the New Testament, who is a loving God, who looks with favor on all people, and would never do anything to hurt or punish any of them. Years ago, in order to disprove this theory, I made a survey of all the verses in the Old Testament that spoke of the love, kindness, mercy of God, and in the New Testament all the verses containing allusions to the wrath of God and His punishment on people. To my surprise, yet satisfaction, I discovered almost exactly two verses per chapter in the Old Testament that told of God's love, kindness, and mercy toward people, and in the New Testament likewise almost exactly two verses per chapter concerning God's wrath and punishment. Not fully satisfied with these results, I made a second complete survey, this time looking for verses in the Old Testament that spoke of God's wrath, anger, condemnation, and punishment; and in the New Testament verses concerning God's love, mercy, and kindness. This time, to my surprise, I found again almost two verses per chapter in each Testament of what I was seeking. That proved conclusively, to me at least, that it is both false and ludicrous to claim that there are two different kinds of Gods revealed in the Bible.

With regard to this dispute, we ought to be reminded, if not informed, of the many instances in the New Testament in which our Savior spoke of the wrath of God against those who do evil, including both warnings and threatenings of the judgment to come, and the punishment in hell for those who reject God's merciful salvation by His grace through faith in the Lord Jesus Christ. Large sections of the Sermon on the Mount, found in Matt. 5-7, are devoted to the threat of punishment upon those who disobey God's stringent law. People who are supposed to be the "salt of the earth," if they have lost their "saltiness," are worthy to be "thrown out and trampled by men" (5:13). Un-

---

[21] O. Michel, article, μισέω, TDNT, Vol. IV, page 687.

less people's righteousness exceeds the righteousness of the Pharisees, they "will certainly not enter the kingdom of heaven" (5:20). Murder is forbidden by the commandment, but a person who is angry with his brother is "subject to judgment"; or who speaks contemptuously of his brother is answerable to the "Sanhedrin"; and anyone who says to his brother "You fool!" "will be in danger of the fire of hell" (5:22). Jesus warns of the dangers of hell several more times, in 5:29, 5:30 in the Sermon on the Mount; and in 10:28 "be afraid of the one who can destroy both body and soul in hell." He warned the people in the cities where He had performed most of His miracles that unless they repented of their sins, they would be worse off than Tyre and Sidon "on the day of judgment" (11:22), and even than Sodom (11:24). In speaking of Himself as the Rock on which the Church would be built, He promised that "the gates of Hades will not overcome it" (16:18), implying that all those remaining outside the true Church would be punished in Hades. In 18:6 He says that if anyone causes a little child who belongs to Jesus to sin, "it would be better for him to have a large millstone hung around his neck and to be drowned in the depths of the sea;" and in 18:8-9, Jesus warns that the end is "eternal fire" and "the fire of hell" for those who allow hand or foot or eye to cause them to sin. Finally from Matthew's gospel, we read in chapter 23 a series of eight woes upon the lawyers and Pharisees who were following their own traditions rather than the laws of God. Parallels exist in Mark and Luke. John does not mention "hell" in his gospel, but one of the strongest statements of God's judgment on unbelievers is found at the end of the chapter that contains the "Golden Text" of the Bible, John 3:36: "Whoever believes in the Son has eternal life, but whoever rejects the Son will not see life, for God's wrath remains on him." John's gospel is sprinkled with similar warnings.

### "...therefore, God, your God...."

For what follows, we must recognize that God the Father is still speaking to God the Son, as we noted at the beginning of the quotation from Psalm 45. Let us emphasize again that Jesus Christ is God, the Son. The Father, in speaking to Him, calls Him God. In addition, the One who is speaking is also God in saying, "therefore God, your God." In all this we must remember, however, that there is only one God. So God the Father and God the Son are but one God. Confirmation for this comes from an important source, Deut. 6:4, where we read, "Hear, O Israel: The LORD our God, the LORD is one." This has been called the great "Shema" by Jews from the time Moses wrote it. It still is important to Jews today. I have seen the words, in Hebrew, carved on the bullet-pock-marked stone wall next to the Zion Gate in Old Jerusalem. Jesus in the New Testament reaffirms that God is one, as was mentioned earlier from John 10:30, "I and the Father are one."

If one looks for a place where the Bible calls Jesus "God," we have not far to look wherever we find ourselves in scripture. In the first chapter of the

47

Bible, Gen. 1:26, we see the trinity indicated. God is named in the verse by the Hebrew word, אֱלֹהִים, which is a plural form in that language. God, speaking within Himself, says, "Let us make man in our image, in our likeness...." And that is exactly how God made man in the first place. Mankind is in the likeness of God in two respects: he is a spirit being, like the Father and the Spirit; and he has a physical body, like the Son. Later in Genesis (18:1), we read that God appeared to Abraham; we have already discussed how that had to be God the Son. In Ps. 2:12 the author talks about the Son, who certainly must be more powerful than a mere human:

> Kiss the Son, lest he be angry
> and you be destroyed in your way,
> for his wrath can flare up in a moment.
> Blessed are all who take refuge in him.

Moving further in the Bible, we read of Jesus who is called Immanuel in Is. 7:14, which Matthew has translated for us as "God with us" (Matt. 1:23). And in Is. 9:6, even those who claim the "Mighty God" is not Jehovah God Almighty but another God, admit that Isaiah writes there of Jesus, which is certainly true. But it is not at all true that Isaiah is writing about a second God, because at least some acknowledge that Rev. 1:8 is speaking of Jesus, God the Son, who describes Himself as "the Alpha and the Omega...who is, and who was, and who is to come..," but the amazing thing here is that He continues to describe Himself as "...the Almighty." We also have already discussed the string of verses at the beginning of John's gospel (verses 1, 14, and 17) when linked together demonstrate indubitably that Jesus is God Himself. And when Jesus heals the paralytic let down by four friends (Mk. 2:1-12), teachers of the law objected to Jesus' saying, "Son, your sins are forgiven." Their reaction was, "Why does this fellow talk like that? He's blaspheming! Who can forgive sins but God alone?" Jesus in effect claimed to be God in His response to them: "But that you may know that the Son of Man has authority on earth to forgive sins...I tell you, get up, take your mat and go home." These references are but a sample of places in the Bible which tell without obfuscation that Jesus is God the Son.

### "...has set you above your companions...."

Here is another indication that Jesus is "better than" anyone else. The enigmatic term "companions" might be interpreted in several ways: non-human beings on earth; humans themselves; angels; or even the false deities, objects of pagan nations. A good case might be made for people as Jesus' companions here. He calls them "servants" and "friends" in John 15:15, and speaks to them in diminutive form as "little children" in John 21:5 (παιδία in Greek, not the loose translation "friends" in the NIV). However, this whole chapter has been comparing Jesus to angels, so surely they are meant by the "companions" here.

Companions are almost always compatible in important ways, to keep

48

them together. However, seldom are they equals in every way. For instance, a beautiful young woman and a plain-looking young woman may be very comfortable walking down the street together. What draws them to each other is this: the beautiful girl says to herself, "I will look more beautiful beside my companion, so I will certainly attract more handsome men;" while the other thinks, "If I walk beside her, she will attract handsome men, and I may benefit from the fall-out." Jesus, of course, needs no such incentive to draw people to Himself; His attraction is far different (John 12:32): "I, when I am lifted up from the earth, will draw all men to myself."

### "...by anointing you with the oil of joy."

Anointing was a special act in biblical times, to honor and/or set apart a person, usually for a special task. The Hebrew word "to anoint" is מָשַׁח, from which our English "Messiah" is derived. That same Hebrew word is translated into the New Testament Greek as χρίω, "to anoint," and its derivative χριστός, that is, Christ (which without the definite article is usually a noun used as a name, but with the definite article usually is a verbal adjective).[22]

In Old Testament times people such as these were routinely anointed: priests, and especially the High Priest; kings of Israel and Judea; prophets; and peculiarly Cyrus King of Persia (Is. 45:1). Also, in Ps. 105:15, we read that the early descendants of Israel, who wandered in the Wilderness, were anointed:
> Do not touch my anointed ones;
>   do my prophets no harm.

There is a beautiful picture, in Ps. 133, of the anointing with oil of the first High Priest; and even more beautiful is the situation which it symbolizes, the peaceful existence of God's people together. Here is that whole Psalm, written by David:
> How good and pleasant it is
>   when brothers live together in unity!
> It is like precious oil poured on the head,
>   running down on the beard,
> running down on Aaron's beard,
>   down upon the collar of his robes.
> It is as if the dew of Hermon
>   were falling on Mount Zion.
> For there the LORD bestows his blessing,
>   even life forevermore.

For most of those who were anointed, there was a specific event in which it took place. However, in the case of Cyrus, and of the early Israelites, there is given no specific event, but rather those people seem to have held a status with respect to God, in which He considered them set apart as

---

[22] This according to A. T. Robertson, A GRAMMAR OF THE GREEK NEW TESTAMENT IN THE LIGHT OF HISTORICAL RESEARCH. This reference is on page 795.

peculiar people to do His will.[23]   Therefore, when the author of Hebrews informs us that the Father had exalted the Son "by anointing you with the oil of joy," it is not necessary for us to search for a specific event when this occurred.  The Father had simply established this special relationship between His beloved Son and His companions.  However, it might be appropriate to consider that the Son was anointed by the Father at Jesus' baptism, which could be a symbol of anointing.  It was in God the Son's baptism that the Holy Spirit as a dove came upon Jesus, and the voice of the Father from the heavens was heard to say, "This is my Son, whom I love; with him I am well pleased" (Matt. 3:17; Mk. 1:11; Lu. 3:22).  Jesus was selected by the Father for the specific task of dying on the cross for the salvation of those who would believe on Him.  Surely the "oil of joy" is likewise a symbol of the special kind of anointing the Father awarded to His Son.   In a great sense, then, Jesus was in agony in the Garden of Gethsemane when, with sweat like drops of blood fell from His brow, He pleaded with the Father (Matt. 26:39; Mk. 14:36; Lu. 22:42), "Father, if you are willing, take this cup from me; yet not my will, but yours be done;" and when He cried out as forsaken (Matt. 27:46; Mk. 15:34), "My God, my God, why have you forsaken me?"  But even in that agony, Jesus must have been filled with joy at the knowledge that He had obeyed the Father even unto death.  We might consider what joy it is for us to do the will of the Father, just as Christ did.

**Heb. 1:10.   He also says,**
**"In the beginning, O Lord, you laid the**
**foundations of the earth,**
**and the heavens are the work of your hands."**

This quotation from Ps. 102:25-27, as found in the book of Hebrews, is almost identical to what the Psalm says.  Although some words are different, especially in verse 12, the meaning is virtually the same.  It is important to realize that the author of Hebrews is affirming that Jesus, God the Son, is the Creator of the heavens and the earth.  What is said by the Psalmist is the same thing we read in the very first verse of the Bible: "In the beginning, God created the heavens and the earth."  The major difference is that in Gen. 1:1 it is Moses, the author of the book who is making a statement; while in the Psalm it is God the Father who is declaring the same act of creation as performed by the Son.  Surely it is proper to assume that if God the Son created the heavens and the earth, He also created all that is in them.  If this is so, then Jesus created the angels among all the other things created.  It goes without saying that the Creator is "better than" the things created.

**Heb.  1:11.**
**"They will perish, but you remain...."**

---

[23]  Walter Grundmann, article χρίω, TDNT, Vol. IX, page 504.

There is unfortunate division of opinion among people who call themselves Christians over the exact meaning of the term "perish." Some think it means to be annihilated, that is, entirely to cease to exist. Others think it means something less drastic than that. To try to solve the dispute, it is well to discover just what the original words in Hebrew and Greek mean; and to survey at least some of the important places in scripture where the term is used.

Let us learn what the original Hebrew word means. That word for "perish" in Ps. 102:26, is אָבַד, and is transliterated as 'abhadh; phonetically it would sound "avádh." This phonetic knowledge is important because of a Hebrew proper noun derived from the verb root. That noun is "Abaddon," which in Job 26:6 is a simile for the more familiar "Sheol," and it means "a place of destruction." The basic meaning of the Hebrew verb, however, is simply "to perish," which in itself is not helpful to settle the dispute among Christians. A more intimate study of the term[24] shows us that to perish means "to die." In Num. 17:12 and 13 (which is Num. 17:27 and 28 in the Hebrew Bible), the word under study here is equated to two other Hebrew words, גָּוַע, and מוּת, both of which mean simply "to die." It can mean for a group of people "to be exterminated," as in Lev. 26:38, where the NIV translates, "You will perish among the nations..," which means that Israel as a nation will no longer be considered a nation among the others. It can also mean "to be ruined, or to be destroyed, or to vanish" such as riches or houses; or, as in Deut. 12:3, where God commands the Israelites to blot out all evidence of idols, He commands the people, "cut down the idols of their gods and wipe out their names from those places." Among beasts it can mean "to be lost or strayed," which certainly is not a permanent "annihilation." For instance, in I Sam. 9:3 we read, "Now the donkeys belonging to Saul's father Kish were lost...." All these thoughts are supported by an article on the term by Benedikt Otzen in TDOT.[25] In both these authorities, the idea of "annihilation" is almost totally absent. The whole idea is that people, animals, or things, disappear from the sight of man and from the face of the earth, but they still exist in another place God has prepared for them.

Virtually all this can be said of the Greek translation of the Hebrew verb, both in Heb. 1:11, and in the LXX of Ps. 102:26 (Ps. 101:27 in the LXX). One verse used as illustration by Louw and Nida[26] is Matt. 10:28. Here Jesus is warning His disciples about the relative authority of the the the enemies of believers, "those who kill the body but cannot kill the soul;" and God alone, "the one who can destroy both soul and body in hell." This is not annihilation, but just what John in the Revelation (20:14) calls "the second

---

[24] This information is from Brown,Driver and Briggs under the definition of the Hebrew verb.

[25] THEOLOGICAL DICTIONARY OF THE OLD TESTAMENT. This will be known hereafter as TDOT (to be distinguished from TDNT).

[26] Vol. 1, item 20:31.

death" in the lake of fire which burns "for ever and ever" (verse 10).

When the Father tells the Son, "they will perish, but you will remain," we must remember that He is talking about the earth and the heavens; this is how the quotation begins. However, to mention earth and heavens implies the inclusion of everything contained in them. They all will not be annihilated, but will be changed into different forms, and at least some of them will be moved to different places. It is well to remember also that none of us can predict when this "perishing" of the heavens and earth will occur. Jesus Himself made that clear, in His statement recorded in Mk. 13:32: "No one knows about that day or hour, not even the angels in heaven, nor the Son, but only the Father." Nor should we be like those scoffers who will be living just before it happens who deny its possibility (II Pet. 3:4-5):

> They will say, "Where is this 'coming' he promised? Ever since our fathers died, everything goes on as it has since the beginning of creation." But they deliberately forget that long ago by God's word the heavens existed and the earth was formed out of water and with water. By water also the world of that time was deluged and destroyed.

Although it is important for us to know that angels will be "destroyed," it is much more important to be aware that Jesus "will remain," making Him, in this sense, once again "better than" the angels. If Jesus "will remain," that means that Jesus has no end; He exists eternally. In the other direction, Jesus had no beginning; since He was God, He existed in whatever "beginning" there was. Only will Jesus "remain" unchanged, unlike the angels, the earth and the heavens, which will "perish."

### "...they will all wear out like a garment."

God is able to keep things from wearing out if He wants to do so. For instance, He preserved the Israelites' clothing from wearing out during their forty years in the wilderness (Deut. 29:5). But He is going to let the universe wear out one day. Although all created things are going to "wear out," including the angels, Jesus Christ will never wear out. The end of this quotation from Ps. 102 assures us of that.

### Heb. 1:12.
### "You will roll them up like a robe;
### like a garment they will be changed."

When you are ready to discard a worn-out garment—whether a robe or otherwise—you usually roll it up into a bundle, and throw it into the trash, or into your mother's rag bag, to be cut up and used for cleaning and then thrown out. Once you have discarded it, it no longer encumbers your home.

The Greek word for "changed" is ἀλλάσσω, which means "to cause a difference by altering the character or nature of something.[27] This surely does not mean merely a change of clothing (the quotation has been talking about a

---

[27] Louw and Nida, item 58.43.

52

robe), for that would be a quite superficial change. It also means more than a change of appearance (expressed in Greek by the term μεταμορφόω), which although usually a greater transformation than a mere change of clothing, is still not a change of *character*, as the term used here expresses.

Scientists tell us that the universe is wearing out. By the process of entropy, heat is being dissipated until finally the whole thing will cool off. However, the Bible tells us that the end will be quite different, probably through a special intervention of God. We read in II Pet. 3:7, "...the present heavens and earth are reserved for fire, being kept for the day of judgment and destruction of ungodly men." In other words, God will destroy the universe because of the sinfulness of the human race, and along with the elements and humans will come the destruction of angels as well. When the heavens and the earth are worn out and rolled up, they will no longer be the same, but will have been transformed by God into "a new heaven and a new earth, the home of righteousness" (II Pet. 3:13).

Let us note that it is Jesus Himself, the Creator of the heavens and the earth, who at the end will "roll them up like a robe" and change their very character, while He remains the same forever. Further, it is most comforting to note that since Jesus will not change, even in His character, He also will never change His promises to us, especially the promise of eternal life with Him in heaven forever, by believing on Him.

### "But you remain the same, and your years will never end."

Apart from His changing His clothes from time to time while He walked the earth, or from the time He was transfigured before His three disciples (Matt. 17:1-8, and parallels) Jesus never changed His nature. We often refer to what the author said in Heb. 13:8, "Jesus Christ is the same yesterday and today and forever."

All time will cease in eternity, from our understanding of God and His creation. Time is one of the four dimensions within which we are trapped now. When the world ends, however, and we are ushered into the presence of the Great Triune God, there will no longer be such a thing as time.

### Heb. 1:13. To which of the angels did God ever say....

Here is a repetition of what we read in verse 5. Again, the author's purpose is to show that the Father *never* said such things to even one of the angels. The Father loved His Son, and desired to show that the Son is "better than" the angels.

Of all the quotations from the Old Testament which we find in the first chapter of Hebrews, only one speaks directly to, or about, angels; all the rest are spoken about the Son. Even this quotation, which is introduced by asking about angels, does not have angels as its subject, but rather the Son. Even the quotation in verse 6, "Let all God's angels worship him," although it is not a direct statement about the Son, still decidedly contrasts Jesus and angels, by saying that angels worship the Son. So, since six of the seven quotations are about Jesus, even this preponderance implies that Jesus is preeminent.

### "Sit at my right hand...."

This begins a quotation from Ps. 110:1. God the Father is speaking to God the Son once again, introduced this time in the words: "The LORD says to my Lord..," which was used by Jesus to confound His opponents near the end of His earthly life (Matt. 22:41-46; Mk. 12:35-37; and Lu. 20:41-44). We will study another exceedingly important part of this Psalm when we get to Heb. 5:6 through chapter 7. It is prefaced by the same Psalm used earlier in this chapter, Ps. 2:7, "You are my Son; today I have become your Father."

To sit at anyone's right hand is to be given the most favored position. We remember again the request made by James and John, through their mother, that Jesus place the brothers at His right and left hands in His kingdom (see Matt. 20:20-23), but Jesus said He had no authority to make such a promise. However, when Peter and John were defending themselves before the Sanhedrin after preaching in the temple area, Peter said (Acts 5:29-31):

> We must obey God rather than men! The God of our fathers raised Jesus from the dead—whom you had killed by hanging him on a tree. God exalted him to his own right hand as Prince and Savior that he might give repentance and forgiveness of sins to Israel.

We also noted in Heb. 1:3 that even the angels are required to either stand or lie prostrate before the triune God, while apparently only the twenty-four elders are allowed to sit surrounding His throne. This ties together the whole chapter, whose prime theme is that Jesus is "better than" the angels.

### "...until I make your enemies
### a footstool for your feet"?

Who are Jesus' enemies? We find a convenient list in these verses of Psalm 2:

1. Nations that rage against God.
1. People who plot, yet in vain.
2. Kings who take a stand against the Lord.
2. Rulers who conspire against the Lord and His Anointed One.
3. They determine independence from God's rule.
4. God laughs and scoffs at them.
5. God rebukes and terrifies them.
6. God establishes His King over them all.
8. The Father gives the nations, the whole earth, to Jesus.
9. Jesus will rule with an iron scepter, dash them like pottery.

Jesus' enemies will be made a footstool under His feet. A footstool is as far removed from a seat at the right hand as any two things can be placed.

The Father never promised to do that for the angels, but the Son receives the full inheritance. Incidentally, the loyal angels are not to become Jesus' footstool, but only Satan and his cohorts will be thus dishonored.

### Heb. 1:14. Are not all angels ministering spirits sent to serve those who will inherit salvation?

This is the purpose for which angels were created by God. He destined them to serve us who belong to Christ, as well as all other human beings whose names are also written in the Lamb's book of life. In this sense, then, angels were made lower than people, because they are our servants. In Lu. 17:7-10, Jesus gave His disciples an illustration to show that the servant is lower than his master. He talked about a servant who comes in from the field, doubtless tired from the day's work. The master does not invite him to sit at table with him and dine; rather, he orders the servant to put on his apron and serve the master, and when he is done, only then can he sit and eat by himself.

Christ died to save the lost, but He died only for people. Angels who have rebelled against God have no Savior: neither Jesus nor anyone else will save them. What a tremendous blessing it is that we of the human race, although universally sinful, still have access to heaven because God became a Man in order to die for us. There is a song that declares the difference between angels and humans in this respect; it ends, "Angels never know the joy that our salvation brings."

### Heb. 2:1. Therefore....

The author of Hebrews indicates a transition in what he wants to say at this point, but he shows by this single word that what he adds is to be linked to what he has said before. We may summarize what he wrote in chapter 1 this way: Jesus Christ is "better than" all of the angels; the angels are exalted high above mere humans; angels were created to be servants of human beings, to minister to all people who have inherited eternal life through faith in Jesus Christ as their Savior and Lord.

### We must pay more careful attention to what we have heard....

First, we must recall what we discussed about the irreducible minimum of the very first sentence, especially as it applies to the core of this sentence at the beginning of chapter 2. The opening words of this letter say, "God has spoken;" now the author adds "We have heard." At the beginning of human history, God went to great lengths to send a message out to all people "at many times and in various ways." He walked with Adam and Eve in the Garden of Eden, and spoke directly to them. He spoke similarly to prophets and seers, even to Moses "face to face" (Ex. 33:11). He spoke through those prophets and seers to all the people. He spoke not only to His chosen people, the nation of Abraham, Isaac, and Jacob, but He spoke to every human of every race and language in the world (Ps. 19:1-4):

> The heavens declare the glory of God;
> the skies proclaim the work of his hands.
> Day after day they pour forth speech;
> night after night they display knowledge.
> There is no speech or language
> where their voice is not heard.
> Their voice goes out into all the earth,
> their words to the ends of the world.

He performed miracles, signs and wonders through His servants Moses and Aaron, as well as through others like Elijah and Elisha, and the whole world heard of those events (Rahab told the spies that her people had already heard of the miracles in Egypt that had delivered the people from bondage, in Josh. 2:9-11). God spoke to people like Judge Gideon through His messengers the angels (Jud. 6, beginning at verse 11). God spoke through natural phenomena, like intense winds, shattering rocks, earthquakes, fires, and even through a gentle whisper (the Hebrew says "a voice of silence") to people like Elijah (see I Kings 19:11-13). After the Old Testament times, God spoke to the people through His Son, and through His apostles and prophets, and through further miracles and wonders.

For all this, communication does not occur unless the people hear what is being said. Several decades ago, the people of the mission radio station HCJB in Quito, Ecuador wanted to get God's word out to the third-world Indians in Central and South America. They were frustrated because, although they had spent money and energy building their radio transmitter, they knew the people would not receive the message because they had no radio receivers. So the mission designed and built many very cheap radios and gave them to the Natives. However, many of the Natives discovered other radio stations they could pick up on their little receivers. The mission solved that problem by designing radios built to receive only their own station HCJB. After that, they got the information that many Indians were receiving the message of the gospel. For communication to take place, there must be not only a transmitter, but also a receiver. In this case, God is the Broadcaster, transmitting through a variety of means; while the spirits of human beings are the receivers. Even all that is not sufficient to guarantee the successful communication of the message; the "receivers" need to be turned on. If people refuse to listen to the message God so painstakingly sends to the whole world, God should not be faulted if the people do not hear.

You have just read an excellent, though perhaps incomplete, answer to the question many people ask: "Are the heathen lost? Would a loving God send any of them to hell, if they have not had an opportunity to hear the message of salvation?" I would like to add two answers to what has just been said about that question. The first answer is, "Let's not worry about the 'heathen' yet. The important detail is that *you have heard*." Every one who has read this treatise so far cannot escape the fact that you have heard the gospel message. Therefore, if you go to hell, it is not God who has sent you there, but your own refusal to listen to, and heed, the message God has so fully broadcast to you from the beginning. My second answer to the question is simply, "All the 'heathen' *have* heard." There is no one alive today, nor has there been anyone who has lived in the world before now, who has failed to have the message sent to him. The quotation from Ps. 19, recorded just above, is absolute proof that every person has had the opportunity to hear. Besides Ps. 19, we may turn to Rom. 1:18-24 in the New Testament for a similar statement. That passage reads in part:

> For since the creation of the world God's invisible qualities—his eternal power and divine nature—have been clearly seen, being understood from what has been made, so that men are without excuse. For although they knew God, they neither glorified him as God nor gave thanks to him, but their thinking became futile and their foolish hearts were darkened.

We see then that the whole Bible, both Old and New Testaments, aver that "we have heard;" and not only we, but the whole world in all times has heard.

Next comes the practical application: *if* we have heard, "we must pay more careful attention." The *why* of the demand that we pay more careful attention is found in verses 2 to 4; and the *result* of failure to pay such careful attention is told at the end of verse 1.

### ...so that we do not drift away.

What factors are there that might cause us to drift away? One of the main things is the tug of the world and worldly things. We are caught between two poles of a spiritual magnet. The Holy Spirit tends to draw us to the spiritual world; while the opposite pole, the world, uses all its strength to pull us away from God and His realm. The poet, William Wordsworth, said it aptly:

> The world is too much with us; late and soon,
> Getting and spending, we lay waste our powers:
> Little we see in Nature that is ours;
> We have given our hearts away, a sordid boon!

Our scripture says the same thing. The apostle John wrote (I John 2:16): "For everything in the world—the cravings of sinful man, the lust of his eyes and the boasting of what he has and does—comes not from the Father but from the world." Most of the time the world does not tear us away violently or rapidly from God, but does it slowly and in subtle steps. We are like the frog placed in a pan of cool water on a stove. The water gets warmer, but the frog does not recognize it until it is too late, and he is cooked. So also the world tries to ease us away from the Spirit without our sensing that something is wrong. The antidote for this is to spend time daily meditating on God's word, to draw us closer to Him.

How far it is possible for a person to drift away is a thorny question; we shall reserve a discussion of that until we get to Hebrews: 6:4-6, and all of chapter 10; disputes over both have contributed to the sundering of the body of Christ over the centuries. For now, let us simply think about why we ought not to drift away.

We all know the old proverb: Absence makes the heart grow fonder. Although this may be true in certain instances, it is not universally true. When two people in love are separated through work or travels, it is possible that one will find someone else who will steal the other person's affections. On the other hand, sometimes someone wants to be separated. During my studies in Edinburgh, our son John was born. He had digestive troubles, so he slept sporadically during the daytime and screamed throughout each night. His mother took him to visit friends for a few days, during which time she called our private hotel where we were staying to see if everything was all right. One of the spinster ladies who operated the home replied, "Oh, peace, perfect peace, with loved ones far away!"

We ought to want to remain as close to the Lord as we can at all times. The psalmist wrote (Ps. 42:1-2):

> As the deer pants for streams of water,
> so my soul pants for you, O God.
> My soul thirsts for God, for the living God.
> When can I go and meet with God?

The saintly Morris Hanson, an Elder in a church I served, once told how he learned to stay close to God: "When I was a boy, I learned that when my daddy had to spank me, if I tried to pull away from him as he held my hand, the spanking would hurt much more than if I tried to squeeze as close to his knee as possible. When I was far away, he could swing in a larger arc so the blow was much heavier; but when I kept close to him, he couldn't swing nearly as strongly." Morris would always go on to relate that story to our keeping close to our heavenly Father. "When we stay close to Him, His chastening is much less severe." He also said that the sheep that stayed closest to the shepherd always were the best fed. The shepherd would reach up with his crook, and pull down the branches that had the best, most tender leaves, and the most lush ripe fruit, so the sheep close to him could feed on what the other sheep could not reach.

Years ago, there was a great pianist who said, "If I fail to practice just one day, I know it. If I fail to practice two days in a row, my friends know it. If I fail to practice three days in a row, the whole world knows it." If you fail to have your daily devotions, how many days does it take for your friends to be aware of it? One day a high school girl named Sue came to my study and complained, "All my friends have stopped talking to me. When I walk down the hall in school, they walk on the other side of the hall and won't speak to me." What Sue didn't know was that a few days before that, her best friend Carolyn had come to see me with this story, "Mr. Teply, something has happened to Sue. When we, her old friends from the Youth Group, meet her in school, she walks down the other side of the hall and turns her head the other way, and talks to her new friends, and they aren't the right kinds of friends. We try to talk to her, but she won't talk to us." As I was talking to Sue, it was obvious that she wanted me to call in all her old friends and urge them to become friendly with her again. Instead, I asked Sue, "Tell me, Sue, when did you stop having your daily devotions?" She looked startled for a few moments, and then slowly replied, "I guess about a month ago." I said, "That's what I thought. I could tell it, and your friends know that something is wrong too." I urged her to begin the practice of daily devotions again, and she did. Her fellowship with her Christian friends was restored, as well as her relationship to her Lord.

The author of Hebrews does not really tell us what it is from which we can drift away. He may be saying merely that we drift away from what we have heard. He may be encouraging us not to drift away from the Lord. After all, He is the ultimate Source of all that can bless us, especially our salvation.

### Heb. 2:2. For if the message spoken by angels was binding....

We now turn to the "why" of the importance of paying careful attention to what we have heard. At this point we return to the principal argument found in chapter 1, that Jesus Christ is "better than" the angels. It is important to remember, though, that the author spoke very highly of angels and their status in the hierarchy of creatures, in order to catch the full impact of what he is seeking to tell us here. Why the author said these things is because the Jews of New Testament times held angels in exceedingly high regard. Therefore, whatever message the angels bore was of utmost importance to them. Whether the Jews in Old Testament times heeded the messages of angels (and usually they did not), they still knew they ought to pay very careful attention.

In all this, we need to recognize that it is not the messenger that validates the message, no matter how greatly or meanly the recipient holds the messenger. For instance, it may be the United States Congress that makes a law, but a less-important official, the County Sheriff, can arrest a lawbreaker. Likewise, the written law may be bound in leather in an attorney's posh office, but if it is written on newsprint and stapled to a telephone pole, it carries the same weight. However, most of us would more likely cringe if it was not the County Sheriff but an FBI agent who arrested us. At any rate, the message given to the Jews before Christ's time was just as valid as any message given by God to men.

### ...and every violation and disobedience received its just punishment....

I emphasize again that it is not the messenger who lends force to the message, but the authority who creates the message and has power to enforce it. Let us remember that legal matters require four major elements: someone in authority must make the law; that authority must make the law known to his subjects; he must give fair warning regarding the consequences for disobedience of the law (and the rewards for obedience); and he must carry out the punishment upon anyone who breaks the law. God was careful to follow every step of this in all His dealings with His creatures—not only human beings, but angels as well.

Some people seriously question God's wisdom or justice in His dealings with Adam and Eve. After all, the thinking goes, all they did was eat a piece of fruit which they found in the garden where they lived; and for that God put them to death! That was such a mighty punishment for such a tiny infraction. (Incidentally, Adam and Eve did in fact die, on the very day they ate the fruit. They did not die physically that day, for they lived many years and had children after that; but they did die spiritually, which is much worse than physical death.) But God was in no way unjust in what He did to our first parents. He had made the law; He had clearly communicated the law (so well that Eve not only remembered the law verbatim but elaborated on it unnecessarily); He had warned of the consequences of disobedience; and when the couple broke the law God punished them according to His word. Today we hear much talk about "cruel and unusual punishment," and many people recoil at the thought of what the Bible says God did to Adam and Eve; some go so far as to say it didn't happen—a loving God could not have done such a thing. But the Bible says that it did happen, so those who believe the Bible is true must accept it.

If, then, Adam and Eve received their "just punishment" for their single infraction, then every other instance of lawlessness against God's Ten Commandments and other ordinances He gave to men was treated utterly justly by God in His punishing the people in Old Testament times, whether they were Jews or Gentiles. And the messengers who conveyed God's statutes, although mere angels, who were considered great by the Jews, were sufficiently able to carry God's will to the people.

We could multiply cases through the Old Testament where, from our perspective, we might think God was unduly harsh in His punishment of people for their seemingly petty sins. Think of Moses' exclusion from the Promised Land, merely because he struck the rock (the Rock) instead of speaking to it as God told him to do (Num. 20:1-13). King Saul and his heirs lost the kingdom, only because he spared the life of Agag of the Amalekites, and saved the best of the enemies' sheep and cattle, ostensibly to sacrifice them to God (I Sam. 15). King David lost his first son born of Bath-sheba "merely" because of his adultery with her (II Sam. 11). The first king of the northern kingdom, Jeroboam, saw his right hand wither instantly just because he pointed to God's prophet and threatened him (I Kings 13). Even the young prophet, although he obeyed God in carrying out his dangerous mission to Jeroboam, himself failed to arrive home, but died a wretched death on the way, simply because he delayed his journey to eat a meal with an older man of God (also I Kings 13). As I mentioned, this is but a sampling of what we can find in the biblical record of God's punishment on people who flaunted his laws.

How can we reconcile such dealings by God upon His people, when we think of Him as an infinitely and everlastingly loving God? The only way to accept the record is to realize that God is not only loving, He is also just; and because He has made His law known along with the punishment for its disobedience, He has every right to wreak that punishment upon every lawbreaker. Let us begin at the beginning again, and see how from the start God made clear His intentions to every person who transgressed His word. He established Adam and Eve in the Garden of Eden, a perfect place, with every need for sumptuous living easily accessible without even working for it. Neither original human had the slightest need of any kind, material or emotional. They did not need to strike for higher wages. They were not deprived of a good education—God had taught them everything they needed to know. They did not need to fight for land or food or clothing to have enough. They had no enemies (save Satan). There was no conceivable reason why they needed to turn their backs on the multitudes of varieties of food trees in the garden to select the fruit of the forbidden tree. And I say again, what is really so bad about merely eating a piece of fruit? I have eaten many apples in my lifetime, and so have you. Actually, there was but one thing wrong about what they did. It was not the eating the apple that killed them. It was their disobeying God's command not to eat the fruit of that tree. God had warned them (Gen. 2:16-17): "You are free to eat from any tree in the garden; but you must not eat from the tree of the knowledge of good and evil, for when you eat of it you will surely die." In reality, there is but one sin that any person in the world can commit: to disobey God's clearly transmitted command. Likewise, there is but one punishment for every sin of disobedience (no matter how heinous or mild that infraction may be): instant spiritual death. If it is not enough to read that in the Old Testament, we have it reiterated in the New: "the wages of sin is death" (Rom. 6:23). Again, examples could be multiplied to show the law and the threat repeated throughout scripture. Therefore, God is totally just in putting to death *every* sinner, including you and me.

But here of course is where the gospel enters the picture. Not every human being will remain spiritually dead, even though every one of us deserves to die and stay dead forever because of our sins. Even though God has required that every sin must be punished for justice to be met, still He has arranged a way of escape for us who believe in Jesus as our Savior and Lord. Paul explains it to us, in part in Rom. 8:1-4:

> Therefore, there is now no condemnation for those who are in Christ Jesus, because through Christ Jesus the law of the Spirit of life set me free from the law of sin and death. For what the law was powerless to do in that it was

weakened by the sinful nature, God did by sending his own Son in the likeness of sinful man to be a sin offering. And so he condemned sin in sinful man, in order that the righteous requirements of the law might be fully met in us, who do not live according to the sinful nature but according to the Spirit.

Earlier in the same letter to the Romans (3:25-26), Paul also made clear that God's justice was satisfied by the death of His Son, who died on behalf of all of us who trust in Him:

God presented [Christ Jesus] as a sacrifice of atonement, through faith in his blood. He did this to demonstrate his justice, because in his forbearance he had left the sins committed beforehand unpunished—he did it to demonstrate his justice at the present time, so as to be just and the one who justifies the man who has faith in Jesus.

### Heb. 2:3.  ...how shall we escape....

It is easy to understand that this is a rhetorical question. The obvious answer is, "There is no possibility of escape." The author of Hebrews has already established that the message spoken by mere angels was absolutely binding; he has already established that we have heard the message; he has already established that the Son as Messenger was "better than" the angels as messengers. So when the question comes, "How shall we escape?" we are hemmed in on every side, so that the only possible answer is, "We have no escape route whatsoever."

### ...if we ignore....

It is important to repeat for emphasis here, "We have heard." Having heard God's message, we have two options for our response: we can heed it; or we can ignore it. What is the content of the message which is deemed so important by the author?

### ...such a great salvation?

It is not merely the message itself we should be concerned about. It is the importance of the message; which is without doubt the most amazing message the world has ever heard or could even dream up. Anyone who would attempt to refute this idea makes it obvious that he has not an inkling of the meaning of the message. Such a person may search all the religions of the world, and will fail to find even one that makes such a promise to people. The promise is so great because the benefit offered is not based on the works of the person hoping to receive it. Rather, it is based on the very death of the Deity who offered it. And since that Deity has already died, the promise is secure to every person who meets the criteria designated by Him. (Again I say, one of the criteria is definitely *not* the righteous works of the recipient.) Even the Old Testament salvation was not a complete salvation in itself, as we shall see later on in our study—see especially chapter 9 for now. The animal sacrifices were but a shadow of the true, final sacrifice made by God Himself on our behalf.

We ought to add a note about atheists here. Their belief system prevents them from acknowledging that there is any God or god who can do them good. Their refusal to acknowledge the existence of a God, however, does not to the slightest degree affect the fact that there is a God. We have already shown that such people do know that God exists (see especially Rom. 1:18-23). So no one can ever rightly claim not to know God; such a person can only refuse to acknowledge that God is. Since we who know Christ as our Savior and Lord know that nothing this world offers can compare with the glories of God's salvation, we know that atheists may cling to something they consider important from the world, but their minds are darkened to the awareness of God's salvation through Christ.

**This salvation, which was first announced by the Lord....**

There may be just cause for disagreement about when this announcement was first made. There are two possibilities. One is that it was the Lord God, the Father, who announced this salvation to Adam and Eve. After all, salvation was announced to them in God's providing the lamb's skins to cover their nakedness after their disobedience in the Garden. We are also sure that salvation was proclaimed to people throughout Old Testament history. Abraham knew that it was coming, when he responded to Isaac's inquiry where was the lamb for the sacrifice (Gen. 22:8): "God himself will provide the lamb for the burnt offering, my son." Moses was given instructions regarding making sacrifices for sin throughout Leviticus. King David demonstrated that he knew that only God could save him, when after his heinous sin he cried out (Ps. 51:1-2):

> Have mercy on me, O God,
>     according to your unfailing love;
> according to your great compassion
>     blot out my transgressions.
> Wash away all my iniquity
>     and cleanse me from my sin.

Isaiah also knew of God's salvation (Is. 61:10):

> He has clothed me with garments of salvation
>     and arrayed me in a robe of righteousness.

This is but a sample of instances scattered through the Old Testament of people who had heard of God's great salvation, and trusted in Him to save them.

However, all those instances of the knowledge of salvation were but figures, types, portents of the great salvation which would be wrought by Christ Himself when He came in bodily form to the world. We shall study this in greater depth when we get to Heb. 8:6, which puts it all in perspective: "But the ministry Jesus has received is as superior to theirs as the covenant of which he is mediator is superior to the old one, and it is founded on better promises." Not only was Jesus' ministry superior, but the results were far greater as well (Heb. 9:9-10): "...the gifts and sacrifices being offered were not able to clear the conscience of the worshiper. They are only a matter of food and drink and various ceremonial washings—external regulations applying until the time of the new order." Therefore, it is my opinion that "the salvation, which was first announced by the Lord" is the message given by Christ to His disciples during His earthly ministry. After all, the author of Hebrews is making a distinction between the message given to men by angels and the superior message given by Jesus. In addition, I believe the following clause in the letter adds weight to this opinion.

### ...was confirmed to us by those who heard him.

The author of Hebrews is saying here that he and those to whom he is writing had received this stupendous message of "such a great salvation" only secondhand. It may be important for more than one reason to emphasize that it was no more than secondhand, however. What he means is that the people who originally heard the message directly from the mouth of the Messenger then spoke it without other intermediary to the author, to his companions, and perhaps as well to the recipients of his letter. If this is what he means, then it had to be Jesus who is "the Lord," who first announced "this salvation."

Another reason this may be important is to realize that the author of Hebrews was not himself one of the original apostles or disciples, since he did not hear this great salvation directly from the lips of the original Transmitter. In fact, it could not have been anyone who had known Jesus or heard Him in His earthly ministry. This is because the original apostles and first one hundred twenty disciples were insistent that there be made a fine distinction between those who had followed Jesus and heard His message and all other people. This is evident in Peter's admonition to those one hundred twenty when they prepared to select one of their number to replace Judas Iscariot as the twelfth apostle. Peter said (Acts 1:21-22):

Therefore it is necessary to choose one of the men who have been with us the whole time the Lord Jesus went in and out among us, beginning from John's baptism to the time when Jesus was taken up from us. For one of these must become a witness with us of his resurrection.

This kind of reasoning may even exclude Paul as a possible author of Hebrews, for two reasons. First, although it is not certain whether Paul ever heard Jesus *before* His crucifixion, yet he claimed to receive the gospel message *directly* from the Lord Jesus. Paul says this in two places, first in Gal. 1:15-16: "When God, who set me apart from birth and called me by his grace, was pleased to reveal his Son in me so that I might preach him among the Gentiles, I did not consult any man...." Then in Paul's enumeration of Jesus' appearances to the disciples after His resurrection, he concludes the listing thus (I Cor. 15:8): "and last of all he appeared to me also, as to one abnormally born." Therefore Paul heard about salvation directly from Jesus, not

64

secondhand.

Through all this, let us be confident that although the author acknowledged that he received this message secondhand, that is still close enough to the original to have full confidence that his report is fully accurate. We need not fear any corruption of the message from him.

### Heb. 2:4.   God also testified to it....

It was God the Son (as we have claimed above) who gave this message of salvation to the world. Now the author claims that "God" testified to it by various means. Now it is possible for us to try to decide whether it was God the Father who confirmed the message by such signs, or whether it was God the Son who did so. In this case, I believe it really doesn't matter, since God the Father, God the Son, and God the Holy Spirit are one God immutable. It is important for us to remember that the message must be heeded since it is God Himself who delivers it. What the author thinks important is that the verbal message was supported by the different means he lists here.

### ...by signs, wonders and various miracles, and gifts of the Holy Spirit....

We may think of various Old Testament signs given to the people of those generations, confirming the limited vision of salvation they received from God. Here are a few samples gleaned from those pages.

Signs: we think of the rainbow given to Noah as a sign that the earth would never be destroyed by flood again (Gen. 9:12-13). Another sign was the pillar of cloud by day and pillar of fire by night, to guide and guard the Israelites as they wandered through the wilderness for forty years: see especially Ex. 14:19. The pillar of cloud was itself even an instrument of Israel's salvation, because it stood between the Israelites and the Egyptian army until God opened the way through the Red Sea.

Wonders: God offered wonders of blessings for obedience to His word in Deut. 28:1-14; and wonders of cursing and troubles for disobedience in Deut. 28:15-46, especially the last verse. God also offered wonders to the children of Israel in Ex. 34:10.

Miracles: Some people may consider that the parting of the Red Sea so the children of Israel could escape from the Egyptian army (Ex. 14:21) was no miracle, since God merely used a natural cause—a great wind—to part the waters so His people could pass unharmed, while the army that chased them was drowned when the waters returned. But it took some pretty miraculous fine-tuning for God to cause the wind to blow with proper strength when Israel was nearly swallowed by Egyptian hordes; and like fine-tuning for the water to remain backed up until the last Israelite was safely on the other shore, and then return to swallow the enemy army.

Gifts of the Holy Spirit: We think of the Spirit given to King Saul in

I Sam. 10:10-11, so he could prophesy with other prophets of God, although the Spirit was withdrawn from Saul later (I Sam. 16:14). Then there is the great prophecy of the Holy Spirit who was to be given to the Messiah later, but may have been a prophecy of His coming upon either Isaiah or some other person of that time in Is. 61:1-3.

It should not be necessary to enumerate the signs, wonders, miracles, and gifts of the Holy Spirit about which we read in the New Testament. The gospels are literally filled with Jesus' special deeds; further, we read in them about miracles wrought by His apostles and disciples when He sent them out to preach, teach, and amaze the people. The book of Acts adds to the long list of special things wrought by God through apostles, disciples, deacons, and other people. The works and gifts of the Holy Spirit are expounded and made evident, not only in I Cor.12-14 and Eph. 4, but other passages as well. You are urged to study those three chapters in I Corinthians and other relevant passages regarding the Holy Spirit, so you can know these things for yourself.

### ...distributed according to his will.

It is the gifts of the Holy Spirit that are distributed according to His will, claims the author of Hebrews here. There is no equivocation, no confusion in this statement; nor is there any need for interpretation or questioning what the author means here. It is by the Holy Spirit's own will that He distributes His gifts to people. No human chooses which gifts he will receive from the Holy Spirit. No human being chooses what gifts the Holy Spirit must give to any other human being. The Holy Spirit *alone* decides whether any individual person will receive any gift from Him, or how many gifts, or which gifts. You are encouraged to ask for gifts from the Holy Spirit; you are even permitted to ask for specific gifts, according to I Cor. 12:31. But your asking does not guarantee that your request will be fulfilled according to *your* will, but only according to *His* will which may be entirely different from yours. Simon the Sorcerer (Acts 8:18) asked for the gift of the Holy Spirit, but was utterly rejected. Of course he asked for the gift from Peter, but Peter was guided by the Holy Spirit in his answer. Also, James warns us (James 4:2-3), "You do not have, because you do not ask God. When you ask, you do not receive, because you ask with wrong motives, that you may spend what you get on your pleasures." The Holy Spirit knows our inner thoughts, so He is able to make the right decisions regarding our gifts. Paul makes this matter clear at the beginning of his dissertation on the gifts of the Spirit when he says (I Cor. 12:3): "No one who is speaking by the Spirit of God says, 'Jesus be cursed,' and no one can say, 'Jesus is Lord,' except by the Holy Spirit." The author of Hebrews echoes, and makes utterly unambiguous, what Paul said in his dissertation on the gifts of the Spirit, that it is the Spirit Himself who distributes His gifts to people, according to His own will (I Cor. 12:11): "All these are the work of one and the same Spirit, and he gives them to each man, just as he determines."[28]

The opening statement of the author of Hebrews, although difficult to understand, is still a very important message. It challenges us to listen carefully to what he has to say, because it may affect our eternal destinies. It is difficult to understand because it is so convoluted. This is one reason why many people think Paul is the author of this book, because he often wrote extensive sentences in his thirteen letters. In the Greek, the opening sentence actually covers all four opening verses of the book. Mercifully it is broken down into several sentences in many modern versions in English; that helps us grasp it better. But the KJV slavishly follows the original and keeps the statement as one sentence, as does the American Standard Version (ASV) of 1901. The New International Version (NIV) breaks up the sentence into four, but it is still complicated. I intend to use the NIV throughout this study, except where I indicate some other translation is quoted.

---

[28] This theme is spelled out fully in my book, THE SPIRIT OF SCRIPTURE, pages 73 to 77.

# CHAPTER II
## JESUS IS BETTER THAN PEOPLE.  HEB. 2:5-18.

**Heb. 2:5.  It is not to angels that He has subjected the world to come....**

The author of Hebrews continues his theme that Jesus is "better than" the angels, with an interesting twist.  He develops the idea that since our Savior became a man, therefore in one sense at least He was made for a brief time even lower than angels, since humans are lower than angels.  Still, even in His humanity, Jesus is superior to angels.

We have already seen that Jesus is the sovereign of the present universe, since He created all things that exist (Heb. 1:10, the quotation from Ps. 102:25-27), and is King over them all, since the throne and the scepter (Heb. 1:8, the quotation from Ps. 45:6-7) are His.  But in addition, the world to come is Jesus' domain as well.  This is the thought the author emphasizes here, making clear that the angels will not match Jesus' position even after this universe disappears.

Many people stumble over the idea of being "subjected" to someone or something.  It is human nature for us to want to be in control of our lives with no interference from any outside influence.  We do not want our teacher to give us homework; we hate to stop when the traffic light turns red just before we get to the corner; and we grit our teeth in outrage when it rains on our football game.  Our experience in this life makes it abundantly clear that many factors are capable of changing, even ruining, our plans.  My brother fully intended to go to his sixth grade closing picnic, but the day before the event he fell ill with chicken pox.  One need not even consider God in such a happening (although we Christians know God's hand was in it) to realize that our choices are truncated at almost every step of our lives.  But if Jesus is sovereign over the world now, we can see that He decides when we get sick and when we stay well.  A good biblical example of that is the final illness of Herod who was king in the early days of the apostle Paul, when he was struck by "worms" and died, because he attempted to usurp God's glory (Acts 12:21-23).

The Greek verb root translated here "has subjected" is ὑποτάσσω, which according to Delling[1] means "to place under," or "to subordinate."  In connection with sovereigns it means to be subject to.  The submission can be either voluntary or enforced.  The word in Greek does not necessarily carry the idea of "obedience," although that is implicit in the whole idea of submission.  It is the same word used by Paul in Eph. 5:21, 22, and 24, in his discussion of the mutual submission of Christians to one another, the submission of a wife to her husband, and the submission of the Church to Christ.  Paul also tells us that Adam caused the world to be "subjected to frustration" because of his original sin (Rom. 8:20).  We find the verb also in I Cor. 15:26-27, where we read, "The last enemy to be destroyed is death. For 'he has put everything un-

---
[1] Gerhard Delling, in article ὑποτάσσω in TDNT, Vol. VIII, pages 39-46.

der his feet.'"

What will be the extent of the "world to come" that will be subjected to Christ? The Greek word used here for "world" is οἰκουμένη, which means basically "the inhabited part of the earth." It could have meant the whole Greek world, that is, the realm of civilized people; or it could mean the dwelling-places of all humans wherever they lived. It is from this Greek word that we get our English term "ecumenical" which ordinarily means "whole" or "worldwide," and refers to the Church as a single body in the world.

John, in his visions (Rev. 21:1), wrote, "I saw a new heaven and a new earth, for the first heaven and the first earth had passed away, and there was no longer any sea." Peter says the same thing in his discussion of the destruction of the present world in II Pet. 3:1-13, and ends with these words: "That day will bring about the destruction of the heavens by fire, and the elements will melt in the heat. But in keeping with his promise we are looking forward to a new heaven and a new earth, the home of righteousness." Therefore, we assume that the "world to come" will include a heaven and an earth. The whole Bible gives us sufficient evidence that there will be an eternal hell as well. Whether that hell will be integrated somewhere into the new heaven, or completely separate from it, we cannot be sure. But there is no doubt of its existence. Jesus speaks of it often in the gospels, and John tells about it in the Revelation, especially chapters 19 and 20. Whether there is such a place called purgatory is a matter of dispute, particularly between Roman Catholics and Protestants. Such a place is neither mentioned nor hinted at any place in scripture except in one of the Old Testament apocryphal books. The Apocrypha is accepted as canonical by the Roman Catholic Church, but is rejected by all Protestants as having such authority, although it is included in some Protestant versions of the Bible; normally for historical purposes only.

It is in the book of II Maccabees that we read about purgatory. But Goodspeed, in his preface to that book, writes in part:

Second Maccabees...is professedly an abbreviation of the lost history of the events of 175-160 B.C., written by Jason of Cyrene. It thus parallels the most significant part of First Maccabees, but does it in a very affected, exaggerated, and stilted way. It has no such claims to historical worth as First Maccabees.[2]

The passage which supposedly speaks of purgatory is II Maccabees 12:38-45. The gist of the passage, which is too long to quote here, is that Judas Maccabeus gave command to the soldiers, after a battle near Adullam, to gather the bodies of their fallen comrades. In doing so, the soldiers "found amulets of the idols of Jamnia, which the Law forbids the Jews to wear." Judas urged the living soldiers to avoid sin, because he believed the other soldiers died because of this infraction. The survivors believed that the dead would rise one day, otherwise "it would have been superfluous and foolish to pray for the

---

[2]   Edgar J. Goodspeed, THE APOCRYPHA, AN AMERICAN TRANSLATION, page 443.

dead....Therefore he made atonement for the dead, so that they might be set free from their sin." Although the term "purgatory" is not mentioned here, the concept is made clear: those who die with unforgiven sins are relegated to a special place; the living must pray for their release from those sins and their punishment; and atonement must be made for them before they can enter heaven. Since the Bible nowhere else hints at such a place or such transactions, Protestants reject the present or future existence of purgatory.

### ...about which we are speaking.

The author is simply tying these subsequent thoughts to what he has already written in the first part of his letter to the Hebrews. We may agree that what he is talking about is the world to come, or the fact that Jesus is the sovereign over whatever world exists or has existed or shall exist. We need not belabor that point here.

### Heb. 2:6. But there is a place where someone has testified....

This clause is a good reminder to us that the author of Hebrews bases all his argument on the scriptures of the Old Testament, which he unquestionably considered to be the infallible word of God. He is not interested in putting together a logical argument which some more logical mind might refute. His writing is not a mere history lesson of what happened to Israel in days gone by, or even his (perhaps) twisted interpretation of that history. His only purpose is to show what God had said of the ministry in Old Testament times, and to compare that ministry and its participants with Jesus Christ and His ministry, as expressed in the life of Christ and reported accurately to him and to all who would listen. So what follows is a long quotation from Ps. 8:4-6, attributed to David in its introduction, which shows the proper relationship among Jesus Christ, angels, and human beings. It is a doxology to God for His majesty revealed in His acts of creation of everything.

David makes a great contrast between God's majesty and man's humility. In spite of man's humble status, David points out, he as a mere creature has been appointed by God to have dominion over all else in earth (and perhaps even in the whole universe, which man is now exploring). This thought is an echo of what God promised to Adam in Gen. 1, verses 26 and 28-29:

> Then God said, "Let us make man in our image, in our likeness...." God blessed them and said to them, "Be fruitful and increase in number; fill the earth and subdue it. Rule over the fish of the sea and the birds of the air and over every living creature that moves on the ground." Then God said, "I give you every seed-bearing plant on the face of the whole earth and every tree that has fruit with seed in it. They will be yours for food."

All this is said of mankind in general. But the author of Hebrews is using this passage to show a mighty contrast between man the creature and the God-man Jesus Christ the Creator of all things.

70

## What is man that you are mindful of him?

David begins by stating the abject insignificance of man in comparison to God. There really is no valid comparison. In spite of this, God *is* mindful of mere man. At the very least, He knows the most prominent people. In Is. 43:1 we read what God says to the father of the nation of Israel:

> But now, this is what the LORD says—
>> he who created you, O Jacob,
>> he who formed you, O Israel:
> "Fear not, for I have redeemed you;
>> I have called you by name; you are mine."

In like manner, God not only knew Jeremiah before he was born, He made him to be the man he became (Jer. 1:4-5):

> The word of the LORD came to me, saying,
>> "Before I formed you in the womb I knew you,
>> before you were born I set you apart;
>> I appointed you as a prophet to the nations."

More than just famous people, God knew all about common people as well. To His disciples in the Sermon on the Mount, which probably included more than just the twelve apostles, Jesus assured them (Matt. 6:26): "Look at the birds of the air; they do not sow or reap or store away in barns, and yet your heavenly Father feeds them. Are you not much more valuable than they?" Later on, Jesus said to His twelve (Matt. 10:30): "...even the very hairs of your head are all numbered."

Consider this illustration. Suppose you were walking through your living room at home. As you were walking, you saw a needle lying on the carpet. You didn't want anyone to step on it to get hurt, so you stooped to pick it up to discard later. Do you suppose that act of picking up the needle would be too insignificant for God to notice? Many people would give a strong affirmative answer. But now suppose an additional factor. A sniper was outside your window with his rifle pointed at your head, and just as you stooped to pick up the needle, the sniper pulled the trigger. But because you had stooped at that instant, he missed you. Now, do you suppose God would be interested in whether you lived or died at that instant, especially if He had some great mission for you to perform yet in your life? Most certainly if God cares for the sparrow's welfare, surely He is concerned whether you live to carry out your assigned mission.

All of the portion of Psalm 8 quoted here continues to exalt mankind above the creation. But the author of Hebrews relates the quotation to more than mere men; he refers it as well to Jesus Christ, God who became a Man. It is important for us to know this distinction in what the author says, and to recognize when he is talking about man in general and when he means God who became Man, Jesus. First of all, if God knows all about each human being, surely He can have no lack of knowledge about Himself as the God-Man.

71

So when the Psalmist says, "What is man that you are mindful of him?" he is saying that the Father is fully "mindful" of the Son.

### ...the son of man that you care for him?

This clause really says the same thing as the previous one. Again, this is an example of synonymous parallelism, which we mentioned before.

The perpetual blessings we all receive from God (including the rain that falls on the unrighteous as well as the righteous, and the sun that rises on the evil and the good, Matt. 5:45) unfortunately become so commonplace that we forget that James (1:16-17) reminds us , "Don't be deceived, my dear brothers. Every good and perfect gift is from above, coming down from the Father of the heavenly lights, who does not change like shifting shadows." When we sit down casually to our breakfast each morning, how many of us think of the infinite number of details God pursued to get the breakfast to us? The cereal we eat was grown as grain by a farmer in Iowa, who needed machinery, gasoline, farm hands, not to mention fertilizer and sunshine and rain as well as God's life-giving power to grow the plants. Then God saw to it that a trucker took the grain to a factory in Michigan, where the grain was processed by many people to whom God had given wisdom to do their work in a factory built by materials God had provided. Packaging materials came from several sources to keep the food edible. Someone else shipped it to your grocery store, where the wife God gave you purchased it with money you earned through the talents God gave you. She also set it on the table for you, placed in dishes made of ceramic by someone else, and brought to you through God's providence. Do not forget that God gave you a healthy body that can assimilate the nourishment from the food. We could proceed with a like litany for the milk and sugar you put on your cereal, or the bacon and eggs you eat, or the pancakes, the bananas you slice on the cereal, and the orange juice you drink, and Juan Valdez' coffee. And that is only breakfast. Jesus said more about that in His Sermon on the Mount, reminding us not to worry about food, or clothing, but rather to seek God's kingdom and righteousness first, and God will provide the rest for you. At least God thinks you are worth more than birds, or grass, or flowers (Matt. 6:25-34). Peter echoed the same thing when he wrote (I Pet. 5:7): "Cast all your anxiety on him because he cares for you."

If God is willing to extend Himself for us humans, how much more was He willing to care for His dear Son while He walked the earth? One of the vast differences between Jesus and the rest of us is that He never wavered from His assurance that the Father would care for Him, even through the agony of death. Jesus knew He was already the victor over death, so He faced the cross with equanimity.

* * *

72

**Heb. 2:7.**
## You made him a little lower than
## the angels....

The word translated here as "angels" is the Greek word ἀγγέλους, which was used by both the author of Hebrews and the translators of the LXX version of Psalm 8. However, the Hebrew word used in this passage is אֱלֹהִים, one of the principal words for either "God" or "gods" in the Old Testament original. Actually, either term is appropriate here, since there is no argument that God made mankind lower than angels in the hierarchy of creatures. Likewise, only a fool who would say "There is no God" (Ps. 10:4; 14:1; and 53:1), or a devotee of New Age religion would deny that man is infinitely lower than God.

Having said that about mankind in general, however, we must remember that this is a quotation from Psalm 8 to Jesus the Son. Therefore, we must see that even Jesus, the Son of God, was *made* a "little lower than the angels" for a time. At this point we must be cautious to distinguish between the concept of Jesus Christ as the eternal God who never ceased to be God even in His incarnation, and Jesus Christ as the Son who was made a man by being born of the virgin Mary. Paul makes this distinction very well in the opening words of his letter to the Romans (1:3-4), when he wrote of Jesus as God's "Son, who as to his human nature was a descendant of David, and who through the Spirit of holiness was declared with power to be the Son of God by his resurrection from the dead: Jesus Christ our Lord." The Almighty God, the Eternal One, at one point in human history "became" or "was made" a man, and thus for a while "was made" a little lower than the angels—without, however, for a moment losing His status as the God of the universe. Further, although Jesus never lost His human body once He was conceived and born, He did not remain "a little lower than the angels," as the following clause of the quotation shows.

The fact that Jesus was willing to be made a little lower than angels demonstrates His humility. Such humility is worthy of our emulation, says Paul in Phil. 2:6-8:

> [Christ], being in very nature God,
>> did not consider equality with God something to be grasped,
> but made himself nothing,
>> taking the very nature of a servant,
>> being made in human likeness.
> And being found in appearance as a man,
>> he humbled himself
>> and became obedient to death—
>> even death on a cross!

Further evidence of Christ's humility is found in His own statement to the Pharisees (John 8:29): "I always do what pleases [my Father]." Moreover, Peter adds his thought (I Pet. 2:23-24):

When they hurled their insults at him, he did not retaliate; when he suffered,
he made no threats. Instead, he entrusted himself to him who judges justly.
He himself bore our sins in his body on the tree, so that we might die to
sins and live for righteousness; by his wounds you have been healed.

These words remind us of what Isaiah said of Jesus in his chapter 53, which is
probably the greatest passage expressing Jesus' humility.

### ...you crowned him with glory and honor....

We have already discussed the kind of "glory and honor" God gave to
the human race by giving man dominion over all the creation in the world.
However, in referring this passage to all mankind, the author of the Psalm,
David, is pointing out, and the author of Hebrews is affirming, that although
man in his created estate (even before he fell into sin in Eden) was made lower
than angels, yet many shall be exalted above the angels in time to come. Peter encouraged us to become part of this great assembly (I Pet. 5:6): "Humble
yourselves, therefore, under God's mighty hand, that he may lift you up in due
time." The measure of that "lifting up" is spelled out in Peter's next letter (II
Pet. 1:4):

Through these [spiritual blessings] he has given us his very great and precious promises, so that through them you may participate in the divine
nature and escape the corruption in the world caused by evil desires.

Such participation certainly does not mean that any of us becomes a god, or
even an infinitesimal part of the living God. We understand this better because John spelled out the new nature more carefully in his first letter (I John
3:1-2):

How great is the love the Father has lavished on us, that we should be called
children of God! And that is what we are!...Dear friends, now we are children
of God, and what we will be has not yet been made known. But we know
that when he appears, we shall be like him, for we shall see him as he is.

One of these days, humans will be exalted even above the angels. Paul assures the church members in Corinth (I Cor. 6:3), "Do you not know that we
will judge angels?" That event will not occur in this world though, but in the
next.

In applying these words to Jesus, there is a magnificent contrast between the two halves of this verse: what *was* for a time in the middle of
eternity, and what *continued to be* without interruption throughout eternity.
Although in His humanity Jesus was made lower than angels, He was exalted
above everything else except Himself. In His High Priestly Prayer in John
17, Jesus invited His Father to glorify Him then, because His time for exaltation had come, through His death and victory over death. He said (verses 1, 5,
10, 24),

Father, the time has come. Glorify your Son, that your Son may glorify
you....And now, Father, glorify me in your presence with the glory I had
with you before the world began....Glory has come to me through [those
whom you gave me out of the world]....Father, I want those you have given

74

me to be with me where I am, and to see my glory, the glory you have given me because you loved me before the creation of the world.

In the first chapter of Colossians, after Paul prayed on behalf of the people there, he penned a soaring doxology to Christ in verses 15-20. It is too long to copy here, but you would benefit greatly by reading those six verses which honor and glorify the Savior. Likewise, the book of the Revelation is laden with songs of praise, both long and short, to Jesus Christ the "Alpha and the Omega...who is, and who was, and who is to come, the Almighty" (Rev. 1:8), beginning with the introduction to the letters to the seven churches in 1:12 to 18. Songs of praise are sung by angels, the twenty-four elders, the living creatures, the redeemed people, together with heavenly hosts, singing such wondrous hymns as these found in chapter 5, verses 12 and 13:

Worthy is the Lamb, who was slain,
to receive power and wealth and wisdom and strength
and honor and glory and praise!

and:

To him who sits on the throne and to the Lamb
be praise and honor and glory and power, for ever and ever!

A moment ago we read Paul's words in his letter to the Philippians how Jesus was willing to be humbled. Following that passage, Paul continues with His exaltation (Phil. 2:9-11):

Therefore God exalted him to the highest place
and gave him the name that is above every name,
that at the name of Jesus every knee should bow,
in heaven and on earth and under the earth,
and every tongue confess that Jesus Christ is Lord,
to the glory of God the Father.

Peter explicitly states that at Jesus' exaltation He will be superior to angels (I Pet. 3:22): "[He] has gone into heaven and is at God's right hand—with angels, authorities and powers in submission to him."

Here is a practical thought with regard to Jesus' exaltation. If you know Jesus Christ as your own Savior and Lord, then you will be delighted to bow down and worship and exalt Him. On the other hand, think of those who have denied Him in this life. Because every knee shall bow down, they also will be required to do so, we may even say "forced" to bow down and worship Him; but with every fiber of their beings they will hate the requirement and hate Him who requires it.

### Heb. 2:8.

#### ...and put everything under his feet.

In applying this statement to the human race, we refer once again to Gen. 1:26 and 28-29. No mention is made there, however, that humans will have dominion over angels. Reference has been made already to I Cor. 6:3, which implies that the situation will be reversed one day, when men shall

75

judge angels.

Once again we look at this part of the quotation from Psalm 8 in reference to Jesus. Now if men are not superior to angels at this time, it is clear that Jesus always has been superior to them, and will continue so through eternity. The doxology in Colossians 1, also referred to above, proves that Jesus is superior to everything that exists—with the exception of God Himself. Because of its great importance, here is a portion of that doxology (verses 18 to 20):

> [The Son] is the head of the body, the church; he is the beginning and the firstborn from among the dead, so that in everything he might have the supremacy. For God was pleased to have all his fullness dwell in him, and through him to reconcile to himself all things, whether things on earth or things in heaven, by making peace through his blood, shed on the cross.

The opening words of Ps.110 have been quoted by the author of Hebrews, to show specifically that everything has been put under Jesus' feet. We must understand further that everything has been put under the feet of Jesus *alone*. We humans may have dominion over the world and the things in it, but Jesus' domain covers everything, including men and angels.

**In putting everything under him, God left nothing that is not subject to him.**

If you bake a pie, you have a right to decide whether to serve it to your family for dinner tonight, or to give it to a friend who is ill and cannot cook. Since you made it, you have full control over it, and that is as it should be. By the same token, if God the Son made the universe, He rightly is sovereign over His whole creation. The scripture tells us that Jesus is the Creator of all things (John 1:3): "Through him all things were made; without him nothing was made that has been made."

We probably take comfort in the knowledge that our Savior has control over our enemies—even over such a powerful enemy as Satan. He is able, when He wills, to keep evil ones from harming us. Asaph the hymn writer knew this; he wrote (Ps. 76:10, KJV): "Surely the wrath of man shall praise thee: the remainder of wrath shalt thou restrain." Paul showed that he also was aware of it (I Cor. 10:13):

> No temptation has seized you except what is common to man. And God is faithful; he will not let you be tempted beyond what you can bear. But when you are tempted, he will also provide a way out so that you can stand up under it.

The author of Hebrews is thinking specifically about the angels, who are lower than Jesus; and they, with all creation, are subject to Him. Peter makes that idea explicit in I Pet. 3:21-22. He was writing about Noah and his family who were saved through the flood of waters, the water being a symbol of baptism: "It saves you by the resurrection of Jesus Christ, who has gone into heaven and is at God's right hand—with angels, authorities and powers in submission to him."

God does care for us in this way, but only if we are willing to let Him control us as well as our enemies. During the United States' involvement in the Viet Nam conflict, a young lady brought her boyfriend to my study one day to talk about getting married. During our preliminary discussion, Mary blurted out, "Why doesn't God step in and stop all the evil people who are causing so much trouble and sorrow in Viet Nam?" My response was not what she wanted to hear: "I'm sorry, young lady, but you simply can't have it both ways. If you want God to stop the evil people over there from committing sin, you have to be willing to let Him intervene in your life as well. You know that your mother believes that you intend to commit serious sin in marrying this young man, since he by his own confession is not a Christian, and you claim to be one. You know the biblical rule as well as I do, 'Do not be yoked together with unbelievers'" (II Cor. 6:14). They left my study quite sad, and later traveled to another state to be married by someone else. A short time later, I heard that they had been divorced. God is able to stop us from sinning, but if we are stubborn, He often lets us do as we please, and we pay the consequences, just like Adam and Eve did.

### Yet at present we do not see everything subject to him.

Although Jesus has been glorified by His death and resurrection (as He discussed with His Father in John 17, the High Priestly prayer), yet the Father has chosen to let the world continue in sin for a time, until Jesus returns and everything will be restored as it was at the creation before sin entered. In saying all this, we must be very careful to distinguish between the idea that the sinful world is rebellious against Christ during this present age, and the idea that He still has absolute authority over all His creation. Just because God the Son allows sin to continue does not mean that He has either lost or abandoned control over the creation. Paul the apostle may have alluded to this when in his sermon at the Areopagus in Athens he said of man's idolatry (Acts 17:30): "In the past God overlooked [KJV says "winked at"] such ignorance, but now he commands all people everywhere to repent."

Another way to look at the idea that not everything is subject to Jesus just yet is to remember what Paul says to husbands about their relationship to their wives in Eph. 5:25-27:

> Husbands, love your wives, just as Christ loved the church and gave himself up for her to make her holy, cleansing her by the washing with water through the word, and to present her to himself as a radiant church, without stain or wrinkle or any other blemish, but holy and blameless.

The Church, the Body of Christ, most certainly is not yet perfect. I, as an ordained clergyman, am more particularly aware of this than the ordinary worshiper in the pew, even more than most elected church officers. On the other hand, virtually every person in the world who has heard of the Church, knows of the infightings, the hypocrisy within every segment of the Body.

But if this is really so, then did Christ die in vain to make the Church perfect in every way? In my normal counseling sessions with couples seeking marriage, I point out the fact that just as the Church is not perfect in Christ's sight, so also the wife-to-be is not yet perfect in the groom's sight. But just as Christ loved the Church so much that He was willing to die to make her perfect, knowing that it would be at least two millennia before she became such in His sight, so also a husband must love his wife sufficiently to make her perfect in *his* sight. It will happen, but only if he is willing to give himself to the very point of death for her sake. Too often men see imperfections in their wives as the wives' fault, when they should realize instead that it is their own fault for not loving their wives sufficiently. Back to the Church, most if not all the members of churches I have served have recognized that I as their Minister was a large part of the imperfection they found in their church. By the same token, each of them is at least partly responsible for the stains, wrinkles, and blemishes in their church. There is the story of the pharisaical Christian who boasted to his friend that he had never joined a church, because he had yet to find a perfect church. His friend said, "When you find the perfect church, do me a favor and don't join it." The other asked in surprise, "Why not?" The friend added, "Because then it would no longer be perfect."

The wonderful truth is that one of these days the whole Church *will* be utterly "radiant, without stain or wrinkle or any other blemish." The beloved apostle John reported a vision in Rev. 21:2: "I saw the Holy City, the new Jerusalem, coming down out of heaven from God, prepared as a bride beautifully dressed for her husband." That is when we will see "everything subject to him."

### Heb. 2:9.  But we see Jesus....

We see Him only with our spiritual eyes now, of course. It is possible to have a vision of Christ, just as John did. One of the most saintly of my seminary professors was Dr. J. Christy Wilson, Sr. His family reported this event: they were all gathered around his death-bed, knowing that his breath was about to cease. Dr. Wilson, although very weak, suddenly cried out in a loud voice, "I see Jesus! I see Jesus!" With that he lay still on his bed, and was gone. There is no better way to die than that.

But even without supernatural events we can see Him now. The important question is not whether you are able to see Jesus now, but rather, "Are you eager to see Jesus now?" We may not always want to see a police officer, especially when we have just broken a traffic rule. Several years ago in Anchorage there was reported a peculiar situation, where a young fellow called the police to report that his car had just been stolen. The strange part of the story was that the man was calling from a home from which he was trying to steal a television set. If we truly love Jesus, and are seeking the aid of the Holy Spirit to do His will, we will have unmingled feelings about wanting to

see Jesus. Paul yearned to get a glimpse of Jesus, and told his young t.
Timothy that the great motivating factor for Christians to lead holy lives
this (II Tim. 4:8): "Now there is in store for me the crown of righteousnes
which the Lord, the righteous Judge, will award to me on that day—and no
only to me, but also to all who have longed for his appearing."

**...who was made a little lower than the angels, now
crowned with glory and honor....**

We have already discussed at length these two clauses, and noted their
relationship, in our discussion of the quotation from Psalm 8 found in Heb.
2:7. It may be profitable for you to go back to that discussion before you
proceed. This outline may aid you in putting the whole matter together:

1. Jesus was the Eternal Creator, the absolute Sovereign over all.
2. Jesus humbled Himself as a man, even a servant, to the point of death.
3. Jesus was exalted above all His creation, despite the moment of
   humbling.

Why did Jesus have a *right* to be exalted? The answer is found in the
next clause.

**...because he suffered death....**

This was the ultimate act of obedience on the part of the filial Son in
His relationship with His Father. Near the end of our study we will look further at the attitude Jesus had toward His death, when we consider these words
in Heb. 12:2: "...who for the joy set before him endured the cross, scorning
its shame, and sat down at the right hand of the throne of God." Still, never
has the world seen such a mingling of joy and sorrow, exaltation and scorn,
euphoria and pain, well-being and shame, as Jesus experienced through His
earthly dying.

The Old Testament contains numerous passages which speak by way of
prophecy about Jesus' suffering. You are invited to search for them, after we
copy just two here.

My God, my God, why have you forsaken me?
　　Why are you so far from saving me,
　　so far from the words of my groaning?
I am poured out like water,
　　and all my bones are out of joint.
My heart has turned to wax;
　　it has melted away within me.
My strength is dried up like a potsherd,
　　and my tongue sticks to the roof of my mouth;
　　you lay me in the dust of death. [Ps. 22:1; 14-15]

He was pierced for our transgressions,
　　he was crushed for our iniquities;
the punishment that brought us peace was upon him,

and by his wounds we are healed. [Is. 53:5]

The New Testament is so freighted with discussions of the death of Christ that is it impossible to do justice to them by quoting just a few. We read about His suffering and death not only at the end of each gospel, but also by way of prophecy of Jesus and others leading up to the actual events. The rest of the New Testament is founded on the two-pronged base of Christ's death and His resurrection. The next clause in Hebrews, and other scriptural attestation, make that clear.

**...so that by the grace of God he might taste death for everyone.**

Here is the culmination of all Jesus did in coming into the world. We have already noted I Tim. 1:15, which gives the purpose of the incarnation: "Here is a trustworthy saying that deserves full acceptance: Christ Jesus came into the world to save sinners—of whom I am the worst." Of course it was by His death that He saved us. Another passage which makes this clear is Rom. 5:8-10:

> God demonstrates his own love for us in this: While we were still sinners, Christ died for us. Since we have now been justified by his blood, how much more shall we be saved from God's wrath through him! For if, when we were God's enemies, we were reconciled to him through the death of his Son, how much more, having been reconciled, shall we be saved through his life!

I would call to your mind just one other passage, which is one of my favorites (Phil. 3:9-11):

> [I want to] be found in him, not having a righteousness of my own that comes from the law, but that which is through faith in Christ—the righteousness that comes from God and is by faith. I want to know Christ and the power of his resurrection and the fellowship of sharing in his sufferings, becoming like him in his death, and so, somehow, to attain to the resurrection from the dead.

These passages ought to be self-explanatory to anyone who reads them. Beyond that, they ought to be taken at face value. That is why Paul wrote what he wrote, and he intended for us to understand what he meant by what he wrote.

We may question one matter contained in the words from Hebrews. Did the author really mean that Christ actually tasted "death for everyone;" or did He taste death merely for "everyone who believes on Him"? This happens to be an exceedingly controversial matter which unfortunately tends to estrange Christians from one another. My readers have a right to know where I stand on the issue. I believe that Jesus Christ died for every human who ever lived or who shall live. I hasten to add that the whole of scripture makes abundantly clear that even if that is true, not everyone for whom Christ died will arrive in heaven. There are many passages which state quite clearly that Christ died for everyone. In addition, as a practical matter, I would find it very

80

difficult to be an evangelist to anyone if I could say to him nothing more encouraging than, "Jesus may or may not have died for you; I really don't know. If He didn't, then you are going to hell." I would much rather say, "Jesus died for you; if you repent and trust in Him as your own Savior and Lord, you are going to heaven." Actually, it really doesn't matter whether Christ died for the lost; He knows who they are. Every Christian has this responsibility to carry the message of salvation to the world so every one we speak to has full opportunity to receive Christ. Then God will take care of the proper results.

**Heb. 2:10.    In bringing many sons to glory, it was fitting that God....**

I am not sure that I understand some parts of this verse as fully as I ought. I may not understand it fully even after I get to heaven.

Regarding the clause, "it was fitting," many people question the wisdom of God in causing His own Son Jesus Christ to suffer in order to save people from the penalty of sin so they could go to heaven. They say specifically, "Couldn't God have planned some better way to do it?" One possible answer surely is, "Most certainly, God could have done it in any one of an infinite number of ways, ways we could not dream of by means of our finite minds. Surely the omniscient God is not limited in what He can do, or in how He chooses to do it."

We humans are filled with many such silly questions. After telling us that "God has mercy on whom he wants to have mercy, and he hardens whom he wants to harden," Paul talks about one of them in Rom. 9:19-21:

> One of you will say to me: "Then why does God still blame us? For who resists his will?" But who are you, O man, to talk back to God? "Shall what is formed say to him who formed it, 'Why did you make me like this?'" Does not the potter have the right to make out of the same lump of clay some pottery for noble purposes and some for common use?

It is foolish for us to think that God, who made everything according to His own plan and for His own purpose, should need to consult us creatures regarding whether we want to go to heaven or not.

Surely our time could be better spent in avoiding such a question; rather, we should acknowledge, "God chose to do it this way. Blessed be the name of the Lord."

The author of Hebrews says briefly, "it was fitting" for God to work salvation in this way. My best guess as to why it was fitting is that since the Old Testament is filled with information about making sacrifices for sin, it "fits" quite well into the picture for God to plan that a Sacrifice be made for sin in the New Testament as well. But this brings up the question, "Why was it 'fitting' for God to arrange for sacrifices for sin from the beginning of human history until the time of Jesus?" To me, that question is imponderable. We cannot go further back without attempting to open the mysteries of God's ways which He has chosen not to reveal to us, at least not yet. It would be more sensible for us to ask God, "Why did You make me with ten toes, instead of six, or fourteen? After all, a horse has but four toes on all four feet." It would be better simply not to ask such a question. I, as the writer of this discussion, certainly am not trying to hide the truth from you; nor is God trying to hide the truth from you either, at least not any truth which you need to know. After all, if God could have wrought our salvation in any one of an infinite number of ways, He was free to choose whichever way He wanted, without any interference from us.

### ...for whom and through whom everything exists....

We have already discussed at length the matter of "through whom everything exists." God is the Creator of whatever exists, with the exception of Himself, since naturally the Creator did not create Himself. We have noted further that it was each person in the Godhead who participated in the act, or acts, of creation. Certainly the Father was not the sole Creator, but the Son and the Holy Spirit took part in the creation.

We have not yet discussed as fully the matter of "*for* whom everything exists." From his first breath outside the womb, man has demonstrated that he considers himself the very center of the universe. Not only is he its center, but it exists for his exclusive benefit and enjoyment. Nothing else, either living or inorganic, is significant or has any rights in itself, but is obliged to satisfy every whim of man. Not even any other man has a right to self-satisfaction, but is there to feed his foibles. Certainly in the beginning of man's life, there is no thought of bringing any shred of satisfaction to his Creator; he does not even consider the existence of a Creator, especially one who might make demands upon the man. Evidence of this all-consuming self-centeredness is the first wail coming from the lips of the newborn babe. It does not take a spank from the attending physician to cause the infant to cry. Immediately he senses needs and wants: food, warmth, cleansing, freedom from pain, safety. The new human does not care who or what provides for him, whether it be the exhausted and pain-wracked mother, some other person, or any inanimate object; he wants what he wants, and he wants it immediately.

But God did not make man just to wallow in his own desires, either good or evil. God had an entirely different purpose for the creation. The author of Hebrews tells us that everything exists for God Himself ("for whom...everything exists"). When He finished creating, "God saw all that he had made, and it was very good" (Gen. 1:31). In God's dealings with His creation, and especially with human beings, all His purposes are entirely arbitrary, that is, they do not depend in the slightest degree on the feelings or desires of man, but solely on His own design. For instance, when God was bringing the Jewish nation into the Promised Land under Moses, He informed the people that His decision to choose them over all other nations was totally subjective. Moses told them (Deut. 7:6-9):
The LORD your God has chosen you out of all the peoples on the face of the

earth to be his people, his treasured possession. The LORD did not set his affection on you and choose you because you were more numerous than other peoples, for you were the fewest of all peoples. But it was because the LORD loved you and kept the oath he swore to your forefathers that he brought you out with a mighty hand and redeemed you from the land of slavery, from the power of Pharaoh king of Egypt. Know therefore that the LORD your God is God; he is the faithful God, keeping his covenant of love to a thousand generations of those who love him and keep his commands.

Scripture further shows that God at all times is arbitrary in His dealings with all of creation, and especially with humankind, in two parallel illustrations, each of which is repeated in both Old and New Testaments. One is the example of the domesticated olive tree (representing the Jews), from which branches have been broken off; and wild olive branches (representing the Gentiles), which have been grafted into the tame olive tree. God is the one who has control over this whole process. This is found in Rom. 11:11-24, and is alluded to in Jer. 11:14-17. The other illustration is about the potter and the clay in Rom. 9:19-29, in Jer. 18:1-12; and in Is. 64:8, mentioned above.

In commenting on God's selecting the Hebrew nation simply because He wanted to, a wag wrote:

> How odd
> Of God
> To choose
> The Jews.

The first question and answer in the Westminster Shorter Catechism has summarized God's centrality and man's dependence quite well. To the question, "What is the chief end of man?" the answer is, "Man's chief end is to glorify God, and to enjoy him for ever." Similar to that is question 39, "What is the duty which God requireth of man?" and its answer, "The duty which God requireth of man is obedience to his revealed will." One of the scripture "proofs" appended to question 1 is Paul's statement in I Cor. 10:31: "Whether therefore ye eat, or drink, or whatsoever ye do, do all to the glory of God" (the Catechism quotes the KJV).[3]

### ...should make the author of their salvation....

The term "author of their salvation" may sound foreign to us, or at least seem fuzzy in meaning. It should be helpful to dig into the meaning of the Greek word for "author" here. That word is ἀρχηγός, and has several different but related meanings. Thayer gives a set of general meanings: "leading, furnishing the first cause or occasion." He adds three specific definitions, the first of which is "the chief leader, prince," and gives as reference Acts 5:31, which is part of Peter's defense before the Sanhedrin about Jesus, slain by the religious leaders but raised to life by the Father: "God exalted him to his own right hand as Prince and Savior that he might give repentance

---

[3] CONSTITUTION OF THE PRESBYTERIAN CHURCH, page 207, footnote a.

and forgiveness of sins to Israel." Thayer's second specific definition is "one that takes the lead in any thing...and thus affords an example, a predecessor in a matter," and points us to Heb. 12:2: "Let us fix our eyes on Jesus, the author and perfecter of our faith, who for the joy set before him endured the cross, scorning its shame, and sat down at the right hand of the throne of God." Finally, Thayer adds this third definition of the Greek term, "the author," and cites the only other (two) verses in the New Testament where this word is used. One is the verse we are studying now, and the other is Acts 3:15, where Peter called Jesus the "author of life."

It may aid our understanding if we note that in Heb. 12:2, cited just above, that Jesus is called not only the ἀρχηγός, but also the τελειωτής of our faith. We shall examine more carefully a derivative of this second Greek word as we look at the next phrase in the verse. But for now, let me simply state that that word has two related meanings: one has to do with perfection, and the other with completeness. If Christ is the ἀρχηγός and τελειωτής of our faith, we could comfortably translate the idea as "the origin and completion of our faith." This then would be synonymous to the term we see several times in the book of Revelation, where Jesus is called the "A" and the "Ω" or the "Alpha and the Omega," which are the first and last letters in the Greek alphabet. So Jesus is the beginning and the ending of all that exists.

Gerhard Delling[4] adds ideas for the definition of our Greek word from secular Greek literature. He mentions that an ἀρχηγός was a hero who conquered a city, and then gave the city his name, as Athens was named for Athene. This leads us into the idea that the term means "originator" or "author." Another idea connected with the Greek term would be that of "captain."

From all this information we gather that Jesus, the "Author" of our salvation, is He who designed it, provided the means to carry it out, and then performed the act Himself. He was therefore far more than someone who simply wrote about it (as an "author" would), but He thought of it and did it—for you and me.

### ...perfect through suffering.

Is it conceivable that Jesus could be imperfect? Obviously, many people have thought so throughout Christian history. There can be no question that the members of the Sanhedrin, as well as many other Jews in Jesus' day, believed powerfully that Jesus was not perfect. Otherwise they would not have called Him a tool of the Devil, sought to kill Him, railed at Him during His several trials, and finally watched in grim satisfaction as He was nailed to the cross. Surely each of us can think of individuals or groups of people whom we know today, who believe Jesus was as much a sinner as the rest of us. However, there are many passages in scripture that assert boldly that Je-

---

[4] In TDNT, Vol. I, in the article on ἀρχηγός, pages 487-488.

sus was indeed perfect. We shall develop this difference of opinion more fully when we come to Heb. 4:15, which is perhaps the *textus classicus* on this theme.

There is one more matter that must be presented here. That is the idea, as some people see it set forth in this verse, that Jesus was at one time in the past imperfect, but later on became perfect. This is how this verse says it: "...God...should make the author of their salvation perfect through suffering." The problem can be resolved easily by looking more carefully at the meaning of the Greek word for "perfect" used here. It is the verb τελειόω, and the preponderance of meaning, according to Thayer has to do with completion rather than perfection, although the idea of perfection is very important also. Louw and Nida tend to multiply layers of fine distinction in their definitions of words, which is often helpful to obtain a broad band of related meanings in words. They give the following nuances of meanings to τελειόω: to make perfect in the moral sense; to make genuine or real, as opposed to phoniness; to complete as a task, or to finish as a race; to be completely successful in reaching a goal; to admit or initiate into as a religious rite; to make happen or accomplish or fulfill; and to attain a goal.[5] In presenting these various definitions, Louw and Nida do not attempt to set forth one concept above another, but simply state the various meanings that may be ascribed to the Greek term.

Gerhard Delling,[6] who also wrote the article on ἀρχηγός discussed above, emphasizes the idea of completeness, wholeness, and fulfillment as primary meanings of the τελειόω; although he adds the ideas of "moral 'perfection,' perfect, blameless, free from stain" as legitimate meanings as well.

The purpose of citing these references is to show that the author was less likely to refer to Jesus' moral perfectness than to the completion of His work of salvation through His suffering. Therefore, the author certainly did not intend to intimate that Jesus had been at some time sinful or imperfect in any respect; he only intended to show the finality of Jesus' work on our behalf by means of His death on the cross.

### Heb. 2:11. Both the one who makes men holy and those who are made holy are of the same family.

Here we find a new, exhilarating thought. The author of Hebrews avers that Jesus and some people have become one family. There is no more exalted state for creatures to achieve than this.

As we examine this grand statement, we must be certain, first of all, who the author is talking about. Surely "the one who makes men holy" can be none other than Jesus Christ, God the Son. He is the subject of all that the author has written so far. Not one human being can be compared to Him,

---

[5]  I give credit to Louw and Nida for the terms used in these definitions.

[6]  In TDNT, Vol. VIII, in the article on τελειόω, pages 79-84.

nor can any other creature. Paul states clearly in Rom. 3:25-26 that God the Father used Jesus (God the Son) as the instrument of salvation for people: "God presented him as a sacrifice of atonement...to demonstrate his justice at the present time, so as to be just and the one who justifies the man who has faith in Jesus." In truth, there is no Greek word in the New Testament that can be translated as "atonement," but the "sacrifice of atonement" here is ἱλαστήριον, which technically means "expiation" or total expungement of the blot of sin.

It is even more critical to denote the exact population identified by the term, "those who are made holy." This population does not include every member of the human race, both living and dead and yet to live. It includes only a certain segment of that population, identified as each "man [person] who has faith in Jesus" according to Paul's statement in Rom. 3:25-26. Jesus in no way makes holy anyone who does not have faith in Him, and no one is made holy in any other way.

Just because we who have believed in Jesus are "of the same family," that does not mean that we are identical with Him, that is, we have not become Gods (which the Mormons claim), nor have we become little parts of God with the rest of creation (which the Pantheists claim). We have already dealt with Jesus' quotation from Ps. 82:6 (which says, "You are 'gods'") in our discussion of Heb. 2:7 above.

What the author of Hebrews does claim for believers, however, is still more marvelous than we have any right to expect from God. What he says is that as part of the family of God, we have been made greater than angels. I repeat: the author of Hebrews never implied that angels were not great creatures, but in implying their greatness he is now saying that we who believe will be even greater than they. No angel will ever achieve our status.

The scriptures are sprinkled generously with allusions to our familial relationship to God the Father, Son, and Holy Spirit. According to John 1:12 we have the "right to become children of God." John says the same thing over and over in a variety of ways in I John 3:1-3:

How great is the love the Father has lavished on us, that we should be called children of God! And that is what we are!...Now we are children of God, and what we will be has not yet been made known....when he appears, we shall be like him, for we shall see him as he is.

In II Sam. 7:14 God says of Solomon, "I will be his father, and he will be my son." This is one of those prophecies with a double meaning, so it refers also to Jesus as well as to Solomon. Paul uses this quotation in a different sense in II Cor. 6:18, by applying it to all believers who have separated themselves from the uncleanness of the world: "I will be a Father to you, and you will be my sons and daughters, says the Lord Almighty." Jeremiah says Israel is God's child (Jer. 31:9):

I am Israel's father.

and Ephraim is my firstborn son.

Isaiah says the same thing of Israel (Is. 43:6):

> Bring my sons from afar
> and my daughters from the ends of the earth.

Hosea echoes the theme as well (Hos. 1:10): "In the place where it was said to them, 'You are not my people,' they will be called 'sons of the living God.'" Peter says almost the same thing in I Pet. 2:10: "Once you were not a people, but now you are the people of God; once you had not received mercy, but now you have received mercy."

### So Jesus is not ashamed to call them brothers.

Here is another amazing statement. God the Creator is willing to call some of His creatures "brothers!" Here the author of Hebrews adds several quotations from the Old Testament, showing that Jesus would call His followers "brothers." Before we look at them, let us note several places in the New Testament where Jesus actually does just that. It is at least implied in Matt. 25:40, in Jesus' parable of the sheep and the goats, where He will say to the righteous people, "...whatever you did for one of the least of these brothers of mine, you did for me." Jesus said in Matt. 12:48-50, when He was told His mother and (natural-born half-) brothers were seeking Him, "'Who is my mother, and who are my brothers?' Pointing to his disciples, he said, 'Here are my mother and my brothers. For whoever does the will of my Father in heaven is my brother and sister and mother.'" The same is said in Mk. 3:35, and in Lu. 8:19-21. When Mary was in the Garden and finally saw the risen Christ, He said to her (John 20:17), "Go...to my brothers and tell them, 'I am returning to my Father and your Father, and to my God and your God.'" Matthew reports that several women saw Christ in the Garden, and said to them (Matt. 28:10): "Do not be afraid. Go and tell my brothers to go to Galilee; there they will see me."

Please note the progression of thought through which the author of Hebrews is leading us here:

1. Jesus was the Creator of all, including angels and men.
2. Jesus was made lower than the angels; He was made a man.
3. Jesus died so that:
    a. He would be exalted.
    b. He would exalt people, so that:
4. Jesus (now), and men (later) will be above angels!

The author of Hebrews then gives three Old Testament quotations to prove his point.

### Heb. 2:12. He says

> "I will declare your name to my brothers;
> in the presence of the congregation
> I will sing your praises."

This first of the three quotations comes from Ps. 22:22. The Psalm written by Jesus' ancestor David, is the greatest passage of the Old Testament which describes in agonizing detail what happens to a person at crucifixion. Once again the author of Hebrews draws our attention to the all-important fact that Jesus' death is the means of our exaltation as His brothers. Further, Jesus is not ashamed to express this relationship of brotherhood openly to His Father; conversely, He is glad to continue to declare the Father to His brothers.

All this is done "in the presence of the congregation." There is an unfortunate tendency in our day for Christians to neglect gathering together for worship and support. This is not a new phenomenon, however, because even the author of Hebrews noted it in chapter 10, verse 25, on which we will comment further when we get there in our study. Though there have been varied forms of corporate worship throughout the history of mankind, gathering together is more helpful and important than many people wish to acknowledge. Early in my ministry, I was calling door to door in the community, inviting people who had no church home, or for some reason were not going to their churches, to attend our start-up congregation to test its benefit to them. As I approached one home, I drank in its beauty, along with that of the whole neighborhood. Huge maple trees shaded most of the area; lush grass covered every lawn; beautiful hedges, shrubs, and flowers were visible everywhere. To the side of the freshly-painted house I was approaching there was a manicured sunken garden, with wrought iron benches at intervals around it. I operated the door-knocker, and prayed while I waited for a response. A pleasant woman of middle age opened the top of the Dutch door and greeted me. I made my little speech: "Hello. I'm Tom Teply, from the Loudonville Presbyterian Church. If you do not attend church or have a church home, I invite you to visit our worship service, and hope it will be helpful to you." The lady answered immediately, "Oh, I don't need to go to church to worship God. I can go right into my garden to worship just as well there!" My comment to her was, "Yes...do you?" Startled, the woman stood motionless for several seconds, then slammed the door in my face. One benefit of going to church regularly is that you are certainly more likely to worship God than if left to yourself. In addition, the instruction, encouragement, fellowship and admonition you receive when you worship together is something you can never receive when you go it alone, as Elijah found out when he fled from Jezebel and thought he was the only God-fearing person left in Israel (I Kings 19:14-18).

Jesus has even promised to "sing the praises" of the Father in the presence of the congregation. An important part of every worship service is the singing of hymns by all the people. Often in addition, one or more choirs, a soloist or small group, and/or an instrumental ensemble will present an anthem and other special music. Martin Luther attributed the great success of the Protestant Reformation in large part to joyful singing of God's praise by the whole congregation. Apart from the Psalm quoted here, there is at least one additional reference to Jesus' singing praises in the midst of the congregation. When Jesus and His disciples had completed their celebration of the Passover Feast and the first sharing of the Lord's Supper in the upper room, Matthew records the way they concluded the service (Matt. 26:30): "When they had sung a hymn, they went out to the Mount of Olives." Some scholars believe that more of Jesus' followers than the original apostles were present at the observance, while others believe only the inner circle of the eleven remained to its end.

### Heb. 2:13. And again,
### "I will put my trust in him."

Here is the second of the author's three Old Testament quotations to prove that Jesus was above (better than) even the angels. This statement is found in Is. 8:17. That chapter in Isaiah is sandwiched between two chapters Christians hold significant as Messianic passages we love to quote at Christmas time.

Isaiah 7 is the story of the invasion of the land of Judah by Syria and Israel in the days of Ahaz King of Judah. God promised Ahaz through the prophet Isaiah that He would protect the country through this most recent threat. Because Ahaz was not convinced, Isaiah invited Ahaz to ask for a sign from God to prove that the land would remain intact at that time. The sign was to be fulfilled twice in history, once for Ahaz, and once seven centuries later as a sign to the whole world of their deliverance from the great enemy of men, sin and its punishment. The sign is found in Is. 7:14: "Therefore the LORD himself will give you a sign: The virgin will be with child and will give birth to a son, and will call him Immanuel." For Ahaz the sign was carried out in the birth of Isaiah's son, Maher-Shalal-Hash-Baz (Is. 8:1), born of Isaiah's prophetess wife, who was not a virgin but a "young woman of marriageable age, whether a virgin or not," which is the proper definition of the Hebrew word עַלְמָה. Brown, Driver and Briggs gives this technical definition: "young woman (ripe sexually; maid or newly married)." If Isaiah had wanted to use a more restrictive word here, which could mean only "virgin," he could have used the word בְּתוּלָה, but then his prophecy could not have referred to the sign to Ahaz. Of course, Isaiah's wife was not a virgin, or she would not have had a child, and no sign then could have been given to King Ahaz. On the other hand, to translate the Hebrew word as "virgin" in the right context is also entirely proper, as when it refers to the birth of Jesus, Son of the heavenly Father by the power of the Holy Spirit and of the virgin Mary. This, of course, is the second fulfillment of Isaiah's prophecy.

It is entirely proper, therefore, and probably preferable, to translate the Hebrew word עַלְמָה in Is. 7:14 as "young woman." However, when Matthew quotes Isaiah's verse and applies it to the birth of Jesus in Matt. 1:23, he translates the Hebrew word for "young woman" using the Greek word παρθένος, whose meaning is restricted to "virgin," not just any young woman whether a virgin or not. Our NIV rendering of that verse is: "'The virgin will be with child and will give birth to a son, and they will call him Immanuel'—which means, 'God with us.'" This is the proper translation of the word under discussion. Unfortunately, not all translators into English were aware of these nuances of meanings. In 1950, Charles B. Williams had his translation of the New Testament[7] published. His translation reads:

> The maiden will become pregnant and have a son,
> And they will call Him Immanuel.

I understand that shortly after that book was published, a revision was published which used the proper translation "virgin" in place of the ambiguous "maiden."

That the Jews, long before the time of Jesus, believed that a "virgin" would conceive and bear a child who would be "God with us," is given clear evidence in the fact that the LXX (Greek) version of the Old Testament translates Is. 7:14 with the Greek term παρθένος, just like the quotation in Matt. 1:23. Alfred Edersheim affirms this, adding the thought that it was Jews who interpreted Isaiah's word to mean a virgin:[8] "The quotation of St. Matthew follows, with scarcely any variation, the rendering of the LXX. That *they* [the Jews] should have translated the Hebrew, עַלְמָה by παρθένος, 'a Virgin,' is surely sufficient evidence of the admissibility of such a rendering" (Edersheim's emphasis). The LXX was completed at least a century before Jesus was born,[9] so that they had believed in the virgin birth of their Messiah for many years before the event. It may well be that they accepted the concept of the virgin birth shortly after (if not from the time that) Isaiah wrote his prophecy in the seventh century BC. Delitzsch[10] affirms that Isaiah was surely referring to Jesus when he wrote the prophecy here: "It was the Messiah whom the prophet saw here as about to be born, then again in ch. ix. as actually born, and again in ch. xi. as reigning,—an indivisible triad of consolatory images in three distinct stages...." In addition, Jennings[11] adds another refer-

---

[7] Charles B. Williams, THE NEW TESTAMENT: A TRANSLATION IN THE LANGUAGE OF THE PEOPLE, p. 12.

[8] Alfred Edersheim, THE LIFE AND TIMES OF JESUS THE MESSIAH, Vol. One, page 156, footnote 3.

[9] Alfred Rahlfs, in his introductory article "History of the Septuagint Text" in his edition of the LXX, SEPTUAGINTA, Vol. I, page xxii: "The Pentateuch...was translated...during the rule of Philadelphus (285-247 B. C.)....there was in existence towards the end of the 2nd century B. C. a Greek translation of the whole, or at least of the essential parts, of the O. T. There is no reason for us to doubt that the LXX text of that period was in general agreement with our present-day text."

[10] Franz Delitzsch, KEIL AND DELITZSCH: BIBLICAL COMMENTARY ON THE PROPHECIES OF ISAIAH, Vol. I, page 218.

[11] Jennings, F. C., STUDIES IN ISAIAH, p. 85.

ence next to Isaiah's prophecy that shows the he meant a dual fulfillment of what he predicted (Jennings agrees that the first fulfillment was accomplished in Isaiah's son):

In the next chapter [after chapter 7] Isaiah becomes the father of a child, who is also a sign (as we are divinely told in chap. 8:18, and the fact that God tells us that the child is a sign justifies this interpretation), the mother being an unmarried young woman, the prophetess.

George Adam Smith[12] puts a different twist on the interpretation of Is. 7:14. He claims that in the first part of Is. 7 God promises (through Isaiah) to give King Ahaz a sign that He would deliver Judah from the twin enemy, that is, Syria and Israel. But because Ahaz rejected God's gracious offer and chose rather to seek the aid of Assyria, God then promised to give the unwilling king an entirely different sign, that of the child born of a virgin or young woman of marriageable age. This interpretation, of course, negates the idea of a Messiah to be born later of a virgin.

The other Christmas passage surrounding Is. 8:17 is the very familiar saying in 9:6-7:

For to us a child is born,
to us a son is given,
and the government will be on his shoulders.
And he will be called
Wonderful Counselor, Mighty God,
Everlasting Father, Prince of Peace.
Of the increase of his government and peace
there will be no end.
He will reign on David's throne
and over his kingdom,
establishing and upholding it
with justice and righteousness
from that time on and forever.
The zeal of the LORD Almighty
will accomplish this.

There can be no doubt that this is one of the great Messianic passages, not only in Isaiah, but in the whole Old Testament. The four mighty names given Him in verse 6 prove that He is to be identified as God Himself. The two middle terms especially show this. "Mighty God" ought never be doubted as the one true living Creator God. Some people would claim that since Jesus is called merely "Mighty" and not "Almighty," then He must be another God, since the one great original God is called "Jehovah Almighty." However, even those who would make such a claim, and have translated the Bible in such a way as to attempt to make it fit their peculiar doctrines, have correctly translated Rev. 1:8 this way:[13] "'I am the Alpha and the Omega,' says Jehovah God, 'the One who is and who was and who is coming, the Almighty.'"

---

[12] George Adam Smith, THE BOOK OF ISAIAH, Vol. I, pages 114-115.

[13] NEW WORLD TRANSLATION OF THE HOLY SCRIPTURES, page 1324.

Throughout the Revelation, the "One who is and was and who is coming" refers explicitly to Jesus Christ, the second Person in the Godhead who will one day return to receive His elect to take them to heaven with Him forever. The other special name given to Jesus in Is. 9:6, "Everlasting Father," shows how closely allied to the First Person of the Godhead He is.

As mentioned above, sandwiched between Isaiah's prophecies of Jesus as Immanuel in 7:14, and His fourfold name in 9:6 is the statement, "I will put my trust in him" (8:17). In deriving my own translation of Hebrews, I made the statement say this in English: "I shall be faithful to Him." If this quotation repeated in Heb. 2:13 is put in context with the others in that passage, and is parallel to them, then it is Jesus who is saying, "I, Jesus, will put My trust in Him, the Father," or, as the thought my translation would convey, "I, Jesus, will be faithful (obedient) to My Father."

It is possible that Isaiah's prophecy in 8:17 lends itself to a double fulfillment, just like the one in 7:14 refers either to Isaiah's son or to Jesus the Son of God. If that is the case, then in the historical setting, Isaiah was terrified at the thought of Syria and Israel's invasion of Judah, so he promised God that he would be both trusting and faithful to Him if He would deliver Judah from the two-pronged enemy. And in the context of the author of Hebrews' situation, it was Jesus who trusted the Father to care for Him through the agony of the cross, and promised to be faithful and obedient to His Father, setting His face steadfastly to all the suffering and terror the occasion brought, so He could be the Redeemer of His brothers. We ought to add in our thoughts that if Jesus our great Brother was willing to do that for us, then we also ought to be perfectly trusting and obedient to God as well.

**And again he says,**
    **"Here am I, and the children God has given me."**

It is possible to understand three different ways in which this prophecy may have been fulfilled. It may have been fulfilled in Isaiah's son Maher-Shalal-Hash-Baz (besides other children Isaiah had). Or, it may be a reference to all the people of Judah at that time, as God's children. Finally, it may refer to Jesus and to all those who are saved by His blood. This third possibility is the intent of the author of Hebrews. This is the final quotation in the series of three from the Old Testament which the author of Hebrews quotes to prove his point that Jesus suffered for people so that He could become better than even the angels. We should note that this quotation comes from Isaiah again (8:18), immediately following the one the author has just quoted. In this way, Isaiah linked Jesus to those for whom He died. This thought will be developed next in Hebrews, because he has something important to add.

**Heb. 2:14.   Since the children have flesh and blood....**
One of the characteristics of human beings is that they are made up of

flesh and blood. There should be no argument about that point. Of course, the other animals also possess flesh and blood, but humans' physical makeup is different from that of any other creature, as Paul says in I Cor. 15:39: "All flesh is not the same: Men have one kind of flesh, animals have another, birds another and fish another." The reason the author of Hebrews makes this point is because of what he says immediately following.

### He too shared in their humanity....

God became a man, as God the Son, Jesus Christ. We have already set forth many passages from scripture to prove that. Therefore, to avoid belaboring the subject, I will remind you of one representative example, that of John 1:1, 14, and 17.

Now the author begins to reveal the *purpose* of Jesus Christ's being human, now that he has clarified once more the *identity* of Jesus our Savior. What follows are four tremendous reasons why Jesus had to become a man.

### ...so that by his death he might destroy him who holds the power of death—that is, the devil....

Here is the first great reason why Jesus had to become a man: *so that He could die.*

As God alone, Jesus could not have died, for God never dies. But Jesus, in His human nature, was as capable of dying as any human. We may not understand this fully, but this had to be the situation. Jesus, as God, did not in fact die. This is proven by what Jesus told His disciples in His conversation about His being the Good Shepherd and His followers the sheep of His fold, in John 10. He said in verse 15, "I lay down my life for the sheep." No one else had the power to take His life from Him, because He said (verse 18), "No one takes it from me, but I lay it down of my own accord." Having said that, He added what is greatly more important than that: "I have authority to lay it down and authority to take it up again." Thus Jesus did what no mere human being could do: after He was dead, He raised Himself up from death, with no help from His Father or from the Spirit. We all are positive that as soon as we are dead, we are totally incapable of performing any lively function whatsoever, because life has departed from us—and it is life itself that makes us able to move about. Of our own power, not one of us can make any dead person come back to life, even before we die, let alone after we are dead. But Jesus, who is vastly superior to any ordinary man, was able, as God, to raise His human body from the dead.

Jesus' death accomplished the conquest over death. If He had not died, He could not have risen from the dead, to demonstrate to the world—to all creation—that He had won the victory over death. Paul tells us in I Cor. 15:26, "The last enemy to be destroyed is death," and Jesus has already destroyed that enemy, in time for Himself, and in effect for us. His death also

93

accomplished the conquest over Satan. He told His disciples in Matt. 10:28, "Do not be afraid of those who kill the body but cannot kill the soul. Rather, be afraid of the one who can destroy both soul and body in hell." Although Satan is able to kill a person's body, Jesus has conquered Satan, and so is able to protect from harm anyone who flees to Him for refuge from Satan's power. It is my impression that only God is able to "destroy both soul and body in hell," although there may be some people who would hope that God is not that kind of God. From the beginning, the Father had predicted that Jesus would be the Victor over Satan, when He gave sentence to the serpent in Gen. 3:15:

> he will crush your head,
> and you will strike his heel.

and the ultimate fulfillment is expressed in Rev. 20:10: "And the devil, who deceived them, was thrown into the lake of burning sulfur, where the beast and the false prophet had been thrown. They will be tormented day and night for ever and ever."

**Heb. 2:15.  ...and free those who all their lives were held in slavery by their fear of death.**

*Free* indeed!  What a turn of events will occur at the judgment. Satan will be imprisoned forever in the lake of fire, while those faithful to Christ whom Satan tormented during their sojurn on earth will be free from the pains of sin, and the consequence of sin—death itself.  Paul said exactly the same thing in expanded form in his classic theological treatise, his letter to Rome (Rom. 6:16-18):

> Don't you know that when you offer yourselves to someone to obey him as slaves, you are slaves to the one whom you obey—whether you are slaves to sin, which leads to death, or to obedience, which leads to righteousness? But thanks be to God that, though you used to be slaves to sin, you whole-heartedly obeyed the form of teaching to which you were entrusted.  You have been set free from sin and have become slaves to righteousness.

Paul adds one factor in his statement that deserves our careful notice: he says that when we are set free from Satan and his bonds of sin and death, we become "slaves to righteousness."  In other words, we can never be free from all masters; but our decision to forsake Satan and his ways leads us to a voluntary subservience to Christ and His ways.  Jesus assured us, "...my yoke is easy, and my burden is light" (Matt. 11:30).  So such bondage is not onerous, but constitutes the greatest freedom.

We find the same thoughts regarding freedom from sin to righteousness in Christ in Jesus' own words, found in three statements near each other in John, chapter 8. In verses 31 and 32, we read, "To the Jews who had believed him, Jesus said, 'If you hold to my teaching, you are really my disciples. Then you will know the truth, and the truth will set you free.'"  In verse 34, Jesus warned, "I tell you the truth, everyone who sins is a slave to sin."  He concludes in verse 36, "If the Son sets you free, you will be free indeed."

For many a man, the greatest fear possible is the "fear of death." Much wailing at the side of a deathbed is not so much the prospect of the loss of a loved one's companionship as the renewed stark encounter with the absolute reality of death which the mourner himself will face one day. Further, the death which people fear the most is different in different people. The reason this is so is because some people either unwittingly or willfully exclude the existence of the "second death," or spiritual death, which is to be distinguished from physical death. That there are two distinct deaths is made clear in the Bible. The book of Revelation speaks explicitly of the "second death" (Rev. 20:6 and 14), which will occur after the first resurrection and the second resurrection have taken place. That passage shows the division of all humankind into two parts. There are those whose names have been written in the Lamb's book of life, who will take part in the first resurrection and upon whom the second death will not light. The other group of humans are the rest of all the people of the world from all time whose names are not written in the Lamb's book of life; they will be revived in the second resurrection, and after they are judged they will be thrown fully conscious into the lake of fire that burns forever and ever, and their torment will never end.

The fact of two different deaths is found, implicitly at least, in the story of the fall of Adam and Eve. God had commanded them not to eat of the tree of the knowledge of good and evil, warning them (Gen. 2:17, KJV) "in the day that thou eatest thereof thou shalt surely die." We know that the human couple did not die physically on the day they ate the forbidden fruit, because they lived many years after and had children. But if they did not die in some fashion, then either God did not mean what He had said, or else He failed to carry out His threat. Since neither of these options is possible with God, we must look for a third option; that option is that there is a death different from that which is physical; it is called spiritual death, or the "secod death."

It is hard to believe that no person has had at least some measure of trepidation at the thought of death. After all, there is a vast chasm between life in this world, and the cessation of that life—even without regard to what may follow it. We are aware that death may be preceded by much physical pain. We all think about when death may occur for us, or how it will come about: either from a long, drawn-out, painful illness, or from a shot in the back of the head from a concealed intruder. Some stoics, at least outwardly, face death with no concern. Other people shout and writhe in their deathbeds from the terror in their hearts. But physical death holds scant fears compared to spiritual death when a person knows that he has no hope of deliverance from the punishment of his sins.

It is that kind of fear from which Jesus our Savior has delivered those who have believed the gospel and know that they "...would prefer to be away from the body and at home with the Lord" (II Cor. 5:8). Paul, who wrote those words, made it emphatic in his love letter to the Philippians, when he said, "to me, to live is Christ and to die is gain" (1:21); and "I desire to depart and be with Christ, which is better by far; but it is more necessary for you that I remain in the body" (1:23-24). Even people in Old Testament times had that same assurance: King David in his best-known Psalm (23:4) wrote:

> Even though I walk
>> through the valley of the shadow of death,
> I will fear no evil,
>> for you are with me.

Jesus gave full assurance of spiritual life without the second death in his conversation with his beloved friend Martha as they faced her brother Lazarus' grave (John 11:25-26): "I am the resurrection and the life. He who believes in me will live, even though he dies; and whoever lives and believes in me will never die." Paul gives a ringing affirmation of this in Gal. 2:20, where he points out that he has already died (spiritually), and since Christ has given Paul His own spiritual life which is eternal, then Paul no longer needs to look forward with fear to death, because now it is impossible for him to die. Here is how he says it in the KJV:

> I am crucified with Christ: nevertheless I live; yet not I, but Christ liveth in me: and the life which I now live in the flesh I live by the faith of the Son of God, who loved me, and gave himself for me.[14]

We have concluded our discussion of the first great reason why Jesus had to become a man. The next verse tells us the second great reason.

### Heb. 2:16. For surely it is not angels he helps, but Abraham's descendants.

Jesus had to become a man, *so that He could save mankind, not angels.* Although the scriptures make it plain that some of God's angels fell into disobedience (see Jude 6, and Rev. 12:7-12) along with Satan, the chief rebel angel, there is no hint throughout the Bible either that Jesus did anything to save fallen angels, or that angels once fallen have any other means of salvation.

That some angels did fall into sin is recorded in II Pet. 2:4: "God did not spare angels when they sinned...." Also Jude says (verse 6): "...angels...did not keep their positions of authority but abandoned their own home." Satan fell together with his followers who were fallen angels (Rev. 12:7): "There was war in heaven. Michael and his angels fought against the dragon, and the dragon and his angels fought back. But he was not strong enough, and they lost their place in heaven." Each of these three passages

---

[14] This is from the KJV, which I prefer here over the NIV. The difference between the two translations comes from two different manuscripts, merely in the placement of the comma in the Greek text. Punctuation, however, did not exist in the originals.

adds that Satan and his angels will be punished for their disobedience to God. Peter said, "[God] sent [the fallen angels] to hell, putting them into gloomy dungeons to be held for judgment." Jude agrees: "...these he has kept in darkness, bound with everlasting chains for judgment on the great Day," although this does not mean that those fallen angels, sometimes called demons, are not active in the world now, seeking to turn people away from God, as we see often in the gospels. Finally, John in the Revelation passage adds, "The great dragon was hurled down—that ancient serpent called the devil or Satan, who leads the whole world astray."

The case for Satan and his angels is hopeless. Christ has already won the victory over them, by His death on the cross. Paul said this in Col. 2:15, "And having disarmed the powers and authorities, he made a public spectacle of them, triumphing over them by the cross." In discussing Jesus' total victory by means of His resurrection from the dead, Paul also said (I Cor. 15:24), "Then the end will come, when he hands over the kingdom to God the Father after he has destroyed all dominion, authority and power."

Because humans have been chosen over angels to receive the gift of salvation through Christ's sacrifice, we will have even greater cause for rejoicing when we take our places in heaven. God Himself died for us, not for angels, so our presence with Christ in heaven will be infinitely more meaningful to us than to them. In fact, whenever any person who has strayed from God is brought back into His circle of influence, as Jesus said in the parables in Lu. 15, "There is rejoicing in the presence of the angels of God over one sinner who repents." Someone has written a hymn whose last line reads, "Angels never know the joy that our salvation brings."

Following the theme that Jesus is "better than" the angels, we learn additionally that those whom Jesus redeems will also become "better than" angels. We may recall that the author of Hebrews said at the very end of chapter 1, "Are not all angels ministering spirits sent to serve those who will inherit salvation?" Not only will angels be subservient to those humans who are saved; the angels also will be judged by the saved people, as Paul says in I Cor. 6:3: "Do you not know that we will judge angels?"

### Abraham's descendants.

Some Gentiles may be concerned that the author of Hebrews mentions exclusively "Abraham's descendants" as the recipients of God's favor through Jesus' death on the cross. It is true that the book we are studying is called "Hebrews," as if it were written exclusively to them and that no Gentiles are affected in any way by what is said to Jews. True enough, the gospel ought to be proclaimed to the Jews first (Rom. 1:16). But it was Paul who wrote those words who claimed to be the prime messenger of this fabulous offer to the Gentiles of the world. So the Gentiles surely are not excluded from the benefits of the gospel. More than that, Paul avers that every Christian is in fact a descendant of Abraham. Here is how he said it in Rom. 4:16-17:

> Therefore, the promise comes by faith, so that it may be by grace and may be guaranteed to all Abraham's offspring—not only to those who are of the law but also to those who are of the faith of Abraham. He is the father of us all. As it is written: "I have made you a father of many nations."

Therefore, we Gentiles need not fear being excluded from any of the wonderful things promised to the Jews in the book of Hebrews, as long as we hold the same faith which Abraham held.

**Heb. 2:17. For this reason he had to be made like his brothers in every way, in order that he might become a merciful and faithful high priest.**

The third great reason Jesus had to die was *to be our High Priest.* Jesus became like us, so that we could become like Him. Paul said it this way (I Cor. 15:49): "Just as we have borne the likeness of the earthly man, so shall we bear the likeness of the man from heaven." And you can almost hear the exultation flowing from the heart of John when he wrote the same thing in his first small letter (I John 3:2): "We know that when he appears, we shall be like him, for we shall see him as he is."

It is not necessary for us to discuss further here the idea that Jesus was willing to call us His "brothers," because our exposition of Heb. 2:11 did it well enough. Suffice it to say here that Jesus had to become a man, like us, in order to minister to us in our infinitely great needs.

By the working definition of a priest, God could not be a Priest between Himself and mankind, because a priest is a spokesperson between God and man. This is one of the reasons why the Levitical priesthood was inadequate. Every priest, even every high priest, was a mere man, a sinful man at that, so he could never properly stand between God and the rest of mankind. This concept of Jesus as our High Priest is the heart of the whole argument of Hebrews; much is said about the nature of Jesus, and about his sinlessness, in future chapters, to qualify Him to be our High Priest. So we will discuss all that when we arrive at the appropriate passages.

In human relations, it is wrong for a person on one side of an argument to be a mediator between his side and the opposition. In such a situation, we would say that the feigned mediator would be utterly disqualified because he was "biased." However, when God became a man, we might say He "biased" in both directions, and thereby would be the fulcrum between both sides. That is precisely what Jesus did: "For there is one God and one mediator between God and men, the man Christ Jesus, who gave himself as a ransom for all men" (I Tim. 2:5-6).

**...in service to God....**

It is God who makes the appointment of the High Priest. No one else has authority either to make the appointment or even to participate in that decision. In human relations this is not so. When there is a dispute between management and labor, for instance, each side is allowed to choose at least one arbitration panelist, so each side has opporlunity for favorable representation. But when God is one of the disputants, He alone chooses the Arbitrator. In that way, God is certain that justice is done. It is probable that many humans cannot see this as guaranteeing justice, but we who know that God is justice itself, have no qualms about such an arrangement. Jesus is the Mediator, the Arbitrator, "in service to God."

Here we see a pattern already emerging in Hebrews, that will continue throughout the book. There are two intensely important themes. One theme is that Christ's death, His sacrifice for sin, is infinitely better than the death of sacrificial animals in the Old Testament pattern; the second is that the act of making the sacrifice was done infinitely better by Christ as the Great High Priest than was done by any or all of the Levitical priests together in Old Testament times.

### ...and that he might make atonement for the sins of the people.

We now come to a doctrine that is fraught with uncertainty, but even more laden with ignorance; still, multitudes of people write and speak dogmatically about it. The English word used here for the doctrine is "atonement," but even translators cannot agree on whether this is the right term to apply. Books have been written, and ecclesiastical battles have been fought (and continue) about the matter. Much of the discussion becomes highly technical. I have been involved in the struggle recently, but now I have changed my mind radically, because I have searched more diligently for answers to my own questions. It is important for us to study the question; perhaps we can come to some agreement before we proceed in our study of the rest of Hebrews. It will be impossible to avoid some technical matters in this discussion, but I will try to keep our thoughts easy to understand. Those readers who want to pursue the subject may look at the sources I will point out here, as well as more of the rich fund of literature available.

The Greek root verb translated as "atonement" here is ἱλάσκομαι. As mentioned above, even translators cannot agree on the best English word to use. The KJV reads "reconciliation," while the ASV uses the term "propitiation," and the RSV differs from all these, employing the term "expiation." To complicate matters, the new Testament uses this Greek word only once more, in Lu. 18:13, where the tax collector cried out "God, have mercy on me, a sinner." There is slightly more agreement among translators here. The KJV says, "be merciful," the ASV has "be thou merciful," while the RSV agrees with the KJV.

This Greek word is one of a family of related terms, four of which are used in the New Testament, each one just twice. The second of these four terms is ἵλεως, found in Matt. 16:22 and Heb. 8:12. Thayer[15] gives two definitions for this term, "propitious, merciful." It takes some grammatical gymnastics to make sense from this word in Matthew's use. Our NIV translates Peter's objection to Jesus: "Never, Lord! This shall never happen to you!" We might think of Peter's words in this more literal way, "Let mercy keep it from you, Lord!" The KJV and ASV both are like that: "Be it far from thee, Lord." The RSV reads here, "God forbid, Lord!" The other New Testament location of ἵλεως, is Heb. 8:12, which is near the end of a rather long quotation from Jer. 31:31-34. Verse 12 is translated by the NIV translators this way:

> For I will forgive their wickedness
> and will remember their sins no more.

The Greek word in question is the English word "forgive." The KJV translators chose the term "be merciful," which is copied by the ASV and RSV.

The final two Greek terms in this family of four used in the New Testament I have kept together, because in my mind they are related more closely together than any other combination of the four. One of these last two is ἱλασμός, and is found in I John 2:2 and in I John 4:10. Except for the NIV, there is rather close agreement among the other three translations we have been noting: in both passages the Greek word is translated either "propitiation" or "expiation," while the NIV translates the word in both places as "atoning sacrifice." The other of these last two words is very similar to the one; it is ἱλαστήριος. This word is found in Rom. 3:25 and Heb. 9:5. This word has one meaning in the Romans passage, which is very similar to the meaning of ἱλασμός, but unfortunately has a quite different meaning in Hebrews. In Romans 3:25, the KJV, ASV, and RSV all translate the word as either "propitiation" or "expiation," as if ἱλασμός and ἱλαστήριος were identical in meaning, while the last word is translated in the NIV virtually the same as in the other: "sacrifice of atonement." In Heb. 9:5, where ἱλαστήριος is used the second time, it is a noun which Thayer says is "the well-known cover of the ark of the covenant in the Holy of holies." The translation we are using in this study, the NIV, calls it "the place of atonement." The KJV calls it the "mercyseat," by which it was known by Christians until recent years. The ASV also calls it the "mercy-seat," separated as "mercy seat" in the RSV.

Now that we have before us this cluster of related Greek words, together with their various English translations, let us attempt to make sense of the overall matter. It appears that there are three principal English terms we need to understand, atonement, propitiation, and expiation, if we are to get at the heart of the matter. We may look at some of the other terms later as well, if they can be helpful.

In our attempt to understand what atonement means, we ought to begin with the concept in the Old Testament. We all have heard of the Jewish "Day

---

[15] Thayer, page 301. All references to Thayer in this study about atonement are found on this page.

of Atonement," and we have a vague idea of what it is about. Jews faithful to their understanding of the law and the prophets set aside that day as the most holy day of the year, when they gather together to acknowledge their sins committed during the past year, seek God's favor in prayer, and hope that God in some way will forgive their sins. In Old Testament times, and until 70 AD when the Roman army destroyed the Temple, the altar of sacrifice, and all their appurtenances, the High Priest made a sacrifice for himself and all the people. A proper animal was slain; the High Priest took some of the blood, entered the Holy of Holies, and sprinkled the blood on and in front of the mercy seat where God sat for this transaction. This was the act of making "atonement" for the people, as well as for the High Priest himself. The people believed that God would forgive their sins through this procedure.

The "Day of Atonement" comes from the Hebrew words, יוֹם הַכִּפֻּרִים, and is pronounced "Yom Kippur" by today's English-speaking Jews. "Yom" means "day," and the "Kippur" part comes from the Hebrew root verb כִּפֶּר, which literally means "to cover over." Brown, Driver, and Briggs adds the meanings "pacify, make propitiation." Here we have a beautiful picture of what God is able to do for us humans: He wants to cover our sins with the blood of the Lamb, His Son, so that He will never look at them again. The procedure for observing the Day of Atonement is found in Lev. 16.

The author of the article on כִּפֶּר, B. Lang,[16] points out that the syntax related to the Hebrew term causes variations in meaning. For instance, in Ezek. 16:63, it is God Himself who performs the act of atonement: "When I make atonement for you for all you have done, you will remember and be ashamed and never again open your mouth because of your humiliation, declares the Sovereign LORD." In Ex. 32:30, Moses promises to try to make atonement for the people: "Moses said to the people, 'You have committed a great sin. But now I will go up to the LORD; perhaps I can make atonement for your sin.'" And when a man was unclean, he performed certain rituals; then he brought two birds to the Tent of Meeting, where the priest "is to sacrifice them, the one for a sin offering and the other for a burnt offering. In this way he will make atonement before the LORD" (Lev. 15:15).

In the same place, Lang, by quoting Lev. 17:11, points out that atonement could be made only by shedding the blood of a sacrifice: "For the life of a creature is in the blood, and I have given it to you to make atonement for yourselves on the altar; it is the blood that makes atonement for one's life."

The idea of "substitution" in the context of atonement must be important, because Hanse Herrmann[17] says this in his portion of the article on ἱλάσκομαι: "In the light of כִּפֶּר and the non-cultic כפר, it would be useless to deny that the idea of *substitution* is present to some degree" (emphasis added).

Let us attempt to bring all this information together, and apply it to

---

[16] TDOT, Vol. VII, pp. 290-291.

[17] TDNT, Vol. III, p. 310.

the term in Heb. 2:17. To begin with, we ought to say something which will be developed fully in the book of Hebrews as we proceed through its chapters. That is that Jesus Christ, in our New Covenant system, is not only the High Priest who performs the act of making the blood sacrifice for sin; He is also the sacrifice itself. Therefore, Jesus is not only the One who is propitiated, but also the one who makes the sacrifice; and to complete the picture, we must add that Jesus is the Sacrifice whose blood was shed to accomplish the package. In order to explain our thought in Heb. 2:17, we read that it was Jesus, God Himself, who became a man, so that He "might make atonement for the sins of the people." Our sin, our guilt, is gone, when we receive this accomplished work of Christ. Christ propitiated, or appeased, the Father by His sacrifice; He also appeased Himself, since He is God. Jesus had to become a man so that He could do His work for us humans, not for angels. Further, because He became a man, He was able to reach down to us in order to do His work on our behalf.

I must add a note regarding the matter of a distinction between the terms "propitiation" and "expiation." Some people fear that by claiming that Jesus died for every human who has ever lived, the door is opened to admit universal salvation, while to limit the "atonement" of Jesus obviates that problem. However, I believe that I John 2:2 should include the term "propitiate," since Jesus' death fully satisfied God's opposition to receiving even some people into heaven. That verse says that Jesus is the "propitiation not only for our (Christians') sins, but for the sins of the whole world." That means that God will accept anyone who accepts His atoning sacrifice. On the other hand, we read in Rom. 3:25 that by Jesus' blood sacrifice God has expiated (or expunged) all the sins, not of the whole world, but of an elite group consisting of those who have "faith in his blood." For practical purposes, however, we humans, not being omniscient, cannot know who has been "elected" by God and who has not. But Rev. 22:17 assures us all, "Whoever wishes, let him take the free gift of the water of life." Thus we who claim to want to work to see people brought into the kingdom need only to seek to obey the Great Commission, which is to go into all the world and proclaim the good news. That eliminates the necessity for us to debate the question of "Limited atonement."

**Heb. 2:18. Because he himself suffered when he was tempted, he is able to help those who are being tempted.**
Here, now, is the fourth and final reason why Jesus had to become a man: *so He could help us in our temptations.* This verse tells us that why Jesus was able to help us was because He *suffered* in the times He endured His temptations. Jesus could not have suffered physically when He was tempted unless He had had a body.

The scriptures make clear that Jesus was tempted. Just two chapters beyond this spot we read that He was tempted (4:15): "...we have [a high priest] who has been tempted in every way, just as we are—yet was without sin." It is not recorded there precisely how Jesus was tempted, but we have evidence from other places in the New Testament that He was tempted; and the Old Testament predicts the same. Matthew 4 is the first place to report the temptation of Jesus by Satan in the wilderness, at the beginning of His ministry. Verse 1 says it specifically: "Then Jesus was led by the Spirit into the desert to be tempted by the devil." Mark 1:12 tells us the same thing, in slightly different words; and the first two verses in Lu. 4 echo the other gospel accounts.

We learn in scripture how God divides temptation of humans into three catagories. John makes the separation in I John 2:16: "For everything in the world—the cravings of sinful man, the lust of his eyes and the boasting of what he has and does—comes not from the Father but from the world." Bible students have pointed out that the three temptations Satan poured on Jesus in the wilderness fit these categories. As you review those temptations, you can see that when Satan invited Jesus to change stones into bread to satisfy His forty-day fast in the wilderness, that was akin to what the KJV called "the lust of the flesh," or the NIV calls "the cravings of sinful man." Next, when Satan took Jesus to a high place to show Him all the kindgoms of the world, and offered them to Him if only He would bow down and worship Satan just once, that temptation was part of the "lust of the eyes." Finally, when Jesus was taken to the pinnacle of the temple and invited to jump off so that the people could see that the angels would catch Him, that was "the pride of life," or the "boasting of what he has and does." In these temptations by Satan we see that Jesus was "tempted in every way, just as we are." If that is so, and it is, then none of us is ever tempted in any way outside the temptations which Jesus endured for us. If He endured them, then He is able to "help [us] who are being tempted."

Dr. Howard T. Kuist, my English Bible professor at Princeton Seminary, explained in class one day how temptation works. He invited us to think back over our own experiences of temptation (and I invite you to do the same right now), and think of some of the times we had been tempted and resisted those temptations. He reminded us that as we resisted some specific temptation, that temptation did not vanish just because we resisted it; rather, it returned immediately with greater force. When we resisted again, and again, the temptation continued to grow stronger. As a matter of fact, if we were tempted infinitely, the temptation would grow to infinite strength. In a case like that, one of only two things could happen: either we would succumb to the temptation and commit the sin, or we would flee to a Power greater than our own (only the power of Jesus would suffice), and that Power would deliver us from the bondage of that temptation. Since Jesus never submitted to any temptation, He was tempted infinitely more than we have ever been tempted, until He delivered Himself from the temptation. In like manner He can do the same for us, if we ask for His help.

The apostle Paul gives us another word of assurance with regard to the temptations we all suffer. In I Cor. 10:13, he gave us this familiar promise, "No temptation has seized you except what is common to man. And God is faithful; he will not let you be tempted beyond what you can bear. But when you are tempted, he will also provide a way out so that you can stand up under it."

The reason why "He is able to help those who are being tempted" is because He has already been there and knows all about it. An Indian proverb says something like this: You must walk in your brother's moccasins for one moon. So just as Jesus is able to help us in our temptations, we also must be willing to help others when they are tempted, by offering words of encouragement to them, especially words directing them to our Savior who is able to help them. This is one reason why we must suffer in this life, according to Paul in his words to the flock in Corinth (II Cor. 1:3-5):

> Praise be to the God and Father of our Lord Jesus Christ, the Father of compassion and the God of all comfort, who comforts us in all our troubles, so that we can comfort those in any trouble with the comfort we ourselves have received from God. For just as the sufferings of Christ flow over into our lives, so also through Christ our comfort overflows.

And from where did God in the flesh receive His comfort? He received it from the Holy Spirit (Lu. 4:14), and even from angels (Matt. 4:11 and Mk. 1:12), even though they were inferior to Him. Jesus' comfort from the Holy Spirit was a sign to us that we also can be comforted by Him; that is why Jesus promised "another Comforter" or "Counselor" (John 14:16). The Spirit-Comforter is not a replacement for Jesus as our Comforter, but a supplement, for He promised at the very end of Matthew's gospel, "And surely I will be with you always, to the very end of the age."

Let us summarize in outline what we have discovered in these first two chapters of Hebrews. Jesus was, and always is, better than angels. Jesus had to be made lower than angels for a time (in His human form), so that He could do four things for us: 1) He could die on our behalf; 2) He could help men (but not angels); 3) He could be our Great High Priest; and 4) He could comfort us in our afflictions and especially in our temptations. After Jesus' abasement, He was exalted above all things because He was willing to suffer for our sakes.

# CHAPTER III
## JESUS IS BETTER THAN MOSES OR JOSHUA.
## HEB. 3:1 to 4:13.

Chapter 3 of Hebrews portrays Jesus as "better than" Moses. Why Moses? There are many characters in the Old Testament, from whom the author of Hebrews might have chosen one to compare with Jesus. But Moses was held in high esteem by most Jews, even ahead of King David or the prophet Isaiah whom we as Gentiles exalt. One great reason why Moses was almost revered was because he was the person chosen by God to receive the law through the ministry of angels, so that God's people, the Jews, could receive the law, and thereby consider themselves superior to Gentiles.[1]

The Pharisees had spent their lives studying the minutiae of the law; they had compiled a list of 613 rules they claimed to have derived from the ten original commandments. However, in making their studies, they wandered far from the law itself, and in the process changed it radically in many ways. Their departure from the law is shown by their argument with Jesus on at least one occasion, recorded in Matt. 15:2-3. The Pharisees accused Jesus: "Why do your disciples break the tradition of the elders? They don't wash their hands before they eat." Jesus' response demonstrated their error: "And why do you break the command of God for the sake of your tradition?"

Here is the step-by-step departure of the Jews from the law God originally delivered to them through Moses.[2]   First came the Targum, composed of paraphrases, written by Onkelos on the Pentateuch; and by Jonathan ben Uzziel on the Prophets. Next came the Mishnah, or the "Second Law," written to interpret and supplement the first law, or the law of Moses. After this was written the Midrash, meaning the "Investigation." This was a set of commentaries on the law, divided into two parts. The first was the Halakah, the "Rules of the Spiritual Road," by Hillel of Babylonia; and the second part was the Haggadah, intended to be the "Sayings of the Sages," written by Eleazer the Mede in the first century AD. Although the Haggadah had no authority, it became popular and authoritative, so that the life of the synagogue was guided by it.

This progression of documents, and subsequent departure from the law of Moses, as given to him by God, may be understood by reminding ourselves of a parlor game many of us played years ago, called "Gossip." People would sit in a circle; the leader would whisper a statement to the person beside him. The second person would turn and try to whisper the same statement to the person on his other side. This sequence continued until the last person in the circle told the leader, and everyone present, what he had heard. Invariably it was different, sometimes radically different, from the original message. Such

---

[1]  Paul accuses the Jews of this in Rom. 2:17, telling them "you rely on the law and brag about your relationship to God."

[2]  This information is found in Edersheim's LIFE AND TIMES OF JESUS THE MESSIAH, Vol. I, pp. 11-12.

sequential transmission of any information always gets corrupted in the process.

At this point, we ought to be well warned not to fall into the same trap that beset the Jews. It is far too easy for someone to comment on a passage of scripture, after which a friend or someone who reads his popular work quotes him instead of the original scripture. Then another person refers to the last one, and slightly changes what he said, until after several steps of quoting, mis-quoting, and intentional alteration, it is impossible to recognize the original scripture or know its meaning.

Although Moses was to a large degree superseded by subsequent writings, still he was held in high esteem by nearly all Jews. That is the main reason the author of Hebrews chooses Moses as the man with whom to compare Jesus.

Another reason why the Jews of New Testament days held Moses in high esteem was because he was chosen by God to lead the children of Israel out of Egypt into the Promised Land. Although the people who were actually delivered murmured almost continuously against Moses for taking them away from their garlics, melons, leeks, and other good foods, future generations were thankful that they finally made it into the land of their inheritance.

**Heb. 3:1.    Therefore, holy brothers, who share in the heavenly  calling....**

Who are these people, called by the author "holy brothers"? Surely he refers to the recipients of his letter. Beyond that, it is impossible to know with certainty whether they were actually Christians, or mere hangers-on, or even wolves in sheeps' clothing attempting to infiltrate the body of Christ. Merely to add that these people "share in the heavenly calling" does not prove that they must be Christians. After all, the "heavenly calling" is offered to everyone in the world in all times, but not everyone responds to that calling. The referents likely are assumed by the author of Hebrews to be Christians, yet aware that some have not yet become true followers of Christ. There is a similar ambiguity in chapter 6, verses 4 and 5, where the author surely is writing about a larger population of people than the recipients of this letter, but surely include them as well. In the passage in chapter 6, the people are called "those who have once been enlightened, who have tasted the heavenly gift, who have shared in the Holy Spirit, who have tasted the goodness of the word of God and the powers of the coming age." Still, the author continues to report that it is possible for them to "fall away," which leads some people to believe that they can become lost.

This matter is more complicated than we can discuss effectively here, but when we come to chapter 6, we will elaborate more fully on the several parts the whole question engenders there. Let us now be content with the hypothesis that the author is writing to a group of people, nearly all of whom are at least considered to be saved.

## ...fix your thoughts on Jesus....

There is no better subject in the universe on which or on whom to
think and meditate. Later in his letter, the author of Hebrews urges (12:2):
"Let us fix our eyes on Jesus, the author and perfecter of our faith." In Phil.
4:8, Paul admonishes us (after talking about God who guards our hearts and
minds in Christ Jesus): "Finally, brothers, whatever is true, whatever is noble, whatever is right, whatever is pure, whatever is lovely, whatever is
admirable—if anything is excellent or praiseworthy—think about such
things." All those "things" are centered in Christ Jesus. The Psalmist in the
very first Psalm (verse 2) reminds us that it is the Lord who makes blessed the
man who meditates on His law day and night. Remember, it is Jesus who is
Lord, who also is the Word of God, or the Law of God.

It is proper for us to "fix our thoughts on Jesus" because in doing so
we lavish praise and honor on Him. The first question and answer in our
Westminster Shorter Catechism teaches us that the reason God created us was
for us "to glorify God and enjoy Him forever." It is not only proper for us to
do this, but it is also beneficial to us. According to the man of God who
came and spoke condemnation to Eli for failing to discipline his sons with regard to their evil procedures in sacrifices, "Those who honor me I will honor,
but those who despise me will be disdained" (I Sam. 2:30). Further, scriptures far too numerous to catalog here inform us that God will bless those
who obey Him, and will destroy those who disobey.

## ...Jesus, the apostle and high priest whom we confess.

Just who is an apostle? There is some confusion about the term, and
especially about whether it ought to be used with reference to anyone alive
today. Some thoughts on the precise definition of the term, as well as how it
has been used in the past two millennia, may help us grasp its meaning more
fully, and help us in the way we use it.

The English word "apostle" comes from the biblical Greek word
ἀπόστολος, whose basic meaning is, "a delegate, messenger, one sent forth
with orders."[3] The Greek noun is derived from the verb ἀποστέλλω. The
verb is composed of two parts: the first part is a preposition which means
"out from" or "away;" the second part is the common verb which means "to
send." From the definition of the term then, and excluding the possibility of
limiting the term to a particular technical meaning, the word "apostle" can be
used properly to anyone who is sent out by another person to carry out a task
or carry a message.

In Christian writings, the term "apostle" is usually limited to designate
the original twelve chosen by Jesus to be His principal followers during His

---

[3] Thayer's definition.

107

three-year ministry on earth. However, two things need to be pointed out with regard to the use of the word referring to to those twelve men. First, not everyone, even in New Testament times, favored the use of the title "apostle" for even the twelve. J. B. Lightfoot, D. D., Bishop of Durham, a preeminent commentator on several New Testament books, has pointed out that of the seventy-nine times the Greek word is used in the New Testament, sixty-eight of them are found in the writings of Luke and Paul.[4] Matthew, Mark, and John more often referred to the apostles as "disciples," or sometimes simply "the twelve," so the term "apostle" must not have been used commonly in the early days of the Church's history after Pentecost. Matthew uses the term only once, where in chapter 10, verses 1 and 2, he lists the twelve by name, calling them "disciples" in verse 1, and "apostles" in verse 2. Likewise, Mark uses the term only once in his gospel, calling them "apostles" in 6:30, when they returned to Jesus to report what the Holy Spirit had done through them; but when they were "sent out" Mark called them merely "the twelve" (verse 7). John in his gospel, never refers directly to the twelve as "apostles," but uses the term only once in a general sense for anyone sent, quoting Jesus in 13:16, "no servant is greater than his master, nor is a messenger (ἀπόστολος) greater than the one who sent him."

John's use of the term "apostle" in his gospel points up the second thing, which is that the term is used in reference to followers of Jesus in general, not just the twelve, who have been sent out to serve Him. Luke uses the term in this way in Lu. 11:49, where it is highly unlikely that Jesus intended the term to be limited to the twelve He had chosen: "God in his wisdom said, 'I will send them prophets and apostles, some of whom they will kill and others they will persecute.'" Besides this one instance, Luke calls the twelve "apostles" only five times throughout his gospel, but he uses the term in his book of Acts twenty-nine times, with two exceptions referring to the original twelve. Here are the exceptions: in Acts 1:26, Luke included Matthias among the "twelve" after he is voted into the group by the disciples; in Acts 14:14, Barnabas and Paul together are called apostles. Other people in the New Testament are also specifically called apostles, who were not among the twelve. Paul calls Epaphroditis an apostle (Greek ἀπόστολος, NIV "messenger") in Phil. 2:25; in Rom. 16:7 he also calls Andronicus and Junius apostles; and Paul may imply that Silas and Timothy are apostles in I Thes. 1:1, where he links them both with himself in the salutation of the letter, one of few where Paul fails to call himself an apostle.

In the six times the term "apostle" is used in Acts 15:2 to 16:4, a group of people mentioned is called "apostles and elders," so sometimes the term "apostles" should be understood in the restrictive sense of the original twelve which then included Matthias.

We often refer to Paul as "the apostle Paul," and rightly so, since he

---

[4] Thayer, page 68, under his definition of ἀπόστολος.

claims that title for himself. He introduces himself as the author as well as "an apostle" in all thirteen of his letters except Philippians, I and II Thessalonians, and Philemon. In addition, Paul calls himself an apostle in I Tim. 2:7 and II Tim. 1:11.

Once again we think about the use of the term "apostle" as it is used with various people or with an indeterminate group of people, as it is used in parts of the New Testament other than the writings of the gospel authors. Paul uses the term broadly in I Cor. 12:28 and 29 and a parallel passage in Eph. 4:11; Eph. 3:5; in I Thes. 2:7 (English, or verse 6 in the Greek); in II Cor. 8:23 (translated "representatives" in NIV); and in John's Rev. 18:20. In II Cor. 11:13 Paul talks of false apostles, similar to its usage in Rev. 2:2.

Since biblical times certain outstanding Christians have been called "apostles." The great Baptist missionary, Adoniram Judson, was called the "Apostle to Burma" for his work of translating the Bible into the Burmese language. Charles Chiniquy, a Canadian Roman Catholic Priest, converted to Protestantism at age fifty, was known as the "Apostle of Temperance" because of his labors to stop the liquor trade. In the twentieth century, the Reverend Richard Benjamin was designated an "apostle" by his church board because of his building a huge Christian ministry in Anchorage, Alaska and his planting numerous daughter churches not only in Alaska but in other parts of the United States.

What has all this to do with Jesus? Just that He is called in our present verse in Hebrews the "Apostle...whom we confess." If anyone in the world has a right to be called an "apostle," that is, "one sent with a message," it is Jesus Himself. Paul puts it most clearly in Gal. 4:4-5: "...when the time had fully come, God sent his Son, born of a woman, born under law, to redeem those under law, that we might receive the full rights of sons." Jesus may not have been the very first person sent into the world with His message, but He was both the Supreme Messenger and the Message Itself. The Psalmist says virtually the same thing when he writes in Ps. 8:4 (KJV):

What is man, that thou art mindful of him?

and the son of man, that thou visitest him?

It is acknowledged that this verse does not say that God sent Jesus into the world; the implication is that God Himself paid a visit on mankind to show His interest in him and to bring a message. But since Jesus is God, we may say that Jesus sent Himself into the world with His message.

It is important to add one step to the ideas that an apostle is "a delegate, messenger, one sent forth with orders," and that Jesus is the the Great Apostle who was sent with His infinitely gracious message. He has designated us all to be His "sub-apostles." On the evening of His Resurrection Day, Jesus appeared to the "disciples" to comfort and encourage them. The people present are not identified by John, but they were the ten original men called to follow Jesus (Judas Iscariot had already committed suicide, and Thomas was absent for some reason). It is possible that many if not most or all of the one hundred twenty mentioned in Acts 1:15 were present. To all who were there, and to all of us who claim to follow Christ, He said (John 20:21), "As the Father has sent me, I am sending you." Therefore, messengers, followers of Christ, indeed, all of us who call ourselves Christians are appointed to be apostles. This is not an option in our Christian life; it *is* our Christian life.

### High Priest.

The theme of the high priesthood of Jesus was already introduced by the author of Hebrews—in 2:17, where the author explained that Jesus had to be made a man so He could minister to us as distinct from angels. This theme is elaborated extensively in chapters 4 through 8, and indeed continues into the very last chapter of the book.

The author renews the subject of Jesus as High Priest because he now wants to talk about Moses, and how much better Jesus is in every respect. The connection between Moses and the high priesthood is that Moses was the younger brother of Aaron the original high priest in the hierarchy designated as Levitical high priests "according to the flesh." Therefore, the author has begun this all-important dissertation on Jesus as the High Priest, working up to it gradually, laying a foundation for all he has to say about it. We will pursue the matter further in the rest of the book.

### ...whom we confess.

In using the first person plural here, the author is assuming that not only he, but all his hearers, are already converted to the Christian faith. We have already mentioned the tenuous quality of that assumption, and will delve into it further at least twice more in our study.

The idea that we "confess" Jesus, it should be emphasized, goes far beyond merely "believing" in Jesus. Belief is a state of mind, in which one passively holds to some proposition, and accepts it as valid in every way. The term "confess," however, is an action verb. It involves conversation with other people: it can be with one or many people at once; it can be either oral or written, or even demonstrated in one's individual actions and lifestyle.

Incidentally, the term "confess" as it is used here has nothing to do with the idea of "confessing our sins" either to God or to another person. The KJV uses the term "profess" here, and the meaning of that term today is closer to what the author was thinking when he wrote the word.

Are you a person who merely claims to believe in Jesus without doing anything positive about it? Or do you consciously spend time and energy in *confessing* Christ before others in an attempt to get them converted to your faith? Jesus made us "apostles" to do just that, and He is our Great High Priest to help us in our efforts. It is an easy task for us, if we "fix our eyes on Jesus, the author and perfecter of our faith, who for the joy set before him endured the cross, scorning its shame, and sat down at the right hand of the throne of God" (Heb. 12:2).

**Heb. 3:2.    He was faithful to the one who appointed him....**

Jesus is faithful. Unfortunately, there is a vast contrast between Jesus' faithfulness and the faithfulness of much of the world. Nations break treaties when they no longer benefit the ones who break them. Statistics tell us that the vast majority of spouses are unfaithful to the ones to whom they have pledged their troth, despite the fact that they have taken solemn vows—if not before God, at least before a Justice of the Peace, in either case accompanied by two or two hundred witnesses.

Our faithlessness to one another is but a pale outward sign of our faithlessness toward God which is much more critical than any relationship to one another. What we do to one another is but a reflection of our deepest attitudes toward God and what we are willing to do for Him. We are so unlike Jesus in all this. Opposed to His faithfulness is our vile existence, whose outward acts sprout from our faithless evil within our hearts and minds and spirits. Jesus said it this way to His disciples (Mk. 7:20-23):

What comes out of a man is what makes him "unclean." For from within, out of men's hearts, come evil thoughts, sexual immorality, theft, murder, adultery, greed, malice, deceit, lewdness, envy, slander, arrogance and folly. All these evils come from inside and make a man "unclean."

Jesus knew we humans would be like that. Before He left the earth in anticipation of His return one day, He told His disciples the parable of the unjust judge, and concluded it by asking them (Lu. 18:8), "...when the Son of Man comes, will he find faith on the earth?" Surely Jesus will find a faithful remnant then, because He also told the story of the talents given to servants, and two of them will hear His commendation for their labors (Matt. 25:23): "Well done, good and faithful servant! You have been faithful with a few things; I will put you in charge of many things. Come and share your master's happiness!"

It was the Father "who appointed him" to His work on earth. Jesus was always willing to remain faithful to Him. Some people are confused at the idea that Jesus had to be obedient to His Father, in light of the scriptural declaration that the Son was equal to the Father. For Jesus Himself said, "I and the Father are one" (John 10:30). Still, it was also Jesus who boasted, "I always do what pleases him" (John 8:29). It is important to notice that both previous quotations are from the same author; he would be quite unlikely to contradict himself in his writing, especially in two passages so close together. Therefore, we must somehow reconcile the two statements together. One likely explanation is that Jesus, as God, was one with the Father, but because He was called God the Son, He demonstrated to us all that filial obedience and obeisance to our earthly fathers ought to be the norm. Especially in His human form Jesus was fully willing to give place to His heavenly Father.

111

**...just as Moses was faithful in all God's house.**

This statement is virtually a quotation from Num. 12:7-8, right after God has said that He spoke to prophets other than Moses in visions and dreams, but then contrasts His conversations with Moses:

> But this is not true of my servant Moses;
> he is faithful in all my house.

This is a sweeping, comprehensive statement, and we need to understand that it does not mean that Moses never was diverted from faithfulness to God in thought or deed, but that he was faithful in every area of God's house. After all, Moses was a mere human, and as such he was tainted by the tendency to sin that has infected every human being since Adam and Eve (with the exception of Jesus, God the Son). Probably the most glaring shortcoming Moses ever demonstrated in his life was on the occasion of God's call at the burning bush (Ex. 3:1 to 4:17). At that time Moses conjured up five objections why he should not answer God's call to be the deliverer of his people from bondage in Egypt. Here are his excuses:

1. Who am I? (3:11);
2. Who are you? (3:13);
3. What is my authority? (4:1);
4. I cannot talk. (4:10);
5. Send someone else. (4:13).

Several years after I received God's call to serve Him with my life, I was reading these chapters in Exodus once again. Suddenly, I realized that in my struggle to escape God's will for my life, I had expressed every one of these excuses that Moses had attempted to use against God's will. But God answered me as well as He had answered Moses. I had done better than Moses at making excuses; I had dreamed up an additional excuse: "God, it's too late; I already have a career established." God's answer to that was as devastating as the other five: "Tom, it's never too late to *begin* to serve the Lord."

Probably the most egregious error Moses committed against his faithfulness to God was the third time the people complained to Moses that they had no water to drink. The first was at Marah (Ex. 15:22-27); the second was at Rephidim (Ex. 17:1-7); and the third was at Kadesh, in the Wilderness of Zin (Num. 20:1-13). When Moses pleaded with God, each time He graciously provided water in abundance for all the people and their flocks. In the third instance God instructed Moses to speak to the rock to cause the water to flow. Moses, however, because of his great anger at the children of Israel for their almost constant murmuring and complaining, disobeyed God, and struck the rock instead of merely speaking to it. Moses' disobedience was evil in itself, but Paul in the New Testament points out that Moses' sin was especially heinous this time. This is what Paul said in I Cor. 10:3-4, in writing of God's gracious provision for the people in the wilderness, "They all ate the same spiritual food and drank the same spiritual drink; for they drank from the spiritual rock that accompanied them, and that rock was Christ." In other words, Moses' disobedience was made exceedingly sinful because what he struck—not once but twice—was our Savior Himself.

Moses was aggrieved numerous times during the forty-year trek from Egypt to the Promised Land, as the people murmured against him as well as against God. One more instance when Moses was upset, and this time rightly so, was when he came down from the top of Mount Sinai and found the people eating, drinking, and participating in what well might have been sinful pleasures, in celebration of the molten calf which Aaron had made for them. Moses was willing to perish on the spot, unless God forgave them for their great sin against Him. Moses said (Ex. 32:32), "But now, please forgive their sin—but if not, then blot me out of the book you have written." What Moses said here is like what Paul expressed with regard to the children of Israel in his day. Paul wrote to the church at Rome these words about his own people (Rom. 9:2-4): "I have great sorrow and unceasing anguish in my heart. For I could wish that I myself were cursed and cut off from Christ for the sake of my brothers, those of my own race, the people of Israel."

Despite the times Moses became upset with the people, his faithfulness to God was more exemplary than the rest of Israel during that trying time. I'm certain the trials I endured as a Minister were small compared to those of Moses, but I recall numerous instances when I became upset and even angry at some of the people. It is possible that you also have failed to be faithful to God during your years as a Christian. This is the reason why the author of Hebrews selects Moses as the man with whom to compare Jesus as "faithful in all God's house." If Moses was faithful in God's house, how could there be found anyone who could better that record? Such a person would need to be very good indeed, and the recipients of this book of Hebrews knew they could not meet such a high standard of faithfulness. But there was indeed someone found who was "better than" Moses, and He is revealed in the next verse.

### Heb. 3:3.    Jesus has been found worthy of greater honor...

Here the author begins immediately with his thesis; he will prove it in what follows. We recall that the theme of the whole book is that Jesus is "better than" anyone or anything else to be found in the Old Testament ministry.

### ...than Moses.

We have already discussed how great a man Moses was. He was great in himself. He was head and shoulders, spiritually speaking, above any other people in his generation. It would be difficult to discover anyone in any other Old Testament era to compare with Moses. He was not only great in himself; he was greatly esteemed by all the Jews of all time. Perhaps those he led from Egypt gave him only grudging respect, since he made decisions they often did not understand. Nevertheless, they recognized him as a great leader and man of God. Therefore, if you can be greater than Moses, you are at the top of the heap. But *is* there anyone greater than Moses? How could such a thing be? Yet the author is eager to give the answer.

**...just as the builder of the house has greater honor than the house itself.**

The author of Hebrews now offers two different contrasts between Jesus and Moses. The first is found here, and we will observe the second in verse 6.

This may be called a "homey" illustration by the author. Certainly no one would argue with this statement. Anyone who makes anything must be better than his product. For instance, Henry Ford could build a Model T car that was able to travel along a road, make turns, and stop. But the Model T was not able of itself to start its own engine, back out of the driveway, travel over several different roads, pull into Harvey Firestone's driveway, then stop and chat with him. Only Henry Ford could make his Model T take him to call on his old friend. Similarly, I firmly believe that no human will ever be able to build a computer that will do more than a man can do. Surely, the computer may process information faster, as we already see; but the computer will never be able to think and make moral decisions like the human can. To take this illustration one step further, only God can make a man who is able to live, think, grow, and reproduce. And this, after all, is exactly what the author of Hebrews is driving at when he says that the Builder of the house (God our Savior) is worthy of greater honor than the house itself (the Church).

**Heb. 3:4.   For every house is built by someone, but God is the builder of everything.**

We see here two steps leading to Christ's grandeur. The contrast is only implied in each case, but is supported by the last clause in verse 3. The first step to Christ's grandeur is that a human being is better than a house he may build, however elaborate. Step two is that God is better than any human He has built (created); in fact, God is better than anything else that exists or can be imagined, since He is the "builder of everything." In this figure, Moses is the house, which God built.

Let us not move beyond this point without observing an important fact that is hidden rather subtilely in this passage. The fact is that Jesus is God, and here is how the author makes the statement. We see that the whole theme of the book is that Jesus is better than Old Testament things, and that Jesus is better than Moses. However, the author has suddenly shifted from talking about Jesus, and is pointing out that it is God who is greater than Moses. But it is in this way that the author is proffering the argument, as he does several times in his book, that Jesus is God. We will see more of this near the end of chapter 4 of Hebrews.

This is the first of two illustrations which contrast Jesus and Moses: Jesus is the Builder of the house, while Moses is that house. Do not become confused because of two different kinds of contrasts which both use the same elements for the illustration.

**Heb. 3:5. Moses was faithful as a servant in all God's house....**

In this second illustration, we still see the "house" mentioned, but now Moses is not set forth as the house itself, but now as a servant in that house. This is the beginning of the second great contrast mentioned in verse 3, the first being between the house and the Builder. However, we must wait until we get to verse 6 to see the other part of this second contrast.

**...testifying to what would be said in the future.**

Moses did a tremendous work in leading the Chosen People from their slavery in Egypt. However, no matter how great that work was, we must remember Moses for another immeasurably great work he performed during his lifetime. This greater work affected not only the people of his day, but it has had an impact on every succeeding generation of people who have read the word of God. That work is his writing what we now call "the five books of Moses," or "the Law." Those writings are a record of God's creation of the universe; the beginnings of human life in the world; the origin of the Hebrew nation in the person of Abraham; and God's dealings with Israel through the end of their wanderings in the wilderness after their deliverance from bondage in Egypt.

The author of Hebrews adds that what Moses wrote was a "testifying," not only of what God had done up to the death of Moses, but a "testifying" concerning future events and messages. That is to say, Moses wrote not only history and law; he also wrote prophecy. In fact, Moses wrote of that "Better One" who would take his place at some future date. We recall that Jesus put His stamp of approval on Moses as the author of the Pentateuch, when He said of Moses, "He wrote about me" (John 5:46).

Here is a sampling of the things Moses wrote about Jesus in his five books. For one thing, Moses testified that both he and Jesus are prophets in Deut. 18:15 and 17-18:

> The LORD your God will raise up for you a prophet like me from among your own brothers. You must listen to him....The LORD said to me: "What they say is good. I will raise up for them a prophet like you from among their brothers; I will put my words in his mouth, and he will tell them everything I command him."

Moses showed that God even testified to the two original people that Jesus the Savior would come (Gen. 3:15):

> I will put enmity
> between you and the woman,

> and between your offspring and hers;
>> he will crush your head,
>> and you will strike his heel.

This was God's message to Satan after Adam and Eve were enticed to eat the forbidden fruit. The "offspring" to which God refers here is just one Person, Jesus, as is evidenced by the singular pronoun "he" in "he will crush your head."[5] In another place, Moses gave great promise to Abraham, that his descendants would become a great nation, and that Abraham himself would be a blessing to other nations (Gen. 12:2); and that some descendant of Abraham would be a blessing to many (verse 3): "...all peoples on earth will be blessed through you." It is possible, though unlikely, that God meant that the whole Jewish nation would be a blessing to the world; rather, He surely referred to Jesus the Son of God and of Abraham. Next, when Moses quotes Jacob's final blessing to Judah, Jacob tells this head of the tribe from which Jesus came (Gen. 49:10):

> The scepter will not depart from Judah,
>> nor the ruler's staff from between his feet,
> until he comes to whom it belongs
>> and the obedience of the nations is his.

Who could doubt that this prophecy refers to Jesus the Savior, especially since it is reinforced by a similar quotation from the lips of Balaam in Num. 24:17-19, where Balaam blessed Israel instead of cursing that nation as was demanded by Balak:

> I see him, but not now;
>> I behold him, but not near.
> A star will come out of Jacob;
>> a scepter will rise out of Israel....
> A ruler will come out of Jacob
>> and destroy the survivors of the city.

As noted above, these verses are but a sampling of the messianic prophecies that could be gleaned from the first five books of the Bible. You may search them out for yourself, rather than to have them all repeated here.

There remains the question about all these quotations from the "Books of Moses." That is, did Moses write all these things, or were they written by another person, or by other persons? For many decades now certain scholars have made extensive study of the text of the Bible, not limited to the Old Testament. In their studies, they have designed what they call the "Documentary

---

[5]   There is a strange switch of gender in earlier Roman Catholic English translations of this verse. Ronald A. Knox renders the portion thus in his translation of the Bible, "she is to crush thy head, while thou dost lie in wait at her heels." Knox explains the switch in a footnote to the verse: "For 'she' and 'her' the Septuagint Greek has 'he' and 'him'; the Hebrew text also, as it has come down to us, gives 'he', or perhaps 'it'. But most manuscripts of the Latin version have 'she'..." (the punctuation is Knox'). Because of this, at least some Roman scholars interpret God's words to Satan as referring to Mary who will defeat Satan.

Hypothesis." The idea, in brief, is this: many people were involved in writing each book of the Bible, especially the first books of the Bible ordinarily attributed to Moses as author. These people came from varied backgrounds: some were priests, others were perhaps prophets, some may have been ordinary folk. They lived in different places: they were from Judea, others from the northern kingdom, called either Israel or Ephraim, and some perhaps even from more remote lands. Some of these people actually wrote parts of the record as we have it, while others were called "redactors," people we might call "editors," who put other people's writings together to make the whole flow better. All these people lived in different times, some of them rather early, and others centuries later. If this "hypothesis" has any truth in it, then Moses could not have written the "five Books of Moses." Some scholars even as late as the twentieth century argued that Moses could not have written those books since, they say, writing was not invented until far after Moses lived in the world. Scholars have since discovered writing in many places in the world dating as early as six or more millennia before Christ, long before anyone believes Moses existed.

What are we to say to this "hypothesis"? Did Moses write these things, as the author of Hebrews claims, "testifying to what would be said in the future"? If the book of Hebrews has any credibility as part of the infallible word of God, then we ought to believe that Moses wrote the Books of Moses.

Still, there are additional arguments against the authorship of Moses with regard to these books. One of them is that near the end of the set of books, there is a record of the death of Moses; could he have been able to write about his death before it happened? Certainly: if God could cause Moses to write about Jesus who would come into the world hundreds of years after Moses' time, then surely that same God could cause Moses to predict the details of his own death which would occur a very short time after Moses wrote them.

Other evidence against the "Documentary Hypothesis" is that it is still in its formative stage, after more than a century and a half of struggle to make it seem plausible. No two scholars seem able to agree on any details, but only on a very broad outline of the theory. In other words, no scholar has any concrete evidence to support the hypothesis; it is based totally on conjecture. Honest scholars would therefore agree that the whole idea is still rightfully called nothing more than an hypothesis.

The very most convincing evidence that Moses wrote the books of Moses is the testimony our Savior Himself gave to that fact. In John 5, Jesus sets forth six witnesses to the truth He has been telling the people about His deity: Himself (verse 31); John the Baptist (verse 33); the works Jesus had performed before them (verse 36); Jesus' Father (verse 37); the scriptures (that is, the Old Testament, verse 39); and the final witness in verse 46, where Jesus said, "If you believed Moses, you would believe me, for he wrote about me." If you believe that the Bible is infallible, and especially if you believe that Jesus' words are utterly true, then you must believe Jesus' statement that Moses wrote the books of Moses.

### Heb. 3:6. But Christ is faithful as a Son....

Here is the second contrast between Jesus the Better and Moses the lesser: Christ is the Son and Heir in the house of the Father, while Moses is merely a servant in that house. The first contrast was introduced in the last half of verse 3, where Jesus as God is called the Builder of the house, while Moses was merely the house that was built. You may wish to review what was said there as an introduction to this second contrast.

We should note that the contrast is not between Moses' faithfulness and Christ's; rather the contrast is in the status of the two. Moses' great though flawed faithfulness has already been noted in comparison to Christ's utter faithfulness. So now as we think about "Christ is faithful as a Son," we are concerned only with His Sonship in comparison to Moses' servanthood. There should be no question in the mind of anyone that the position of a Son/Heir/future Master in a house is vastly superior to that of a mere slave in the same household. What a person does in life is not to be denigrated, but a person's status in life counts for much more. Dr. W. Robert Smith, of late a Professor of Philosophy in Bethel College, St. Paul, MN, once made a statement which should help us to understand this truth. Dr. Smith said, "There is a difference between a person's *practice in life*, and his *position in Christ*." He was pointing out that we all fail to achieve the requirement of total perfection set out for us in scripture "Be perfect, therefore, as your heavenly Father is perfect" — Matt. 5:48); therefore we can never get ourselves to heaven by our good works. Instead of relying on our practice in life, we must receive Christ as our Savior, and then we will be taken to heaven by Him, because of our position in Him as our Savior.

It is essential to add here that there must be a relationship between our position in Christ and our practice in life. If we have truly received Jesus Christ as our Savior *and* Lord, then our activities will reflect that new position in which we find ourselves. Please note, I did not say that our activities should match our position, or even that our activities *must* match that position. It is not a matter of ignoring the direction of our new life, or of trying, however valiantly, to live up to our new position in Christ. It is totally automatic, like a baby's beginning to breathe as soon as he is born; if he does not breathe we know he is not alive. So also in our Christian lives, it is ridiculous for a person to try to claim that he has received Christ as Savior and thus has new life, if there is no new life present in him. It is true that our practice in life will always fall short of our new position in Christ, because we never become perfect in the flesh. For a dissertation on that truth, read the last half of Rom. 7, to see that even Paul the apostle did not achieve perfection in this life. This is the case for all Christians, even though we have available the power and guidance of the Holy Spirit to help us overcome sin; unfortunately we do not always make use of His gifts.

### ...over God's house.

We would all do well to remember that it is truly *God's* house with which we have to do, not ours. Too often we try to manage it our own way; we fail even to consult God before attempting to change things to suit ourselves. The habit of tampering with other people's property is probably a common trait of all human beings, but I see it evident in the lives of my grandchildren. When they come to visit, some of them snoop in my desk drawers and other places, perhaps looking for hidden candy or simply out of curiosity. They like to handle everything they see, and try to operate them or to take them apart. I'm sure one grandchild will grow up to become a great engineer or inventor, because he has to see what is inside everything that has parts. Sometimes things get irreparably broken in the process; unfortunately we see God's house, the Church, in such a plight today.

### And we are his house...

Jesus has built God's house, and we, like Moses, are slaves in that house. In another picture described by Peter (I Pet. 2:5), we are "like living stones...built into a spiritual house to be a holy priesthood...." In this sense, Moses is a step above us all: he was a servant in God's house; each of us is merely a part of the house itself. For that reason, Moses is greater than us all, so he is worthy to be compared with Jesus. Jesus, however, is supreme; Moses is under Him; we all are less than Moses.

The Old Testament clearly states that Moses was a huge cut above the people of his day, and surely nobody since then has equaled the exalted position he received from God. This is how the scripture puts it (in Num. 12:8):

> With him I speak face to face,
> clearly and not in riddles;
> he sees the form of the LORD;

and in (Ex. 33:11), "The LORD would speak to Moses face to face, as a man speaks with his friend." This was such a stupendous meeting that in the following chapter, verses 29 to 35, we learn that when Moses returned from the top of Sinai, his face shone so brightly that the people could not look on him, so he put a veil over his face to accommodate them. I am not aware that anyone else is reported to have seen or talked with God face to face. A close likeness is found in Judges 6:22, where Gideon cried out, "Ah, Sovereign LORD! I have seen the angel of the LORD face to face."

### ...if we hold on to our courage and the hope of which we boast.

Other English versions of this clause, such as the KJV and RSV, put

119

the words in slightly different order, more in keeping with the original Greek: "...if we cling to the boldness and boasting of our hope" (my translation). This order of words shows that our hope is supported in two ways: first, our hope gives us boldness; and secondly, our hope gives us something of which to boast.

This clause imposes a condition on the previous statement, "And we are his house." That is to say that not one of us is automatically connected to or part of God's house; we are part of that house only if we have hope in Him, the kind of hope that gives us boldness to live for Him, and qualifies us for a righteous boasting in our salvation. We must "hold on to" both our courage and our boasting of our hope.

Lest we be led astray to a false hope, we must recognize that this statement says nothing about how we *become* a part of God's house; rather it tells how we *demonstrate that we are* a part of His house.

The Greek word translated here as either "courage" or "boldness" is παρρησία. It is a powerful and wonderful word. Too many Christians seriously lack the boldness to expose their relationship to Christ, so much that most of the time the world cannot tell whether they are Christians. In addition to this passage, we are encouraged to have boldness in our Christian lives in three other places in this book. The first is in chapter 4:16, where another English synonym is used: "Let us then approach the throne of grace with confidence, so that we may receive mercy and find grace to help us in our time of need," after the author has spoken about our weakness in temptation. The second place is in 10:19 (where the NIV again uses the English "confidence"): "Therefore, brothers, since we have confidence to enter the Most Holy Place by the blood of Jesus, by a new and living way opened for us through the curtain, that is, his body...." How wonderful it is to know that we can approach God intimately because Jesus shed His blood to pave our way to God's very throne! The third place this strong Greek word is used in Hebrews is also in the tenth chapter, verse 35: "So do not throw away your confidence; it will be richly rewarded." This is said after the author reminded his readers that they had already suffered various kinds of persecution, and had been brought through safely by God.

The matter about boasting is more difficult to understand or even to accept. The Greek word καύχημα is translated by Thayer as "that of which one glories or can glory, matter or ground of glorying...a glorying, boasting." As one reared in a Christian home, I was taught repeatedly that I should not brag or boast about myself, my abilities, or my possessions. Whatever I have is a gift from God; therefore I have no right to take credit for any of it. Paul warned us with regard to our salvation especially, "It is by grace you have been saved, through faith—and this not from yourselves, it is the gift of God—not by works, so that no one can boast" (Eph. 2:8-9). Despite this teaching, Paul disregarded his own counsel at least once, with two demurrers:

he said everyone was doing it, and he claimed to do it as a fool and not as a sensible man (II Cor. 11:16-18):

> Let no one take me for a fool. But if you do, then receive me just as you would a fool, so that I may do a little boasting. In this self-confident boasting I am not talking as the Lord would, but as a fool. Since many are boasting in the way the world does, I too will boast.

Paul then spends the next paragraph listing all the things he had done for Christ and the miseries he had suffered for his efforts. But he warns us, first in I Cor. 1:31, and again in II Cor. 10:17, "Let him who boasts boast in the Lord," which is a quotation from Jer. 9:24. In a slight variation, Paul seems almost to chide himself in his boasting by telling the people of the churches in Galatia (6:14): "May I never boast except in the cross of our Lord Jesus Christ, through which the world has been crucified to me, and I to the world."

The author of Hebrews does not mention boasting elsewhere in his letter except here. In this instance, he is not urging his readers to brag about how great they are, but to boast in the God who gives us such great hope of rescue from sin and its results.

The author now turns from Moses to you and me who are God's house.

### Heb. 3:7.   So, as the Holy Spirit says....

Here the author reminds us of a most important detail about the quality of scripture: the Holy Spirit is the author of it all. We have noted at the beginning of this study that nobody today is certain as to the authorship of this book; but it does not matter, since the Holy Spirit Himself is the true Author. That is the sole reason why it is profitable to study it now. The reason the author raises this matter now is to emphasize that the words he is about to quote from Ps. 95 make an impact on us today, since the true Author is the Holy Spirit and not some famous man, and because God wanted future generations to heed it carefully and take its admonition to heart.

### Today, if you hear his voice....

Thus begins the extended quotation from the last half of Ps. 95. The first part of the Psalm is a great song of adulation and praise to the God of the universe ending with an urgent call to worship Him because He is the sovereign God and we are His cherished subjects. The rest of the Psalm follows as a warning to any who would dare to rebel against that great God, that their end would be most disastrous.

How does this Psalm fit into the scheme of what the author of Hebrews has been trying to say? Simply put, he has been talking about our right as followers of Christ to have "boldness and boasting of hope," and now he is urging his hearers/readers[6] to continue in that hope without faltering. In the

---

[6]   According to Heb. 5:11, it is evident that the author of Hebrews initially delivered his words as a sermon to a congregation. It was later transcribed both for their benefit and for ours.

quotation from the Psalm, the author reminds us of what happened to the children of Israel who abandoned their hope in God in the wilderness wandering.

### Today....

Psalm 95 has no title. Many other Psalms do, so we can tell with some certainty just when they were written, who the author was, and under what circumstances they were composed. So if we had only the Psalm itself to instruct us, we could only conjecture what "day" was meant, whether it was very early in the history of the Jews, or near the end of the writing and compilation of the Old Testament in its canonical form. We do have, however, some clear information about the origin of this Psalm, in what the author of Hebrews says in 4:7, that "God spoke through David." Since Hebrews is part of scripture, what it says is sufficiently authentic for us to be certain that David was the author, and he wrote approximately 1000 BC.

In writing his Psalm, David was writing to the people of his day, so his "today" was an admonition to his compatriots to keep up their hope in the God who delivered their ancestors from bondage in Egypt.

In saying that David was giving a message to the people of his day, we ought to broaden our scope of understanding of what day is important in comprehending the extent of the population to whom this message has been given directly through history. I like to think of four specific "todays" in this regard. Beginning with the first instance historically, we remember that God gave His warning to the Israelites who spent forty years marking time between their departure from Egypt until their entry into the Promised Land. Actually, it was two generations who heard the message then; the generation of people twenty years old and upward, all of whom died during those forty years except the two faithful spies, Caleb and Joshua; and those twenty years and under who survived and actually entered Canaan.

The second "today" we identify is the "day" during the life of King David. He wrote the Psalm to warn the people not to turn from their God. But since many in David's time rejected God and His promises, there was yet much room to be filled by faithful people when the author of Hebrews was living. Therefore, the third important "today" was the period during which that book was spoken and written. The author was concerned for their eternal welfare, so his message to them was the same warning the people received from Moses in the wilderness, and the same warning from David several hundred years later.

There is surely a fourth "today:" the day you and I read Hebrews. Since heaven is not yet filled because of the defection of people in generations past, there is still room for us. We, however, must remain faithful to God, and continue to hope in Him if we are to receive His blessings. This is a brief outline of what we will learn from continuing our discussion of this quotation from Ps. 95.

## Today, if you hear his voice....

Had the people heard God's voice? We must agree that most assuredly they had heard. They may not have heard it directly, but they did hear it sufficiently, through the voices of His spokesmen which He provided to every generation. For evidence we recall the opening words of Hebrews: "In the past God spoke to our forefathers through the prophets at many times and in various ways, but in these last days he has spoken to us by his Son." Beginning with our first parents, God spoke to them as they took their ease in the Garden of Eden. He spoke to and through Abraham, Moses, Joshua, Samuel, David, Elijah and Elisha, and more than all the prophets whose names grace the sixteen books of prophecy in the Old Testament. This is but a sampling of the people through whom God spoke, not to mention angels. Jesus was the supreme voice of God in the world. Since His day there have been apostles, and disciples beyond counting, who have walked, ridden horseback and train, spoken in churches in nearly every corner of every city and village, and have spread the word of God by means of radio, television, and the more recent and increasingly exotic media.

If all those voices have not reached the ears of the people of the world, we should remember that another medium of communication has spoken God's voice to every creature that has ever lived in the world. David said it this way in Ps. 19:1-6:

> The heavens declare the glory of God;
> > the skies proclaim the work of his hands.
> Day after day they pour forth speech;
> > night after night they display knowledge.
> There is no speech or language
> > where their voice is not heard.
> Their voice goes out into all the earth,
> > their words to the ends of the world.
> In the heavens he has pitched a tent for the sun,
> > which is like a bridegroom coming forth from his pavilion,
> > like a champion rejoicing to run his course.
> It rises at one end of the heavens
> > and makes its circuit to the other;
> > nothing is hidden from its heat.

Since the word of God has overwhelmingly blanketed the earth throughout history, the apostle Paul has every right to say without equivocation, "Since the creation of the world God's invisible qualities—his eternal power and divine nature—have been clearly seen, being understood from what has been made, so that men are without excuse" (Rom. 1:20). Paul makes an even more bold assertion in the very next verse, where he states that "they knew God." The refusal of anyone to acknowledge God therefore is not a matter of ignorance, but of outright rejection of Him.

Now, what is the admonition spoken by Moses, David, and the author of Hebrews? Here it is.

### ...do not harden your hearts
### as you [they] did in the rebellion....

Do not be confused by whether the author of Hebrews meant to identify the people of Moses' day or those in David's day. Actually, he followed the exact wording of the Psalm in the LXX version (Ps. 94 in the LXX); and both Greek renderings follow the sense as set forth in the original Hebrew. It would be better to translate both Hebrew and Greek in this manner, to make the people referred to indeterminate: "Do not harden your hearts as in the rebellion." To me, "they" would be more appropriate, since David obviously refers to the people who wandered in the wilderness long before his time, although his warning in the Psalm, of course, was to his contemporaries.

In a spiritual sense the children of Israel who lived in David's day also lived in Moses' day. We read often in the Old Testament that people existed "in the loins" of their ancestors. Further, Jesus Himself expressed the same sense in His discussion with the Pharisees and others regarding their part in persecuting the prophets of old (Matt. 23:29-32):

Woe to you, teachers of the law and Pharisees, you hypocrites! You build tombs for the prophets and decorate the graves of the righteous. And you say, "If we had lived in the days of our forefathers, we would not have taken part with them in shedding the blood of the prophets." So you testify against yourselves that you are the descendants of those who murdered the prophets. Fill up, then, the measure of the sin of your forefathers!

David was admonishing his people not to be stubborn in their defection from God; the author of Hebrews adds this idea as the opposite to what he has just said about clinging to our "boldness and boasting of our hope." Moses was condemning his people for doing something much more serious than merely turning away from God; he was accusing them of turning against Him. The distinction between turning away from God and turning against Him may be very small. They are both sin, and ought to be avoided at all cost. The distinction may be similar to two things Jesus said to His disciples. I am not certain whether they are comparative or contrasting statements. One is in Matt. 12:30, "He who is not with me is against me;" and the other is in Mk. 9:40, "...whoever is not against us is for us." In inspecting these two verses together, it seems as if there are three groups of people, not just two: one group truly belongs to Jesus; a second group truly is against Jesus; and a third group might be called "neutral," but Jesus implies that they are actually supportive of Him and His cause although not part of His group.

### ...in the rebellion,
### during the time of testing in the desert....

The context of these words in Psalm 95 makes it obvious that the people referred to are those who wandered in the wilderness for forty years, before God finally allowed them to enter the Promised Land. That historical period of time is outlined in the books of Moses, beginning in Ex. 13:17, and continuing through the book of Deuteronomy. It truly was a time of "testing", a time of rigorous and austere living. The people moved often, but never were certain when they would be required to move again. Conditions throughout the desert were painful at best, considering the almost constant heat and drought. The people had children and flocks to oversee; surely they had aged and/or ill relatives to care for. They often had no idea where their next meal was coming from, and the sources of water for themselves and their animals were scarce. There were natural hazards, such as asps, thorn-bushes, wild animals, not to mention "wild" men who sought to destroy them.

At first thought, we may consider it no wonder that the people rebelled against Moses and God. If we were called to such hardship today, who of us would "cling to the boldness and boasting of our hope"? Moses records fifteen separate instances of rebellion on the part of the people, and he may have omitted others, but these are surely typical:

| | | |
|---|---|---|
| 1. | Ex. 14:10-14 | There were no graves in the wilderness |
| 2. | Ex. 15:22-27 | No water at Marah |
| 3. | Ex. 16:1-36 | They had no food |
| 4. | Ex. 17:1-7 | No water at Rephidim |
| 5. | Ex. 32:1-6 | Moses had left them |
| 6. | Num. 11:1-3 | Murmurers were burned |
| 7. | Num. 11:4-15 | People coveted meat |
| 8. | Num. 12:1-3 | Miriam and Aaron were jealous |
| 9. | Num. 14:1-5 | Ten spies brought an evil report |
| 10. | Num. 16:1-3 | Korah & Co. revolted |
| 11. | Num. 16:41-50 | People were killed in the plague |
| 12. | Num. 20:1-13 | Moses struck the Rock for water |
| 13. | Num. 21:4-9 | The plague of serpents |
| 14. | Num. 25:1-5 | The people worshiped Baal-peor |
| 15. | Num. 25:6-9 | God punished the idolaters |

God tested the people in the wilderness for two reasons. First, He tested them to see whether they would remain faithful to Him after He delivered them so gloriously from their bondage in Egypt. Secondly, God tested them in relation to their rebelliousness. The people's acts of rebellion most certainly were a wrong response to God's testings. It was never necessary for them to rebel, or to doubt God's promise of faithfulness to them, to take care of all their needs. But, just like our human failure, they often had wants far beyond their mere needs, and the wants often became so powerful that they began to seem like real needs.

The people almost never responded positively to God's testings. We do find two examples of their adherence to God, however. One example is in Ex.

33:4-6, after the incident of Aaron's forming the golden calf for the people to worship during Moses' absence on Mount Sinai. Moses treated them roughly. In Ex. 32:20 we read that Moses "took the calf they had made and burned it in the fire; then he ground it to powder, scattered it on the water and made the Israelites drink it." Moses also commanded the Levites to go among the people with their swords and kill some; three thousand died. God also threatened to refuse to go with them to the Promised Land. Because of this punishment, the people obviously repented of their great sin. The scripture tells us the evidence of their repentance: "When the people heard these distressing words, they began to mourn and no one put on any ornaments....So the Israelites stripped off their ornaments at Mount Horeb."

The second instance recorded of the repentance of the children of Israel is more by way of a statement of compliance than an actual deed, and as such is almost laughable if it were not so seriously false. After Moses had died, just as the people were ready to enter the land under Joshua's leadership, they made a promise to him and confirmed it by a pitifully erroneous boast. It is recorded in Josh. 1:16-17: "Then they answered Joshua, 'Whatever you have commanded us we will do, and wherever you send us we will go. Just as we fully obeyed Moses, so we will obey you.'" The memories of the people seemed to have been very short (like ours often are), because they forgot the multiple times they rebelled against Moses and God in the wilderness.

### ...where your fathers tested and tried me....

Aha! It is important to recognize that "testing" can work both ways. It is not only God who tests us to see whether we will remain faithful to Him; we also test Him with our rebellions, but for no good purpose. When we test God, He often reacts in ways not pleasant to us. We think again, for instance, of the scene at the foot of Sinai, where Moses dealt violently with the people, and God threatened to abandon them (Ex. 33:3): "Go up to the land flowing with milk and honey. But I will not go with you, because you are a stiffnecked people and I might destroy you on the way." Still, God would not utterly forsake them, because He had just promised them (verse 2), "I will send an angel before you...."

Each complaint and rebellion of the people tested God's longsuffering. How thankful we should be that He *is* longsuffering. If He were not, we all would have perished long ago. In fact, we would never have begun to exist, because our ancestors would have been wiped out for their murmurings against the longsuffering God. Right after the incident at Sinai, just as Moses returned to the top of the mountain with the tablets of stone which this time Moses had to carve into shape, God assured him (Ex. 34:6-7):

> The LORD, the LORD, the compassionate and gracious God, slow to anger [KJV "longsuffering"], abounding in love and faithfulness, maintaining love to thousands, and forgiving wickedness, rebellion and sin. Yet he does not leave the guilty unpunished; he punishes the children and their

children for the sin of the fathers to the third and fourth generation.

This is but a sample of the many times God declares His faithfulness and longsuffering toward His people in the Old Testament. Here is a sample of the New Testament instances where the same thing is said of Him (Rom. 9:22):

> What if God, choosing to show his wrath and make his power known, bore with great patience [KJV "longsuffering"] the objects of his wrath—prepared for destruction? What if he did this to make the riches of his glory known to the objects of his mercy, whom he prepared in advance for glory—even us, whom he also called, not only from the Jews but also from the Gentiles?

### ...and for forty years saw what I did.

Forty years is a long time (in human time) for God to suffer testing by His chosen people and yet retain His longsuffering. Naturally the people saw that length of time as interminably long, especially since that span of time was composed of one year of punishment for each day the spies were searching out the land (Num. 14:34). In fact, that length of time was in a sense interminable for the older generation, because God caused all those twenty years of age and older to die in the wilderness before His people could enter the Promised Land (Num. 14:28-30). In spite of the almost constant murmuring of the people, God took good care of them by supplying all their needs: He fed them quail on occasion; He gave them manna constantly; He brought water out of the rock not once, not twice, but three times; and He kept them fully clothed. That amazing feat is stated this way in Deut. 29:5-6:

> During the forty years that I led you through the desert, your clothes did not wear out, nor did the sandals on your feet. You ate no bread and drank no wine or other fermented drink. I did this so that you might know that I am the LORD your God.

In today's throw-away society, some people would be unhappy at being prevented from obtaining the latest fashion in clothing, or from purchasing a new car that is faster and sleeker than last year's. But during that forty years, God took specially good care of His chosen leader Moses, in this way (Deut. 34:7): "Moses was a hundred and twenty years old when he died, yet his eyes were not weak nor his strength gone." Moses knew that his vision and health were miraculous gifts from God, because it was he who wrote in Ps. 90:10 that our normal span of life is only seventy years; and it if continues another decade it becomes neither pleasant nor profitable, and it ends soon.

If God dealt so graciously with the children of Israel in the wilderness—and does the same for us today—we have no reason to rebel against God or be upset with Him when He gently chastises us. God continually loads us with good gifts, demonstrating to us His divine power as well as His goodness. Thus Paul says of people like us, in Rom. 1:20, "Since the creation of the world God's invisible qualities—his eternal power and divine nature—have been clearly seen, being understood from what has been made, so that men are without excuse."

### Heb. 3:10.

**That is why I was angry with that generation....**

Why? Let us review why, lest having hearts too hard, ears too heavy, and eyes too slitted, we like they should forget what God had done for them as well as for us. Let us never think only in terms of a history lesson when we read and study God's word; let us apply it to our own lives, lest we falter and fall like they fell in the wilderness amidst all God's wealth of provisions. God was angry with the ancient Jews because, in spite of the miracles He worked for their deliverance from bondage in Egypt, and in spite of all His tender care for them in their journeys through the wasteland between fertile Egypt and more fertile Canaan, they almost constantly murmured and rebelled, forever wanting either a return to what they had left behind, or a superabundance of luxuries and leisures which God knew would not be good for them. When your grandchild fails to send you a thank-you note for the birthday gift you sent, you are at least disappointed—if it happens often enough you even may become angry enough to withhold a future gift. But if your grandchild complains to you that instead of the twenty-five dollar costume jewelry you sent her she really wanted the thousand dollar necklace, you might even consider erasing her name from your will. God loves to be thanked, appreciated, for all He has given His chosen people the Jews as well as for all He has given you.

Have you meditated lately on even just a few of the things God has given you? You who live in the United States may not have absolutely all the things I now mention, but surely you have virtually all of them, or at least very good substitutes for them: a comfortable home overstuffed with furniture and "labor-saving" appliances; loving family and/or friends living nearby who show constant concern for you; food on the table, including exotic fruits from Central America, New Zealand, Africa and Asia (not to mention chocolate candies and drinks and other desserts); exquisite scenery whether oceans, lakes, mountains, rich farmland, even desert which has its own special beauty, all created by God for your enjoyment and benefit; the sun for energy and light; the air for breathing; the rivers and lakes for drinking; the boundless minerals under the ground. The children of Israel were sometimes glad that they had sandals that did not wear out in the wilderness; have you thanked God for shoes rugged as combat boots, not to mention autos, ocean liners, and airplanes? We might say we are already in our earthly "Promised Land," without having to wander in a wilderness to get here. Have you thanked God for any of these things, or others I have not mentioned? Have you shown your appreciation to Him by anything you have done lately? Is God pleased with us and our generation, or is He as angry with us as He was with the wandering Jews?

**...and I said, "Their hearts are always going astray...."**

Here is an interesting matter, which occurs occasionally, but about which we seldom think. Here in one passage of the Old Testament we have a quotation from another passage of the Old Testament. Let us sort it out. This Psalm 95 was, according to the author of Hebrews, written by King David. In Heb. 3:10, David quotes God as having quoted Himself from Num. 14:21-23. If we compare this quotation in Numbers with what David wrote in the Psalm, it seems to be quite inexact. However, the sense given in both passages is the same. Let us compare the two here. In Ps. 95:10-11 we read:

> I said, "They are a people whose hearts go astray,
> and they have not known my ways."
> So I declared on oath in my anger,
> "They shall never enter my rest."

And this is the parallel passage in Num. 14:21-23:

> Nevertheless, as surely as I live and as surely as the glory of the LORD fills the whole earth, not one of the men who saw my glory and the miraculous signs I performed in Egypt and in the desert but who disobeyed me and tested me ten times—not one of them will ever see the land I promised on oath to their forefathers. No one who has treated me with contempt will ever see it.

God in His great mercy and compassion does reserve for Himself a remnant in every generation. So although "all" those Israelites over twenty years of age when they left Egypt would never enter the Promised Land, yet many of those under twenty would enter. We read that promise in Deut. 12:8-10, spoken through Moses:

> You are not to do as we do here today, everyone as he sees fit, since you have not yet reached the resting place and the inheritance the LORD your God is giving you. But you will cross the Jordan and settle in the land the LORD your God is giving you as an inhertitance, and he will give you rest from all your enemies around you so that you will live in safety.

The hearts of the people surely did go astray, and the extent of their wanderings is only slightly exaggerated by the modifier "always." Fifteen times of murmuring, dissent, and desire to defect are only the times recorded by Moses. Surely there were many more during that forty years in the wilderness. The word for "going astray" is also well translated as "wandering." It is the Greek verb πλανάω, from which we derive our English word for planets, so called by the ancient astronomers because they did not stay in their proper places in the heavens among the other "fixed" stars, but wandered perpetually.

Surely it was the hearts of the wanderers that led them astray, as the author of Hebrews says. The thought always comes first, then the intent, and finally the action takes place. Jesus affirmed this sequence in His conversation with the Pharisees in Mk. 7. We may sum up what He said as recorded in verses 15, 21 and 22:

> Nothing outside a man can make him 'unclean' by going into him. Rather,

it is what comes out of a man that makes him 'unclean....' For from within, out of men's hearts, come evil thoughts, sexual immorality, thefts, murder, adultery, greed, malice, deceit, lewdness, envy, slander, arrogance and folly.

We may say that some actions of people are spontaneous or automatic, but that is not true. Even quickly withdrawing one's hand from a hot object is not strictly "automatic," because it is something we have learned to do through experience. Likewise, feeding a poor person is not something a philanthropist does simply because a poor person is at hand. The philanthropist must first take note of the poverty; then he must somehow be motivated to act in behalf of the hungry person. That is why liberal churches fail in their objectives of giving help to needy people. They try to get people to contribute only because the need exists, and few people are willing to act merely on the basis of obedience to some churchman. This is why it is of utmost importance first to preach the gospel, so that God will change people's hearts. Only then will they be willing to help those less fortunate than they. In fact, I am sure studies would show that churches where the gospel is faithfully preached contribute far more per capita for the needs of others around the world than churches that neglect the preaching of the word of God and emphasize doing good.

### ...and they have not known my ways.

People who claim to encourage helping the needy without first seeking to establish changed hearts often go another step further in violating God's will. They often urge people to do things which they claim are the right things, although they are utterly contrary to God's directions in scripture. One horrendous example of this in our day is the promotion of legalized abortion. It is claimed that some women would be harmed if they were required to carry their babies to term, so they need to be freed from the burden of the pregnancy and the requirement to care for a child for two decades. The scriptures contain not one indication that the personal desire of the mother is of greater importance than the life of the child. This is especially true when the woman has become pregnant through an act contrary to God's law. Jesus spoke of this pattern of men's evil actions as He was talking to the Pharisees in the incident noted earlier. In Mk. 7:6-7, Jesus quoted Isaiah on disregarding God's ways:

> These people honor me with their lips,
>> but their hearts are far from me.
> They worship me in vain;
>> their teachings are but rules taught by men.

Isaiah had something further to say about the wanderings of men from God's ways (Is. 55:9):

> As the heavens are higher than the earth,
>> so are my ways higher than your ways

We must be sure to note that these "wanderings" mentioned by Isaiah are not the "wandering" of the children of Israel those forty years in the wilderness. That wandering was ordained by God, and was not in itself sinful. But the wanderings which are people's "going astray" are probably the most heinous in God's sight in that they abandoned Him in favor of other gods. When men go their own way instead of God's, the punishment is most severe (Prov. 14:12):

> There is a way that seems right to a man,
> but in the end it leads to death.

### Heb. 3:11.
### So I declared on oath in my anger....

We are not supposed to swear, that is, make an oath; because doing so brings dire consequences to anyone who breaks his oath. Jesus warned us in His Sermon on the Mount (Matt. 5:34-37):

> You have heard that it was said to the people long ago, "Do not break your oath, but keep the oaths you have made to the Lord." But I tell you, Do not swear at all; either by heaven, for it is God's throne; or by the earth, for it is his footstool; or by Jerusalem, for it is the city of the Great King. And do not swear by your head, for you cannot make even one hair white or black. Simply let your "Yes" be "Yes," and your "No," "No"; anything beyond this comes from the evil one.

The sin does not consist in making the oath, but in breaking the oath once made. Jesus knew full well that all people find it extremely difficult to keep an oath. We are surrounded by evidence of this difficulty. People seem to forget that when they marry, they make solemn vows, or oaths, to remain married to that same person, to live in selfless love, to do everything to support the partner in all of life, and in particular to abandon even the thought of having sexual relations with any other person. The fact that the divorce rate in the United States has hovered around fifty per cent for decades does not begin to expose the state of faithlessness among people; studies consistently show that the rate of adultery is closer to ninety per cent, give or take a few per cent. Another example of breaking oaths is the large number of perjury convictions in our courts, where every attorney, every witness, every juror, must take a solemn oath with hand held on a copy of the Holy Bible, ending with the words, "...so help you God."

Very few people today seem to be as respectful of the laws of oath-taking as was Judge Jephthah, who kept the vow he made to the Lord, "If you give the Ammonites into my hands, whatever comes out of the door of my house to meet me when I return in triumph from the Ammonites will be the LORD's, and I will sacrifice it as a burnt offering" (Jud. 11:30). Of course Jephthah was sure that his dog, or a pet lamb or other such animal would be first to meet him, but tragically it was his beautiful daughter, his only child,

131

who ran out gleefully to meet and congratulate him. Jephthah had caught himself on the horns of a great dilemma: either he could break his vow to God, or he could commit murder which would be breaking one of the ten commandments. Either decision would be dastardly. Jephthah chose to keep his vow, and sacrifice his daughter (Jud. 11:39). It is my opinion that Jephthah would have been no less culpable in God's sight if he had taken the other choice, but that is beside the point here. Jephthah had made a vow, and he considered keeping a vow to be more important than keeping one of the commandments. As Jesus urged us, we would do well never to make a vow, so we would not think we had forced ourselves to break it.

There is another instance in Hebrews where God takes an oath; it is found in Heb. 6:13-20. Further implications of oath-taking will be discussed when we get to that portion of scripture.

If you are now thinking that God does not set us a very good example when He freely makes oaths, even in anger, you need to remember that God is in an infinitely different category from us humans. First of all, God is supreme, so He has a right to do whatever He pleases. His decision could be illogical or unjust in our minds, but no decision of God's could be wrong since He is sovereign. Secondly, God *is* just in all His dealings with men, as with all His creation. Further, when God swears He will do something, He *always* does it. This is far different from the practice of humans; we often make promises to others which we fail to keep.

Not only does God have a right to make oaths, He also has a right to be angry. When we rebel against Him, and disobey His commandments, He is free to feel anger and to discipline us for what we have done against Him. But for our part, we do well not to get angry for any cause whatever, because when we become angry, we often think, say, or do something which ought not to be done. The apostle warned us in Eph. 4:26, "Be ye angry, and sin not" (KJV). This is the way the Greek ought to be translated, rather than the NIV "In your anger do not sin." Robertson[7] tells us that the Greek word used here, ὀργίζω, is in what he calls the "permissive imperative" mood. That is to say, Paul uses the imperative because he says there are times to be angry, but we are not required to be angry always, or ever. My own experience has most often been that whenever I get angry for any cause I invariably harbor evil thoughts or even commit sinful acts. But Paul has said that sinning is not at all allowed, even in the state of anger. My counsel to you, reader, is to avoid anger at all times and you will be less likely to sin against your Lord and Savior. Paul's statement is a quotation from Ps. 4:4, which reads in the NIV exactly the same as Eph. 4:26; but the KJV has a different rendering of the Psalm, "Stand in awe, and sin not." Paul quotes the LXX verbatim. The Hebrew word in the Psalm (verse 5 in both LXX and Hebrew Bibles) is רָגַז, which, according to BDB, can mean "be agitated, quiver, quake, be excited,

---
[7] WORD PICTURES IN THE NEW TESTAMENT, Vol. IV, p. 540.

perturbed." Some commentators add that the word could even mean, "be provoked to wrath, be enraged."[8] The Hebrew word is also in the imperative mood.

Paul adds to his admonition to avoid sinning in anger (Eph. 4:26b-27), "Do not let the sun go down while you are still angry, and do not give the devil a foothold." It is bad enough to fall into sin as a result of anger, but it is much worse to let the anger last beyond sundown. Sin engendered by anger, like a sliver in one's skin, will fester and grow if left untended.

God has a right not only to swear, but to be angry. It may be appropriate for us to mention here a third matter of mental reflection although it is not mentioned in this passage. God is a jealous God, and has every right to be jealous. Probably the most memorable passage where God's jealousy is noted in scripture is in the second Commandment, Ex. 20:4-6. This commandment has been lost to Roman Catholics, for all intents and purposes, since they integrate this commandment with the first commandment. In order to arrive at a total of ten commandments, they split the tenth (all of which has to do with covetousness) into two commandments, the first of which is the prohibition to covet one's neighbor's house, and the final commandment then becomes a word against coveting anything else belonging to one's neighbor. I say the true second commandment is lost, since most Roman Catholics, when studying the Catechism, learn only the initial part of each commandment without ever learning the rest of any of them. Thus the prohibition against making false gods with one's hands and bowing before them is totally lost to most Roman Catholics.

That second commandment can be divided into two important parts. The first forbids us to fashion a deity of any material, a deity that is similar to anything that God has created in His universe, while the second part forbids us to bow down before or worship those things. God's warning to those who dare to defy this edict is that His punishment will be meted out not only on them but also on their children "to the third and fourth generation of those who hate me." The reason God gives for threatening such punishment is that He is a "jealous" God.

We may be troubled by two matters connected with this stringent action God warns will come upon those who disobey Him. One is that He says He will bring punishment upon even the children of those who "hate" Him. But do we not read in such passages of scripture as Ezek. 18 that no son will die for the sins of his father, neither will the father die for the sins of his son? The whole chapter is a discussion of this matter, but these verses are especially appropriate: (17-18) "He will not die for his father's sin; he will surely live. But his father will die for his own sin, because he practiced extortion, robbed his brother and did what was wrong among his people;" (and 20) "The soul who sins is the one who will die. The son will not share the guilt of the

---

[8] Quoted in the definition by BDB.

father, nor will the father share the guilt of the son." I may misunderstand how to reconcile these two thoughts best in the Bible, but here is how I put them together: it is my opinion that a father who commits idolatry such as is described in the commandment is such a force for evil that his abominable life makes such an impact on his children that they also fall into the same or similar sin, and so they are also guilty. That taint is so strong, in fact, that it is not vitiated until a third or fourth generation comes and goes in the world. Perhaps we can see this idea more clearly when we look at the examples of evil kings of Israel and Judah. Especially appropriate is that of the first king of the Northern Kingdom, Israel, who was Jeroboam. The record of his reign begins in I Kings 12:25; the remainder of that chapter tells of his awful idolatry. He made two golden calves for the people to worship. He placed one in Bethel and the other in Dan, so the people would not be moved to go to Jerusalem any more to worship the true God. For Jeroboam's efforts, God sent a young prophet to speak against Jeroboam and the altar in Bethel (this story is in I Kings 13). Later, God sent another prophet, Ahijah, to prophesy against the king and all his descendants, all because of Jeroboam's idolatry (I Kings 14:9-10):

> You have done more evil than all who lived before you. You have made for yourself other gods, idols made of metal; you have provoked me to anger and thrust me behind your back. Because of this, I am going to bring disaster on the house of Jeroboam. I will cut off from Jeroboam every last male in Israel—slave or free. I will burn up the house of Jeroboam as one burns dung, until it is all gone.

Part of Ahijah's prophecy at that time was that Jeroboam's son who was then ill would die; its fulfillment is recorded in I Kings 14:17. The rest of the prophecy came to pass all too soon afterward. Jeroboam had only one descendant who ascended the throne of Israel, Nadab, who reigned only two years, and was killed. We are told that Nadab "did evil in the eyes of the LORD," so he was killed not for the sins of his very wicked father, but for his own sins, but he was a true son of his father in this respect. In this particular case, God saw the sin of Jeroboam as so greatly evil that He did not allow Jeroboam to have children as far as the third or fourth generation, but all were cut off with Nadab (I Kings 15:28-29):

> Baasha killed Nadab in the third year of Asa king of Judah and succeeded him as king. As soon as he began to reign, he killed Jeroboam's whole family. He did not leave Jeroboam anyone that breathed, but destroyed them all, according to the word of the LORD given through his servant Ahijah the Shilonite.

It would be fruitless to continue with examples of evil fathers who had evil sons from the list of kings of Israel; surely you see the point that sons do not die for their fathers' idolatry, but the sons of idolatrous fathers follow in their footsteps. Therefore, God has every right to punish sons whose fathers are idolaters to the 'third and fourth generation."

The other matter that may trouble us with regard to God's punishing people for idolatry is His jealousy. Normally, we humans think we are doing something amiss when we are jealous; that is true. So why then does God have a right to be jealous?

First, we ought to come to grips with the correct understanding of what jealousy really is. Both the Hebrew verb for jealousy, קָנָא, and its New Testament Greek counterpart, ζηλόω, can mean either to be jealous or to be zealous. It is permissible for people to be zealous for God, to want to glorify or serve Him. For instance, Paul had a great desire for the Corinthian Christians to be devoted to Christ; in other words, he was zealous for them to be zealous for their Savior (II Cor. 11:2): "I am jealous for you with a godly jealousy. I promised you to one husband, to Christ, so that I might present you as a pure virgin to him." On the other hand, the desire to possess something another person has, or to envy him for his status, is, like covetousness, a terrible sin that leads to further sin. An example of that is Cain's jealous rage against his brother (Gen. 4:6-16), because Abel's offering was accepted by God but Cain's was not. The result was that Cain committed the first murder in human history. (The Hebrew word for jealousy does not occur in this story, but the mental attitude is surely there.) Elwell[9] points out that jealousy is just the opposite of love, as Paul says in I Cor. 13:4, "Love is patient, love is kind. It does not envy [is not jealous], it does not boast, it is not proud."

Here I express my own opinion why jealousy is wrong for humans and right for God. Since God is the Creator of all things, then He possesses all things by virtue of His creation. No person, no angel, no demon, or any other creature has a right to claim possession of anything. But when someone dares to usurp ownership of anything from God, whether it be some physical possession or whether it be worship and adoration rightly due to God alone, then God has absolute right to be jealous and to punish the offender. This is why idolatry is so sinful, because the idolater wrongfully removes worship from the true and living God, and seeks to give it to part of God's creation, a part that has been fashioned into the shape of something else by the offender. Isaiah points out how utterly absurd such activity is. His comments in this regard cover much of his book of prophecy, but it can be summed up in Is. 44:15-17:

> [A tree] is man's fuel for burning;
> > some of it he takes and warms himself,
> > he kindles a fire and bakes bread.
> But he also fashions a god and worships it;
> > he makes an idol and bows down to it.
> Half of the wood he burns in the fire;
> > over it he prepares his meal,
> > he roasts his meat and eats his fill.
> He also warms himself and says,

---

[9] EVANGELICAL DICTIONARY OF THEOLOGY, p. 577.

"Ah! I am warm; I see the fire."
From the rest he makes a god, his idol;
   he bows down to it and worships.
He prays to it and says,
   "Save me; you are my god."

Man, on the other hand, is the possessor of nothing, by virtue of God's possession of all things. Therefore, it is utterly senseless for man to be jealous of anyone or anything. If, for instance, someone steals my wife's affections from me, I surely ought to be sad because of my loss, and because of the sin committed by her and her paramour. But God gave my wife to me in the first place; she belongs ultimately to God. Therefore, God ought to be the one to straighten the matter out, because of their sin against Him, and I ought to leave it to God to mete out the right punishment in His good time. The same is true not only of spouses; it is true of everything we think we possess. We are "jealous" of all those things when we ought to acknowledge that they all belong to God. God, then, is the only one who has a right to be jealous.

### ..."They shall never enter my rest."

In the original Hebrew text this clause is couched in a Hebraism that is different from Gentile thought. There it reads, "...if they shall enter into my rest," but our translation is a faithful expression of God's intent. God was so angry with His people in the beginning of their wilderness journey that He determined to exclude them from His rest forever.

We could probably find many instances of this particular Hebraism in the Old Testament. Let one example suffice. In just one verse, Is. 62:8, the same structure is used twice:

The LORD has sworn by his right hand
   and by his mighty arm:
"Never again will I give your grain
   as food for your enemies,
and never again will foreigners drink the new wine
   for which you have toiled...."

It is important to define what is meant by the term "rest." One reason it is so important is that it has two entirely different meanings in its usage through the times in which it is operative. I have mentioned earlier the four different periods in history we must consider, to which this quotation from Psalm 95 applies. Let us review those four periods: the wanderings through the wilderness under Moses; the warning given to God's people in the days of David the Psalmist; the warning renewed by the author of Hebrews to his listeners; and the warning transmitted to us today as we read these words.

First, on behalf of those who traveled from Egypt to Canaan, the "rest" was their cessation from wandering and their final settlement in the Promised Land. For them it should have been truly a rest in several respects. It would have been such a rest if only they had dispossessed the inhabitants as God had

136

ordered them to do. They would live in permanent homes instead of having to pitch and break down their tents continually. There would be no more setting up of the Tabernacle, which must have been an arduous task. They would have a steady source of food from the land they could till and use for pasture: meat to eat, grain, fruit, honey, olives, figs, grapes and wine. They would remain in familiar surroundings rather than wondering what terrain they would encounter today and tomorrow. They would possess the inheritance God had promised their fathers Abraham, Isaac, and Jacob; and could pass the deed to their children, to remain in their family always.

The nomadic life must have been excruciating for the people, especially for the aged, the children, the wives, the ill and handicapped. Certainly many tribes in the world, some even today, are used to living in such a way. But to us who live in the United States such a life seems unthinkable. We tend to complain when our company moves us from one city to another because the factory has moved, or the husband gets a better job with a new company. Still, all that is as nothing compared to the life of the Jews in Sinai.

That "rest" we have just been discussing was really the portent of another "rest" which God was even then providing for all those who love Him and are willing to make Him their Lord and Savior. That other rest is heaven itself, and is infinitely more glorious than the one God offered the children of Israel in the land of Canaan. We shall see more about the new rest as we continue our study of Hebrews.

The relationship between Old Testament events and New Testament promises encompasses much of the book of Hebrews. Not only do we see it in Hebrews, but the apostle Paul affirms this as part of the overall plan of the Bible. He tells us in I Cor. 10:6 and 11, "Now these things occurred as examples, to keep us from setting our hearts on evil things as they did....These things happened to them as examples and were written down as warnings for us, on whom the fulfillment of the ages has come."

David had quoted God as saying of the older generation of Jews who traveled through the wilderness, "They shall never enter my rest," and they did not enter. We read the record of God's threat in Num. 14:22-23:

...not one of the men who saw my glory and the miraculous signs I performed in Egypt and in the desert but who disobeyed me and tested me ten times—not one of them will ever see the land I promised on oath to their forefathers. No one who has treated me with contempt will ever see it.

But for four exceptions, which God had explicitly named in His threat of punishment, the warning of God was carried out to the last detail. When God makes a threat of punishment, we can be certain that the threat will be fulfilled to the letter. Of course, God's threats of punishment also carry promises of forgiveness under certain conditions. But that is not what we are talking about here. If a person disobeys God and does not repent, the punishment is more certain than the assurance that the sun will rise tomorrow. Let no man think he can escape God's wrath by any means. God will not change

His mind. God will never become unable to carry out His threats. God is no respecter of persons, to let someone go scot free just because of who he is. God really did mean what He said, throughout mankind's history. God will not let disobedience go unpunished.

If this is true of God's threats of punishment, it is equally true of His promises of blessing to those who fulfill His requirements to obtain His "rest." The previous paragraph contains no scripture passages to support the statement, nor does this. The Bible is so filled with promises and threats, and their fulfillment, that it is superfluous to begin to list them. Let the reader search the scriptures for himself to see that this is so.

I mentioned that God had set forth four exceptions to His threat to the children of Israel that "they shall never enter my rest." The first two exceptions are those of the two faithful spies whom Moses sent into the Promised Land to prepare the people to conquer it. The first two of these were Joshua the son of Nun, and Caleb the son of Jephunneh. The story of the spies' trek into Canaan, and their evil report, is found in Num. 13. The next chapter, verses 6 to 9, tells of Joshua and Caleb's positive report, urging the people to invade the land and take it; and God's promise to the two good spies is found in verses 30 and 38 of chapter 14. By contrast, the ten evil spies not only failed to enter the Promised Land but they were struck with a plague and died, verses 36 and 37.

The third exception to God's destruction of the people of Israel for refusing to enter the land when God commanded them to, were those twenty years and younger at the time they left Egypt. Here is how God said it, as recorded by Moses (Num. 14:29-36):

> In this desert your bodies will fall—every one of you twenty years old or more who was counted in the census and who has grumbled against me. Not one of you will enter the land I swore with uplifted hand to make your home, except Caleb son of Jephunneh and Joshua son of Nun. As for your children that you said would be taken as plunder, I will bring them in to enjoy the land you have rejected. But you—your bodies will fall in this desert. Your children will be shepherds here for forty years, suffering for your unfaithfulness, until the last of your bodies lies in the desert. For forty years—one year for each of the forty days you explored the land—you will suffer for your sins and know what it is like to have me against you. I, the LORD, have spoken, and I will surely do these things to this whole wicked community, which has banded together against me. They will meet their end in this desert; here they will die.

This extended passage tells us clearly not only that those twenty years old and upward would die before entering the Promised Land, but that those twenty and under would be permitted to enter and to enjoy the land.

The fulfillment of God's threat is clearly recorded in Num. 26:63-65:

> These are the ones counted by Moses and Eleazar the priest when they counted the Israelites on the plains of Moab by the Jordan across from Jericho. Not one of them was among those counted by Moses and Aaron the

priest when they counted the Israelites in the Desert of Sinai. For the LORD had told those Israelites they would surely die in the desert, and not one of them was left except Caleb son of Jephunneh and Joshua son of Nun.

The age of twenty years seemed to be an important cut-off point in that part of Israel's history. In both Ex. 30:13-15 and Ex. 38:26 we discover that each male person of twenty years and over was required to pay an offering or poll tax of half a shekel. The silver that was offered was melted into parts for the construction of the Tabernacle. Those two passages in Exodus, and Num. 1:2-3, tell us that the people twenty years old and older were not only to pay the tax designated, but those men were counted at the time of collecting the tax, so that each one would be drafted into the army. In most of the rest of Num. 1 the tribes (excluding Levi) are named in order, and the number of men in each tribe is given, with the total given in verse 46 as 603,550.

The fourth exception among those destined to die in the wilderness is not exactly a true exception, but still is worthy of note. That exception is Moses himself. If Moses had been utterly "faithful in all God's house" (Heb. 3:2), he probably would have had the privilege to lead the people into the Promised Land. Instead, God condemned Moses for just one infraction (striking the Rock at Meribah instead of speaking to it), and forbade him to enter with the others who did go in. God's words of condemnation are in Num. 20:12: "Because you did not trust in me enough to honor me as holy in the sight of the Israelites, you will not bring this community into the land I give them." Actually this statement was made to both Moses and his brother Aaron, but of course Aaron had committed at least one other grave sin, when he made the molten calf for the people to worship while Moses was atop Mount Sinai receiving the Ten Commandments from God. The death of Aaron occurred soon after the incident at Meribah; the account of his death and the transfer of his High Priesthood to his son Eleazar is recorded in the same 20th chapter of Numbers, verses 22-29. But Moses continued to lead the remaining people through the desert up to the very entrance to Canaan. We read of Moses' end in Deut. 32:48-52:

On that same day the LORD told Moses, "Go up into the Abarim Range to Mount Nebo in Moab, across from Jericho, and view Canaan, the land I am giving the Israelites as their own possession. There on the mountain that you have climbed you will die and be gathered to your people....Therefore, you will see the land only from a distance; you will not enter the land I am giving to the people of Israel."

We see then that Moses, although he did not actually enter the Promised Land, did get to see virtually all of it from a high vantage point east of the Jordan River. He saw it from the top of Mount Nebo, also called Mount Pisgah, where Balak sought to entice Balaam to curse Israel for him (Num. 22-24).

We are sad to think that Moses, who had been faithful to his God with one exception, was not allowed to enter the Promised Land, what King David in Ps. 95 and the author of Hebrews called God's "rest." The verdict upon

Moses was final; there could be no reversal from the sentence once God had passed judgment. According to David, God had said, "They shall *never* enter my rest." It has been noted that the word "never" is absent in the Hebrew, as well as in the Greek translations, but the idea most certainly is understood by the authors. Once God has made His final decision with regard to the eternal destiny of each person, that decision is unalterable. We must remember this fact as we continue our study of Hebrews; it is certainly imperative that we remember it as we seek to live out our daily lives, to be sure that we have cast our vote with the Savior.

**Heb. 3:12. See to it, brothers, that none of you has a sinful, unbelieving heart that turns away from the living God.**

Here the author turns from the Old Testament historical reality to the lesson his hearers/readers needed to receive. It was the same lesson King David sought to convey to his people, and is as valid for us today as it has ever been. The word "you" is all-important in his sentence. The author wanted to make sure the people of his day noted, and understood, and obeyed what was being taught. And the same "you" applies to each of us today as well. Years ago I read that the word used most commonly in all advertising today is that word "you." It is personal, it is individual, it catches one's attention. Therefore, my message to you today is as urgent those of of Moses, David, and the author of Hebrews.

**Heb. 3:13. But encourage one another daily....**

The Greek word for "encourage" here, παρακαλέω, is a complex word, with two quite different basic meanings; the second of the two has several nuances of meaning. The term is composed of two parts. The first part is the Greek preposition παρά, whose root meaning is "a preposition indicating close proximity." The second part of the term in Greek is the verb καλέω, which basically means "to call," that is, "to call aloud, utter in a loud voice." Therefore, the primary meaning of the whole Greek word is "to call to one's side, call for, summon."[10] An example of this is found in Acts 28:20, where we read that Paul has invited the Jewish leaders in Rome to visit him in order to defend himself before them. The literal translation of that verse is, "On account of this then I *called you to me*, to see you and to converse with you...."

The second basic meaning of the Greek word is "to address, speak to (call to, call on)."[11] The finer meanings of this general idea are these: 1. to admonish or exhort. 2. to beg, entreat, beseech. 3. to console, encourage by consoling, comfort. 4. encourage. 5. the combined ideas of exhorting, comforting and encouraging. 6. to instruct, teach. In this verse in Hebrews, the older English versions (KJV and ASV) chose the word "exhort" as the translation here. The more recent NIV translators preferred the term

---

[10] All these definitions are from Thayer, under the Greek words.

[11] *Loc. sit.*

"encourage," probably following the modern trend in many theological circles to attempt to soften any harsh thoughts throughout scripture. For instance, exhortation may carry the idea of browbeating in the minds of some people, and they do not like that. There is also the idea of attempting to ignore, squelch, or "reinterpret" words of judgment or condemnation. Perhaps the most glaring example of this is the content of the lectionary selections used by many churches and denominations today. A casual reading of the context around many of the passages will show that they stop short of including references to God's punishment upon people for disobedience. To me this is an intentional rejection of an important part of God's revelation to people today. And as far as our present passage is concerned, the context ought to convince us that the author of Hebrews meant for the people to warn each other of the consequences of having a "sinful, unbelieving heart." Encouragement may be a part of the warning, but simple encouragement is not sufficient.

The author of Hebrews urges the people to exhort one another "daily." It is not sufficient to exhort and encourage one another only on Sundays at 11:00 AM. It is too easy to slip into old customs and thoughts the other six days of the week. The author could not perform that task alone, so he solicited the aid of all the members of the congregation to carry out the task among themselves. When I was the Minister of a church that included seven hundred members plus the members of their families, as well as adherents who chose not to become members, and occasional visitors, I knew it was impossible for me to see each of them daily to urge them on to fidelity with the Lord. I believed it was important for me to do regular visitation, but most of my visits were on people who had special needs at the time. We tried to establish different kinds of visitation programs among the people, and had many week-day activities, but that never began to cover the whole territory. A young Army Chaplain's Assistant, named Stan, began attending our church; he was very intent on reaching other young people for Christ. As soon as he met another young person in church, he would telephone that person each day (along with the rest of the youth he had met), to ask how he was, what he was doing, what spiritual problems he might be having, and how he could overcome such problems. The Young Adult Ministry of that church grew by leaps and bounds during Stan's time in the church. Exhorting one another daily is not only imperative, it is spiritually profitable.

### ...as long as it is called Today....

Here the author of Hebrews links his teaching to his hearers with what went on in Old Testament times. What he says, in effect, is that the "today" of which David wrote in his Psalm is a continuous, open-ended "today." Therefore, the option that was available to the Jews in Moses' day was still available to the people in David's time, and remained a possibility for the people of his day also. It is essential for us to accept the fact that we have now received the same invitation that was given to all generations before us. The only people for whom the option is no longer available are the ones who rejected God's invitation through their "sinful, unbelieving hearts," and died in their rejection. So the warning must be included with the invitation every time it is offered, so that people will realize that it is their choice (within God's sovereignty) to enter the Promised Land or to withdraw from it.

The reasons the invitation remains available to us are two. First, God has left it open by renewing it in His word. Secondly, we may accept God's offer because our Promised Land, that is, heaven, is not yet filled; there is still much room left for people to enter and to enjoy it forever. There is no way God could have miscalculated and failed to provide space for all those who through the centuries embrace His gracious invitation.

> Soft, loyal hearts entered the "rest," the "Promised Land,"
> Hard, rebellious hearts lost that rest forever.
> Righteous, believing hearts will enter into God's rest.
> Sinful, unbelieving hearts will lose the eternal rest of heaven.

"Today" may fade into "tomorrow" for you, as it did for those who wandered in the desert, unless you flee to God and gladly follow His guidelines for entrance into His eternal rest.

The Reverend Carl Naumann was a great saint of God. He had been a Presbyterian missionary in China for twenty years before I had the privilege to meet him. The summer before I entered seminary studies, Mr. Naumann graciously spent time with me, teaching me the rudiments of biblical Greek and Hebrew. In our study together, he often told me, "Hebrew is truly God's language. It was the language of His chosen people, the Jews. He spoke to His prophets in that language. His word is recorded in that language. Most of all, the Hebrew language has no verb tenses as such; therefore, Hebrew is a timeless language, just like God is a timeless God, existing outside the confines of the dimension we call 'time.'" Therefore, when God says, "Today," He means His "today," which is every today time. But your today, my today, will end, and after that there is no further opportunity for decision. Be sure you have decided for God *today*.

**...so that none of you may be hardened by sin's deceitfulness.**

Here is a great secret. At least, virtually nobody admits knowing this secret. But if perchance anyone does admit knowing it usually denies that it is true. The secret? Sin is so deceitful that it hardens one's heart.

Now you know why nobody knows, or at least affirms this great secret: its truth is so deceitful that one's heart is hardened so that he cannot declare it.

None of us likes to confess sin. That is one of the hardest things for a human being to do. We prefer to devise multiple excuses for what we have done wrong, rather than to admit the wrong. You need not look around to find someone who has sinned to demonstrate that confession is practically impossible. You only need to look within and see the sin that is harbored there. If you do acknowledge that something there is truly sin, you can review what you have done about it. In most cases, you find that you have skirted the option of confessing your sin.

The way we act usually tells us we are aware that we are committing a sin, but we try to deceive our own hearts that it is all right for us to do it. When I was a child, my mother taught me not to drink any alcoholic beverage. She was reared in Christian Endeavor, which was a strong temperance organization for church youth, and wanted me to be a teetotaler, because she was sure drinking alcohol was a grave sin. She often said that saloons had only small windows, and they were perpetually covered with curtains, so no one could look in and see who was drinking at the bar. She said that proved they knew they were committing sin, because they did not want anyone to see them there. We need not think of those who frequent bars, however. We only need to look inward, and see the blinds we have drawn on much of our lives, to try to hide our sinfulness, not only from other people, not only from God, but even from ourselves.

An excellent biblical example of this is found in the experience Moses had in the wilderness, when he returned from the top of Sinai after meeting God face to face. In Ex. 34:29-35, we read of Moses' radiant face because he had been in God's very presence. But that radiance frightened the Israelites, so Moses put a veil over his face, so the people could not see that it was shining. Paul comments on this situation in II Cor. 3:12-18, where he points out the reason the people wanted Moses to don the veil was because (verse 14) "their minds were hardened" (ASV, RSV), "blinded" (KJV), "made dull" (NIV). The Greek word differently translated here is πωρόω, which according to Louw and Nida[12] has the root meaning "to harden," but in the New Testament usage it means "to cause someone to be completely unwilling to learn and to accept new information—'to cause to be completely unwilling to learn, to cause the mind to be closed.'" In this story of Moses and his veil, we see that the children of Israel were totally unwilling to be reminded that Moses had been in the very presence of God, because if they thought about that, they would surely be faced with their sins, and they could not stand the thought of such a confrontation.

### Heb. 3:14. We have come to share in Christ....

The author of Hebrews now comes about on a positive tack, and in it he shares another seemingly well-kept secret: *Christ* is the key to entrance into God's rest. Neither hiding our sins from ourselves, or from others, or from God (if that were possible) will get us into heaven: only trusting in Jesus Christ as our Lord and Savior will get us there. After all, it is *Jesus* who

---

[12] Vol. 1, p. 333.

is "better than" Moses.

## ...if we hold firmly till the end....

The problem with the people of Ancient Israel was not "never having belief," but "turning from belief." This is the problem we see pictured in the pages of the Old Testament. Numerous times the Children of Israel, having at first trusted in their God, turned from Him to alien deities. It happened thirteen times in the days of the Judges. And we remember the defection already noted, when the people suddenly did an about face while Moses was on the mountain top to receive the Law from the hand of God.

On the other hand, this problem of the Jews could not have been related to our doctrine of eternal security, for these reasons. First, their "belief" was not really belief because it dissipated so quickly in the burning heat of God's refiner's fire of testing. Secondly, what is spoken of here is a corporate matter, a national defection from God. A remnant of individuals has remained faithful in every generation while the bulk of people in the nation prostituted themselves to the gods of the nations surrounding them.

Jesus admonished His disciples to cling to their faith without ceasing, and to do it despite all opposition (Matt. 10:21-22): "Brother will betray brother to death, and a father his child; children will rebel against their parents and have them put to death. All men will hate you because of me, but he who stands firm to the end will be saved." You also must believe this: if you hold your faith in Christ firmly to the end, then you will continue to "share in Christ."

We have several words of comfort from scripture that assure us that once we are on the road to heaven, there is nothing that can prevent us from reaching that destination. One of the most important thoughts we receive from various verses is that when we receive Jesus Christ as our Savior and Lord, we receive a gift which the Bible (see, for instance, John 3:16) calls "eternal life." By very definition of the word "eternal," we have assurance that that life cannot end. If it could end in a day, it would be called daily life. If it lasted until death, then it could be called merely temporal life. But if it is eternal life, it is impossible for it to end, or it cannot rightly be called eternal. Jesus affirms this by what we read in John 10:28: "I give them eternal life, and they shall never perish; no one can snatch them out of my hand." He affirms this even more strongly at the end of the next verse: "No one can snatch them out of my Father's hand." Next, Paul tells us in that soaring passage of expectation in Rom. 8:38-39:

> I am convinced that neither death nor life, neither angels nor demons, neither the present nor the future, nor any powers, neither height nor depth, nor anything else in all creation, will be able to separate us from the love of God that is in Christ Jesus our Lord.

To me one of the most forceful arguments to support the fact that we cannot possibly lose our eternal life once we have it is found in I John 5:11-

13. The first two verses explain how we receive eternal life to begin with: "This is the testimony: God has given us eternal life, and this life is in his Son. He who has the Son has life; he who does not have the Son of God does not have life." How to have the Son is explained in the gospel of John 1:12: "To all who received [Jesus Christ], to those who believed in his name, he gave the right to become children of God." To receive Jesus Christ can be understood in a simple analogy: if you eat a morsel of food, it enters your body and nourishes it and sustains its life; so also if you allow Jesus to enter your spirit, He not only sustains your spiritual (eternal) life, but imparts that life to you in the first place.

Then comes the last of those three verses in I John 5, verse 13, in which I must emphasize four important words. We read, "I write these things to you who believe in the name of the Son of God so that you may know that you have eternal life." The first is the word "believe." We have already discussed that from verses 11 and 12. I add here that only one factor is required for a person to receive eternal life: he must believe in Jesus as Savior and Lord. He is not required to change his lifestyle, or perform great or mighty or spiritual deeds in order to receive eternal life; but when he does receive that life he begins to *live* that life, that is, he puts away his sins and does God's work as the Holy Spirit gives him power and encouragement to do so.

The second important word in verse 13 is the word "know." That is to say that you can have absolute certitude that you will live forever. It is not a matter of mere hope, or wishing, or wondering, or of waiting to see; you can *know without question* that you have eternal life.

The third important word is "have," and the important thing about that word is the tense of the verb. Note carefully that it is the present tense. You need not wait until you die to see whether you go up or down. In addition, the eternal life you receive is not something that displaces your physical life when you die. Rather, the moment you believe in Jesus (receive Him, have Him) you receive the gift of eternal life.

The fourth important word in that verse is "eternal." That word is the sum of the whole matter. Again, I appeal to the definition of the word. If God has given you eternal life, then nothing, not even God, can wrench it from you.

### ...the confidence we had at first.

The Greek word for "confidence" in this verse is the same as that used in chapter 1:3; we discussed it at length there. To sum up what we discussed, it seems the basic meaning of the Greek word is "being," or "essence." For an easily comprehended way to translate verse 3 was to say simply, "Jesus is God." That is what the author of Hebrews was driving at in all he wrote in his introduction. But here the use of the English word "confidence" to translate the Greek word seems to be an entirely different thought.

I find it difficult to believe that the author means to urge his readers to cling to a certain "thought process" that they had earlier, in order to be assured of salvation. It seems more certain that he is continuing his effort to encourage people to trust fully in Christ alone for salvation and everything else they need. In my struggle to make sense of this verse by translating it for myself, while remaining faithful to that central purpose of the author of Hebrews, I settled on these words for verse 14: "...we have become partakers in Christ, if indeed we cling tenaciously—to the end—to the real thing like the real thing [they had] in the beginning." In other words, we do not cling to our confidence, we cling to the eternal Christ.

We must cling to that without wavering. To persist is urged upon us in several different ways in scripture. Here are three. "Let us not become weary in doing good, for at the proper time we will reap a harvest if we do not give up" (Gal. 6:9). "I hold this against you: You have forsaken your first love....Because you are lukewarm—neither hot nor cold—I am about to spit you out of my mouth" (Rev. 2:4, and Rev. 3:16); "...there is no discharge in that war" (Eccl. 8:8, KJV).

### Heb. 3:15.   As has just been said, "Today...rebellion."

Here the author of Hebrews repeats, for emphasis, the first part of Ps. 95. Besides the element of emphasis, I believe the author tries to drive home the idea that this quotation now applies to his hearers equally with the people to whom David had written a millennium earlier. With that in mind, let us recall the various times to which this "today" applies. First, there were the days when Israel was plodding through the wilderness; unfortunately virtually all those twenty years old and over flunked their test. The second "today" was during the days of King David, when he admonished his people not to be like the sinful, unbelieving people under Moses. The Old Testament record shows that the people in that day were more or less faithful, but the people's faithfulness did not last long, because ten of the twelve tribes defected the second generation later. Thirdly, the "today" applied to the people to whom the author of Hebrews was writing. When we get to his chapter 5, we will see how difficult was his job to keep their attention as he gave them his message. But for us, the most important "today" is in your lifetime and mine. And without doubt it does apply to us, because of what the author said in the beginnings of the first two chapters of his book. He said, "God...has spoken to us by his Son;" and "We must pay more careful attention, therefore, to what we have heard, so that we do not drift away." By reading the words written here, you cannot escape the fact that *you* have heard the message; so you therefore are obligated to heed it.

Following these admonitions we read a series of six rhetorical questions, meant by the author to emphasize strongly the result of ignoring the warnings he has just given. We also do well to give heed to the warnings.

146

Here follows my translation, so you can more easily see the three pairs of questions.

> **16. How many who heard, rebelled?**
>> was it not all those who departed from Egypt under Moses?
> **17. And by how many "was he provoked forty years"?**
>> was it not by those who sinned, "whose corpses fell in the desert"?
> **18. And to how many did he "swear that they would not enter into his rest"?**
>> was it not to those who disobeyed?

As already mentioned, we have three linked pairs of rhetorical questions—that is, each has an obvious answer, implied either by the question itself, or at least implied by the context of the questions. However, although no question needs an answer, the second question in each pair is the answer to the first. It should be obvious that the correct answer to the second question in each pair is a resounding "Yes!"

All this is pretty much by way of review of what the author has already said. But since review is one of the best ways to remember a matter, we do well to follow the review as well.

How many people rebelled in the wilderness? The author does not bother to list the exceptions we have already pointed out, but he makes a blanket statement which is, for all intents and purposes, correct. At least one place in the Old Testament makes the same universal statement, which may be considered an Oriental exaggeration (Ex. 17:1-2): "The whole Israelite community set out from the Desert of Sin, traveling from place to place as the LORD commanded....So they quarreled with Moses...."

How many people provoked God? Again, it was all but the few select exceptions. Their end was as predicted in the Old Testament record (Num. 14:29): "In this desert your bodies will fall—every one of you twenty years old or more who was counted in the census and who has grumbled against me."

How many people were the objects of God's oath that they would not enter His rest? The oath was against all those who were disobedient, as the Old Testament declared (Num. 14:22-23): "Not one of the men who saw my glory and the miraculous signs I performed in Egypt and in the desert but who disobeyed me and tested me ten times—not one of them will ever see the land I promised on oath to their forefathers. No one who has treated me with contempt will ever see it." One of the great tragedies among human beings is that most of us are so utterly indifferent to God that we do not consider the possibility that we are "treating Him with contempt."

147

The Greek word for "disobeyed" deserves special consideration. It is the word ἀπειθέω, and is used one other time in Hebrews (11:31), as well as thirteen other times through the New Testament. A brief exposition of its use in John 3:36 ought to help us understand its complete meaning. The NIV translation we are using in this study translates the verse thus:

> Whoever believes in the Son has eternal life, but whoever rejects the Son will not see life, for God's wrath remains on him.

The Greek word we are considering is ἀπειθέω, and in the NIV is translated "rejects." The same Greek word is translated a variety of ways in other versions: the KJV reads "believeth not;" the ASV has "obeyeth not" in the text with a marginal reading of "believeth not;" the RSV has the phrase "does not obey." The New English Bible (NEB) of 1970 agrees with the thought of the ASV and RSV with the translation "disobeys." There is a division among these translations, whether to use the basic thought of "believing," or that of "obedience." The ASV comes nearest the full meaning of the Greek word if one combines its text with its marginal reading.

The English translation I have which most nearly translates the Greek term correctly is THE LIVING NEW TESTAMENT PARAPHRASED; it employs the phrase "don't believe and obey." My standard authorities for definitions of Greek words are Thayer,[13] and Louw and Nida.[14] Thayer gives several separate definitions: "not to allow oneself to be persuaded; not to comply with; **a.** to refuse or withhold belief...to be disobedient....**b.** to refuse belief and obedience...." Thayer's several definitions seem to combine belief and obedience as parts of an overall definition. Louw and Nida, on the other hand, seem to separate the verses in the New Testament where this term is found, and to attribute the concept of belief to one set of verses and the concept of obedience to the other set. For instance, in Vol. 2, they have two categories of definitions: their first definition is "disobey," under which they place John 3:36; and their second definition is "reject belief," and use as an example of that idea Acts 14:2, which they translate: "but the Jews who would not believe stirred up (the Gentiles)."

We may get some help in sorting out these two ideas innate in the Greek word by noting what is said in the TDNT discussion of the term.[15] Bultmann writes, "ἀπειθεῖν has acquired...the sense which is now characteristic, namely, that of refusing to believe the Christian *kerygma*; for faith is obedience to the divinely appointed order of salvation....Hence ἀπειθεῖν often stands in antithesis to πιστεύειν [to believe], Ac. 14:1-2; I Pt. 2:7-8; Jn 3:36. It is also synonymous with ἀπιστία [unbelief]." The core of this statement, I think, is Bultmann's three words, "faith is obedience." In other words, faith and obedience are inseparably linked. That is to say: a person who believes will act on the basis of his belief. The converse is also true: a person who

---

[13] THAYER'S GREEK-ENGLISH LEXICON OF THE NEW TESTAMENT.

[14] GREEK-ENGLISH LEXICON, 2 volumes.

[15] TDNT, Vol. VI, p. 11, article on ἀπειθέω by Rudolf Bultmann.

does not believe will act like an unbeliever. It is justifiable to say that a person who acts like an unbeliever but claims to be a believer makes a patently false claim.

An illustration from everyday life may help us to understand the relationship between belief and refusal to obey. Suppose you and I were traveling along the highway from Anchorage to Wasilla, AK. Just beyond halfway there we come to a bridge over the Knik River which is fed by Knik Glacier a few miles up the mountains. During the summer the melting glacier fills the river higher than usual. As we approach the bridge you begin to slow down and stop short of the bridge. I ask why you have stopped, and you answer that you are not sure the bridge will hold you. I point to a sign beside the road, placed there by the State Highway Department, which reads: "Bridge capacity 20 tons." I ask, "Your car weighs no more than a ton and a half, with us both in it. Don't you believe the sign?" You answer, "Oh, yes, I believe the sign all right. But I really don't want to take a chance." So you turn around and head back to Anchorage. Did you really believe the sign? Not unless you acted on the basis of your belief. Your verbal claim is negated by your action.

One further notation from Ps. 95 may help us to see that belief and its resultant action are inseparable in what we read in Heb. 3:10, where God said of the Jewish rebels in the wilderness, "Their hearts are always going astray." We do not think of one's heart leaving the body and wandering away. What God said was that the people's hearts and minds had forsaken Him, and their wandering hearts had caused them to "go astray."

**Heb. 3:19. So we see that they were not able to enter, because of their unbelief.**

The author sums up his whole argument from his quotation from Ps. 95 in this statement. We may distill what he said further by noting that there is but one crucial element required for entering God's rest: faith.

It is important for us to see that the children of Israel "were not *able* to enter" the Promised Land. We recall that God instructed Moses to send twelve spies into the land to check it out. When they returned to report, ten of them grudgingly acknowledged that the land was fruitful and exceedingly livable in every way, but they emphasized their terror at the inhabitants of the land, and urged the people not to attempt the invasion. Only Joshua and Caleb urged them to trust God to win their inheritance for them. When the people refused to obey God, the Lord sentenced them to wander in the wilderness one year for every day the spies had been on duty. At that, the people began to worry and decided to try to take the land. Their paltry efforts ended in disaster, because God refused to go with them to conquer the land for them after their disobedience. That is why the author of Hebrews now says, "they were not able to enter."

Certainly our whole life must be an expression of the faith that results

149

in obedience to God's will, but as the author of Hebrews says in 11:6, "without faith it is impossible to please God."

Without a pilot (or ground controller today) a plane doesn't fly.

Without a hoe a farmer doesn't farm.

Without a brain a body doesn't live.

So also, without faith a person doesn't enter into God's rest. Do you have faith in Jesus Christ for your salvation?

**Heb. 4:1.  Therefore, since the promise of his rest still stands....**

What follows now is predicated on what has gone before in chapter 3, especially the promise God gave to the children of Israel. He promised them rest, not once but twice. What David said strongly implies that God's offer of rest is an open-ended promise, waiting only for willing followers to enter.

In our discussion of verse 15 of chapter 3 we already affirmed the availability of God's rest to us. However, the author of Hebrews expresses it more firmly here. The "rest" of God is still available, and will continue to be available. The rejection of that rest by multitudes in Old Testament times does not negate God's promise of rest to generations following them. Our scriptures record two large bodies of people who turned from God's gracious offer: first, the people of Israel in Moses' day, when he urged them to move forward to take the land; and secondly, the people in David's day who were exhorted not to reject the eternal "rest" of heaven which God held out to them.

**...let us be careful that none of you be found to have fallen short of it.**

The author of Hebrews repeats himself, saying the same thing several times in different ways. He knows that what he says is crucial to the eternal salvation of his hearers, and of us. He urges us to "be careful." We know that we must take care in our everyday lives, lest we have an accident. We tell our children to "stay within the lines." When cutting an apple, always point the knife away from your hand. When you are driving, keep away from the edge of the road, and avoid the potholes. The only way to avoid many accidents is through "eternal vigilance."

It is not only the author of Hebrews who ought to shoulder the responsibility. He says, "let *us* be careful that none of *you*" fails. In other words, I need to look out for my own welfare. But that does not begin to fulfill my responsibility. I must be careful to see that you also should avoid disaster. The author of Hebrews yearns for all his hearers to arrive safely in God's "rest." My deep desire is for you to achieve that same goal. This has been the driving force throughout my ministerial career, toward all who have come near my influence of witness; it has been my goal in writing this devotional commentary for you.

The idea of "falling short" has intrigued me ever since I learned the Greek verb for it, which is ὑστερέω. The reason for my interest came from my study of magnetism in college physics, where I saw a curve describing the fact that the level of magnetism in a core of soft iron always lags behind the number of amperes added to the magnetic field and then again lagged behind as the amperage was diminished. The curve was called the "hysteresis" curve; its name comes from this Greek verb.

A less technical illustration may help you to grasp the idea of "falling short." Suppose a frog fell into a well twenty feet deep. He laboriously began to climb the wall of the well to get out. Suppose he got nineteen feet above the water level, but was too tired to climb farther. Would he escape from the well? Even nineteen feet and eleven inches would not get him out. He would not escape, but would have "fallen short" of his "salvation" because he did not get all the way to the top.

By the same token, if you try to get to heaven by being good, and doing good works, you will fall short of arriving, because you lack faith. The reason why righteousness and doing good works cannot get you to heaven is because your acts are at best faulty. In Romans 3:9-18 Paul quotes more than half a dozen verses from the Old Testament, all of which state emphatically that not one person has ever lived a perfect life, but all human beings (except Christ, of course) "have sinned and *fall short* of the glory of God." In Matt. 5:48 Jesus commands us all, quoting from or alluding to Gen. 17:1, Lev. 19:2, and Deut. 18:13: "Be perfect, therefore, as your heavenly Father is perfect."

We must avoid misunderstanding something Paul once wrote concerning Christ's suffering to make up what is lacking when we "fall short" of God's requirement of perfection in us. In Col. 1:24 Paul said, "Now I rejoice in what [I] suffered for you, and I fill up in my flesh what is still lacking in regard to Christ's afflictions, for the sake of his body, which is the church." After a casual glance at this verse, some might think that Paul is saying that Christ's sacrifice on the cross was not sufficient penalty to pay for our sins, but that Paul also had to suffer to make Christ's work complete. Paul was not thinking about the completeness of our Savior's work for us, but instead he said that he, Paul, needed to suffer in his flesh in order to be able to present the tremendous message to the "body, which is the church."

### Heb. 4:2. For we also have had the gospel preached to us, just as they did....

If you still are in doubt that you have had sufficient opportunity to hear the gospel, please return to the beginning of this study and review the first and second verses of Hebrews: God...has spoken...to us." Add to these words the first words of chapter 2: "we have heard," and the warning connected to them: "We must pay more careful attention...." Should this fail to be sufficient evidence for you, then recall what Paul said in Rom. 1:20: "God's invisible qualities...have been clearly seen, being understood from what has been made, so that men [including you] are without excuse." Surely Paul wrote these words with Psalm 19 in mind:

> The heavens declare the glory of God;
>> the skies proclaim the work of his hands.
> Day after day they pour forth speech;
>> night after night they display knowledge.
> There is no speech or language
>> where their voice is not heard.

God has used every conceivable means to get His message across to every human who has lived in the world and will live in the future. "No excuse" will be the fatal words to every unbeliever who stands before the judgment throne.

We may like to think that in these latter days we have an advantage over those who lived before the incarnation of Christ, in two ways. First of all, Jesus was born and has lived in the world. People could see Him, hear His words, witness His miracles, and more than five hundred people[16] saw Him after He rose from the grave. Secondly, the canon of scripture has now been completed; so besides the living Word, Christ, we also have the written word, the Bible containing the Old and New Testaments, fully available to us. What additional witnesses to the gospel we now have in no way diminish the responsibility of those who lived before the time of Christ, because God had revealed Himself sufficiently to them, as outlined above.

### ...but the message they heard was of no value to them....

What an astounding statement! Such a thing is impossible, you say. But such a thought is the result of but a superficial glance at these words. We must look more carefully at what the author actually said here.

He did not say that the message itself was valueless. What he said was that the message, though precious in itself, brought no benefit to the hearers. The message in itself is infinitely valuable. It was the hearers who destroyed its benefit to themselves. And what was the one element by which they excluded themselves from its benefit?

### ...because those who heard it did not combine it with faith.

The ingredient they lacked was faith. Without faith, eternal life was missing.

The first car my father owned was a used Model T Ford. On cold winter days on the Nebraska farm, dad would crank and crank the engine by hand to try to get it to start. He would check the settings, and make sure there was gas in the tank. Sometimes he would wear himself to a frazzle cranking, with no result. The reason the engine would not start was because the cold batter-

---

[16]  I Cor. 15:6.

ies could not create a spark to ignite the fuel in the cylinders. Everything else was fine: the engine was in good condition; there was gas in the tank and oil in the pan; the controls were set right. They were good, but they were useless, because there was no spark. So also, we may think everything is all right in our lives, and we may expect to enter the gates of heaven with no trouble. But without the "spark" of faith, there is no life. That is the way Henry Ford made an engine to work, and that is the way God made us to work. Do it His way; He is the Maker.

### Heb. 4:3.   Now we who have believed enter that rest....

We may take great comfort in the present tense of the verb "enter" here. We need not wait forty years (like Israel in the wilderness), or until we die, or until some great judicial trial is ended; rather, we who have believed *now* enter that rest. God blesses us abundantly all through this life, despite the trials and sorrows and disappointments, because we know that we already have entered His rest and will remain there forever.

It is quite evident that none of us has fully achieved God's rest. The Greek verb for "enter" is in the present tense here, and has a progressive connotation. Many of you who are reading this commentary are still employed. You go to work daily, yet you work with the expectation that some day you will retire and continue to live from your accumulated wealth and retirement benefits. You fully expect to "live happily ever after," but you are not there yet. It may be said that you are in the process of retiring. So also, with regard to God's rest, none of us has achieved it fully yet, but because we have trusted in Jesus Christ as Savior and Lord, we "are entering" into that rest.

A flood of memories fills our minds as we think of those in days past who did not enter God's rest. Moses' followers wandered aimlessly and waited in the wasteland between the melons and leeks and garlics of Egypt, and the fertile vineyards of the Promised Land. But their carcasses dropped in the wilderness, never to arrive. After them came the subjects of King David. They spent their days thinking only of their victories over the Philistines and other enemies. They grew into a more affluent and flabby society (which peaked in Solomon's reign), yet they too fell by the wayside without approaching the eternal goal.

The "rest" was available, freely offered to every generation, to every person. They failed to grasp it, but we (at least some of us) have arrived and already entered. The determining factor, the author continues to emphasize, is faith. True, the people offered myriad sacrifices, but God no longer desired to eat them or smell them:

> "The multitude of your sacrifices—
>     what are they to me?" says the LORD.
> "I have more than enough of burnt offerings,
>     of rams and the fat of fattened animals;
> I have no pleasure

in the blood of bulls and lambs and goats."[17]

It was all because of their lack of faith that God rejected their offerings. We may think we are doing good in order to gain God's favor, but Isaiah warns us (64:6) that "all our righteous acts are like filthy rags."

One further truth from scripture demonstrates that it is impossible for us to enter God's rest by our own efforts is found in Rom. 8:8, where Paul warns us, "Those controlled by the sinful nature cannot please God." It is not what we do, but who we are (our sinful, human nature), that prevents us from getting to heaven. We cannot change our own beings; only God can do that. Peter tells us how at the beginning of his second little letter: that we can "participate in the divine nature" (II Pet. 1:4). In its context Peter tells us how we may become such participants. He tells it in verse 3, "His divine power has given us everything we need for life and godliness through our knowledge of him who called us by his own glory and goodness."

Lest I be accused of rejecting the idea that we must live godly lives after we have received this new nature through faith, allow me to point out what Peter says right after his information in verses 3 and 4:

> For this very reason, make every effort to add to your faith goodness; and to goodness, knowledge; and to knowledge, self-control; and to self-control, perseverance; and to perseverance, godliness; and to godliness, brotherly kindness; and to brotherly kindness, love(verses 5-7).

Our faith in Christ gives us a new nature, the very nature of God, which is eternal life; and when we possess that life we begin to live it. That life always bears fruit for God, as Peter tells us in the following verse (verse 8): "For if you possess these qualities in increasing measure, they will keep you from being ineffective and unproductive in your knowledge of our Lord Jesus Christ."

> **...just as God has said [in the negative],**
> **"So I declared on oath in my anger,**
> **'They shall never enter my rest.'"**

It is both a promise and a threat. God gave all the people fair warning, but through all generations, most people rejected both the promise and the warning.

We have already seen how the people in Moses' day and in David's day rebelled against God. But is the same true of the people in New Testament times, during which the author of Hebrews wrote his book? Did the people then living have faith, and fully populate heaven? A cursory look at the New Testament shows that although there were many followers of Jesus and the disciples, many more turned from the message of hope. Here are several examples:

1. Acts 5 had its Ananias and Sapphira, who lied to the Holy
   Spirit.

---

[17] Is. 1:11.

154

2. Paul told the people of the church in Rom. 2:1, "You, therefore, have no excuse...."

3. To the Corinthians (first letter 1:12) Paul said, "...there are quarrels among you....One of you says 'I follow Paul'; another...'Apollos';...'Cephas';...'Christ.'"

4. People in the Galatian churches (1:6) were castigated: "I am astonished that you are so quickly deserting the one who called you by the grace of Christ and are turning to a different gospel." And in 3:1: "You foolish Galatians! Who has bewitched you? Before your very eyes Jesus Christ was clearly portrayed as crucified."

5. Paul warned the Ephesians (4:17): "So I tell you this, and insist on it in the Lord, that you must no longer live as the Gentiles do, in the futility of their thinking."

6. Even in his love letter to the Philippians Paul had to say (4:2): "I plead with Euodia and I plead with Syntyche to agree with each other in the Lord."

7. But not all there responded, for Paul told another group (I Thess. 2:2): "We had previously suffered and been insulted in Philippi, as you know, but with the help of our God we dared to tell you his gospel in spite of strong opposition." In telling them of what had happened elsewhere, Paul had to note that the Thessalonians opposed him and his work also.

8. Paul reminded the people of Colossae of their faithless past (and probably some never were converted) in Col. 1:21-23: "Once you were alienated from God and were enemies in your minds because of your evil behavior. But now he has reconciled you by Christ's physical body through death...if you continue in your faith, established and firm, not moved from the hope held out in the gospel." Even in his commendation, Paul knew it was necessary for him to urge them to continue in their faith without wavering.

9. To some on the fringe of the church, Paul wrote in I Thess. 4:8: "He who rejects this instruction does not reject man but God, who gives you his Holy Spirit."

10. Paul singles out some slackers in II Thess. 3:11-12: "We hear that some among you are idle. They are not busy; they are busybodies. Such people we command and urge in the Lord Jesus Christ, to settle down and earn the bread they eat."

11. In I Tim. 1:3-4 Paul urged his young friend Timothy to "command certain men not to teach false doctrines any

longer nor to devote themselves to myths and endless genealogies. These promote controversies rather than God's work—which is by faith."

12. Paul set forth other sinners and defectors in II Tim. 3:2-8:
"People will be lovers of themselves..," and continues with a long list of sins common to mankind. He compares them to Jannes and Jambres who "opposed Moses.., men of depraved minds, who, as far as the faith is concerned, are rejected," and ends in verse 9, "But they will not get very far because, as in the case of those men, their folly will be clear to everyone." Such people, implies Paul, will never enter God's rest. Paul notes by name several egregious sinners in II Tim. 4:9-14: Demas, Crescens, Titus (a good man who temporarily defected), and Alexander.

13. There must have been unbelievers in some if not all churches then, so Paul had to instruct Titus (in 3:10): "Warn a divisive person once, and then warn him a second time. After that, have nothing to do with him."

14. Finally, we learn that many "wolves in sheeps' clothing" had infiltrated the churches in those days (and still do so today), whom John identifies in this way in I John 2:19:
They went out from us, but they did not really belong to us. For if they had belonged to us, they would have remained with us; but their going showed that none of them belonged to us.

From these references we see that of Israel in Moses' day, *none* of them entered God's "rest," save for a very few faithful ones. In David's day, many were defectors—even Joab the general.[18] Then in New Testament times the author of Hebrews pleads with his hearers to enter into God's "rest" by faith; but we've just reviewed how many in those days failed to get there. Now I say to you the same thing: "Take heed that you do not fall short because of lack of total faith in Jesus."

**And yet his work has been finished since the creation of the world.**

Now the author takes a different tack on the same subject. He says that God entered into His "rest" after He created all things. A string of ideas springs from that fact:

There must be such a thing as a rest.
That rest is accessible, not only to God but to us.
God entered His rest.
You too can enter that rest—

---

[18] See I Kings 2:5.

If you fulfill the condition, which is faith.

Before a rest, there must be work. There was work for God to do, and He did it in the six days of creation. Then the author of Hebrews says God's work "has been finished since the creation of the world." If this is so, does that mean that God has done absolutely nothing since He created the universe, or has God had many "days" of rest since then? I'm not sure any of us can speculate on whether God has created anything more since His work of creation "has been finished." But we know He has not ceased to do anything. Even Jesus said in John 5:17, "My Father is always at his work to this very day, and I, too, am working." Also, God truly watches over us without lapse, so the scriptures quote God as saying to us (Heb. 13:5):

> Never will I leave you;
> never will I forsake you.[19]

How do we reconcile these seemingly contradictory differences: that God rests, and that God still works after His creation? One possible way is to say that God has rested from His *creation* because it is finished, but that He does other things now in order to *sustain* His creation. I cannot be sure how to reconcile the question, but since I have offered at least one possible solution, no one can claim that there are irreconcilable differences here. Thus the Bible remains without contradiction.

**Heb. 4:4. For somewhere he has spoken about the seventh day in these words: "And on the seventh day God rested from all his work."**

There is great controversy today over the question whether the six "days" of creation are literal twenty-four hour periods of time, or whether those six "days" actually covered a period of more then ten billion years in human reckoning. My opinion on the matter is that to interpret the "days" literally, it is not necessary to adhere to the concept of twenty-four hour solar days. The main reason I hold this idea is that all people acknowledge that the word "day" has several different definitions throughout the Bible. One certainly is a twenty-four hour solar day. But that cannot be the definition of the term in Gen. 2:4. The NIV evades the issue in its translation by omitting the word for "day" found in the original Hebrew with this paraphrase: "When the LORD God made the earth and the heavens...." The KJV translates the verse correctly: "...in the day that the LORD God made the earth and the heavens...." The ASV says virtually the same: "...in the day that Jehovah God made earth and heaven...." The RSV also uses the term "day:" "In the day that the LORD God made the earth and the heavens...." Now we who accept the Bible as true and without contradiction, the word "day" in Genesis 1, and the word "day" in 2:4 must mean some period of time undefined with regard to its length. It may be but an instant in our time, or it could be billions of years; neither of these interpretations is patently false, but both are "literal" interpretations of

---
[19] Quoted from Deut. 31:6; 31:8; and Josh. 1:5.

what the Bible says. The same is true also, in the second verse of Gen. 2 (which the author of Hebrews quotes here almost verbatim), "And on the seventh day God rested from all his work." If God rested on the seventh day, was that a solar day if each of the six days was a solar day? And if so, has God rested one day in seven—of our solar days—forever; and has He continued to do so to the present and will He continue to do so for all eternity? Few believe that God has limited Himself to our time dimension.

Further, Moses said in Ps. 90:4:

> For a thousand years in your sight
> are like a day that has just gone by,
> or like a watch in the night.

Virtually the same idea is set forth in Ex. 20:11 (the fourth commandment): "For in six days the LORD made the heavens and the earth, the sea, and all that is in them, but he rested on the seventh day. Therefore the LORD blessed the Sabbath day and made it holy."

Incidentally, some people may think that our English words "Sabbath" and "seventh" must come from the same Hebrew root word, but that is not so. There is no connection between them, except that they sound similar in both languages. Our word for Sabbath comes from the Hebrew verb שָׁבַת, which means to rest, or to desist from labor. The English word for the numeral seven is the Hebrew שֶׁבַע. You can recognize that the last (leftmost) letter of one word is different from that of the other. The same can be true in our English words; that is, the word "heat" is quite unrelated to the word "hear," although the words are very similar except for the last letter in each. The Spanish language has complicated the matter by calling the seventh day of the week (our Saturday) by the name "Sabado," which is the English term Sabbath. It is quite clear that the Old Testament intends to indicate that the seventh day of the week (which we call Saturday) is to be identified as the Sabbath. If this is so, then why do not all Christians follow certain groups such as the Seventh Day Adventists in reserving Saturday as their Sabbath?

There are four good reasons why I accept Sunday instead of Saturday as my day to worship God. First of all, it is utterly impossible to determine now which day of our week is actually a multiple of seven days from the first day of creation. The early children of Israel reckoned their weeks by the phases of the moon (see Amos 8:5; Hos. 2:11; and Is. 1:13 ), and that is not an exact multiple of seven days. In the Christian era the calendar has been revised several times. For instance, George Washington was born on what would be our February 11 instead of the 22nd, because the calendar has been changed since his day. Therefore, our Saturday may actually be the fourth day of the week, counting from the first day of creation.

My second reason for not following Saturday as my Sabbath is because the original disciples worshiped the risen Savior on the "first day of the week" (Acts 20:7; I Cor. 16:2; and Rev. 1:10), probably because it was on the first day of the week that Jesus rose from the dead; the first day of the week on which He appeared alive again to the women (Matt. 28:1; Mark 16:1), to ten apostles that very day (John 20:19), and to the eleven remaining apostles a week later (John 20:26). Therefore, if the apostles believed it was proper to worship God on Sunday, it should be all right for me as well.

I believe it is not necessary to reserve Saturday as the day of rest for my third reason, which is that since we do not know which day is actually the seventh day of the week, surely God will not hold us guilty for selecting one of the days of seven to set aside for rest and worship. I do believe that it is important for every person to save one day in seven, whether it be Tuesday or Saturday or Sunday, as God's special day. As a Minister who worked on Sunday, I reserved Mondays as my day of "rest." Nurses, policemen, and utility workers ought also to reserve one day in seven, if their workday schedule includes Sunday.

The fourth reason why I believe it is not necessary for me to reserve Saturday for my day of "rest" is that Jesus spent much time debating with the Pharisees over whether the letter of the law was more important than its spirit. He chided the Pharisees for criticizing His disciples for plucking and eating grain on the Sabbath (Lu. 6:1-2). He reminded them that "The Son of Man is Lord of the Sabbath" (verse 5); and said, "I ask you, which is lawful on the Sabbath: to do good or to do evil, to save life or to destroy it?" (verse 9). Jesus even criticized the Pharisees for their own Sabbath practices (Lu. 13:15): "You hypocrites! Doesn't each of you on the Sabbath untie his ox or donkey from the stall and lead it out to give it water?" He asked them virtually the same question in the very next chapter (Lu. 14:5). In summary of this reason of mine why I am free to worship and rest on Sunday is because Jesus said we ought to do what is right and not to be concerned exclusively with the minutiæ of the law.

Both the Old Testament and the New teach us that to argue about such trivia is worse than to ignore the matter. For instance, Isaiah (in 1:10-15 lashes out at the people who are legalists in their activities, but their worship is not heartfelt:

> Hear ye the word of the LORD,
>> you rulers of Sodom;
> listen to the law of our God,
>> you people of Gomorrah!
> "The multitude of your sacrifices—
>> what are they to me?" says the LORD.
> "I have more than enough of burnt offerings,
>> of rams and the fat of fattened animals;
> I have no pleasure
>> in the blood of bulls and lambs and goats.
> When you come to meet with me,
>> who has asked this of you,
>> this trampling of my courts?
> Stop bringing meaningless offerings!

> Your incense is detestable to me.
> New Moons, Sabbaths and convocations—
> I cannot bear your evil assemblies.
> Your New Moon festivals and your appointed feasts
> my soul hates.
> They have become a burden to me;
> I am weary of bearing them.
> When you spread out your hands in prayer,
> I will hide my eyes from you;
> even if you offer many prayers,
> I will not listen."

And why was God displeased with rituals of His people, even though He had ordained them? We find the reason in Is. 29:13:

> The LORD says:
> "These people come near to me with their mouth
> and honor me with their lips,
> but their hearts are far from me.
> Their worship of me
> is made up only of rules taught by men."

The apostle Paul echoes these sentiments, and even some of Isaiah's words, in Col. 2:16: "Therefore do not let anyone judge you by what you eat or drink, or with regard to a religious festival, a New Moon celebration or a Sabbath day." Paul elaborates on this in Rom. 14:5-6:

> One man considers one day more sacred than another; another man considers every day alike. Each one should be fully convinced in his own mind. He who regards one day as special, does so to the Lord. He who eats meat, eats to the Lord, for he gives thanks to God; and he who abstains, does so to the Lord and gives thanks to God.

In light of the controversy over the right day to worship God and rest, examine your own heart now, to see how you balance your seven days of each week God has given you. The Pharisees thought they were "religiously correct" in their thoughts, observations, and actions. But Jesus condemned them for emphasizing the letter of the law to the exclusion of meditating on the Spirit of God. We ought to avoid a high "PQ" (Pharisee Quotient).

**Heb. 4:5. And again in the passage above he says, "They shall never enter my rest."**

It is important to note the pronouns here. The word "they" refers to the unbelievers; the word "my" points out that it is *God's* rest we are discussing, in which all humanity is invited to participate. However, the author of Hebrews continues to reiterate the necessity of relying solely on faith in Jesus Christ as Savior to enter that rest.

* * *

### Heb. 4:6. It still remains that some will enter that rest....

In spite of the fact that the offer of God's rest is universal, the receipt of that rest is partial. Only "some" will enter. Some may quibble over whose fault it is that not all receive it. But we must remember that it was God who prepared the rest, and it was God who offered it to the people; further, God used every means conceivable to inform the people of the rest and its availability. Still, some have not entered the rest. Why? It is solely because it was they who persisted in unbelief (from man's point of view).

Merely because some in ancient times failed to enter the rest does not bar entrance to others in later generations. God's design for entrance to heaven is not like that of the Japanese who bombed Pearl Harbor on the 7th of December 1941. They tried to sink American ships in the channel that provided entrance to the Harbor, so that ships that were not bombed would be unable to leave, to escape to the open sea or to fight the Japanese ships. In fact, others have entered heaven even though some have failed to enter. The invitation remains open. There is room for all who qualify. And the sole qualification for entrance is faith.

### ...and those who formerly had the gospel preached to them did not go in because of their disobedience.

Some were excluded from the rest, not (I repeat *not*) because they did not have a chance. They "had the gospel preached to them," as we have noted already in this study. They were like those "who disobeyed long ago when God waited patiently in the days of Noah while the ark was being built. In it only a few people, eight in all, were saved through water..." (I Pet. 3:20). In our discussion of 3:18 we noted the relationship between unbelief and disobedience. And we should remember that Jesus testified (in Lu. 24:44) that He had been clearly revealed throughout the Old Testament: "Everything must be fulfilled that is written about me in the Law of Moses, the Prophets and the Psalms." Jesus meant that all of Hebrew scripture contains adequate evidence of Him and His ministry of salvation through His own sacrifice, so the Jews more than anyone else were without excuse for not having faith in Him.

### Heb. 4:7. Therefore God again set a certain day....

God provided it "again" ! What a gracious, longsuffering God! David said it well in Ps. 86:15:

> But you, O LORD, are a compassionate and gracious God,
> slow [longsuffering] to anger, abounding in love and
> faithfulness.

Likewise, in Romans 9, Paul talks about the patriarchs (verses 5, 7, 8, 10, and 12); Moses (verse 14); Pharaoh (verse 17); and the twins (in verse 13, quoting Mal. 1:2-3): "Jacob I loved but Esau I hated." After discussing these diverse Old Testament people, he concludes (verses 22-24):

161

What if God, choosing to show his wrath and make his power known, bore with great patience [longsuffering] the objects of his wrath—prepared for destruction? What if he did this to make the riches of his glory known to the objects of his mercy, whom he prepared in advance for glory—even us, whom he also called, not only from the Jews but also from the Gentiles?

### ...calling it Today....

For God, time is the eternal present tense (remember, the Hebrew language has no past, present, or future tense).

### ...when a long time later he spoke through David, as was said before....

Let us summarize what we have been saying about God's "Today:"

> The first Today was for Israel and Moses in the wilderness.
> The second Today was in David's time.
> The third Today was in apostolic times.
> The fourth Today is the one you and I live in.

However, all those "Todays" are not separate, unique, periods in history. God's Today is a continuum. No one has ever been excluded from God's—

### "Today, if you hear his voice,
### do not harden your hearts."

Never in history has there been a valid question whether God has spoken, the correct question is whether anyone has listened. When I attended the U. S. Naval Academy, there was a harsh rule, strictly enforced, "Get the word!" All the information a Midshipman needed regarding what uniform to wear; where to form in companies to march to classes or meals; what materials to read before each class; and any other extraneous data required to obey every activity was either posted on a bulletin board; read over a loudspeaker; repeated by Midshipman deck watchmen; or published in class outlines. It never was a valid excuse to say, "I didn't get the word." Punishment for any infringement was instantaneous and merciless. Thanks be to God that He is not that harsh, but He repeats His commands, cajoles, even begs His people to "Get the word."

Some people have gone to great lengths to try to get God's word to every soul in the world, in accompaniment with God's natural means of communication (the heavens, the stars, in fact all His creation). About fifty years ago the people of the mission radio station HCJB in Quito, Ecuador devised a special way to get people within range of their station to hear the gospel broadcasts. They knew that it was not enough for them to transmit the message by their radio station; it was necessary for the people to have receivers to pick up the sound. However, people in remote regions, and poor people in the cities, had no radios. So the mission designed and built small, cheap, but adequate battery-operated radios and distributed them free to as many people as they could. Soon many people were hearing the gospel message on their radios. A problem arose almost immediately, however. The missionaries quickly discovered that many people had learned how to tune their gift radios to other stations, and were listening to the secular programs of other stations. The mission soon solved that problem by building radios with only their station locked in so no other station was heard. God is the ultimate Transmitter of His message, and we are the receivers. We still are able to tune God out and listen to the siren voices of the world and the Devil. The choice is ours to hear and heed, or to ignore God's word. Again I say, no person has ever had a valid excuse to turn from God's promised rest. God has done His part, long-sufferingly.

### Heb. 4:8.  For if Joshua had given them rest....

The King James Version unfortunately translates the name in this verse as "Jesus." Technically, that is a correct translation, but it is also misleading.

To set the record straight, the Old Testament Hebrew word for Joshua is יְהוֹשׁוּעַ, which comes from two Hebrew words: one word is "the Lord", and the other is the verb "to save." Thus the root meaning of both the Old Testament Hebrew word and its New Testament (and LXX) transliteration Ἰησοῦς is "The Lord Saves." The context in this book of Hebrews demands that we understand the term here to mean Joshua, who led Israel into Canaan, God's "rest" for them.

Now the author plants a question in our minds about achieving the rest. He says, "If Joshua had given them rest..," implying that the people in Joshua's day did not enter the rest God intended for them, even though the chosen few did arrive in Canaan finally.

Therefore, we see the two different "rests" the author has been talking about; the rest from wilderness wandering for a limited number of Jews, and the eternal rest in heaven for all generations and peoples who have faith in Christ. Certainly we understand that it is Jesus who by His sacrifice provided the eternal "rest" in heaven, not only for those ancient Jews, but for all humanity.

It is important for us to relate what the author of Hebrews says about Joshua here to the main theme of his message. That message is that Jesus is "better than" any other person in the Old Testament, and that His ministry is "better than" any ministry we find there.

It may be difficult for some to see an improvement in Jesus' ministry over that of his Old Testament namesake. After all, although Joshua was not able to lead all the children of Israel into the Promised Land, he did in fact bring all those who had been twenty years old and under when they left Egypt. In addition, both he and Caleb were permitted to enter, because they were the two faithful men who gave a good report to Moses and the people after they had spied out the land. Not only that, but we must parallel that with Jesus' ministry, whereby although He died for the sins of all the world, only those of faith will enter heaven.[20]   However, we note the vast difference between Joshua's ministry and that of Jesus when we realize that Joshua did not "save" the remnant of Israel who entered Canaan, but merely led in those who were left after God had winnowed them. Jesus, on the other hand, died on the cross to provide the way of salvation to those who believe on Him. The difference between Joshua's and Jesus' ministries may be compared to the difference between Moses' and Jesus' in that Moses was merely a servant in God's house and obeyed the Master, while Jesus was the Son and Heir who governed the house.

Some may wish to debate that since Jesus did not cause all humans for whom He died to enter the "Promised Land" of heaven, then His ministry was no more powerful than Joshua's. But in one sense it is not Jesus who decides who goes to heaven. Every individual must decide whether he wants to go, for Jesus said (Rev. 22:17), "...whoever wishes, let him take the free gift of the water of life." Jesus said it even more clearly in His lament over the Holy City (Matt. 23:37): "O Jerusalem, Jerusalem, you who kill the prophets and stone those sent to you, how often I have longed [have willed] to gather your children together, as a hen gathers her chicks under her wings, but you were not willing [willed not to be gathered]." Many people do not understand that this concept does not obviate the fact of predestination, but it does show that every individual must decide whether to receive Jesus Christ as Savior and Lord, without considering God's plan.

### ...God would not have spoken later about another day.

Here we make an important digression from the main theme, to emphasize once again a matter we have discussed before, but which never can be overemphasized for those seeking the truth contained in the Bible. The author is revealing his high view of the inspiration of scripture again when he says, "*God* would not have spoken...." He has just said (in verse 7) that "[God] spoke through David." Although it was David who wrote down the words of Psalm 95, it was God who spoke through the spokesman-king. We also recall that in 3:7 the author  began the whole series of quotations from Psalm 95 by saying "So, as the Holy Spirit says...." By the same token, since the author of Hebrews was likewise inspired by the Holy Spirit to write his book, we need not be concerned to know the identity of the human author of Hebrews, except for curiosity's sake.

* * *

---

[20] I am fully aware that there is a large dispute among scholars of salvation theology:  some believe that the sins of only the "elect" were paid for by Christ's death on the cross; while others believe He died for all, although only the "elect" will be saved.  The issue is far too large to expound here, but for a hint of my position I would invite the reader to study carefully I John 2:1-2, and accept the correct definition of the term "world" there.

**Heb. 4:9. There remains, then, a Sabbath-rest for the people of God....**

First, the author says "there remains," so he is reiterating the fact that there are still vacancies to be filled in God's rest, and he wants to be sure that none of his hearers misses that rest through unbelief.

Secondly, we must be sure to accept the fact that it is a most *select group* that enters God's rest; that select group is called here "the people of God." And for emphasis we add that the ones selected are the ones who have faith in Jesus.

Lest we dislike the concept of the selection of people for admission to heaven, let us remember that the Bible, from beginning to end, describes a process of selection on the part of God throughout the course of the existence of the universe He created. Here is the pattern of God's selectivity:

| | |
|---|---|
| Gen. 1:1 | God "created the heavens and the earth;" earth was chosen. |
| Gen. 1:11 | Plant life; living beings were chosen. |
| Gen. 1:26 | Living beings; Adam/man was chosen. |
| Gen. 5:3 | Adam's children; Seth was chosen. |
| Gen. 6:9 | All humans; Noah was chosen. |
| Gen. 10:31 | and 11:10    Noah's children; Shem was chosen. |
| Gen. 12:1 | Semites; Abraham was chosen. |
| Gen. 22:2 | Abraham's many children; Isaac is called his "only" son. |
| Gen. 25:23 | Isaac's twins; Jacob chosen. |
| Ex. 28:1 | Jacob's twelve sons: Levi; Aaron chosen for priesthood. |
| Gen. 49:8-10 | Jacob's twelve sons: Judah chosen to be ruler. |
| Gen. 38:29 | Judah's sons; Perez, the bastard twin of incest, chosen. |
| Ru. 4:18-22 | Perez' descendants; David chosen to be king. |
| I Kings 1:30 | David's many sons; Solomon chosen. |
| I Kings 11:43 | Solomon's many sons; Rehoboam chosen. |
| Lu. 1:32 | David's descendants; Jesus chosen (to be King, High Priest, Sacrifice/Savior). |
| Gen. 17:7 | Abraham's physical descendants; God's chosen people. |
| Rom. 4:16 | Abraham's spiritual descendants; all who have faith. |

Regarding Abraham's physical descendants, God promised: "I will establish my...everlasting covenant between me and you and your descendants after you for the generations to come." Also, regarding Abraham's spiritual descendants, Paul wrote to the mixed (Jewish and Gentile) congregation in Rome (4:16): "Therefore, the promise comes by faith, so that it may be by grace and may be guaranteed to all Abraham's offspring—not only to those who are of the law but also to those who are of the faith of Abraham. He is the father of us all." Paul says here that the Jews as an ethnic group are still ("not only") God's chosen; but his illustration of the olive tree with wild branches grafted in (Rom. 11:17 and following) shows that we who are Gentiles are added to God's chosen—if we have faith.

Not only is selectivity enunciated in scripture, but also it is demonstrated in nature (Darwin called this—erroneously, I believe, "natural selection"). The farm on which I was reared in Nebraska had two rows of huge, stately cottonwood trees. In springtime, literally billions of cottonwood seeds floated through the air under their down-like umbrellas. Although they were scattered for miles by the breezes, virtually none of them sprouted or became trees that also reproduced. So also there are many human beings in the world, but not many of them become saved souls or soul-savers. Jesus said (Matt. 22:14), "Many are invited, but few are chosen." Even among the original apostles whom Jesus chose, not all of them went to heaven (John 6:70): "Have I not chosen you, the Twelve? Yet one of you is a devil!"

**Heb. 4:10.  ...for anyone who enters God's rest also rests from his own work, just as God did from his.**

Perhaps I was just a slow worker, but during most of the later years of my ministry, I regularly worked more than eighty-three hours a week. Many times I would think, "Boy! I'm looking forward to my retirement, when I won't have to do anything, unless I want to." Of course, that thought applied only to my retirement from work in this world. The real rest will come when I leave this world, and enter heaven.

But wait! Am I going to do absolutely nothing when I get to heaven? Is that the kind of "rest" I must look forward to? I can think of nothing more boring than that. On the contrary, I am sure I will have multitudes of things to do there; I will be kept happy and excited to do just what God wants me to do, without fear of drifting to do something contrary to His will. However, by comparison with what I do on earth, even during these days of retirement, what I do there will be entirely restful. Maybe then this is a partial answer to the conundrum we posed at verse 3 of Heb. 4 and what we read in John 5:17. You are invited to turn back to our discussion there.

After all, even on the Lord's day now, you breathe, you digest your food, you walk around the house and in church. You probably do not need to lift your ox out of the ditch on Sunday, but if you drive anywhere and see an accident, surely you would do the right thing to stop and help someone escape from a burning wreck, regardless of the exertion. You do not become inanimate on Sunday; you "rest" from your regular work. And that is what this verse says to do.

**Heb. 4:11. Let us, therefore, make every effort to enter that rest....**

What "effort" is required on our part to enter that rest? The answer is in the next clause.

**...so that no one will fall by following their example of disobedience.**

In the desert, except for the select few, *all* fell. Here, the author wants just the opposite for his hearers: he urges them to heed, so that "no one will fall." He labors, so that all of them may enter their rest. One day that will be universally true for the Jews, because Paul promises in Rom. 11:26, "And so all Israel will be saved." I doubt Paul means that every physical descendant of Abraham will go to heaven, since there are far too many instances in scripture that make it clear that certain ones will not be saved. I have not found a clear statement in the Bible that explains it, but my opinion is that Paul means that all Jews who are alive at the coming of the Lord will be saved by faith. But to whomever it applies, what a glorious "Today" that will be! On the other hand, I find no evidence in scripture that implies that the same promise is true for Gentiles. The promise did come near fulfillment, however, to some people of whom I read years ago. The story was in the mission autobiography of John G. Paton, a Scottish missionary to the New Hebrides Islands in the South Pacific. After much struggle with the native people, during which time he was almost killed, he finally saw some results of his proclamation of the gospel. After several years, Paton could report that nearly every person on at least one of the islands where he ministered had made a commitment to Jesus Christ as Savior and Lord.

With regard to the word "disobedience" here, please remember our exposition of it when we thought about its use in Heb. 3:18.

Now we read a great paean to scripture:

**Heb. 4:12. For the word of God is living and active.**

We must be sure to understand that the author is speaking about the verbal (both written and uttered) word, not Jesus God's Son, the Word of God.

All the author says here about the word of God is a personification. Although it is an inanimate object, he gives to it some of the characteristics and abilities of a living intelligence. In truth, this is how he begins: "the word of God is *living* and *active*" We might say that the word of God is "vital," which gives a slight variation to the meaning, but is essentially the

167

same.

Surely the author is referring to what we call the Old Testament, which had become canonical by his time. It had been locked in, with its books included and all others excluded, since before the Greek translation (the LXX) was completed before the end of the second century BC, and was agreed upon universally except for the handful of books and parts of books added in the Greek, commonly called the Apocrypha. The author recognized that God was speaking powerfully among people in apostolic times as well. He must have been acquainted with the four written Gospels as we know them, and (if he was not Paul) he probably knew at least some of Paul's writings, and considered them to be inspired by God. After all, it was he who started this message we are now studying with the words "God spoke...by his Son."

If the word of God is truly living, and active, then it is able to sustain life and activity in all who "consume" it. Think now of your favorite food. If you see it on the grocery shelf or counter, and take it home, prepare it, and eat it, it keeps you alive by its nourishment. But if you leave it in the grocery store, it provides you no benefit.

### Sharper than any double-edged sword....

When I think of God's word in this imagery, I think of the founder of the world's Presbyterian family of churches, John Knox, who in December 1545 carried a two-handed (and probably double-edged) sword in front of George Wishart for his protection, as he went about Dundee, Scotland, preaching.[21]

A sword is used for slashing or piercing, ultimately for killing. But is that what we want the word of God to do to us? or to our loved ones? or to our friends and fellow church members? or to people we are trying to reach with the gospel of Christ? or even to people like Hitler or Stalin?

On the other hand, are these the right questions to ask about the word of God? Should we not rather ask, "Is this what God really wants His word to do, either to us or to anyone else in the world?" Is there not some other way, *any* other way, to interpret it? As you ponder the matter, you will realize that there is really no other way, because that is precisely the way the author interprets it in the rest of this verse. Read on.

### ...it penetrates even to dividing soul and spirit, joints and marrow....

Here is the interpretation. This is exactly the image the author of Hebrews wants us to visualize as we meditate on the word of God. The word of God slashes, pierces, and kills rebellious souls.

By the way, since mention of the sword is a figure of speech, so also the sundering of soul and spirit, joints and marrow is also a figure of speech.

---

[21] A. R. MacEwen, A HISTORY OF THE CHURCH IN SCOTLAND, Vol. I, p. 477.

No one should commit suicide, or tear his physical body apart because of what this verse says.

The phrase "dividing soul and spirit" as it is translated here may be slightly misleading. The KJV renders the phrase as "piercing even to the dividing asunder of soul and spirit." The Greek word for "dividing" or "piercing" is διϊκνέομαι. It can mean "to go through, penetrate, pierce;" in classical Greek, Homer used it of "going through in narrating."[22] Louw and Nida make a helpful suggestion regarding the use of the word. They suggest[23] that the word means in essence "to move through a three-dimensional space," and suggest further that it is a close synonym to the Greek διέρχομαι, which means to go through. That word is used in Acts 12:10 where we read that Peter and his rescuing angel passed through the first and second guard stations of the prison where Peter had been. If this is so, we could translate our verse in Hebrews thus: "...penetrating into the dividing place between soul and spirit, and joints and marrow." Rather than stabbing to make a hole in something, the author would mean that the word of God enters into the deepest nooks and crannies of our innermost beings. Such an act would be much less violent than tearing into and sundering flesh and other body parts.

If we do think of the separation of soul and spirit, a theological question arises regarding the relationship between those two entities. Some scholars say that the soul and spirit are identical; the same substance merely has two names. I have no proof to refute that idea, except for several passages which at least seem to imply that soul and spirit are two distinct entities in a person. The verse we are discussing is one of them. If the word of God can go between soul and spirit, then they must be separate though connected in some way. Paul talked about "spirit, soul, and body" as three distinct parts of a person in I Thess. 5:23. Dr. Donald Grey Barnhouse,[24] for many years Minister of Tenth Presbyterian Church in Philadelphia, made an interesting observation (which he made no effort to substantiate) about different kinds of living things. He said that plants have physical bodies, animals have bodies and souls, but humans in addition have spirits with which to commune with God. In I Cor. 15:44, Paul talks about a "soulish body" and a "spiritish body" (the NIV calls them a "natural body" and a "spiritual body"), one controlled by worldly things and the other controlled by heavenly things. Some people think that this verse teaches that in this life we have a physical body, but that in the resurrection we have no such body but only disembodied spirits. That cannot be so, else Christ had not risen bodily from His tomb. Paul uses the same kind of terminology found in this resurrection chapter near the beginning of the same letter. In I Cor. 2:14 Paul says, "The man without the Spirit does not accept the things that come from the Spirit of God," where he

---

[22] According to Thayer.

[23] In their GREEK-ENGLISH LEXICON, VOL. 1.

[24] In a video of a Bible class years ago.

uses the same word for "soulish body" in 15:44 as he does for "man without the Spirit" in 2:14.

Why would God want to cause His word to penetrate so deeply into our innermost beings? The author of Hebrews gives the answer in his next words.

### ...it judges the thoughts and attitudes of the heart.

This may not be the sole purpose for the existence of the word of God, but we dare not try to escape from it. The word of God exposes, slashes, penetrates, judges all our innermost thoughts, intentions, and motives, such as: What are you doing? Why are you doing it? What causes you to want to do it? The Holy Spirit sees and knows everything that is in your heart; if so, then the world might as well know it. If so, does that bother you? If you do not want the world to know all that your heart contains, that may be the best indication to you that you are harboring some sin there. When you realize that, it may be the very best way in your life to help you to confess your sin, turn in disgust from it, and seek the guidance of the Lord to overcome it.

By what means of penetration, communication, gathering of information the Holy Spirit via His word has, we are not aware. Technically, we are more ignorant of His process than is an uncivilized aboriginal would be aware of how we know his every move and word if we had a TV camera focused on him at all times. We really need not know *how* the Holy Spirit does this; it is important for us to be aware of it.

What else does the word of God do for us, besides discover our innermost thoughts, intentions, and motives, and judge them? Here is a selection of other things the word of God does (this is by no means a complete listing):

| | |
|---|---|
| Ps. 119 | It is a lamp to our feet and a light to our soul, verse 105. |
| | It is a deterrent to sin, verse 11. |
| Ps. 16:7 | It counsels us, and instructs our hearts, even at night. |
| Deut. 8:3 | It feeds our spirits, like bread feeds our bodies. |
| Jer. 15:16 | "When your words came, I ate them; they were my joy and my heart's delight." |
| Jer. 23:29 | It consumes and crushes whatever opposes it: "like fire...like a hammer that breaks a rock in pieces." |
| Josh. 1:8 | Whoever clings to it becomes prosperous and successful. |
| Ps. 19:11 | "By them [ the word, law, ordinances of God] is your servant warned; in keeping them there is great reward." |
| Matt. 7:24 | "Everyone who hears these words of mine and puts them into practice is like a wise man who built his house on the rock." |

170

| Lu. 11:28 | "Blessed...are those who hear the word of God and obey it." |
|---|---|
| John 5:24 | "Whoever hears my word and believes him who sent me has eternal life and will not be condemned; he has crossed over from death to life." |
| Rev. 1:3 | "Blessed is the one who reads the words of this prophecy, and blessed are those who hear it and take to heart what is written in it, because the time is near." |
| John 17:17 | "Sanctify them by the truth; your word is truth." |
| Rom. 15:4 | "...through endurance and the encouragement of the scriptures we might have hope." |
| I Cor. 10:11 | "These things happened to them as examples and were written down as warnings for us." |
| I John 5:13 | "I write these things...so that you may know that you have eternal life." |
| Gal. 3:24 | "So the law was put in charge [KJV reads 'was our schoolmaster'] to lead us to Christ." |

Let us summarize these and other passages in the Bible that tell us what the word of God does for and to us. The word of God does many wonderful things for us, when we heed it. But we dare not ignore or spurn the surgical side of the word; for if we do, we shall be punished without remedy or appeal.

### Heb. 4:13. Nothing in all creation is hidden from God's sight.

Does this statement bother you, or even frighten you? Surely you know why you may feel uneasy if you consider that God knows every thought in your innermost being, not just your outward actions which others may or may not discover. If you do not like to have God know some of the things you have hidden within yourself, there is only one way you may divest yourself of them: get rid of all you do not want God to see or know. John has told us how to do that, in I John 3:3: "Everyone who has this hope in him purifies himself, just as he is pure." And how does one go about purifying himself? Surely he cannot do it by himself, any more than Lady Macbeth was able to wash away her "damn spot." Paul tells us that we must allow God Himself to eradicate it all from us (Tit. 3:5): "...through the washing of rebirth and renewal by the Holy Spirit."

Here are some ways by which many people try to get rid of their uneasiness over knowing that God is aware of their hidden sins, but be sure that none of these methods works. They try to ignore the fact of God's surveillance; they deny the truth that God does this; they try to claim that what they did or thought isn't all that bad, at least no worse than what others do; or they say that they really do not care who sees their thoughts and actions, even God. However, as I already said, none of these excuses works. It is said that this country's counseling rooms are filled with patients who know their sins are not forgiven.

What do you want God to see within you? It is more important to ask, What do you think God wants to see within you? Finally, are you convinced that your answers to those two questions are correct?

This concept must be exceedingly important to God, and to the author of Hebrews, because he repeats the same idea, this time in a positive way:

**Everything is uncovered and laid bare before the eyes of him to whom we must give account.**

In the days far gone when doctors made house calls, the President of the local bank in her small midwestern town came to my Great-grandmother's home, and as gently as possible informed her that her checking account was overdrawn. Great-grandma protested strongly several times that it could not be overdrawn. As the bank President persisted in his statement, Great-grandma finally rose, went into her bedroom, and returned with her checkbook. She showed it to the man, "I can't be overdrawn. See, I still have several checks left!" Guess who won the argument?

Not one excuse we dream up for God is good enough. He sees through every ruse, every plot we design, to make Him think that sin has not stained us. He not only knows all that is within us, He also knows by the measurement of His standard whether what He sees is so or not.

Just as my Great-grandmother could not prove to the bank President that she still had a balance in her checking account, so also we cannot convince God we have not sinned. There is only one way to change His mind, and that is to change what is in our spiritual account. Examine yourself, by the standard God has set in His word for you. When you measure what you find there, what will the piercing word of God judge? Will God give approval of what is in your spiritual account? Does your account contain His spiritual money, or spiritual garbage? Whatever your answers are now, you *will* give an accounting to God one day.

We began this whole discussion at the beginning of chapter 3 of Hebrews, and the beginning of chapter 3 of this devotional study. We said then that Jesus is better than Moses, and His rest is better than the rest which Moses and Joshua offered the people. We saw that the people in Moses' day rejected the offer of rest. Then King David half a millennium later repeated the offer, but apparently the people of his day largely rejected it as well. So the author of Hebrews promised us that the offer of rest is still available to all those who pass God's test of faith. Now we return to Jesus, the "Better One," but here we begin an extended dissertation on the comparison between the Old Testament priesthood and the Priesthood of Jesus. Jesus as High Priest has already been mentioned in Hebrews, in 2:17, and in 3:1. Now that theme continues in several sub-themes, beginning in 4:14 and continuing through chapter 8.

# CHAPTER IV
## OUR SINLESS JESUS.   HEB. 4:14-16.

**Heb. 4:14.    Therefore, since we have a great high priest....**

The concept of Jesus as the Great High Priest seems to lie supreme in the mind of the author of Hebrews. The priesthood was the focus of all the Old Testament ministry. Without a high priest, the people were hopeless in their sins. The high priest was the people's visible link with God.

The author states that the priesthood as expressed in the Old Testament is gone, at least for the purposes required by those who trusted in Jesus as their High Priest. Hebrews probably was written late in the seventh decade AD,[1] and the Roman armies destroyed all Jerusalem including the Temple in 70 AD. By then it was impossible for anyone to perform the sacrificial rituals demanded by the Old Testament, because although there were priests still living, there was no altar on which to offer the sacrifices. That situation has existed continuously ever since those terrible days, and never will be renewed as long as the world exists. Some students of prophecy claim the Bible teaches that near the end days the Temple will be rebuilt on the site of Solomon's Temple, where the Muslim Mosque called the Dome of the Rock now stands, but nothing done there will separate anyone from his sins or get him to heaven.

We interpose here a note on the authorship of Hebrews. Since, as some scholars claim, the apostle Paul died in the summer of 67 or 68 AD,[2] or even earlier,[3] likely before Hebrews was written, the likelihood of Paul's authorship diminishes.

With the cessation of the Old Testament priesthood, there is only one link left between the people and God. Jesus is that link, according to what Paul told his young friend in I Tim. 2:5-6: "There is one God, and one mediator between God and men, the man Christ Jesus, who gave himself as a ransom for all men—the testimony given in its proper time."

How wonderful! We *have* a High Priest! Today, Jews who do not receive Jesus no longer have a high priest. They have not had access to a high priest, or any priest who can perform the priestly function for them, ever since the Temple was destroyed in 70 AD. But we who have received Jesus Christ as Lord and Savior (whether Jew or Gentile) do have a High Priest.

Neither in Old Testament times, nor in the Christian Era, could there be as many as two High Priests at the same time. Do not be confused by the mention in Lu. 3:2 of two High Priests, Annas and Caiaphas. It is possible that during the ministry of John the Baptist, of which this passage speaks,

---

[1] Merrill F. Unger, UNGER'S BIBLE DICTIONARY, p. 465. Unger estimates the date of writing between 67 and 69 AD.

[2] Unger, p. 838; Gehman's DICTIONARY, p. 464.

[3] Metzger and Coogan, THE OXFORD COMPANION TO THE BIBLE, p. 576, "...beheaded during the persecution of Nero in the mid 60s CE."

both those men were High Priests, one after the other. More likely is the fact that Caiaphas was the High Priest during that time, but Annas was both his father-in-law and the preceding High Priest. Further, Annas was a domineering man, so although his High Priesthood had ended, he was the puppeteer who pulled the strings on Caiaphas; so people in general considered them both to be co-High Priests. There was much confusion about the High Priesthood during the Roman occupation before the fall of Jerusalem. There was not a succession of High Priests from father to eldest son as in the days of Aaron and as ordered by God. Instead, the Roman authorities appointed High Priests from among those who willingly submitted to their authority. The appointments were made annually, not for life as was the Aaronic priesthood.

Neither be confused by the designation of the High Priest as "Chief" Priest at times in the Gospels. The Greek term for the top priestly position is ἀρχιερεύς. Sometimes it is translated as either "Chief Priest," or "High Priest." All that confusion was swept away by the emergence of Jesus as the sole, enduring, Great High Priest.

### ...who has gone through the heavens.

Prepositions are notoriously difficult to translate from one language to another, as you know if you have studied any language different from your native tongue. It is difficult even to decide which preposition to use when you limit yourself to your own language. When translating something as important as the Bible, it is necessary for the translator to make every effort to delve into the actual meaning of the original author in order to make his sense known to the translator's reader. The present clause from Hebrews is one of those difficult instances. A brief review of some of the more common English prepositions of position, motion, and direction may help us to think more clearly about the problem. (See the diagram on the next page.)

What we are considering in this clause is the preposition "through." If the author used the preposition he really wanted in order to convey his intended meaning, he was saying that Jesus did not merely go "into" heaven on our behalf; rather, He went even "beyond" the heavens, to the very end of whatever exists past our known universe, away from what biblical authors considered to be all the heavens, to places totally incomprehensible to our finite minds. Surely He went far beyond the last place any of the Old Testament High Priests were able to go. Therefore, Jesus our Great High Priest is far greater than any of them. Remember, this is the theme of the whole book of Hebrews. Jesus is "better than" anyone or anything the Old Testament ministry had to offer.

Jesus was raised bodily after three days in the grave, never to die again. No Old Testament high priest was raised bodily, although other people in those ancient times were raised, but every one of them died again.

* * *

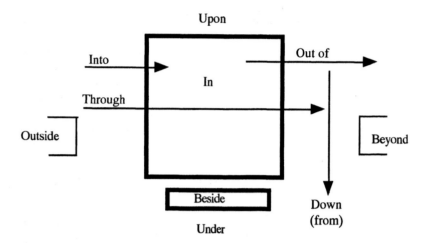

**...Jesus, the Son of God.**

We find here the echo of what the author spoke about in chapter 1, verse 2, where he said that in these last days God has spoken to us "in a Son." None other is a son of God like He. We who have eternal life are children of God by virtue of the new spiritual life He has given us, but that is a different category. There is a third category of relation between God and humans. Paul, in his sermon on Areopagus in Athens quoted two Greek philosophers in Acts 17:28, showing their understanding of the filial relationship between all humans and God. The first quotation, "For in him we live and move and have our being," is from *De Oraculis* by Epimenides the seventh century BC Cretan poet; and the second, "We are his offspring," is found both in *The Phenomena* by Aratus of the third century BC, and in the *Hymn of Zeus* by Cleanthes.[4] Thus the pagan philosophers said, and Paul quoted them favorably, that all humans are children of God by virtue of His creating them.

Some people are confused apparently by the use of the two terms, "Son of God," and "God the Son." When Jesus is spoken of as merely the "Son of God," they conclude that He is not really God, but some lesser being since He is only a Son. At least they hold to a strong monotheistic view, while still holding Jesus as a very important Person though not God. It may be easier for some people to understand that God is one God yet understood in three ways by calling Jesus "God the Son." One of the most famous people who thought of Jesus as less than God was Michael Servetus, whom some consider to be one of the founders of the Unitarian movement. He bitterly opposed the idea that Jesus is God while upholding Him as a very important spiritual leader. Servetus was burned at the stake in the days of the Reformer John Calvin.

---

[4] I gathered this information from an article, "Plundering the Egyptians," by Wesley J. Callihan, in the newsletter VERBUM of Veritas Academy in Lancaster, PA for September 2000.

Many people accuse Calvin as the ringleader in Servetus' death, but actually Calvin sought to lessen Servetus' punishment, although he strongly opposed his anti-trinitarian stance. Some people find it difficult to see how Calvin and Servetus disagreed on the being of God. After all, as Servetus felt the flames, he said something like, "Lord Jesus, Son of the Eternal God, have mercy on me." If you find it difficult to see what is wrong with what Servetus said, compare that with what a trinitarian ought to say: "Lord Jesus, eternal Son of God, have mercy on me." You see, Servetus denied both that Jesus was God and that He was eternal. The Bible teaches clearly that Jesus is God who became flesh (John 1:1-17); not that Jesus was a man who one day became a god, nor yet a man who never was a god but merely a "son" of God.

### ...let us hold firmly to the faith we profess.

The first implication of this statement is from the theme of Hebrews, that this faith which we profess is eminently worth clinging to without cessation. The reason is because this faith is "better than" anything else in which we might believe. You may study all the religions the world has ever offered, but you will never find another that assures you that the Creator of the universe willingly became one of us in order to bear our punishment by His death on the cross, so that by merely believing on Him we have total assurance of eternal life in heaven with Him. Other religions offer no such absolute assurance of glory, and most of them make absurdly impossible requirements in order to attain even the meager blessings they offer.

Here is a second implication. We must be aware of the disastrous results from letting go of that faith, or of failing or refusing to grasp it in the first place. The author of Hebrews spent chapters 3 and 4 reminding such people that "they shall never enter my rest."

What does it mean to "profess" our faith? The original Greek says that we must hold firmly to "our confession," one word translated here by "the faith we profess." That Greek word is ὁμολογία. It is the same word used in 3:1, where it is also a noun that is translated as a verb in the NIV. Thayer says that the noun means a profession or a confession; the idea of confession here has nothing to do with acknowledgment of sin, but rather as the related verb means, "to declare openly, speak out freely."[5]

Our faith in Christ therefore must be an active faith, not merely a passive mental assent to some doctrine. If we have that faith, we must tell others we have it; further, we must invite, encourage, urge, even admonish them to acquire that same faith. As one of the objectives of the Navigators is: we are not asked merely to win souls to Christ; we are required to win soul-winners to Christ.

* * *

---

[5] This is contained in Thayer's definition of ὁμολογέω in his LEXICON.

**Heb. 4:15.** **For we do not have a high priest who is unable to sympathize with our weaknesses.**

The idea contained in this statement does not imply a contrast between Jesus and the Old Testament string of earthly high priests with respect to the ability to sympathize with human weakness. The members of the Aaronic priesthood were aware of their inability to deal with temptations. However, the earthly high priests, being human and therefore fallible and sinful, would not be able to sympathize with our condition as Jesus the God-man could. By contrast, Jesus was perfectly capable of such sympathy because He is the infinite God.

The author wants to convey that Jesus, who is able to sympathize with our weaknesses, is human as well as God. If He were not, He could have no appreciation of our weaknesses, but because He is the Creator God who made us and knows all about us, He could experience all our feelings. This is what the author wants to bring out regarding the ministry of Jesus, none of which could He have done without His becoming "flesh" as we note in John 1:14.

**...but we have one who has been tempted in every way, just as we are....**

The thought of the temptation of Jesus causes us to recall the account in all three Synoptic Gospels (Matthew 4:1-11; Mark 1:12-13, and Luke 4:1-13) of the three-fold temptation of Jesus by the devil. Commentators have pointed out that those temptations cover every conceivable enticement that could come to mankind. Further, my English Bible professor in seminary, Dr. Howard T. Kuist, led our class in a comparison of the temptations of Jesus as set forth in Lu. 4:1-13, and the three kinds of temptations mentioned by the fourth Gospel writer, John, in his first little letter, I John 2:16. I use here the KJV English.

| I John 2:16 | Luke 4:1-13 |
|---|---|
| Lust of the flesh | Stone...be made bread |
| Lust of the eyes | Showed...all the kingdoms |
| Pride of life | Cast thyself down |

It is easy to see that the specific temptations to sin which Satan presented to Jesus were representative of the categories of sin John listed in his first letter. I suppose someone could think of some temptation in this life which he would consider outside the three categories listed above; on the other hand, someone else could refute the idea and show how even that sin could be subsumed under one of those categories. Let us not miss the point by inventing trivia; let us agree with the all-inclusive assertion that the temptations Jesus experienced in His earthly journey covered every temptation.

**...yet was without sin.**

Here is the greatest contrast between Jesus and every other human being that will have ever existed in the world: Jesus never committed a sin, but every other person has sinned and thus deserves to be banished in the lake of fire that burns forever and ever. Paul reminded us in Rom. 3:23 that "all have sinned and fall short of the glory of God." In that passage, Paul quotes many verses from a variety of places in the Old Testament which assert that not one human being is guiltless but all deserve the same fate. In our present comparison between Jesus and the Old Testament high priests, we point out for emphasis that every one of them committed sin (Heb. 5:3), therefore Jesus and His ministry are "better than" the others.

If Jesus had sinned, then He could not be God. It is God who made all the laws, so He made them according to His own wishes and determination. Since He made all laws, He automatically exists according to them.

That brings up an interesting question: Was Jesus not able to sin; or was Jesus able not to sin? I think it would be a waste of time to debate that issue, although it might be interesting to try to think of reasons why one part of the question is correct and the other wrong. Much better time would be spent in acknowledging that Jesus *did not* sin, because that is the all-important point.

Is it really so that Jesus did not sin? Does every part of the Bible agree with such a statement? A woman who was a member of one of the churches I served once tried to prove to me that Jesus must have sinned because He even admitted as much. She pointed me to the story of the Rich Young Man in Matt. 19:16-26. The man asked Jesus, "Teacher, what good thing must I do to get eternal life?" A different reading from some of the ancient Greek manuscripts makes his question more apropos of the sense of Jesus' answer, which reads in the KJV, "Good Master, what good thing shall I do, that I may have eternal life?" Jesus' answer, according to some Greek texts, and our NIV, was, "Why do you ask me about what is good?" Again, the KJV agrees with other Greek manuscripts in Jesus' reply: "Why callest thou me good? there is none good but one, that is, God." Actually, if we follow the NIV text, the issue of whether Jesus denied that He was good evaporates. But for the sake of argument, let us agree that the King James translators were correct. Then we must ask the crucial question, Did Jesus actually *say* that He was not good, but that God alone was good? If that is what Jesus meant to imply, then He would have not only admitted that He was a sinner, but also that He is not God because He was making a distinction between Himself and God. However, from all other data we find in scripture, Jesus is God and Jesus is sinless. What Jesus was saying, according to the variant Greek readings, is, "Do you call Me good? You certainly know and agree that no one but God is good [that is, sinless]; so if you choose to call Me Good, then you are agreeing that I am the true God." So, contrary to the opinion of at least one unbeliever, Jesus did not admit that He is a sinner, but that He is the eternal, sinless God.

This story as recorded in Luke's Gospel, 18:18-30, is more apropos of our question whether Jesus was sinless. There we read of the rich ruler who said, "Good teacher, what must I do to inherit eternal life?" Jesus' answer was, "Why do you call me good? No one is good—except God alone." In my edition of the Greek Testament, I find no indication of a variant reading in Luke's account, so that is probably more accurate than Matthew's. As an aside, we find in Lu. 10:25 the beginning of a very similar story, in which a lawyer asks Jesus the same question, but without calling Jesus "Good."

Important as it is, I shall not belabor the point that Jesus is God, since we can seek elsewhere for passages that give clear evidence for it. But I shall set forth at least ten of the passages that declare Jesus to be sinless. We begin with Matt. 27:4. This verse in itself is not conclusive evidence, since it is the testimony of Judas Iscariot who betrayed Jesus. But added to other evidence in scripture, it adds weight to the argument. When Judas returned the thirty pieces of silver to the priests in the temple, being "seized with remorse" (not repentance, by the way), he told them, "I have sinned, for I have betrayed innocent blood." Even Judas was aware that Jesus did not deserve to die, since He was sinless.

A second passage is Lu. 23:41. This testimony comes, like the first, from a person we might call a non-theologian; but his testimony likewise adds weight to the whole. The thieves who were crucified with Jesus had an argument. One railed on Jesus for not rescuing them from their excruciating end, since He claimed to be the Savior. But the other said, "We are punished justly, for we are getting what our deeds deserve. But this man has done nothing wrong." If such a man, especially in that predicament, had discernment about Jesus' sinlessness, it must have been obvious to all but those who hardheartedly refused to believe.

The next verse I have chosen shows without question that Jesus was sinless. In the passage where Paul discusses the important matter of reconciliation, he ends his presentation with this clinching argument (II Cor. 5:21): "God made [Christ] who had no sin to be sin for us, so that in him we might become the righteousness of God." It is evident that Paul believed firmly that Jesus "had no sin." However, although He was sinless in Himself, the Father imposed upon Him the burden of the sin of the whole world, the Father knowing that no one else could lift that burden of sin from even one person. But Jesus, being the infinite God, was able to provide forgiveness for an infinite number of people's sins, which He did by His death on the tree. Still, although Jesus paid the price for all people's sins, the purchase transaction was efficacious only for those who have faith in Him, as we have seen repeatedly in chapters 3 and 4 of Hebrews.

As an aside, there is the idea that by some actions or thoughts we humans can reconcile ourselves to God, so that He then must accept us into His family. That is far too boastful! The whole thrust of II Cor. 5 is that people are utterly passive in the process of reconciliation between God and man. The correct understanding can be summed up in verse 20 of that chapter, where the passive tense of the verb is used: "We implore you on Christ's behalf: Be reconciled to God." We do not reconcile ourselves to God; we allow Him to reconcile us to Himself, through Jesus Christ, whom we receive by faith alone.

I have selected I Pet. 2:22 as the next bit of evidence that Jesus was sinless. There Peter quotes from Isaiah's great chapter on the Suffering Servant, Is. 53:9:

> He committed no sin,
> and no deceit was found in his mouth.

Isaiah said it slightly differently, not emphasizing Jesus' innocence:

> ...he had done no violence,
> nor was any deceit in his mouth.

The way Isaiah said it affirms our contention that Jesus was sinless, because the whole of Is. 53 points toward Jesus as the One who bore the sins, the iniquities (verse 11) of the world on the tree; no one could have done that who had been required to bear his own burden of sin.

John affirmed our contention in terms equally clear with those of Peter in his quotation from Isaiah. In I John 3:5, the apostle was speaking of Jesus and said, "...you know that he appeared so that he might take away our sins. And in him is no sin."

That statement alone is sufficient evidence to prove our point. However, I shall add five additional statements, all of which come from the book of Hebrews. The first we have studied already in our thoughts on 2:10, where we saw that God made Jesus' work complete, or perfect "through suffering," that is, by His death on the cross. We noted there that the Father transferred Jesus from imperfection to perfection; He declared that act of suffering to be the final act required of Jesus, the completion (perfection in that sense) of all He had set out to do.

A similar idea is found in Heb. 5:8-9, where the author says, "Although he was a son, he learned obedience from what he suffered and, once made perfect, he became the source of eternal salvation for all who obey him...." Some people find it difficult to believe that Jesus was equal to the Father in every way, if He was required to obey His Father. But as God the Son, Jesus was willing to be obedient, and in that sense He lived as a perfect example of filial submission for all children. It is in John 8:29 that we read what Jesus said of this relationship with His Father, "He has not left me alone, for I always do what pleases him."

In the next passage from Hebrews we look at, we see term after term the author uses to emphasize that Jesus is perfect, sinless. The passage is Heb. 7:26: "Such a high priest meets our need—one who is holy, blameless, pure, set apart from sinners, exalted above the heavens." Not one of those epithets can rightly apply to any created being; every one of them cries out with the idea of utter perfection, total sinlessness. And only Jesus' being fits them, one and all.

Verse 28 of that chapter tells us the same thing about Jesus. The author has been pointing out that all the Old Testament priests, being sinful creatures, were required to make sacrifice for their own sins before they were able acceptably to offer sacrifices for the sins of the people. Jesus, on the other hand, made just one sacrifice, not for His own sins, but for the people: "For the law appoints as high priests men who are weak; but the oath, which came after the law, appointed the Son, who has been made perfect forever."

Before I turn back to Heb. 4:15, our verse now under consideration, I shall point out two additional verses that tell of Jesus' sinlessness by means of a different Greek word. Those verses are Heb. 9:14 and I Pet. 1:19. The Greek word in each of those verses is ἄμωμος. Its basic meaning is set forth by Thayer in these ethical terms: "without blemish, faultless, unblamable." The KJV translates the word as "without spot" (Heb. 9:14), or "without blemish" (I Pet. 1:19). Peter, in his statement, uses two Greek words, ἄμωμος and ἄσπιλος, the second of which is more correctly literally translated as "without spot." The sense of both passages is that Jesus as our sacrifice for sin was perfect morally, ethically, legally, spiritually, physically, in every way, just as every Old Testament sacrificial animal was supposed to be whole and without blemish physically, the best of the flock; none other was acceptable to God.

Hebrews 4:15 is my last sample of the Bible's indication that Jesus was utterly sinless, the *textus classicus* from all scripture for this assertion. The simplicity of the statement does not detract from the power of its implications. Even though Jesus was "tempted in every way, just as we are," He was totally different from us: He "yet was without sin." One statement, so unambiguously stated, should be sufficient to prove to everyone that Jesus never committed any act, or had any thought, that could even remotely be considered as sin. Even with such a pristine character, Jesus, because He was human as well as divine, was capable of sympathizing with our weaknesses.

### Heb. 4:16. Let us then approach the throne of grace with confidence....

Here is the author's hortatory conclusion: Let us act on what we have heard and now know of Jesus. This is what good preaching is all about, in three steps: This is the truth. You must accept the truth. You must act on the truth.

Our first act, after learning that the perfect Jesus is capable of sympathizing with our weaknesses, we must "approach the throne" where Jesus is now seated at the right hand of the Father. There is no better place to go in all the universe. In our country, psychiatrists' waiting rooms are filled with people who no longer can cope with their guilt feelings. After seeing the expert, they may feel good for a day or so, until they realize that he has done nothing to eradicate their struggle with sin, but only has tried to palliate them with such ideas that they are no different from anyone else, so they should quit blaming themselves for their guilt feelings. But after a few days the spell wears off and they find themselves back in the doomsday-filled waiting room.

When we wait upon Christ before His throne, what do we find there that is so different from the psychiatrist's office? We find that it is the throne "of grace." Here is no empty jargon containing only false hope, but we find the healing grace of God. How shall we define "grace"? Perhaps the best way is to illustrate it. Suppose you are invited to a mansion for dinner. The hostess has set out the finest white linen tablecloth and napkins, beautiful china tableware, gold flatware, crystal goblets. The food is prepared by a great chef, and served by impeccable waiters. You did nothing to be invited, and the hostess expects no meal in return because she knows you could not afford to respond to her invitation in kind. For such an experience you call the lady of the house a "gracious" hostess. She is gracious for three reasons: she has the wherewithal to be so lavish; she gives you a valuable gift which in no way you deserve; nor are you expected to repay her. Translating the story, Jesus Christ, who sits on His throne of grace, confers on you a peace of mind which only the assurance of forgiveness can provide, and grants to you the full knowledge of your possession of eternal life with Him in heaven. You probably did not expect those gifts until you heard about them in the recitation of the gospel; you did not know you could receive them until you heard that He offered them freely simply by receiving Him as your Savior and Lord; and throughout eternity you can never pay Him back although you might strive perfectly to do so. The throne of grace is the place to go, nay, it is the *only* place to go "in our time of need."

Nor need we approach His throne stealthily, as if we might get caught doing it. We are encouraged to make our approach "with confidence." The Greek word for confidence is παρρησία. Thayer offers these terms as translations: "freedom in speaking...free and fearless confidence, cheerful courage, boldness, assurance." Heinrich Schlier[6] notes that when Jesus was on trial before the high priest on the night of His betrayal, He said (John 18:20), "I have *spoken openly* to the world," and Paul averred in his defense to Agrippa (Acts 26:26) that what Jesus did and said "was not done in a corner," which is the opposite of "openly." Likewise, at the Feast of the Dedication, the Jews asked Jesus (John 10:24-25), "How long will you keep us in suspense? If you are the Christ, tell us *plainly*." Jesus, in His answer, showed them that it was not obscurity but unbelief that caused them not to believe: "I did tell you, but you do not believe." Schlier adds that the Greek word is used for our relationship toward God, as in I John 3:21 and 5:14-15, where the apostle tells the "little children" to whom he is writing, "Dear friends, if our hearts do not condemn us, we have *confidence* before God;" and "This is the *assurance* we

---

[6] In his article on παρρησία in TDNT, Vol. V, pp. 879-886.

have in approaching God: that if we ask anything according to his will, he hears us. And if we know that he hears us—whatever we ask—we know that we have what we asked of him." Schlier also points out that in many places in Acts the disciples spoke with "candour [British spelling] or boldness" to the people, most of whom were unbelievers.

This Greek word for what I like to translate mostly as "boldness" is found not only here at the end of chapter 4, but three additional times in Hebrews. We already noted in 3:6 that the author encouraged us to "hold on to our *courage*." Then in 10:19 we read, "Therefore brothers, since we have *confidence* to enter the Most Holy Place by the blood of Jesus..," and in 10:35, "so do not throw away your *confidence*...." We will examine these verses more fully later.

**...so that we may receive mercy and find grace to help us in time of need.**

Only a few moments ago we studied the meaning of grace. If now we do the same with the term "mercy," we may be able to grasp a better understanding of "grace" as well, as we compare the two. We all remember stories of the olden days when pirates roamed the seas. When a pirate was captured, he would fall on his knees before the captain and cry out, "Have mercy on me!" The pirate was well aware that for his evil life he deserved only death, but he pleaded for his life. If, as was occasionally the case, the captain was merciful, the pirate's life was spared, again not because he deserved it. We may therefore define mercy as the withholding of punishment we so richly deserve. This is contrasted with grace, which is the granting of rich blessings which we in no way deserve. So our Lord extends both grace and mercy to those of us who come boldly to His throne of grace, which is also His throne of judgment, and His throne of mercy for believers.

When is our time of need? Probably all of us would agree without much thought that our "time of need" is every moment of our lives. Even when on occasion we find ourselves at a picnic on a perfect sunny day in the midst of a grassy field of flowers surrounded by lovely maple shade trees with the closest loved one alive, we never fully escape from the dual fact that we are mere creatures in need of God's supply of everything although we deserve nothing good from His hand, and that we have sinned continuously throughout our lives in need of God's forgiveness. It is not merely during especially stressful times that we acknowledge our helplessness. We must come to God's throne of grace for our help; and how wonderful it is to be assured that He delights in our coming to Him with boldness, knowing He will receive us because we come in the name of our Intercessor, Jesus Christ.

# CHAPTER V
# THE OLD TESTAMENT PRIESTHOOD. HEB. 5:1-10.

**Heb. 5:1. Every high priest is selected from among men....**

From where else would the high priests be selected? Since they ministered to people, it is natural that they would be selected from among people. And that was so, at least in virtually every case. However, there are two glaring exceptions to this rule, and that is what this part of Hebrews is all about. Aaron and his descendants were the "normal" high priests, but since they were faulty, there was a need for a better superior high priest to be installed.

Let us begin with a description of those high priests. We have already observed that they were "selected from among men." This statement may not have excluded women necessarily; on the other hand, the record shows that every high priest was a male person. Other passages of scripture to teach us that women were not to be included among the high priests, or of any of the legitimate priests throughout biblical history.

It is important to note that the selection of those high priests was not made by men, or by any man. Exodus 28:1 tells us quite simply and clearly what the process was. In that verse God is speaking to Moses and gives the order: "Have Aaron your brother brought to you from among the Israelites, along with his sons Nadab and Abihu, Eleazar and Ithamar, so they may serve me as priests." Since God was their Master and they His servants, it was His prerogative to choose His priests. In fact, God selected all the leaders of every category He wanted to serve Him.

There are two instances in the Old Testament where people attempted to force themselves higher on the scale of leadership, and the attempt in each case ended disastrously. One instance was when Aaron, whom God had already appointed to the high priesthood, and his sister Miriam, confronted Moses. Each of them hoped to be elevated to a position even higher than they then occupied. Apparently their desire was triggered by Moses' choice of a Cushite to be his wife. But as is often the case, Aaron and Miriam probably only used that circumstance as an excuse to gain more power and fame for themselves. We read about it in Num. 12, the whole chapter. In the first verse we read the setting: "Miriam and Aaron began to talk against Moses because of his Cushite wife...." Their real purpose in opposing Moses, however, appears in what they said to him next, "Has the LORD spoken only through Moses? Hasn't he also spoken through us?" Miriam wanted to be a prophet of God, equal to Moses; and apparently Aaron thought his position as high priest was inferior to that of Moses. But God had heard their complaint, and ordered the three of them to meet Him before the Tent of Meeting. There God reminded them of how honorably He had elevated Moses, even above all other prophets (verses 6-8):

> When a prophet of the LORD is among you,
> I reveal myself to him in visions,

> I speak to him in dreams.
> But this is not true of my servant Moses;
> > he is faithful in all my house.
> With him I speak face to face,
> > clearly and not in riddles;
> > he sees the form of the LORD.
> Why then were you not afraid
> > to speak against my servant Moses?

For the evil efforts of Aaron and Miriam, God smote Miriam with leprosy (verse 10), and caused her to die in Kadesh (Num. 20:1), long before the children of Israel entered the Promised Land. Aaron also died in the wilderness, partly because of this rebellion, but mostly because both he and Moses "did not trust in me enough to honor me as holy in the sight of the Israelites, you will not bring this community into the land I give them" (said God to both Moses and Aaron, Num. 20:12). The record of Aaron's death is in Num. 20:22-29, along with the transfer of the high priesthood to Aaron's third son Eleazar.

The second of the two great attempts by people to exalt themselves to high positions of leadership is found in Num. 16:1-50. That is the story of Korah, Dathan, and Abiram, along with two hundred fifty other "well-known community leaders who had been appointed members of the council" (verse 2). They objected to the exclusive leadership of Moses and Aaron, saying (verse 3): "You have gone too far! The whole community is holy, every one of them, and the LORD is with them. Why then do you set yourselves above the LORD's assembly?" There were two gross errors in the people's complaint. First, they considered themselves equal to Moses and Aaron ("the whole community is holy"). The rebels themselves proved that to be untrue through their conduct. No one as holy as Moses or Aaron would have vied for leadership in the way these men did. The second error of the people was even more gross than the first: they claimed that Moses and Aaron had "set [them]selves above the LORD's assembly." It was God who had chosen the two leaders. Moses certainly was a reluctant leader. His battle with God in an attempt to avoid the leadership position is spelled out in his objections, listed and refuted in Ex. 2 and 3. It is not so clearly stated in scripture that Aaron was also unwilling to serve as a leader. In fact, he was only a distant second choice for God, selected only because Moses claimed he could not speak sufficiently well. But it is very clear that it was God who had selected both Moses and Aaron to be His leaders of the Israelites: Moses in Ex. 2 and 3; and Aaron in Ex. 28:1. For all the efforts of Korah and Company to usurp the leadership from Moses and Aaron, God caused them and their families to be swallowed up by a rift in the ground; further, when the people murmured against Moses and Aaron for the death of the usurpers, saying "You have killed the LORD's people" (Num. 16:41), God sent a plague among the people for their rebellion, and 14,700 people (verse 49) perished. God set up the Old Testament priesthood and selected Aaron to be the first high priest.

### ...and is appointed to represent them....

The high priest was established in his office for a special purpose. We usually think of a priest as a person who leads the people in worship. The author of Hebrews tells us there is a more important task for him: he is appointed to *represent* his people. Most often we think it is an attorney who represents his client in court. Sometimes the attorney is appointed by the court to represent an indigent defendant. When we think of that, how wealthy are we with respect to God's court? Can we afford a lawyer to represent us before God? Hiring a lawyer in a people's court can be expensive, so much so that many people believe our whole system of justice is corrupt because rich people can escape punishment by hiring an expensive, corrupt attorney. It is comforting to know that money is not involved when we select a representative before God. On the other hand, should we be concerned that the attorney who represents us has been appointed by our Adversary, God?

Many years ago, my wife and I were scheduled to meet with a group of people in order to close on the purchase of a home. The realtor had assured us that he would find a competent attorney to represent us at the closing. When we arrived at the meeting-room, we looked around and saw the realtor, the husband and wife who were selling the property, and their attorney who was obviously a close friend of theirs. Seeing no one else in the room, we asked the realtor where our attorney was. He pointed to the only attorney in the room and said he would represent us. We objected strenuously, believing that an attorney who was a close friend of the sellers could not possibly represent us fairly also. We left the room immediately, and sought an attorney in whom we had confidence, and set another date for the closing. If God were corrupt, such a situation before Him would be most irregular as well as dangerous. But since God is perfect, and honorable in every way, we could never find an advocate to compare to Him.

### ...in matters related to God....

Apart from "matters related to God," how many matters are important enough in our lives for us to need a "representative"? In this world we have our quarrels, and sometimes we think we need to go to court, or someone else hauls us before the magistrate. But when life in this world is ended, what is left to contend but "matters related to God"? For such important matters we need the best representative we can find. How wonderful it is to know that God has supplied us with the greatest Attorney, Advocate (I John 2:2), Lawyer, and Paraclete/Comforter (John 14:16)! We are in safe hands when it comes to "matters related to God."

* * *

### ...to offer gifts and sacrifices for sins.

Although gifts are among the things we are expected to present to God, the Bible ordinarily uses the term "sacrifices" for only things acceptable to Him that will expiate sin. Several kinds of gifts that are outlined in the Old Testament please God when people offer them to Him. But to sacrifice an animal, specifically including the shedding of the animal's blood, was the only thing that could remove the guilt of a sinner and make him right with God.

Some people see a difference between what Cain presented to God and what his brother Abel gave as the difference between a mere gift and the sacrifice of an animal. However, in the story in Gen. 4:2-5, the Hebrew term מִנְחָה, a gift, tribute, or offering (usually called a "meal-offering," because it consists of some grain or flour) is used for what both brothers gave to the Lord. There is no indication that either of them meant his offering to be a sacrifice for sin, but simply a gift to God. Those who see the difference in what they gave think that Abel's presentation was accepted by God because it consisted of an animal, while Cain's was "fruits of the soil," probably garden produce, or fruits from trees, or grapes, or grain from the field. Therefore, they think that God was pleased with what Abel brought because it was an animal "sacrifice," and displeased with Cain's bloodless presentation.

There are several reasons why that difference was not the reason for God's reaction to the two men's gifts. The first reason is that the Genesis story puts them on equal terms by calling the gifts by the same name, as spelled out above. The second reason is that each man offered what he had, since Cain "worked the soil;" and Abel "kept flocks." Certainly God is not so unjust as to require of a person anything he does not have. A third reason is that neither of the gifts is linked in the story to any response to sins committed, but only something offered to God. Finally, a reason why it was not the nature of the gift that was offered is because in Heb. 11:4 we read of the "sacrifices" made by both Abel and Cain to God. Since they were identified as identical, both here and in the Genesis account, it could not have been what was offered that changed God's attitude. What the author of Hebrews says is that "by faith [Abel] was commended as a righteous man, when God spoke well of his offerings."

By means of the story of Cain and Abel we see that the terms "sacrifice" and "offering" are sometimes exchanged in scripture, so we ought not make too much of that difference. Rather, we should look behind the terms to see what God intends for us to do.

That a priest is required to make sacrifices on behalf of people's sins is evident in the outline of sacrifices given in Lev. 4. The priest was required to make a sin-offering for his own sins (verse 3); for unwitting sins of the people (verse 2); for the whole congregation (verse 16); for a ruler (verse 22); for a common man (verse 27). Succeeding chapters list additional sacrifices, all of which must have been made by priests.

Saul, the first king of Israel, forgot that even a king was forbidden to make sacrifices. In a story in I Sam. 13, we read that Saul waited impatiently for Samuel to arrive to make sacrifices on behalf of the army of Israel, when confronted by the Philistines. Some of Saul's soldiers became frightened, and began to slip away to avoid the conflict. Samuel had promised to come within seven days (I Sam. 10:8), but on the seventh day had not showed up. So Saul took upon himself the task of making burnt-offerings and peace-offerings (I Sam. 13:9). As he completed the sacrifices, Samuel showed up, confronted him with his sin, and predicted that for his rebellion the kingdom would be taken from him and from his descendants and given to someone else (verses 13 and 14).

Without a priest, therefore, no one can offer a sacrifice for sin; and if no sacrifice is made for sin, there is no forgiveness. We shall see this more profoundly as we continue in the next verses and chapters of Hebrews.

**Heb. 5:2. He is able to deal gently with those who are ignorant and are going astray, since he himself is subject to weakness.**

We are still talking about the Old Testament priests here, not yet about Jesus as our Great High Priest. The priests of old were in the same boat, spiritually, as the rest of the people. The reason is that both had sinned. It was for this very reason that a priest was "able to deal gently" with the rest of the people; he had sinned their sins, he had sensed the same guilt, he knew the only escape from guilt and its punishment was to make a sacrifice acceptable to God. Look again at the first few verses of Lev. 4, and renew your understanding that the priest had to make a sacrifice for his own sins before he was capable of making a proper sacrifice for the sins of the people.

The author of Hebrews wrote that the ancient priests were "able" to deal gently with the people when they had sinned. Surely because of their sinful nature they did not always deal gently with others. Sometimes they succumbed to the temptations of the people, as did Aaron when the people urged him to make a golden calf for them to worship (Ex. 32). More than that, Aaron attempted to pass all the blame on the people in response to Moses' accusation, when he said (Ex. 32:23-24): "They said to me, 'Make us gods....' They gave me the gold, and I threw it into the fire." Aaron's plea was most ridiculous when he blamed even the calf for forming itself: "out came this calf!"

A further example of evil priests was in the lives of Eli's sons, who demanded extra meat from the people's sacrifices (I Sam. 2:12-17). An almost identical story is told about Samuel's sons in I Sam. 8:1-3. Although they were appointed judges and not priests, their leadership was not exemplary.

The author talks about people who "are ignorant and are going astray." We must note carefully that in God's economy ignorance does *not* erase the sin. When I was a child I learned this truth about civil law from my parents: "Ignorance before the law is no excuse." The truth of this is found in Lev. 4:2 which begins the discussion of sins and sacrifices by talking about "When anyone sins unintentionally." A practical exhortation is appropriate for us. When we come to God by prayer in confession and repentance, we certainly ought to express the sins we know we have committed and ask God to cleanse us from guilt. At the same time we should not neglect to ask God to reveal to us any sins we have committed unknowingly, and ask Him to forgive them also. He has promised to forgive us when we confess our sins (I John 1:9). But "If we claim to be without sin, we deceive ourselves and the truth is not in us" (I John 1:8). Any claim of ours to be without sin is like failing or refusing to confess our sin. It most certainly is not acceptable to God for us to claim that what we have done is not sin if God has declared in His word that it is sin.

"Going astray" is from the Greek word πλανάω, the word from which we get our name for planets, "wandering stars" as the ancients called them. There is only one right path as far as God is concerned. To deviate from the path by ninety degrees surely is gross sin. But to turn away by only a fraction of a degree makes us just as culpable in God's sight as committing the most heinous sin.

The author completes the comparison between a priest and other people by saying that the priest is also "subject to weakness." In the original Greek he says it more colorfully: the priest is surrounded by weakness, totally hemmed in, without hope of escape from the malady. He has just named the two important elements of that weakness. First, the priest is ignorant—perhaps not as ignorant as the rest of the people, but still he is ignorant with respect to all there is to know about God and His will. Secondly, the priest also goes astray—he steps from the pathway paved by God wherein we must walk according to His will. The priest, then, is little if any better able to deal with the people's needs than the people themselves. The only difference, in fact, is that the priest is appointed by God to do the work.

The priest, then, is in need of a large measure of compassion from the people whom he represents before God, because he is like them. This brings up an important point for today's churchgoer. Although your Minister, Pastor, Priest, or whatever you wish to call him, no longer is burdened with the function of making sacrifices for the sins of his people, still he has an equally great task of informing the people of the Sacrifice that has already been made for their sins by Christ. Your Minister is subject to the same weaknesses as you, and sometimes is tempted even more powerfully than you. Therefore, your Minister needs your understanding and compassion; more, he needs your prayers. I have been grateful throughout my ministry for the prayers of the people who prayed for me. It was their prayers that made a large contribution to whatever success I had in fulfilling my task as their Minister.

**Heb. 5:3.  This is why he has to offer sacrifices for his own sins....**

Just because a priest was appointed by God, he was no more acceptable to God than the most humble garbage collector or most heinous sinner. Like any other person, a priest had access to God's throne of grace only through sacrifice and everything which sacrifice implied, that is, repentance, and offering one's self as a gift to God. Once again I remind you of the beginning words of Lev. 4, detailing rules for sacrifices for sins.

Every high priest was a sinner. There was no exception. For evidence, please go back to the discussion on the last part of Heb. 4:15.

**...as well as for the sins of the people.**

No one is excluded from God's demand that sacrifice be made for the expiation of sin. Are you better than your Priest, or Minister? Actually, you may be far better, as the headlines during 2002 trumpeted the great misconduct that many priests had been involved in over the past several decades. But the proper question is not whether you think you are better than your Minister or even may actually be more righteous than he. The proper question anyone must ask for himself is, "Am I totally innocent of any sin or disobedience in God's sight?" It is vain to try to compare yourself with any other human being. It is only fair to compare yourself with God's ultimate standard, that is repeated by Christ (Matt. 5:48): "Be perfect, therefore, as your heavenly Father is perfect."

Years ago I was conversing with an Elder in an attempt to make clear to him what he needed to do in order to receive eternal life. I asked him if he was sure he was going to heaven when he died, and he assured me that he had never done anything bad enough to keep him out of heaven. When he said that, I was convinced that his very statement was sufficient to keep him out of heaven, because surely he was a sinner along with every other person. I tried to convince him of this through a story. One day I was walking toward the business district of the city when suddenly the earth began to shake beneath me. It was a significant earthquake. A block ahead of me was a new building going up. The steelwork was ten stories in the sky; and a steelworker was walking on one of the top girders. When the earth began to shake, naturally it caused the top of the structure to sway measurably. The man's piercing scream carried to where I stood, and he dropped to his belly and clung tightly to the girder. As the man lay there, a thought struck me. Suppose that man had been one day shy of retirement, and was looking forward to receiving his pension payments for the rest of his life, while he mowed his grass, went fishing, and did whatever he wanted to do for the rest of his retirement years? He had worked hard for perhaps forty years to earn the retirement. But if he had made one misstep and fallen from the girder, would he have begun to receive his retirement the next day? Sadly, no. All the good he had done all his life would be erased by just one mistake. So also, in our spiritual lives, it takes only one sin to banish us from heaven forever. The Elder objected to my story, and said that it was only what happens in the world, and not spiritually. But I was reminded of the story of Adam and Eve. They were in a paradise already, and could have stayed there forever, but they did not. What did it take for God to exclude them from Eden? We think of eating a piece of fruit freshly plucked from a tree as an exceedingly insignificant matter, but God thought it was serious enough to drive both Adam and Eve from the Garden, and to put them to death instantly, spiritually, as He had threatened to do. God's standard is utter perfection, for both priests and people.

### Heb. 5:4. No one takes this honor upon himself....

It was God who appointed Aaron and his sons to the priesthood. They did not choose it for themselves. All others were utterly forbidden to offer sacrifices, unless they were specifically elected by God in some other kind of selection.

We have already reviewed the cases of people or groups of people who attempted by themselves to usurp the position of the priesthood in Israel, in our discussion of verse 1 of this chapter. I would remind you that they all claimed "equality" with the leaders as sufficient authority for them to take over leadership or priestly roles. Miriam and Aaron claimed (Num. 12:2), "Has the LORD spoken only through Moses? Hasn't he also spoken through us?" Similarly, Korah and Company said (Num. 16:3): "You have gone too far! The whole community is holy, every one of them, and the LORD is with them. Why then do you set yourselves above the LORD's assembly?" Saul claimed (I Sam. 13:12), "I felt compelled to offer the burnt offering." How often our desires become demands!

We might add other instances where people claimed the right to act as priests apart from God's appointment. There is the case of Jeroboam, who wrested ten tribes of the kingdom of Israel from Solomon's son Rehoboam. In the last part of I Kings 12, we read how Jeroboam attempted to keep the people of the northern kingdom from defecting to Judea and Jerusalem by erecting altars in Bethel and in Dan. At the end of the chapter (12:33), we read that Jeroboam "instituted the festival for the Israelites and went up to the altar to make offerings." As a matter of fact, God indeed had appointed Jeroboam to be the first king of the northern kingdom, but to offer sacrifices as a priest was not part of God's package of leadership for him.

I shall add a seemingly strange case, but it shows how rigidly God enforces His dictum of appointing only His chosen ones to be leaders of the people. It is the case of Uzzah, of whom we read in II Sam. 6:3-8. The Philistines had captured the ark of God, but God had done terrible things to them for possessing it (I Sam. 5:1-12). So they decided to return it to Israel. God had decreed that only Levites, specifically descendants of Kohath one of Levi's sons, should handle the ark (Num. 3:31), but seventy curious people decided they wanted to see what was in the ark, so they looked inside, and God killed them (I Sam. 6:19). The ark was sent to the property of Abinadab in Kiriath Jearim, where it stayed for twenty years. King David wanted to bring it to Jerusalem which he had conquered, so they had a great festival when the journey began. However, the ark was on a new cart, and two of Abinadab's sons, Uzzah and Ahio, walked beside it. But along the way, the oxen drawing the cart stumbled, and Uzzah put out his hand to steady the ark so it wouldn't fall. However, he was not appointed by God to touch the ark, so God struck him dead. Apparently Uzzah was not a Levite, and only Levites were permitted to touch the ark. That is what we read in I Chron. 15:2. After Uzzah's death, David attached at least some blame on the Levites for Uzzah's death. He said (I Chron. 15:13): "It was because you, the Levites, did not bring [the ark] up the first time that the LORD our God broke out in anger against us." We think that Uzzah was trying to do a good thing in protecting the ark from falling, but God's appointment is infinitely more important in His view than any human attempt to do good on one's own.

I labor this point to show that scripture is very emphatic in God's insistence that only a person specifically chosen by Him should serve Him in special ways. There are people today who claim that although they are of a certain group designated by God to be excluded from ministry, think they are "as good as" anyone else and therefore have a right to become leaders. In many instances their claim to have received God's "call" to service is simply a cover-up for a strong desire for leadership, power, and fame. In fact, leadership in all the denominations is filled with people who have been ordained to high positions whose motive was not a call from God. In the seminary class ahead of me there was a man ready to graduate, who when asked "Just why are you going into the ministry?" replied after some thought, "Well, it's a soft job, with lots of prestige." Today the leaders of our denomination are crying out for more people to enter seminary and the ministry because of a critical "shortage" of Ministers. The truth is that there are now one hundred eighty-eight ordained Ministers for every one hundred churches, and not all the "extras" are either retired or missionaries. The rest do not feel "called" to become Ministers of congregations of only forty people; they must have a larger flock and a higher salary. If the church leaders would make certain that only those who are truly called by God could be ordained to leadership positions, though the number might be smaller than at present, the results would be huge by comparison. Granted, I have pursued no million-dollar study to make such conclusions, but I am sure this is what God's word directs us to do. Have you ever consulted God in prayer and Bible meditation whether He wants you to serve Him in some specific way? That is the only way to be certain you are doing what He wants.

*   *   *

193

**...he must be called by God, just as Aaron was.**

This statement not only continues the emphasis on the necessity that a call to ministry must be made by God alone. It also leaves the door open for the possibility of the existence of a priesthood other than that of Aaron. There was, in fact, another order of priesthood which God alone instituted, and the discussion of that comes next.

**Heb. 5:5. So Christ also did not take upon himself the glory of becoming a high priest.**

This is so, even though Christ was the eternal God Himself, as we saw clearly in our discussion of 4:14-15 near the end of our last chapter. Please return to that part of our study, and refresh your thinking about it if you now have the slightest doubt. It is hard for us to understand how God (the Son) required God's (the Father's) endorsement to become a High Priest. The fact may be beyond our understanding, but that does not necessarily make it beyond the realm of possibility. One of the part-time professors at my seminary once said something about the story of Jonah and the whale in the Bible that helped me to accept its truth. He said, "The story of Jonah may be beyond our powers of reasoning, but that does not make it unreasonable. We are asked to believe that a whale swallowed Jonah, not that Jonah swallowed a whale!" So also we are asked to believe that God the Father appointed God the Son to be a High Priest, even though both are God. We have already mentioned that Jesus was a filial Son, as He said of His relationship to His Father in John 8:28-29, "I do nothing on my own but speak just what the Father has taught me....I always do what pleases him."

**But God said to him....**

The author of Hebrews never says anything on his own authority; he simply states what God has caused to be written in His word. What we read of God's statement to His Son, therefore, is to be accepted and believed.

**"You are my Son;**
**today I have become your Father."**

Here the author reaches back to the very first quotation he made from the Old Testament. We find it in Heb. 1:5, and the quotation comes from Ps. 2:7. In chapter 1 the author quoted it in the context of the comparison between Jesus and angels, that He is better than them all. Now the author quotes the same Psalm to prove that Jesus is better than all the Aaronic priests. That verse, of course, is not directly related to a comparison of Jesus with priests. But the next verse gives a clue to the direction his argument will take.

\* \* \*

**Heb. 5:6.** **And he says in another place,
"You are a priest forever,
in the order of Melchizedek."**

This quotation is from Ps. 110, verse 4. Its first verse was quoted by the author in his first chapter, at the very end. We note that in chapter 1, the author is pointing out the superiority of Jesus over the angels. Now the author is quoting from the same Psalm to show that Jesus is superior to the Aaronic priests as well. In this passage he gives several reasons why Jesus is better than they:

1. Jesus went "through the heavens," not just into heaven, 4:14
2. He is God, not a mere man, as the Priest, 4:14
3. He is sinless, 4:15
4. Although He is God, He is also man, selected from among men, 5:1
5. He was chosen by His Father, 5:4
6. His priesthood endures forever, 5:6
7. His priesthood is in the order of Melchizedek, 5:6

We have yet to study, in 6:20 and following, why the Melchizedek priesthood was so much better than that of Aaron; there are many differences.

We may be more familiar with the different orders of priesthood in the Roman Catholic Church. We have heard of the Franciscans, the Jesuits, and the Dominicans among others. However, although they are different organizations, they are still under the umbrella of that Church; they pledge obedience to the Pope; they are all men; so there is very little difference among them. In the Old Testament economy there were also "orders" in the Aaronic priesthood. We read, for instance, in Lu. 1:8 that Zecharia the father of John the Baptist was a member of a particular division of Aaronic priests. In the Old Testament we note that King David had separated the priests of his day into orders or "divisions" (I Chron. 24:1-19). Also, Ezra talks about "priests in their divisions and the Levites in their groups" (Ezra 6:18).

Following this brief discussion of the Aaronic high priests, the author narrates some of the things Jesus began to do as our Great High Priest.

### Heb. 5:7. During the days of Jesus' life on earth....

Sometimes we discover some very important things through statements that are made by authors from time to time, even though those things may be tangential to the main thrust of the discussion. Often we would lose much knowledge if these little details were omitted. Here are two important things.

First, when the author speaks of Jesus' "life on earth," he implies that there is life elsewhere. You know of people who torment themselves with the question whether there is life somewhere in the universe other than on our Earth. Astronomers search the skies for evidence of other planets that might be capable of supporting life as we know it, and geologists examine in detail every piece of celestial debris to see if they can find a plant or animal fossil, or some kind of organic matter. So far hopes have been dashed after initial clues have been proved faulty. But Christians not only believe, but know for certain, that there is life elsewhere, not only in the universe, but far beyond it as well. God is out there, filling more than the space we are aware of; His angels and the fallen angels roam freely through the heavens; and people who have left the earth continue to live in heaven which may be far more vast than we can imagine. Surely God could have put life on other planets if He wished, but then why would He? He has had trouble enough with us.

Secondly, if the author of Hebrews talks about Jesus' "life on earth," the implication is that Jesus was alive before He came to earth, and continues alive after His death. We know both these things are true. He lived before He came to earth, because (John 1:2) "he was with God in the beginning;" He as God (John 1:14) "became flesh and lived for a while among us." Jesus also lives after His death on the cross: the resurrection stories give ample evidence of that. King David predicted that Jesus' body would not remain in the grave; he said in Ps. 16:10:

> ...you will not abandon me to the grave,
> nor will you let your Holy One see decay.

Peter, in his Pentecost sermon (Acts 2:24-32) affirmed that when David wrote those words he was not speaking of himself, but of Christ whose body God would raise from the dead.

By the way, all that the Bible says about the resurrection has nothing to do with people's thoughts about "reincarnation." There is no connection whatever between those two concepts; one is true and the other is not. We search in vain for even a hint of reincarnation in scripture. Interestingly, there must be such a thing as "pre-incarnation." At least that is the best way I can interpret the story in Gen. 18 (the whole chapter) about God who appeared to Abraham by the trees of Mamre, to inform Abraham that he would have an heir, and to discuss the fate of Sodom and Gomorrah. That chapter begins, "The LORD appeared to Abraham." John in two places assures us that "No one has ever seen God" (John 1:18; I John 4:12), but John could not have meant that no one had seen God the Son, because he affirms that Jesus is God, and he is the beloved disciple who leaned on Jesus' breast at the institution of the Lord's Supper. So if Abraham saw God, it must have been a "pre-incarnate" sight of Jesus.

As for ourselves, we do not expect that we existed for all time before the creation, except as thoughts in the mind of God, because He knew even the end from the beginning. Now that we have lived in the world, our spirits are immortal, and our bodies will die for a brief time and then will be raised to newness of life, and we will continue to exist forever. All scripture assures us of that; because Jesus lives, we too shall live.

Now the author of Hebrews begins to enumerate all the things Jesus has done for us as our Great High Priest.

### ...he offered up prayers and petitions....

If I were a lawyer, or were interested in proper legal procedure, I could write a whole dissertation on this subject. Jesus offered up prayers and petitions on our behalf. There is a multitude of things Jesus has done for us, all encompassed in these few words. His prayers for us began even while He was in the flesh. In what is called the "Great High Priestly Prayer" in John 17, part of His prayer was, "My prayer is not for [those disciples now living] alone. I pray also for those who will believe in me through their message, that all of them may be one, Father, just as you are in me and I am in you" (verses 20-21).

All our lives Jesus has been interceding for us before the Father's throne. We have needed every plea He has made on our behalf. It is impossible for us to begin to enumerate the sins each of us has committed. During Billy Graham's great New York 1957 Crusade, he often pointed his finger at us and said, "Every one of you has broken every one of the Ten Commandments every day." When I first heard him say that I was offended. But as I pondered his words over the next few days, the truth began to soak into my mind. Especially if we interpret the commandments the way Jesus did in His Sermon on the Mount in Matt. 5:17-48, we know that we have broken every law at least in thought if not in word and deed, as some church confessions remind us. So I am sure for myself at least that Jesus' intercessions for me must be constant; and I suspect the same is true for you as well. Jesus began to offer prayers and petitions for us even before He died on the cross ("during the days of Jesus' life on earth"), just as He prayed for those who crucified Him when He said, "Father, forgive them, for they do not know what they are doing" (Lu. 23:34). My sins are the more heinous, because most often I do know what I do. Jesus' pleas for us never cease, nor are they interrupted for a second. His promise to us is as sure as His promise to Moses in the wilderness (Ex. 33:14): "My Presence will go with you, and I will give you rest."

### ...with loud cries and tears....

Jesus' prayers on our behalf were not perfunctory, rote, thoughtless, like those of the Pharisees, but were charged with emotion; they were real, pleading prayers. Jesus shed tears, not for Himself alone, but for us too. He did weep for Himself. As He stood before Lazarus' tomb "Jesus wept." We are not sure why He wept then. Much dispute has been bandied over whether He was weeping for Himself because He was sorry to see the anguish of Lazarus' sisters; sorry at the loss of His own dear friend; sad because He knew it was sin initially that caused Lazarus' death; anger because the Pharisees and others did not believe in His healing or saving power. It is possible that all those factors caused Jesus to weep.

197

Jesus wept, surely for Himself, when He knelt in the Garden of Gethsemane just before His trial and crucifixion. Doubtless those same tears were shed on our behalf as well, for Jesus knew better than we that He was dying for us. In this respect, Jesus set us a great example. We too should weep on behalf of the world; and if we must suffer in our efforts to win the world to Christ, we may weep for ourselves. The Psalmist tells us that this is what we should do (Ps. 126:6):

> He who goes out weeping,
> > carrying seed to sow,
> will return with songs of joy,
> > carrying sheaves with him.

### ...to the one who could save him from death....

Jesus, you see, did pray for Himself, not only for us. When He prayed for Himself, however, it was not for His own salvation. Rather, He prayed for matters concerning His death, that is, for our salvation.

Did Jesus pray for Himself to escape from death? Yes, surely that was at least one of the reasons He prayed and wept. We read His prayer in Matt. 26:39: "My Father, if it is possible, may this cup be taken from me. Yet not as I will, but as you will." We must note that Jesus' petition was contingent on the Father's will; while Jesus was praying He already knew what that will was. In fact, Jesus had known the Father's will from before the time of His birth. Later we read the amazing fact that Jesus was able to speak to His Father at the moment of His birth when He said (Heb. 10:5):

> Sacrifice and offering you did not desire,
> > but a body you prepared for me;
> with burnt offerings and sin offerings
> > you were not pleased.
> Then I said, 'Here I am—it is written about me in the scroll—
> > I have come to do your will, O God.'

When Jesus prayed in the Garden to be delivered from the "cup," was His prayer answered? Some think yes, and others think no. It depends on what they think Jesus prayed for. Donald Grey Barnhouse thought Jesus was praying to be delivered from eternal death, so he said Jesus' prayer was answered. On the other hand, if Jesus was praying only about His physical death, His prayer was not answered, but He endured that death for only three days. Some may argue that if Jesus' prayer was not answered, then His prayer was flawed, and He was not perfect. Perhaps we should consider more carefully the *whole* of Jesus' prayer, and in that consideration we may find a better pattern for our own prayers, especially when we want to pray for some blessing or benefit to ourselves. How much happier we would be if each of our petitions ended with, "Yet not as I will, but as you will."

\* \* \*

198

**...and he was heard because of his reverent submission.**

Here is what makes Jesus throughout His life, and in particular in his prayers, so great: His "reverent submission." Too often we humans want what we want, and we want it now; then we are disappointed and even angry when we fail to get it. It was precisely because Jesus prayed "not my will" that the Father heard Him. Lord, teach us to pray!

What do you ask for? More importantly, how do you make your petitions? Do you believe God hears you? If not, it may be well worth your while to think carefully through the whole pattern of your prayer life.

One sad situation I encountered in my ministry was that of a lady I barely got to know after I had moved to a different church to serve. I had seen her only a few times before I was called to the hospital by her husband to visit her. She had been diagnosed with a malignant brain tumor. After the surgery to remove the tumor, she began to pray earnestly with copious tears for God to take her out of the world, so she would be spared the agony of radiation therapy. She lived, however, and had the therapy. Months later, when she began to slip after the radiation failed to cure her, she began to pray earnestly that God would let her live. Just before she slipped into a weeks-long silence before her death, she asked me, "*Why* doesn't God answer me?" I did not have the heart to answer, "Why don't you make up your mind what you want? First you pray for God to take you; then you pray for Him to keep you alive."

It may be that you have wondered why God doesn't answer your heart-felt requests. Consider the possibility that you really don't know what you want. It may be that you want what God knows is not good for you. To solve your prayer problem, consider what Jesus taught us in His prayer life, "reverent submission."

**Heb. 5:8. Although he was a son, he learned obedience from what he suffered....**

Some people are like clay, others are like tar. When a brick freshly made from clay is set out in the sun, it bakes dry and becomes very hard, which is just what the contractor wants for a solid house. But when the tar filling the cracks in a pavement is exposed to the sun for a short time, it becomes soft, pliable. So also when the sunshine of God's love comes down, people whose hearts are like clay grow hardened, like the children of Israel who basked in the warmth of God's blessings thirteen times over as reported in the book of Judges, but their hearts were hardened and their necks became stiff, and they turned from God. Jesus was just the opposite in His reaction to the Father's love. He was made pliable, and obedient, even though He knew He must suffer in His obedience.

We have already discussed the matter of Jesus' Sonship, so we need not pursue that again here.

Was it necessary for Jesus to "learn" obedience? The Greek word here may help us to understand what the author was driving at. The word means to learn by use and practice.[1] In His nature as God, surely it was not necessary for Jesus to "learn" anything, since as God He not only knew everything; He had made everything. But in His human nature, Jesus developed in every way like any human (except for His sinlessness). Luke puts it this way in describing Jesus' boyhood (Lu. 2:40): "And the child grew and became strong; he was filled with wisdom, and the grace of God was upon him."

Here is a good reason why suffering exists. Many people question why there must be suffering if God is really in charge. If Jesus learned *obedience* through suffering, it may be that you should look back at your pathway of obedience and see how God has been trying to bring you back onto His pathway by allowing suffering to put potholes in your path of life.

### ...and, once made perfect....

Does this phrase mean that at one time Jesus was imperfect? That is hard to believe if we think of the common understanding of what "perfect" means. There must be a difference in meaning between "sinless" and "perfect" as it is used here. The Greek word is τελειόω, and means to be complete, or to make complete, so it has less to do with moral perfection than with completion of tasks. In fact, Jesus used this Greek word in His sixth "word" or statement on the cross. John 19:30 tells us that Jesus said, "It is finished," and after one further word, He died. He was saying that the work for which He had been sent into the world by the Father was ended in every detail.

### ...he became the source of eternal salvation....

This is the all-encompassing theme for Jesus' incarnation. Without His coming into the world in human form, He could not have saved us, as we shall see more clearly in a detail in chapter 10.

There is an interesting small detail in the Greek of this statement: there is no definite article to limit the source of salvation to Jesus, as some might think. But what source is there besides the One Source, Jesus Christ? No other religion offers an alternate. Paul makes this clear in Gal. 1:6-8:

> I am astonished that you are so quickly deserting the one who called you by the grace of Christ and are turning to a different gospel—which is really no gospel at all. Evidently some people are throwing you into confusion and are trying to pervert the gospel of Christ. But even if we or an angel from heaven should preach a gospel other than the one we preached to you, let him be eternally condemned!

As a matter of fact, the definite article is not needed to assure us that "source" is definite. Greek scholars agree that "As a rule the predicate is without the article, even when the subject uses it."[2] So the author cannot be interpreted as implying that there is a source of eternal salvation other than Jesus.

---

[1] This is one of Thayer's definitions for the word μανθάνω.

[2] Robertson, GRAMMAR OF THE GREEK NEW TESTAMENT, p. 767.

**...for all who obey him....**

The Greek word for "obey," ὑπακούω, means to hearken, that is, to obey a command. That word is used only once more in Hebrews, in 11:8: "By faith Abraham, when called to go to a place...obeyed and went, even though he did not know where he was going." It is not obedience that gives a person access to heaven, but faith. However, the faith that saves is the faith that works. James spends many words elucidating that in his small epistle. And Paul, the great exponent of faith, agrees (Gal. 5:6): "The only thing that counts is faith expressing itself ["which worketh," KJV] through love." Also, remember our discussion on the word in John 3:36, which has the combined meaning of believing and working. The songwriter said it this way:

> I'll go where you want me to go, dear Lord;
> I'll be what you want me to be.

**Heb. 5:10.     ...and was designated by God to be high priest in the order of Melchizedek.**

How tantalizing for the author to lead us to this point in our discussion of Jesus as our Great High Priest, and then to break away to a long, seemingly irrelevant, parenthesis! That parenthesis continues in the rest of chapter 5 and concludes at the end of chapter 6, where the words are virtually the same: "He has become a high priest forever, in the order of Melchizedek." Let us now study the parenthesis, to see how it supplements the author's argument.

**Heb. 5:11.     We have much to say about this....**

The author of Hebrews alludes here to what he has been talking about, that is, that Jesus was designated by the Father to be a High Priest in the order of Melchizedek.  But before he continues with that theme, he senses the need to chide his hearers.  He begins his gentle admonitions here, and continues with them through chapter 6.  This parenthesis is the subject of our study now.

**...but it is hard to explain....**

What the author is saying here, according to the Greek word he uses, is that the subject of Jesus as a High Priest in an order other than that of Aaron is "hard to interpret."  For those of you who want to know the Greek word, it is δυσερμήνευτος.  The first part of the word, δυς, according to Thayer, conveys the "idea of difficulty, opposition, injuriousness or the like."  The rest of the Greek word comes from the verb which Thayer says is "1. to explain in words, expound;" or "2. to interpret, i. e. to translate what has been spoken or written in a foreign tongue into the vernacular."  The Greek verb for interpreting is used only three times in the New Testament; and the combined word used here in Hebrews is found nowhere else in the New Testament.

The author's use of this Greek word gives me opportunity to discuss a matter that has troubled me greatly throughout my  ministry.  Many Bible teachers, professors, and others acknowledged to be theological scholars make extensive studies on words, thoughts, and passages in the Bible in order by theological manipulation to attempt to make the portion they are studying mean something other than what it clearly means to any casual reader.  Thus they change the word of God to their own words.  At best they confuse, at worst they deny, what God is saying to the world.

An example of this is found in a report to the 1991 General Assembly of the Presbyterian Church (USA), titled, "Keeping Body and Soul Together." The report was written in defense of homosexual activity, and purports to prove that the Bible does not state that such activity is sin.  In a discussion of Rom. 1:26-27 and I Cor. 6:9-10, the article states in pages 101-102, "Both passages require careful linguistic and contextual analysis, because the original Greek is not as clear as one would like."  However, the original Greek could not be more clear.  Neither passage contains any variant reading among the ancient manuscripts.  All the words in the passages are easy to translate and understand in either Greek or English.  There is no way to change the meaning of those passages.  The only reason why anyone would want to search for a different meaning would be to change what God has said to something He has not said.  The attempt, for instance, to change the meaning of these biblical passages by so-called "careful linguistic and contextual analysis" is nothing more than a not-so-subtle attempt to make the Bible say just the opposite.

Why was the author's proposed discussion of Jesus as High Priest so "hard to explain"? Certainly it was not because the author himself did not grasp its meaning. Nor was the concept so very difficult to understand. It was not because he was a poor speaker. On the contrary, the sole reason the message was so "hard to explain" was because the people were not receptive.

### ...because you are slow to learn.

The first time the author gives his reason the people were not receiving his message, he says it gently, you are "slow to learn." The author uses the same Greek word in 6:12, where the NIV translates it to "become lazy." The Greek word is νωθρός, which means according to Thayer, "slow, sluggish, indolent, dull, languid."

The KJV and ASV both translate the last part of this sentence as "dull of hearing." The reason is because the sentence does not end with the Greek word noted above, but adds the word ἀκοή, which has to do with hearing, not seeing. In other words, the original recipients of this sermon or lecture were listening to the message as the author gave it; they were not reading it as we do now. It is for this reason we have been alluding to the idea that this New Testament book was first presented as a speech. Surely it was recorded by a stenographer who later published it, so we have its benefit.

### Heb. 5:12. In fact, though by this time you ought to be teachers....

Apparently the original hearers had had many opportunities to learn well the details concerning the Gospel of Christ, but the author knew they had not availed themselves of those opportunities. He must have been well acquainted with them to know their Christian background and training. He may not have been their only instructor, but that was not his concern.

Here I will make another practical point, with a pointed question. How well have *you* learned the facts and teachings of the Bible? If you have read this far in this book, then you certainly have received a significant measure of teaching already. But have you intentionally absorbed enough of God's word that you are prepared to be a teacher? I ask this question understanding that not all people are equipped, either naturally or spiritually, to be teachers. On the other hand, we all spend much of our lives in conversation with other people, and thus unconsciously are teaching others what we know of God and His word.     One of my basic objectives throughout my ministry (including the writing of this book) has been to encourage, even entice, those in my care to become teachers in their turn. Paul knew that in order to keep the Gospel alive and fresh, it was necessary to have an unbroken chain of teachers through the generations, to carry the message faithfully to the next group. He said it to his young friend in II Tim. 2:2: "The things you have heard me say in the presence of many witnesses entrust to reliable men who will also be qualified to teach others."

**...you need someone to teach you the elementary truths of God's word all over again.**

Repetition is a good teacher; by it you not only learn, you retain what you have learned. It is said that aged people remember things they learned in their childhood, but cannot remember what happened yesterday. You probably recall many things you learned as a child, mostly because you repeated them multiple times, so much so that your parents despaired of your finding something else to say.

The Navigators is an organization founded by Dawson Trotman in the early 1930s to encourage people to practice scripture memory. In their early years they distributed packets of small cards, each containing a verse of scripture. People were invited to carry packets in their pockets or purses, take them out during lull times, and go through them over and over again until they had committed them to memory for the rest of their lives. Numerous packets were prepared, each with an increased number of verses. If the people to whom the author of Hebrews had had such a program available, and had used it, there would have been no need to chide them for their lack of knowledge. Later on, the Navigators expanded their encouragement of grasping scripture truths by means of a five-point program of receiving and retaining the word of God. People were urged to: 1) hear; 2) read; 3) study; 4) memorize; and 5) meditate on the word. These elements were likened to the fingers of a hand that could grasp a copy of the Bible: each finger, beginning with the little finger, could hold an increasing weight of the word; but it took the "thumb," meditating on the word, to grasp it fully. Repetition was the key to success.

There comes a time in every Christian's life when he has absorbed a sufficient amount of the word that he "ought to be a teacher." This is the final objective of learning more of God's word.

Once again, I emphasize that it is God's word that is the only valid source of truth, the only basis for legitimate teaching about God and His will.

The people to whom the author was speaking had been taught the word already; he knew it, and he knew they also were aware of it. Remember what he said to them in chapter 2:1: "We have heard!" Therefore, they were without excuse. They were just lazy.

**You need milk, not solid food!**
These words remind us of what we read in Ps. 34:8:
Taste and see that the LORD is good.
When we encounter a food that is strange to us, we begin by gingerly tasting a very small morsel to see whether we will like it or not. Sometimes the first taste is unpleasant, because it is new. If, however, we try it further, we often begin to like it better and then are ready to fill ourselves with it.

Perhaps more to the point of what the author of Hebrews is driving at is what Peter said in I Pet. 2:2: "Like newborn babies, crave pure spiritual milk, so that by it you may grow up in your salvation, now that you have tasted that the Lord is good." In our physical lives, we know that infants are able to digest only their mothers' milk or a substitute that is virtually the same. But as a child grows to adulthood, milk no longer suffices; more powerful food is necessary to sustain physical life. So also in one's spiritual life; a newborn babe in Christ can handle only the rudiments of doctrine until he grows stronger, then he can absorb stronger, more advanced doctrine. Henrietta Mears, the great Christian educator, used to say, "Milk for babes, bread for youth, solid meat for adults." The author of Hebrews had deduced that his hearers were still in the infant stage, spiritually.

**Heb. 5:13. Anyone who lives on milk, being still an infant, is not acquainted with the teaching about righteousness.**

This is pretty harsh criticism of the author's listeners. He was saying that they were not acquainted even with righteousness yet. We all probably think that righteousness is a fundamental topic in our theological understanding. So if his people did not even know about that, they were almost totally ignorant, and as the Psalmist said, they may have needed to limit their intake to mere tasting. Of course, milk does not hurt adults if they drink it, but milk is for infants specifically: they cannot survive without it. Adults need something stronger, more nourishing. And after his admonitions, the author is prepared to give them much more than spiritual milk which he begins in the next chapter.

**Heb. 5:14. But solid food is for the mature....**

The author has already implied this above. Milk will not hurt adults, but solid food will give indigestion to infants.

**...who by constant use have trained themselves to distinguish good from evil.**

It is impossible to over-emphasize this concept. Constant use is the only way you can retain, and make use of, the spiritual knowledge you have already gained in your lifetime. One of the very best ways, perhaps the only way, to be sure you make "constant use" of your spiritual possessions is by a rigid discipline of daily devotions consisting of Bible absorption and prayer. By "rigid" I do not mean to keep a set time of devotions every day even if your house is burning down or you are coming out of the anesthetic following surgery. But surely you ought not to neglect your devotions to prepare for a picnic or because you have company in the house. After all, you think you are treated very badly if someone or something prevents or even delays you from one of your three regular physical meals a day. The world is filled with spiritual anorexics who are unaware they are starving.

Let us not forget that the purpose of taking in "solid food" is not simply to soak it up like a sponge, but for scrubbing the crusted pot which is the world spoiled by sin.

It is exceedingly important for us to be able to "distinguish good from evil." The only way to know that is to know what God has set forth in His commandments, statutes, laws, and ordinances. Many people practice evil deeds and harbor evil thoughts, because they have not tried to learn what God has revealed in His word. It is not enough for us to think we are doing the right thing, especially not just to please ourselves, or to think we are doing good or helping our friends or someone in need. We may be doing ourselves and them more harm than good if we are not sure from God's word that we are in His will.

I am assuming that your sole desire is to do good and not evil, and not be like church members I know who considered themselves pillars of their churches, but apparently had never really thought through all they did and said, whether they were good or evil. There were those whose business practices were shady; there were others whose tongues cut like razors at the most godly people in the church. If they really considered what they were doing, they had to know their lifestyle was contrary to God's purpose. Therefore, I admonish you, and myself, to think carefully about all we do and say, and compare those things in the light of God's word. It is a great omission not to know God's will; it is terrible sin to know it and flout it.

Now, the author makes a brief listing of six rudimentary doctrines, so he can jog the memories of his hearers and then go on to the important subject of Jesus as our Great High Priest in the order of Melchizedek.

**Heb. 6:1.    Therefore, let us leave the elementary teachings about Christ....**

What the author calls teachings could be called literally the "first things of Christ," a foundation for all we need to know about Him. They are the "milk" of the word of God that he spoke of at the end of chapter five. When the author calls them the "first things" or "elementary teachings" of Christ, we must not assume that all teachings about Christ are rudimentary while all other teachings are advanced. He means that these six things about Christ he mentions here are the most basic ones, but the matter of Christ's high priesthood is above these six, and must rest on them.

**...and go on to maturity, not laying again the foundation of....**

The author continues to chide his hearers of having lazy minds. He has already said that they ought to be sufficiently mature spiritually to be able to teach others. He fears they do not know the most simple things about Christ and His will for them and the world. Let us note carefully that the author reminds them that they have been taught these things already. He must have been well acquainted with them to know this. He may have been their teacher, or he was a friend or companion of their former teacher.

Such dullness of hearing is a continuous part of human history. Once two ladies were talking about their Minister's last sermon. One commented, "Yes, he said something about being 'born again.' I don't know what that means." The other said, "Why, he has been talking about that all the time." The questioner said, "I've never heard him talk about that before. I've been coming to church every Sunday for the past twenty-five years, and I never heard him say anything like that." Actually, the same Minister had been there at least twenty-five years, and he never failed to talk about the necessity to have new life in Christ in order to get to heaven. He may not have used the words "born again" in every sermon, but he did so sufficiently often that only a person very dull of hearing could have missed it.

Here follow the six beginners' doctrines that even an immature Christian ought to know and understand. As you read them, check your own thoughts about them, and think how well you would do if you were given a pop quiz on them. After I list them, we will discuss them briefly, so you can explain them to someone else.

**Repentance from acts that lead to death**
**Faith in God**
**Instruction about baptisms**
**The laying on of hands**
**The resurrection of the dead**
**Eternal judgment**

### Repentance from acts that lead to death.

What are the acts that "lead to death"? They are the acts which God considers to be sin. And how may we define sin? According to the Westminster Shorter Catechism's answer to question 14, "Sin is any transgression of, or want of conformity to, the law of God." Mankind's first sin was not eating a piece of fruit, but the disobedience of Adam and Eve contrary to God's command to them. Further, God had warned them that if they disobeyed, they would die on that very day—and they did (Gen. 2:17). They did not die physically that moment, but they did die spiritually. Ezekiel warned the people the same thing in these words (Ezek. 18:4), "The soul who sins is the one who will die." The warning is found sprinkled throughout scripture.

Sins are not merely acts of disobedience, but also failure to obey instructions. He who is instructed by God to do something and fails to do it has sinned just as much as one who has broken one of the ten commandments.

This is stated not only in the Catechism quoted above, but James says the same thing in his little letter (James 4:17): "Anyone, then, who knows the good he ought to do and doesn't do it, sins." James even goes beyond that to say (James 2:10), "For whoever keeps the whole law and yet stumbles at just one point is guilty of breaking all of it."

We may ask, "What are 'acts that lead to death'?" in the light of what we read in I John 5:16-17:

> If anyone sees his brother commit a sin that does not lead to death, he should pray and God will give him life. I refer to those whose sin does not lead to death. There is a sin that leads to death. I am not saying that he should pray about that. All wrongdoing is sin, and there is sin that does not lead to death.

Commentaries are not helpful at this point. They argue about whether it is the sinner or the one who prays who receives life. They wonder how to distinguish between a "sin unto death" and a "sin not unto death;" how heinous must the sin be before it leads to death? The best way to solve the problem is to acknowledge that all scripture is uniform in warning that every sin, no matter how trivial, deserves the punishment of spiritual death; and the only way to escape that punishment is to repent, ask for forgiveness, and seek the help of the Holy Spirit to avoid that sin. The Bible makes room for intercessory prayer, and such prayer often causes God to lead the sinner to penitence, and life.

We must be very careful at this point lest we blame God for failing to answer one of our prayers of intercession for someone else. The Bible does not promise that God will fulfill positively every prayer we make on behalf of another person. God's answer to prayer comes on one condition: the prayer must be in accord with what God has determined to do already. John puts it this way (I John 5:14): "This is the assurance we have in approaching God: that if we ask anything according to his will, he hears us." Too many earnest Christians prefer not to read those critical words, "according to his will." But those are the operative words in this case.

This brings us to the first word of the first doctrine, repentance. It is a most important word, but a most neglected word in our society today. Repentance requires first an acknowledgment that sin has been committed (we have just defined what sin is). But to see the immense importance of repentance, we need only remind ourselves that the first word in the first sermon which John the Baptist preached was "Repent!" (Matt. 3:2). The first word in the first sermon which Jesus Christ preached was "Repent!" (Matt. 4:17). In the very beginning of Mark's gospel, we read that repentance is for "the forgiveness of sins" (Mk. 1:4). This is an exceedingly important teaching: that forgiveness of sins from God is found only after repentance on the part of the sinner. No one is forgiven unless and until he repents. The summary of Peter's great sermon at Pentecost, when the people asked him what they must do, was "Repent!" (Acts 2:38). Paul told Agrippa that his commission to the

Gentiles was to "preach that they should repent...and prove their repentance by their deeds" (Acts 26:20). Peter tells us of God's infinite mercy, "not wanting anyone to perish, but everyone to come to repentance" (II Pet. 3:9). Repentance is the first step in the pathway from death as a result of sin to life through faith in Christ.

### Faith in God.

A good definition of faith is found later in the book (Heb. 11:6): "Without faith it is impossible to please God, because anyone who comes to him must believe that he exists and that he rewards those who earnestly seek him." A good example of faith in God's promises is found in Abraham, who was promised many descendants by God (Gen. 15:6, quoted in Rom. 4:3): "Abram believed the LORD, and he credited it to him as righteousness." And Abraham demonstrated to the world his faith in God through an act of obedience (Heb. 11:8): "By faith Abraham, when called to go to a place he would later receive as his inheritance, obeyed and went, even though he did not know where he was going."

True faith is not the kind that demons possess (James 2:19): "You believe that there is one God. Good! Even the demons believe that—and shudder." They shuddered because they knew their simple mental assent would not save them (Matt. 8:29): "'What do you want with us, Son of God?' they shouted. 'Have you come here to torture us before the appointed time?'"

### Instruction about baptisms.

Let us think about the significance or results of baptism. Some people believe in baptismal regeneration, that is, the act of water baptism automatically and immediately imputes salvation to the person baptized. Among those in Christendom who believe this are the Roman Catholics, Episcopalians, and Lutherans. There are other groups, like the Churches of Christ and some Baptists, who believe that without water baptism a person cannot go to heaven. They rely on words found in the epilogue of Mark's gospel, Mk. 16:16: "Whoever believes and is baptized will be saved." There are two problems with their understanding of this. First, the epilogue is not found in the best ancient manuscripts, and therefore may not be a true part of the Christian canon of infallible teachings. Secondly, that is only the first part of the verse; the second adds, "but whoever does not believe will be condemned." This part of the verse omits entirely anything about baptism, which leads us to reason that belief is more important than baptism. There is another important reason why water baptism is not required for salvation, and it will be discussed when we think about the number of baptisms that actually exist.

There is another group of Christians, those of the Reformed and Presbyterian tradition, of which I am a part, who hold to different significance and results of water baptism. These people think of water baptism as symbolic;

it neither imparts salvation to the person baptized, nor does withholding water baptism prevent a person's entrance into heaven. Matthew 3:15 lends support to this view. There we read about John the Baptist's reticence in administering baptism to Jesus, who responded, "Let it be so now; it is proper for us to do this to fulfill all righteousness." Jesus did not need to be baptized with water in order to be saved; as God He was never lost. He submitted to baptism as symbolic of His true status as a Citizen of heaven.

In thinking about whether it is necessary to be baptized with water in order to be saved, we may wonder when any of the original twelve apostles was baptized? It is hazardous to argue from silence, but that silence implies at least that water baptism was not as significant as to imply it is essential for salvation. Another argument from silence, which is more likely true, is the case of the thief on the cross. After he expressed his belief in Jesus, Jesus assured him (Lu. 23:43): "I tell you the truth, today you will be with me in paradise." It is impossible that after this conversation the thief was taken down from the cross, immersed in a pool of water, let alone the Jordan River, then nailed back on the cross before the soldiers broke his legs and he expired. Yet Jesus assured him he was bound for heaven.

There are other groups within Christianity which do not observe the practice of water baptism; these include the Salvation Army and the Quakers. Surely they are not all relegated to hell merely because they are not baptized with water.

The second thing we should know about baptism is which mode is proper. Some believe that immersion is the only biblical mode, and nothing else is acceptable. A German Baptist Pastor once told his Presbyterian Minister cousin, "Ve don't zbringle dem; ve *buptize* dem!" Some groups practice pouring water over the heads of those being baptized, while others normally sprinkle a few drops of water on their heads. These two groups do not argue with one another, nor does either usually criticize Immersionists for their practice.

Which mode of baptism then is scriptural? Once I was waiting to talk with a Baptist Pastor, and was in his church library. As I scanned the shelves I came upon a book title that intrigued me. It had to do with baptism, and I thought I might get some definitive instruction on why Baptists hold so rigidly to immersion. One chapter listed and explained the seven "biblical" reasons why immersion was the only proper mode of baptism. Six of the reasons given were very general, like, "Immersion is the only sensible way to baptize," but did not refer to any passage of scripture to support the contention. A seventh reason was, "Immersion is the only biblical way to baptize," but not one verse of scripture was given in the brief explanation to prove it. I must confess I was somewhat amused at the failed effort to prove the point.

But if that book gave no biblical proof, what proof is there in scripture to show the proper mode of baptism? To begin with, the Greek verb used for the idea "to baptize" sounds very similar to our English word; it is βαπτίζω. In a search for the meaning of that word, we find that it can mean any one of three different things: to immerse, to pour, and to sprinkle.[1] Its meaning cannot be proved to be limited to immersion. In fact, the New Testament uses the Greek word twice outside the ritual idea, where the meaning cannot be immersion. We read in both Mk. 7:4 and Lu. 11:38 of an instance where the Pharisees criticized Jesus for not requiring His disciples to wash their hands before eating food. The word βαπτίζω is used in both verses; neither can mean that the Pharisees immersed their hands to wash them. Instead, a servant poured water over their hands and the water fell to the ground. Otherwise, the pan would have been ritually defiled irreversibly, and would have had to be destroyed. We must note that wherever the Greek word is used in the New Testament with regard to the ritual of baptism, in not one place is it spelled out what mode is to be used. We must conclude that any mode is acceptable, as far as scriptural direction is concerned, so we ought to accept another person's mode as equally valid with our own.

Another issue in baptism that divides Christians is the age at which baptism is appropriate. Some say that the only biblical time for a person to be baptized is after a public profession of faith in Christ is made. They claim (erroneously) that all baptisms mentioned in the New Testament follow that pattern. In saying that, it must be remembered that Christianity and baptism were just beginning, so it would be expected that new adult Christians, principally, would be baptized.

Others believe that the baptism of infant children of believing parents is in accordance with New Testament teaching. They cite the three examples in the book of Acts[2] where a new believer and his household were baptized together. In those days a household consisted of a person, his spouse, his children of all ages, his servants, and their children as well. It can hardly be supposed that in those three households there were no children under the age of accountability, or who were too young to make a valid profession of faith. So they were baptized on the basis of the new-found faith of at least one of their parents. Many people who accept infant baptism set forth another argument, that is, the analogy of the Old Testament covenant of circumcision, by which male infants were inducted into the number of God's chosen people. That may not be proof, but it is an analogy with which to be reckoned.

The final matter to discuss with regard to baptism is the question of

---

[1]  Thayer defines the Greek verb with such terms as to dip repeatedly, to immerse, submerge, cleanse by dipping or submerging, to wash, to make clean with water, to wash oneself, to bathe. Louw and Nida say it means to wash (in some contexts, possibly by dipping into water). Albrecht Oepke, in his article on the word in Vol. II of TDNT, uses such English words as to dip in or under, to dye [he refers to Rev. 19:13, where Jesus is spoken of as "dressed in a robe dipped in blood"], to immerse, to bathe, to wash.

[2]  Acts 10:47 (Cornelius); 16:15 (Lydia); and 16:33 (the Philippian jailer).

how many baptisms there are. We must remember that the author of Hebrews listed "instruction about baptisms," in the plural, as if there are more baptisms than just one. This question touches on the issue of the significance of baptism with which we began our discussion. Surely we can dismiss as irrelevant the pagan idea of putting a religions initiate in a pit under a platform on which a bull is slaughtered and the blood rains down on the person; this was referred to as "baptism" sometimes. We do find in scripture, however, two distinct kinds of baptism: water baptism, and baptism of the Holy Spirit. We should not be confused by Paul's statement in Eph. 4:4-6: "There is one body...one Spirit...one hope...one Lord, one faith, one baptism, one God and Father of all...." It was Paul who both baptized people with water (I Cor. 1:14-16), and writes much about the baptism of the Holy Spirit, especially in I Cor. 12-14, and specifically in 12:13. So when Paul speaks in the Ephesian passage about "one baptism," surely he means that one is of so much more importance that the other pales into virtual insignificance. That there are two distinct baptisms in scripture is attested by words Mark puts into John the Baptist's mouth (Matt. 3:11): "I baptize you with water for repentance. But after me will come one who is more powerful than I, whose sandals I am not fit to carry. He will baptize you with the Holy Spirit and with fire."

John the Baptist, then, even more specifically implied that one baptism is superior to the other, the baptism of the Holy Spirit. And Paul said that it is the baptism of the Spirit that initiates us into the body of Christ, saying, "For we were all baptized by one Spirit into one body...and we were all given the one Spirit to drink" (I Cor. 12:13). If this is so, we ought to claim biblical basis, as we did at the beginning of our discussion of baptism, that it is the baptism of the Holy Spirit that imparts eternal life to us, and not baptism by water, since water baptism is not required for salvation. If that is the case, then Christians have wasted precious time arguing about what water baptism does or does not do, or how or when it ought to be performed. I therefore plead with you to desist from debating this matter with others.

### The laying on of hands.

This is one topic that non-Charismatics seldom discuss; most avoid it. When they do mention it, they do so in a very limited sense. It has become a rote, a formality. Virtually the only time it is practiced is in a worship service when one or more persons are ordained to some special office like that of Minister, Elder, or Deacon. The person being ordained kneels before the congregation, and the Ministers and Elders present place their hands on his head during the prayer of ordination. This form is a way of saying that God must have selected this person for a special kind of work in the Church and in the world. Further, when the Elders lay their hands on a person to set him apart for a particular work for God, something ought to happen in the life and spirit of that person: God should endow him with some special gift or gifts to equip him for the work God has given him to do on behalf of the Church. If nothing like that happens, then the laying on of the hands of the Elders has no meaning, and bears no fruit for God's glory.

Charismatics, on the other hand, lay hands on people often, and for various reasons, such as for healing or for imparting gifts. Years ago Mike came to my study to talk about a public program of worship his group was planning to present in a park near the church I served. At one point our conversation drifted into the subject of the gift of tongues. After Mike learned that as far as I knew I had not spoken in tongues, he offered to lay his hands on me so that I would have the gift. Some discussion ensued, and finally Mike said, "In the past month I have laid my hands on one hundred twenty-seven people, and not one has failed to receive the gift of tongues." I replied, "Mike, thanks for the offer, but no thanks. I am aware of the gift of tongues, and I agree that it is biblical. I also believe that if God wants me to have the gift of tongues, I should not shy away from it, but be willing to receive it and use it for His glory. But I also believe strongly that the gift of tongues must be imparted by the Holy Spirit. So if I receive the gift of tongues, I want to be sure it is truly from the Holy Spirit and not from any other source." I was grateful that Mike saw my point, and dropped the subject.

There are several places in scripture where we read of the laying on of hands. In Acts 8, we read how Philip preached in Samaria, and many people believed. Peter and John went there to pray for the new converts, because they had not yet received the Holy Spirit. Verse 17 tells us, "Then Peter and John placed their hands on them, and they received the Holy Spirit." Simon the Sorcerer was in the group, and when he saw that the people received the Holy Spirit by the imposition of the disciples' hands, he wanted to purchase that power. But Peter had to rebuke him, "...you thought you could buy the gift of God with money" (verse 20). In Acts 19:6 we read how Paul in Ephesus "placed his hands on them, the Holy Spirit came on them, and they spoke in tongues and prophesied." Paul reminds Timothy in I Tim 4:14 that he had been given a gift "through a prophetic message when the body of elders laid their hands on you." And in II Tim. 1:6 Paul urges Timothy to "...fan into flame the gift of God, which is in you through the laying on of my hands." In all this, Paul warns Timothy that the practice of laying on of hands can be abused by over-use (I Tim. 5:22): "Do not be hasty in the laying on of hands, and do not share in the sins of others."

Jesus Himself practiced the laying on of hands. When His disciples tried to shoo away parents who were bringing their children to be blessed by Jesus, He told them (Matt. 19:14-15): "'Let the little children come to me, and do not hinder them, for the kingdom of heaven belongs to such as these.' When he had placed his hands on them, he went on from there." Jesus laid His hands on other people for a different purpose (Lu. 4:40): "...the people brought to Jesus all who had various kinds of sickness, and laying his hands on each one, he healed them." In noting this instance, we must remember that Jesus did not make a practice of laying hands on people for the purpose of healing them. A brief review of His acts of healing will make that clear.

There are several interesting examples of laying on of hands in the Old Testament. In Ex. 29, the procedure for the consecration of Aaron and his sons, and of the altar was outlined. One bull and two rams were utilized in the process. To consecrate the altar, Aaron and his sons were instructed in verse 10, "Bring the bull to the front of the Tent of Meeting, and Aaron and his sons shall lay their hands on its head." Then Moses was to slaughter the bull, anoint the altar with some of the bull's blood and pour the rest of the blood on the ground before the altar. Then he burned part of the bull on the altar and the rest he burned outside the camp (verses 11-14). For the consecration of the priests, they were to lay their hands on the head of one of the rams; then Moses would slay it, sprinkle its blood on all sides of the altar, and burn the whole ram on the altar. Also, they were to lay their hands on the other ram, Moses would slay it, and touch some of its blood on the right ear lobe, the right thumb and right big toe of each priest, then sprinkle the rest of the blood on all sides of the altar; then with the residue of the blood together with some anointing oil Moses would sprinkle the mixture on Aaron, his sons, and their clothing. Then the second ram was to be burned, and it is then said (verse 22), "This is the ram for the ordination." All this was much more complicated than the process by which Presbyterians ordain their Ministers, Elders, and Deacons. But what is considered crucial is the laying on of hands.

When anyone in Israel needed to have his sins forgiven, he was required to bring an animal for a burnt offering to the priest. Then the penitent laid his hands on the sacrificial animal, and "...it will be accepted on his behalf to make atonement for him" (Lev. 1:4). Similarly, if the whole community of Israel unintentionally committed a sin and then discovered the sin, then a sacrificial bull was to be brought to the priests, and (Lev. 4:15) "The elders of the community are to lay their hands on the bull's head before the LORD, and the bull shall be slaughtered before the LORD," and after several other procedures the people's sin would be atoned for.

A similar procedure was directed for the consecration of the Levites, who were set aside from all other Israelites for special work for the Lord. Two young bulls, and other offerings, were to be brought to the priests. We read in Num. 8:10, "You are to bring the Levites before the LORD, and the Israelites are to lay their hands on them." Then verse 12 says that the Levites were to lay their hands on the heads of both bulls, and they were to be sacrificed, one for a sin offering and one for a burnt offering, to make atonement for the Levites, to consecrate them for their work for the Lord.

Joshua was made Moses' successor in this way, according to Num. 27:18-19:

The LORD said to Moses, "Take Joshua son of Nun, a man in whom is the spirit,[3] and lay your hand on him. Have him stand before Eleazar the priest and the entire assembly and commission him in their presence."

Let us now turn back to the matter of laying on of hands as it is described in the New Testament. As we do so, we ought to ask ourselves whether every time Jesus or a disciple laid hands on someone, that person received the gift of tongues, as some claim; similarly, did they always receive the Holy Spirit whenever hands were laid on them? We also may ask ourselves this pair of questions: Did people lay hands on others at God's specific direction? Or did people lay hands on others in order to force God to respond by imparting the gift of tongues or the gift of the Holy Spirit?

We have already noted above that on at least some occasions, such as in the story in Acts 8:17-19, people received the Holy Spirit when Peter and John laid hands on them; also in Acts 19:6 when Paul laid his hands on the little congregation in Ephesus, not only did they receive the Holy Spirit, but they were able to speak in tongues. From these two incidents we see that people did not always receive the gift of tongues every time they received the Holy Spirit by the laying on of hands. Further, in Mark 16:17 we read that Jesus told His disciples that at least some people who believe "will speak in new tongues." In this context Jesus does not mention that any human was required to lay hands on such people, nor that the Holy Spirit would be given to the people who were enabled to speak in tongues, but every other place in scripture where a spiritual gift is given, it is given through the instrumentality of the Holy Spirit, so we presume the same here.

Probably the most prominent passage of scripture where both the Holy Spirit and the gift of tongues were given is in the classic description of the descent of the Holy Spirit at Pentecost, in Acts 2. When that great event occurred, however, there was no man equipped to lay hands on the one hundred twenty people gathered there, but the gifts were given nevertheless. In like manner, what may be the first instance of the imparting of the Holy Spirit to Gentiles, along with the gift of tongues is found in Acts 10, when Peter preached to Cornelius, his household, and his neighbors. The Holy Spirit came upon them, and they were able to speak in tongues (verses 44-46). When Paul had his experience on the road to Damascus, Acts 9:17 tells us that Ananias "placed his hands on Saul," and said to him, "Brother Saul, the Lord...has sent me so that you may see again and be filled with the Holy Spirit." It is not recorded that Paul received the gift of tongues on this occasion; however, we know that at some time Paul did receive that gift, because he boasted in I Cor. 14:18, "I thank God that I speak in tongues more than all of you."

There is at least one occasion in scripture where a person had received the Holy Spirit before anyone laid hands on him. This is found in the story of the election of the first Board of Deacons in the apostolic church, recorded in Acts 6. Beginning in verse 5 we read that "They chose Stephen, a man full

---

[3] A marginal reading capitalizes "Spirit."

of faith and of the Holy Spirit;" and in the next verse, "They presented these men to the apostles, who prayed and laid their hands on them." Therefore, it was not necessary for anyone to lay hands on Stephen for him to receive the Holy Spirit. In addition, we note that although Stephen preached to a diverse group of people in Jerusalem ("Jews of Cyrene and Alexandria as well as the provinces of Cilicia and Asia" Acts 6:9), there is no indication that he spoke, or was able to speak, in other tongues. Nor was it necessary, because all those people were able to understand, and even speak, the Greek language.

From all these passages we must conclude that it is not necessary for a human intermediary to be used by God either to confer the Holy Spirit on another person or to transmit the gift of tongues to him. Nor is it necessary to suppose that every person who has received the Holy Spirit also must have received the spiritual ability to speak in tongues.

Earlier we asked another pair of questions about laying on of hands, whether disciples were always moved by the Holy Spirit to lay hands on people to impart gifts or for any other spiritual purpose, or whether there were occasions when people, on their own initiative, laid hands on others in order to try to force God to impart gifts He may not have wanted to give. This may be more difficult to discuss than the question whether the laying on of hands was necessary in order for God to impart spiritual gifts. However, we may attempt to answer this question by referring again to the incident when Peter and John went to Samaria to lay hands on the new believers there (Acts 8:9-24), after Deacon Philip had preached to them. We read that Simon the Sorcerer was one of those who "believed and was baptized" (verse 13). After Peter and John had laid hands on the believers, Simon saw that the Holy Spirit was given to the people and great "signs and miracles" (verse 13) occurred, so he offered money to receive that power to impart such things, but Peter rebuked him sharply for thinking such a thought. This seems sufficient evidence that the ability to give the Holy Spirit and spiritual gifts is reserved for God alone, and He has never given that authority to anyone else. Therefore, if anyone claims today to be in control of his own spiritual gifts, to turn them on or withhold them at will is under the same stern warning that Peter gave to Simon the Sorcerer.

### The resurrection of the dead.

One severely neglected thought among Christians is that every person is raised from the dead, both Christians and non-Christians. Of course most non-Christians do not believe in the resurrection, so this is not a problem for them. Some Christians think that non-Christians die and go to hell, and others believe that non-Christians are annihilated at death, so there is no more life for them nor even existence. But the Bible teaches that every human that dies will be raised from the dead.

The best way to approach this little-acknowledged fact is to see that the

216

Bible speaks of two separate resurrections. They are conveniently noted together in the same chapter, Revelation 20. In verses 4-5 we read of what John calls the "first resurrection." Those who are raised from the dead at that time are described as

> those who had been beheaded because of their testimony for Jesus and because of the word of God. They had not worshiped the beast or his image and had not received his mark on their foreheads or their hands. They came to life and reigned with Christ a thousand years....This is the first resurrection.

All other people are lumped into a second category, consisting of those not included in the "first resurrection." It is not stated explicitly in the rest of the chapter that they are the "second resurrection," but that is surely implied by verse 5, "The rest of the dead did not come to life until the thousand years were ended;" and by verse 12, "I saw the dead, great and small, standing before the throne, and books were opened."

Please be aware that all humans who have ever lived or shall live are named in these two categories; there is no third category. Years ago I heard a theory that those described in verse 4 are in some fashion an elite group of Christians, and these alone participate in the first resurrection while the rest of Christians must wait until the end of the thousand years (the millennium), when they will be raised to life along with all those who will be relegated to the Lake of Fire although they themselves will finally arrive in heaven "but only as one escaping through the flames" (I Cor. 3:15). We must be careful, however, to recognize that John does not mention such a division between Christians whereby only a fraction of Christians will be raised to enjoy the blessings of the presence of Christ for that millennium.

An additional caution is necessary as we study this matter of resurrection in Rev. 20. In the first ten verses John is speaking about those who are physically dead and will be raised from the dead. But in verses 11-15 his attention is given to those who not only were dead physically but also were and are dead spiritually. This, incidentally, is one of the best ways to describe all those in the second category: "the dead."

At this point it is most important for us to agree on the definition of the term "resurrection." Here is one: *Resurrection means the bringing back to life of something that had been alive and had died.* That is, there is a succession of three states of an object for resurrection to occur. Two illustrations ought to help us understand this. For one, a stone can never be resurrected because it had never been alive. (God could make stones come alive, as Jesus implied at His triumphal entry into Jerusalem. The Pharisees urged Him to rebuke His disciples for praising Him, and He replied [Lu. 19:40], "I tell you...if they keep quiet, the stones will cry out.") The second illustration is you, the reader. You are alive now, but you have not yet died, so you cannot now be resurrected; you may be only after you have died.

It is now important to point out specifically the practical result of this definition. You are now alive, body, soul, and spirit. When you die, it is your body that dies and goes to the grave. Your spirit, however, does not die. Rather, it goes immediately to heaven to be with the Lord. Paul makes this clear in Phil. 1:22-24:

> If I am to go on living in the body, this will mean fruitful labor for me. Yet what shall I choose? I do not know! I am torn between the two: I desire to depart and be with Christ, which is better by far; but it is more necessary for you that I remain in the body.

If what Paul says is true, then you see that when you die, it is not your spirit that dies, but like the thief on the cross, your spirit will go immediately to Paradise when you die. Therefore, if it is only the body that dies, and not the spirit, then the spirit cannot be resurrected since it did not die; only the body can be resurrected. This should be proof sufficient for anyone, but here is one more scripture reference to prove the point. In Rom. 8:11, Paul talks about life from the dead, and says, "If the Spirit of him who raised Jesus from the dead is living in you, he who raised Christ from the dead will also give life to your mortal bodies through his Spirit, who lives in you." Paul specifies that it is your "mortal body" that is raised from the dead, not your spirit.

There is as great confusion about the definition of resurrection as there is about how many people will be raised, as we mentioned at first. Surely the confusion about how many are raised is caused principally by the dispute over the definition of the term. But the dispute is aggravated further in large part by two issues.

First, there is confusion over what Paul meant when he spoke about the nature of the resurrection in I Cor. 15:42-44:

> So it will be with the resurrection of the dead. The body that is sown is perishable, it is raised imperishable; it is sown in dishonor, it is raised in glory; it is sown in weakness, it is raised in power; it is sown a natural body, it is raised a spiritual body.

The confusion is totally dissipated when one notes carefully that in this passage Paul is speaking throughout about a body, not a soul or spirit. That point must be remembered and imposed on the statement that a person's body "is sown a natural body, it is raised a spiritual body." Paul does not say that when a person dies his body is "sown" (buried) in the ground while his spirit is raised. This is a stumbling block for many people, however. They believe that because Paul speaks of a "spiritual body," he really means "a spirit, not a body." Paul is talking about a body in both instances, but he uses two modifiers to show that the nature of that body is changed in the resurrection. It should be helpful to see the two Greek words Paul uses as those modifiers. The first modifier, translated "natural," is ψύχικος, which is difficult to translate into English, but we might coin a term for it: "soulish," a soulish body, nevertheless a physical body. The second Greek modifier is πνευμάτικος, which we could call "spiritish," a spiritish body, nevertheless still a physical body. This is supported by the rest of I Cor. 15, the great resurrection chapter in the Bible. Especially in verses 12-20 Paul repeatedly reminds us that because Christ was raised from the dead, we who believe in Him shall be raised from the dead also, and that if Christ was not raised then we have no hope of resurrection. Since every Christian believes that it was Christ's body that was raised from the dead (His tomb was empty), then "when he appears, we shall be like him" (I John 3:2). Thus we see that the Bible speaks indubitably of a bodily resurrection.

Secondly, many people have an almost insuperable problem with God's ability to gather a dead physical body back together and make it alive again. They even ask many misleading questions in order to avoid the fact of physical resurrection. Some people, for instance, don't like the nose God has given them, and they do not want to think of living through eternity with such a nose, even though they may have had surgery to change its appearance. Others worry whether a person must spend eternity with a missing arm if they lost it in an accident in the world. Or worse yet, will a "thalidomide baby" be forced to live forever with no arms at all, because he was born without them? Such doubters ought to remember that Jesus said,[4] "If your right hand causes you to sin, cut it off and throw it away. It is better for you to lose one part of your body than for your whole body to go into hell" (Matt. 5:30). Let me propose an even more perplexing question. Suppose a Christian missionary should go to a tribe of cannibals and be eaten by two of them. Will his body take their bodies to heaven, or will their bodies cause his body to burn in hell forever? To complicate the matter, suppose one cannibal subsequently becomes a Christian. Will half the missionary's body go to heaven and the other to hell? Of course, it is utterly foolish to ask such questions. If God could take the dry bones mentioned in Ezek. 37 and bring them back to whole, living bodies in the world, surely He could do the same for all bodies that are bound for heaven—as well as all those bodies bound for hell. Also, if God could create Adam's body in the first place, surely He can simply remake it at the resurrection.

Probably the very best proof that can be produced regarding whether it is the body that is raised from the dead and not the spirit is to be found in the details of Jesus' own resurrection. Surely you are familiar with that historical event. If you are not, or if you care to review the story, I invite you to read carefully the whole matter found in the four Gospels, namely, Matt. 28 (the whole chapter); Mk. 16 (the whole chapter); Lu. 24:1-49 (especially verses 36-43); and John 20:1-21:14 (especially 20:26-28). In those narratives it is impossible to conceive that the four Gospel authors intended anything but to express in the most impressive terms that it was Jesus' body which was raised from the dead, and not merely His Spirit. So Jesus, who is God, did raise up

---

[4] Lest anyone, in a fit of despondency over his sinfulness, should literally cut off his hand or foot, or pluck out his eye, let me urge you to consider a much better alternative: repent of your sin, ask God to forgive it, and determine with the help of His Spirit to turn in disgust from whatever sins plague you.

His own physical body from the dead (as He claimed He would, in John 10:17-18). The argument of the whole of I Cor. 15 (the great Resurrection Chapter of the Bible) is predicated on the assumption that if Jesus rose bodily from the dead, then all His followers would experience the same event.

Another proof that because Jesus Christ was raised bodily from the dead we believers shall also be raised bodily from the dead is found in the very important passage that describes exactly what will happen when Jesus makes His second appearance in the world. That passage is I Thess. 4:13-18; I urge you to read that passage carefully also. There you will note that as Jesus begins His return trip to the earth, God will bring with Him all believers who have already died. As Jesus and the saints approach the world, however, Paul says that the dead in Christ shall rise first, that is, before the living Christians are caught up to meet the Lord in the air. Here it is most important to realize that the believers who return from heaven with Christ are the very same persons who will rise (first) from the earth. The only way to understand that is to realize that it is the spirits of the saints who will return with Christ; and their dead bodies will be raised from the ground, made alive again, and reunited with their spirits, "and so [or, 'in this manner'] we will be with the Lord forever."

For our purposes in this study, it is not necessary to examine the events surrounding the time of the resurrection. But for those who are interested, you are invited to turn to the *textus classicus* regarding this matter, which is I Thess. 4:13-18.


### Eternal Judgment.

We come now to the final "rudimentary" doctrine mentioned by the author of Hebrews in 6:1-2. Later in his sermon, the author tells us (9:27), "...man is destined to die once, and after that to face judgment." All Christians will be judged, as well as all non-Christians. Some people tend to think that Christians will not be judged. But Paul shows us in I Cor. 3:10-15 that the works of Christians will be judged. He talks about Jesus Christ as the foundation for our faith, and about the works of Christians that are built on Christ. Some Christians' works will endure the test, but others' works will be consumed. Within these verses we read:

> If any man build on this foundation using gold, silver, costly stones, wood, hay or straw, his work will be shown for what it is, because the Day will bring it to light. It will be revealed with fire, and the fire will test the quality of each man's work. If what he has built survives, he will receive his reward. If it is burned up, he will suffer loss; he himself will be saved, but only as one escaping through the flames.

The implication of these words is that people who have established their lives on the foundation which is Christ Jesus have already been justified, or judged righteous by God, so their eternal destiny in heaven is assured. However, what they have done for Christ in their Christian lives will be judged for the purpose of determining their reward.[5]

For evidence that those who have not received Jesus Christ as Savior and Lord will be judged and condemned to eternal punishment, we return to Rev. 20:7-15. We read in verses 7 to 12 about the end of Satan, the beast, and the false prophet, who are thrown into the lake of fire. And verse 15 talks about all unbelieving humans: "If anyone's name was not found written in the book of life, he was thrown into the lake of fire," where Satan and his underlings already exist.

That the punishment of all these wicked people is eternal is shown by what the end of Rev. 20:10 says, "They will be tormented day and night for ever and ever." There are no better words than these to prove that there is an "eternal judgment," as the author of Hebrews avers. Even Jesus affirms the everlastingness of the fires of hell in His discussion of caring for little children, where He says in Matt. 18:8, "If your hand or your foot causes you to sin, cut it off and throw it away. It is better for you to enter life maimed or crippled than to have two hands or two feet and be thrown into eternal fire." Jesus reaffirms this in his parable of dividing good and bad people like dividing sheep and goats, and said (Matt. 25:41): "Then he will say to those on his left, 'Depart from me, you who are cursed, into the eternal fire prepared for the devil and his angels.'"

Some people question whether the "lake of burning sulfur," or the "lake of fire," is not merely the same kind of symbolism which fills the book of Revelation, implying that it must not be nearly as bad as it sounds. If those words are mere symbolism, someone has remarked, then how much more horrible must be the reality behind the symbolism! There is no escape from the stark reality of what the Bible teaches about "eternal judgment."

Many soft-hearted souls cringe at the thought of such horror. They cannot believe that a loving God would do such a thing to any of His creatures. I have heard people say, "I cannot possibly believe in a God who would do or even plan such a thing." To those who think such thoughts, I must respond, "Whether you like it or not, the God of the Bible has not only thought to do such a thing; He is even now carrying it out."

Consider this side of the issue. Suppose God did relent some day, and allow such unrepentant scoundrels into heaven after only five years in the lake of fire, or after a thousand years. If that happened, then heaven would immediately cease to be heaven for those who sincerely had repented of their sins. For the rest of eternity, they would shudder in fear of experiencing the same kinds of molestations they had endured through life in this wicked world. I think those with soft hearts should think what kind of God would do that to His beloved saints.

So much for the "rudiments" of the faith as outlined in the first two verses of Hebrews 6.

[5] For scriptural evidence that there is a scale of rewards in heaven, remember Jesus' parables of the talents, and other like passages.

**Heb. 6:3.  And God permitting, we will do so.**

What is it that we will do now?  After such a long dissertation on the rudiments, the author has encouraged us to go on to "solid food...for the mature" (5:14).  He echoes the same sentiment in 6:1, saying, "...let us leave the elementary teachings about Christ and go on to maturity...."

Before you scan the next paragraph, try to determine for yourself the identity of those the author describes in verses 4-5.  Is he talking about Christians or non-Christians?  Your answer may help you to determine how you interpret verse 6.  The truth contained there is highly important; it is one of the watersheds of Christian doctrine.  So read, and think, carefully, before you give your final answer to that question.

**Heb. 6:4-5.  It is impossible for those who have once been enlightened, who have tasted the heavenly gift, who have shared in the Holy Spirit, who have tasted the goodness of the word of God and the powers of the coming age....**

First, let us simply list the five qualities or characteristics of the people the author is talking about, and note briefly the two possible ways they might be interpreted.  Then we will try to answer the question whether the author is talking about Christians or non-Christians, before we tackle verse 6.

### 1. once been enlightened.

These people have been given enlightenment, so we would think, or hope, that they were enabled to see something of God's truth.  On the other hand, although they may have been privileged to see the truth, they may not have looked carefully enough to understand or absorb what they saw.  Isaiah said about such people, in 6:9:

> Be ever hearing, but never understanding;
>
> be ever seeing, but never perceiving.

Is one "enlightenment" sufficient to make them Christians?

### 2. tasted the heavenly gift.

There is a difference between tasting something then spitting it out, and devouring large quantities of it.  A taster would gain no benefit from the food, while a devourer would be nourished for a long time to come.  For instance, when Jesus was about to be crucified, someone "offered him wine to drink, mixed with gall; but after tasting it, he refused to drink it" (Matt. 27:34).

### 3. shared in the Holy Spirit.

We remember that King Saul was so possessed of the Holy Spirit that he was able to prophesy among the prophets of Israel, but on more than one occasion the Spirit departed from him (I Sam. 16:14; and by implication I Sam. 28:6).  So Saul had but fleeting experiences with the Holy Spirit, and at the end of his life he committed such an abominable act (inquiring for news from the witch of Endor) that it is possible that he did not get to heaven. Paul urges us that we ought to "be filled with the Spirit," instead of being intoxicated with wine. Would a Christian have only a casual brush with the Spirit of God, or must he at least possess the Spirit?

### 4. tasted the goodness of the word of God.

Here is the idea of "tasting" again. How many Christians merely taste or nibble at the word of God? Do we spend as much time grasping and consuming the God's word as we do in working for and eating physical food? Which is more beneficial in the long run? Would we be called Christians by this criterion?

### 5. [tasted] the power of the coming age.

Again, is it enough for a Christian to merely brush by a thought or two about his destiny? The apostle Paul thought not, when he said that there is a crown of righteousness to be given to him and "to all who have longed for [Christ's] appearing" (II Tim. 4:8).

What, now, is your verdict? Is the author of Hebrews referring to Christians, or to non-Christians here? I think you will agree with me that his description is rather nebulous and not a clear definition of what is a "Christian." Now that you have struggled with this question, let me invite you to assume, at least for the sake of our argument, that the author is talking about Christians. I believe this will make my task harder as I seek to interpret the real meaning of verse 6, but let me try.

### Heb. 6:4, 6. It is impossible for those [described by these five characteristics]... if they fall away, to be brought back to repentance, because to their loss they are crucifying the Son of God all over again and subjecting him to public disgrace.

Here is the whole issue before us compressed into three verses of scripture. Let us sort out its parts, in order to accomplish two things: first, to discover what the controversy is; and secondly, to see what is the best settlement for that controversy.

### It is impossible....

This is a very strong statement. And for at least the part of the question to which it applies, it is total, final, irrevocable, irreversible. We need to remember this as we study the next few parts of the issue.

### ...if they fall away....

It is important for us to determine, insofar as possible, *from what* it is said they fall away, and *toward what* they fall. In attempting to do this, we seem to be left completely on our own to supply those objects. In our attempt to answer what those objects are, we must be perfectly honest and admit that every one of us is biased in one direction or another, from our parents, our Minister or Priest or church, our denomination, and other people we have heard or their books we have read on the subject.

What are some of the things you have heard? Surely you have heard that some people claim that the people described in these verses have fallen away from salvation and to a state of lostness or perdition. Some say that those people have fallen away from the five qualities which here describe them. But if that is so, to what have they fallen, to perdition? And if so, what is entailed in their falling away from those qualities? How do you fall away from being *enlightened*? By forgetting what you saw, or by erasing it from your memory? How do you reverse or eliminate a *taste* for a heavenly gift? (Studies show that a fleeting odor or taste can bring back memories after decades have elapsed.) If you have *shared* in the Holy Spirit, how can you excise Him from your being? Can you eliminate the *taste* (again) of either the word of God, or of the powers of the coming age? Unfortunately, many people think that what falls away is salvation itself. But by a careful study of what the rest of these verses say, we shall see they contradict themselves.

**...it is impossible [I repeat] to be brought back to repentance....**

Aha! Here is the author's answer to the question we asked above! If a person must be brought back to *repentance*, then he must have fallen away from *repenting*.

This happens to be one of two crucial matters we must acknowledge, if we hope to understand aright what the author is saying. The author did not, I repeat emphatically, *did not* say, "it is impossible to be brought back to *salvation*," but, "it is impossible to be brought back to *repentance*." Therefore, the author is not talking about whether a person can lose his salvation. If it were so, such a thing must be proved by some other passage of scripture.

**...because....**

On this single word hangs the second of the two most important points to be made in order to understand what the author of Hebrews is saying. Therefore, please do not be offended at our deliberating over one word. You will see how important this word is to the whole argument.

The Greek sense used here is translated in a variety of ways in our English versions. Older people grew up on the KJV, and it, along with the ASV, translate the word as "seeing." Several translations use the highly ambiguous English word "since," including the RSV, NASV, Weymouth, and Williams. Three versions, the Amplified Bible, NEB, and Phillips use the word "for." The Living Bible chose the word "if." Finally, the TEV and NIV translate the Greek sense as "because." In my estimation, all these translations are at best inadequate, and at worst very misleading. The translation closest to the Greek sense is in a footnote in our NIV, "while."

Now look at what our Greek Testament actually says. You may have noticed that I omitted the use of "Greek word or term" in the paragraph above; I did that intentionally, as you will see. I need to get rather technical to explain the situation, and your recollection of English grammar should help you follow my argument.

Verse 6 of chapter 6 of Hebrews contains three Greek participles each of which describes some action of the people identified in these verses. The first is at the beginning of the verse, and is παραπεσόντας, and is translated as "if they fall away." This word is what is called a present aorist participle, and the important thing to know about it is that it identifies an action that is punctiliar in nature, something that happens in a moment, not something that takes a period of time to do. It is like falling off a wagon: the fall itself is instantaneous, although you may remain off the wagon for a long time. So also, the act of falling from repentance happens in an instant, but the lack of repentance may continue.

The other two participles in verse 6 are found near the end of the verse. Unlike the first one, these are present active participles instead of aorist, which means that they are durative[6] rather than punctiliar. In other words, instead of their identifying an instantaneous event, they speak of things that continue to happen over a period of time, but not necessarily forever. They can be terminated by a new act, which in this case is to repent.

For your information, the first of these two Greek participles is ἀνασταυροῦντας, and means "to crucify again or afresh." In Greek secular writings the term means more like "to raise up on a cross," and we do well to keep this idea in mind as we think about what the author of Hebrews is saying.

I must add a parenthesis. We will see it pointed out and reemphasized later in Hebrews that Jesus Christ died but once for the sins of the world. He did not die twice or many times, nor is it necessary for Him to die one or more times daily for our sins to be forgiven. The author implies here that whenever we commit a sin, that sin is another cause of Christ's dying on the cross to pay the penalty for that sin. The effect is that every time I sin, that sin caused Christ to die for sin. This thought is one of the most powerful deterrents to my sinning. If I love my Savior, I certainly do not want to be the cause of His crucifixion again and again; and I do love Him.

The last of these Greek participles is παραδειγματίζοντας, which speaks of "putting to open shame, or subjecting to public disgrace." If this term is divided into its two Greek components, it basically means "beside"

---

[6] Lenski, HEBREWS AND JAMES, p. 186, admits that the last two participles are durative, but he treats them as causal, but they cannot be both. The durative is what the author of Hebrews intended, or else he would have selected a different tense for the terms.

plus "show or exhibit," and that leads to the idea of setting forth as an example, and especially "holding up to infamy." This means in practical terms that whenever I commit a sin, even when no person ever learns of that sin, still Jesus Christ is demeaned by people in the world. The Savior is put to ridicule by people. Again I say, if I truly love my Savior I certainly will not want that to happen to Him.

The English word which is the prime key to a correct understanding of this passage actually has no Greek word in the text as a counterpart. Why then should we have spent so much time discussing the importance of a word that does not even exist in the original text? The reason is that without including the word in an English translation, it is impossible to make a correct or sensible translation of the three Greek participles we have been discussing. That important English word is the word we earlier saw variously translated as "seeing," "since," "if," "for," and "because."

What makes this English word so important? It connects two related thoughts, and the relationship must be established properly, or we may find ourselves caught in a doctrine few Christians want to entertain, and which is totally untrue as well. One thought precedes the important word, and the other succeeds it. The first thought which the author presents is, "...it is impossible...to be brought back to repentance." Although we have noted that some people believe this passage refers to one's losing his salvation, let me emphasize that the thought of salvation is not implicit here. The author is talking about repentance, stated so clearly that the author uses that word.

Now, if the English word used here is "seeing," or any other word commonly used in our English translations as noted above, then the author would have been saying that once a person becomes a Christian, that is, he has salvation, it would be impossible for him ever to get saved again, *because*, or *seeing*, he has fallen away from salvation. And if that were so, we all would agree[7] that it were better for nobody ever to get saved and then lose his salvation, because that would condemn him to eternal damnation without hope of remedy.

Thankfully, neither the idea of losing salvation, nor the permanency of whatever loss there is, is to be found in this passage. In order to make clear what the author is driving at is to use some English term such as "as long as," or "during which time," the person crucifies Christ again and puts Him to open shame. Let me put the whole sentence together, so you can see all of what the author was saying in this sentence. "[It is impossible] to restore them to repentance again, during which time they are crucifying again for their own sakes the Son of God, and are exposing him to public shame."

So you can be certain that you understand correctly what the author is

---

[7] One exception to this universal agreement is found in the LIVING BIBLE, verses 4-6, "There is no use trying to bring you back to the Lord again if you have once understood the Good news and tasted for yourself the good things of heaven...[plus the other 3 things]...and then have turned against God.

saying, please participate in the following exercise, which I am sure will make you see it clearly. First of all, think in your innermost being of some sin you have committed in the past. (Do not speak to anyone about what you are thinking. Let it be solely within yourself.) As you think about that sin, try to recall how much time was spent in committing it. While you were committing that sin, did you find any remorse, sorrow, or repentance creeping into your mind, before the sinful act or thought was completed? Surely you will find that repentance was totally absent from you. However, after the sin had reached its end (if you were a Christian at that time), there came a flood of grief that you had once again disappointed your Savior, as when Peter denied Christ. In other words, while you were sinning, you were not repenting. After the sin was ended, you were filled with repentance and realized that it was your sin that caused your Savior to go to the cross and be mocked, spat upon, and derided by the angry crowd.

To summarize, when you "fell away," that is, when you committed a sin, your mind was so filled with the thoughts of sinning that it was impossible for you to repent during that time. But when your godly senses returned, you immediately repented.

In all this there is no hint in Hebrews that you lost your salvation. Since, however, any argument from silence is no proof, we must turn to other passages of scripture to show us whether a person also loses his salvation when he commits a subsequent sin. Please refer to Rom. 8:38-39, which tells us that not one thing in heaven, on earth, or in hell, can "separate us from the love of God that is in Christ Jesus our Lord." Again, see I John 5:13, "I write these things to you who believe in the name of the Son of God so that you may know that you have eternal life." If it is eternal, then it cannot end; if it can end from any cause whatsoever, it cannot be called "eternal." John tells us in I John 1:9, "If we confess our sins, he is faithful and just and will forgive us our sins and purify us from all unrighteousness." Jesus Himself said the same thing even more powerfully, in John 10:28-29, "I give them eternal life, and they shall never perish; no one can snatch them out of my hand...no one can snatch them out of my Father's hand." Thirty-seven times the New Testament says that new life given to those who trust in Christ and commit their lives to him is called either "eternal" or "everlasting" life.

**Heb. 6:7. Land that drinks in the rain often falling on it and that produces a crop useful to those for whom it is farmed receives the blessing of God.**

This verse is like a parable in a way; yet it contains reality as well. The author is talking about inanimate land, an entity that makes no choices for either good or evil; to work and produce or to loaf and waste. The fact is that some land produces much fruit, while other land produces little or no fruit. See Jesus' parable of the sower ( Mk. 4:1-20 and parallel passages in

Matt. 13:1-23 and Lu. 8:4-15) to confirm this. Naturally, that land which produces fruit benefits the farmer, but the author goes on to say that the land "receives the blessing of God." This I find intriguing: that inanimate land, of which nothing is said of its doing anything for God, and which has no sense of pleasure or pain, is blessed by God.

What do we suppose is the author's point of this parable? We may get a clue from the fact that this verse follows on verse 6. That clue seems to be that a person who remains faithful to God will first of all bear fruit *for God*, and will be greatly blessed *by God*. The converse thought of the next verse should aid in our interpretation.

**Heb. 6:8. But land that produces thorns and thistles is worthless and is in danger of being cursed. In the end it will be burned.**

We easily recognize that this is in fact the converse of verse 7 in general, yet with a significant difference. Verse 7 says that fruitful land "receives the blessing of God," with no equivocation whatever beyond the condition of fruitfulness. Verse 8, on the other hand, equivocates on the result of land that gives useless produce (thorns and thistles); it "is *in danger of* being cursed." That is to say that useless land may some day become useful. The verse does not make it explicit, but it is implicit that if land in the future does become fruitful, it also will be blessed by God. The final sentence of the verse is not necessarily a final judgment. Only if a piece of land persists unfruitful to the end, then it is cursed by God and will be burned.

About the year 1920, my father inherited an eighty-acre farm from his uncle. The farm was right on the edge of the Colorado River near the southeastern corner of California. The whole farm supported nothing but sagebrush and a few other weeds, hardly fit for a few sheep to graze. The uncle realized, however, that the land was rich loamy soil. If it could be irrigated it should be excellent farmland. An attempt had been made at the beginning of that century to divert some of the river water for irrigation, but the attempt failed. Many years later a means of irrigation was devised, and a group of businessmen began to buy up all the land in the area. My father finally sold his acreage, and the enterprising people tilled the land, washed out the salt, and irrigated it. My wife Claire and I drove past the area in 1988, and as far as eye could see, the irrigated land brought forth lush crops of corn, alfalfa, and other beautiful crops. The land was transformed by the water brought to it. So also, a person who is filled with the sacred moisture of the Holy Spirit will be transformed, will become fruitful for the Lord, and will receive eternal blessing in heaven.

Let us tie these thoughts into the teaching of verse 6. Verse 7 says nothing about a particular piece of land's becoming unfruitful after it has borne fruit. Of course, that is possible, in agriculture. But every parable has its limits beyond which we must not stretch our analogies. So from the parable we obtain the corroboration with our conclusion from verse 6 that once a person becomes a fruitful servant for Christ, he will remain that way, and will be ushered into heaven ultimately, because he has received Jesus Christ as Savior and Lord, and has the Holy Spirit within him to bear fruit for the Master.

### Heb. 6:9. Even though we speak like this, dear friends, we are confident of better things in your case—things that accompany salvation.

In the passage from 5:11 through 6:8, the author has been chiding his listeners/readers. You may think the admonitions either gentle or rough, and your evaluation surely depends on your own level of commitment to Jesus Christ. If his words apply to you in but a small measure, then you will think them to be very light. On the other hand, if your walk with Christ is minimal, then these words ought to hit you with much strength.

Beginning here however, the author changes his thrust from exhortations and warnings for the people to words of confidence in their security in Jesus, and in their perseverance toward Him. He says, "we are confident of better things in your case," almost as if he had been talking about other people previously. It is as if he was saying, "I believe you all are saved, although I do not have the final say or insight with regard to that. But I will assume it is so. However, I want to warn you about the symptoms both of unfruitfulness and of unbelief, and remind you of their consequences."

### Heb. 6:10. God is not unjust; he will not forget your work and the love you have shown him...

Now the author presents them with an even greater compliment, and a further promise. He must have loved them dearly in order to speak so lovingly to them.

We are fully aware of God's justice (which balances His love), but we often neglect to remind ourselves of that justice. We need to be fully aware of His justice in this context, so that we do not deceive ourselves into thinking that it is God's love alone which covers all our sins, when it is His forgiveness based on our confession of sin and repentance that makes the way for His forgiveness.

That God never forgets their work and love (or ours) is a source of great comfort. He keeps accurate records (the books noted in Rev. 20 contain those records). I am sure God really does not need written records; He is able to remember everything from beginning to end, not only of creation but of all eternity. He is not a slave to what is written as was King Xerxes (biblical Ahasuerus) who had to have the court records read to him before he remembered Mordecai's warning of a plot against his life (see the story in Esther 2:21-23 and 6:1-10).

What was the "work and love" which God remembered about the author's hearers? The author answers that question in the next clause.

**...as you have helped his people and continue to help them.**

We may not know the specific details of the works of mercy and love in which those people participated, but they must have been significant. We know, however, that throughout scripture we are reminded to lend aid to those in need. Before the children of Israel entered the Promised Land, Moses gave them this strong injunction (Deut. 15:11): "There will always be poor people in the land. Therefore I command you to be openhanded toward your brothers and toward the poor and needy in your land." James defines "religion" by allusion to helping those in need (Jas. 1:27): "Religion that God our Father accepts as pure and faultless is this: to look after orphans and widows in their distress and to keep oneself from being polluted by the world." In fact, there seems to be but one exception to this universal admonition; that is when Jesus was incarnate, residing with His disciples. A woman with an alabaster jar of very expensive perfume broke it and poured it on His head, but the disciples objected, thinking the perfume ought to have been sold and the money given to the poor. But He said, "The poor you will always have with you, but you will not always have me" (Matt. 26:6-13).

In taking care of the physical needs of the poor, Jesus' disciples ought not to neglect making spiritual offerings to them also; after all, spiritual life is infinitely more important than physical life, since it lasts so much longer. When Jesus was teaching in the synagogue in Nazareth, He read from the scripture for the day, which happened to be Is. 61:1-2, and applied it to Himself. Among the things He was sent to do was this: "...to preach good news to the poor" (Lu. 4:18). If Jesus thought this was important for Him to do, surely it should be one of our principal tasks as we live for Him.

The people in New Testament times were urged to give aid to those in need, both physical and spiritual need, and were commended when they did it. If it was important for them to do so, it is equally important for us to follow suit.

**Heb. 6:11. We want each of you to show this same diligence to the very end....**

Here the author of Hebrews continues to urge constancy in demonstrating their faith in Jesus, so he would be reassured of their faith in Christ and of their salvation. Jesus knows the hearts of the people; therefore He knows whether they have remained faithful to Him; but it is important for us to show our faith so the world will know we belong to Him. In Jas. 2:18, 20 he said, "Show me your faith without deeds, and I will show you my faith by what I do....Do you want evidence that faith without deeds is useless?"

One of the greatest rewards a Minister (or any Christian worker for that matter) can receive is to have assurance that his labors for the Lord are bearing fruit in the lives of those to whom he ministers. When Jim Vaus, a great evangelist to youth, was reaching the New York gang members around 1960, one young man began to appear a likely candidate for conversion. Before that event occurred, Jim said to the youth, "When you accept Christ as your Savior, don't tell me; I'll tell you." A few days later, Jim said to him, "You've become a Christian, haven't you?" Surprised, the lad said, "How did you know? I didn't tell you." Jim replied, "I could tell by the change in your life."

The words "to the very end" are exceedingly important. Many Christians grow weary of serving the Lord, and begin to shed their harness to stop pulling their load. Jesus said with sorrow to the people of the church in Ephesus (Rev. 2:4), "You have forsaken your first love." Wise Solomon reminded us that "no one is discharged in time of war" (Eccl. 8:8); and we know that our spiritual warfare will not cease until the end of the world.

### ...in order to make your hope sure.

We do well to remember that once we are in the fold of the Savior we cannot be abandoned. But it is reassuring for us to have confirmation that this is so, lest we become discouraged in our efforts. So the people to whom the author of Hebrews wrote were able to reaffirm their own relation to God through their faithfulness in bearing fruit, and that same assurance is available to us who remain constant for the Lord in His work.

### Heb. 6:12. We do not want you to become lazy....

The Greek word translated "lazy" here is the same word used in 5:11 for "slow to learn." We mentioned there that Thayer gives this series of synonyms for the Greek: "slow, sluggish, indolent, dull, languid." It seems to me that the translators tried to soften the meaning in both verses, to make it seem like the author was not too upset with his hearers. We have already mentioned what Solomon said about continuing to serve the Lord. Paul put it rather well when he said in II Thess. 3:13, "never tire of doing what is right." Paul said the same thing to the people in the Galatian churches, and added a promise to them (Gal. 6:9): "Let us not become weary in doing good, for at the proper time we will reap a harvest if we do not give up." The author of Hebrews also makes a promise at the end of what he says here:

### ...but to imitate those who through faith and patience inherit what has been promised.

It should not be difficult to find people to imitate; there seem to be so few throughout history that we need not be confused by an overload of information. How sad it is to know that this is true. Jesus told us in His teaching

231

(in Matt. 7:13-14) about the narrow gate and road that leads to life which few people find; but the road that leads to destruction beginning with a wide gate and broad road is traveled by many people. We dare not attempt to determine numerical percentages for the two ways, but it remains that the large majority do not receive the blessings of eternal life. For example, remember what we read in Hebrews of the quotation from Ps. 95, where God told Moses that "all" the people died in the wilderness save the youth under twenty years, and Joshua and Caleb. Not even Moses was allowed to enter. And David made a pitying plea in his day for people to let God soften their hearts, but most of them apparently fell by the wayside. We have a long list of faithful people in Heb. 11, the great "faith" chapter of the Bible; but compared to the millions, they are precious few. But "to imitate them" is to share in their destiny; to receive the "inheritance of what has been promised!"

The rest of chapter 6 emphasizes the absolute validity of God's promises. The author does it in these steps:

    1. By an example of a promise to Abraham fulfilled
    2. God's double seal of His promise
        a. His nature (verses 13-14)      A Person
        b. His oath (verse 17)          A Promise
    3. Mediated through an out-of-this-world High Priest

Now let us see how these steps are explained by the author.

### Heb. 6:13. When God made his promise to Abraham....

God *does* make promises. He made one (in fact, many more than one) to Abraham, which we shall note soon. And what a glorious promise it was! God makes promises to other people as well. The amazing thing is that the promises of God are not limited to His followers. Jesus told His disciples that "He causes his sun to rise on the evil and the good, and sends rain on the righteous and the unrighteous" (Matt. 5:45).

Sometimes we tend to think solely of what God has promised us, and neglect almost entirely the instructions He has given us as well, and even the threats of punishment He makes to those who fail or refuse to obey Him without repentance. During the early years of my ministry, I suddenly realized I had been underlining many verses in the Bible (as is the custom of many who study it diligently), but only verses containing what I believed to be precious promises from God to me. I had failed to underline verses containing instructions or warnings. Such a practice leads to a false sense of security. There is no fault in clinging to God's promises, but holding only to His promises leads to death-dealing error.

### ...since there was no one greater for him to swear by, he swore by himself....

We are taught in scripture that we are not to swear; Jesus explained that in Matt. 5:33-37. The main reason, I believe, why we should avoid swearing, is because too often we find ourselves in a situation where we think we must break our oath. Unfortunately, these days people think nothing of breaking their marriage vows, which are made to God as well as to spouses, so they are as sacred and important as any vow can be. Others routinely break ordination vows, when they refuse to accept the whole Bible as the word of God and utterly true (rightly interpreted), and by both actions and words they demonstrate publicly that they have broken their vows. Other vows are made by people daily in courts of law; they not only break their vows at will, but also by court routines are forced to break their vows.

God, on the other hand, has every right to swear. Probably the best reason why He can do so with impunity is because He knows the end from the beginning, so no circumstance can surprise Him to keep Him from keeping His vows.

When a person swears or makes an oath, he must swear by something greater than himself, or else what he says is no oath. Jesus, then, had to criticize the Pharisees about their oaths, because they spent much time bickering over what was best to appeal to for oath-taking (Matt. 5:33-37).

Consider this. Many people make oaths constantly, almost with every sentence, and fail to recognize that they are in fact swearing. During my youthful days, we had a neighbor whose English was poor because he had come from another country. He began nearly every sentence with the words, "By Gott...." Likewise, many Spanish-speaking people have the thoughtless custom of beginning each sentence by saying, *"Por Dios...."* Just because people speak thus thoughtlessly does not mean that their speech is excusable.

Since nothing is greater than God, whenever He swore, He had to swear by Himself, and He did.

### Heb. 6:14. ...saying, "I will surely bless you and give you many descendants."

This was the oath referred to by the author of Hebrews. It comes from Gen. 22:16-18, and we note that there God says He swears by Himself:

I swear by myself, declares the LORD, that because you have done this and have not withheld your son, your only son, I will surely bless you and make your descendants as numerous as the stars in the sky and as the sand on the seashore. Your descendants will take possession of the cities of their enemies, and through your offspring all nations on earth will be blessed, because you have obeyed me.

God promised to bless Abraham with "many descendants." That was a great blessing in those days. The Psalmist Solomon affirmed this in Ps. 127:3-5:

Sons are a heritage from the LORD,
children a reward for him....
Blessed is the man
whose quiver is full of them.

Today, many people are not so sure that such a promise would be a great blessing. Thirty years ago there was an organization called the "Club of Rome," whose members at that time were making dire predictions that within a very few years there would be mass starvation throughout the world, and civilization as we know it would disappear, unless people took drastic steps to cut down and almost eliminate the procreation of people in the world. China, for one, took the warning to heart, and even today only a few rural families are allowed to have more than one child each; all others who have one child must abort all other children before they are born. Birth control has become popular in most of the world, partly because people are fearful of overpopulation. Still, the prediction of the Club of Rome has not yet come to pass.

Although God promised Abraham many descendants, in number as the stars in the sky or the sand on the seashore, yet in God's reckoning he had but one child, Isaac. By human count, Abraham had numerous children. Sarah's Egyptian maid bore Ishmael to Abraham (Gen. 16:1-12). After Sarah died, Abraham took another wife, Keturah, and had at least six additional sons by her (Gen. 25:1-2; I Chron. 1:32). Further, we read in Gen. 25:6 that Abraham had a number of concubines who bore him additional sons, whom he "sent...away from his son Isaac to the land of the east." So although the patriarch gave gifts to those sons, he counted them neither heirs nor descendants in comparison to Isaac who was kept at home.

It was not only Abraham who reckoned Isaac as his only son, but God said as much. At the beginning of the story of Abraham's figurative sacrifice of Isaac (Gen. 22:1-19, see especially verse 2), God gave him this directive, "Take your son, your only son Isaac, whom you love, and go to the region of Moriah." God also promised Hagar, Sarah's handmaid, that her son would be the father of many descendants "too numerous to count" (Gen. 16:10).[8] Further, in Gen. 17:19-21, God limited His covenant relationship to Isaac (although He promised to bless the descendants of Ishmael):

Your wife Sarah will bear you a son...Isaac. I will establish my covenant with him as an everlasting covenant for his descendants after him....But my covenant I will establish with Isaac, whom Sarah will bear to you by this time next year.

It is not always physical children who are a blessing to their parents. Nor is it physical children who are counted as heirs. I knew a devout couple

---

[8] If anyone wonders why terrible turmoil exists in the Middle East today between the Jews (descendants of Isaac) and the Arabs (descendants of Ishmael), the answer is found in God's prediction at the time they were born, noted in Gen. 16:12, where God says of Ishmael:

He will be a wild donkey of a man;
his hand will be against everyone
and everyone's hand against him,
and he will live in hostility
toward all his brothers.

in Schenectady, NY, Harry and Anna Meahl, who were in their fifties when I met them. They had no children of their own, but they loved children. They were instrumental in starting a Christian camp for Junior age children, and every summer they worked diligently with others to reach for Christ the children who came to camp. One Wednesday evening Harry and I were talking after the mid-week prayer meeting at church. He told me with a glow of blessing on his face about the many new births that had taken place at camp that week already. I could not think of any of the women camp workers who had been pregnant, so Harry had to explain to me that many Junior boys and girls had received Christ as their Savior and Lord that week, and so had been born again. They were the new births; and Harry and Anna could rightly call them their children, just as Paul called Timothy "my true son in the faith" (I Tim. 1:2). Such children are often a greater blessing to their spiritual parents than are physical children to their parents.

Incidentally, God promised Abraham many other things, all of which were fulfilled: He promised to give him the land of Israel for him and his covenant descendants in Gen. 12:7; He promised a Descendant (who, of course, is Jesus Christ) who would be a blessing to all nations in Gen. 12:3; and He promised that Israel would become a great nation in Gen. 12:2.

### Heb. 6:15.  And after waiting patiently, Abraham received what was promised.

"Patiently"? I must laugh at that. After God has promised Abraham a son and heir, after waiting a while, Abraham was sure he would have no child, so he thought perhaps God meant that Abraham's faithful servant Eliezer would be his heir (Gen. 15:2). Then when the promise was renewed, Sarah thought to help the situation by offering her slave girl Hagar to Abraham so he could become a father (Gen. 16:2). Finally, when God gave full assurance to Abraham, the poor man actually laughed at such a preposterous promise (Gen. 17:17). But in spite of those three faltering steps, Abraham was patient for ninety-nine years before the true son, Isaac, came along. Not only that, but when God told Abraham to leave his home in Ur and go to a place God had not yet revealed to him, Abraham faithfully pulled up stakes and started his long journey westward, in total obedience and faithfulness to God. So we ought not to judge him too harshly.

At any rate, the important thing is that God did make the promise, and Abraham did receive it and wait for its fulfillment. So here we have the example in Abraham of God's fulfillment of His promises. That is the point the author of Hebrews is making here. So if God did everything He promised to Abraham, then He will do the same for us, as long as we are faithful to Him, and patient.

* * *

**Heb. 6:16.    Men swear by someone greater than themselves....**

This is part two, if you will, of the outline of the validity of God's trustworthiness to keep His promises to all people.

There is no point for a human being to swear by himself, because then a simple yes or no would do as well. So why is there need for a person to swear at all? The need exists because far too often when a person gives a simple "Yes, I will," or a "No, I won't," he fails to keep his promise because it has little meaning and is too easy to forget. The people in biblical times no doubt encountered many broken oaths, just as happens today. So others did not believe their simple promises.

**...and the oath confirms what is said and puts an end to all argument.**

In our age, our system of making promises demands not an oath, but a signed legal document. For us, that is supposed to end all argument. We think what we have done is written in granite, but unfortunately not even a notarized legal document ends all arguments between either individuals or nations. Someone finds a loophole in the statement; someone else disputes the meaning of a word or a phrase; still others simply walk away from their agreement. However, in general a sworn statement takes care of the matter at hand.

But now we go on to study the nature of God's oaths, and the reasons why He never breaks them.

**Heb. 6:17. Because God wanted to make the unchanging nature of his purpose very clear to the heirs of what was promised, he confirmed it with an oath.**

Some people cannot believe that God never changes either His being or His purposes. They cite various passages of scripture which they think proves that God changes His mind from time to time. For instance, they read Gen. 6:6, which says, "The LORD was grieved [He repented] that he had made man on the earth." In other words, God was angry at the humans He had made, and was determined to wipe them from the face of the earth. But God had other sentiments about people, as we read in Jud. 2:18, "...the LORD had compassion [KJV "repented"] on them as they groaned under those who oppressed and afflicted them." Both these ideas of one's changing his mind, and being sorry for, are found in Ex. 13:17: "When Pharaoh let the people go, God did not lead them on the road through the Philistine country, though that was shorter. For God said, 'If they face war, they might change their minds and return to Egypt.'"

My explanation for these seeming contradictory actions on the part of God is this. God neither changed His mind to begin to punish the people; nor

did He change His mind to begin to bless them. Rather, from the very beginning of human existence He laid out His complete plan: "If you obey Me I
will bless you, and if you disobey I will curse you." This is made evident in
the antiphonal choir readings of the people from Mounts Ebal and Gerizim,
which we read in Deut. 27. Half of Israel stood on Mount Gerizim and affirmed the blessings God had promised the people through Moses on condition
of their obedience to God's law and their faithfulness to follow Him; the other
half stood on Mount Ebal to acknowledge the curses God threatened against
them if they should disobey.

Therefore, God does not really change His mind. He merely responds
to man's action based on what God from the beginning laid down as conditions for life. Paul assures us that when God makes a promise for good to us,
He will surely keep it. He said in II Cor. 1:20, "So no matter how many
promises God has made, they are 'Yes' in Christ." And the biblical clincher
for my argument is in I Sam. 15:29, "He who is the Glory of Israel does not
lie or change his mind; for he is not a man, that he should change his mind."
It is interesting to note that the Hebrew word used here for changing one's
mind is נחם, which according to BDB means basically "to be sorry," which
can be either "to be moved to pity, have compassion for others," or " to rue,
suffer grief, repent of one's own doings." That same Hebrew verb is found in
Gen. 6:6, translated "grieved;" in Ex. 13:17 for the people's "changing their
minds;" and in Jud. 2:18 when the Lord "had compassion" on His oppressed
people.

One of the infinitely different characteristics that separates God from
mankind is that man changes his mind continually, but God never changes
His mind. Even such a staunch, firm character as Margaret Thatcher, former
Prime Minister of Great Britain, had changed her mind, according to a TV
news report of the 14th of February 1985.

### Heb. 6:18. God did this so that, by two unchangeable things....

The author of Hebrews now adds that God's promises are sure forever
because of two things. As we search the context of this verse, we may find it
difficult to discover to what the author is referring. I think I have discovered
the two, but you may find one or two different from my choices.

The first unchangeable thing is God's very Person (verse 13), where it
is said of God that "there was no one greater." I can think of no better definition for God than to say that of all that exists there is nothing greater than
God; if there were, then that person or object (or concept) would be God, and
the god we had been thinking of would be relegated to a no-god status. It may
be well for a moment to consider what this means in our own personal relationship to God. If I, for instance, am able to tell God what I want Him to do
and He is forced to do it, then I have become God and He has become my mere

slave. How wrong it is, then, to pray as if by merely praying for something we can not only get His attention, but also get His humble acquiescence. But God is God by His very nature. So the first unchangeable thing that proves the validity of God's promises is His *Person*.

The second unchangeable thing which validates God's promises is His oath, sworn by Himself, as we read in verse 17, "confirmed it with an oath." As we said, a mere statement is often neglected or forgotten; but an oath makes any promise more sure. But what can we say more than when God promises something with an *oath* made by Himself, because of His very Person there can be no better Promise?

**...in which it is impossible for God to lie....**

A moment ago we alluded to I Sam. 15:29, where we read that God "does not lie or change his mind." Although God Himself does not lie, and since there is lying in the universe, and since God is able to use anything He wants to use in any way He pleases, He can take the lies of men or even of angels and bring glory to His name through them.[9]

**...we who have fled to take hold of the hope offered to us....**

We may ask, "From what have we fled?" The author does not tell us in so many words, but we presume from what he has been discussing, especially with regard to the quotation from Ps. 95, that we have fled from unbelief, that kind of faithlessness that results in our disobedience, and ends in our exclusion from God's eternal rest.

We also may ask, "What then is the hope?" And again we stretch ourselves to provide an answer since the author does not. Perhaps that hope is the rest we just mentioned. What a tremendous hope it is! Paul talked about "Christ in you, the hope of glory" (Col. 1:27), and about a crown of righteousness for all who "long [hope] for his appearing" (II Tim. 4:8).

**...[we] may be greatly encouraged.**

We often become discouraged, and want to cry with the saints under the great altar (Rev. 6:10), "How long, Sovereign Lord, holy and true, until you judge the inhabitants of the earth and avenge our blood?" We would do well to acknowledge, however, that the Lord may be waiting for us to see the beams in our own eyes and ask Him to remove them from us so that we may be assured of our full reward in heaven, even before we see more clearly the sins of those around us. We want "consolation, comfort, solace,"[10] which the Holy Spirit of God is ready to provide for us when we seek His help.

\* \* \*

---

[9] See the story of the angel who offered to lie to King Ahab for God, in I Kings 22:19-23.

[10] This is part of Thayer's definition.

**Heb. 6:19.    We have this hope as an anchor for the soul, firm and secure.**

This warm encouragement brings strong images to my memory from my Navy days. On my first summer cruise at the Naval Academy, we were sailing to Port of Spain, Trinidad on the ancient battleship New York. It was said that only the many coats of paint on the hull were holding her together. Another myth was that when the fourteen-inch guns were fired to starboard, then another salvo had to be fired to the port side to push the turrets back to the center of the ship. The reality was that while we were anchored in the harbor at Port of Spain, one of the four huge screws came loose; divers were sent down to secure the screw to the hull by tying it on with a length of anchor chain. Then a hurricane developed and the Captain was not sure our ship could survive such a storm, or that the anchors would hold us in our place in the harbor. So we got up steam and started out for New York City at whatever flank speed we could muster, considering we had but three of four screws to push us, and the fourth was a terrible drag on us. Mercifully, the chain holding the sick screw broke and let it fall to the bottom, and we could flee faster. The point of that story is that a ship's anchor is supposed to help hold the ship in place against currents, waves and winds. But man-made anchors often fail to do their job.

God's anchor is not like ours. "We have...an anchor for the soul," and God's anchor never fails. It is not made with the hands of men, but by God Himself. We can depend on it utterly, despite whatever storms of life may assail us.

> Though the angry surges roll On my tempest-driven soul,
> I am peaceful, for I know, Wildly though the winds may blow,
> I've an anchor safe and sure, That can evermore endure.
>
> Troubles almost 'whelm the soul; Griefs like billows o'er me
> roll;
> Tempters seek to lure astray; Storms obscure the light of day:
> But in Christ I can be bold, I've an anchor that shall hold.[11]

You may ask, "Just what is our "anchor for the soul"? I presume it is the hope which we have been considering; and we also noted that what we hope for is that eternal rest God promises to all who believe in Him without wavering.

### It enters the inner sanctuary behind the curtain....

What is "it" that enters? Surely the author is still talking about the hope of the future rest of which Christ assures us who remain faithful to Him to the end.

We are now nearing the conclusion of the outline we began at verse 13

---

[11] "My Anchor Holds," Copyright 1930, by Ada P. Towner, Renewal. Hope Publishing Co., owner.

of this chapter. The outline details the reasons why God's promises are utterly sure. And now we come to the most important point which validates those promises. It has to do with God's High Priest, whom He sent to be our Savior.

The sanctuary in the Tabernacle or in the Temple was the place where the priest ministered on behalf of the people to present them to God. Beyond that was the Holy of Holies, or the "inner sanctuary" spoken of here; only the high priest was allowed to enter, and he could enter no more than once a year, on the Day of Atonement.

That was then. But now *you*, because you have hope, may enter that Most Holy Place, and with boldness, to find yourself in the intimate presence of the Most Holy God.

Let us note that when Jesus was crucified, scripture tells us (Matt. 27:51) that the heavy veil that separated the Most Holy Place from the Sanctuary was rent from top to bottom (the direction it was torn hints that it was God who split it), so that then it was possible for any person to peek into that forbidden place. This, however, did not give anyone but the high priest permission to enter. This was true in the physical sanctuary in Jerusalem, and may also be true of the "inner sanctuary" spoken of here, as we will discuss with regard to the next verse.

### Heb. 6:20. ...where Jesus, who went before us....

Here finally is the introduction of the High Priest, whom we have been waiting to discuss since the beginning of this long parenthesis which started in 5:11. Remember, it was only the high priest who was able to enter the Holy of Holies, so if Jesus entered He had to be a High Priest.

The author says that Jesus "went before us." But where did Jesus go "before us"? For one thing, Jesus went before us in all our experiences in life except in the matter of sin. We saw that Jesus went before us into temptation in Heb. 4:15, where we reviewed Jesus' broad band of temptations by Satan in the wilderness. Surely Jesus experienced times of joy; He must have had pleasant feelings at the wedding feast at Cana of Galilee. Also, we read in Lu. 10:21, after the seventy-two disciples returned to report what great things had been done through them, that "Jesus, full of joy through the Holy Spirit, said, 'I praise you, Father, Lord of heaven and earth, because you have hidden these things from the wise and learned, and revealed them to little children.'" On the other hand, Jesus often was sorrowful, and even angry, when He saw the unbelief of people and the burdens they were required to bear, as when He wept at Lazarus' tomb (John 11:33): "When Jesus saw [Mary] weeping, and the Jews who had come along with her also weeping, he was deeply moved in spirit and troubled." Jesus has gone before us in two important ways where we have not yet gone, that is, through death and the resurrection. Specifically, we read here that Jesus went "behind [beyond] the curtain."

**...has entered on our behalf.**

When I was about to graduate from the Naval Academy, it was announced at dinner one evening that our yearbooks were ready and could be picked up at a certain room after dinner. As soon as the bell sounded for our release, my roommate and I made a dash down the hallways, each to try to be the very first in our class to pick up his book. Surely neither of us had any thought of being of help to anyone else by being first. All we were interested in was to bask in the glory of receiving the first yearbook. It was not so with Jesus, in His preceding us into the Most Holy Place. True, He rode with great pomp on the first Palm Sunday into Jerusalem, but even that was not to glorify Himself, but to demonstrate His royal status as the King of kings and Lord of lords. And He did it all "on our behalf."

### He has become a high priest forever....

Here finally we enter the apex of the book of Hebrews, the discussion of Jesus as our Great High Priest, who is *better than* all the foregoing high priests, or any who might have followed. The following discussion, which fills the next several chapters, is the very most important, most significant contrast of the whole book of Hebrews, or of any book that could be written.

The high priesthood was the greatest office attainable in Hebrew society. Not Moses, or David, or anyone else you care to think of, could compare with the high priest in importance to the welfare of the nation. After all, it was the high priest who anointed the king to his office.

Not only was the office of high priest the highest imaginable, but the duration of Jesus' tenure was far longer than that of any other officeholder, infinitely longer in fact. For Jesus "has become a high priest forever." Each of the Aaronic priests lasted far less than one lifetime, a matter of a few years at most. But Jesus was a High Priest from before the beginning, and will continue in that office forever. This is one of the reasons why Jesus as High Priest was "better than" any other high priest.

### ...in the order of Melchizedek.

Who, pray tell, is this Melchizedek? It will be profitable for us to get somewhat acquainted with the man and his office before we begin our deeper study beginning in the next chapter.

Melchizedek is mentioned in only three places in scripture. The first instance is in Gen. 14, in the story of Abraham's defeat of four kings and their armies by means of his paltry crew of three hundred eighteen servants. Melchizedek met Abraham after his victory, and blessed him, and received tithes of all the loot.

The second place where we read of Melchizedek is in the great Psalm 110 where King David is talking about the Lord, the heavenly Father, and his Lord, the Son, the Lord Jesus Christ, David's descendant. Verse 4 of that

Psalm tells us:

> The LORD has sworn
> and will not change his mind;
> "You are a priest forever,
> in the order of Melchizedek."

Here is God's great statement of ordination of His only Son to be a Priest, a Priest in an entirely different category from that of the Aaronic priesthood.

The only other place in scripture where Melchizedek is mentioned is in the book of Hebrews. He has been named already twice (where the author quotes Ps. 110:4), in 5:6 and 5:10, just before the long parenthesis which we are now concluding. In chapter 7 the author begins the large explanation of the person of Melchizedek, how Jesus became a High Priest in Melchizedek's order, and how Jesus as our great High Priest is infinitely better than any of the priests in the order of Aaron, better than all of them put together, better than anyone who might come after Jesus.

## CHAPTER VII
## A BETTER MINISTRY.[1]
## THE MELCHIZEDEK PRIESTHOOD. HEB. 7:1 to 8:6.

**Heb. 7:1.  This Melchizedek was king of Salem and priest of God Most High.**

At the end of chapter 6, we introduced Melchizedek. There is much more to be said about this important person. We need as full a picture of him as the scripture affords.

First, let us see what is important about Jesus' priesthood as being in the "order" of Melchizedek. In the Bible, we find two distinct orders of priests in Israel. One was that of Aaron, of the tribe of Levi. God had designated the descendants of Levi to care for the Tabernacle, its fixtures and implements, and for whatever was necessary to carry out the priestly office. This is spelled out in Num. 1:47-54. Further, from among the Levites God chose Aaron and his descendants to be the priests, as we read in Ex. 28:1. Aaron's priestly order was confirmed through God's response to the rebellion of Korah, Dathan, and Abiram; see Num. 16. Those three rebels, along with two hundred fifty other leaders in Israel, thought Moses and Aaron were too bold in assuming political, military, and spiritual leadership of the people, and demanded equal rights to power (people are the same today). But God confirmed the leadership He had assigned to Aaron as high priest, and caused the earth to open and swallow the households of Korah, Dathan, and Abiram (Num. 16:31-34); and caused fire to consume the other two hundred fifty rebels (verse 35).

Another act of rebellion against God's appointment of Aaron to the high priesthood is recorded in I Kings 12:31. At the beginning of the divided kingdom, Jeroboam, the first king of the northern kingdom was afraid that his subjects might defect if they thought it necessary to return to Jerusalem to fulfill the rules for feasts and sacrifices. The king's solution is recorded in that verse: "Jeroboam built shrines on high places and appointed priests from all sorts of people, even though they were not Levites." Verses 32-33 add that Jeroboam had made calves for the people to worship, and he and his priests offered sacrifices to those calves on the altars he had built. Then chapter 13 tells us how God warned Jeroboam of His displeasure at his turning away from God's appointment of priests and plan for their service.

The only other legitimate priesthood established by God is that of Melchizedek. All others are false priests, and their service is an abomination to Him. In saying this, I recall that Peter called Christians a "royal priesthood" (I Pet. 2:9), and four verses before that he called Christians "living stones...built into a spiritual house to be a holy priesthood, offering spiritual sacrifices acceptable to God through Jesus Christ." Further, Paul urged us to make sacrifices (as only priests should do) in Rom. 12:1. But there is a great

---

[1]  The chapter divisions for chapters VII to X in this study follow logically (in broad terms) from what the author of Hebrews says in 8:6 about a BETTER MINISTRY, a BETTER COVENANT, and BETTER PROMISES.

difference between the priesthood of believers, as Christians are called, and either the Aaronic or Melchizedek priesthoods. The sacrifices of believers are "living" sacrifices according to Paul, and "spiritual" sacrifices in what Peter said. The only sacrifices that make atonement for sins are blood sacrifices, like those Aaron and Melchizedek made. The author of Hebrews emphasizes this necessity for blood sacrifices in 9:22.

The author begins to describe Melchizedek. We noted at the end of our last chapter that Melchizedek is mentioned in only two places in the Bible outside the book of Hebrews, Gen. 14, and Ps. 110.

The name "Melchizedek" will instruct us in a measure just who this person is. The author of Hebrews informs us that his name means "king of righteousness" (verse 2). The first part of his name is the Hebrew word for king, מֶלֶךְ, which may be transliterated as "Melek." The last part of his name is the Hebrew word for righteousness, צֶדֶק, which sounds like "Tsedhek." Probably there was not any geographical place called "Righteous" or "Righteousness," so this king should be understood to be sufficiently righteous in his character to be called the "king of righteousness."

In the same verse 2, the author of Hebrews calls this king by another name, that is, "king of Salem." Unlike the priest's other name, this name does designate a particular place, a city called Salem. We know that this city was also called the city of Jerusalem, and this is likely how the name evolved. In early days, the city was inhabited by a group of Canaanites called Jebusites. After King David had ruled Israel from Hebron for seven and a half years, he determined to go up to Jerusalem and establish it as his center of power. In I Chron. 11:4-7 we read that the Jebusites dwelled there, and boasted that David could not take their city. But David promised that whoever conquered the city would become the commander-in-chief of his army. It was Joab who won the battle. Because the city had been occupied by Jebusites, it was called Jebus (I Chron. 11:4). They may have wanted to call their home the "City of Peace." The Hebrew word for peace is שָׁלוֹם, transliterated by the familiar "Shalom," which is the Arabic "Salaam." In some way the first word "Jebus" became "Jerus." This could be a very easy mistake or intentional shift, because the Hebrew letter ב for our "b" looks like the Hebrew ר (our letter "r") with a line on its bottom. So the city of the Jebusites was transformed first into the city of the "Jerusites," and then with the word for peace added it finally became Jerusalem, and remains such today.

Melchizedek was given two titles, "king," and "priest." We recall that this whole study of Hebrews is designed to show that Jesus and His ministry are "better than" any other person or ministry revealed in the Old Testament. Although Melchizedek was such a special person, Jesus was even greater than His antetype, in that Jesus is well-known by not two but three titles. First, Jesus is called not merely King, but King of kings and Lord of lords (Rev. 17:14). Secondly, although mention of Jesus as High Priest or even Priest is made only in Hebrews, there are other indications in the New Testament that Jesus was marked for the priesthood. He was to perform the most important role of a priest, that is, to offer a sacrifice for sins. This He claimed He would do, when He said (John 10:14): "I lay down my life for the sheep."

The third title given to Jesus but not to Melchizedek was that of Prophet. Moses predicted His coming as a Prophet in Deut. 18:15: "The LORD your God will raise up for you a prophet like me from among your own brothers. You must listen to him." In addition, in verse 18 Moses quotes the Father as saying the same thing: "I will raise up for them a prophet like you from among their brothers; I will put my words in his mouth, and he will tell them everything I command him." These predictions of Moses and God can refer only to Jesus, because Peter said so in his second great sermon after Pentecost; Peter even quotes Deut. 18:18, recorded in Acts 3:22-23. In support of this, Stephen, the first martyr, in his defense quotes that same passage from Deuteronomy, recorded in Acts 7:37, because Stephen's whole message was of Jesus who came to die for sinners.

### He met Abraham returning from the defeat of the kings and blessed him....

Melchizedek had two claims to fame, the second of which flows from the first. The first claim is that he met Abraham. We have already discussed that story. There is no doubt that Abraham was an extremely important person, because he became the father of all Jews, but more importantly because God promised to bless him, to bless his descendants, and to make one of his Descendants a blessing to the whole world. We read of God's promise of blessing to Abraham and to his descendants in Gen. 22:17: "I will surely bless you and make your descendants as numerous as the stars in the sky and as the sand on the seashore. Your descendants will take possession of the cities of their enemies." The blessing of the world through one of Abraham's Descendants follows in verse 18: "...through your offspring [literally, seed] all nations on earth will be blessed, because you have obeyed me." The promises to Abraham were reiterated to his singularly blessed son Isaac in Gen. 26:4.

We are assured that Jesus is the one Descendant, or Offspring, or Seed, to whom God alluded when He made those promises to Abraham. The assurance is written by Paul in Gal. 3:16, where he says, "The promises were spoken to Abraham and to his seed. The Scripture does not say 'and to seeds,' meaning many people, but 'and to your seed,' meaning one person, who is Christ."

It was not just God who blessed Abraham after the defeat of the four kings, but Melchizedek also blessed him. The words of the blessing are in Gen. 14:19-20:

> Blessed be Abram by God Most High,
> Creator of heaven and earth.

And blessed be God Most High,
who delivered your enemies into your hand.

**Heb. 7:2.   ...and Abraham gave him a tenth of everything.**

In Gen.14 we learn about God's standard of giving for His people, which is the tithe. Many people today object to being held to that standard, because, they claim, we no longer live under the Old Testament law. They say that not only the ritual law but the whole of the moral law is totally irrelevant, since Paul said in Rom. 6:14, "...you are not under law, but under grace." (It is both interesting and rather humorous that people who espouse that idea usually adhere to the moral law more closely than many other Christians.) Paul did not say that it is safe to ignore the law, because in the next verse he adds, "What then? Shall we sin because we are not under law but under grace? By no means!" The law still exists for our instruction, so we may know what God expects of us. Christ tells us, "Be perfect, therefore, as your heavenly Father is perfect." Nor will it do to ignore that commandment simply because we know we cannot become perfect in this life. With the help of the Holy Spirit we must make every effort to do God's bidding as revealed in the law.

We are sure that many people in Old Testament times failed to give God a tithe of what He gave them. A Minister once asked his people, "Would you be satisfied if God gave you exactly ten times as much as you have given Him?" The priesthood suffered miserably because the people forsook their responsibility to God. If the people of the eleven tribes had given a tenth of their goods to God, the Levites would have had ten percent more than anyone else; instead they were invariably the poor outcasts. In fact, if the people had given not only the tithe, but also all the offerings stipulated for the feast days, the new moon days, and other specified offerings, one Old Testament scholar estimated that each person would have given not merely a tenth, but one-third of all he had.

God has assured us that as we give willingly and gladly to Him, He will repay in ever greater abundance. He made this promise in Mal. 3:10:

"Bring the whole tithe into the storehouse, that there may be food in my house. Test me in this," says the Lord Almighty, "and see if I will not throw open the floodgates of heaven and pour out so much blessing that you will not have room enough for it."

Some people quibble about the basis on which they ought to reckon their tithe. They often ask, "Should it be before taxes, or after?" A man in a church I served revealed to me that his offering to the church was fifty cents per Sunday. It was unusual for me to know this, because my practice was to avoid learning how much any person gave. In our conversation I questioned whether he was earning only five dollars per week in his good job, since he had assured me that he was a tither. He continued to protest that what he gave

246

was a tithe, but not on his salary. He said that the Bible said that you should tithe your "increase" and not your income. He figured his increase was what he was able to put in his savings account after all his expenses including food, clothing, housing, auto expense, business expense, incidentals and recreation.

To be obedient to what God expects me to give is to increase my desire to give back to Him more and more of all He has given me, based on how much I love Him for giving me all that I have in the first place, and especially for the eternal life He purchased for me by dying for me on the cross.

This emphasizes that the scripture says that Abraham gave to Melchizedek a tenth of everything. We may assume that Abraham's giving was not based solely on the loot he gained from victory over the four kings, nor was it based on what he thought he could spare after expenses. He gave a tenth of "everything,"[2] and God blessed him and his descendants, and the peoples of the world, forever. God said His blessing came to and through Abraham "because you have obeyed me" (Gen. 22:18).

**First, his name means "king of righteousness"; then also, "king of Salem" means "king of peace."**

We have covered these matters in our introduction to this chapter. Please review it in this context.

**Heb. 7:3. Without father or mother, without genealogy, without beginning of days or end of life....**

Some things said about Melchizedek are hard to understand, and harder to believe. It may take some speculation to understand what the author means to tell us, but let us seek the guidance of the Holy Spirit in our search for the truth. I do not know assuredly what is meant, nor do I ask you to accept all I have to say. I have a sense of peace in what I have learned, and trust it will help encourage you in your search.

If we read about Melchizedek only in the two Old Testament passages, Gen. 14 and Ps. 110, we could not conclude what is written in Hebrews concerning Melchizedek's ancestry or progeny.

Where the author of Hebrews got his information about Melchizedek we could not know, at least from a human standpoint. But at the beginning of this study we emphasized that although we cannot identify the human author, we do know that the real Author is the Holy Spirit. So I conclude that the human author received his data from the Spirit of God, and I accept it as true, however difficult it may be to comprehend.

The information we have of Melchizedek is peculiar indeed. He must have been especially created by God for a very limited role to perform in the world. The author of Hebrews says he was "without father or mother, without

---

[2] I acknowledge that the author says in verse 4 that Abraham tithed "the plunder," but it is likely that he extended his giving to Melchizedek to a tithe of all his possessions.

genealogy," so he was not a human. This must be a critical point in our overall Christian theology, because if there were humans not descended from Adam and Eve, they might not have inherited the sinful nature, and thus either would not need a Savior or could not have Jesus for their Savior and thus would be lost forever. Therefore, I conclude that Melchizedek was not human, but was much like a human. It is possible that he was another of God's angels, created for one particular task, to minister to Abraham.

Our thinking about the special creation of Melchizedek is reinforced by the next thing the author of Hebrews says about him: "...without beginning of days or end of life." From this we could easily gather that Melchizedek was created before the rest of universe. If he had no beginning of days, he had to be created before time came into existence. And if he had no end of life, he is in the limited category occupied by Enoch (Gen 5:24 and Heb. 11:5) and Elijah (II Kings 2:1-12), since he did not die.

It seems logical to me that if Melchizedek was the forerunner of a line of two priests separate from the Aaronic priesthood, and if the second of that line was Jesus Christ the God-man, then Melchizedek ought also to be something more than a mere man among all other people. Having said that, it is important to avoid going so far in our speculation as to presume that Melchizedek was God Himself, or more precisely Jesus Christ who was the second in this line of priests. Melchizedek was the forerunner of Christ, not Christ Himself.

### ...like the Son of God he remains a priest forever.

Let me emphasize the point: Melchizedek is "*like* the Son of God;" he is in fact *not* "the Son of God." It is interesting to note that at the end of chapter 6, the author of Hebrews implies that Jesus came to be "like" or "after" Melchizedek. So each of the two is like the other—but only in limited ways. Melchizedek was not God, but Jesus was. Melchizedek was not the Son of God, but Jesus was. Melchizedek was like Jesus in one tremendously significant way: *both* of them "remain a priest forever."

The fact that Melchizedek remained a priest "forever" is one of the most important facts about him. This distinguishes him from all the Aaronic priests; none of them lived more than a century as a priest of God; they faded into history while successors took their place. Melchizedek had no predecessor, nor did he have a successor. We may think of Jesus' high priesthood more as complementary than supplementary to Melchizedek's.

Here is a word of encouragement for those who feel discouraged now, thinking that we are pretty insignificant in light of the two great personages, Melchizedek and Jesus. We may buoy up our spirits by remembering that just as Melchizedek was "like" Jesus, we too one day shall be "like" Jesus. John assures us in I John 3:2, where he says, "We know that when [Jesus] appears, we shall be like him, for we shall see him as he is." John  gives us further assurance that this will happen in verse 3, "Everyone who has this hope in him purifies himself, just as he is pure." We who seek to be like Jesus in eternity should spend our days trying to purify ourselves, with the help of the Holy Spirit.

From learning who Melchizedek was, we discover his mission in the world.

### Heb. 7:4.  Just think how great he was.

The author is talking about Melchizedek, not Jesus. It is important to establish the fact that Melchizedek was exceedingly great. He was great, great in comparison with anyone else in the world. He was greater than Abraham who was considered great by all Old Testament Jews. It is difficult today, especially for Gentiles, to comprehend how great Abraham was in the eyes of his descendants for at least two thousand years, until the coming of Jesus. Abraham, Moses, and David were probably tops in the list of any Jew. The author now tries to show how great Melchizedek was by comparing him to the Levitical[3] priests, by showing how much greater those priests were than even Abraham.

### Even the patriarch Abraham gave him a tenth of the plunder!

This is the one factor which made Melchizedek so great: he received tithes from the great Abraham. Abraham was great not only in the eyes of his biblical descendants, but also in the eyes of God, because God had chosen Abraham to be the first Jew, the father of all God's Chosen People. Later, the author makes a strong point that it is the greater person who receives tithes from the lesser, so Melchizedek was greater than Abraham. The next step in the argument is that since Levi was a descendant of Abraham, the author implies that Abraham was greater than either Levi or any subsequent high priest. The author would put those who filled these roles, in their descending order of importance:

> Jesus
> Melchizedek
> Abraham
> Levi
> Any Levitical priest

More of this schedule of important people will unfold as we proceed.

---

[3] Most people interchange the designation of the Jewish priesthood by using two terms, the "Levitical" and the "Aaronic" priesthood. Aaron was one of the descendants of Levi, and it was only male descendants of Aaron who became priests. All other descendants of Levi were ministers and caretakers of the Tabernacle, the Temple, and all things related to the priesthood, but they could not be priests. So the descendants of Aaron were the Aaronic priests, but because Aaron was a Levite, his descendants were sometimes referred to as "Levitical" priests.

**Heb. 7:5.** **Now the law requires the descendants of Levi who become priests to collect a tenth from the people—that is, their brothers—even though their brothers are descended from Abraham.**

What we understand in this verse is that all the sons of Jacob ordinarily would be considered equal (with the possible exception of the firstborn, who was Reuben and not Levi). However, the children of Levi were selected by God to be *above* "their brothers" given the fact that the Levites received tithes from the rest. Therefore, we can now add another item to our list:

> Jesus
>
> Melchizedek
>
> Abraham
>
> Levi
>
> Any Levitical priest
>
> Any tribe besides Levi

"The law requires" others to give a tithe to Levi. Is this law in effect for us today, especially Gentiles? God makes a very strong statement about tithing in the very last book of the Old Testament. In Mal. 3:8-10 we read this powerful admonition:

> "Will a man rob God? Yet you rob me.
>
> "But you ask, 'How do we rob you?'
>
> "In tithes and offerings. You are under a curse—the whole nation of you—because you are robbing me. Bring the whole tithe into the storehouse, that there may be food in my house. Test me in this," says the LORD Almighty, "and see if I will not throw open the floodgates of heaven and pour out so much blessing that you will not have room enough for it."

Some Gentiles might try to escape this admonition by claiming that the tithe is to be given to Levi, but here God says that it is to be put into "my house," which today is the Church, the body of Christ.

Some people think they are excused from the "law" of tithing, but the New Testament always talks about tithing as if it was inadequate. When Jesus, for instance, chided the Pharisees about their strict adherence to tithing their mint, dill, and cummin, He did not say they were not required to do that, but that in addition they ought not to have "neglected the more important matters of the law—justice, mercy and faithfulness. You should have practiced the latter, without neglecting the former" (Matt. 23:23, see also Lu. 11:42). Paul said in II Cor. 9:7, "God loves a cheerful giver." In Matt. 5:17, Jesus said, "I have not come to abolish [the law or the Prophets], but to fulfill them." When the Pharisees came to Jesus to ask whether He thought it was right to pay taxes to Caesar, He replied, "Give to Caesar what is Caesar's, and to God what is God's" (Matt. 22:21; Mk. 12:17; Lu. 20:25). And when Peter was confronted with the people who collected the temple tax, Jesus told him not to offend them, but to go catch a fish, open its mouth, and there find a four-drachma coin. He told Peter, "Take it and give it to them for my tax and yours" (Matt. 17:27).

**Heb. 7:6.   This man, however, did not trace his descent from Levi....**

We ask why this is important. The author's purpose is to continue his objective to show that Melchizedek was superior to Levi or to all the Levitical priests. Remember that Melchizedek was not in the line of Levitical priests, who truly were exalted by having been appointed by God as His priests. Melchizedek was of an entirely different order and calling from Levi.

**...yet he collected a tenth from Abraham and blessed him who had the promises.**

We assume that only a rich man can "bless" a poorer man with material possessions. So, by the same token, only a more blessed, or more spiritual, man may "bless" a less spiritual person. (When Solomon dedicated the temple, he prayed {I Kings 8:56 KJV}, "Blessed be the Lord...." He was not blessing God, but acknowledging that God is blessed or worthy of praise.) Therefore, Melchizedek, since he blessed Abraham, was greater spiritually than Abraham. Further, Abraham was under obligation by God's law to give him a tithe. Thus the author continues to build his case that Melchizedek was better than Levi.

**Heb. 7:7.   And without doubt the lesser person is blessed by the greater.**

The author came to the same conclusion that we did. Then the author presents another reason why Melchizedek was better than Levi:

**Heb. 7:8.   In the one case, the tenth is collected by men who die....**

All the Levitical priests died before they were one hundred fifty years old. Surely an immortal person would be greater than a mortal, simply because of his longevity which he could receive only as a gracious gift from God. Mortal priests had need for the same ministry as they were attempting to dispense to others. So, although the Levitical priests did receive tithes from their brothers (and thus were greater than the rest), still they left the world with nothing in their hands.

**...but in the other case, by him who is declared to be living.**

Melchizedek was not merely "living," he was immortal. Remember the author's statement in verse 3 that Melchizedek was "without beginning of days or end of life...he remains a priest forever." We may wonder where the author got his information about the immortality of Melchizedek in his inter-

251

pretation of Gen. 14, but we dare not dispute it since we have no other data to show otherwise. Surely the author was inspired by the Holy Spirit to learn all this about Melchizedek, just as he has already averred that David was inspired to write Ps. 95 (Heb. 3:7 compared with 4:7). Our only conclusion from what the author says here is that a person who is perpetually living is better than any mortal.

### Heb. 7:9.   One might even say....

Here the author seems to be hedging somewhat in his interpretation. But I see this argument as valid as anything else he has written.

The apostle Paul also said something like this. In I Cor. 7 when he said it was better for a person not to marry, he said in verse 25, "Now about virgins: I have no command from the Lord." However, Paul merely acknowledges that God had not told him to say this, nor had God told him to say anything contradictory to it. Rather, Paul added, "...but I give a judgment as one who by the Lord's mercy is trustworthy." So Paul here rides on his credentials, which were both voluminous and noteworthy. Further on, Paul ends his whole discussion of the matter in verse 40 in this way, "...and I think that I too have the Spirit of God."

Now, what was it that the author of Hebrews "might even say"?

### ...that Levi, who collects the tenth, paid the tenth through Abraham....

The author, we may think, seems to be stretching the point, but it is nonetheless valid. If we were left with only this statement of the author's, we might do well to challenge it. But he continues with an explanation of his logic in the very next verse.

### Heb. 7:10.   ...because when Melchizedek met Abraham, Levi was still in the body of his ancestor.

What the author says here is that Levi, being a direct descendant of Abraham, with no intervening miraculous leap from one category to another, was in the same class as Abraham. Certainly he was in no better category than Abraham, because he was "still in the body" of his great-grandfather.

We come again, then, to the conclusion that if Melchizedek was better than Abraham, because Abraham paid tithes to him, then Melchizedek was also better than Levi, who as a (yet unborn) son of Abraham, *also* paid tithes to Melchizedek, his superior.

After this, we begin a new paragraph that contains an additional argument why Melchizedek is better than Levi. Upon reflection, we see in the preceding argument that Melchizedek was superior to Levi because Levi paid tithes to Melchizedek. Now we will see how the Levitical priesthood was flawed in comparison to the Melchizedek priesthood.

**Heb. 7:11.    If  perfection  could  have  been  attained through  the  Levitical  priesthood  (for  on  the  basis  of  it  the  law was  given  to  the  people)....**

First, the Levitical priesthood had to be very good, in the eyes of both God and man. It is not our purpose here, and it was not the author's purpose, to denigrate the Levitical priesthood, especially since it was the instrument of administering the law to God's Chosen People.

We remember how highly the Jews regarded the law:
- •It came down from God, written by His own hand (Ex. 32:16: "The tablets were the work of God; the writing was the writing of God, engraved on the tablets.")
- •It was mediated by angels (Acts 7:53: "...you who have received the law that was put into effect through angels....")
- •It was given by Moses at Sinai (Ex. 19:20: "The LORD descended to the top of Mount Sinai and called Moses to the top of the mountain.")
- •It was administered by Moses' brother Aaron, the first in the line of priests.

In spite of all this spoken in favor of the Levitical priesthood, still it was not perfect, nor could it not bring perfection to the people. This is what the author claims here, and we dare not think his claim is spurious. But why could not such a priesthood bring perfection? After all, we cannot accuse the law of being imperfect; it was designed and even written by God Himself. Nor can we accuse the people of preventing the priesthood from being perfect; for although the people were not perfect, they were the ones being ministered to in order to bring them to perfection. The most obvious answer is that the Levitical priesthood itself was not perfect.

**...why  was  there  still  need  for  another  priest  to  come....**

Why indeed? Could God not have been satisfied with what He had established in the first place? Could He not have foreseen that such a priesthood would be flawed and therefore need to be replaced? And after all, since the fall of man, what else in all God's creation is perfect? God made all things good (Gen. 1:31: "God saw all that he had made, and it was very good." But when Adam and Eve rebelled, the whole universe fell into chaos. "The LORD was grieved..,his heart was filled with pain. So the LORD said, 'I will wipe mankind, whom I have created, from the face of the earth—men and animals, and creatures that move along the ground, and birds of the air—for I am grieved that I have made them'" (Gen. 6:6-7).

One day a street urchin approached a pompous wealthy businessman on the street to beg for money. The man dismissed the child with a sneering remark about not throwing good money to trash. The urchin defended himself:

"God don't make no trash!" That is true, but the boy forgot one detail; man has "trashed" not only himself but the universe because of his sin. For instance, I once saw on a road bank beside Highway 9 south of Albany, NY. It was a sleek, spotless brand new Buick, loaded with bells and whistles. It had just been purchased by a man who celebrated his new toy by getting drunk. As he raced merrily down the highway at ninety-five miles per hour, he suddenly swerved, inexplicably, across the divider and was hit broadside by two huge trucks that happened to be traveling neck and neck in parallel lanes. When I saw the car, almost no part of it was wider than six inches, good for nothing but "trash." So we can not blame God for making trash, but we see that man has spoiled, ruined, corrupted, perverted God's creation by his rebellion and sin.

The important thing is that God was not satisfied with the Levitical priesthood. He demands perfection, and nothing less, from all His creation. So He wanted to replace the flawed priesthood with a priesthood that was not merely superior, but perfect.

In connection with this, I am struck with an amazing thought. That is that God is also unsatisfied with me, since I also am a mortal sinner. But contrary to God's dealings with the corrupt priesthood, He in His mercy does not discard me for a perfect model. Rather, He has promised to remodel me, so that in heaven I will be incorruptible, both physically and morally (I Cor. 15:53: "For the perishable [corruptible, subject to rust] must clothe itself with the imperishable [incorruptible, stainless], and the mortal with immortality.")

At any rate, God *will* have a perfect priesthood. And He has provided it in the two-person Melchizedek priesthood.

### ...one in the order of Melchizedek, not in the order of Aaron?

The lines of demarcation are drawn. They are not really battle lines, although the high priests in Jesus' day did fight mightily to retain their place in opposition to what they saw as the Usurper.

As an aside, I have often wondered why the author of Hebrews refers to the purely human priesthood almost exclusively as the Levitical priesthood rather than the Aaronic priesthood. In fact, Aaron is mentioned only twice in all the book of Hebrews, here and in 5:4. I discussed the relationship of those two titles in a footnote earlier in this chapter. Surely the author thought the question was immaterial, at least as long as we all understand that we are always speaking of the one priesthood established by God for the Jews at the Temple in Jerusalem.

* * *

**Heb. 7:12. For when there is a change of the priesthood, there must also be a change of the law.**

At first I balk at this thought. My problem with it is logical. Just because the priesthood changes I do not see why there must be a change of the law as well. Then, I ask whether the law actually did change. There must have been a change, since the author of Hebrews said so, and what he wrote is part of infallible scripture. Jesus said (Matt. 5:17): "Do not think that I have come to abolish the Law or the Prophets; I have not come to abolish them but to fulfill them." Surely Jesus' sayings are infallible as well. Perhaps we may reconcile these two seemingly contradictory statements by believing that the law has stayed the same in one sense or part, and has changed in another sense or part. Let us proceed and look for an answer.

**Heb. 7:13. He [Melchizedek? or Jesus?] of whom these things are said belonged to a different tribe....**

Levi was one of the tribes of Israel. Melchizedek came from no tribe of Israel, and Jesus was of the tribe of Judah.

The term "tribe" is a common term for descendants of one of Jacob's twelve sons. The Old Testament Hebrew has two common, interchangeable words which are translated into English as "tribe." One Hebrew word is מַטֶּה, pronounced "má-teh," and the other is שֵׁבֶט, pronounced "sháy-vet." The root meaning of both Hebrew words is "rod, staff, scepter," and ordinarily is a sign of leadership or authority.

Both Hebrew words are translated into our New Testament Greek as φυλή. It is used mostly of the tribes of Israel, but it can also refer to a nation, people, ethnic group, or any distinct group. So the author of Hebrews could be saying that Melchizedek came from a different φυλή, that is, a group outside any of the tribes of Israel, for he existed before Israel, or Isaac, or even Abraham. He was not one of Abraham's descendants. But the next clause makes us believe the author was not speaking about Melchizedek, but of Jesus.

**...and no one from that tribe has ever served at the altar.**

Melchizedek must have served at an altar to God in Jerusalem, since he was the King of Salem, that is, Jerusalem, although it is not specifically mentioned in scripture. And since Melchizedek was the lone member of his "tribe," it is easy to track down in scripture whether he did serve at the altar there. It is not said in Gen. 14 that Melchizedek made any sacrifices in connection with Abraham's giving him tithes, and Ps. 110 says nothing about his making offerings either, even though that was the specific role of a priest. If the author is referring to Jesus here, we can easily see that His ancestors were not priests at God's altar. Jesus descended from Judah, as the genealogies in Matthew and Luke both attest. Even the spurious priest whom Micah appointed in the days of the Judges (Ju. 17, especially verse 9) was a Levite. Jeroboam also appointed priests who had nothing to do with the ministry of God's altar, and although they were specifically not of the tribe of Levi (I Kings 12:31), even if some of them had been of the tribe of Judah, they did not serve at God's altar, but at Jeroboam's false altars in Bethel and Dan (I Kings 12:29). So, anyone who truly served the Lord as a priest had to be chosen by God, and the two in the "tribe" outside Levi, Melchizedek and Jesus, both were so chosen.

**Heb. 7:14. For it is clear that our Lord descended from Judah....**

We have already mentioned that Jesus' genealogy in both Matthew and Luke are traced back through the tribe of Judah. The list in Matthew begins at 1:2: "Abraham was the father of Isaac, Isaac the father of Jacob, Jacob the father of Judah and his brothers...." That genealogy ends in verse 16 with "...and Jacob the father of Joseph, the husband of Mary, of whom was born Jesus, who is called Christ." Luke's record of Jesus' genealogy is in Lu. 3:23-38, and begins "[Jesus] was the son, so it was thought, of Joseph...," goes through Judah (verse 33), and ends with God. Moses affirms the perpetual royalty within the tribe of Judah by quoting Jacob's blessing on that son, "The scepter will not depart from Judah" (Gen. 49:10). Jesus is that eternal King of kings, as well as our Great High Priest.

**...and in regard to that tribe Moses said nothing about priests.**

In order to confirm this, it would be necessary to skim the whole Pentateuch to discover whether Moses did mention any such thing. Actually, such a task would be made much easier if we merely find a place where Moses said that the priesthood was exclusively for members of the tribe of Levi. It is an easy search, for we find several such passages:

- •Ex. 29:9 "...Aaron and his sons. The priesthood is theirs by a lasting ordinance."
- •Num. 3:10 "Appoint Aaron and his sons to serve as priests; anyone else who approaches the sanctuary must be put to death."
- •Num. 16 Korah and others' attempt to take over the priesthood ended in death for them all.
- •Num. 18:7 God said to Aaron, "But only you and your sons may serve as priests in connection with everything at the altar and inside the curtain."

Numerous other places in the Old Testament affirm the same truth. Here are some:

- •I Sam. 13:9-14 We remember what happened to Saul who

made sacrifices instead of Samuel.

- •I Kings 12:31  We just mentioned Jeroboam's appointing priests who were "not Levites."
- •I Kings 13:33-34  "Even after this [warning], Jeroboam did not change his evil ways, but once more appointed priests for the high places from all sorts of people. Anyone who wanted to become a priest he consecrated for the high places. This was the sin of the house of Jeroboam that led to its downfall and to its destruction from the face of the earth."
- •Ju. 17:1, 5  Micah, who was of the tribe of Ephraim, appointed one of his sons as a priest. We also have mentioned the story of Micah and the Levite he appointed as priest, who probably was not a descendant of Aaron.
- •Ju. 17:7-13  A young Levite came by (although a Levite, probably not a descendant of Aaron), Micah made him his private priest, not a priest for all Israel as he should have been if he were from Aaron's house.
- •Ju. 18  Six hundred soldiers (verse 11) of the tribe of Dan took Micah's priest as their own. And in verse 31 we read, "...they continued to use the idols Micah had made, all the time the house of God was in Shiloh."
- •II Chron. 26  King Uzziah (who ordinarily was a good king) burned incense on the altar. Azariah and other priests confronted him. He got angry. God struck him with leprosy until the day he died.

Surely that is enough evidence from the Old Testament to prove that neither Moses nor anyone else said anything about priests from the tribe of Judah; then Jesus came along in the New Testament.

**Heb. 7:15. And what we have said is even more clear if another priest like Melchizedek appears....**

Verse 14 begins "It is clear that our Lord descended from Judah...." The author wants us to comprehend that Jesus had no connection of any kind with the tribe of Levi, to make sure we are positive that none of the weaknesses and failures of the Levitical priesthood was able to contaminate the priesthood of Jesus. He does this first in a physical sense by emphasizing that Jesus was entirely separate from that Old Testament priesthood by having proceeded from the tribe of Judah instead of the tribe of Levi. Now secondly the author shows that Jesus' priesthood was different in a spiritual sense in that He was "like Melchizedek," and not like the temporal descendants of Aaron.

* * *

257

**Heb. 7:16.   ...one who has become a priest not on the basis of a regulation as to his ancestry....**

This clause confirms what we have just said about making a distinction between the Levitical priesthood and that of Melchizedek. One defining feature of the Levitical priesthood was that it was a succession of men who were chosen exclusively on the basis of their ancestry. It was a dynasty, established (in Aaron) in the first place by God, and deemed by Him to continue through the generations of Aaron. Jesus, on the other hand, was not chosen by the Father because of any physical ancestry, but purely at the behest of the Father.

**...but on the basis of the power of an indestructible life.**

The criterion, then, for selecting Jesus as High Priest was not that He was the son, or descendant, of any particular person. The choice of Jesus was made rather on the basis that He lives eternally. This one factor in the nature of Jesus is sufficient to separate Him from all the Levitical priests.

The relative greatness of Jesus' priesthood should be obvious. An eternal priest could serve much more effectively: he would know the tasks; he would have no fear of eviction, and thus could concentrate on his work; and he would not need to seek ever-increasing power, because he would have the "power of an indestructible life."

If Jesus' life was indestructible, did not Satan know that? It is impossible to conceive that he did not, although he acted as if he were unaware of it. His treatment of Jesus at the temptation in the wilderness (Matt. 4:1-11; Mk. 1:12-13; Lu. 4:1-13) seemed like he was unaware of Jesus' indestructibility. After all, Satan exists in the spirit realm, so he could hardly fail to know it. On the other hand, if Satan did not know that Jesus could not be destroyed, how could he be so foolish as to rebel against Him? There is really no answer to that question, because all sin is totally irrational. Unfortunately, it is not Satan alone who acts irrationally in the matter of sin and rebellion against God. Every one of us acts precisely the same way. We know what sin is. We are born with a knowledge of good and evil; we inherit that knowledge, and we are taught it in a multitude of ways throughout our lifetime. Further, we know that whatever sin we commit, it will not escape the attention of God. Next, we know that God has condemned anyone who sins. But even when we know what sin is, and its consequences, we still fall into sin. Finally, there is no way to explain why we sin, any more than we can explain why Satan tried to displace Jesus Christ.

**Heb. 7:17.   For it is declared,**
**"You are a priest forever,**
**in the order of Melchizedek."**
We recall that this quotation from Ps. 110:4 was already stated by the

author in chapter 5:6; there he quoted it right after he quoted Ps. 2:7. In chapter 5, the author is emphasizing the fact that Jesus' position as High Priest came only by appointment by God the Father. Here, the author puts emphasis on the High Priest's eternal existence. These two facts, Jesus' appointment by God, and His endless existence, are two powerful indications of the vast superiority of Jesus' priesthood over the Levitical priesthood.

True, Aaron and his descendants were chosen by God to be priests, but their succession to the priesthood was flawed almost from the beginning. Aaron himself was not without sin. In Num. 12:1-16 we read how Aaron and his sister Miriam condemned Moses for marrying a Cushite woman; more brazenly, they considered themselves to be equal to Moses in authority: "'Has the LORD spoken only through Moses?' they asked. 'Hasn't he also spoken through us?'" (verse 2). For their attempted usurpation, God condemned them both, and Miriam became leprous for a week (verses 9-15).

Aaron had four sons, all of whom were to be priests, but the eldest was to become the successor to Aaron as high priest. However, Nadab the eldest and his next oldest brother Abihu committed great sin before God. They "offered unauthorized fire before the LORD, contrary to his command," and for that God burned them up with fire. The story is recorded in Lev. 10:1-11, and the judgment on the brothers is repeated in Num. 26:61.

Virtually the same scenario, with merely a few details different, occurred within the priesthood again. The instance concerns Eli and his sons Hophni and Phinehas. They were priests in Israel when Samuel was born and was given to God for ministry under Eli. But Eli's sons were "wicked men; they had no regard for the LORD" (I Sam. 2:12). Their practice was to steal meat from the sacrifices and offerings the people brought to God at the worship place in Shiloh. God predicted to both Eli (I Sam. 2:27-36) and Samuel (I Sam. 3:11-14) that He would destroy the wicked priests and terminate Eli's line so that no descendant of his would be a priest. God's prediction was fulfilled in a battle with the Philistines shortly afterward. Both sons of Eli were killed in the battle which Israel lost. When he heard the news, Eli fell backwards off his chair and died of a broken neck. And Eli's only other descendant, according to the biblical record, was a son of Phinehas who was born (probably prematurely) when Phinehas' wife heard the news from the battleground. The unnamed mother of the child died in childbirth, after naming her son Ichabod, which is a combination of two Hebrew words, אִי(say "Ee"), and כָּבוֹד("ka-vódh"), translated literally as "where is the glory?" and interpreted by the mother as "The glory has departed from Israel." This tragic story is recorded in I Sam. 4:1-22.

**Heb. 7:18. The former regulation is set aside because it was weak and useless.**

The "regulation" probably was the manner of selecting a priest. If that is so, then it had nothing to do with a possible change in the moral code, or even in the necessity for making sacrifices or for having a priesthood. On the other hand, by "regulation" the author may mean the whole gamut of priestly ministry in the Old Testament. At least this is what the author has been talking about, and continues to discuss not only through the rest of this chapter, but also continuing through chapter 10. I will not try to list here all the reasons why that former regulation was weak and useless, since there are many. But I will point out two matters here to give you an idea of what to expect as we discuss the matter in the next two and a half chapters of Hebrews.

First, in 8:6, the author asserts that Jesus

"has obtained a *better ministry*,
as much as he is the Mediator of a *better covenant*,
which is regulated by *better promises*" (my translation).

The other matter is found in 10:4, where the author states boldly that "it is impossible for the blood of bulls and goats to take away sins."

The author here uses emphatic words in the Greek to show how unfit the old ministry was. The word he uses for "weak" is ἀσθενές, whose basic meaning is "sickly." We all have experienced the enervation, almost impotency, of a debilitating illness. That is what the author is implying here about the ministry of the Levitical priests. For the idea of uselessness the author uses the Greek ἀνωφελής. In a phrase, we would say, "It cannot do anything." That word is used only once again in the New Testament, in Tit. 3:9, where Paul warns his young friend to "avoid foolish controversies and genealogies and arguments and quarrels about the law," because Paul calls those things "unprofitable [weak] and useless."

We wonder how and why the author could use such strong language, to defame the Old Testament priestly ministry, since it had stood the test of time from about 1500 BC to the middle of the first century AD. He explains his position beginning in the next verse, and continues extensively.

### Heb. 7:19. ...(for the law made nothing perfect)....

But then, we may add, it was not the purpose of the law to make anything perfect. The purpose of the law is pretty well summed up in Paul's writings. We may think Paul was biased in his opinion; and he *was*. He had obtained an overwhelming impression of the value of what had replaced the law, beginning with his experience on the road to Damascus, and that experience was fortified immensely as he continued his walk with Christ. But we dare not negate Paul's opinion for that reason; after all, Paul was well acquainted with the old covenant long before he encountered the living Savior. He lists his credentials to the church in Philippi (3:5-6) this way: "circumcised on the eighth day, of the people of Israel, of the tribe of Benjamin, a Hebrew of Hebrews; in regard to the law, a Pharisee; as for zeal, persecuting the church; as for legalistic righteousness, faultless." Probably more than any other human who has ever lived, Paul was expert with the details of both sides of this issue.

Paul tells us what the law existed for. In Gal. 3:19, 24 he wrote, "What, then, was the purpose of the law? It was added because of transgressions until the Seed to whom the promise referred had come....So the law was put in charge [was our schoolmaster, KJV] to lead us to Christ that we might be justified by faith." Paul also adds his bit in emphasis on the uselessness of the law in Rom. 8:3: "What the law was powerless to do in that it was weakened by the sinful nature, God did by sending his own Son in the likeness of sinful man to be a sin offering."

### ...and a better hope is introduced....

What is that hope? The great hope of the Christian is the return of Jesus Christ in His Second Coming, at which time we who have trusted in Him for salvation will rise with Him to participate in His glory forever. Paul says it this way in Tit. 2:13-14: "...we wait for the blessed hope—the glorious appearing of our great God and Savior, Jesus Christ, who gave himself for us to redeem us from all wickedness and to purify for himself a people that are his very own, eager to do what is good." John, the beloved apostle, says the same thing in even more loving terms in I John 3:2-3: "Dear friends, now we are children of God, and what we will be has not yet been made known. But we know that when he appears, we shall be like him, for we shall see him as he is. Everyone who has this hope in him purifies himself, just as he is pure." When human beings were first created, the triune God spoke (Gen. 1:26) within Himself and said, "Let us make man in our image, in our likeness." However, when all humankind began to sin, as it is recorded in Gen. 3, the image of God in him was marred. It is that image that will be restored to us who trust in Christ and hope for His return.

### ...by which we draw near to God.

It is our hope that causes us to want to draw near. Likewise, the same hope causes us to want to serve our Savior and be more like Him, not because we think we can work for our salvation, but because we love Him intensely for the salvation He wrought for us.

Therefore, one reason why Christ's priesthood is better than the Levitical priesthood is because it supplies us with a better hope for eternity.

### Heb. 7:20. And it was not without an oath!

We conclude that the author of Hebrews believes oaths are very important, especially those made by God. In Heb. 6:13-18, he talked about a doubly-supported oath which God made to Abraham. Review that now, before we look at this new oath of God's. The author pointed out (for the first time in his argument regarding priests) that the appointment of Melchizedek to the high priesthood was accompanied and affirmed by God's oath. The quotation containing God's oath to Melchizedek appears in the next verse. The fact of God's oath of appointment to Melchizedek is strengthened by contrast with the negative oaths imposed on the Israelites in the wilderness because of their rebellion, which the author repeated three times, in 3:11, 4:3, and 4:5.

### Others became priests without any oath....

Here is a second instance where it would be difficult to prove or disprove an assertion made by the author of Hebrews without at least skimming the whole Torah. (The first instance is in verse 14). Rather than trying to examine all five books of Moses to search for an oath regarding establishing the Aaronic priesthood, let me say that I do not recall any such statement. If it is true that God did not establish that priesthood by means of an oath, this is another reason why the Melchizedek priesthood was superior to the Levitical priesthood.

Let us summarize the reasons the author has given why the Melchizedek priesthood was superior to the Levitical priesthood. The Melchizedek priesthood was:

> 5:6 made by divine appointment, not by human succession
> 5:6 and 7:3 unending, eternal
> 7:16 powerful, indestructible
> 7:20 sealed with God's oath

### Heb. 7:21. ...but he became a priest with an oath when God said to him:
> **"The Lord has sworn**
> **and will not change his mind:**
> **'You are a priest forever.'"**

The first two lines of this part of Ps. 110 are quoted by the author of Hebrews for the first time here. It contains the words affirming that God deemed it important to appoint Melchizedek by means of an oath. The oath, then, is the focus of the author's thrust as he continues his discussion of the superiority of the Melchizedek priesthood over that of the Levites.

Not only is God's oath the center of attention, but added to it is the fact that if it is God who makes an oath, He *will not* back down, He *cannot* back down on what He has promised, else He would deny His most basic nature. How wonderful it is to be utterly certain that when God makes a promise to someone He will never renege on that promise, whether it be made to His own Son, or to Moses, or to you and me. If God has promised us that He will take us to heaven to be with Him forever under certain conditions He has stipulated, there is nothing that will keep us out of heaven. In connection with that thought, I always recall the assurance we have in I John 5:13: "I write these things to you who believe in the name of the Son of God so that you may *know* that you *have* eternal life."

Here the author simply repeats the clause, "you are a priest forever," to tie together the whole argument. We have already discussed the eternal nature of the Melchizedek priesthood. I merely mention it for emphasis, as did the author of Hebrews.

### Heb. 7:22. Because of this oath, Jesus has become the guarantee of a better covenant.

Up till now, the author has been referring to Melchizedek primarily, but now he affirms that it is Jesus who is the core of his discussion regarding the superiority of priesthood. He has been talking about Melchizedek merely to lead up to the status of Jesus as our Great High Priest.

Here is the argument. Melchizedek was a better priest than any one, or all together, of the Levitical priests. This being so, then Jesus also as a member of the order of Melchizedek priesthood must be better than any or all of the Levitical priests. Now the author turns specifically to Jesus as the subject of his argument.

When we think of a guarantee, we think of something we have purchased. When you buy a new car, it may be guaranteed for five years or 50,000 miles. But the car still wears out, and we joke that it is "guaranteed" to last just beyond the time or distance of the guarantee. About a year after I had purchased a new Ford station wagon about 1960, one of its two mufflers burned out. I had it replaced with a new Midas muffler, guaranteed for the life of the car as long as I owned it. Unfortunately for Midas, either one or both mufflers burned out annually for as long as I owned the car, and they were replaced. We see ads about the Maytag man who is the most lonely person in the world, because he is never called on to repair a Maytag appliance. But the company does have a repairman, just in case. God's guarantee is better than any guarantee on something we purchase, for two excellent reasons. First, God's guarantee never needs to be called on, because what God guarantees never needs repair. Secondly, God's guarantee does not expire in five years, or at the end of your earthly life; it lasts into eternity.

The Greek word for "guarantee," ἔγγυος, is used only here in the New Testament, and "guarantee" is probably the best English word we can find to translate it. In classical Greek, the word has to do with surety, one person's promise to pay a debt for a friend or relative if that person fails for any reason to fulfill his obligation. On occasion the guarantor may need to go so far as to pay with his own life.[4]

Since God's guarantee is forever, He supplies the guarantee of a "better covenant." Now if the priesthood is the major theme in Hebrews, especially this middle part of the book, to demonstrate that Jesus is "better than" the old way of redemption, then the "covenant" is an inseparable but distinct part of

[4]  The information in this paragraph about the Greek word comes from the article by Herbert Preisker in TDNT, Vol. II, p. 329.

263

that theme. That is to say, although the high priesthood of Jesus is the highlight of chapters 7 through 10, the covenant is interwoven with the priesthood throughout the same passage. To change the figure of speech, it is like a symphony that contains two interplaying themes: a better priesthood, and a better covenant.

**Heb. 7:23.  Now there were many of those priests....**

Here the author takes us back to the idea of the perpetuity of Jesus' priesthood. For one thing, this proves that the adage "more is better" is not always true. There were many priests, both high priests and regular priests, from the time of Aaron in the fourteenth century BC; to the leadership of Annas and Caiaphas (see Lu. 3:2) during Jesus' days on earth; to Phanas (or Phannias)[5] the last high priest, who ministered during the days of the destruction of the Temple in 70 AD. During that time there were many priests, first because they were imperfect, and secondly because they served only during their lifetimes on earth.

**...since death prevented them from continuing in office....**

Every one of the priests died. Scripture records the names of the only two humans who never died: Enoch, who lived 365 years, and "who walked with God; then he was no more, because God took him away" (Gen. 5:24); and Elijah who was walking with Elisha one day, when "suddenly a chariot of fire and horses of fire appeared and separated the two of them, and Elijah went up to heaven in a whirlwind" (II Kings 2:11). Surely Elijah was not a priest, although we cannot know from which tribe of Israel he came. Although Elijah presided over a sacrifice (in the story of the contest between him and the prophets of Baal and of Asherah, I Kings 18:16-40), it was not he who made the sacrifice, but "the fire of the LORD fell [from heaven] and burned up the sacrifice." Aaron, on the other hand, died when he was 123 years old (Num. 33:39), which means that by the year 2000 AD he had been dead more than 3,420 years. His approximately forty years of high priesthood was relatively brief compared to the rest of time up until now if he had remained alive. But since death came to Aaron, there had to be a succession of priests to continue his dynasty; all of them also perished.

**Heb. 7:24.  ...but because Jesus lives forever, he has a permanent priesthood.**

Incidentally, there is no hiding the fact that Jesus also did die, just like Aaron and his successors did. Further, Jesus was only thirty-three years old when He died. But there is a vast difference between the death of Jesus and the death of all the Aaronic priests. After all, every one of the priests in the course of Levi still lie moldering in their Middle East graves. On the other

---

[5]  See Davis/Gehman WESTMINSTER DICTIONARY OF THE BIBLE, page 247.

hand, Jesus not only rose bodily from the grave, but He actually raised Himself from the dead, as He foretold in John 10:17-18. Further, Jesus not only rent the bonds of death for Himself, but He conquered death itself; this is what Paul declares in a verse of that great resurrection chapter, I Cor. 15:25-26: "For he must reign until he has put all his enemies under his feet. The last enemy to be destroyed is death." To be certain of Jesus' conquest, we realize that He will never taste death again, unlike Lazarus, for instance, whom Jesus raised from the grave, but then Lazarus had to die again some time after that (John 11). Also, there were doubtless many priests after Aaron who had no spiritual right to be priests, but were made so only because they were part of the dynasty. One example is of the two oldest sons of Aaron who, as we saw earlier, were put to death by God because of their "unauthorized" fire made before God (Lev. 10:1-2). Since it is quite unlikely that they repented of their sin before God destroyed them, they were subject to the "second death" and eternal punishment in the lake of fire described in Rev. 20:14.

The fact of Jesus' death is highly important to one aspect of the covenant God made with people through Jesus. That covenant is God's "last will and testament" made to humanity, and without the death of the one who made the will, it does not become effective. We shall study this more fully when we come to the author's discussion of it in Heb. 9:16-17.

Although Jesus died, still He "lives forever." This is another of the great contrasts between the Levitical priesthood and the Melchizedek priesthood, and another reason why the priesthood of Jesus is "better than" that of Aaron.

And because Jesus "lives forever," that means that He "has a permanent priesthood." The English word "permanent" is almost wholly inadequate to convey the full, important meaning of the Greek term. Actually, "permanent" implies the important idea that Jesus' priesthood cannot be superseded; He can have no successor. The Greek term the author of Hebrews uses here is ἀπαράβατος; this is the only place it is used in the New Testament. The most important meaning of the word has to do with the idea that something is "unchangeable," that is, "valid and unalterable."

### Heb. 7:25.  Therefore he is able to save completely....

"Completely" is one of the superlative terms the author of Hebrews uses in connection with Jesus and His ministry. Our NIV adopts a single word for what in the Greek is a phrase: εἰς τὸ παντελές. The KJV parallels the form of the Greek with a phrase, "to the uttermost." Delling[6] expresses the all-encompassing nature of the term by telling us that "...the saying about the 'totality' of the saving work can hardly be expounded in only a single direction." To describe the term, Delling uses these words:  with regard to amount, "completing all;" with regard to omnipotence, "fully effective" or

---

[6]  The exposition of this Greek phrase is by Gerhard Delling, found in TDNT, Vol. VIII, pages 66-67.

"all-powerful;" ethically "unblemished;" in the sense of totality "completely" or "altogether;" in point of time "for ever" or "permanently."

Several years ago a man and his son were flying in a small airplane over the glaciers in Alaska. A friend of theirs was flying in company with them in his own plane. Suddenly, the friend saw that the other plane was in trouble and had crash landed on the glacier. The friend therefore tried to land to help them out, but in attempting to land, he crashed his plane as well. Fortunately no one was seriously injured in the double accident, but unlike Jesus he was of no help to his friends.

Jesus does not strike a bargain with anyone by saying, "I'll do this for you if you do that for Me." Nor does He yet say, "I'll do this much for you if you do the rest." John puts it well in I John 1:7, when he writes, "the blood of Jesus, his Son, purifies us from every [or 'all'] sin." I take that to mean that when Jesus cleansed me from all my sin, He cleansed me from my past, present, and future sins; He cleansed me from my big and little sins, that is, my mortal as well as my venial sins; He cleansed me from my heinous and innocuous sins; He cleansed me from my wilful and unwitting sins; He cleansed me from my known and unknown sins. Praise be to God forever for saving me eternally, totally, in every way thinkable. If Jesus' salvation were incomplete, we still could never save ourselves, nor could anyone else help to save us. It is not a matter of degree; Jesus saves "to the uttermost."

### ...those who come to God through him....

Although Jesus' salvation is "to the uttermost," that does not mean that it is universal. In other words, the salvation of Jesus for those who are saved is total, complete. But the salvation of Jesus for those who are lost does not exist. Jesus' atoning work on the cross is *sufficient* for every person who ever will have lived in the world, but not every person *applies* that salvation to himself. Again I turn to John the apostle for his wisdom, and this matter is exceedingly important, lest anyone think he is going to heaven and later discovers he does not qualify. We read in I John 2:2, "[Jesus] is the atoning sacrifice for our sins, and not only for ours but also for the sins of the whole world."[7] The Greek word John uses here for "atoning sacrifice" is ἱλασμός, and means merely the "availability of salvation," and not "actual salvation." That is, Jesus offered the gift of salvation to the whole world, but not all the world received or accepted that salvation. In contrast, Paul writes about salvation in Rom. 3:25, and makes it clear that the salvation Christ wrought on the cross was limited to a certain group of people. Paul wrote,

---

[7] Unfortunately, some who fear that the Bible might teach universalism here, intentionally mistranslate the term for "whole world," that is, ὅλου τοῦ κόσμου, as "the world of the saved" or some such escape. But the term here must mean exactly what it is translated to say. For proof, verses 15 and 16 of that same chapter in I John use the same Greek word κόσμος in a sense that is totally meaningless if the part of the world which includes the lost sinners is excluded from the definition.

"God presented [Christ] as a sacrifice of atonement, through faith in his blood." The Greek word Paul uses for "sacrifice of atonement" (which is similar to John's "atoning sacrifice") is very much like John's ἱλασμός, it is ἱλαστήριον. Close observation will show that the two Greek words begin just the same. But they have different meanings. John's word means merely "availability of salvation" while Paul's word means "the actual expiation of sin." Why, then, is Paul's statement not universal? The difference is that John is talking about the whole world, but Paul is speaking about those who come to Christ "through faith in his blood." The whole world then is divided into two groups (and in this case, only two groups) of people, those who have trusted in Jesus Christ as their Savior and thus are saved; and those who have not trusted in Jesus Christ as their Savior, and although they have been offered salvation they are not saved.

God truly does love the whole world (John 3:16), but not the whole world will be saved. Here are other verses that tell of God's universal love which does not result in universal salvation.

II Pet. 3:9: "He is patient with you, not wanting anyone to perish, but everyone to come to repentance." The sad fact is that not everyone is willing to come to repentance.

Matt. 23:37: "O Jerusalem, Jerusalem, you who kill the prophets and stone those sent to you, how often I have longed to gather your children together, as a hen gathers her chicks under her wings, but you were not willing." Jesus willed to receive them, but they willed not to seek shelter.

Matt. 18:14: "...your Father in heaven is not willing that any of these little ones should be lost." Some people think that this verse means that every baby who dies in infancy will automatically go to heaven, but that is no more necessarily so than what Jesus said in Matt. 23:37 makes it so.

John 14:6: "I am the way and the truth and the life. No one comes to the Father except through me." This is another way of saying that Jesus is the Door, the only Door, to heaven (John 10:7, KJV and original Greek).

John 6:44: "No one can come to me unless the Father who sent me draws him, and I will raise him up at the last day." It is God who draws us, but "...whoever wishes, let him take the free gift of the water of life" (Rev. 22:17, but far too few actually "wish" to drink of it).

John 3:18: "...whoever does not believe stands condemned already because he has not believed in the name of God's one and only Son." This comes close after John 3:16.

John 3:36: "Whoever believes in the Son has eternal life, but whoever rejects the Son will not see life, for God's wrath remains on him." This was written by John the *beloved* and loving apostle, and in the same chapter as John 3:16.

Acts 4:12: "Salvation is found in no one else, for there is no other name under heaven given to men by which we must be saved."

### ...because he always lives to intercede for them.

Here we return to the main point in this portion of the author's argument: the reason why Jesus Christ as our High Priest is better than all the Levitical high priests put together is because He has an eternal priesthood, "he always lives."

Jesus' purpose in living forever is so that He can intercede for us at any time we need His intercession. The Greek word the author uses here, ἐντυγχάνω, may have two quite different, almost opposite, meanings. Otto Bauernfeind, in his article on the word,[8] says that on the one hand it can mean "to approach someone with a complaint," and refers to Rom. 11:2-3, where Elijah complains to God against Israel, saying, "Lord, they have killed your prophets and torn down your altars; I am the only one left, and they are trying to kill me." On the other hand, Bauernfeind points out that Paul uses the term three times in a brief space near the end of Rom. 8, in verses 26, 27, and 34. In the first two verses, Paul says that the Holy Spirit intercedes for us before the Father; and in verse 34 Paul says it is Christ Jesus Himself who, rather than condemning us, intercedes for us because of His resurrected state. The article on the Greek word says, with good reason, that this intercession is very much like the intercession suggested by the term παράκλητος, the Comforter, Advocate, Attorney we find spoken of in John 14:16 and 26; 15:26; and 16:7 (all referring to the Holy Spirit, the Comforter); and in I John 2:1 (referring to Jesus Christ Himself, the "one who speaks to the Father in our defense"). Bauernfeind concludes his exposition of the use of the word in the New Testament with this encouragement to us who believe:

In relation to the last things and the judgment (R. 8:34) as well as the present unattainability of the life of prayer (8:26f.) the believer may know that he is not left in helpless isolation. There is an ἐντυγχάνειν for him which reaches up to the very top.

Why is it that we need someone to intercede for us? Lest we forget the answer to that question, let us remind ourselves that we need a lawyer, a very good one. The more heinous the crime committed, the more expert the attorney needed. Since disobedience to God is the most despicable sin that can be committed by anyone, then we need the very best Advocate available to us, if we expect to win our cause, especially since our cause is entirely hopeless.

### Heb. 7:26. Such a high priest meets our need....

Again I emphasize: How needy we are! When we think of the legal system in our country, we like to point out how unjust it is. We talk about

---

[8] In TDNT, Vol. VIII, pages 242-244.

someone who has committed a vicious crime, and the whole world knows he is guilty. However, he retains a crafty attorney who finds some obscure loophole in the law, and the guilty man goes scot free, utterly unpunished in any way. We all agree that such a situation is inexcusably unjust. However, when we turn to our own vile guilt as God sees it, we know there is only one hope for us if we would escape the wrath of God our Judge and the condemnation of eternal punishment in the fires of hell. That one hope is Jesus Christ the "high priest [who] meets our need." Any other lawyer on whom we might depend for our appeal would be either a novice, or incompetent, or expert in some other field from what we need, or (as would be the case always) one whose sympathies would be for the plaintiff, that is, Satan our great accuser. We do not need a slave of Satan's to defend us before the Father; we need the best Attorney we can get, and we know that is His Son, Jesus. There is no kind of disability in Jesus. Here follows a list of His peculiar qualifications and qualities.

**...one who is holy, blameless, pure, set apart from sinners, exalted above the heavens.**

Let us examine each of these qualities carefully.

The first quality named here is "holy," whose Greek term is ὅσιος. When we think of a person as holy, we probably think of him as like God and not like men in his moral character. In the New Testament, this term for "holy" is sometimes paired with the word for "righteous." We should not think, therefore, that the two words are identical in meaning; rather, it is more likely that the sense of the words is so close that it is almost impossible to think of one without thinking of the other. That is, a person cannot be thought of as holy without also being acknowledged as being righteous, and vice versa. In I Tim. 2:8, we are commanded to lift up "holy hands" when we pray to God; and in Tit. 1:8, one of the qualifications of a bishop is that he must be holy as well as righteous. Of course, we must acknowledge that not one human can be utterly holy, because we have all sinned. Christ on the other hand "in mind and conduct...perfectly fulfills the divine requirements. Hence, as one who is wholly free from sin, He does not need to bring an atoning offering for Himself, like the imperfect priests of the OT."[9]

Just as the word "righteous" is linked closely with the word "holy," there are other Greek words that seem to be in a close-knit family with these two. One of the other words is ἅγιος, also translated as "holy," as in John 6:69, where Jesus is called the "Holy One of God." In Rev. 4:8, we see the four living creatures chanting,

Holy, holy, holy
is the Lord God Almighty,

---

[9]   This quotation, and other information in this paragraph, is from the article on ὅσιος by Friedrich Hauck in TDNT, Vol. V, pages 490-492.

As God is holy, we are called to be holy, although we must acknowledge that utter holiness is beyond our reach in this life. Despite the impossibility, we are commanded to be holy. We see it said in I Pet. 1:15-16: "But just as he who called you is holy, so be holy in all you do; for it is written: 'Be holy, because I am holy.'" Another word in this family of terms related to "holy" is ἀγνός, which means "pure," mostly in a sexual sense. Peter urges wives to be good witnesses to their unconverted husbands by showing "the purity and reverence of your lives" (I Pet. 3:2). Two more words in this family are ἀκέραιος and ἄμωμος. The first of these two means "unmixed" or "pure" in the sense of being without fault; while the other means "without a blemish," as a beautiful red apple has no scar or rotten spot visible on it. Both these words are used in Phil. 2:15, "...so that you may become blameless and pure (ἀκέραιος), children of God without fault (ἄμωμος) in a crooked and depraved generation, in which you shine like stars in the universe...." One more word is in this family: ἄσπιλος, "without spot." Paul uses the root of this word in his admonition to husbands in Eph. 5:27, where he says that a husband can make his wife look in his sight as "without stain (μὴ ἔχουσαν σπίλον) or wrinkle or any other blemish" simply by loving her as much as Christ loved the Church and gave Himself for her.

The author next calls Christ "blameless." For this he uses the Greek word ἄκακος. This is one of those Greek terms that is made up of a word which is preceded by the negative letter "alpha." Therefore, whatever the Greek κακός means, then ἄκακος means just the opposite. The first of these words means bad or evil; it can mean bad things brought onto a person by God, or the bad things a person brings on himself by his disobedience of God. Walter Grundmann says it this way, "Human guilt and divine action are thus combined in the question of the origin of evil."[11]

The third term the author of Hebrews uses to describe Jesus as our Great High Priest is "pure," which is ἀμίαντος in the Greek. Do not be confused by the fact that the Greek word is a negative , although it is translated into English by a positive word such as "pure." This is so, because the Greek word is derived from another Greek word, or set of words, that have a positive although bad sense. The Greek verb in the group is μιαίνω, and the Greek noun is either μίασμα or μιασμός. By simply looking at the Greek cluster, you can tell that they are related.

Following this word of characterization of Jesus as High Priest, the author next says He is "set apart from sinners." Although Jesus lived in close proximity to His disciples, as well as to multitudes of people many of whom were considered gross sinners, He kept His distance from their sinful natures,

---

[10] This cry of the four creatures echoes the doxology of the seraphs in Is. 6:3. Isaiah uses the Hebrew word commonly used for "holy," קָדוֹשׁ.

[11] The information about ἄκακος and κακός is found in the article by Walter Grundmann in TDNT, Vol. III, pages 469-487.

except only to wash and purify those who would come to Him in repentance so they could be forgiven and be made free from the guilt of sin. Paul talks much about their being "justified" in his letters, especially in such passages as Rom. 3.21-26. Otherwise, we read that He kept Himself separate from unbelievers; an example is John 2:24-25: "But Jesus would not entrust himself to them, for he knew all men. He did not need man's testimony about man, for he knew what was in a man." Jesus not only kept Himself from sinful men, but this is why God throughout the Old Testament urged the Israelites to eradicate totally all the people in the land of Canaan as they began to possess it, so that they would not be defiled by the pagan practices of those idolaters and sinners. Here is one prime example of God's instruction:

> When the LORD your God brings you into the land you are entering to possess and drives out before you many nations—the Hittites, Girgashites, Amorites, Canaanites, Perizzites, Hivites and Jebusites, seven nations larger and stronger than you—and when the LORD your God has delivered them over to you and you have defeated them, then you must destroy them totally. Make no treaty with them, and show them no mercy. Do not intermarry with them. Do not give your daughters to their sons or take their daughters for your sons, for they will turn your sons away from following me to serve other gods, and the LORD's anger will burn against you and will quickly destroy you. This is what you are to do to them: Break down their altars, smash their sacred stones, cut down their Asherah poles and burn their idols in the fire. For you are a people holy to the LORD your God. The LORD your God has chosen you out of all the peoples on the face of the earth to be his people, his treasured possession.[12]

Today, in our pluralistic, non-theistic society, we are forbidden by both God's law and the law of the land to harm non-Christians or any of their property, no matter how evil they may be. Paul summarizes our proper relation to them by both the civil law (Rom. 13:1-7) and God's law (Rom. 16:17-18). In his admonition about God's law Paul says simply, "Keep away from them," that is, "those who cause divisions and put obstacles in your way that are contrary to the teaching you have learned..,serving their own appetites. By smooth talk and flattery they deceive the minds of naive people."

The author's final word of description of Jesus as our Great High Priest is "exalted above the heavens." If Jesus is that high, then there is no one, nothing, that can approach Him in exaltation. With our finite minds we can hardly conceive of anything above even one heaven, not to say many. When we get to heaven, we will be made aware of just how high above us our glorious Savior is forever. But as we think about the possibility, we wonder where else He could go, in order to be totally separated from sinners. There is a non-Christian cult, the Mormons, one of whose well-known statements is: "As God was, so you are; as God is, so you may become." There could hardly be a more false statement. Before creation existed, God was there to make His creation. He had neither a beginning nor a development of any sort; He re-

---

[12] Deut. 7:1-6.

mains God. We never become gods in any true sense of the word. Finally, Jesus is that God, the Almighty God, the only God who has ever existed or ever shall exist. This is what Jesus said of Himself: "'I am the Alpha and the Omega,' says the Lord God, 'who is, and who was, and who is to come, the Almighty'" (Rev. 1:8). Even the Jehovah's Witnesses admit that this verse is about Jesus, not God the Father whom they call God Almighty; for no other Person in the Godhead is called the One "who is, and who was, and who is to come." It is the Son, not the Father, who "is to come," who "will appear a second time" (Heb. 9:28). Jehovah's Witnesses seem unable to reconcile the fact that Jesus is here called "Almighty," and not merely "Mighty" as it is said of Him in Is. 9:6.

In saying this about Jesus, we are in danger of believing He is untouchable, totally alienated from humanity, unable to come near enough to us either to help us in this life, or to transmit to us eternal life. But none of that is the reason why Jesus is so highly exalted above us. For earlier in Hebrews, the author told us, after saying (in 4:14) that Jesus is our "great high priest who has gone through the heavens," that (4:15), "we do not have a high priest who is unable to sympathize with our weaknesses, but we have one who has been tempted in every way, just as we are—yet without sin." Jesus' compassion and helpfulness are near at hand, even within us, but it is our sin that separates Him morally and spiritually from us.

I want to point out once again that Jesus is totally without sin. We discussed this fact at length in connection with 4:15, and noted the many places in scripture that make this fact clear. But we need to be reminded that Jesus is sinless, perfect in every way. And each of the five terms in this verse by which the author describes Jesus add to the all-encompassing truth of this: Jesus is "holy, blameless, pure, set apart from sinners, exalted above the heavens."

### Heb. 7:27. Unlike other high priests, he does not need to offer sacrifices day after day, first for his own sins, and then for the sins of the people.

Now that he has wrapped up his dissertation on the qualifications for perfection for the priesthood, the author begins to show the contrast in ministry between Jesus our High Priest and all other high priests. He states that earthly priests must make sacrifices for their own sins when Jesus needed to make no sacrifice for Himself since He was sinless; then showing that the priests needed to make sacrifices every day, first for themselves and then for the people, when Jesus made just one sacrifice which was valid for eternity.

The whole book of Leviticus is filled with the huge variety of sacrifices the priests needed to make for themselves, for the rulers of the people, all the way down to the most humble of Israelites. A cursory glance at Leviticus will expose the plethora of sacrifices, offerings, and gifts, which the priests needed to make. Here is but a sample.

| | |
|---|---|
| Lev. 4:3 | The anointed priest needed to make sacrifices of young bulls for his own sins, even those sins he committed without knowing he had committed a sin ("unintentionally," verse 2). |
| Lev. 4:13 | A young bull must be sacrificed for the whole congregation if they sin unintentionally. |
| Lev. 4:22 | If a ruler sins unintentionally, the designated sacrifice is a male goat. |
| Lev. 4:27 | If a common man sins unintentionally, the designated sacrifice is a female goat. |
| Lev. 6:20 | When Aaron was anointed high priest, he had to offer a grain offering (whether he had sinned or not, apparently, although he was a sinful man). |
| Lev. 8 | The whole chapter is devoted to the offerings that had to be made when Aaron and his sons were ordained to the priesthood. |
| Lev. 9:8 | After Aaron was ordained, he first had to sacrifice a calf as a sin-offering for himself. Following that, he made sacrifices and offerings for all the people. |
| Lev. 16:1-5 | When Aaron was ready to enter the sanctuary, there were several animals he had to sacrifice. |
| Lev. 16:6-14 | These verses tell of the sacrifices Aaron had to make for himself. |
| Lev. 16:15-34 | We read about the requirements for the annual Atonement. |

Now let us examine what Jesus had to do by way of contrast with the requirements for the Levitical priests.

**He sacrificed for their sins once for all when He offered himself.**

The first thing we must take into account is not a contrast; instead, it is part of a continuum. It is true that Jesus "sacrificed for their sins," just like the Old Testament priests did. Jesus, a High Priest, performed the one necessary priestly act: He made a sacrifice for sin. That is how He affirms His priesthood, and how He becomes our Intercessor. This is how Paul said it to his young friend Timothy: "There is one God and one mediator between God and men, the man Christ Jesus, who gave himself as a ransom for all men—the testimony given in its proper time" (I Tim. 2:5-6).

Unlike all other lawyers, mediators, counselors, Jesus did not simply spew out words, words, words; Jesus *did* something tangible for those He represented. He took their punishment upon Himself by putting Himself in their place of punishment. He made a sacrifice for them.

Sacrifice is not out of date today. Some people dislike the book of Hebrews; they are offended by its talk about bloody sacrifices. But sacrifice is the only way, God's only way, for any human being to get to heaven. You, today, in this twenty-first century AD, cannot hope to even see heaven without a sacrifice having been made for you. And the only valid sacrifice which God accepts, or has ever accepted (as we shall see soon) is the sacrifice of His only Son Jesus on the cross at Calvary. You *will* fulfill all the Old Testament law of sacrifice, or you will go to hell forever. The only difference is the kind of sacrifice that is made for you by the High Priest who has ascended high above all the heavens.

The first of two great contrasts between the Old Testament sacrifices and Jesus' sacrifice found near the end of verse 27 is expressed in the one word "once." As we think about this term, we must be careful to avoid misunderstanding a peculiarity of our English translation of the Greek word. Our NIV (as well as the RSV) uses the phrase "once for all," which erroneously might tend to cause some readers to think the author of Hebrews meant "one time for all people," or "one time for all people's sins," but this is not so. The Greek word, which is an emphatic form of the word that means simply "once" is ἐφάπαξ; so the emphatic would mean for us something like "one time only," or "not more than once." Incidentally, the KJV translates it most nearly correctly, using the single word "once."

The theme that Jesus offered Himself just once ought to be divided into two important points. The first is that in Old Testament times one sacrifice had to be made for each sin, that is, every sacrifice, no matter how large or expensive, was sufficient to cover the guilt of only one sin for one person (or in the case of corporate sin, for the sin of the congregation or group of people who had sinned). Jesus' sacrifice, on the other hand, was efficacious, sufficient, satisfactory, able, to cover *all* sins of all people who lived at all times (although only those who receive His sacrifice for their sins receive forgiveness and eternal life). Why Jesus' sacrifice was fully adequate was because as the infinitely great God His sacrifice was infinitely capable of paying for the sins and cleansing the sinners of their guilt. Even if an ordinary human being was able to pay for the sins of others, his sacrifice could pay for only one sin for only one friend. But without Christ, each person must die for his own sins, and therefore cannot die for the sins of anyone else.

The second important point about Jesus' single sacrifice is that Jesus did not and does not need to die more than once for all the sins of the world. If you should commit another sin tomorrow, it will not be necessary for Jesus to die another time to cover that sin. When we discussed Heb. 6:6, we covered that matter, although from a slightly different perspective. In addition, the beloved apostle John said in his first little epistle (I John 1:7), "the blood of Jesus, his Son, purifies us from every [all] sin." There is, however, a denomination that demonstrates its unwillingness to believe that every sin is covered by the one sacrifice of Jesus Christ. Each of its priests throughout the world is required to perform a ritual at least once daily, called "the sacrifice of the Mass." That is why every church in that denomination has prominently displayed at the front of the sanctuary a table that is called the "Altar." An altar, as you know, is a place to make a sacrifice for sin, to appease God. But if Jesus made one sacrifice, once, on the cross at Calvary, there is no need for another sacrifice and therefore no need for an altar today. That is why people in Protestant churches correctly call such a table their "Communion Table," where we remember the one sacrifice Jesus made for our sins as we celebrate Communion. Communion is not a sacrifice for any sin, but a memorial by which to remember Jesus' single sacrifice for all sin.

This idea that Jesus needed to die but once for all sin recurs several times in the book of Hebrews, therefore it must have been exceedingly important in the mind and heart of the author.

We said that the end of verse 27 has two great contrasts. We have just finished discussing the first. We are ready to discuss the second contrast, which is that Jesus offered Himself as the sacrifice for the sins of the people, whereas the Old Testament priests never offered even themselves but rather a variety of animals and birds as sacrifices for the sins of the people. Therefore, we see that Jesus was not only the Great High Priest who performed the act of sacrificing an appropriate offering for sin; He also was the Sacrifice Itself. Truly, Jesus has done absolutely everything for us:

> Jesus paid it all, All to Him I owe;
> Sin had left a crimson stain, He washed it white as snow.

John the Baptist spoke of Jesus as our Sacrifice in these words (John 1:29 and 35): "Look, the Lamb of God, who takes away the sin of the world!" The apostle John wrote of Jesus in the Revelation (13:8), whom he called "the Lamb that was slain from the creation of the world." Paul said the same thing in I Cor. 5:7, "Christ, our Passover lamb, has been sacrificed." All this was presaged in Isaiah's soaring passage on Christ the Suffering Servant in Is. 52:13-53:12, especially 53:7:

> He was oppressed and afflicted,
>> yet he did not open his mouth;
> he was led like a lamb to the slaughter,
>> and as a sheep before her shearers is silent,
> so he did not open his mouth.

When we come face to face with the enormous love Jesus showed to us by dying for us, even while we were still enemies and sinners against Him, we ought to weep copiously for two reasons: for our inexcusable sinfulness and rebellion against Him, and for our uncontainable gratitude for His loving sacrifice to save us for eternal glory!

* * *

**Heb. 7:28.** **For the law appoints as high priests men who are weak....**

The law is considered here as the scapegoat, blamed for the imperfection of the old covenant administered by the Levitical priests. Paul supported that harsh judgment on the law in Rom. 8:3-4:

> What the law was powerless to do in that it was weakened by the sinful nature, God did by sending his own Son in the likeness of sinful man to be a sin offering. And so he condemned sin in sinful man, in order that the righteous requirements of the law might be fully met in us, who do not live according to the sinful nature but according to the Spirit.

When the author talks about men who are weak, he uses the word ἀσθένεια, which in the Greek can mean either "physical frailty" or "sickness." Both ideas are appropriate here. In addition, the idea could well be extended to the moral and spiritual weakness of all the Old Testament priests. They all were men, mere, ordinary men, nothing more.

**...but the oath, which came after the law....**

We could probably get into some very convoluted arguments with this clause. For instance, did God's oath designating Jesus as a High Priest after the order of Melchizedek really come after the law, or did it come at the time, probably before the creation, when God created Melchizedek to be the forerunner of Jesus? After all, the law is itself the old covenant, but God's oath brings in the new covenant. Yet this new covenant that appoints Jesus Christ a High Priest like Melchizedek is an everlasting covenant: it is everlasting backward before the earliest days of the universe, as well as forward into the endless future. So we may ask ourselves, when did the Father for the very first time swear, "You are a priest forever"? That oath is first recorded in the words of King David who wrote Ps. 110 in about 1000 BC, five hundred years after Moses brought the tablets of the law down from Sinai. Of course that was not the very first time God made known His law to any people either. It was the codification of the law for the sake of God's chosen people who were on their way to the Promised Land. David implies in the introduction to those words that God had made the oath before David wrote it. How long before is anyone's guess.

Perhaps we should simply agree that with God everything is in the eternal present. He, even more than Melchizedek, has no beginning or end. God is eternal, and He knows the end from the beginning, as the Psalmist says in Is. 46:10:

> I make known the end from the beginning,
> from ancient times, what is still to come.

In our human system of timing, however, the people were governed by the law (including the ritual sacrifices) before Jesus came in the flesh to introduce the New Covenant in which Jesus is both High Priest and Sacrifice for sin. Perhaps the timing relationship between the law and the oath is not so crucial as the fact that God's oath was made to establish Jesus as our Great High Priest in place of the Levitical priests.

### ...appointed the Son, who has been made perfect forever.

Here we have the same grammatical construction we find in the second verse of the book of Hebrews. The author says literally that the oath appointed "a Son." There can be no confusion as to who is the One designated, since God had but one "only-begotten" Son. The rest of us, who are designated as "children of God," are His children only through adoption, as Paul explains in Rom. 8:15: "You did not receive a spirit that makes you a slave again to fear, but you received the Spirit of sonship [the Greek word here is 'adoption'];" Gal. 4:5: "...to redeem those under law, that we might receive the full rights of sons [again, the Greek word is 'adoption'];" and Eph. 1:5: "...he predestined us to be adopted as his sons through Jesus Christ, in accordance with his pleasure and will." The reason the author omits the definite article "the" here (as he did in 1:2) is that he is not concerned about being specific about the Person (since that cannot be confused anyway), but rather he is drawing our attention to the contrast in categories between the Levitical priesthood and the Melchizedek priesthood. Jesus is the Son, and apart from Melchizedek there is no other person in this category; Jesus is unique after the prototype Melchizedek.

The phrase "has been made perfect" may imply to us that Jesus at one time was not yet perfect, but through some process was "made perfect." Nothing could be further from the truth. We have already studied the passages in Hebrews and other places that state unequivocally that Jesus is perfect, has always been perfect, and always shall continue to be perfect.[13] The Greek word is a perfect passive participle, which simply means that Christ was perfect. For clarification, we ought to point out that the Greek verb from which this participle comes, τελειόω, can mean either "perfect" or "complete." For instance, when Jesus was on the cross, He cried out (John 19:30), "It is finished" (using a form of that Greek word), meaning that by His death He had accomplished everything for which He had been sent into the world by the Father. In applying Jesus' statement to ourselves, we can say with confidence that because Jesus' work was completed, the debt for our sins has been paid in full. How grateful we ought to be to our loving Savior that He paid it all!

When the author says that Jesus had been made perfect "forever," he is saying that the old covenant has been superseded by the new one, so the old covenant will never be reinstated at any time by any person for any purpose. That is an extremely important thought, especially for some Jews who might think they should look for a day when the altar will be rebuilt in Jerusalem on the spot where Abraham sacrificed his son Isaac and where Solomon built his lavish Temple. But although someone may some day indeed build an altar on

---

[13] See our discussion of Heb. 4:15.

that spot, it will never be used to make sacrifices to God; at least God will not accept any.

There is a second matter with regard the the eternity of the new High Priesthood. It is that there will never be any successor thought to be supreme to Jesus as our Great High Priest. That is fully set forth in chapter 10 of Hebrews, and especially in the climax of that chapter, verses 26-27. Be sure to read that discussion for elaboration on this subject.

In our study of chapter 7, we have noted that Jesus is a better High Priest than those of the Levitical priesthood, and that He ministered under a better covenant than they did. Next we turn to the fact that Jesus' place of ministry was a better tabernacle.

### Heb. 8:1. The point of what we are saying is this....

With these words we may expect to read a summary of what the author has been teaching us in chapter 7. What he has to say is more than a summary; it is a transition from what he wrote about in the previous chapter to what he wants to talk about now. In brief, here is the transition. He told us about Jesus as the better High Priest; now he wants to expound on the better tabernacle, the place where Jesus' priesthood is practiced. The author begins his talk about the tabernacle here, in verses 2-6; then after more details about the new covenant he continues his discussion of the tabernacle in chapter 9.

### We do have such a high priest....

The author wants us to be sure to believe that his description of the new high priesthood is not just a fairy tale, or a wish; it is a firm reality: "We *do* have such a high priest," amazing as it may seem to those who have been used to the Aaronic priesthood not only throughout their own lives, but through nearly all the history of the Jews, beginning with Moses and Aaron.

### ...who sat down at the right hand of the throne of the Majesty in heaven....

These words are almost identical to those the author used in chapter 1, verse 3; here he adds the words "of the throne." This phrase does not change what the author said earlier, but it does indicate that the Father is sovereign because He sits on a throne.

The earlier reference to Jesus as the One who sat down beside His Father introduced the discussion of Jesus as "better than" angels. His argument was supported by the first verse of Ps. 110. Now he has been discussing Jesus as "better than" high priests. This second argument is supported by the same Ps. 110, but verse 4:

> You are a priest forever,
> in the order of Melchizedek.

We turn (in this transition) to Jesus' tabernacle as "better than" the wilderness tabernacle. We may not be sure why the author chose to discuss that tabernacle instead of the more beautiful and permanent temple which Solomon built. It may be that since he has been contrasting Jesus with the first priest Aaron, he decided to use the tabernacle in which Aaron ministered rather than its replacement in which another priest in Solomon's time (probably Zadok, I Kings 4:4) ministered. At any rate, the author will surely prove conclusively that Jesus' tabernacle was infinitely "better than" either the tabernacle in the wilderness or any temple that replaced it.

### Heb. 8:2. ...and who serves in the sanctuary....

There must be an appointed *place* at which to make sacrifices to God. So this discussion follows logically after talking about the High Priest and His Sacrifice. It is a fact that there was such a place set up for Jesus and the sacrifice of Himself, a place entirely separate and different from the tabernacle in the wilderness. We begin to see what and where that place of sacrifice was.

### ...the true tabernacle set up by the Lord, not by man.

Moses' tabernacle was the rustic forerunner of Solomon's temple. Still, the tabernacle served as well as the later elaborate place; they both served as the place designated to make sacrifices for sins. We already noted that it is appropriate for the author to speak of the tabernacle rather than the later temple, since his argument so far has rested heavily on Moses and Aaron in the wilderness.

The main point is that Jesus' tabernacle was made by God Himself, without the aid of the hands of men. The wilderness tabernacle, although it was designed by God, was built by skilled artificers under the direction of Bezalel and Oholiab (see Ex. 31:2 and 6), who were set apart by God specifically for that purpose. These men were tops in their trade, master craftsmen in their guild. No human could have been more cunning in the creation of the tabernacle and all its parts and equipment. The reason the men were so great in their craft was that they possessed the Holy Spirit. God said to Moses (Ex. 31:3), "I have filled [Bezalel] with the Spirit of God, with skill, ability and knowledge in all kinds of crafts...." God continued (verse 6), "I have given skill to all the craftsmen to make everything I have commanded you," and enumerated all the things related to the tabernacle in the next five verses. Still, for all their innate abilities spurred on by the indwelling Holy Spirit, what they built in the wilderness was as nothing compared to what God built. The Greek word used here for "build" or "set up" is πήγνυμι, which means to fasten together, to build by fastening together. As you read the directions for building the tabernacle in the wilderness in Ex. 26:1-37, you see that it was designed so that literally it was fastened together so ingeniously that it could be taken apart and put together very easily, whenever the pillar of cloud began to move or to stay still, indicating that the children of Israel were to travel or encamp. At any rate, the tabernacle in the wilderness was a marvelous piece of craftsmanship. Lest we get enamored of such a tabernacle, we must ask ourselves: Why settle for something excellent, when you can have something perfect?

### Heb. 8:3. Every high priest is appointed to offer both gifts and sacrifices....

We have repeated this fact often, that the main function for a priest is to make sacrifices for people's sins. The author of Hebrews adds the idea that a priest also offers gifts. Although the ordinary term used to denote making atonement for sins is "sacrifice," scripture sometimes uses the term "gift." Just as we noted that there are many kinds of sacrifices for sin, we see in the Bible several different kinds of gifts that God required, such as meal offerings, drink offerings, and poll taxes. However, it was only the blood sacrifices (by whatever name they were called) that were efficacious to remove sin and its punishment.

### ...and so it was necessary for this one [Jesus] also to have something to offer.

Jesus' prototype, Melchizedek, made offerings to God on behalf of Abraham, although this idea is rather obscure in the Genesis record. That record does say, however (Gen. 14:18), that "Melchizedek king of Salem brought out bread and wine...and he blessed Abram." It is quite unlikely that Melchizedek brought out the food and drink because Abraham and his servants were hungry after the battle. Abraham was far from destitute, because "Abram gave him a tenth of everything" (verse 20). Nor does the text say that Melchizedek made an offering or sacrifice of what Abraham gave him, but surely it was an offering, probably a thank offering, made by Abraham to God through His high priest-servant.

In the same way, Jesus made an offering to God just as His forerunner had done. Jesus offered Himself, His body, as we shall see in Heb. 10:10, which says, "...we have been made holy through the sacrifice of the body of Jesus Christ once for all."

### Heb. 8:4. If he were on earth, he would not be a priest....

What is the author saying here? Surely he cannot claim that Jesus did not die on a physical cross on Calvary outside the wall of Jerusalem, where two ways met. He could not mean to say that, because in 9:22 he says, "without the shedding of blood there is no forgiveness." All four gospels make clear that Jesus did die at Golgotha, in the world.

There is, however, another sense in which Jesus made a sacrifice and offering, and the place for that was heaven itself. This is what the author is trying to prove in this chapter, and in the next, where he contrasts the earthly tabernacle and the heavenly. That Jesus did make His sacrifice in heaven is proved by what John wrote in Rev. 13:8, when he talks about "the Lamb that was slain from the creation of the world," that is, even before the world or the tabernacle existed.

**...for there are already men who offer the gifts prescribed by the law.**

The author is making reference again to the Levitical priesthood that had existed in the world from the time of Moses and Aaron until the destruction of the temple in 70 AD. That marked the end of sacrifices there, because the altar was destroyed as well. Since the author used the present tense for the verb here, it is possible that he wrote before that date, when the Levitical priesthood was terminated. However, such a signal is merely a possibility, not a proof of the date of authorship for the book of Hebrews.

**Heb. 8:5. They serve at a sanctuary that is a copy and a shadow of what is in heaven.**

The Greek word for "copy" is ὑπόδειγμα, which can mean a "sign...delineation...representation, figure, copy."[14] Most certainly it is not the real thing, not even a good substitute. What the priests served at on earth was no better than a blueprint, or photograph, or hand-drawn sketch, or word picture of the real thing in heaven. Surely you would not want to sail the high seas on the drawings of an aircraft carrier, but on the ship itself. This is a bad illustration, however, in that the drawings came before the ship, while the sanctuary in heaven existed from eternity before Moses received the plans for the Tabernacle built in the wilderness, which was the "copy" of the real thing.

When the author of Hebrews added the word "shadow" in this verse, he was no more complimentary than when he called it a "copy." The Greek word for "shadow" here is σκιά and needs no further translation into English. We all are sufficiently familiar with a shadow to know that it provides no details of the object beyond a mere distorted outline of the outermost parts of the real thing. It would be impossible for anyone to design the real object from a mere shadow. One must wait for vastly more information even to comprehend the real thing. So also, the sanctuary, or tabernacle, around which Aaron and his successors ministered does not help our imaginations until we arrive in heaven to see for ourselves exactly where our Savior offered Himself for our sins.

The word "sanctuary" is not found in the Greek of this verse. Do not be confused by its use here, however. The English word "sanctuary" means a "tent" or "tabernacle," words that are usually used for the place of worship

---

[14] From Thayer's definition.

281

which Moses had built in the wilderness. The word "sanctuary" is added by the translators to complement the meaning of the first part of the verse.

The way the author described the Levitical tabernacle in this verse is far from complimentary: he never intended it to be so. It was his purpose to make as glaring a distinction as he could between the tabernacle in the wilderness and the true tabernacle in heaven in which Jesus ministered for us all. The "real thing" was in heaven; Aaron's tabernacle was nothing better than a representation. What does this do for the efficacy or validity of the sacrifices and offerings made by the priests in the sight of God? We would conclude, rightly, that the earthly ministrations were not very valuable. A discussion of that point will be opened in the middle of chapter 9 of Hebrews.

**This is why Moses was warned when he was about to build the tabernacle: "See to it that you make everything according to the pattern shown you on the mountain."**
The Word for "tabernacle" here is the Greek word σκηνή, which is the Old Testament LXX translation of the Hebrew words אֹהֶל (the word ordinarily used for the tabernacle), מִשְׁכָּן (a tent), and סֻכָּה (a little shelter of boughs made for families during the Feast of Tabernacles). You may notice the large similarity between the Greek word for "tabernacle" and the one for "shadow" in this verse; they are closely related in Greek.

I would have difficulty understanding and commenting on the first part of this verse, "This is why..." if those words were all I had to depend on for a proper understanding of the verse. I choose to translate the phrase this way: "...[examples and shadows of the heavenly things] just as when Moses was given the divine blueprint...." To me there are two possibilities for understanding the thought of this verse correctly.

First, the author may have been strongly emphasizing that God wanted His directions to be carried out to the letter in Moses' building of the tabernacle. Since the tabernacle in the wilderness was at least a representation of that in heaven, God wanted no flaw to be built into it which would either detract from its utility or lead an observer astray from any important detail in the real Tabernacle.

Secondly, the author may have wanted us to be sure that what Moses built was truly a replica of the heavenly Tabernacle. In one sense I find this argument difficult to accept. After all, how could that prefab construction in the desert ever be considered comparable to the true Tabernacle? Was the heavenly one no better than that? Of course the heavenly one was infinitely better, but although the earthly one was so rudimentary, still it was not flawed, as long as Moses took care in its construction. In another sense, this possibility seems more plausible to me, because the author has been talking about the heavenly Tabernacle by comparison to the earthly one. We understand fully that there is an infinite difference in quality between the two although the pattern for each is the same pattern.

Perhaps most importantly, God's orders for Moses to build the tent in the wilderness with no deviation whatsoever from the pattern sent down to him from heaven were very insistent. We read the original directive in Ex. 25:40.

**Heb. 8:6. But the ministry Jesus has received is as superior...as the covenant of which he is mediator is superior to the old one, and it is founded on better promises.**

If we rewrite this sentence in a pictorial form, we will see more clearly how the author of Hebrews here presents a three-fold summary of reasons why Jesus' ministry is "better than" anything the Old Testament can offer:

> Now he has obtained a *better ministry*,
>
> as much as he is the Mediator of a *better covenant*,
>
> which is regulated by *better promises*.

As we think about the "better ministry," it is most likely that we are looking at the material elements of the ministry of the Old Testament, such as the altar, the tabernacle, the animals and birds dedicated for sacrifice, and perhaps even the fire in the altar. The Greek word for "ministry" is λειτουργία, which is defined as "the service of ministry of the priests relative to the prayers and sacrifices offered to God."[15] In considering the material elements, we do not find the altar in heaven defined or described anywhere in scripture, as far as I recall, but whatever it was, it must have been far superior to the piece of furniture made of acacia wood and bronze (Ex. 27:1-8) by the hands of Bezalel and Oholiab and their assistants in the wilderness (Ex. 31:1-6, 36:1-5). The sanctuary on earth was the tabernacle in the wilderness, while Jesus' sanctuary was heaven itself, not made by the hands of even the most skillful men. The animals and birds sacrificed on earth surely ought to be considered the most diverse of all elements of ministry from the one great Sacrifice made in heaven, our Savior, God Himself, who gave Himself for our sakes, who "while we were still sinners" against Him (Rom. 5:8) still died for us. And if we think of the fire as part of our consideration here, we may contrast the fire under the sacrifices on the altar with the third person of the Trinity, the Holy Spirit, described as fire often in scripture (the tongues of fire at Pentecost, Acts 2:3-4; Lu. 3:16 is another indication of the Holy Spirit as fire in the act of baptism; the Holy Spirit is doubtless the Person of the Godhead who passed between the parts of the sacrifices for Abraham in Gen. 15:17; and the seven burning lamps in Rev. 4:5, which are the seven Spirits of God), who not only burns the sacrifice, but also in a figure brands our spirits and consciences in order to identify us as children of God.

Jesus' covenant is the second detail by which Jesus' work is better than that of the Levitical priests. The Greek word for "covenant," διαθήκη, is

---

[15] Thayer's definition.

translated in addition as "will" and "testament" in scripture, and is "used to denote the close relationship which God entered into...with...the people."[16] The idea of "covenant" is not mentioned by the author of Hebrews until 7:22, but there he introduces the matter as a prelude to his greater exposition of the idea, not only as "covenant," but also as "will" and "testament" in chapter 9, and further sprinkled through chapters 8, 10, 12, and 13. As defining the relationship between God and His people, the covenant is made distinct from the "ministry," which as we said was the discussion of the outward physical elements of the work.

A covenant can be of two kinds. One is unilateral, such as was made by God with Abraham in the Gen. 15 passage we noted a moment ago. The covenant was that God would in truth give Abraham an heir, from his own loins, born of his wife Sarah, so that Abraham would be the father of a nation of God's people forever. There God the Spirit made promises to Abraham and confirmed His role in the covenant by passing between the two piles of the sacrificial animals and birds. God also affirmed the promises of the covenant without regard to a single promise on the part of Abraham or his children-to-be. For evidence of that, read that whole chapter which contains the story.

The other kind of covenant is a bilateral one, in which God promises to do certain things, but only based on the response of the people with whom the covenant is made. Such a covenant is elaborated in Deut. 26:16 through 28:68, the covenant recited antiphonally by the children of Israel on Mounts Ebal and Gerizim, in which God promised blessing in return for their obedience to His law, and cursing in case of their disobedience. Parallels to these two kinds of covenant in the New Testament may be illustrated by God's covenant to love the whole world (John 3:16) regardless of the response of any individual, as a sample of unilateral covenant; and God's act of salvation based on a person's faith in Christ as Lord and Savior, as Paul says in Acts 16:31: "Believe in the Lord Jesus, and you will be saved—you and your household."

The author talks about a single covenant in each case, Old and New Testaments, but it takes little search to find multiple covenants in the Old Testament. What the author quotes here from Jeremiah is, without doubt, his expression of the two covenants he intends to discuss next.

The third thing the author means to show us is "better than" what the Old Testament offers is the "better promises," which he presents through the rest of his letter, or sermon. I like to summarize whatever promises there are with what he wrote in Heb. 10:11, "Day after day every priest stands and performs his religious duties; again and again he offers the same sacrifices, *which can never take away sins*" (I added the emphasis). The "better promises" relate to the assured taking away of sin through the sacrifice of Jesus Christ our Lord.

---

[16]  Again, Thayer's definition, in part.

**Heb.  8:7.   For if there had been nothing wrong with that first  covenant....**

The author has written, and we have elaborated at length, on the several things wrong with "that first covenant." The priests were not appointed by divine oath as was Christ; the priests were all sinful while Christ was "without sin;" each priest died only a few years or at most decades after his appointment, but Christ was a "priest forever" (Heb. 7:21, quoted from Ps. 110:4). In addition, the sacrifices of the first covenant were at best inadequate. All the animals and birds put together could not compare with Christ as the great Sacrifice. Every Old Testament sacrifice was flawed in some way, while Christ was perfect, without blemish, sinless.

**...no place would have been sought for another.**

God Himself determined to make the change. It was not man's idea to abandon the old covenant and draw up a new one. It would be especially ridiculous to assume that the Aaronic priests wanted a new program. After all, they were the ones who benefited most from the sacrifices and offerings the people brought to the temple; they would never want to give up such a plush position. In fact, when they realized that Jesus was about to sweep away the whole system, they cried out in both fright and bitter anger (John 11:47-48):

Then the chief priests and the Pharisees called a meeting of the Sanhedrin. "What are we accomplishing?" they asked. "Here is this man performing many miraculous signs. If we let him go on like this, everyone will believe in him, and then the Romans will come and take away both our place and our nation."

Apart from the Sanhedrin, and especially the priests among them, it would be difficult to find any other person or group who would cry out against a change in regime; most would have welcomed the relief from oppression attained by the change. Ordinarily people like to make changes in their lives. They want to live in a different house or country; they seek a different kind of job; far too many trade in their old spouses for new ones. Too often, however, the changes we make for ourselves are more detrimental than beneficial. Only God invariably makes changes for the betterment of mankind.

**Heb.  8:8.   But God found fault with the people and said....**

Suddenly here we face a new twist on the idea of God's intention to establish a new covenant because the old one was faulty. Heretofore He has chided the priests for their failure to live up to what was required of competent priests. Now the author turns to the people in general, and says that their lives of transgression have alienated them from God, so that the old covenant was impracticable.  So now we are faced with two major reasons why the old covenant had to be abandoned and replaced with one that would accomplish its purpose in God's loving intention to save multitudes of people from the pains of hell and deliver them into a blissful heaven forever.  How amazing is the extent to which God goes to accomplish His purpose in showing kindness to those whom He has chosen!

Now we come to a very long quotation from Jeremiah, who was called the "Weeping Prophet," because he was deeply sorrowful over the utterly sad prophecies God required him to declare to the people.  Among all his unsettling and hated messages, there are at least a few bright spots to relieve the pain.  One of his greatest notes of encouragement is found in the very middle of the arguably saddest of all books, Jeremiah's "Lamentations."  We read in Lam. 3:21-24:

> Yet this I call to mind
> and therefore I have hope:
> Because of the LORD's great love we are not consumed,
> for his compassions never fail.
> They are new every morning;
> great is your faithfulness.
> I say to myself, "The LORD is my portion;
> therefore I will wait for him."

The author of Hebrews quotes another of his words of encouragement (Jer. 31:31-34), to show that God not only established a new High Priest, but also created a new people who somehow had to be better than those who lived under the old covenant.  You may read the full quotation; here we shall divide it into its clauses, to study each as it comes.

### The time is coming, declares the Lord....

When Jeremiah wrote (about 629 BC), these prophecies had not yet been fulfilled.  God would see that they happened in His "fullness of time."

### ...when I will make a new covenant....

It is God who took the initiative to make the change.  Further, He did it regardless of people's preferences.  He did not wait for them to vote, to see which group would win.  He is the sovereign creator God, who does as He pleases, and it is always for the best for all people, not just what the majority want, whether it is right or wrong, beneficial or detrimental.

### ...with the house of Israel
### and with the House of Judah.

At these phrases we Gentiles will prick up our ears, if we are alert enough to notice the intention of what we are reading.  What first catches my attention is that I thought this new covenant of which the author of Hebrews speaks is for all people, not just for the tribes of the divided House of Israel.  I

286

initially ask myself two questions: Am I confused by what this new covenant is? or, Am I confused by who Israel and Judah are? Perhaps at this point we can remember that the Bible book we are studying is called "Hebrews" in our English translations; however, we have no clue to that identity in the introduction of the book.

In considering this problem, we may be sure of at least one thing: the new covenant was intended for all Jews, whether for anyone else or not. After all, the first covenant Jeremiah is talking about here seemed limited to Jews, so the prophet may have wanted to draw a parallel in this respect between the two covenants. On the other hand, must we assume that Gentiles were totally excluded from the first covenant? A careful study of the Old Testament shows that many Gentiles were assimilated, in one way or another, into the Jewish community; further, some Gentiles received God's blessings without being connected to the Jewish nation at all. For instance, a large number of Egyptians, and perhaps people of other nations as well, were more than mere "camp followers" when they accompanied the Jews out of Egypt to wander with them forty years before arriving at the Promised Land, as we read in Ex. 12:37-38: "The Israelites journeyed from Rameses to Succoth. There were about six hundred thousand men on foot, besides women and children. Many other people went up with them...." We read of an enemy of Israel, Naaman, army general of the King of Syria (Aram), whom God blessed with healing from leprosy (II Kings 5:1-19). We cannot miss the fact that several of Jesus' Old Testament ancestors were Gentiles: Rahab the Harlot was an inhabitant of Jericho, but was married to Salmon the father of Boaz; Ruth the Moabitess was married to Boaz the great-grandfather of King David; Bath-sheba David's wife and mother of Solomon was first married to Uriah the Hittite, so she may not have been an Israelite herself. (See Matt. 1:1-17 for the genealogy, and related Old Testament stories in Josh. 2 and 6 for Rahab; the four chapters of the book of Ruth for her; and II Sam. 11 and 12, and I Kings 1 for Bathsheba.) A further consideration is that Paul claims that all Christians who believe in Jesus Christ as Savior and Lord in the same way Abraham did are in fact spiritual children of Abraham and thus spiritual Jews. Paul explains this in Rom. 4:11: "And [Abraham] received the sign of circumcision, a seal of the righteousness that he had by faith while he was still uncircumcised. So then, he is the father of all who believe but have not been circumcised, in order that righteousness might be credited to them." Paul continues this line of argument through verse 17 of chapter 4. I invite you to read it all, and note carefully that the children of Abraham are those who believe like Abraham believed in Jesus Christ; for that reason Abraham is the "father of many nations."

**Heb. 8:9.**
**It will not be like the covenant**

> I made with their forefathers
> when I took them by the hand
> to lead them out of Egypt,
> because they did not remain faithful to my
> covenant,
> and I turned away from them, declares the
> Lord.

Certainly God's new covenant with His people would be quite different from the one He had made with them in the wilderness. The first covenant was established at the beginning of the Exodus ("to lead them out of Egypt"). What, then, was that first covenant? We may call it a covenant of law, or obedience to God's law. In connection with the argument of the book of Hebrews here, it had to do mainly with the sacrifices stipulated in Leviticus, and the ritual of the tabernacle of which we read in Ex. 25-40. One other major factor in the old covenant was the requirement that the people seek only the help of God in the difficulties which they encountered.

The people were quick to break God's first covenant, however. Shortly after they began their trip into the wilderness, they turned from God to Aaron to make them a golden calf in which they could trust (Ex. 32:1): "Come, make us gods who will go before us." And after the calf was set up, the people declared (Ex. 32:8): "These are your gods, O Israel, who brought you up out of Egypt."

We must note that it was the people who broke God's covenant, and not God who broke covenant with them. Jeremiah tells us this in Jer. 11:7-8:

> From the time I brought your forefathers up from Egypt until today, I warned them again and again, saying, "obey me." But they did not listen or pay attention; instead, they followed the stubbornness of their evil hearts.

Again, in Jer. 44:17-19, Jeremiah points out the people's unfaithfulness:

> "We will certainly do everything we said we would: We will burn incense to the Queen of Heaven and will pour out drink offerings to her just as we and our fathers, our kings and our officials did in the towns of Judah and in the streets of Jerusalem. At that time we had plenty of food and were well off and suffered no harm. But ever since we stopped burning incense to the Queen of Heaven and pouring out drink offerings to her, we have had nothing and have been perishing by sword and famine."
>
> The women added, "When we burned incense to the Queen of Heaven and poured out drink offerings to her, did not our husbands know that we were making cakes like her image and pouring out drink offerings to her?"

How utterly false were the deductions of the people! They were exactly 180° out of phase with reality in their relationship with God. They blamed God for their troubles, and gave credit to the "Queen of Heaven" for what they considered their blessings. On the contrary, it was God who gave them whatever blessings they did possess (although they did not always recognize them as blessings), and it was God who punished them for their rejection of Him. The "Queen of Heaven" had nothing to do with any of it, because she was but a figment of their vain imaginations (see Ps. 2:1 in the KJV). Yet this is the kind of topsy-turvy world many people live in today: they boldly "do their own thing" despite all admonitions from God or His messengers, and then blame God for the ills they encounter.

There is a great contrast in all this. It was the people who strayed from God and His covenant, but it was God who adhered rigidly to His bargain. It may take a few moments of careful thought to agree with this, at least the second part of the statement. It will be helpful if you remember that God's part in the covenant was two-fold: He promised to bless the people as long as they remained faithful to Him; but He threatened to curse them if they turned their backs on Him. So when the people rejected God by their unfaithfulness, if God was to keep covenant with them, He was obliged to shower curses upon them. Here is a continuation of the quotation from Jer. 11:7-8: "So I brought on them all the curses of the covenant I had commanded them to follow but that they did not keep." Ultimately, God completely abandoned them (at least for the seventy years of exile which Jeremiah predicted) when He allowed Jerusalem, the last stronghold of the Promised Land, to be overrun and destroyed by Nebuchadnezzar King of Babylon in 586 BC. Read all about it at the end of II Chronicles, chapter 36:11-23.

**Heb. 8:10.**
**This is the covenant I will make with the house**
**of Israel**
**after that time, declares the Lord.**

Even in the face of flaming retribution, God delivered to Jeremiah and his people the outline of the new, perfect covenant which would replace the old, flawed one. Here it is.

**I will put my laws in their minds**
**and write them on their hearts.**

First, God promises a new kind of writing material on which to inscribe the laws of His new covenant. We may assume that it was not just the laws of the old covenant that were faulty; the recording material, that is, the stone tablets, were also faulty, so they failed to do what was required for men. The original tablets were stored in the ark, which resided in the Most Holy part in the tabernacle. For that reason, only one person was allowed to look at them, and he had access to them only once a year, on the Day of Atonement, when he entered the inner room to offer blood for his own sins first and then for those of the people. It is possible that copies of the law were made, so they could be read by others than the high priest, but it is unlikely that many of the people could read anyway. Today with libraries filled with billions of books, and computers hooked to the internet, it is incomprehensible that the word of God was unavailable to the people. On the other hand, although the Bible has been on the top of the best seller list for decades, or perhaps centuries, we know that most people are ignorant of the message it contains. However, God chooses to write His new covenant on the very minds and hearts of all people. How gracious He is to donate such a huge gift. Those who reject God's covenant are without excuse before Him, because the message is inescapable to them who see churches on every fourth corner, and hear and see Christian programs on radio and television, and have neighbors who lovingly urge them to take heed to God's word, all of which merely reinforce what is written on their hearts.

Some people think here is another clue that Paul who the book of Hebrews. A strong link to this idea of writing God's new covenant on people's hearts is found in II Cor. 3:3-10. After commending the people of the church in Corinth, Paul boasts, "You show that you are a letter from Christ, the result of our ministry, written not with ink but with the Spirit of the living God, not on tablets of stone but on tablets of human hearts." Paul continues in verse 6, "[God] has made us competent as ministers of a new covenant—not of the letter but of the Spirit...." The next four verses argue that the blessings brought by the new covenant are far superior to those supplied by the old one: "If the ministry that condemns men is glorious, how much more glorious is the ministry that brings righteousness!" (verse 9).

### I will be their God,
### and they will be my people.

This promise is not new, but the rebellious people had turned away from God's promise and His relationship to them. But God, who is longsuffering toward those He loves, provided a new avenue by which they could make their way back to Him. This is an absolute promise. God would not utterly forsake His people, but we see scattered through the prophets God's assurance that "a remnant will be saved." Even Jeremiah, whose words are recorded here, speaks of the remnant nearly a score of times, with such words as these in Jer. 23:3: "I myself will gather the remnant of my flock out of all the countries where I have driven them and will bring them back to their pasture, where they will be fruitful and increase in number." And the author of Hebrews ends his quotation from Jeremiah on a high note, "...they will all know me, from the least of them to the greatest. For I will forgive their wickedness and will remember their sins no more." The apostle Paul affirms this truth in his letter to the Romans, 11:26, "And so all Israel will be saved." We rejoice in the knowledge that there is no more beneficial relationship for us humans, than to have God as our God, and for Him to enfold us as His people!

* * *

## Heb. 8:11.

### No longer will a man teach his neighbor,
### or a man his brother....

The teaching about God was, at certain ancient times, prevalent. The Jews from Moses' time onward were urged to make such teaching a large part of their daily lives. Jews even today have memorized the Shema, Deut. 6:4-9:

> Hear, O Israel: The LORD our God, the LORD is one. Love the LORD your God with all your heart and with all your soul and with all your strength. These commandments that I give you today are to be upon your hearts. Impress them on your children. Talk about them when you sit at home and when you walk along the road, when you lie down and when you get up. Tie them as symbols on your hands and bind them on your foreheads. Write them on the doorframes of your houses and on your gates.

In those days, the responsibility for teaching was upon the fathers. There is no indication in scripture that that guideline has been abrogated since Moses wrote it. So when a people defects from the knowledge and ways of God, the fault invariably lies with the fathers. As through most of history, the tragedy is that fathers have shunned their role in teaching. Today, fathers are noticeably absent from church. If they have not learned the word, how can they be expected to transfer it to the next generation? In my ministry, many wives have testified that their husbands not only refuse to go to church, or read the Bible; they actually forbid their wives and children to do so. Once a teenage girl in Chicago was converted through a friend's testimony. Shortly afterward, in an attempt to live the Christian life at home, she asked her father if she could thank the Lord for the food before they ate. In a fit of anger the father responded, "No, you may not! If you want to thank anyone for the food, you can thank me, because I worked hard to provide that food for you."

The verse we are considering does not say that teaching the word of God is unnecessary; it emphasizes that such knowledge will be general, and generally accepted. People will no longer need to teach others, because all will have been taught already. New generations certainly will need to hear the words so they can believe.

### ...saying, "Know the Lord;"
### because they will all know me...

How that knowledge of the Lord gets disseminated I am not sure, if not through teaching. Perhaps Jeremiah was making it clear that "neighbors" and "brothers" would know the word, so they would not need to be taught. But when new people come into the world, they surely need to be taught, unless he is saying that God will make Himself known in supernatural ways.

Actually, Paul says the same thing, but in a different sense, when he says that the knowledge of God is already universal. Here is what he wrote in Rom. 1:19-21:

> ...since what may be known about God is plain to [godless and wicked

men], because God has made it plain to them. For since the creation of the world God's invisible qualities—his eternal power and divine nature—have been clearly seen, being understood from what has been made, so that men are without excuse. For although they knew God, they neither glorified him as God nor gave thanks to him, but their thinking became futile and their foolish hearts were darkened.

What Paul is saying is that every human is born with an innate knowledge of God in his heart and mind. His sinful nature causes him to turn from that knowledge, and to fill the vacuum created thereby with gods of his own making, like images of animals, birds, fish, people, and other things. Thus their knowledge of God is useless to them. James says the same thing in his letter, only with regard to the knowledge of God which fallen angels possess, but it applies to people equally (Jas. 2:19): "You believe that there is one God. Good! Even the demons believe that—and shudder." Simply to know God is inadequate. The only "knowledge" that helps a person is to receive Jesus Christ as both Savior and Lord. Only then will a person receive eternal life.

### ...from the least of them to the greatest.

Choose any category of people: aged or child; wealthy or poor; a member of Mensa or with a low IQ; an Ivy League graduate or one totally unschooled; a blue-blood or an "untouchable;" all of them will be equal in their knowledge of the Lord in the era of the new covenant. All people will be like the gatherers of manna in the wilderness, "...he who gathered much did not have too much, and he who gathered little did not have too little. Each one gathered as much as he needed" (Ex. 16:18, quoted by Paul in II Cor. 8:15).

### Heb. 8:12.
### For I will forgive their wickedness
### and will remember their sins no more.

"Forgiveness" is just about the greatest word in my vocabulary. The absolute assurance of forgiveness means absolute peace. As I write these words, the United States is sending tens of thousands of military people to the Middle East to confront Iraq in the battle against terrorism and against the possibility of Iraq's deployment of nuclear missiles, or chemical or biological "weapons of mass destruction." Some people seem to be more terrified of the onset of war than they are of terrorist attacks by those who hate America. They are staging demonstrations on the streets of cities around the country. Others, although they deplore the possibility of war, are determined to promote peace even if the price of peace is war itself. World War I was fought with the motto, "The war to end all wars." That proved futile, because World War II was begun almost exactly two decades from the end of the first. Since then the world has been wracked by dozens of wars, both small and large, many being waged at the same time. So another war will not bring lasting peace, nor will political negotiation, which was tried by people such as Neville Chamberlain before the second great war started.

The cause of war is "wickedness" and "sin," as the author of Hebrews implies. And the only way to peace is for men's wickedness and sin to be eliminated. That can be accomplished only by God's forgiveness. And forgiveness comes only by man's confession of sin, repentance, and the desire to turn from sin to God's righteousness. People have attempted a variety of ways to eliminate their sin. Our first parents tried two oft-copied methods. First, they tried to cover their disobedience by sewing fig-leaves together to fashion aprons (Gen. 3:7). Next, when they were confronted by God with their sin, they tried to blame someone else for forcing them to sin (Gen. 3:13). But God accepted none of their lame attempts. Instead, He slew a lamb and took its skin and covered their nakedness. That lamb was a symbol of the "Lamb of God, who takes away the sin of the world!" (John 1:29).

Other methods by which people futilely attempt to eliminate the guilt of their sins are many. Lady Macbeth tried to wash away the stain of her murder with water, but the strongest detergent will never cleanse a person's soul from guilt. A friend of mine tried to escape the consequences of his sin of assaulting a nurse with a knife by telling me, "I am not guilty of the crime of which I am accused," attempting to change the name of his crime, as if a sin by any other name would make him guiltless. Several years ago, a homosexual man and a lesbian woman, speaking to a group of teenagers at a church conference, when asked whether they thought the Bible said that homosexual living is a sin replied, "No we don't think so," in the face of numerous clear, unambiguous statements that God utterly condemns such a lifestyle. To deny that a sin is sin is abomination to God. The only way for God's forgiveness to come upon anyone is for that person to confess his sin, ask God for forgiveness, and ask the Holy Spirit's help to overcome the temptation to sin further. John wrote (I John 1:9), "If we confess our sins, he is faithful and just and will forgive us our sins and purify us from all unrighteousness."

There is one further factor required of us in order to receive God's forgiveness. After teaching His disciples the Lord's Prayer, Jesus warned them that God will not forgive a person who has not forgiven other people their sins against him. In Matt. 6:14-15 we read, "For if you forgive men when they sin against you, your heavenly Father will also forgive you. But if you do not forgive men their sins, your Father will not forgive your sins."

Evangelical Christians are accused of saying that people are bad, liberal Christians are accused of saying that people are good. Each group is right, but only to a degree. It would be better to set the whole idea into a three-step formula: 1) All people are partly good; 2) All people are partly bad; 3) God forgives and perfects all who come to Him confessing and repenting.

Some thirty years ago, the passing fad of Transactional Analysis was espoused in a book by Thomas A. Harris entitled I'M OK--YOU'RE OK. The author posed four possibilities for different relationships between people:

"I'm not OK--you're not OK; I'm not OK--you're OK; I'm OK--you're not OK; and I'm OK--you're OK." All these are pretty self-explanatory, but they do not really help anyone make the grade from the first to the last state. Shortly after I read the book, I preached a sermon I titled, I'M OK--BUT WHY? In that message I pointed out my thesis that psychotherapy will not guarantee anyone a place in the fourth category. I can never make myself OK, only God can make me OK, through my faith in Him as my Lord and Savior. Further, only by God's grace in forgiving me can I account my neighbor as OK because I have forgiven him.

### Heb. 8:13. By calling this covenant "new," he has made the first one obsolete....

Incidentally, we ought to recognize that the author of Hebrews strongly implies here that God has made only two covenants with men: the first; and this. If this verse were all we had to try to prove such an assertion, we would be lost in the attempt. However, when we get to chapter 10, we will see the author makes such a proposal, and he makes it one of the most important points of his whole argument.

We might say that the "new" covenant is like a a new car off the assembly line. It is fresh, it is perfect, there is not a dent in it anywhere. It is ready to be of service to the new owner, and ought to be useful for a long time into the future. The very fact that this is called a "new" covenant means that the other covenant is either much less useful or of no use whatsoever.

The first covenant is here called "obsolete." The Greek word used is παλαιόω, which means to be old and worn out. In the LXX, that Greek word is used as the translation of the Hebrew word בָּלָה, which means to be worn out by use. Actually, our English word "obsolete" had an additional connotation. The old covenant was not merely old and worn out, but even if it were useful as a used-car, it has been replaced by something more up-to-date, much better because it has replaced the "old model." Anyway, the new covenant is "better than" the old; it has replaced the old. The old covenant has gone the way of the "wonderful one-hoss shay."

### ...and what is obsolete and aging will soon disappear.

The Greek word for aging here, γηράσκω, is used only one other time in the New Testament. When Jesus was talking to Peter by the Sea of Galilee after His resurrection, He told something about the end of Peter's life. He said (John 21:18): "...when you were younger you dressed yourself and went where you wanted; but when you are old you will stretch out your hands, and someone else will dress you and lead you where you do not want to go." This is what happens when a person grows old: he no longer can choose his own clothes to wear today nor even put them on for himself; neither can he take a walk down a pleasant path if he so desires, but someone else will carry him to a nursing home where he would rather not be. Finally, the old person "fades away" as we say, until he is gone. That is what happened to the first covenant. It became the worse for wear, caused mostly by the sinfulness of the priests who administered it, until finally it was totally useless; its "clothing," the tabernacle, was destroyed, and its instruments of ministry were carried off as the spoils of war, leaving no altar on which to offer sacrifices for the sins of the people. It lingered for a while, like a sunset, and finally disappeared beneath the horizon of people's sight. What a sad ending it was for what seemed to be a brilliant ministry. But God had something better to take its place.

### Heb. 9:1. Now the first covenant had regulations for worship and also an earthly sanctuary.

Two things are necessary for practically everything to happen: rules are needed for guidance; and a site must be provided. In the case of the "first" or "old" covenant, the rules were the law of Moses. We are thinking not so much about the moral law as expressed in the Ten Commandments, found in Ex. 20 and Deut. 5. Rather, we are thinking about the ritual practices performed in and around the tabernacle and the altar before it. You may read those rules, in Leviticus, and in other parts of the Books of Moses (the first five books of our Bible) to acquaint yourself with their substance.

Despite what I just said, the moral law is an integral part of the "first covenant." It was because of the transgressions of the moral law (including laws regulating man's relationship to God) that the ritual law was established in order to mitigate the results of those transgressions.

As for the place where the rituals were to occur in the wilderness, God directed Moses to build the tabernacle with all its appurtenances, and especially the altar of burnt offerings before it. After the Children of Israel began to occupy the Promised Land, God designated Shiloh as the place for the tabernacle to stay (Josh. 18:1), until Solomon built his great temple in Jerusalem, which God had specifically appointed as the permanent place for people to worship Him and offer sacrifices for their sins (see I Kings 8:44 as one indication that God had chosen the place of worship).

### Heb. 9:2. A tabernacle was set up.

The author begins to describe the tabernacle and its implements. The "blueprints" or plans for the tabernacle are described in detail in Ex. 26:1-37. It was about forty-five feet long, fifteen feet wide, and fifteen feet high, assuming one cubit to be half a yard in our measurement. It therefore was not a large structure—certainly not large enough to house all the children of Israel at one time for a worship service. In times of worship, the people stood either in the courtyard of the tabernacle, or remained by their tents which surrounded the tabernacle by tribes, three on each side. The building was constructed so it could be assembled and disassembled quickly and easily, when the people were directed by the pillars of cloud and fire to move from place to place. Also, the tabernacle had to be built strong enough to withstand the desert winds.

### In its first room....

The details of the tabernacle are found in chapter 26 of Exodus. Before thinking about the furniture and elements of worship, we should note that the tabernacle was divided into two rooms. The first room entered from outside was called "the Holy Place," and was twice as long as the other room, called the Most Holy Place. Only priests could enter the Holy Place, and only the high priest could enter the Most Holy Place. Those who were not priests might be able to peek into the Holy Place from the outside, but no one was able to even get a glimpse of the inside of the Most Holy Place. The one exception was that, when the tabernacle was to be moved, the Levites, each of whom was assigned a specific task in caring for, packing, and moving parts of the tabernacle, naturally had to see and handle those furnishings.

### ...were the lampstand, the table and the consecrated bread....

Each element in the tabernacle had a spiritual significance, and took on special significance with respect to the things in the heavenly tabernacle.

The biblical description of the lampstand is found in Ex. 25:31-36. Ornate as it was, the lampstand was to be fashioned from just one piece of gold. The light from the lamps which burned continuously, as well as the light from the pillar of fire that stood over the tabernacle at night, was symbolic of our Lord Jesus, who in John 8:12 said, "I am the light of the world."[1]

The table had no great significance in itself, but the bread placed on it was of note. How the table was to be built is described in Ex. 25:23-30. Not only was it covered completely with gold, but the bars with which to carry it were overlaid with gold.

The "consecrated bread" has several names throughout scripture, and names vary from one English version to another. In the KJV, the bread is called "shewbread" in both Heb. 9:2 and in Ex. 25:30, and in sixteen other places in scripture. our NIV calls it "consecrated bread" here, and "bread of the Presence" in the Exodus passage. In Keil and Delitzsch' COMMENTARIES[2] we read their explanation for their translation of the Hebrew words, לֶחֶם פָּנִים, "These loaves were called 'bread of the face' (shewbread), because they were to lie before the face of Jehovah as a meat-offering presented by the children of Israel (Lev. xxiv.8), a figurative representation of the calling it had received from God...." The commentary continues to point out that the bread and the wine connected to the same offering to God symbolized the people's laboring

---

[1] Some of this information about the significance of the parts of the tabernacle is from Soltau and his TABERNACLE, THE PRIESTHOOD, AND THE OFFERINGS. This information about light is on page 330.

[2] Vol. II of the Pentateuch commentary, page 171.

in the fields for their food, just as they were supposed to labor spiritually to bear fruit for God.

The author of Hebrews fails to mention here the golden altar on which incense was burned. He does mention it, however, in verse 4, in connection with the ark which was in the Most Holy Place. There is some question as to whether it was supposed to be in the Holy Place or the Most Holy Place. We will discuss that in our comments on verse 4. Otherwise, there were no other pieces of furniture in the Holy Place.

### ...this was called the Holy Place.

We would think that this place was a pretty odd place of worship, since we normally think of a church as our sanctuary, where God's people gather at set times to worship God together. Even today Jews have synagogues as places of worship, and the people meet in those buildings. But remember, the tabernacle was hardly large enough to have seated forty or fifty people comfortably. Even Solomon's temple, although it was larger than the tabernacle, would have been too small to accommodate more than a hundred worshipers at a time. It was not designed to contain worshipers. Instead, it was the place where God met the priests as they ministered on behalf of the people. After God met with the representatives of the people, they went outside and carried on their ministrations in view of the whole congregation, as many as were willing to observe. Surely there were some even in those days who had no interest in worshiping God and occupied themselves in other ways during the priestly procedures. This part of the tabernacle was called the "Holy Place" because the Holy God met with the priests to sanctify them for their tasks.

### Heb. 9:3. Behind the second curtain....

There was a "first curtain" in the tabernacle, but the author of Hebrews does not mention it in this context. That first curtain covered the only outside door of the tabernacle, and its design is described in Ex. 26:36-37. The design of the second curtain is found in Ex. 26:31-33. Both curtains were to be made of "blue, purple and scarlet yarn and finely twisted linen," and the inner or second curtain was to be decorated further with "cherubim worked into it by a skilled craftsman" (verse 31). Both curtains were to be hung with gold hooks on acacia wood posts overlaid with gold. The first curtain was carried on five posts, while the second curtain had only four. It is my conjecture that the outer curtain was divided, so the priests could part them and easily enter the first room. However, if the curtain (or veil) of the later temples was patterned after that of the tabernacle, then it was not divided at all (remember the veil was rent from top to bottom at Jesus' crucifixion {Matt. 27:51}. This would have made it difficult, to say the least, for the high priest to enter the Most Holy Place with his sacrifice of blood, even once a year. The posts were to stand in metal bases; bronze bases for the outer curtain and silver bases for the inner one.  Because of differences in detail between the two curtains, the inner one was considered more precious than the other.

### ...was a room called the Most Holy Place....

We have seen that this room was only half the size of the Holy Place, so it could have held even fewer people.  In addition, the Most Holy Place was almost filled with the Ark of the Covenant with the two huge cherubim overshadowing it.  One wing of each cherub touched a wall and its other touched the second wing of the other cherub.  We should recall also that not more than one person, the high priest, was allowed to enter the Most Holy Place, and then only once a year.

### Heb. 9:4.  ...which had the golden altar of incense and the gold-covered ark of the covenant.

The construction of the golden altar of incense is described in Ex. 30:1-5.  Its purpose was to burn incense as a sweet-smelling odor to please God.  We read in Rev. 8:3-4 that an

> angel, who had a golden censer, came and stood at the altar.  He was given much incense to offer, with the prayers of all the saints, on the golden altar before the throne.  The smoke of the incense, together with the prayers of the saints, went up before God from the angel's hand.

The formula for compounding the incense is in Ex. 30:34-38.  That passage says some of the incense was to be ground fine and sprinkled "in front of the Testimony in the Tent of Meeting."  The rest was probably burned on the altar of incense.

Now it is time to discuss the placing of the altar of incense, a question we raised in our comments on verse 2.  We read the full description of the placement of all the furniture in the tabernacle in Ex. 40:17-33.  The placement of the altar of incense is in verses 26-28, which says that the altar was placed "in front of the curtain," which most people have interpreted to mean in the Holy Place, not in the Most Holy Place.  Since the author of Hebrews says it was in the Most Holy Place, commentators have tried to solve the discrepancy in a variety of ways.  Lenski, for instance, evades the issue with some grammatical gymnastics by saying that μετά plus the accusative which the author of Hebrews uses here is not a "locative" use but rather is the common use of "after," which would then make the author say, "after seeing the lampstand and table, then they would see the incense altar farther behind, against the curtain blocking off the Holy of Holies" (my interpretation of what Lenski wrote.)[3]  In the INTERNATIONAL CRITICAL COMMENTARY volume on Hebrews, Moffatt says that the Samaritan text of the Pentateuch moves some verses in Exodus regarding the tabernacle and its furniture, and inserts the words "before the LORD" instead of "before the veil" in Ex. 40:27, thus placing the ark of incense in the Holy of Holies, at least at some point in

---

[3] Lenski, INTERPRETATION OF HEBREWS AND JAMES, page 276.

the history of the tabernacle.[4]   However, Moffatt adds that if the ark was inside the Holy of Holies, then no priest could have burned incense on it daily as was required: "...no other position was possible for an altar which required daily service from the priests."[5]   Robertson[6] tries to solve the issue by pointing out that the author of Hebrews uses the Greek word θυμιατήριον, which is the word for "censer" in the Old Testament LXX, but probably means the golden ark of incense here in the book of Hebrews.  But if the author of Hebrews meant a "censer" which was also used to burn incense to God, then it could have been in the Holy of Holies.  Robertson concludes, "Apparently the altar of incense was in the Holy Place, though in Ex. 30:1-10 it is left quite vague....So we leave the discrepancy unsettled."  There is further information in Lev. 16, where Moses describes the Day of Atonement.  There he says in verses 12-13 that Aaron must "take a censer full of burning coals from the altar before the LORD and two handfuls of finely ground fragrant incense and take them behind the curtain.  He is to put the incense on the fire before the LORD, and the smoke of the incense will conceal the atonement cover above the Testimony, so that he will not die."  This passage does not say that the altar of incense is behind the curtain, but the incense is to be burned there, to cover the Mercy Seat, so Aaron will not see God sitting there, apparently.  It is still uncertain whether the altar of incense is in front of the curtain or behind it; but at least the burning of the incense is behind the curtain, so if it is burned on the altar of incense, then the altar must be there.  I have heard or read that a few people think the altar of incense was placed behind the curtain, but that the ends of the poles attached for carrying it stuck out through the curtain, so the priests who went into the Holy Place could see the poles and know the ark was there.  At any rate, it is impossible to prove that the author of Hebrews made a mistake in his placement of the ark of incense; surely he was right in his statement for at least part of the history of the tabernacle.

The gold-covered ark of the covenant is mentioned next.  There is no question about where it was placed.  It was in, or near, the very center of the little room, the Holy of Holies.  Its construction is found in Ex. 25:10-16.  According to our NIV translation, this ark is called merely "the gold-covered ark."  The author of Hebrews was more emphatic: the "ark of the covenant [was] covered completely with gold" (my translation).  The instructions to Moses were that it was to be covered "both inside and out," with "a gold

[4]   In Ezek. 9:1-3 and 10:1-3, we read of Ezekiel's vision of six armed guards and a man with a writing kit who entered the temple and "stood beside the bronze altar."  Ezekiel adds that "the glory of the God of Israel went up from above the cherubim" which were in the Most Holy Place, as if that was where the altar of incense (the bronze altar) was.

[5]   James Moffatt, the INTERNATIONAL CRITICAL COMMENTARY on Hebrews, page 114.

[6]   Robertson, WORD PICTURES IN THE NEW TESTAMENT, Vol. V on John and Hebrews, page 395.

molding around it." The rings to hold the carrying poles were of solid gold, and even the poles for carrying it were covered with gold, and were never to be removed from the ark (verses 13-15).

**This ark contained the gold jar of manna, Aaron's rod that had budded, and the stone tablets of the covenant.**

The ark of the covenant, precious as it was, was merely the box built to house three even more precious artifacts saved to remind the children of Israel of their relationship with their God and what He had done for them. Also, atop the ark sat the Mercy Seat, which was named by the NIV in Ex. 25:17 the "atonement cover," and in Heb. 9:5 the "place of atonement." We will study about that when we get to verse 5.

The first artifact in the ark the author of Hebrews names is the "gold jar of manna." The manna was the food God provided miraculously for all the children of Israel while they were wandering in the wilderness for forty years. The name "manna" comes from the question the people asked (Ex. 16:15), "What is it?" when they first saw it lying on the ground. The Hebrew words for the question are מָן הוּא (it sounds like "mahn-who?"). Afterward (Ex. 16:31), the people began calling it מָן, (pronounced "mahn"), transliterated into English as "manna." Moses commanded Aaron to gather a jar of the manna and keep it before the Lord, verse 33, as a remembrance to future generations of the people of God.

It was a miracle of God that the manna in the pot did not spoil, because when He gave instructions to Moses regarding gathering the manna, He gave specific guidelines (Ex. 16:15-30). They were to gather approximately one omer per day for each person to eat that day (verse 18), "And when they measured it by the omer, he who gathered much did not have too much, and he who gathered little did not have too little. Each one gathered as much as he needed." If they gathered more than they needed, the manna would rot and breed maggots (verse 20), so they would have to throw it out and gather more manna the next day. However, on Friday, they were to gather enough for two days, and save half for the sabbath, so they would not have to work on the sabbath (verses 22-26); the remainder did not spoil that day. Some people refused to gather enough on Friday for two days, and when none appeared on the ground on the sabbath, they went hungry (verse 27).

God began providing the manna for the people after they began to murmur against him and Moses for bringing them out of Egypt where they had plenty of food and a great variety. At least they made that claim after they had got into the wilderness, but while in Egypt they complained about their harsh treatment, and probably had complained against the food as well. God first gave them quail in the evening to eat (Ex. 16:1-13); and the next morning the first manna appeared.

The people remembered about the manna which the Lord provided, even long after the gold pot of manna was lost or destroyed when Solomon's temple was devastated in 586 BC. You may recall that when Jesus began talking about His being the bread which came down from heaven to feed them, the people said (John 6:31-33), "Our forefathers ate the manna in the desert; as it is written: 'He gave them bread from heaven to eat.'" Jesus responded by saying it was not Moses who gave bread to the people, but God Himself; and that Jesus is the "true bread from heaven" that "gives life to the world."

The second amazing artifact kept in the ark was Aaron's staff (rod in the KJV) that budded. We read about that in Num. 17:1-12. This event occurred after the brief rebellion and extinction of Korah, his henchmen, and their households, as recorded in Num. 16. God knew that the children of Israel needed further confirmation that He had chosen Moses and Aaron to be the leaders of the people, so He told the head of each tribe to bring a branch, with the tribe's name inscribed on it, to Moses to place before the Lord in the Tent of Meeting overnight. The Hebrew name for "branch" was מַטֶּה, which could be either a rod, staff, branch, or shaft, without regard to the kind of wood used. The same Hebrew word was used for a tribe of Israel, because a tribe was headed by a man carrying a "staff." Aaron's staff was inscribed with his name, not Levi the name of the tribe. And we know that Aaron's staff was from an almond tree, because the next morning it had not only budded, but had flowered and borne almonds (verse 8). Aaron's staff was kept in front of the ark at first, perhaps to let the people know that God had appointed him to be the first high priest.

The final precious artifact in the ark was the pair of stone tablets on which God had written the Ten Commandments. We read in both Ex. 25:16 and 21 that Moses was commanded to place the tablets in the ark. Those stone tablets could not have been very large, for two reasons. First, the inner dimensions of the ark (three feet nine inches long and two feet three inches wide) limited their size. In addition, since Moses was required to carry them down from Sinai where he met God and received them, it would have been difficult for him to carry very heavy tablets down the rugged terrain. Moses may have been strong, but surely he was not as strong as Samson, who carried a pair of wooden city gates together with their posts and locking bars on his shoulders from the Philistine city of Gaza to Hebron, a distance of sixty miles as the crow flies (Jud. 16:1-3).

Surely you recall the stories which told why Moses had to carry two sets of stone tablets down the mountain. After Moses had been up the mountain the first time to meet with God and receive the tablets, he came down and saw the people worshiping the golden calf Aaron had made in his absence. Moses was so angry he smashed the tablets on the ground. This story is recorded in Ex. 31:18-32:20. After that, Moses went back up the mountain to converse with God, and carried back down the second set of stone tablets. We read of this in Ex. 34:1-29. It was God in both instances who wrote the commandments on the tablets on both sides of each (Ex. 32:16 and 34:1). You may have noticed that these same two verses tell us that the first set of tablets were carved by God Himself, while Moses was required to "chisel out" the second set. Perhaps this was God's temporal punishment on Moses for being angry and destroying God's workmanship. That possibility should give us pause, and make us more careful with what God has placed in our hands to use for His glory.

### Heb. 9:5. Above the ark were the cherubim of the Glory....

The KJV uses the word "cherubims," which is a reduplication of the Hebrew plural. In Hebrew, the singular is "cherub," and the masculine plural is formed by adding an "i" and an "m." The word for "cherub" is כְּרוּב., an unusual Hebrew noun because it has no verb root.

For centuries, scholars have been speculating what the cherubim looked like. You may have an image of a cherub in your mind. I have always thought of a cherub as a sort of huge bird with outstretched wings, but my thoughts have not wandered beyond that basic idea to fill in other details of its features. The scholars[7] cannot agree on what a Hebrew cherub ought to look like. Ezekiel in his chapters 1 and 10 describes a variety of cherubim, probably none of which is like the ones overshadowing the ark in the tabernacle. All we know about them is that they were made of solid gold, and made one with the underlying Mercy Seat, which itself covered the ark. Since Moses gives only one hint as to the looks of the cherubim, that is, that they had wings, it must be left up to each person's imagination what they looked like. We must be careful not to be dogmatic about our fancied description.

### ...overshadowing the place of atonement.

I just mentioned that the cherubim were made one with the Mercy Seat which is called here the "place of atonement." We shall study the significance of that artifact in a moment.

First, let us think about the matter of "overshadowing." The Greek word is κατασκιάζω, and is only here in the New Testament. It is compounded from σκία, "shade" or "shadow." A σκία is just the opposite of what Jesus is as God in relation to the Father, as we saw in Heb. 1:3, where Jesus is called the χαρακτήρ, the "precise representation of his full being" (see our discussion of that verse). A σκία is no more than a bare outline with no details of the real thing represented.

The "place of atonement" was a most important part of the furniture of

---

[7]  I have read the article on cherubim in TDOT, Vol. VII, pages 307-319 by D. N. Freedman and M. P. O'Connor. They tell of a wild variety of creatures from Near Eastern pagan religions, and offer ideas for possible images for biblical cherubim, but they conclude, "there is no single persuasive identification of the cherubim" (page 318).

the tabernacle, and we must get as clear an understanding as possible of what it was and its significance in the lives of the people who lived in the wilderness and before Solomon's temple was built. As mentioned in our discussion in verse 4, different English versions of the New Testament use a variety of translations for the Greek word used here. That Greek word is used only twice in the New Testament, here and in Rom. 3:25, where although it is used in an entirely different sense, that use will be helpful in our understanding of its significance here.

We have noted that the NIV calls this artifact the "atonement cover" where it is mentioned in Ex. 25:17. The KJV calls it the "Mercy Seat" in both those places. The RSV also calls it the "mercy seat" in both places, but in Ex. 25:17, in a footnote calls it a "cover." Both Ken Taylor's translation [8] and that of J. B. Phillips [9] use the term "mercy seat," so that has been the almost universal name for it in our English language. Now we ought to find out why that has become its common name. To discover that we can go to the Hebrew and Greek names as well as words related to them.

Let us begin with the Hebrew name, because that is the origin for whatever names are used in other languages, including Greek and English. The Hebrew word for the Mercy Seat is כַּפֹּרֶת (ka po reth´). That noun is derived from the verb כִּפֶּר (ki pear´). The verb means to "cover over, pacify, make propitiation." [10] That is to say that the idea of forgiveness in the Old Testament is expressed by a word picture of God's *covering* the sins of the person. The first instance of this in the Bible is the both wrenching and beautiful story in Gen. 3, where after the first couple broke God's commandment to avoid eating the forbidden fruit, they tried to hide their sin by covering themselves with fig leaves. Any attempt of theirs was utterly futile. But God "made garments of skin for Adam and his wife and clothed them" (verse 21). Another similar beautiful picture is painted by Isaiah in his prophecy, Is. 61:10, which we discussed in our thoughts on Heb. 1:3. When God met the high priest in the Most Holy Place, the priest sprinkled blood from the sin-sacrifice on the Mercy Seat and on the floor in front of it. The blood covered the Mercy Seat in a figure as a symbol of God's covering the sins of the people on whose behalf the high priest ministered.

One use of the Hebrew word that is familiar to most of us is the name of today's Jewish most sacred day, which they call "Yom Kippur," and we translate it into English as the "Day of Atonement." The idea is that God obscures our sins, or we can say He makes atonement for our sins, by covering them with the blood of the sacrificial animal. It is very important to retain the idea that the shed blood, sprinkled on the "Mercy Seat" is essential to the whole transaction. Without the blood, nothing happens. However, the Ara-

---

[8] THE LIVING NEW TESTAMENT PARAPHRASED.

[9] LETTERS TO YOUNG CHURCHES.

[10] Brown Driver and Briggs' definition.

bic language has a similar word, *kaffara*, which means "to absolve" from sin, but without the need for pouring out of sacrificial blood; it is merely the act of a merciful Allah.[11]    An example of this is found in the KORAN, Sura VIII.29: "O ye who believe! if ye fear God He will make for you a discrimination, and will cover for you your offenses, and will forgive you; for God is Lord of mighty grace."[12]

A good way to move from our understanding of the Hebrew word to the Greek is to recall that Brown Driver and Briggs partly defined the Old Testament word as "propitiatory." That word is seldom used in our language, so we must try to find a good definition for it. Since there seems to be both confusion and disagreement over that definition, we need to take great care in our study.

The Greek word for "place of atonement" or "mercy seat" in Heb. 9:5 is ἱλαστήριον. It is one of a family of four Greek terms, all of which are used in the New Testament, although very sparingly. We have made an extended discussion of these four Greek words in our study of Heb. 2:17. You are invited to refresh your memory on the explanation there.

### But we cannot discuss these things in detail now.

There certainly is much more to be said about these things. However, what is to be said is merely by way of symbolism, for background of the main point he desires to make. Therefore he decided not to expound on the Old Testament tabernacle implements, but to proceed to contrast them with Jesus, His ministry, and whatever implements He used.

### Heb. 9:6.   When everything had been arranged like this, the priests entered regularly into the outer room to carry on their ministry.

The priests and Levites "arranged," that is, set up the sanctuary and its contents after a stint of wandering through part of the wilderness. It must have been a tremendous task, but there were thousands of Levites, so if each did his part, the work was manageable.

When the tabernacle was set up, the priests entered it "regularly," or daily. Their tasks in the first, or Holy, place, included caring for the fresh bread on the table of "Showbread" (spelled thus in some modern translations), trimming the candles; adding oil as necessary, and burning incense if the golden altar of incense was there.

When the high priest went into the Holy of Holies, the Mercy Seat was supposed to be smothered in incense smoke. The incense had to be put on the fire, that is, on the altar of incense, and the high priest was already behind the curtain where he could sprinkle the blood of sacrifice. If all this is so, then it

---

[11] This information is found in TDOT, Vol. VII, page 289, in the article on כִּפֶּר by B. Lang.

[12] THE KORAN (QUR' ÂN), translated by E. H. Palmer.

was only the high priest who burned incense, and that once a year. For background, read Lev. 16:11-14. Also, Ex. 26:35 mentions only the table of Showbread and the lampstand as being outside the curtain.

**Heb. 9:7. But only the high priest entered the inner room....**

No one else could ever enter that room, not even any other priest. This being so, then Jesus our great High Priest enters a place where we can never go in our own merit; His place is at the right hand of the Father on His throne.

**...and that only once a year....**

It was a most uncommon event, but most important as well. Jews still today celebrate the Day of Atonement, which is the anniversary of the day the high priest was authorized to enter the Holy of Holies.

**...and never without blood....**

This may sound curious at first, but it is arguably the very most important factor in the whole system of sacrifices and forgiveness to be found in the Old Testament. Please keep this in mind during the rest of our study of the comparison between the sacrifices of the Old Testament and the great sacrifice which Jesus made for the world. We will elaborate on this point more fully when we study verse 22 of this chapter.

The blood was the life of the animal, as it is in human beings. Therefore, the blood is of utmost importance in the maintenance of life: "For the life of a creature is in the blood, and I have given it to you to make atonement for yourselves on the altar; it is the blood that makes atonement for one's life" (Lev. 17:11). It was for this reason that the ancient Jews were forbidden to drink the blood of the animals they killed for food: "None of you may eat blood, nor may an alien living among you eat blood" (verse 12), and "You must not eat the blood of any creature, because the life of every creature is its blood; anyone who eats it must be cut off" (verse 14). It is therefore for this reason that Christ's blood had to be shed in order for His work to be effective in the forgiveness of sins.

Because of talk of the shedding of blood for the remission of sin, many people dislike the book of Hebrews, especially because it stands in the New Testament. They are highly offended by the subject, perhaps because they hate to see blood coming from wounds, or do not want to think of the blood that poured from animals which they accept for food. But the scriptures make it clear that God's design is for blood to be shed if sin is to be forgiven. Therefore, we have no recourse but to accept the fact if we hope to have our sins forgiven; there is no other way.

\* \* \*

### ...which he offered for himself....

Remember, we now are returning to the discussion of the Levitical high priests; we must avoid confusion with Jesus, who never needed to make offering for Himself since He was sinless. But the high priests of old needed first to present a sacrifice for themselves. Otherwise, they were spiritually incapable of making sacrifices for the people they represented before God. Years ago I was surprised initially when I first learned that even the Pope of Rome has a priest confessor, the priest of St. John the Lateran Church in Rome, before whom he confesses his sins just like any other Roman Catholic. He, like the Jewish priests of old, must acknowledge that he is not sinless, and thus needs forgiveness.

### ...and for the sins the people had committed in ignorance.

This verse reminds us that it is not sufficient for us to confess only our sins which appear glaringly before our minds' eyes. We all have committed other sins of which we are totally unaware. There may be several reasons for our lack of knowing those sins. We may think they are not sins because of some failure to read carefully or completely all the things God calls sin and hates. We may think, as one Elder in a church told me, "I've never done anything bad enough to keep me out of heaven." It may be that we have done something without realizing that we are doing it. For instance, most people who take the Lord's name in vain do it so routinely that they are now unaware of what they say. When they are confronted with their sin, they respond, "Oh, I didn't even know that I was saying that," which statement of course proves the utter "vanity" of their taking His name in vain. Ignorance is no excuse before God's law.

We read about sins committed in ignorance in Lev. 4, which we mentioned before. Remember verse 2: "When anyone sins unintentionally and does what is forbidden in any of the LORD's commands...." The rest of the chapter tells us what are the remedies for such sinfulness. Of course, sinning in ignorance is not the only sin God hates. In Heb. 10:26, the author reminds us, "If we deliberately keep on sinning after we have received the knowledge of the truth, no sacrifice for sins is left." We shall discuss that more fully when we reach that point in our study.

Here is a personal illustration of a sin committed in ignorance. Years ago, my sons John and David, who then were young boys, and I were driving through Utah from Minneapolis to visit my parents in Escondido, CA. We were in rather a hurry, so we had driven late into the night. Finally I pulled off the road a safe distance, the boys unrolled their sleeping bags in the back of the station wagon, and I tried to rest in the seat behind the wheel. About 4:00 o'clock sleep abandoned me, so I slowly pulled back onto the road and began driving again. About 7:30 the boys began to stir, and suddenly John said, "Dad, there's a red flashing light behind us." I pulled over and stopped. The State Policeman came up and asked me, "Do you know what the speed limit is through that town back there?" I didn't tell the policemen that I could not remember that I had driven through a town. I did say, "No sir, I don't." He said, "Do you know how fast you were going?" I replied, "No, but I suppose it may have been about 60." He said, "You are about right." He got out his pad, and began writing, and then asked me my occupation. I hung my head in shame and said, "I'm a Minister." He brightened and said, "Oh well then, I won't give you a ticket, but just a warning. Please be a little more careful after this." I had committed a sin unwittingly, and should have paid the penalty, but the policeman was gracious and let me off. How merciful our God is to let us off when we plead the blood of Jesus as payment for our sins, whether they be intentional or unwitting.

It is not sufficient for the high priest to make offering for his own sin; he must make an additional conscious offering for the people's unconscious sins, lest they be lost in their sins. It was the high priest who was the intercessor, or mediator, for the people in those days. That is no longer so, and not only because the Jewish priestly office has disappeared. Paul has told us what is the case now in I Tim. 2:5-6: "There is one God and one mediator between God and men, the man Christ Jesus, who gave himself as a ransom for all men."

**Heb. 9:8. The Holy Spirit was showing by this that the way into the Most Holy Place had not yet been disclosed as long as the first tabernacle was still standing.**

In a way, what the author says here is perfectly obvious. The physical tabernacle in the wilderness existed for all the people to see. Although they could not enter the Holy Place, it is likely that they could peek in the front door and see the veil hanging between the two parts of the tent. That veil blocked the view of all but the high priest, so the back room was mysterious.

On the other hand, as far as the Holy Spirit's "showing," or teaching, or informing anyone what was the significance of what they saw is more difficult to understand. The people all knew well enough that they could not then look into the Most Holy Place. But I do not recall any place in the Old Testament that told those people that one day the veil would be rent, so that they could not only see into that sacred spot, but that they actually would be able to enter it along with their High Priest. Virtually all that is said of the veil is the instructions to Moses how to make it in Ex. 26; the fact of its construction in Ex. 35, and the fact of the veil in Solomon's temple in II Chron. 3:14 (the NIV calls it a "curtain").

The author's whole point is this: people in Old Testament times were forbidden to enter the Most Holy Place; now, we *may*. How much better is our situation than theirs! This theme will be developed in chapter 11, where the author ties up the list of faithful people by showing that they all were looking forward to the things we experience.

### Heb. 9:9.  This is an illustration for the present time....

We must be careful to acknowledge that what the author has been saying about the Old Testament ministry is not just a story, or fable, or "myth" as some people like to call it today.  We ought to remember what the apostle Paul said about the things written in the Old Testament, how real historically they were.  In I Cor. 10:6, in talking about the events surrounding the wandering of the Children of Israel for forty years, he wrote, "Now these things occurred as examples," and he emphasized the fact of their occurrence in verse 11, "These things happened to them as examples...." But Paul recognized that these happenings were not merely interesting historical data, but all were designed by God to occur as a means of instruction for us who live today.  To show this, Paul followed what is quoted from verse 11 above with these words, "...and were written down as warnings for us, on whom the fulfillment of the ages has come." So God's impeccable design for Old Testament times was at least two-fold:  He caused those things to happen; and He used those events as lessons for us to learn about how He deals with people in all ages.

### ...indicating that the gifts and sacrifices being offered were not able to clear the conscience of the worshiper.

If what the author of Hebrews has reported here is the only indication for his new premise, I would be hard put to see how to jump from the tabernacle's veil to the present order's ability to clear the conscience of anyone.  Fortunately, the author continues with his explanation, so we must wait for him to reveal to us what he is driving at.

Meanwhile, let us note carefully what the author says here:  those Old Testament ritual sacrifices could not "clear the conscience of the worshiper." If that is so, what then were they good for?  Why did God command them, if they could not fully protect the people?  These questions, as well as others, will be answered as we continue our study.

### Heb. 9:10.  They are only a matter of food and drink and various ceremonial washings—external regulations applying until the time of the new order.

The "new order" is translated as the "reformation" in the KJV, ASV, and RSV.  The Greek word, διόρθωσις, is used only here in the New Testament.  Literally it means to make straight or erect.  Preisker[13] tells us the word was used by Hippocrates for "the setting of a dislocated member."

Here is an illustration of the difference between the Old and New Testament practices.  When I was a small boy on our Nebraska farm, if a piece of

---

[13] Herbert Preisker, article on διόρθωσις in TDNT, Vol. V, page 450.

machinery broke in the field, my father could hardly have unhitched the horses, taken them back to the barn, driven the seven miles to town in the old Model T Ford over rough dirt roads, to purchase a new piece. Instead, he took a piece of baling wire to hold the piece together well enough to work properly, until such time as my mother could go to town to get the necessary piece, or he could go after the horses and machine were put away for the day. The baling wire repair was merely a stop-gap measure to try to keep things going until the real thing could be obtained.

So in a figure the Greek word means to perfect what was imperfect. Preisker wrote that the Old Testament ministry "was only a temporary plan in God's dealings with man. It lasted until the setting up of the order of the fulfilled time...the time of the true order....[It] is a witness to the fulfillment of Judaism in Christianity...." The idea is that when Christ arrived with His "new order," the "old order" was no longer needed, and disappeared. As a matter of fact, what is done in Jewish temples and synagogues today does not compare with the Old Testament practices outlined by Moses.

When the author talks about "food, drink, ceremonial washings," the places they are described in the Old Testament are too numerous to copy here. But a cursory glance at the books of Exodus and Leviticus will fill our minds with sufficient information to let us know what the author is driving at. He is talking about sacrificial foods, cleansings for illnesses, washings of sacrifices under "living" water, that is, water that is poured out or running water. We note that these are all physical things, not spiritual; that is what was wrong with them and what made them ineffective.

This idea brings up our present-day emphasis on material things we use and depend on in our worship of God. We think we must have beautiful buildings with stained glass windows, oftentimes stuffed with icons or graven images, and at least with finely carved communion tables (often called altars) and baptismal fonts or tanks. Once an angry young couple who had visited the church I was serving approached me after the service with this outburst: "It is obscene for you to have such an expensive church building with that huge stained glass window in the front, when the world is filled with starving people. You should have bought food with that money." I lamely tried to point out to them that our church did give more money per capita than other churches around us to feed and clothe the poor of the world, but that if we did not have a nice building in which to worship, then those people who lived in multi-million dollar homes would never come to church nor give a penny for the poor. The young people were not satisfied with my explanation, nor was I. I thought of the Hollywood stars who traveled to India, not to take their millions to feed the poor there, but to sit on filthy streets to listen to the gurus who tried to give them a sense of "religion" by assuaging their consciences with regard to the sins of which they felt guilty. Those wealthy, famous people needed no expensive church in which to worship their false gods. I also think of the costly statuary and other artifacts in many churches, all of which appeal to the physical senses, not to the spirit within: idols which appeal to the sight; bells to be heard; burning incense that attracts the sense of smell; the bread and wine which tweak our taste-buds; and the beads of the rosary and the holy water which invoke contentment from the touch.

This appeal to material things in worship is not new. The original apostle Thomas Didymus had the same problem. At first he refused to believe that Jesus was raised from the dead, because he did not see Him alive as the rest of the disciples had seen. He then went one step further in his demand for material proof: "Unless I see the nail marks in his hands and put my finger where the nails were, and put my hand into his side, I will not believe it" (John 20:25). But think what would have been Thomas' reaction if Jesus' wounds had been healed miraculously before Thomas got to see Him? Would he ever have believed? But Jesus was gracious to him, and granted him the proof he claimed he needed. However, Jesus gently reminded Thomas, and us, that we should not need material things in order to believe: "Because you have seen me, you have believed; blessed are those who have not seen and yet have believed" (John 20:29).

As I recall, the only material things the scriptures speak of which are needed either to worship or to believe are the elements of the sacraments: the bread and cup in communion, and the water in baptism. Unfortunately, those three elements have violently separated individual believers and Churches throughout Christian history. When the woman at Jacob's well argued with Jesus about whether it was necessary for people to worship God on Mount Gerizim[14] or on Mount Zion, Jesus responded (in John 4:23-24), "A time is coming and now has come when the true worshipers will worship the Father in spirit and truth, for they are the kind of worshipers the Father seeks. God is spirit, and his worshipers must worship in spirit and in truth." Some wag has put it this way, "The higher the liturgy, the lower the spirituality."

Why do we think we need *things* in order to help us to worship God? Calvin urged people to build stark, plain church buildings with white walls, clear glass in the windows, and no trimmings. You may object to this: "But even the tabernacle in the wilderness was more elaborate than that." I would respond, "That could well be a large part of their problem." The author of Hebrews called those things "external regulations;" the Greek words literally mean "ordinances of the flesh." As we seek to worship God worthily, let us make every attempt to insulate ourselves from everything that appeals to our senses, so that our spirits may approach God's Spirit unhindered.

We have already discussed the meaning of the "new order." I invite you to review that and move to the next paragraph.

\* \* \*

---

[14] The particular mountain indicated by the woman is not mentioned in John's Gospel, but it is spelled out in Josephus' ANTIQUITIES, Book XIII, Chapter ix, paragraph 1.

**Heb. 9:11. When Christ came as high priest of the good things that are already here....**

The author has concluded making his contrast between high priests; now he begins again his discussion of the tabernacles in which they ministered. Having noted that transition, let us proceed.

**...he went through the greater and more perfect tabernacle....**

Here the author uses the Greek word μείζονας, which is the comparative (a grammatical term) of the Greek μέγας, which means great in either weight, size, dimensions, but especially in height. In other words, Jesus' tabernacle was greater than the tabernacle in the wilderness in every respect, but especially it was "higher," as heaven is above the world. The tabernacle built by Moses was (counting a cubit as one and a half feet) but forty-five feet long, fifteen feet wide, and fifteen feet high—and that included both the Holy Place and the Most Holy Place. It is impossible for us to speak of the dimensions of heaven, Jesus' tabernacle. We are told this in scripture, though: one city, the New Jerusalem, will have dimensions of "12,000 stadia[15] in length, and as wide and high as it is long" (Rev. 21:16). Remember, that is only one city in heaven. I presume heaven is even larger than the physical universe in which we dwell, and astronomers are now able to see more than ten billion *light years* in every direction, and they know they have not reached its extremities yet. That is a pretty amazing comparison between the puny tabernacle in the wilderness and Jesus' tabernacle where He offered Himself for us.

The author now says that Jesus' tabernacle was "more perfect" than the one in the wilderness. The Greek word used here can mean either perfection or completeness. Moses' tabernacle in the wilderness was supposed to be made perfect, but because it was made by human, that is, fallible, hands, no doubt there were many flaws in it, although Moses was commanded by God to make it precisely like the pattern given to him (Ex. 25:9). Besides, the earthly tabernacle was made of materials that were subject to decay. We often think of gold as permanent, but even gold is subject to corrosion over time. But the heavenly tabernacle will endure forever, and was not made by human hands.

**...that is not man-made, that is to say, not a part of this creation.**

When the author says "not man-made" he said literally "not made by hand." Anything made by hand, as any craftsman knows, has its imperfections. Not every line is utterly straight, and the curves are far from smooth. The stitches are not even or straight. Objects can be made more nearly perfect by means of machines, but even the machines are man-made, so the machines themselves are imperfect. Further, the materials of which the objects are made

---

[15] Or, about 1,400 miles, according to a footnote in the NIV.

are still subject to mildew, rot, and corrosion. Nothing in this world is permanent, except for the souls of people.

When the author says that Jesus' heavenly sanctuary is "not a part of this creation," he causes me to think, "But God created both heaven and earth." True, but we remember that although God created all things "very good" (Gen. 1:31), man has corrupted the earthly part of that creation by his disobedience against God's commands; therefore God was obligated to fulfill His word by cursing the ground for man's sake. That is unlike heaven, which was created perfect, and the corruption of the earth did not affect heaven. No blemish has come upon heaven, nor can it, because God will not allow any corruption in His presence. That fact is what makes heaven heaven, and so attractive to me. When I get there, I will have been perfected (made imperishable [NIV], that is, incorruptible [KJV], I Cor. 15:52-54), so that my presence will not bring any flaw to heaven. I can think of no better prospect for the future, which is not for me alone, but for all who trust in Christ as their Savior and Lord.

### Heb. 9:12. He did not enter by means of the blood of goats and calves....

Here we make a slight shift in our discussion, from the tabernacle itself to the offerings of the tabernacle.

In order to make his offerings, the high priest had to "enter" the Most Holy Place, once a year, to make atonement for himself and for all the people. This was a special act of atonement, because all the priests made daily sacrifices on the altar outside the front door of the tabernacle for the sins of the people who came in repentance and desired their sins to be forgiven. In like manner, Christ "entered" His Holy of Holies, to make sacrifice, not for Himself, but only for the sins of the people.

All that the high priest of old had to offer was "the blood of goats and calves." He had nothing better available. It is conceivable that the high priest could have offered himself as a sacrifice, and poured out his own blood on the Mercy Seat. Surely that would have been a better sacrifice than the blood of goats and calves. But there are at least two things wrong with that picture. First, God did not order the high priest to sacrifice himself; that was not in God's plan. Secondly and more importantly, if the high priest did in fact sacrifice himself, that sacrifice could have made atonement for the sins of only one person, himself, since he was a mere man, and only one man could benefit from a man's sacrifice. That is the reason why we must acknowledge that Jesus is God, because only the infinite God could be a sacrifice for an infinite number of people's sins, and Christ did it.

### ...but he entered the Most Holy Place once for all by his own blood....

Jesus, as our Great High Priest, had the right to enter the Most Holy

Place, even the one in heaven. We do not have that right, but through Jesus we have the privilege to enter because His righteousness covers all our sins.

Our NIV then adds the phrase "once for all," which is unnecessarily verbose, but also is misleading. If we slur the phrase together, we might get the idea that the author meant to say "just once and that is all." But it is more likely that we would separate the phrase to mean, for the first part, "one time," and for the second part, "for all people," or "for all time." However, the Greek word used here is ἐφάπαξ, which is a compound word derived from ἅπαξ, which means simply "once." But to add the prefix does not change the meaning so much as it emphasizes the basic meaning. Stählin[16] makes that clear in his definition of the word by saying it means "at once (= together)." The author simply means to say that Jesus died once only, despite what he said in chapter 6, verse 6, where he said that we are able to crucify Him "all over again," which is akin to what Paul said in I Cor. 15:31, where Paul said of himself, "I die every day." In other words, we in a figure crucify Christ by each of our sins, but still He died but once for all our sins.

This idea of Christ's dying no more than once for the sins of the world differs from the Roman Catholic concept of the daily "sacrifice of the Mass," in which every priest around the world, at least once every day, for all time of the existence of the Roman Catholic Church, crucifies Christ in his performance of the Mass. Christ's dying only once differs from the Old Testament concept, where the priests made daily sacrifices and offerings of many animals and birds, because none was complete, or even efficacious, as we just saw in verse 9 of the chapter we are studying.

The author continues that Jesus' sacrifice was "by his own blood," which was the medium of sacrifice, while the creatures' sacrifices did not do the job. Jesus was willing to make that sacrifice. He volunteered to do it, as we shall see in 10:5-7.

### ...having obtained eternal redemption.

Today some of us older folks have a skewed view of redemption. We remember the days when we were given S&H Green Stamps, or other kinds of stamps, with our purchases, which we saved in the pages of booklets designed for that purpose. When we got enough stamps, we could look at our "redemption" catalog, or go to the "redemption store," where we could select something and exchange sufficient books of stamps for what we wanted. We "redeemed" the stamps, which of themselves were virtually worthless, for an object of value to us. Scriptural redemption is something like that, especially in the Old Testament. In Lev. 25:26, we learn of a kinsman who "redeems" or purchases the land of a poor relative who had to sell his property either to pay his debts or to feed his family. The kinsman in effect, then, redeemed not only the land by his purchase, but he "saved" his poor relative from the poor

---

[16] Gustav Stählin, article on ἅπαξ, ἐφάπαξ, in TDNT, Vol. I, page 383.

house or from starvation. This is a picture of what Christ does for us: He gives His blood in payment for our sins and their punishment, in order to save us from eternal punishment. In Ps. 103:4, we read that God has redeemed us; the Old Testament does not say very clearly how that redemption is effected, but Christ provided for them the same redemption He has supplied to us.

What a wonderful promise God has made to us, that instead of "eternal" punishment we receive "eternal" redemption from our sins! Once we are sure we have obtained that redemption from our Savior, we can rest assured that our situation will never change. God will never change His mind.

**Heb. 9:13. The blood of goats and bulls and the ashes of a heifer sprinkled on those who are ceremonially unclean sanctify them so that they are outwardly clean.**

Such a multitude of Old Testament sacrifices did only one thing for the participants: it made them outwardly clean. But it failed totally to cleanse any part of their inward beings, and those are the things that needed cleansing more than any outward bathing. Those sacrifices made them outwardly clean, because they were ceremonially (or outwardly) unclean. Nor was it because they were spiritually clean so they did not need spiritual cleansing, but the Old Testament sacrifices did not, could not, touch their most important and persistent uncleanness. But those Old Testament people were not without hope merely because their sacrifices could not clean them inwardly. We will see what glorious hope they had for cleansing when we examine verse 15.

**Heb. 9:14. How much more, then....**

I want to climb to the rooftops, and proclaim this wonderful truth to all who will hear. What the world offers is empty, vain, worthless. The Old Testament sacrifices could do only so much, and that little gave the worshipers no benefit worth having. They could serve only for the cleansing of the flesh. Taking a bath in the Jordan River could have done as much. But Jesus came to do more, much more, infinitely more for us and for the ancients.

**...will the blood of Christ....**

This theme about blood started out at the beginning of verse 13, with "the blood of goats and bulls." But now the author wants to contrast that with "the blood of Christ." Regardless of your possible sensitivities over talk about "blood," Christians should agree wholeheartedly that the blood of Christ is much more valuable, and infinitely more effective for us, than the blood of any or all animals. Further, His blood is infinitely of more worth than the blood of any other human, no matter how great or wonderful he may be. His blood is infinitely of more worth than the blood of all humans who have ever lived and ever will live. The reason is Jesus is not merely a man—and He was that—but He is the infinite Creator-God as well.

I would remind you again that it was the blood that was the essential element in the redemption of anyone. Therefore, it is bordering on blasphemy to snub, or even to feel squeamish about, the blood of Jesus Christ as being shed on the cross at Calvary. You cannot escape the fact that His blood had to be shed for us to be saved. Again, we will see that more clearly when we study verse 22. Blood is essential for the forgiveness of sin, whether it was in the Old Testament with regard to animals, or in the New Testament with regard to Jesus Christ; whether the transaction was nearly fruitless as in the Old Testament, or infinitely beneficial as in our Savior.

Blood was the life of the animal, as we read in both Deut. 12:23 and in Lev. 17:14. Both those passages speak about God's permission for us to eat meat, as much and whatever kind you want, but you must pour out the blood of the animal on the ground and cover it up, because you must not eat the "life" of the animal with its meat. The hymnwriter penned:

> Thy life was giv'n for me,
> Thy blood, O Lord, was shed,
> That I might ransomed be,
> And quickened from the dead.

Three quarters of a century ago, the committee responsible for putting together the hymns for the old Presbyterian HYMNAL of 1933 were aware that some people wanted desperately to avoid talk about the blood in their hymns, while others thought it was essential to acknowledge Christ's blood as necessary for our salvation. They compromised at one point, where although they included the hymn "There is a fountain filled with blood," they had it printed in fine print at the bottom of one page.

Jesus gave His life, His life-blood, if you will, for you and me. What more could He give? What more do I need? What more do you need?

### ...who through the eternal Spirit....

The ministry of the Holy Spirit is much neglected, as well as highly controverted. No matter what else we may think about the Holy Spirit's being and work, must acknowledge that it is He who imbues us with the life that Jesus supplied by shedding His blood on the cross.[17]

### ...offered himself....

Animals were either ignorant or unwilling sacrifices, although we read in Is. 53:7 that "a sheep before her shearers is silent." But Isaiah's reference is merely to the shearing of sheep, not sacrificing them. On the contrary, Jesus "resolutely set out for Jerusalem" (Lu. 9:51), knowing full well what He faced there. He knew His destiny from the beginning of His life on earth, as we

---

[17] In an attempt to lessen the controversy, I published a book in 1998 which contained every reference to the Holy Spirit in scripture, with my comments on what those verses meant. The title of the book is THE SPIRIT OF SCRIPTURE, and may be obtained by contacting me at 94040 Doyle Point Road, Gold Beach, OR 97444.

read in Heb. 10:5; and Rev. 13:8 that in a spiritual sense He "was slain from the creation of the world." Jesus also said (John 10:18), "I lay [my life] down of my own accord." So Jesus' shedding of His blood was not forced upon Him; He gave it willingly and with full knowledge of what He was doing.

### ...unblemished to God....

The Greek word ἄμωμος means "without blemish, faultless, unblamable."[18] Jesus was unblemished both physically and ethically and spiritually. Peter adds to the idea of faultlessness the idea of spotlessness in I Pet. 1:19: "...Christ, a lamb without blemish or defect," where "without blemish" is the Greek ἄμωμος, and "defect" is the Greek ἄσπιλος, which basically means "spotless," and also means "irreproachable," "unsullied."[19] Thus, in every conceivable way Jesus was perfect. We have covered this concept thoroughly in our discussion of 4:15.

It was required of the Old Testament sacrifices that they also be "perfect." At least thirty-five times in Exodus, Leviticus, Numbers, and Deuteronomy we are reminded that all sacrificial animals must be "without blemish." Two examples will suffice. In Ex. 12:5, we read about the Paschal lamb: "The animals you choose must be year-old males without defect...." And in Lev. 1:3, the beginning of the discussion of all kinds of sacrifices, we read of the first sample, "If the offering is a burnt offering from the herd, he is to offer a male without defect." But of course not one of those sacrificial animals was perfect; all were tainted with the earthly corruption caused by man's first sin. God had said to Adam for his punishment, "Cursed is the ground because of you" (Gen. 3:17); and Paul relates the cursing to everything created in Rom. 8:22, "We know that the whole creation has been groaning as in the pains of childbirth right up to the present time." But each animal was to be chosen because no defect could be seen, such as a lame or bent leg, any kind of sore or blemish in the skin, or one which was blind, or deformed.

Both Old Testament sacrifices and our New Testament Sacrifice were made "to God." He was the only One to whom any and all sacrifices were to be made. All other sacrifices were gross idolatry, such as the sacrifices made by the Israelites to the golden calf made by Aaron in the wilderness when Moses was on top of Mount Sinai to receive the Ten Commandments (Ex. 32:6, "So the next day the people rose early and sacrificed burnt offerings and presented fellowship offerings").

### (How much more then will the blood of Christ...) cleanse our consciences....

Now we are getting to the heart of what the author wants us to know. Here is where our need lies: not the cleansing or mere washing of our skins,

---

[18]  Thayer's definition.

[19]  Also Thayer's definitions.

but the cleansing of our innermost beings, our consciences. We appeal again to Thayer for a definition of this word, which in Greek is συνείδησις. Basically, it means "the consciousness of anything." A longer definition by Thayer is, "the soul as distinguishing between what is morally good and bad, prompting to do the former and shun the latter, commending the one, condemning the other; conscience." In effect, we need to know what is right and what is wrong, and we need something to nudge us to turn toward what is right, and to be sorry and repentant when we do wrong. The author of Hebrews now adds an excellent definition of "conscience."

### ...from acts that lead to death....

The author is not talking about things like flying into a storm in your airplane, which leads to physical death; but about immoral acts or acts contrary to God's will that lead to spiritual or eternal death. For instance, when Solomon was admonishing his son about the consequences of consorting with an adulteress, he warned (Pr. 2:18-19):

> For her house leads down to death
> > and her paths to the spirits of the dead.
> None who go [sic.] to her return [sic.]
> > or attain [sic.] the paths of life.

### ...so that we may serve the living God!

The Father caused His Son to die for us:

- •to forgive our sins
- •to give us eternal life
- •to bless us with material blessings
- •to bless us with spiritual blessings
- •to make Himself known to us

But all these things God did for us are subservient to His great purpose in causing His Son to die for us: He gave us the ability to "serve the living God." If God has saved you and blessed you in all these ways, have you proved it to the world by your service to the living God? You have probably heard the very important question, "If you were accused of being a Christian, would there be sufficient evidence to convict you?"

### Heb. 9:15. For this reason Christ is the mediator of a new covenant....

Once again we find the idea of "covenant." We shall continue it into the middle of Hebrews 10. It is of utmost importance.

"For this reason:" what is that reason? Surely it is so that we may serve the living God. All that happens to us, and all that we do and say, ought to be directed toward bringing glory to our Great God. That is why we were created in the first place. And it is for that reason Christ is willing to continue to work with us, by mediating God's new covenant.

It is of extreme importance that we have a Mediator between God and us. Without such a buffer, we all would perish in an instant. God banishes sin, and sinners, from His presence. So Christ, the God-Man, must stand between God and us, in order to keep God's wrath from being vented on us. It is like the children of Israel who were forbidden to approach the foot of Mount Sinai while Moses went up to receive the Ten Commandments, lest they be destroyed by fire in a puff of smoke. But even Moses was not able to be a very effective mediator between God and the people. All perished in the wilderness before they arrived in the Promised Land because of their sinfulness and murmuring. Only Christ is the perfect Mediator between God and man.

### ...that those who are called may receive the promised eternal inheritance....

Here we find that old ogre of a doctrine of predestination again. I say "again" because it is found many times throughout scripture, although admittedly in several disguises. For instance, the very word "predestination" and its derivatives are found only four times in the Bible, and then only in a select few English translations. The KJV includes the term twice in Romans 8 and twice in Ephesians 1. The RSV uses the term in Romans 8, but shies away a bit in Ephesians by substituting the word "destined" in both places. The NIV uses the correct translation in all four places. Ken Taylor seems at best to have been uneasy about the doctrine of predestination, because he tried to hide the concept with a different word and a phrase in his paraphrase of Rom. 8:29: "God *decided* that those who came to Him—and all along He knew who would—should become like His Son...." In the next verse Taylor comes closer to the truth by writing, "And having chosen us...." In the phrase he used in verse 29, Taylor made the mistake many people do by abridging at best and falsifying at worst the true definition of the term. Predestination really means that God decided beforehand who should go to heaven and who should be excluded. But when Taylor wrote that God "knew who would" come to Him, he wrongfully substituted the idea of foreknowledge for the idea of absolute determination. Actually, if you draw the idea of God's foreknowledge to its ultimate result, especially if you believe in the sovereignty of God, you must agree that if God foreknew that one person was not going to heaven but wanted that person in heaven with Him forever, then as Sovereign He would cause it to happen. Most people who reject predestination but hold to foreknowledge are unwilling to think that far. However, Peter in I Pet. 1:1-2 ties the two ideas together to show how predestination is the only possible result of the foreknowledge of God:

> To God's elect...who have been chosen according to the foreknowledge of God the Father, by the sanctifying work of the Spirit, for obedience to Jesus Christ and sprinkling by his blood.

Taylor is still queasy about the word predestination as if it were unacceptable in the two places in Ephesians 1 as well. In verse 5 he talks about God's "unchanging plan" wherein He "adopt[s] us into His own family;" in verse 11 he buries the idea of predestination in another phrase, "...as part of God's sovereign plan we were chosen from the beginning to be His." Other translators, like Phillips[20] and those of the AMPLIFIED NEW TESTAMENT used similar devices to obscure the full meaning of the term "predestinate." In fairness to them, I acknowledge that theirs were not translations, but paraphrases written in modern-day language, so their discomfort may have been more in using an old, little-used term and less in trying to water down the true meaning.

An important part of the concept of predestination is the idea that something happened long ago, or at least before the present situation came into existence. The idea that we are "pre-" destined is made clear by John when he wrote in Rev. 17:8b, "The inhabitants of the earth whose names have not been written in the book of life from the creation of the world will be astonished when they see the beast, because he once was, now is not, and yet will come." If some people's names are not written in the book of life, that surely implies that others' names are so written. In other words, before God created the world, He had already written in His book of life all the names of all who would go to heaven.

If the concept of predestination were found in only four places in scripture, I might sympathize with those who cannot bring themselves to believe it although that ought to be sufficient proof from scripture for anyone who believes that all of it is the word of God. There are many other ways the idea is spelled out in different places in the Bible.

One of the most-used, and perhaps most important, devices is the use of the idea of "election." We all know what election is in politics. We go to the polls, and receive a ballot on which are written the names of candidates for office, as well as blank lines for us to "write-in" another person of our choice. To make sure our favorite candidate is elected, we mark the ballot beside the one we want elected. Please note, that is all we need to do to the ballot. It would be superfluous for us either to take our pencil and obliterate the names of candidates we do not want elected, or snip them off the ballot with scissors. Merely to vote *for* our candidate is sufficient. So also, when God "elected" before time began some people to go to heaven, those are the ones who arrive there. Of course, other factors are involved, like a person's receiving Jesus Christ as Savior and Lord, but even that action depends entirely on God's election of that person in the first place. One additional remark with regard to election is essential here. Please remember my illustration of political balloting, and transfer that idea to God's election: God does not need to "unelect" or banish in any manner all those whom He does not elect to go to heaven. They have already determined their lost estate by their sinfulness. So it is not necessary for us to accuse God of sending anyone to hell through "double predestination." It is not His fault they go there; it is entirely their own. The

---

[20] LETTERS TO YOUNG CHURCHES.

idea of election is used in more than two dozen places in scripture. You may search for them yourself in a good concordance.

The term used in the verse we are studying is not "elect" or any of its derivatives, but rather is "called." The Bible speaks in several places about God's "calling" or "selecting" or "choosing" us. To see that election and calling are very much alike, if not actual similes in these cases, we note what Peter wrote in II Pet. 1:10: "Therefore, my brothers, be all the more eager to make your calling and election sure." This verse almost sounds as if we can accept or reject God's "call" for us to become Christians. But Peter is not talking about whether we are elect, or whether we can change our status as elect; rather, he is urging us to live as Christians because we are Christians.

Besides predestination itself and election, another way the Bible speaks of predestination is to tell of God's choice, or His selecting those who go to heaven. One of the most important of these passages is John 6:44, where Jesus says, "No one can come to me unless the Father who sent me draws him, and I will raise him up at the last day." Jesus echoes the same thought in verse 65 of the same chapter: "This is why I told you that no one can come to me unless the Father has enabled him." A slight twist on this idea is found in Matt. 22:14, at the end of Jesus' parable about the king who prepared a wedding feast for his son and invited many to attend, but they refused. Others were invited willy-nilly from the area; one of them was cast out of the feast for failing to wear proper clothing. The end of the parable is, "Many are invited [ 'called' KJV and RSV], but few are chosen [Greek for 'elected']."

In my zeal to expound on predestination, I nearly overlooked the word "promised" in this verse. For our comfort and total peace of mind, we ought to be "fully persuaded that God had power to do what he had promised" (Rom. 4:21). If God has promised us an "eternal inheritance," there is nothing in heaven or earth that can remove that inheritance from us; no person, no sickness, no sin, no circumstance, not even Satan. Nor will God ever withdraw His promised eternal inheritance from us.

The fact that our inheritance is "eternal" makes it all the more valuable. If one heir should inherit Bill Gates' one hundred billion dollar estate, that would pale into almost total insignificance for two reasons. First, even that sum would be infinitesimally smaller than our inheritance, which is the inheritance which Christ Himself receives: "Now if we are children, then we are heirs—heirs of God and co-heirs with Christ, if indeed we share in his sufferings in order that we may also share in his glory" (Rom. 8:17). Secondly, any heir of Bill Gates will die not too long after he dies, and so the inheritance will be lost to him forever.

The author notes other elements in Jesus and His ministry that are eternal. In the context of this verse about the eternal inheritance, we just studied about the "eternal redemption" in verse 12; and in verse 14 we saw that it is the "eternal Spirit" who ministers Christ's offering for our redemption.

Thus, the substance of our "eternal inheritance" is our "eternal redemption" which is granted to people without addition or omission by the One who is the "eternal Spirit." Earlier, in 5:9, the author spoke of our "eternal salvation" which is tantamount to our "eternal redemption;" and opposite that is the "eternal judgment" which everyone who rejects Christ will receive. It is a proper balance, and stands to reason, that if the saved have "eternal" salvation, then the lost will have "eternal" judgment or punishment, which concept is rejected by many who prefer not to think that God would send to an eternal, conscious perdition any human being, even for the gravest sin.

By way of summary of the author's list of blessings that believers receive, he mentions one final element in his list of "eternal" things. In the benediction, which overflows with wonderful things he has spoken of throughout his sermon, the author says in 13:20 that all these blessings (and judgments) come through God's "eternal covenant." One of the most important things we can think of regarding God's dealings with us is that now in these last days He has established a covenant with the people of the world which will never change, nor will it ever be superseded by another covenant. We have offered to us the very best blessings, established and guaranteed by the very best Donor, Jesus; and no else will ever offer anything better.

### ...now that he has died as a ransom....

We have discussed in detail the matter of Christ's ransom in our comments on verse 12, except that we were talking about redemption there. But ransom, though different, is closely allied to redemption. While redemption, in the word picture I drew, is the exchange of useless stamps for some object of great value, ransom is different in that it involves the exchange of the infinitely precious blood for our precious salvation.

### ...to set them free from the sins committed under the first covenant.

This promise applies both to those saved in Old Testament times and to everyone since Christ died for us. Even Moses, Abraham, David, and Isaiah were saved by Christ's mediatorial sacrifice, because they trusted in Christ for their salvation. The best example of these Old Testament people is Abraham, where in Rom. 4:11 Paul asserts, "So then, [Abraham] is the father of all who believe but have not been circumcised, in order that righteousness might be credited to them." In other words, if you do not have exactly the same faith in Jesus Christ as your Savior which Abraham had, you will not see heaven. Abraham is now in heaven, because he had the same faith in Christ which Paul and other New Testament writers urged you to have.

This promise applies to the Old Testament believers; it also applies to us in these last days. You may object that you thought God had already established a new covenant and put aside the old covenant of the law. This idea is only half true, however. The true part is that God set aside the part of the first covenant which condemned us without hope or mercy if we broke any of the commandments. Instead, we can be forgiven by faith in Jesus Christ as our Savior from sin and its punishment. But the other part of the first covenant is still in effect, whereby if we break even one small part of the law, we stand guilty before God, until we are cleansed by the precious blood of Christ through our faith in Him. The law also makes us know the difference between breaking the law and obeying it. Paul said this in Gal. 3:24-25: "So the law was put in charge ['was our schoolmaster' KJV; 'was our custodian' RSV) to lead us to Christ that we might be justified by faith. Now that faith has come we are no longer under the supervision of the law ('under a schoolmaster' KJV]." That the law and the requirement to obey it is still in effect is shown by what Christ said about it in Matt. 5:17, "Do not think that I have come to abolish the Law or the Prophets; I have not come to abolish them but to fulfill them."

Therefore, we are still committing sins listed under the first covenant, but the means of escape from punishment is different: then the people escaped by making animal sacrifices at the altar, anticipating the great sacrifice Christ was yet to make; now we escape by means of Christ's shed blood made in the tabernacle not made with hands, but in heaven. Because of all this, we ought to rejoice greatly, not only because we are saved by Christ's death on the cross, but also because God in His infinite mercy saved all those in Old Testament times who foresaw that same sacrifice and believed.

### Heb. 9:16. In the case of a will....

The footnote in my NIV Bible tells us that our English words "covenant" and "will" are the same Greek word. That Greek word is διαθήκη. It will be helpful for us to keep in mind both these English words as we study this next portion of Hebrews, and to try to keep separate the meanings of each word to avoid confusion about what the author is driving at each time he uses the Greek word.

A "will" is a special kind of covenant. One important difference is that although a covenant is usually an agreement drawn up by two people or groups of people on behalf of them both, a will is a "legal" document created by only one of the two parties involved, the one who offers some kind of benefit to the other. A father makes a will, and names his eldest son as principal heir of his estate. The son need not participate in the drawing up of the document; he even may be unaware that his father intended to make a will, let alone name him as heir.

It is possible to make a covenant that is not a will, but still is unilateral in that it is made by only one person involved but applies to both parties. Such a unilateral covenant is described in Gen. 15, the one made by God on behalf of Abraham when he was still called Abram. God made a great promise to Abraham that he would be blessed always, and that the blessing would be perpetuated in Abraham's son Isaac and on through Abraham's descendants which would become innumerable as the sand of the sea or the stars of the heavens. Apparently Abraham was not sure God could fulfill such a promise because he was old already and had no heir. But God drew up a covenant with Abraham in the best legal fashion of that day. (Today, we have attorneys write careful documents, anticipating every contingency by means of legalese impossible for most of us to understand, then signed by both parties or their representatives, and affirmed by witnesses who sign their names, and made fully legal by the seal of a notary public.) In ancient days few attorneys were available, so things were established legally in a different way. God commanded Abraham to obtain several animals and prepare them for sacrifice. Then Abraham cut each animal in two and placed the pieces in two piles. It was the custom for the two parties to walk between the piles of sacrifice, and each was to intone the details of the covenant as they walked. In this case, however, it was only God who passed between the piles of animals. We read that "a smoking fire pot with a blazing torch appeared and passed between the pieces" (Gen. 15:17). All this happened while Abraham was sound asleep and dreaming, and "a thick and dreadful darkness came over him" (verse 12). That it was God who passed between the piles of sacrifice is evident in that the Holy Spirit is often spoken of as a flame of fire of one kind or another, such as in the day of Pentecost when He descended on the disciples and gave them the ability to proclaim the gospel, in Acts 2. We note that Abraham did not walk between the pieces of sacrifice, so he was only a passive recipient of the terms of the covenant.

### ...it is necessary to prove the death of the one who made it....

Here is another difference between an ordinary covenant and a specialized will. Such a thing could not be said about an ordinary covenant, because such an agreement takes place immediately on the establishment of the covenant or some other date specified in the agreement. But in a will, the date of execution of the document is never given, because the death of the "testator" is usually uncertain, and the will cannot take effect until he has died. So in this extraordinary case, when God made a special will-covenant with His people, it was necessary for Him to die or the will would never take effect. The author now leads us to the fact that *God died* in order to make His will operative; this he affirms in verse 28 of this chapter.

The author proceeds to point out more fully how it was necessary for God to die, how His death was much more efficacious than that of the Old Testament animal sacrifices, how the proper death was *only* by the shedding of the blood of the Covenant maker in this very special case will or covenant. Otherwise, the will would never have gone into effect. Incidentally, in an ordinary human will, it matters not how the testator dies; the fact of his death is sufficient to effect the will. But in this case, if for instance Jesus had died of cancer, then God's will could never have been executed, because one essential element in this will was for Jesus' blood to be shed.

**Heb. 9:17.   ...because a will is in force only when somebody has died....**

This is a truism; the death of the testator is what makes a will different from every other document. It may be worth mentioning here that a will becomes effective if only one of the parties dies. If the beneficiary dies also, the whole deal is off. And in this special case, which is special from all other special cases, this will is drawn up precisely so that the beneficiary will be able to stay alive; that, after all, is the one great benefit of this will.

**...it never takes effect while the one who made it is living.**

God had to die, in order to make His will operable. And let us note once again that Jesus is God. If He were not God, then God would not have died, and the will would never become effective.

**Heb. 9:18.   This is why even the first covenant was not put into effect without blood.**

There is a difference between mere death from any cause, and death by bloodshed. We might even say that one of the most important stipulations of this will is that the death had to occur by bloodshed. This follows the pattern set by the first covenant (which was a covenant, not a will, because God did not die in that covenant) in that blood had to be shed for that old covenant to become effective. Also, we note again that in the Old Testament, sacrifices were essential and central to the ministry.

In fact, here is one reason why Jesus was angry with the priests of His day. They had set up an elaborate market in the temple area, with pens of sacrificial animals, cages of birds, and tables for money exchange. People who came from long distances went to the temple, selected animals and paid for them with their country's money. The priests were supposed to sacrifice the animals so purchased, but instead they left the animals in their pens and resold them over and over again. Thus the sins of the people were not eradicated, because the priest failed to shed the blood of the animal for them. This is why Jesus cleansed the temple, as we read in Matt. 21:12-13 and in John 2:12-17.

**Heb. 9:19.   When Moses had proclaimed every commandment of the law to all the people....**

The people in Moses' day were not ignorant of the law. They all knew every law. It was not because they did not know that idolatry was gross sin that they urged Aaron to make the golden calf for them to worship while Moses was at the top of Mount Sinai, receiving the commandments from God (they did not need the physical stone tablets in order to be aware of God's law). It was so in Moses' day; it was so in New Testament days; it is so now; it is so for both Jews and Gentiles. Paul told the people in his day (Rom. 2:1): "You, therefore, have no excuse, you who pass judgment on someone else...." Paul wanted to make sure that at least the Jews knew they were without excuse, so he continued in Rom. 3:2 that they "have been entrusted with the very words of God." In this verse, Paul uses a special term for "words," the Greek λόγια (singular λόγιον), which "plainly refers to the OT revelation at Sinai, especially the Torah (or the Decalogue), which was received by Moses," and in Rom. 3:2 "It is obvious that the reference is to the OT promises," it is a "reference to God's speaking."[21] In other words, the whole idea of λόγιον is that it is a very special bit of communication, normally from God, which the KJV translates as "oracle." That is the English word used often for the ancient Greek gods' messages to their people.

If the Jews had no excuse to ignore God's law, the Gentiles had no greater excuse. Paul wrote of them in Rom. 2:14-15:

Indeed, when Gentiles, who do not have the law, do by nature things required by the law, they are a law for themselves, even though they do not have the law, since they show that the requirements of the law are written on their hearts, their consciences also bearing witness, and their thoughts now accusing, now even defending them.

Nearly all who will read this book are Gentiles and have no excuse before the law of God. If the "requirements of the law" were written in the hearts of Gentiles in Paul's day, it is equally true that they are written in your "hearts," "consciences," and "thoughts" today. Claiming that the law does not apply to you today does not let you escape from the consequences of disobedience; only true repentance for your sins and your pleading for God's mercy through Christ's shed blood will free you from eternal punishment.

**...he took the blood of calves, together with water, scarlet wool and branches of hyssop, and sprinkled the scroll and all the people.**

All this is described in Ex. 24:4-8; you are invited to read it. The important element here is the blood of the calf; the rest is the means of applying the blood to the people. Imposing Jesus' blood on believers today is quite a different process, since Jesus' blood is not physically present.

**Heb. 9:20. He said, "This is the blood of the covenant, which God has commanded you to keep."**

We note that receiving the blood of the calf under the old covenant was a commandment people were required to obey. The process is different for us;

---

[21] Gerhard Kittel, article on λόγιον in TDNT, Vol. IV, page 138.

the new covenant requires us only to receive what God has already done for us in the sacrifice of Jesus. Our obedience is our response of thanksgiving to God for His gift of salvation made through Christ's sacrifice.

**Heb. 9:21. In the same way, he sprinkled with the blood both the tabernacle and everything used in its ceremonies.**

This statement is a copy of what the author said in verse 19, except that here he mentions that the tabernacle was also sprinkled with blood. This was not commanded of Moses in Ex. 24:4-8, nor does Ex. 40:9 mention that Moses sprinkled blood on the tabernacle; only anointing oil is mentioned there. In the event in Ex. 24, the tabernacle had not yet been built. In chapter 40 the failure to mention blood was sprinkled on the building does not mean that it was not done. Josephus tells us that the tabernacle was indeed sprinkled with blood at its dedication.[22]

**Heb. 9:22. In fact, the law requires that nearly everything be cleansed with blood....**

We have been discussing this with regard to the last several verses, so we need not repeat it here.

**...and without shedding of blood there is no forgiveness.**

For those of you who are acquainted with the KJV, you may recall that the last word in the verse is "remission." This word and "forgiveness" mean the same thing, and are translations of the same Greek word ἄφεσις.

We have been saying repeatedly that the shedding of blood is a most important concept in scripture. We can talk endlessly about God's infinite love by which He wants to forgive us (II Pet. 3:9, "He is patient with you, not wanting anyone to perish, but everyone to come to repentance"). We can blather about our obligation to confess our sins in order to be forgiven. We can argue that God surely could have planned some other (bloodless) way to eradicate our sins. We can state with disgust that talking about blood is offensive to our socialite sensitivities. For all that, the fact remains that in both Old and New Testaments there is only one way for a person to receive forgiveness, and that is through the shedding of blood. No argument will provide an escape from this eternal truth.

In verse 12 of this chapter of Hebrews, we discussed the importance of understanding that Jesus died no more than one time, that is, He was sacrificed but once physically, although there are people whose liturgical practice is to sacrifice Christ every time (at least once daily) any priest performs the Mass around the world. Perhaps in order to avoid the idea that they needlessly sacrifice Christ during the Mass, they also call what they do a "bloodless sacri-

---

[22] ANTIQUITIES, Book III, Chapter VIII, paragraph 6, "...Moses had sprinkled Aaron's vestments, himself, and his sons, with the blood of the beasts that were slain....The same he did to the tabernacle."

fice." The reason they call the table in front of their sanctuary an "altar" is because that is the place to make sacrifices. But if their sacrifice is a "bloodless" sacrifice, then it avails nothing, because "without shedding of blood there is no forgiveness." Incidentally, some Protestants unthinkingly call the tables at the front of their churches "altars" although they acknowledge they make no sacrifices there. Such tables ought to be called what they truly are: "Communion tables," places where people "commune" with the risen Christ as they remember the one blood sacrifice He made for them at only one place in the world, Calvary. The single act of shedding Christ's blood on the cross outside Jerusalem was sufficient to pay the penalty for all my sins I have ever committed or ever will commit; for all the sins you have ever committed or ever will commit; and for all the sins of every person who receives Him as Savior and Lord has ever committed or ever will commit. Just once was sufficient, because He is the infinite God, so His payment is infinitely available, waiting for repentant souls to accept His one blood sacrifice. How awesome is our God! He has loved us with an infinite love.

For purposes of this study, we have divided Hebrews 7-10 into a trilogy based on what is said in Heb. 8:6: "The ministry Jesus has received is as superior to [the Old Testament priests' ministry] as the covenant of which he is mediator is superior to the old one, and it is founded on better promises." We recall that the underlying theme of the whole book of Hebrews is that Jesus and His ministry are *better than* the ministry of the Old Testament and its people. In 8:6, the author narrows his focus down to three things: a better ministry; a better covenant, and better promises. In 7:1-8:6 we studied the first part of the three; in 8:7-9:22 we investigated the second; and now we have divided the third part, better promises, into two sub-parts, there is one total cleansing, and there is no more sacrifice.

**Heb. 9:23.   It was necessary, then, for the copies of the heavenly things to be purified with these sacrifices....**

We should keep in mind that the heavenly things were *eternal*. They did not come into existence only at the time of the death of Christ on Calvary. Also, the heavenly things did not need to be purified with imperfect animal sacrifices, because those things were not made with impure human hands. By contrast, the tabernacle in the wilderness came into existence long after the universe was created, and because it was man-made, it needed to be cleansed from the impurities of the fallen world.

Because of these things, we must acknowledge that it was the heavenly tabernacle not made with hands that was the reality; the tabernacle in the wilderness with its fixtures was nothing better than a copy of that reality. It is difficult for us to separate our thoughts from the things around us which our physical senses can perceive; they are "too much with us" as Wordsworth reminded us. We are so caught up in "things" that we perceive them as the true reality. However, all these things will cease to exist, and only the spiritual things will remain. What endures is the true reality, and it is those abiding things we ought to embrace with all our beings.

Those old things, says the author of Hebrews, needed to be purified with the Levitical sacrifices of bulls and goats and birds. Then the author makes his contrast.

**...but the heavenly things themselves with better sacrifices than these.**

If heavenly things (the tabernacle, altars, lamps, implements) were "better than" the earthly, then of course the sacrifices used to cleanse or purify them needed to be better also.

We may ask why the plural in talking about "sacrifices" for the "heavenly things"? Have we not been emphasizing that Jesus died only once, and that He is the only sacrifice to be made in heaven? Perhaps the author intended to convey the idea, "however many sacrifices were required to purify the heavenly places," which just happens to be one in number. Also, it is possible that the author was making a parallel between the uncounted number of Old Testament sacrifices needed to cleanse the earthly things and the determinate number needed for the heavenly.

Let us recognize that the sacrifice in heaven was not really needed to make that tabernacle or its equipment perfect, because not having been made with human hands it was already perfect. Again, perhaps the heavenly sacrifice was made to keep that sanctuary free from defilement as Christ brought the sins of the people there for expiation.

**Heb. 9:24. For Christ did not enter a man-made sanctuary that was only a copy of the true one....**

This statement merely recapitulates what we have been saying: each sacrifice had its own proper place to be killed.

**...he entered heaven itself, now to appear for us in God's presence.**

Heaven was Jesus' place of sacrifice, in the spiritual sense. This does not abnegate the necessity for Him to die on the cross at Calvary; that was necessary for Him to shed His blood for the remission of our sins.

The fact that "He entered" means that He had to leave in order to enter. That He left heaven is shown in John's explanation of who He is, in John 1:14, "The Word became flesh and lived for a while among us." Also, King David in his Ps. 68:18 affirmed that Jesus "entered heaven:"

> When you ascended on high,
>> you led captives in your train;
>> you received gifts from men,
> even from the rebellious—
>> that you, O LORD God, might dwell there.

Paul quotes this part of the Psalm in Eph. 4:8, then explains its meaning in verses 9 and 10: "What does 'he ascended' mean except that he also descended to the lower, earthly regions? He who descended is the very one who ascended higher than all the heavens, in order to fill the whole universe."

Jesus entered heaven so that He might "appear for us in God's presence." Jesus has a right to appear there, both because He is sinless, and because He is truly God; that is His rightful place. We, on the other hand, have no right to be found there because of our sinfulness. However, that sinfulness does not necessarily keep us from God's presence forever. If we are covered by Christ's righteousness, then God accepts us into His presence. Isaiah put it this way (Is. 61:10):

> I delight greatly in the LORD;
>> my soul rejoices in my God.

> For he has clothed me with garments of salvation
> and arrayed me in a robe of righteousness,
> as a bridegroom adorns his head like a priest,
> and as a bride adorns herself with her jewels.

Adam and Eve could not walk in the garden in God's presence, until God had clothed them (covered their sin) with the animal skins that He provided. Now we may stand in God's presence if we are covered with His righteousness which is received by faith in Jesus, as we read in Rom. 4:11, where Abraham "received the sign of circumcision, a seal of the righteousness that he had by faith while he was still uncircumcised. So then, he is the father of all who believe but have not been circumcised, in order that righteousness might be credited to them."

Jesus did all this "for us!" His whole being and essence from all eternity was "for us," not for Himself. Is your mind able to grasp that? Jesus' whole existence was not for His own benefit or pleasure, but everything He did, He did for us. If you are able to understand that stupendous truth, then are you willing to try with your whole being to do the same for Him? Say not that such a life is too much to ask of you. Paul exhorted us in Rom. 12:1: "Therefore, I urge you, brothers, in view of God's mercy, to offer your bodies as living sacrifices, holy and pleasing to God—which is your spiritual worship." Christ gave His own "God-life" for you, which is infinitely more than you would be able to do for Him even if you were perfect. Renew your commitment to Him now. Promise Him, out of your love for Him because of all He has done for you, that you will live (and if necessary, die) for Him, now and forever.

I recall an instance in my life when I was in high school. I was walking back to school from lunch at home, and happened to meet Lorraine, a classmate. In our conversation she suddenly said, "Tom, you're a pretty religious guy, aren't you?" Just then I had a perfect opportunity to give witness to my faith in Jesus Christ as my Savior and Lord. Instead, I answered, "Well, no, not really. I'm no different from all the rest." And at that moment, because of my failure to speak for my Lord, I *was* no different from the rest. At our fiftieth class reunion, I was invited to speak to the class because I had been its President. Lorraine was sitting at the head table as another of the officers. Finally, I was able to give witness to my Savior in my speech, but by then it may have been too late for some to hear. How faithful have I been in my life of witness for Christ? How faithful have you been?

**Heb. 9:25. Nor did he enter heaven to offer himself again and again, the way the high priest enters the Most Holy Place every year with blood that is not his own.**

There are two significant contrasts in this verse that put infinite distance between the high priests' sacrifices and Christ's. First, the high priest of old was required to enter the Most Holy Place "again and again," that is, once a year; while Christ entered His sanctuary only once, and that one time was sufficient for Him to accomplish all He had set out to do.

The second contrast is that the Levitical high priests' blood sacrifices were of animals, so no harm came to the priests thereby. In Jesus' case, the blood He offered was His own, and He lost His life because of it.

Few people are willing to give their lives for the sake of others, although it does happen occasionally, according to Paul. Jesus also said, in John 15:13, "Greater love has no one than this, that one lay down his life for his friends." In Rom. 5:6-7 Paul contrasts between Christ's attitude toward giving His life for the world, and our willingness to die for someone else:

> You see, at just the right time, when we were still powerless, Christ died for the ungodly. Very rarely will anyone die for a righteous man, though for a good man someone might possibly dare to die. But God demonstrates his own love for us in this: While we were still sinners, Christ died for us.

One who was willing to die for someone else was Wu Feng,[1] whose Father Wu had fled to Taiwan (then Formosa) with his family in the early 1700s from the onslaught of the Manchu people into Mainland China. After they had lived in the lowlands Wu Feng moved up into the mountains where head hunters lived. There he practiced medicine and helped the people, hoping to find out why they hunted heads and how he might help them stop the practice. He learned they raided other villages and took heads to appease their gods, to bring them prosperity and security. Wu Feng became a trusted counselor to the chief of the villages, by helping all the people with his medicines and selfless assistance. First, he persuaded the chief to save the forty heads taken in one year, and offer only one each year thereafter. When the chief's son succeeded him, Wu Feng persuaded him to offer only one head. One year that did not seem to help, because a typhoon devastated the villages. Finally Wu Feng urged the chief to take one final victim, whom Wu Feng described carefully, and never take another head. Of course Wu Feng had disguised himself as the victim, as well as the place he would be for the villagers to slay. When they discovered it was he they had killed, they honored him by building a memorial to him, More importantly, they determined never to take another head to appease their gods.

### Heb. 9:26. Then Christ would have had to suffer many times since the creation of the world.

The author continues the theme of the uniqueness of Christ's one sacrifice as adequate to forgive all sins for all time. Be sure to understand that if the sins of people in Old Testament times were forgiven, they had to be forgiven by Christ's sacrifice for them. The author points that out here in an oblique way, by saying in effect that Christ did not have to suffer many times "since the creation of the world." The Greek phrase for that (ἀπό καταβολῆς

---

[1] A true story, from the book WU FENG, COMPANION OF HEAD HUNTERS, given to me by my friend Louise Crawford, a long-time missionary to Taiwan.

κόσμου) is identical to that used in Rev. 13:8, where John speaks of the "Lamb that was slain from the creation of the world;" and in Rev. 17:8, where John is talking about the lost people whose names have "not been written in the book of life from the creation of the world."

**But now he has appeared once for all at the end of the ages, to do away with sin by the sacrifice of himself.**

Here again we find the term "once for all" which we noted in 7:27 and 9:12. You may review its meaning there. The only difference is that the simple Greek noun is used here, as opposed to the compound term in both former places, as well as in 10:10.

The author of Hebrews tells us that Jesus has appeared "now...at the end of the ages." I remind you that at the very beginning of this study we saw we are now living in the end times. In fact, those end times started during the days when Jesus walked the earth. This verse tells us that Jesus "appeared" in these times in order to make His sacrifice for our sins. In his saying this, we must be careful to remember that there are two different senses in which Jesus offered Himself for our sins; that is not to say that He made two sacrifices. One of those senses of the sacrifice was spiritual, made in heaven, in the tabernacle not made with hands. That sense of His sacrifice no man could see. The other sense of His sacrifice was on earth, visible, physical, for all then alive to see, so that His blood could be poured out physically. Thus Jesus appeared to confirm to mankind what had been done as a "once for all" thing, an ageless, timeless yet eternally timely, act.

We may make a contrast between the "end of the ages" seen here and the "creation of the world" we read of in the first part of the verse. Jesus' word of deliverance was spoken long ago; but the actual putting away of sin was confirmed at His appearance to offer His body a sacrifice for sin, and will be consummated when He returns to receive all His people to Himself forever.

Jesus made His sacrifice to "do away with sin." What a stupendous promise that is! Surely this is a "better promise" than anything the old order could offer. All the Levitical priests could grant was the cleansing of the flesh (Heb. 9:13); they could not even promise the forgiveness of sins. But now, by the sacrifice of Christ we have the promise not only of the forgiveness of our sins, but the very abolition of sin itself. Jesus has finished His work to accomplish this, but we have not yet received the benefit of it. Paul explains this in Rom. 8:18-23, concluding with these words, we "groan inwardly as we wait eagerly for our adoption as sons, the redemption of our bodies." It is our sin that keeps us from the vital presence of God, as we read in Is. 59:2-3:

> But your iniquities have separated you from your God;
> your sins have hidden his face from you,
>    so that he will not hear.
> For your hands are stained with blood,
>    your fingers with guilt.

> Your lips have spoken lies,
> and your tongue mutters wicked things.

But then when sin will have been effectively abolished, you and I will be able to stand in the very presence of our God and Savior, to have fellowship with Him forever without interruption.

I do not find other places in scripture which state clearly that sin itself shall be abolished. One place that is close to the idea, is I Cor. 15:26, where we read that "the last enemy to be destroyed is death." We have said that we will not, cannot, sin in heaven. It may be that one of the punishments in the lake of fire will be that the people there also will be unable to sin, and thus sin will be no more.

**Heb. 9:27. Just as man is destined to die once, and after that to face judgment....**

This is probably one of the most important sentences in the book of Hebrews; it may be one of the most important in the whole Bible. Contained in this statement are two subsidiary thoughts, each exceedingly important.

The first thought is: There is no such thing as a "second chance" for anyone. Here is the invariable procedure for every human being who has ever existed, or will exist (with three exceptions: Enoch, Elijah, and all Christians who are still alive in the world when Jesus returns). A person, who has been planned and known by God from all eternity, is born into this world in accordance with God's time, place, and circumstances. He lives in the world in every detail determined by God's eternal decrees (His infinitely designed plan for everything that happens). He dies when God wants him to die. He appears before God's judgment throne, where one of two things happens to him: he goes scot free from the penalty of all sin because he has received Jesus Christ as his Savior and Lord, and goes to heaven to be with Christ forever; or he is condemned for all his sins, whether great or small, and is sent to punishment in the lake that burns with fire forever and ever. There is no hint in scripture of anything like a "second chance" upon which some depend for their security. Some people think the Millennium is a time when they can relive their lives and do a better job. That is impossible for two reasons: one is that nobody lives a second time during the Millennium. The other reason is that it is absurd to think that if a person both sinned and rejected the Savior during one lifetime, he would have greater inclination to repent and be saved in a second, or third, or thousandth time. Other people think they will be reincarnated in this world, and each time will be able to build on the experiences of previous lives, until eventually they will become perfect and thus reach "Nirvana." Some people think this "Nirvana" is a place where one feels no pain or remembers no experiences from life in this world; if there were such a place, it would not be much of a heaven without the blessings the presence of God brings.

The second thought in this part of verse 27 is the wonderful assurance that you need never worry about having to die physically several times, not even twice. Of course, such an occurrence is not unheard-of; still it is most unlikely you will be selected for such a grim fate. First of all, there are two people who have never died physically: Enoch (Gen. 5:24), and Elijah (II Kings 2:11). Then Christians who remain alive when Christ returns who will not die, but be "caught up with [the dead Christians] in the clouds to meet the Lord in the air. And so we will be with the Lord forever" (I Thess. 4:17). After these people, we think of those throughout scripture who died, and later were miraculously raised from the dead by God's power working through Christ Himself or some other servant of God. They are:

1. Elijah raised the widow's son, I Kings 17:22
2. Elisha raised the Shunammite's son, II Kings 4:35
3. Elisha's bones raised a soldier, II Kings 13:21
4. Jesus raised Lazarus, John 11:44
5. Jesus raised Jairus' daughter, Matt. 9:25
6. Jesus raised the widow of Nain's son, Lu. 7:15
7. Paul raised Eutychus, Acts 20:10
8. Peter raised Dorcas, Acts 9:40

Besides these eight people, there may be additional people who were likewise raised after dying; that is the group of saints whose tombs were opened during Jesus' crucifixion, and after Jesus' resurrection they walked the streets of Jerusalem. We find that story in Matt. 27:52-53. The uncertainty of whether they had to die again is that Matthew does not tell us whether they reentered their tombs, or were caught up to heaven bodily. If they were caught up, it was "after Jesus' resurrection," so that Jesus could still be called "the firstborn from among the dead" (Col. 1:18).

Actually, these two thoughts of the author's are subsidiary to what he wants to emphasize: that just as you and I must die only once, so Christ needed to die only once—and did. Let us be aware that the parallel with Christ's single death is an additional affirmation that our death is only one time, with the judgment to follow without a second chance to repent or to receive Christ as Savior. Further, the hopeless possibility that no second chance would change anyone's mind and cause him to repent later is affirmed in the story of the Rich Man and Lazarus in Lu. 16:19-31. After a life of debauchery, the rich man died and went to hell. In his torment, he called up to Abraham in heaven, in whose arms Lazarus reclined, and asked for Lazarus to come down and touch a drop of water to his parched tongue. After hearing that was impossible, he asked Lazarus to go back to the world to warn his brothers of their impending doom. But Abraham replied (verse 31), "If they do not listen to Moses and the Prophets, they will not be convinced even if someone rises from the dead." This does not exactly say that if given a second chance, the brothers would not change, but it strongly suggests it.

* * *

**Heb. 9:28.** **...so Christ was sacrificed once....**

The author strongly emphasizes this by his much repetition. If the fact was that important to him, then we do well to take solemn heed to it.

**...to take away the sins of many people....**

Those who think women are given short shrift in scripture ought to take to heart the words of Is. 4:4, where women are specifically selected for blessing: "The LORD will wash away the filth of the women of Zion; he will cleanse the bloodstains from Jerusalem by a spirit of judgment and a spirit of fire." We read further of the cleansing of people in Rev. 1:5-6: "To him who loves us and has freed us [some ancient Greek manuscripts read 'and has washed us'] from our sins by his blood, and has made us to be a kingdom and priests to serve his God and Father—to him be glory and power for ever and ever! Amen." A much greater multitude is indicated in Rev. 7, which speaks of the twelve thousand people from each of the twelve tribes of Israel who have been sealed from the harm coming to the world; plus the innumerable host from "every nation, tribe, people and language" (verse 9), who will be wearing white robes, described by the angel as "they who have come out of the great tribulation; they have washed their robes and made them white in the blood of the Lamb" (verse 14).

That such a great host of people of both Jews and Gentiles is not the totality of humanity is indicated by the author's statement here that it is the sins of only "many people" and not the whole world. We have already discussed the difference between the "all" and the "many" in our exposition of I John 2:2 (where Jesus is indicated as the *propitiation* (or availability) for the sins of the whole world, and His *expiation* or total expungment only for those who believe in Jesus in Rom. 3:25.

**...and he will appear a second time....**

This second appearance of Jesus is variously spoken of as His "second coming" or "second advent" or "coming again," or simply His "appearance." The Greek word the author uses, παρουσία, is best translated as His appearance. Although many people have twisted views of how, when, where, whether Jesus is going to come back, the Bible is amply filled with statements of His return. The angels told the disciples (Acts 1:11), "This same Jesus, who has been taken from you into heaven, will come back in the same way you have seen him go into heaven." Every chapter in I Thessalonians speaks of the return of Christ: 1:9-10: "They tell ...you...to wait for his Son from heaven...." 2:19: "What is our hope, our joy, or the crown in which we will glory in the presence of our Lord Jesus when he comes?" 3:13: "May he strengthen your hearts so that you will be blameless and holy in the presence of our God and Father when our Lord Jesus comes with all his holy ones." 5:23: "May your whole spirit, soul and body be kept blameless at the coming of our Lord Jesus Christ."

I intentionally omitted the reference to Jesus' return in chapter 4 of I Thessalonians, to elaborate on it now. It is probably the most important and extended reference to Christ's second coming in the whole Bible. The return of Jesus is explained in verses 13 to 18. The core of the statement is in verse 16: "For the Lord himself will come down from heaven, with a loud command, with the voice of the archangel and with the trumpet call of God, and the dead in Christ will rise first." Among the details noted in this passage are that the spirits of those who have already died in Christ and have been residing with Him in heaven will be sent back to earth with Him; the bodies of those same spirits from heaven will rise from their graves or from wherever they were placed; surely their bodies and spirits that have been separated since their deaths will be rejoined, never again to be separated; and Christians who have not yet died on earth will be caught up to be with the Lord and His returning saints, to be together with Him for the rest of eternity. What an amazing event that will be!

Better still, that event will be witnessed by every person in the world, living and dead. That is what John tells us in Rev. 1:7:

> Look, he is coming with the clouds,
>   and every eye will see him,
> even those who pierced him;
>   and all the peoples of the earth will mourn because of him.
>   So shall it be! Amen.

That previous generations of people who have already died will witness this event is indicated by the fact that "even those who pierced him" will see His return. Some people think that Jesus' appearance will be secret and only those who are caught up to be with Him will be aware of it for two reasons. They claim that because Paul had said in I Thess. 5:2, "the day of the Lord will come like a thief in the night," those who do not belong to Him will be unaware that He has come. But Paul was not talking about not knowing the thief is there, but in verse 1 when he said "about times and dates we do not need to write to you," he was reminding us of what Jesus had said to His disciples in Matt. 24:36, "No one knows about that day or hour, not even the angels in heaven, nor the Son, but only the Father." When a thief comes, you have no warning; his stirring wakes you and you know he is there.

A reason why other people think non-Christians will not see Jesus' coming is because of what He said after He told His disciples no one but the Father knew the time of His appearance, when He said (Matt. 24:40-41), "Two men will be in the field; one will be taken and the other left. Two women will be grinding with a hand mill; one will be taken and the other left." Those who are left will not be blind or asleep merely because they are "left behind;" it does not mean that they are unaware that Jesus has come, nor will they fail to see Him.

* * *

**...not to bear sin....**

Jesus has accomplished that already. One time was sufficient.

**...but to bring salvation to those who are waiting for him.**

What a terrific contrast this is: Jesus came the first time as a Suffering Servant; He will come the second time as a Glorious Monarch! His purpose in coming both times is to gather to Himself those whom God has chosen from before the foundation of the world. First He died to redeem them; now He will reign to make them co-regents with Him: "They came to life and reigned with Christ a thousand years" (Rev. 20:4).

We who are waiting for Jesus are not doing it passively, just watching the clock. The Greek word the author uses means that we are assiduously and patiently waiting for Him. Also, since He told us to "do business until I come" (Lu. 19:13, my translation), He commands us to keep working for Him until He actually returns.

Jesus told the parable of the "faithful and wise servant...whose master finds him doing [his job] when he returns," who will be blessed because of his faithfulness even in the master's absence; and the wicked servant who "begins to beat his fellow servants and to eat and drink with drunkards," whose master will "cut him to pieces and assign him a place with the hypocrites" (Matt. 24:45-51). We dare not sit in our rocking chairs, refusing to do the work of the kingdom with the excuse that if He should come before we finish the task, all effort will be in vain.

**Heb. 10:1. The law is only a shadow of the good things that are coming—not the realities themselves.**

Once again the author begins a new thought by summarizing what he has already said. The "law" was the set of guidelines for the ministry of the priesthood described in chapter 8, and for the rituals of the tabernacle pictured in chapter 9. Here the author claims that the law in itself is nothing more than a shadow of something much more important. To what could he have been referring when he contrasted the law with "good things that are coming"? I assume that he means to contrast the law not so much with the priesthood and the place of ministry, but with grace. Paul put it succinctly in Rom. 6:14, "...you are not under law, but under grace." Please remember, Paul is not saying here that we need no longer obey the law, but that the law can neither save nor destroy us; rather, we are saved by God's grace, not by our feeble attempt at obedience. Having said this, the author proceeds to explain what he means.

\* \* \*

For this reason it can never, by the same sacrifices repeated endlessly year after year, make perfect those who draw near to worship.

What the author says here has already been said in 9:13, and earlier in 9:9-10; you may review them now.

**Heb. 10:2.  If it could, would they not have stopped being offered?  For the worshipers would have been cleansed once for all, and would no longer have felt guilty for their sins.**

Let us take care in our discernment of the author's logic here. Is he saying that if the Old Testament sacrifices were perfect, then the people would have ceased to sin? That can hardly be his point, because even with Christ's infinitely greater sacrifice made for us, we have not ceased to sin either. John made that clear in I John 1:8 and 10: "If we claim to be without sin, we deceive ourselves and the truth is not in us....If we claim we have not sinned, we make [God] out to be a liar and his word has no place in our lives." Paul was even more emphatic in his assertion that Christians do still sin, referring to his own life in Rom. 7:14-25.  Paul repeats in several ways that the good things he wanted to do he failed to do, and the things he wanted to avoid he continued to do, at least occasionally.  Read the whole passage to get the full force of what Paul says.  You may have heard many people claim that in those two paragraphs Paul is referring to his life before his conversion, so that afterwards he became sinless.  This cannot be so, because Paul uses the present tense throughout the passage.  Further, such a Bible scholar as Donald Grey Barnhouse at first believed Paul was writing of his pre-Christian experience, but later Barnhouse came to accept the fact that Paul acknowledged he was still a sinner.  Some people appeal to I John 3:9, especially because of how it is translated in the KJV: "Whosoever is born of God doth not commit sin; for his seed remaineth in him: and he cannot sin, because he is born of God."  However, our NIV gives the original sense more faithfully: "No one who is born of God will continue to sin, because God's seed remains in him; he cannot go on sinning, because he has been born of God."  The Greek of the verb "to sin" is in the present progressive tense, which means, not that a Christian has ceased altogether to sin, but rather he can no longer sin like he used to, because the Holy Spirit dwells in him.  Otherwise, this verse would contradict I John 1:8 and 10 noted above, and scripture cannot contradict itself, or else we would have no authority on which to base our beliefs except for our own flimsy wishes.  John Wesley claimed it was possible for a Christian to cease sinning altogether.  However, it is said that on his deathbed he confessed to his family and friends that he had not been able to stop sinning in his Christian life.  If such a godly man as John Wesley could not avoid sinning in this life, neither can you.  The apostle Paul recommended in Rom. 6:11, "...count yourselves dead to sin but alive to God in Christ Jesus."  Because the Holy Spirit is in us, we may set our minds to the idea that sin is not accounted to us because we are forgiven, but that does not mean that we have ceased to sin.

If the author is not saying that the people of Old Testament times ceased to sin, then what is his logic? What he is trying to tell us is so grand that many people cannot or will not believe it. He wants us to believe that because Christ died for us, we have been made righteous in God's sight, and *nothing can alter that new standing in Christ we now possess!* It is just as if, when we moved from Alaska to Oregon, it was because we had been banished with no hope of returning there to live. We might go for a brief visit (and we have done that), but we now are citizens of Oregon. Also, if we should travel for a brief visit to California, we do not forsake our citizenship in Oregon, because we return there to live. I shall say it another way. If Christ cannot die for us, then our case is utterly hopeless, *unless* His death took care of all our sins for all time! This to me is at least a collateral proof that those who have been saved cannot possibly be lost. If this verse stood alone in scripture to say that, I am not sure it would be sufficient proof of eternal security; with the many other passages we find about it, this gives heavy support in evidence. Among those additional passages are John 10:28-29; Rom. 8:38-39; and I John 5:11-13. Please study them carefully.

It is because of Christ's sacrifice that His righteousness is imputed to us. Paul says this in Rom. 3:25-26: "God presented him as a sacrifice of atonement...so as to be just and the one who justifies the man who has faith in Jesus." Paul says that God did this for Abraham in Rom. 4:20-25: "...but for us also, to whom God will credit righteousness....He was delivered over to death for our sins and was raised to life for our justification [equals 'righteousness']."

**Heb. 10:3. But those [Old Testament] sacrifices are an annual reminder of sins....**

Of course, the "annual" reminder was just for the sacrifice made by the high priest on behalf of himself first, and then on behalf of the people, especially for their "unwitting" sins. But there were multiple sacrifices made daily for the specific sins of the people. Although those sacrifices were more personal, they may have been, for that reason, less stark as reminders that their sins were not covered by all the efforts of both priests and people.

**Heb. 10:4. ...because it is impossible for the blood of bulls and goats to take away sins.**

Again refer to our discussion of Heb. 9:9-10 and 13. The author then makes another transition, back to his theme of Christ and His one sacrifice.

* * *

**Heb. 10:5.   Therefore, when Christ came into the world, he said....**

Although some people find it difficult to believe, I hold to the idea that on that first Christmas day, Jesus had a conversation with His heavenly Father the moment He was born.  After all, that is precisely what this verse says.  The event spoken of by the author was His birth, "when Christ came into the world."  Is it any less believable that Christ could talk to the Father in 4 BC, the moment of His birth, than that He could converse with the Father in 4004 BC (or whenever the decision was made to create the universe) about the establishment of human beings on the earth (Gen. 1:26)?  Surely Jesus did not lose any of His abilities, intelligence, awareness of all things, or power, just because He took upon Himself the form of a man.  He did not cease to be God when He was born, but in His human form He had the capacity to remain the infinite God.

Let us proceed to what it was that Jesus said.  Appropriately, His message to His Father was a quotation from the Hebrew Bible.  Later, at His temptation by the Devil, all three of His answers likewise came from scripture.  After all, Jesus is the living Word of God, and it was He who, by the instrumentality of the Holy Spirit, caused all those things to be written.  (It may be of interest, though not of great import, to note that Heb. 9 contains not one quotation from the Old Testament, although there are numerous allusions to what is reported there.)  This quotation is from Psalm 40:6-8.

### "Sacrifice and offering you did not desire...."

This statement is not to be interpreted to mean that God did not want or demand, sacrifices of the people when they were appropriate.  But there was always something God preferred greatly over sacrifice, and that was obedience.  We read in I Sam. 15:22 that God caused Samuel to say to King Saul, "Does the LORD delight in burnt offerings and sacrifices as much as in obeying the voice of the LORD?  To obey is better than sacrifice, and to heed is better than the fat of rams."  When I was a little boy, my parents spanked me and in other ways disciplined me quite often (I jokingly say that they spanked me every day and twice on Sundays).   I sometimes believed they took delight in spanking me.  But now that I am a parent, I know they were very sad every time they punished me.  They would have preferred that I had not misbehaved so they could abandon their practice of spanking.  In God's eyes, sacrifices offered insincerely were not only unacceptable, they were an abomination to Him.  For evidence of that, read Is. 1:10-17, the core of which is in verse 13:

> Stop bringing meaningless offerings!
> Your incense is detestable to me.
> New Moons, Sabbaths and convocations—
> I cannot bear your evil assemblies.

But in those days, since people continued in their sinful and rebellious ways, sacrifices continued to be essential to their salvation.

### "...but a body you prepared for me...."

The point here is not whether sacrifices are necessary or must continue, but rather to make a contrast between the animal sacrifices of the Old Testament times and the physical body of Jesus by which He could make His once for all perfect sacrifice.

### Heb. 10:6.
#### "...with burnt offerings and sin offerings you were not pleased."

God was not pleased, for two reasons. First, as we noted above from Is. 1, the people's offerings were often made insincerely, so they did not count in God's estimation. Secondly, as the author has been saying repeatedly, those animal sacrifices were totally inadequate. The problem had nothing to do with the shedding of blood, because that occurred in both the old and new orders. In Old Testament times, the animal was killed by shedding its blood, before it was burned on the altar, or eaten by the priests or the people, or whatever other disposition was made of the body. Nothing like that occurred with Christ's body, because it was placed in the tomb, and after His resurrection He ascended into heaven and thus His body was made inaccessible. It is interesting to note, however, that at the last Passover feast Jesus had with His disciples, He instituted the Lord's Supper, in which He gave the disciples bread and wine as tokens of His body and blood to be received by believers. That they were mere tokens is shown by what Paul said about them in his words of institution of the Lord's Supper (I Cor. 11:26): "For whenever you eat *this bread* and drink *this cup,* you proclaim the Lord's death until he comes." Also, here is a rather strange thing. We have noted earlier in our study that the people were strictly forbidden to drink the blood of any animals, but Jesus invited His disciples to partake, not only of a symbol of His body, but also a symbol of His blood. Whether He meant that to intensify the people's understanding of the validity of His sacrifice over that of the Levitical sacrifices I am not sure. It certainly is a large step ahead of what took place in the old covenant.

### Heb. 10:7.
#### "Then I said, 'Here I am—it is written about me in the scroll— I have come to do your will, O God.'"

Jesus said it, "Here I am."

Abraham said it, "Here I am," before sacrificing his son Isaac, Gen. 22:1.

Abraham said it, "Here I am," again, fortunately, before plunging the knife into Isaac, Gen. 22:11.

Samuel said it, "Here I am," when God called him as a lad, I Sam. 3:5.

*Why* do we not hear it more often today from the followers of Jesus?

The author says this was written "in the scroll." It is impossible to find such a saying in the Old Testament, except by allusion. Perhaps the nearest we come to finding the words is in Is. 53, the great chapter on the Suffering Servant.

Jesus said, "I have come to do your will, O God." Every human being has been called into the world for that same purpose. The vast difference is that Jesus did the Father's will without a flaw. He even boasted that it was so, though not idly, "I always do what pleases him" (John 8:29). On the other hand, the most nearly righteous of people has fallen far short of God's will for him. It is time for us who think ourselves dedicated followers of the Savior to say to Him, "Here I am," and mean it without reservation.

**Heb. 10:8. First he said, "Sacrifices and offerings, burnt offerings and sin offerings you did not desire, nor were you pleased with them" (although the law required them to be made).**

The author here repeats the first part of the quotation from Ps. 40, with some elaboration. It is unnecessary to sort it out bit by bit, because we have already done that. One or two further comments may be helpful.

Here is an interesting thought I have had about the replacement of the Levitical sacrifices with that of Jesus. Perhaps you have thought of it also. That thought is: Why should God order the people of Old Testament times to do something perpetually that did them no good? Perhaps I am asking the wrong question. It is a bit harsh to say that the ancient sacrifices did "no good." We should be able to recall that those sacrifices did at least three things of value:

1. Those sacrifices cleansed the people's flesh, 9:13.
2. They were patterns of the better things to come, 8:5 and 9:23.
3. They were acts of obedience, I Sam. 15:22.

**Heb. 10:9. Then he said, "Here I am, I have come to do your will." He sets aside the first to establish the second.**

The first system of sacrifices was not altogether pleasing to God; it was almost altogether displeasing to Him, as verse 8 says. Nor was the problem an issue of total disobedience, for God had commanded the people to make the sacrifices according to His directions; for the most part the priests and the people obeyed, and sincerely, but not totally. Be that as it may, there is now a replacement for those old sacrifices.

Someone might ask, "Is the sacrifice of Christ truly a replacement, or perhaps merely an alternative option? Must the first be abandoned just because there is another? Could not the two ministries complement one another in some way?" I believe Paul answered this cluster of questions very well in

342

Gal. 1:6-7: "I am astonished that you are so quickly deserting the one who called you by the grace of Christ and are turning to a different gospel—which is really no gospel at all." This is an excellent way of giving the sense of what Paul was trying to say. The KJV does not make it so clear: "...another gospel: which is not another...." The RSV translation is an improvement over the KJV, but is not as good as the NIV. The point is that Paul uses two different Greek words for the words translated "another." Bruce M. Metzger[2] said that ἕτερος, the word used in verse 6, means two objects in two different categories, like a book and a bed. The second word, ἄλλος, means "second, numerically, in the same class." Thus Metzger would translate this passage to say in English, "an opposition gospel which is not an alternative." We can reduce all this technical data to one simple statement: There is but one gospel; anything else is a deadly false gospel. In fact, the first ministry, found in the Old Testament, was not really a gospel; it was merely a textbook at best (or "schoolmaster" in Gal. 3:24) which prepared people to understand and receive the gospel when it came in Christ.

When we asked ourselves a moment ago whether it would be profitable to retain the old covenant while embracing the new, our best answer is that the old covenant is not really a gospel, or "good news." Rather, it should be considered "bad news" because it did not save anyone by itself; it only condemned all who broke God's law, and all had broken it. We may also argue that if you have something most excellent, what profit is there in clinging to something that cannot help you? It is better to abandon it altogether. To attempt to trust in both messages would be as destructive as trying to put one foot in a seaworthy boat and the other in a leaky boat that is rapidly filling with water, hoping that depending on both will provide multiple advantage. Instead, when the leaky boat fills, your foot goes down with it and you tumble into the water and drown.

### Heb. 10:10. And by that will, we have been made holy through the sacrifice of the body of Jesus Christ once for all.

Let us add to what we have already said about these matters.

First, "that will" is the Father's irrevocable decision that His Son Jesus should die to satisfy the law's requirement that all sin should be punished. That is not to say that each person must be punished for his own sins, but that those who trust in Christ as Savior and Lord could lay their sins on Jesus' shoulders and that He should pay the full price for them by His death on the cross. It took an infinitely merciful God to provide such a total cleansing for all who are willing to receive it.

Secondly, we who receive that salvation are not only saved from the punishment due us for our sins, but we are also "made holy." Two things happen in this process to all who believe. One is that God no longer consid-

---

[2]   Dr. Metzger explained this difference between the two words in a class on Galatians at Princeton Theological Seminary in the Fall of 1951.

ers that we have sinned, because our sins have been removed from us. In theological terms, this is called "justification." The other thing that happens is that we are enabled by the Holy Spirit to keep from sinning, if we are willing to utilize His offer. Unfortunately, in this life we do not fully commit ourselves to His keeping power, so we do occasionally fall back into sinful acts. But as we walk with Christ, the Holy Spirit keeps working in our lives to draw us closer to Himself so that we grow more fully into the likeness of the sinless Christ. Theologians call this process "sanctification." Unless we do grow in that way, it is reasonable to question whether we have in fact received Christ as Savior and Lord. The difference between justification and sanctification is that justification is an act of God that happens in an instant, and is done, where God clears us of all guilt and accounts us as sinless; while sanctification is an ongoing process by which God in reality makes us more nearly holy like Himself.

Thirdly, all this is done through a "sacrifice." Nothing else will do, in God's estimation. We recall that Adam and Eve tried to cover their sin by making clothes of fig leaves, but God could see through their puny efforts. So God had to kill the animal (probably a lamb), so He could cover their sin with the skin of the animal. A sacrifice (the animal) had to be made in order to restore Adam and Eve's fellowship with Him. So today, men may use a wide variety of ruses to try to cover their sins, but not one of men's devices, not even a restoration of the Old Testament animal sacrifices, will satisfy God. Only the sacrifice of Christ will do the job.

Next, it took "the body" of Christ to make the sacrifice. Without the incarnation there would be no salvation. That is the one reason why Jesus came into the world, as Paul said in I Tim. 1:15, "Christ Jesus came into the world to save sinners."

Along with this, we recognize that no other body would accomplish what God required. It had to be the body "of Jesus Christ." We read that John the apostle wept copiously "when no one was found who was worthy to open the scroll or look inside" (Rev. 5:4). But one of the elders around the throne of God comforted him (verse 5): "Do not weep! See, the Lion of the tribe of Judah, the Root of David, has triumphed. He is able to open the scroll and its seven seals." Naturally the elder was referring to Jesus. But if no one but Jesus could open the scroll, a relatively easy task, certainly no one else could have made the sacrifice to pay for the sins of the world. That Jesus alone could perform such a feat has been testified by an innumerable host of angels, who sang (Rev. 5:12),

Worthy is the Lamb!

Then every creature in the universe added his voice (verse 13):

To him who sits on the throne and to the Lamb
be praise and honor and glory and power,
for ever and ever!

The final point to make in this verse is from the last three words, "once for all." This theme is repeated so often by the author that he must have considered it exceedingly important. Besides being found here, it is in 7:27, 9:12, and 9:26. Please refer to 9:12 for a full discussion.

**Heb. 10:11. Day after day every priest stands and performs his religious duties; again and again he offers the same sacrifices, which can never take away sins.**

We note here that all the priests offered sacrifices every day for the sins of the people as they came with their animals to the tabernacle. The high priest, however, made the great sacrifice only once a year, on the Day of Atonement, when he entered the Most Holy Place, carrying the blood of atonement for even the unwitting sins of the people. In saying this, we must remember that Jesus is never compared to priests in general, but only to the high priest, although this verse tells us that all priests made sacrifices daily.

The amazing thing about the statement in this verse is that all those daily sacrifices combined from the time of Aaron to the destruction of the temple in 70 AD could "*never* take away sins." Please follow this logical argument: We must conclude that if all the sacrifices under the old order could never take away sins; and without the shedding of blood there is no remission or forgiveness; then it was only by the blood of Jesus Christ that anyone in Old Testament times was saved. If you have any objection to that argument, please remember Rev. 13:8 about the "Lamb that was slain from the creation of the world."

**Heb. 10:12. But when this priest had offered for all time one sacrifice for sins, he sat down at the right hand of God.**

Everything we read in this verse is repeated for emphasis, and to strengthen the next point.

That point is that when Jesus had made His high priestly sacrifice, He had completed at least His work of paying the penalty for the sins of the world. Some people used to think that Jesus' work on the cross was not sufficient to pay the full penalty for sin, but that He was required to remain in hell to continue to make additional payment for sin until His second coming which was not from heaven to earth, but from hell to heaven (that is why nobody saw His return, they claim). That idea of course is contrary to all the Bible says about sacrifice. Sacrifice is understood as death by shed blood to wash away sins. It is true that Christ did descend to hell upon His death, as we read in I Pet. 3:18-20:

> He was put to death in the body but made alive by the Spirit, through whom also he went and preached to the spirits in prison who disobeyed long ago when God waited patiently in the days of Noah while the ark was being built.

That Jesus did not remain in hell is attested to by Peter a few words later when he said (verse 22), "[Jesus Christ] has gone into heaven and is at God's right

345

hand—with angels, authorities and powers in submission to him."

Another scriptural proof that Jesus did not remain in hell an extended time to "pay off" our debt of sin is found in the gospel account of His death. Traditionally, these words of Jesus are the next to last of His seven words from the cross, and found in John 19:30, "When he had received the drink, Jesus said, 'It is finished.' With that, he bowed his head and gave up his spirit." (In case you are wondering why this is not considered Jesus' seventh word, since John seems to make it final, the statement which is counted as the last is found in Lu. 23:46, "Father, into your hands I commit my spirit.")

The discussion of what is said here does not obviate the possibility of some future sacrifice, perhaps by someone else, but we have much to say about that later, near the end of chapter 10 of Hebrews.

The author of Hebrews does declare that Jesus' sitting down at the right hand of God is a fulfillment of the Father's invitation to His Son, which is recorded in Ps. 110:1, and quoted in Heb. 1:13,

> The LORD says to my Lord:
> "Sit at my right hand
> until I make your enemies
> a footstool for your feet."

As far as I know, no one else gets to sit at the right hand of the Father. You will recall that James and John (with their mother's approval) asked Jesus for the right to sit at His right and left hands when He came into His kingdom, and Jesus at best deferred an answer, implying the likelihood that neither would have that privilege (Matt. 20:20-28, and its parallel Mk. 10:35-45).

### Heb. 10:13. Since that time he waits for his enemies to be made his footstool....

This verse continues the allusion to Ps. 110:1 which was started in the previous verse (and was quoted in Heb. 1:13). The statement from the Father to the Son is in two parts. One of them, Jesus' sitting at the right hand of God, has been fulfilled already. The other part, that Jesus' enemies would be made His footstool, has not yet been fulfilled. At least it had not been fulfilled up to the time the words of Hebrews were penned. This fact is shown by the beginning words of the verse, "Since that time he waits...." It appears from what is said in the Revelation that Jesus is still waiting for the fulfillment of that promise. Two separate times this will happen. The first is a brief time during the millennium, when Satan will be bound in the bottomless pit (Rev. 20:2-3), after which he must be released for a short time, when he will be more or less free to roam the earth again to deceive the people. The second and permanent time when Jesus' enemies will be put under His feet will be at the time of the Great White Throne Judgment, when Satan and all Christ's enemies will be cast permanently into the lake of fire (Rev. 20:11-15). Then God will laugh at all His enemies and hold them in derision ("scoffs at them" Ps. 2:4, NIV).

**Heb. 10:14.** **...because by one sacrifice he has made perfect forever those who are being made holy.**

Here is a tremendous truth! It is impossible to express it adequately in human language. This is the "one total cleansing" indicated by the title of this chapter of our book.

Again the author emphasizes that Jesus needed to make only "one" sacrifice. That fact ought to be firmly established in our minds by the time this study is completed.

One of the principal things I am looking forward to when I reach heaven is the fulfillment of the promise that I will be "made perfect forever." I will not make myself perfect; I cannot possibly do it for myself, despite what John says in I John 3:3, "Everyone who has this hope in him purifies himself, just as he is pure." It is only the power of the Holy Spirit working in me that can make me pure or perfect. I am sure John meant that I must be willing to allow the Holy Spirit to do that work, so I will become more nearly perfect in this life, and then be transformed at the resurrection: "...we will be changed. For the perishable must clothe itself with the imperishable, and the mortal with immortality" (I Cor. 15:52-53).

"Those who are being made holy" are the same people whom "he has made perfect forever." I related in connection with our study of Heb. 6:6 that one of my greatest deterrents to sinning in this life is that every sin I commit crucifies my Savior in a sense again, and puts Him to open shame. If I love Him, as I ought to love Him for dying for me, I should want to avoid giving Him pain or sadness. How relieved I will be when the time comes when I will never again, *can* never again crucify my loving Savior.

I am now "being made holy." I am in the process. If that is not happening, then all who know me should seriously question whether I have truly accepted Jesus Christ as my Savior *and* my Lord. How is your life of holiness progressing?

**Heb. 10:15.** **The Holy Spirit also testifies to us about this. First he says....**

This is the third time the author attributes Old Testament writings to the Holy Spirit. The first is in 3:7, just before the quotation from Ps. 95:7-11; and the second is in 9:7, where he writes regarding the entrance of the high priest into the Most Holy Place annually to make sacrifice for the general sins of the people. Many people have refused to acknowledge that the Holy Spirit had anything to do with the writing and preservation of the Bible of the Jews; they prefer to question whether the authority of God supports what is written there. Such people, especially among the scholarly set, prefer to accept the trustworthiness of secular records over the testimony of the scriptures. My Old Testament professor in New College, Edinburgh, for instance, declared in class that because of secular writings he was forced to acknowledge that an historic person named Moses had existed, but added, "his life is so encrustated with saga that we cannot know with certainty any details of his life."[3] Those who reject the validity of the biblical record miss much ancient history.

### Heb. 10:16.
#### "This is the covenant I will make with them...."

When I read these introductory words to this covenant in Jer. 31:38 which God promised to the world, I take it as one of the two most important covenants found in the whole Bible. Because of this, I believe it ought to be emphasized in all theological works regarding God's covenants with the world.

The Dispensationalists seem to downplay the idea of covenants in their discussions in favor of "dispensations." In the Scofield Reference Bible, from a note introducing Gen. 1:28, we find: "A dispensation is a period of time during which man is tested in respect of obedience to some *specific* revelation of the will of God. Seven such dispensations are distinguished in Scripture." (The emphasis is Scofield's.) When Scofield speaks of "some *specific* revelation of the will of God," he ought to refer to some "covenant," because each dispensation is linked to what he calls a covenant. The footnote related to Gen. 1:28 following the definition gives a list of the seven dispensations, each linked with a covenant.[4]

|      |                               |                                  |
| ---- | ----------------------------- | -------------------------------- |
| I.   | Innocency, Gen. 1:28          | Edenic Covenant, Gen. 1:28       |
| II.  | Conscience, Gen. 3:23         | Adamic Covenant, Gen. 3:15       |
| III. | Human Government, Gen. 8:20   | Noahic Covenant, Gen. 9:1        |
| IV.  | Promise, Gen. 12:1            | Abrahamic Covenant, Gen. 15:18   |
| V.   | Law, Ex. 19:8                 | Mosaic Covenant, Ex. 19:25       |
| VI.  | Grace, John 1:17              | Palestinian Covenant, Deut. 30:3 |
| VII. | Kingdom, Eph. 1:10            | Davidic Covenant, II Sam. 7:17   |

The Scofield notes are not clear on which covenant accompanies which dispensation, but I believe I have linked them as they are intended to be. This leaves a covenant without a companion dispensation, the New Covenant, Heb. 8:8. This is the quotation from what I have called the Jeremaic Covenant, the second of the two great covenants.

Why speak of two, and only two, covenants? It is because that thought is the whole point the author of Hebrews makes in drawing his contrast between the Old Testament and New Testament ministries recorded in scripture. He does not always call them "covenants," but he begins in earnest to call them just that in 7:22, in his large and important dissertation on Melchizedek as the forerunner of Jesus whose ministry is better than that of the Aaronic priesthood. The basic Greek word, διαθήκη, for "covenant" and its English counterparts is found, in addition to 7:22, fourteen times in Hebrews: in 8:6,

---

[3] In a class by Prof. O. S. Rankin, Professor of Old Testament, New College, Edinburgh, Scotland, 1950-1951.

[4] This information is also found in Lewis Sperry Chafer's book, DISPENSATION-ALISM.

348

8:8, 8:9, 8:10, 9:4, 9:15 (twice), 9:16, 9:17, 9:20, 10:16 (our present verse under study), 10:16, 10:29, 12:24, and 13:20. The Greek word is found an additional sixteen times in the rest of the New Testament.

When the author quotes God's words about the covenant "I will make with them," we must impress on our minds that it is God who initiates any covenants or any kind of agreement between Him and us. It is He who draws us to Himself, as Jesus said in John 6:44: "No one can come to me unless the Father who sent me draws him." Beyond that, we saw how in Gen. 15 God drew up a unilateral covenant with Abraham which neither he nor any of his descendants could annul.

### "...after that time, says the Lord...."

It is my guess that "that time" is pinpointed in Jer. 30:3, which is part of the preface to the long poem in chapters 30 and 31, from which the quotation in Hebrews 10 comes. In that introduction Jeremiah said, "The days are coming...when I will bring my people Israel and Judah back from captivity and restore them to the land I gave their forefathers to possess." And when did those days occur? They occurred early, still in the lifetime of Jeremiah, who at God's direction had bought land in anticipation of his return to it after the seventy years' captivity noted in Jer. 25:11-12 and 29:10; and noted as well in Ezra 1:1. Then some time after the return of the diaspora of the Jews, the first advent of Christ would occur, which would be the establishment of the "new covenant" mentioned in Jer. 31:33 and quoted in Heb. 10:16.

### "I will put my laws in their hearts, and I will write them on their minds."

We read virtually the same thing in Ezek. 36:26-27:

I will give you a new heart and put a new spirit in you; I will remove from you your heart of stone and give you a heart of flesh, and I will put my Spirit in you and move you to follow my decrees and be careful to keep my laws.

Since God has already done that and we now live under that new covenant, there is no longer a need for the tablets of Moses from which we must read God's law. In that sense, there may be no more need for God's written word in the world, since it at least ought to be written in the minds and hearts of all His people. Still, because we are fallible, it is beneficial to have the written word to help us settle our disagreements and differences when we talk about God and His will for us. Surely we have an abundance of disputes in our day. But when we get to heaven, where we all will be made perfect in every way, then we will need no more paper copies of the word of God. His writing on our hearts will be clear as crystal to us.

### Heb. 10:17. Then he adds....

It may lead only to idle speculation to wonder why the author of Hebrews chose to make this break in his quotation from Jeremiah. My thought

349

is that he may have wanted to add strong emphasis to his report of the bountiful results of God's putting His word into minds and hearts of people.

**"Their sins and lawless acts**
**I will remember no more."**

These words bring to the believer great relief from the overpowering burden of guilt which oppresses everyone who thinks of his moral situation in this life! If God truly has forgotten our sins, these words carry with them the tacit promise that He will never recall them; thus we have confidence we will remain free from punishment forever.

We can have even greater confidence in the truth of these words, because the same idea is conveyed in several additional passages of scripture:

- Ps. 103:12

  "as far as the east is from the west,

   so far has he removed our transgressions from us."

- Micah 7:19

  "You will again have compassion on us;

   you will tread our sins underfoot

   and hurl all our iniquities into the depths of the sea.

- Col. 2:13-14 "God made you alive with Christ. He forgave us all our sins, having canceled the written code, with its regulations, that was against us and that stood opposed to us; he took it away, nailing it to the cross."

- I John 1:9 "If we confess our sins, he is faithful and just and will forgive us our sins and purify us from all unrighteousness."

With regard to the quotation from Colossians above, in New Testament times the custom for giving public notice that a person had made his final payment on a mortgage, the money lender would take the mortgage paper, write "Paid in full" across it, and the former debtor would nail the paper to the doorpost of his home for all passersby to see. In that same way, when Jesus was nailed to the cross, the debt He paid for our sins was in a sense written on His bleeding body, so that all who looked on Him that afternoon could see the price He paid for our forgiveness. Also, let me comment on the last quotation above: I highly recommend that you commit it to memory, to remind yourself immediately after you have sinned and then confessed it to God, that that sin is forgiven, and in fact all your future sins have been cleansed from God's record of your life. Beware, however, lest you think that thereby you are free to sin copiously just because you have already been forgiven. If you truly love your Savior you will not feel free to sin knowing that every sin disappoints Him greatly and in a sense crucifies Him once again.

**Heb. 10:18. And where these have been forgiven....**
Here we have the tremendous climax of this chapter of Hebrews. We

350

have been thinking throughout this chapter of the "one total cleansing" as the first part of God's "better promises" introduced in Heb. 8:6. In this one small verse we have the full presentation in a nutshell. Christ died to forgive us; we who believe have been forgiven; the transaction through Christ's one sacrifice is completed forever.

Forgiveness is a most wonderful, exhilarating feeling. When you know you have done wrong, you are burdened with that knowledge. Piled atop that knowledge is the assurance of certain repayment for the evil you have done. Yet another layer of heaviness is the fearful knowledge that the person you have offended is justifiably offended at you for what you have done. Such a burden is so unbearable to many people that they fill psychiatrists' offices in their search for relief from the load. No one has ever found relief by that route, however. The only escape from that estate is to ask for, and receive, forgiveness from God first and then from the person offended.

Here is one small example from my own life. When our sons were small, we were sitting at the table for a meal, when son John did something I thought was wrong. I rapped his knuckles in punishment, but immediately saw a red welt rise from the middle knuckle. I was instantly mortified at what I had done, to impose such great punishment for what surely was some infinitesimal infraction. I took John's hand and caressed it, and poured out my sorrow at what I had done, and asked him to forgive me. In a moment he answered, "It's all right, daddy. It's OK." It was obvious he was upset, not that I had hit him, but that I was so obviously repentant. But I was relieved beyond measure to know that John had forgiven me for my outburst of anger.

Of course, the repentance must be sincere. A man in church once said to a woman something highly offensive. Later, the man approached the woman after he discovered she was offended, and said, "If I did anything to offend you, I hope you will forgive me," fully expecting she would say, "Oh, no, that's all right. You didn't do anything wrong. There's nothing to forgive." Instead, she looked him in the eye, and said, "I forgive you." The man turned and sneaked away like a whipped dog. He really thought he had done no wrong, and wanted her to agree with him. But when she acknowledged that he had done something wrong by (sincerely) speaking forgiveness, his burden of sin suddenly struck him and remained on his conscience. So it is in our relationship with God. We must be sure to acknowledge the sinfulness of our sins, and be earnest in our repentance. Then the burden is lifted.

### ...there is no longer any sacrifice for sin.

It may take a bit of careful thought to see the logic of this statement. If the sins of the world are paid for by one sacrifice; if all confessed sins are included in the payment; if those sins are wiped out and forgotten by God never to be recalled; and if no unconfessed sin can be forgiven either by sacrifice or by any other means; the only possible conclusion is that there is no necessity for even one additional sacrifice for sin into all eternity. Is there any question about this series of statements? Is there any flaw in the thought, or even an omission? I trust you understand, and believe, and have received that indescribable forgiveness.

This verse begins to reveal the main emphasis in this tenth chapter of Hebrews. The conclusion of that emphasis is that following the sacrifice of Christ, there is no good in abandoning it for some other, future, better sacrifice, because there is no other. We will develop that theme fully in our next chapter of this study.

# CHAPTER X
## BETTER PROMISES II.
## NO MORE SACRIFICE.    HEB. 10:19-39.

As mentioned at the end of our last study chapter, we now come to the main theme of the tenth chapter of Hebrews. Just as in college a student works toward a major goal but has one or more minor interests to work on, so in Hebrews the author has a major theme which is that Jesus and His ministry are infinitely "better than" anything the Old Testament ministry can offer; but in chapter 10 he expounds on a theme which is related but different. This minor theme is that following Jesus and His ministry there will never appear another savior or ministry that will surpass that of Jesus.

Because many people never become aware of this minor theme in chapter 10, there is great controversy over what is actually taught. That controversy is the same one we noted in chapter 6, especially verse 6, which is whether a person who has once been saved can be lost again.

The proper way to understand the author's teaching here is to see the overall thrust of his argument from the very beginning of the chapter. The best way to grasp his purpose is to outline the chapter in brief, and then return to a detailed examination of its last twenty-one verses. Actually, the whole chapter is a summary of what the author has said up to now about Christ's ministry of salvation as better than what the Old Testament priesthood had to offer, with one extremely important addition. Here then is the outline of chapter 10.

Verse 1. OT sacrifices were offered annually, BUT

Verse 4. OT sacrifices could not take away sin.

Verse 10.  Christ died "once for all," and...

Verse 12.  ...that one sacrifice...

Verse 14  ...perfected *forever* those being made holy.

If they are perfected forever, then...

Verse 18  ...there is *no more* (further) offering for sin.

Verse 26  Reiterates verse 18: no more sacrifice for sin, BUT

a certain fearful expectation of judgment...fire.

The one extremely important addition is the fact that although Jesus supplanted the Old Testament sacrifices by His one eternal sacrifice which brings eternal blessing, there is *not one thing* that can ever supplant Jesus' sacrifice. To seek to go beyond Jesus' supreme sacrifice is to rush headlong off the cliff to certain, utter destruction which will be at least as violent as the end of the demons who entered the herd of swine at Gerasa (Lu. 8:26-38). To twist the meaning of the last few verses of chapter 10 to mean that a person can reject Christ once he has received salvation is to do an injustice to the whole teaching of scripture, and especially the teaching of the book of Hebrews. Having said this, it is time now to examine the last part of Heb. 10, to make sure what the author of Hebrews wrote and meant.

\* \* \*

**Heb. 10:19. Therefore, brothers, since we have con-
fidence to enter the Most Holy Place by the blood of Jesus....**

I like that word "confidence." The Greek word παρρησία is translated as
"boldness" in the KJV. It is explained quite fully in our study of chapter 4,
verse 16. The same Greek word is also in 3:6, where the NIV translates it as
"courage." In addition, this last part of chapter 10 is tied together by the author's use of the same word in verse 35, where he urges, "So do not throw
away your confidence" because of persecutions you endure.

Our confidence, or boldness, makes us willing to do what virtually no
Old Testament person was allowed to do: "We...enter the Most Holy Place."
In ancient times only the high priest could enter that sacred room; no one
could accompany him; and he was permitted to enter no more than once a
year. Surely every high priest who entered was filled with awe and trembling.
For you and me to enter that same place should be a most blessed experience.

Such a privilege is available to us, even though we are not high
priests. However, we have been made priests because of our new relationship
to God, as we read in I Pet. 2:9, "You are a chosen people, a royal priesthood,
a holy nation, a people belonging to God." The room which was open only
to high priests is now open to us, to all who have received Jesus Christ as
Great High Priest, Savior, and Lord. Therefore, when we allow Jesus to be
our High Priest, we realize that He has already entered the Most Holy Place
(Heb. 9:12). Therefore, we can follow Him there because we belong to Him.
Let us be careful to acknowledge, however, that we may enter, not because we
deserve it, or because we are better than the people of Old Testament times,
but because Jesus is better than any Old Testament priest, and it is Jesus who
invites us to enter with Him.

Some aggressive people might argue that they have a right to enter the
Most Holy Place simply because Peter calls Christians priests in both I Pet.
2:9 and verse 5. That is a false assumption, however, because although Peter
calls us a "royal" priesthood and a "holy" priesthood, he did not call even one
of us a high priest, and only a high priest had the right to enter simply by his
title. In Old Testament times there was but one high priest at any given time.
Granted, in the New Testament we read occasionally of high priests in the
plural, as if there were more than one at a time.[1]  But in Roman times the
high priesthood was confused. The Roman authorities selected the high
priests, and changed their selections annually. Further, they did not select
them according to lineal descent as Moses' law required. Also, we read in Lu.
3:2 of "the high priesthood of Annas and Caiaphas," which requires some
explanation. Annas had been the high priest earlier; then the Roman authorities selected his son-in-law Caiaphas to be high priest. Apparently Caiaphas
was but a puppet in Annas' hands, so although Caiaphas held the office, An-

---

[1]  John calls them "chief" priests, but they are what the Old Testament calls the
high priests. We see them mentioned in the plural in John's gospel in 7:32, 7:45,
11:47, 11:57, 12:10, 18:3, 18:35, 19:6, 19:15, and 19:21.

nas made the decisions. The same kind of thing happens today in governments both religious and secular.

At any rate, not one of us is a high priest. Truly there is but one, beginning with Jesus' investiture into that office, and that High Priest will never abandon His office for any reason. Since there is, in God's eyes, but one High Priest, none of us needs to apply for the position. Therefore, it is a privilege, not a right, for any of us to enter the Most Holy Place; and we enter only because Jesus has gone before us and invited us to follow.

**Heb. 10:20.    ...by a new and living way opened for us through the curtain, that is, his body....**

The "old way" was just a mental or spiritual path whose ditches on either side were the ten commandments and the rest of the Mosaic law. The new way is astronomically different. It is not just an inanimate path; it is a Person. He had said to His disciples in John 14:6, "I am the Way." He was the Living Way as well, because in that same verse He said, "I am the Life." Beyond that, His life will never end, because the author of Hebrews told us in 7:25, "...he always lives to intercede for them." His body is now the "veil" or "curtain" through which we enter the Most Holy Place. And this "Curtain" was rent, like the veil in the temple at Christ's crucifixion. Christ's body was rent by the nailprints and the sword's mark. There is no question for us who have received Jesus Christ as Savior and Lord that we yearn to enter. There is but one alternative place: that is "outside," the lake of fire which burns forever and ever. Alaskans like to say that everything and everyone beyond the borders of Alaska are "outside." It matters not where that "outside" is, whether New York, or Nebraska, or the Netherlands; they are doomed to the fate of being "outside."

There is no entrance besides Jesus by which we may enter. A slightly different figure of speech was employed by Jesus when He said, "I am the door" in John 10:7 and 9. The NIV employs the term "gate," but the Greek word is θύρα which means "door." I have seen sheepfolds in both Scotland and Israel. They are round walls built of stone, and there is but one break in the whole wall. After the shepherd led his sheep inside at night, he squatted down in that opening, and literally became a "door" so no predator could enter. However, with regard to a gate, we recall that Jesus told the parable of the narrow and wide gates in Matt. 7:13-14, where Jesus meant Himself to be the narrow Gate that leads to life, because He is the "living way."

**Heb. 10:21.    ...and since we have a great priest over the house of God....**

There is nothing new in this verse, but the author repeats it here because our understanding of what follows depends on it.

\* \* \*

355

**Heb. 10:22.  ...let us draw near to God with a sincere heart in full assurance of faith....**

We humans have a one hundred percent obligation to make a conscious effort to "draw near to God," despite what we may believe about predestination.  In expressing this forceful statement, I am not demeaning the fact of predestination; if you have read this far you are aware of my full support of it.  However, everything the Bible says, including what it says about predestination, points to the fact that if I fail to draw near to God I have only myself to blame for the consequences.  Otherwise, it would be a waste of effort to fill scriptures with admonitions and exhortations to come to Christ.  Besides this verse, we have many other passages.  II Cor. 5:20, "We implore you on Christ's behalf:  Be reconciled to God."  Rom. 12:1, "Therefore, I urge you, brothers, in view of God's mercy, to offer your bodies as living sacrifices, holy and pleasing to God—which is your spiritual worship."  Rev. 22:17, "The Spirit and the bride say, 'Come!'  And let him who hears say, 'Come!'"  Only the hyper-Calvinists would argue against this evidence that all we need to do is sit back in our rocking chairs and wait for the Holy Spirit to carry us to heaven if we are "elected," and if we are not among the elect nothing we can do will change matters.  The greatest refutation to that idea is that no one on earth knows who has been chosen and who has not, so we must make every effort to obey our Savior, and enter by Him, the Living Way.

The author of Hebrews warns us that we must draw near with "a sincere heart."  Since God, as He told Samuel in I Sam. 16:7, looks at the heart, there is no way we can deceive Him if we are insincere.  But we must also beware lest we deceive ourselves.  Isaiah pointed out that God was highly offended at the insincere worshipers of his day (Is. 1:12-13):

> When you come to meet with me,
>> who has asked this of you,
>> this trampling of my courts?
> Stop bringing meaningless offerings!
>> Your incense is detestable to me.
> New Moons, Sabbaths and convocations—
>> I cannot bear your evil assemblies.

Jeremiah warned us in Jer. 17:9:

> The heart is deceitful above all things
>> and beyond cure.
> Who can understand it?

Our attempt to come to God must not be half-hearted, but we must come with "full assurance."  The hymnwriter knew how blessed was that full assurance:

> Blessed assurance, Jesus is mine!
> Oh, what a foretaste of glory divine!
> Heir of salvation, purchase of God,
> Born of His Spirit, washed in His blood.

We ought to be fully sure that we are safely in the arms of Jesus.  The first question a worker in the Evangelism Explosion ministry is invited to ask his hearer is, "Have you come to the point in your spiritual life where you know for certain that if you should die tonight, you would go to heaven?" That assurance can be had, without boasting, as we read in I John 5:13, "I write these things to you who believe in the name of the Son of God so that you may *know* that you have eternal life" (emphasis mine).

When the author speaks of "full assurance of faith," we may wonder which of two thoughts about faith he means. He may mean that we have full assurance that we *have* faith; or he may mean that we have full assurance of what our faith supplies to us. It is possible that he intends for us to embrace both objectives for our faith. Our faith gives us assurance, and faith is what we need in order to draw near to God, to receive all His blessings. Let us not forget that the great object of our faith is our Lord Jesus Christ as our Great High Priest with all the results that entails, not least of which are our salvation from the penalty of sin, and our inheritance with Jesus forever.

In speaking of faith, the author names the first of Paul's famous trilogy in I Cor. 13:13. This trilogy is mentioned in our discussion of the authorship of Hebrews. Some people hold to this fact as a firm indication of Paul's influence in the writing of the letter. Further, they emphasize its importance because we see a doubling of the trilogy. First, in verses 22 to 24 we see a mention of faith, hope, and love. Following that, we see that the next three chapters contain at least the flavor of these three thoughts: chapter 11 is the great faith chapter of the Bible; hope is the theme of chapter 12, although the word is not mentioned; and chapter 13 begins with an admonition to have (brotherly) love for one another.

### ...having our hearts sprinkled to cleanse us from a guilty conscience....

Before you glance at the clause following this, please note carefully that the author is speaking in spiritual and/or figurative language. It is impossible physically to have our hearts "sprinkled" with anything, not by me, not by yourself, not by any priest. Yet the author says that we should be "having our hearts sprinkled." The heart is the seat of emotions and the place in which we turn to God, but even this is figurative language.

The author does not specify what is to be sprinkled on our hearts. But he has often alluded to it in many ways. Our hearts are to be sprinkled with the blood of Jesus (remember, some people call this a "bloody" book). For proof of this, refer back to 9:14 for the idea, and to 9:13 for the word "sprinkled." Again I say, the author must be speaking in spiritual terms. How could we obtain the physical blood of Jesus by which to sprinkle our hearts or anything else? Still, the sprinkling of our hearts by the blood of Jesus cleanses our guilty consciences (see again 9:14).

\* \* \*

357

**...and having our bodies washed with pure water.**

Perhaps you would like me to hedge a bit and admit that here at least the author has shifted from spiritual meaning in the previous clause to material meaning. However, such a shift seems inappropriate. My objection to such a change is two-fold. First, it seems more natural to continue in the spiritual mode rather than shifting to a material mode. Secondly, it would be impossible as a practical matter to obtain "pure" water for such washing. The Greek term for "pure," καθαρός, can be used in either a physical or Levitical or ethical sense, according to Thayer. If perchance such water is intended by the author to be water in a material sense (such as baptism by water), then what spiritual benefit does it bring to the person washed? The author was careful, in 9:13, to point out that in Old Testament times the ritual sprinklings made the people outwardly clean but could not touch their inner needs.

Here is a final argument against the idea of being cleansed by physical water: throughout the book of Hebrews the author has exhorted his readers not to revert to the ministry of the old covenant under the Aaronic priesthood. That is not to say that water baptism (by any mode) is wrong; it is simply unprofitable for salvation. We practice baptism out of obedience to Christ (He commanded His disciples to go into all the world and baptize people in the Great Commission, Matt. 28:18-20). Whatever spiritual benefit comes is a result of our obedience. Some of us think spiritual blessing comes, because we call the rite of baptism a "sacrament," that is, a mysterious working of God in the life of the one baptized.

### Heb. 10:23.   Let us hold unswervingly to the hope we profess....

Here is the second word of the trilogy we began to mention in our comments on the previous verse. The trilogy is obscured in the KJV, because this verse is translated incorrectly: "Let us hold fast the profession of our faith without wavering...." In this way, the second word of the trilogy is hidden.

With this word comes a second exhortation: it is your responsibility to hold on; your determination to cling to your hope should not be affected by what God may or may not have ordained beforehand for you. James warns us in his first chapter (1:6-8) that if we vacillate between belief and doubt, we are like a wave in the sea; such a person "is a double-minded man, unstable in all he does." Suppose you are standing beside a lake, and you see a man in a boat far off-shore. While you watch, the wind catches the boat and it overturns. The man bobs up, and clings to the top of the upturned boat, and begins to cry for help. If he holds on for dear life, surely someone with another boat will see his distress and go to rescue him. If, however, the man gets discouraged and lets go, he will drown. He must "hold unswervingly" to the boat to be rescued.

For what do we hope? It is not clearly defined here, nor is it in the previous verses in Hebrews where hope is mentioned: 3:6, 6:11, 6:18, or 7:19. However, I would judge that the tenor of the whole book would lead us to grasp the hope of God's provision for our salvation through the better High Priest.

The author speaks of the "hope we profess." Do you profess your hope? Or have you ever professed your hope at any time in your life? Perhaps you did so when you became a member of your church. I know I did at age twelve, but my profession was a rather perfunctory, mostly meaningless ritual. In fact, the only reason I know I made such a profession is because it was required of each person to become a member of the church. Subsequent to that time, I became fully aware of my salvation, and have sought God's help to make my life a profession of that hope.

### ...for he who promised is faithful.

The Greek word for "promised" here is ἐπαγγέλλω. The form of the verb is punctiliar, that is, it happened but once. God made His promise to you once for all time, and that is sufficient. However, it is necessary for you and me to *profess* our hope constantly, as we seek to draw nearer to Him, and to His will, for our lives. God made His promise to you once, and on the basis of that promise He will not fail to keep it. You may have promised your children that, come Saturday, your family would go on a picnic at some park, and you would have a wonderful time together. But Saturday morning dawned with the rain pouring down, so you abandoned your picnic plans. Your children may have been very disappointed; they may have been angry at you for failing to fulfill your promise. But you did not know, when you promised, that it was going to rain. No such contingency ever confronts God. He knows the end from the beginning, so He never needs to change His mind or fail to make good on His promise to you. Beyond that, God never wants to change His mind with regard to any promise He has made to you. Since that is so, you are urged to cling to your hope in Him, so you may demonstrate to the world the things He has done for you, and will do for you through eternity. We see in Heb. 13:8 that our God Jesus "is the same yesterday and today and forever."

### Heb. 10:24. And let us consider how we may spur one another on toward love and good deeds.

Now Paul's trilogy is complete. But if we are to follow this admonition successfully, we must "consider how we may" do it. We must decide we want to do it. We must plan to do it. We must determine we will do it.

Note carefully that this verse tells us it is not sufficient for us to love one another and to do good deeds; we must in addition "spur one another on" to do the same. The Greek word for "spur" is παροξυσμός, from which comes our little-used English word "paroxysm," which means "any sudden, violent outburst."[2]  The Greek word means either "incitement" or "irritation."[3]  It is used only one other time in the New Testament, in Acts 15:39, where Paul and Barnabas had a "sharp disagreement" over whether to take John Mark with them on Paul's second missionary journey.  We see then that the word the author of Hebrews uses is unusually strong.  That surely means the idea must be very important to him.

We Christians are to urge one another "toward love."  This is something we must all strive toward constantly.  Unfortunately, in this world none of us shall achieve perfect love.  If it ever did happen to anyone, he would be aware of it immediately, because all his fears would evaporate totally, for John told us in I John 4:18, "Perfect love drives out fear."

As we encourage each other to increase our love, we should incite each other to do "good deeds" as well.  I fully believe that if we truly have love for one another, then and only then will we be motivated to do good works for one another.  The same applies to our love for God.  If we love Him perfectly, we will serve Him wholly.

### Heb. 10:25.  Let us not give up meeting together, as some are in the habit of doing....

Steve Blocher came as a summer student intern to the church I served in Anchorage in 1977 (he later became the Associate Minister there).  This verse was his favorite in the New Testament (his Old Testament favorite was Josh. 1:9).  Our verse contains a good and important admonition.

Unfortunately, many people who call themselves Christians ignore the exhortation.  My first responsibility as an ordained Minister was to start a new church in upstate New York.  My habit was to spend afternoons, and some mornings, calling door to door to invite people who did not attend church regularly to visit our fellowship.  One beautiful, sunny day I came to a house surrounded by giant maple trees, flowering shrubbery, and a manicured lawn.  To the back of one side of the house was a sunken garden, with wrought iron benches, where a person could sit and drink in the beauty of the yard and surrounding neighborhood.  I knocked at the freshly-white-painted dutch door, and as was my custom I prayed while I waited for someone to answer.  A pleasant lady opened the top of the door and greeted me.  I told her my mission: "I'm Tom Teply, from the Loudonville Presbyterian Chapel.  If you don't go regularly to any church, I invite you to come to the Chapel on the highway and worship with us."  The lady responded, "Oh, I don't need to go to any church to worship God.  I can worship Him right there in my garden!"  I said, "Yes, you can.  Do you?"  The lady looked stunned at me for five seconds, then angrily slammed the door in my face.  You can guess what

---

[2]  RANDOM HOUSE DICTIONARY.

[3]  Part of Thayer's definition.

her answer was. People need to gather together to worship God, or they will neglect to do so at best, and will fail to do so and turn from God at worst.

Almost nobody is naturally a hermit. We all crave company. Why do you suppose nearly everybody who must be home alone has either the radio or the television on, not really listening but simply aware of someone else's existence? And when we gather together, we like to be with people with whom we are compatible. The proverb puts it, "Birds of a feather flock together." I would encourage you to think for a few moments what kind of "bird" you are. With whom do you prefer to associate? Do you choose Christians, so you may encourage them, and be encouraged by them? Or would you rather be with a more worldly crowd, enjoying the fleeting pleasures of the world, and trying to put from your mind the alternatives of the world to come?

The first time I met my parents-in-law, I was amused at the fact that they belonged to the local golf club. I knew that neither of them played golf (although I learned later that they had played golf in their earlier years), so I thought it strange that they still bothered to belong to the club. I soon realized their reason for keeping up their membership was because they had many close friends in the club, and attendance at various functions there kept them in touch. Incidentally, to keep you from misjudging them, I must tell you that they both were earnest Christians, and they attended their church faithfully.

Why do people stay away from church? Some are embarrassed, because they have no decent shoes to wear. One man almost stopped coming to our church because he had to sit beside the top banker in town, and he was "only" a garbage collector. It took much encouragement to show him that God looks on the soul, not the outward appearance. Others know what the message is, and they do not like it. A few claim the church is full of hypocrites; a Minister responded to one such, "Oh, come to our church. There's always room for one more!" Surveys show that most people do not go to church or to Christian gatherings because no one has invited them to go with them. This idea brings up the next clause in the verse.

### ...but let us encourage one another....

Here is a tremendous reason to go to church: to receive encouragement. That encouragement should not come from the Minister alone. He does not always encourage. One lady who was disappointed with my sermons told me, "Tom, I work hard all week, and have many cares on my mind. When I come to church on Sunday morning, I need to be comforted and be told nice things about myself. I don't get that. You tell us how bad we are, and how much more we ought to be doing. It's very discouraging." I must confess that what she said was true; on the other hand, I like to believe she told only half of what I preached; she may have been too tired to hear the good part. So it is necessary for people who gather together for worship to receive encouragement

361

from each other.

The admonition does not end there. If it does, you have failed to receive the greatest kind of encouragement available to you. You see, if you want to be encouraged by others, you need to be one of those who encourages others. And in doing that, you will discover that as you see others brighten up from your conversation, you are more greatly encouraged yourself.

### ...and all the more as you see the Day approaching.

The author has not spoken of a day, at least in this context. (He did comment on "today" earlier, that is, the day of hearing God's voice when it was important not to harden one's heart, beginning in Heb. 3:7.) But what day does he mean here? No doubt he refers to the end of the world, specifically the day of judgment, for there seems to be a note of fearfulness in what he says. Even more, there is a sense of urgency to gather together, worship God, and encourage each other in our faith, before it is too late to change and be reconciled to God.

We who are Christians and keep clinging to our hope in the Savior need never be fearful of the day of judgment. Paul said, "Therefore, there is now no condemnation for those who are in Christ Jesus" (Rom. 8:1). Not only does that "day" bring an absence of condemnation for Christians, it also brings positive blessing, as Paul relates in II Tim. 4:8: "Now there is in store for me the crown of righteousness, which the Lord, the righteous Judge, will award to me on that day—and not only to me, but also to all who have longed for his appearing." Those who are not Christians, however, have every right to be terrified by the judgment of God. Isaiah said in 2:19-21:

> Men will flee to caves in the rocks
> > and to holes in the ground
> from dread of the LORD
> > and the splendor of his majesty,
> > when he rises to shake the earth.
> In that day men will throw away
> > to the rodents and bats
> their idols of silver and idols of gold,
> > which they made to worship.
> They will flee to caverns in the rocks
> > and to the overhanging crags
> from dread of the LORD
> > and the splendor of his majesty,
> > when he rises to shake the earth.

What follows is the difficult part of this chapter in Hebrews. Unfortunately, it is very controversial. I hope that a careful study of the passage will alleviate at least some of the controversy, as we see precisely what the author had in mind.

* * *

## Heb. 10:26.  If we deliberately keep on sinning....

Some people attempt to escape from the true meaning of the passage that begins here by making an artificial distinction between conscious, deliberate sins and unknowing error or "not sinning wilfully" as the KJV says it. There is, of course, one distinction of sorts to be made between these two kinds of sins. However, that distinction does not carry through to God's reaction to the two. Our scripture, all of it, condemns sin without distinction as to whether it is committed wilfully or not. Not only is God's reaction the same, the punishment due each kind of sin is identical to the other.

One kind of sin is no less heinous than the other, although some like to think their unknown sins are less offensive to God and therefore deserve little or no punishment. However, a case can be made for just the opposite. An unconscious sin actually may be the more heinous, because that means that such a sinner has no desire to discover what is sinful and what is pleasing to God. For instance, you have heard people take the Lord's name in vain with virtually every sentence. Have you ever alerted a person who has just taken the Lord's name in vain? If you have, then you may have heard this response: "Oh, I'm sorry!  I didn't even realize I was doing it!"  But that is precisely what the commandment means when it tells us not to take the Lord's name *in vain*. Vanity is emptiness, contentlessness, thoughtlessness.

Earlier in our study we pointed out Lev. 4:2, where we talked about "unintentional sin."  Remember that such sins were not atoned for unless sacrifice was made for them.  The emphasis is that *every* sin must be covered with sacrificial blood.

## ...after we have received the knowledge of the truth....

Perhaps we should say *"especially* after."  If that is so, some people may claim this as an escape clause from the punishment for their sins, because they sinned before they knew about Christ and His sacrifice for them. But that escape clause was closed.  At the beginning of chapters 1 and 2 of Hebrews we discussed the fact that "God has spoken," and that "we have heard."  Those who have read the book of Hebrews surely have heard; those who are reading this commentary surely have heard.  Beyond that, Ps. 19:1-4 and Rom. 1:18-23 make it abundantly clear that not one person has entered this world, or ever will enter it, without having heard the word of God, thus having "received the knowledge of the truth."

There is another possibility which in apostolic times must have been embraced by some people, and this is what the author of Hebrews is driving at here.  They may have thought that if Jesus and His ministry was one step higher than what we discover in the Old Testament, what is to prevent some further way of salvation that will be a step beyond that of Jesus? as if there is a ladder, perhaps endless, the rungs from which we may choose higher and higher levels of salvation and benefits.  The author shatters all three of these thoughts with his next clause.

### ...no sacrifice for sins is left....

It is difficult to put the Greek words into satisfactory English. Our English word "no" is a pitiful substitute for the Greek word οὐκέτι. That word could be translated as "no longer," "no more," or "no further." To add to the meaning of that Greek word, we might add "additional." That is not really needed, however, because the author adds near the end of the clause his word ἀπολείπεται, a passive verb form from the root ἀπολείπω. That passive form means, according to Thayer, "it remains, is reserved." Let me propose a more literal translation for this clause: "no additional sacrifice is waiting" to be made. This is what the author wrote and what he meant to say.

There is a branch of theology whose adherents are called Arminians (not Armenians, an ethnic group), named after a Dutch theologian Arminius. One of their doctrines is that it is possible for a person who has received Jesus Christ as Savior and Lord to lose his salvation by committing a sin. After that, if he expects to get to heaven, he must receive Christ again. One interesting point in this belief is that those who hold to baptismal regeneration of infants are required by logic and by observation of the human condition to believe that a person once saved can be lost again by sinning. I have already discussed rather fully[4] the fact that water baptism, by any mode, can never save anyone. But this is beside the point we are making here. What the Arminians want this passage to say is that if a person sins, especially if he sins deliberately and badly, since "no sacrifice for sins is left," the person has lost his salvation and will need to be saved again. However, even a superficial reading of verse 26 shows this is not what the author is driving at, but that there is no sacrifice beyond the sacrifice of Jesus by which we must be saved.

There is a logical argument against such a train of thought. Both the Arminians and I believe that according to scripture the only way any person can be saved is by receiving Jesus Christ as Savior and Lord. If this is so (and the Bible says it is), and if it were possible for a person to lose his salvation, then logic would tell us that the only way he could lose his salvation would be by rejecting Christ as his Savior and Lord, not by committing a sin. In I Cor. 6:11-12, after telling the people in the Corinthian church that they had been "washed,...sanctified...justified in the name of the Lord Jesus Christ and by the Spirit of our God," Paul boasts, "'Everything is permissible for me'—but not everything is beneficial. 'Everything is permissible for me'—but I will not be mastered by anything." He repeats himself in I Cor. 10:23: "'Everything is permissible'—but not everything is beneficial. 'Everything is permissible'—but not everything is constructive." In other words, a person who sins after having been saved will not lose his salvation, but it is implied in I John 1:3 and 6 that he will lose fellowship until he re-

---

[4] See my book, THE SPIRIT OF SCRIPTURE, pages 50-53.

pents and confesses his sin:

> We proclaim to you what we have seen and heard, so that you also may have fellowship with us. And our fellowship is with the Father and with his Son, Jesus Christ....If we claim to have fellowship with him yet walk in the darkness, we lie and do not live by the truth.

This logical argument supports what we read in scripture.

Tragically, some people who hold this doctrine of getting lost upon sinning after having been saved grow weary and discouraged at such a see-saw of salvation and lostness. They wonder whether it may be their fate to die suddenly and unexpectedly in a state of lostness after having lived a long life of holiness, so their efforts would be to no avail. Because of that, they decide the whole matter is not worth the effort and constant fear of losing their salvation, so they turn from Christ without ever having really received eternal life through Christ's one sacrifice, and thus are lost forever.

Peter says something related to this idea. In II Pet. 2:20-21 we read:

> If they have escaped the corruption of the world by knowing our Lord and Savior Jesus Christ and are again entangled in it and overcome, they are worse off at the end than they were at the beginning. It would have been better for them not to have known the way of righteousness, than to have known it and then to turn their backs on the sacred commandment that was passed on to them.

In this passage, I am not sure whether Peter means to imply that some people can be saved by "knowing our Lord and Savior Jesus Christ" when he says that they "have escaped the corruption of the world," or whether he merely means that they were freed from the inevitable results of sinful living for a while simply because they tried to live according to what they heard and knew about the Savior. Since I believe that a saved person can never be lost, I tend to believe Peter meant not salvation unto eternal life, but merely a pause in the temporal effects of a sinful life. At any rate, it is certain that Peter meant to say that if a person who has known about God and His ways and then spurns this knowledge, his subsequent condemnation will be more severe than if he had never begun to live a godly life, whether he had obtained salvation or not. Remember: "God has spoken; we have heard."

You may be acquainted with someone you are sure used to be a Christian, but now seems not to be. If you know such a person, there are only two possible things that can be true about him. Either he did in fact receive Jesus Christ as Savior and Lord some time earlier, and through circumstances in his life at present his way of life looks like that of a non-Christian; still before that person dies, God will confront him with his sinfulness and cause him to repent and be forgiven, and take him to heaven. God promises He will do that, in I John 1:9. The only other possibility is that although the person seemed in the past to be a Christian, because he came to church regularly, taught a Sunday school class, sang in the choir, and even was elected an Elder, now he no longer comes to church and is living a seemingly sinful life; he never had actually become a Christian in the first place, but deceived not only other people but himself as well. John talks about such a person in I John 2:19: "They went out from us, but they did not really belong to us. For if they had belonged to us, they would have remained with us; but their going showed that none of them belonged to us."

**Heb. 10:27.** ...but only a fearful expectation of judgment and of raging fire that will consume the enemies of God.

We must paint in our minds a single picture of the content of verses 26 and 27. My translation of the verses may help: "If we deliberately sin after coming to know Christ as Savior as the replacement of the Old Testament sacrifices, there is no third alternative salvation in which to trust. If instead of trusting Christ you seek to trust in something beyond Jesus, then you have not trusted in Jesus. All that is left is judgment and fiery destruction." Therefore, Christ's is the only effective sacrifice.

The judgment spoken of in this verse is what we call the Great White Throne Judgment, which is described in Rev. 20:11-13. Those who have received eternal life through faith in Jesus Christ as Savior and Lord need not fear this judgment. Their judgment will be on an entirely different basis. Paul explains it this way in II Cor. 5:10, "We must all appear before the judgment seat of Christ, that each one may receive what is due him for the things done while in the body, whether good or bad." In I Cor. 3:12-15, Paul lays out the general criteria for deciding the value of what we have "done in the body:"

> If any man builds on this foundation [which Paul laid] using gold, silver, costly stones, wood, hay or straw, his work will be shown for what it is, because the Day will bring it to light. It will be revealed with fire, and the fire will test the quality of each man's work. If what he has built survives, he will receive his reward. If it is burned up, he will suffer loss; he himself will be saved, but only as one escaping through the flames.

Paul obviously is talking about Christians here, because he says that all those to whom he refers will be saved. His point in all he says is that all Christians will be judged, not for the sake of deciding whether they are saved or lost, but of deciding what rewards they will receive in heaven for the work they have done for Christ. Besides this, the fact that they will not be judged to determine whether they will go to heaven or hell is made clear by Paul in Rom. 8:1-2: "Therefore, there is now no condemnation for those who are in Christ Jesus, because through Christ Jesus the law of the Spirit of life set me free from the law of sin and death."

Need we say much about the "raging fire" mentioned near the end of this verse? It is the "lake of fire" described in Rev. 20:10 and 14-15, which we have discussed. The "enemies of God" are those who have failed for whatever reason to receive Jesus Christ as Savior and Lord. God knows who they are, and He alone will divide them from the "children of God" at the judgment.

Let me emphasize once again that neither this passage nor Heb. 6:6 teaches that a person can lose his salvation once he has received it from an eternally gracious and merciful God. On the other hand, there are multiple passages throughout scripture which insist on the absolute certainty that once a person has been saved, he can never lose his salvation by any cause. To me, chief among those passages are Rom. 8:38-39, and I John 5:11-13, both of which state, one by implication and the other in so many words, that the gift we receive when we receive Jesus Christ is called "eternal" life; if it is eternal it cannot be withdrawn.

**Heb. 10:28. Anyone who rejected the law of Moses died without mercy on the testimony of two or three witnesses.**

This verse is the first of two parts of another contrast between the old and new covenants. This contrast was promulgated already in chapter 2, verses 1-4. Regarding the requirement of two or three witnesses, we find its basis in Deut. 17:6: "On the testimony of two or three witnesses a man shall be put to death, but no one shall be put to death on the testimony of only one witness." The author of Hebrews here is not so much trying to protect the innocent from unjust accusation as he is trying to circumscribe every possible argument a guilty person might have in trying to escape from the just condemnation of God. He began the paragraph in verse 26 by showing that no possible future sacrifice will atone for any person's sins. He continues in verse 27 by describing the punishment waiting for anyone who rejects Christ's sacrifice. In verse 28 he shows that accusation, judgment, and punishment were meted even in old times to those whose deeds were witnessed by at least two people. Now (in the next verse) he is ready to aver that since Christ has died for sin there is even more certain punishment waiting for those who reject His work on their behalf.

Of course the punishment executed on people living under Moses' law often was physical death. We see in Deut. 17:1-6, the passage just before the verse noted above about the testimony of two or more witnesses, that God commanded the people to take blasphemers outside the city and stone them to death. In other cases it was God Himself who brought physical death to offenders, as in the case of Korah and his cohorts, of whom we read in Num. 16. However, a much more severe punishment is spiritual death instead of physical death, as in the case of Adam and Eve who disobeyed God and ate the fruit of the forbidden tree, Gen. 3:1-24. God said they would die on the day they ate the fruit (Gen. 2:17), and they did die, spiritually. They were punished in physical ways also, by being banished from the Garden of Eden, by bearing children in great pain, and in hard labor to eke out a living in the land. All these physical punishments that came about in Old Testament times, said Paul in I Cor. 10:11, were "examples and were written down as warnings for us, on whom the fulfillment of the ages has come."

**Heb. 10:29. How much more severely do you think a man deserves to be punished who has trampled the Son of God under foot, who has treated as an unholy thing the blood of the covenant that sanctified him, and who has insulted the Spirit of grace?**

It was an exceedingly serious matter for an Old Testament person to break God's law, and even more serious for him to refuse or fail for any reason to apply for forgiveness through the ritual sacrifices God had established. We who are committed to our faith in Jesus Christ as Savior and Lord may find it difficult to believe anyone would be so foolish as to ignore his fate resulting from such rejection.

But the author says man's stupidity gets far worse. He shows this by noting three ways people now turn away from God's mercies. First, he says that people today "trample the Son of God under foot." They do this by sneering at the law of God and by grinding into the mire our Savior who loved them and gave Himself for them; just as a terrorist stomps on the burning flag of his enemy. But which is greater, the law, or the Savior-God who established the law?

Secondly, the author says that people today "treat as an unholy thing the blood of the covenant that sanctified" them. Paul said the same thing this way in Rom. 1:22-23: "Although they claimed to be wise, they became fools and *exchanged* [my emphasis] the glory of the immortal God for images made to look like mortal man and birds and animals and reptiles." But which is greater, the blood of bulls and goats, or the blood of the God who created the bulls and goats?

Lastly, the author says that people "insult the Spirit of grace." Put into other words, this is the same as committing the unforgivable sin. Jesus warned repeatedly that we must not blaspheme the Holy Spirit: Matt. 12:32, and Mark 3:28-29. Similar stories are found in Matt. 9:32-34 and in Lu. 11:14-26, but Jesus does not state explicitly in them the matter of the unforgivable sin, although it certainly is innate. So which is greater, the soul of the law, or the Spirit of grace?

We may think that the author has used far too strong language in condemning those who merely ignore or even downplay the mighty work which our God wrought to provide for our salvation. But that is exactly what is wrong with those who have rejected Christ and their sympathizers. They think it is a small matter to turn from the God who created them and wants to do them good, and may even think that God does not care or will wink at their "shortcomings." But this is not so in God's eyes: the slightest "cold shoulder" is an absolute rejection in God's sight. Remember the commandment: "I, the LORD your God, am a jealous God, punishing the children for the sin of the fathers to the third and fourth generation of those who hate me..." (Ex. 20:5). The severity of God's wrath and punishment is revealed also in what

Jesus said to His disciples about the unwise servant who thought his master would be gone a long time and began to beat the other servants and live sumptuously in Lu. 12:46: "The master of that servant will come on a day when he does not expect him and at an hour he is not aware of. He will cut him to pieces and assign him a place with the unbelievers." Jesus' condemnation and punishment of a servant we might think less guilty seems even more excessively severe to us: "That servant who knows his master's will and does not get ready or does not do what his master wants will be beaten with many blows" (Lu. 12:47). The person need not have committed any heinous sin; whoever merely neglects to follow his master will be punished severely. So God does to all those who however mildly fail to follow Christ; the "raging fire...will consume" them.

**Heb. 10:30. For we know him who said, 'It is mine to avenge; I will repay," and again, "The Lord will judge his people."**

The first quotation comes from Deut. 32:35; the second is from Ps. 135:14. We note the first quotation in a different setting and usage by Paul, who also quotes it in Rom. 12:19. There Paul urges us not to seek or wreak vengeance on others for wrongs done to us; rather we must depend on God to take care of all wrongs and make everything right. But here in Hebrews we see the certainty of God's punishment on all who have failed to welcome His Son as their Savior and Lord. Again I say, in God's sight all offenders are as fully offensive to Him as those described in verse 29.

The verse from Psalm 135 reads slightly differently in the NIV, but what we read there may make more sense to us than the Hebrews translation:

> For the LORD will vindicate his people
> and have compassion on his servants.

**Heb. 10:31. It is a dreadful thing to fall into the hands of the living God.**

Animists may dread their tree-gods and stone-gods, but need not. The living God is worthy to be dreaded, however. When Jesus had selected His twelve apostles, but before He sent them out to serve Him, He warned them of the hazards they would encounter: opposition, false accusations, physical harm, betrayal by loved ones. But Jesus encouraged them not to be afraid of those things. He told them, "Do not be afraid of those who kill the body but cannot kill the soul. Rather, be afraid of the one who can destroy both soul and body in hell" (Matt. 10:28). Some people think Jesus was referring to Satan as that destroyer, but that cannot be. Only God has the authority and power to relegate people to the pains of hell; Satan only tempts them, trying to get them to disobey God; the final decision does not belong to him. If anyone thinks Jesus' words are ambiguous, let him look at James. 4:12, which makes the issue more clear, "There is only one Lawgiver and Judge, the one

369

who is able to save and destroy."

Some people claim that we ought to love God, not fear Him. But I find it easy to do both at once. Perhaps it is because of my rearing as a child. I loved my parents greatly because they provided me with our home, with warmth, with my clothing and food and all other necessities through hard labor. On the other hand, I feared my parents, because I knew that whenever I did something they thought was bad or wrong, they were quick to punish me. So whenever I thought of doing something against their wishes, I feared them for what surely would happen to me if I did it. So I have no problem with both loving and fearing God, for the same reasons.

Whom do you dread most, the living God, or a bitter enemy? Perhaps you think you ought to dread God more than an enemy, because after all He is able to wreak infinitely greater and more enduring punishment than an enemy can. On the other hand, you ought to dread your enemy much more, because he is merciless. King David was wise in that he chose the wrath of the living God over punishment by either famine or his enemies. In II Sam. 24:14, he told his reasoning to God's messenger Gad: "I am in deep distress. Let us fall into the hands of the LORD, for his mercy is great; but do not let me fall into the hands of men."

**Heb. 10:32.  Remember those earlier days after you had received the light, when you stood your ground in a great contest in the face of suffering.**

We may not be sure to which "suffering" the author refers here. Of this we may be sure, however. He does not refer to the suffering of the Jews in Old Testament times, but to those to whom he is writing. He addresses them by saying "after *you* had received the light," although he reminded them to "remember those earlier days." Here are several possibilities. For one thing, he may have been referring to the persecution of the Jews (including Jewish Christians) under Claudius, as recorded in Acts 18:2. Robertson[5] tells us, "This was about A. D. 49, done Suetonius says (*Claudius* C. 25) because 'the Jews were in a state of constant tumult at the instigation of one Chrestus' (probably among the Jews about Christ so pronounced)." Another possibility was that the author was referring to the persecution of Jewish Christians under Herod in Jerusalem, mentioned in Acts 12:1-4; this was about 42 AD. He may have even referred to the persecution of Jews converted by Paul in Rome in 62 AD, about which we read in Acts 28:17-31. Although the author is not specific on which persecution he meant, he was explicit on the nature of the persecution.  He speaks of four different kinds of persecution in the next two verses.

\* \* \*

---

[5] WORD PICTURES IN THE NEW TESTAMENT, Vol. III, Acts, p. 295.

**Heb. 10:33-34. Sometimes you were publicly exposed to insult and persecution....**

**...at other times you stood side by side with those who were so treated.**

**You sympathized with those in prison...**

**...and joyfully accepted the confiscation of your property....**

Although the author mentions these four types of persecution, he does not say he had included them all. Lenski[6] claims that the persecution in Jerusalem could not be in the author's mind, because it was too early (before 35 AD), and because the author does not mention martyrdom. But Lenski ignores the fact that the author does not claim to have made a complete list of all the kinds of persecution heaped upon the Jews. The only conclusion we can draw is that we cannot be sure what was in the author's mind. In fact, he may have been referring to the ones I have mentioned here as well as others. We can be sure of this, that during the first Christian century after the death of Christ, Jewish Christians endured much persecution in many places and in a variety of ways by other Jews, by Roman authorities, and by Gentiles in general.

**...because you knew that you yourselves had better and lasting possessions.**

Here are some of the indications of future blessings the Jewish converts had.

• Matt. 6:19-21. Do not store up for yourselves treasures on earth, where moth and rust destroy, and where thieves break in and steal. But store up for yourselves treasures in heaven, where moth and rust do not destroy, and where thieves do not break in and steal. For where your treasure is, there your heart will be also.

• Matt. 25:21. Well done, good and faithful servant! You have been faithful with a few things; I will put you in charge of many things. Come and share your master's happiness!

• Rev. 21:9-27. [This is a description of our new home town in heaven.]

• Phil. 3:20-21. Our citizenship is in heaven. And we eagerly await a Savior from there, the Lord Jesus Christ, who by the power that enables him to bring everything under his control, will transform our lowly bodies so that they will be like his glorious body.

• I John 3:2. Dear friends, now we are children of God, and what we will be has not yet been made known. But we know that when he appears, we shall be like him, for we shall see him as he is.

• I Cor. 15:20-57. [This is an extended description of our new, immortal

---

[6] INTERPRETATION OF HEBREWS AND JAMES, p. 363.

bodies, and our victory over all evil, sin, and death.]

Surely this is not an exhaustive list of all the blessings those Jewish converts, and we, have to look forward to. The New Testament is sprinkled with them.

### Heb. 10:35. So do not throw away your confidence; it will be richly rewarded.

Compare this verse with what the author said in 6:11, where he urged his hearers to be diligent to keep hold of their hope. I spoke more fully about the Greek word in connection with 6:19. Please note that the author urged his hearers not to abandon that confidence for any reason. Poor John the Baptist, while he was in prison, seemed to lose his confidence in who Christ was. The account is found in both Matt. 11:2-6, and Lu. 7:18-23. Both of those accounts end with Jesus' words, "Blessed is the man who does not fall away on account of me," which is what the author of Hebrews says to encourage us to cling to Jesus always. That John the Baptist returned to full faith in Jesus is implied by Jesus' highly complimentary words about him afterward: "What did you go out to see? A prophet? Yes, I tell you, and more than a prophet....Among those born of women there has not risen anyone greater than John the Baptist..." (Matt. 11:9, 11).

The author of Hebrews concludes by telling us, "[your confidence] will be richly rewarded." That reward may not be realized in this life, but surely it will be continued throughout eternity in heaven. No greater promise could be given by anyone but God.

### Heb. 10:36. You need to persevere....

In different words the author repeats here what he has just said in verse 35. He continues to urge his hearers: Don't give up. Finish what you start in your faith. Paul said the same thing twice (in Gal. 6:9, and in II Thess. 3:13): "Let us not become weary in doing good," and, "never tire of doing what is right." In connection with this, Paul also reminded us that God never tires of upholding us (Phil. 1:6): "...being confident of this, that he who began a good work in you will carry it on to completion until the day of Christ Jesus."

### ...so that when you have done the will of God, you will receive what he has promised.

Along with the admonition, the author gives us encouragement with the reward we shall receive for being persistent. Only the person who finishes the race receives the reward. See what Paul said about it in I Cor. 9:24-27:

Do you not know that in a race all the runners run, but only one gets the prize? Run in such a way as to get the prize. Everyone who competes in the games goes into strict training. They do it to get a crown that will not last; but we do it to get a crown that will last forever. Therefore I do not run like a man running aimlessly; I do not fight like a man beating the air. No, I beat my body and make it my slave so that after I have preached to others, I myself will not be disqualified for the prize.

Although Paul here makes a valid point that only one person, the winner, receives a crown as his prize, he fails to mention the fact that everyone who completes the spiritual race wins a prize, not merely a corruptible crown but an eternal blessing from God in heaven.

### Heb. 10:37. For in just a very little while, "He who is coming will come and will not delay."

When the author of Hebrews quoted these words, he may have been thinking of what we read in Is. 26:20:

> Go, my people, enter your rooms
> > and shut the doors behind you;
> hide yourselves for a little while
> > until his wrath has passed by.

The author may have been thinking also about Hab. 2:3:

> For the revelation awaits an appointed time;
> > it speaks of the end
> > and will not prove false.
> Though it linger, wait for it;
> > it will certainly come and will not delay.

This promise was both predicted in the Old Testament and promised by Jesus Himself in the New. Jesus is quoted twice as promising His swift return. In Rev. 22:12 He says, "Behold, I am coming soon!" and He repeats Himself in verse 20, "Yes, I am coming soon."

The lives of three American astronauts were tragically snuffed out on the morning of the 28th of January 1986. In one large sense, Jesus came for them that day, to receive them out of the world. That is not the main sense we are considering here. One day, soon, Jesus will return to earth, and as John said in Rev. 1:7:

> Look, he is coming with the clouds,
> > and every eye will see him,
> even those who pierced him....Amen.

Jesus' appearance will be no secret, but every human will see Him come. John says that even all the dead will behold the sight, "even those who pierced him," that is, those soldiers who nailed Him to the cross, and the one who thrust the sword into His side. Both saved and lost will see Him come. Are you ready, now, to see Him should He come this moment?

### Heb. 10:38.

### "...But my righteous one will live by faith."

This is quoted directly from Hab. 2:4:

> ...but the righteous will live by his faith....

This seems to be a popular quotation, because Paul quotes it twice: in Rom. 1:17, and in Gal. 3:11. In the Romans passage, Paul is talking about the gospel, which he describes by means of three qualities: in verse 16 he says it is the "power of God for salvation;" in verse 17 he calls it a "righteousness from God;" and in verse 18 he calls the gospel something that many people close their minds against, "the wrath of God." In the middle of Galatians, Paul is talking about the difference in results between living by the law, and living by faith which alone justifies a person.

A few people may wonder whether the "righteous one" refers to believers in Christ, or in Christ Himself. After all, only Jesus Christ is truly righteous. However, God justifies, or "makes righteous," those who believe in Him, according to Rom. 3:25-26. Perhaps my translation will help to clarify the point that it is the believer who lives by faith:

> And the righteous person will live by faith in me.

### "And if he shrinks back,
### I will not be pleased with him."

This is still part of the quotation from Hab. 2:3-4. The author of Hebrews quotes it in order to emphasize what he has already said in verse 35, but this time in a negative sense. He stated the reward in verse 35: "So do not throw away your confidence; it will be richly rewarded;" while here he warns the one who falters with the fact of God's displeasure in him.

**Heb. 10:39. But we are not of those who shrink back and are destroyed, but of those who believe and are saved.**

The author shows great confidence in those to whom he is speaking. He compliments them for their stand for the Lord. What he said was not to condemn them; he had other purposes. One was to warn them of what dangers exist because of their relationship with God through Christ; the other was to encourage them not to fall into such traps in the future.

I want to review with you now, at the end of this chapter, that the whole chapter was designed to build slowly to the climax in verse 26, which was to warn the people against trying to pass beyond Christ to seek an additional and better Savior. Finally, this wrap-up verse warns the people of the danger of falling back from Christ to recapture the old rituals of offering sacrificial animals through the Levitical priests. This, the main thrust of the whole book of Hebrews, is to show that Christ has supplanted the old ways with the final, irreplaceable, perfect Way.

Years ago I viewed the Billy Graham film "Up," which was a brief prelude to a full-length film. In the clip, we saw a hang-glider sailing among the mountains. He came to a high small pinnacle, and landed gracefully on it. To me this was an apt illustration of "those who believe and are saved." Christ alone is the solid Rock upon whom we must plant our feet. All else is a dark, out-of-focus abyss, both before and behind, as well as on either side.

# CHAPTER XI
## THE FAITH OF THE SAINTS. HEB. 11:1-40.

Chapter 11 is called the great Faith Chapter of the Bible, and rightly so. You will recall that we already mentioned the Pauline trilogy of faith, hope, and love which we find in I Cor. 13:13. It was echoed in Heb. 10:22-24, and is found in extended fashion in the three final chapters of Hebrews. Just as Hebrews 11 is known as the great Faith Chapter, we also know I Corinthians 13 as the great Love Chapter of the Bible. However, I fail to recall that anyone has selected a great Hope Chapter.

Hebrews 11 consists of a brief review of some great people of faith found in the Old Testament. Such a review, including searching the Old Testament for the details of their lives gives a tremendous fund of information about the whole history of humanity up to the time of Jesus. In this study, we will look at each person, as well as the groups of people, and touch on the places we find them described in the ancient scriptures. Since this study cannot give a large commentary on each person, you are urged to look up the Old Testament passages and study them. I assure you, you will profit greatly.

Why did the author of Hebrews insert a chapter on faith here? How does it fit into the author's scheme of showing how Jesus and His ministry are better than anything we find in the Levitical priesthood? My guess is that he had just told us in the previous verse that we are saved by believing. Since this is such an important issue, he wanted to emphasize it. He knew, as we know, that the best way to teach is by illustration, so he gives us a long chapter of illustration. He starts with a definition of faith. The definition is rather obscure and complicated, so I advise you to read it in different English versions. For your convenience, I have supplied several here.

### Heb. 11:1. Now faith is being sure of what we hope for and certain of what we do not see.

These words are from the NIV. The KJV is probably less helpful: "Now faith is the substance of things hoped for, the evidence of things not seen." The ASV, which is probably the most literal English translation, reads, "Now faith is assurance of things hoped for, a conviction of things not seen." The margin of the ASV changes two words: "giving substance to" for "assurance;" and "test" for "conviction." The RSV agrees with the ASV in the two important words. You already recognize those two words: "assurance," and "conviction." The old Roman Catholic Version, the Douay, uses the words "substance" and "evidence." Their Knox translation talks of "substance to our hopes, which convinces us of things we cannot see." The NEB reads, "gives substance to our hopes, makes us certain of realities we cannot see." Phillips writes, "putting our full confidence in the things we hope for, being certain of things we cannot see." The Living Bible talks of the "confident assurance that something we want is going to happen, the certainty that what we hope for is waiting for us, even though we cannot see it up ahead." The TEV says we ought "to be sure of things we hope for, to be certain of the things we cannot see." Weymouth speaks of "confident assurance of that for which we hope, a conviction of the reality of things which we do not see." Williams talks of the "assurance of things we hope for, the proof of the reality of the things we cannot see."

After reading those varying ideas, we ought to turn to the original Greek to see what help we can find there, especially for the two most troublesome words: "substance" or "assurance;" and "evidence" or "conviction" or "proof" or "certainty." The Greek word for the first cluster of English words is ὑπόστασις. This word has been the focus of sometimes bitter debate among theologians for centuries. Therefore, we may do well not to get heavily involved in some precise definition. Thayer may be of some help; part of his definition of the Greek term is: "a setting or placing under... foundation... that which has actual existence; a substance, real being... confidence, firm trust, assurance." The author of Hebrews uses the same Greek word in 1:3 to say that Jesus is the "exact representation of [the Father's] being." Perhaps we could say here that faith is the *greatest reality* we can have at present of all we look for in heaven.

The second troublesome word here, translated by words like "evidence" or "proof," is ἔλεγχος. This Greek word is found nowhere else in the New Testament, so we have no other biblical context by which to compare our thoughts about its definition. Turning to Thayer again, his definition of this word includes "a proof, that by which a thing is proved or tested," and "conviction" as in convicting a person of sin. It is likely that Thayer's first definition here is what the author of Hebrews meant when he used the word in his definition of faith.

In order to summarize what the author is driving at in his definition of faith, we conclude that his idea was that there are some things yet to come for which we have no scientific proof, but we assure ourselves they are part of our future, so we have "faith" they will happen. It is like the contrast between Thomas' attitude toward Jesus' resurrection and ours; Jesus told Thomas (John 20:29): "Because you have seen me, you have believed; blessed are those who have not seen and yet have believed." Actually, what was in Thomas' mind after he saw the risen Christ was not faith but present reality. Faith and hope are much alike in what Paul says about the latter in Rom. 8:24: "For in this hope we were saved. But hope that is seen is no hope at all. Who hopes for what he already has?"

Once I read the signboard outside a Unitarian-Universalist Fellowship building which read, "Faith that is based on authority is not faith." It seems to me that definition of faith lies on the opposite side of the biblical definition, for we do have an authority for our faith, the Bible. Further authority comes from the guidance of the Holy Spirit as He leads us to more proof in the word of God. If faith is based on no authority whatever, then it is merely a figment of one's imagination, and is too nebulous to give confidence.

### Heb. 11:2. This is what the ancients were commended for.

One of those commended was Abraham. We note in Rom. 4:3 a quotation from Gen. 15:6: "Abram believed the LORD, and he credited it to him as righteousness." Also, recall the statement in Hab. 2:4, when we studied Heb.10:38, which speaks in general of all Old Testament people who had faith in God: "...the righteous will live by his faith."

### Heb. 11:3. By faith we understand that the universe was formed at God's command, so that what is seen was not made out of what was visible.

The author of Hebrews puts an interesting twist on the list of Old Testament saints at its very beginning. He does not begin with Adam, the first human, nor even with any Old Testament character, but with us, his readers. By including us, the author intends to encompass all people in all ages and places who have trusted in Jesus Christ their God and Savior. To add to the interest, and even peculiarity, of what the author has to say, it is not so much in God that he speaks of faith, but in one of God's great works, His creation. And that, unfortunately is the center of one of today's raging controversies. There are three different parties to the controversy: scientists who are not Christians, scientists who are Christians, and Christians who are not scientists who discount modern scientific discoveries. It is not my purpose here to settle the sometimes bitter debate; but I would be remiss if I failed to point out salient passages of scripture which bear on the subject.

No human was present when the universe came into being, so we have no human witness to the events. The triune God was there; and Wisdom, who was created by God early on, claimed that she was present and helped Him (Prov. 8:22, 30): "The LORD possessed me [or formed me, or brought me forth] at the beginning of his work, before his deeds of old....Then I was the craftsman at his side." Nothing has more ancient testimony to what happened in the beginning of the universe than the scriptures, God's word. Everything scientists claim about the establishment of the universe and the beginnings of living things is little better than theories based partially on data, but such theories contain liberal amounts of speculation. Some of that speculation may be true, but some surely is erroneous. The best evidence is the Bible.

Here is a very generalized statement of the three major positions held about how the universe came into being. The first position, held usually by scientists who are not Christians, is that everything just happened, and progressed, without any outside power or interference. God had nothing to do with it, since there is no God. Even if there was a God, He would not, or could not, have done anything about it. The second position, held generally by people who call themselves Christians, believe that there is a God, who in some manner directed the events of creation, and then may or may not have had something to do with directing subsequent happenings. The third position, held almost exclusively by Christians, is that it was God who was the Designer and Creator of all things. He planned each detail, even to the creation of each kind of living thing separately. The words of scripture give the bounds of all the details; no idea that goes beyond those bounds is true.

Unfortunately, devout, Bible-believing Christians are seriously divided on one aspect of the manner in which God created the universe. There are those who believe, along with Bishop Ussher of Scofield Reference Bible fame, that God created the universe, the world, and all creatures, in 4004 BC. On the other hand, there are Christians who agree with scientific evidence that the earth has been growing and cooling down and shaped by tectonic plates over a period of millions of years; and that the movement of the heavenly bodies shows that they were created billions of years ago. Most of the controversy centers on the definition of "day" in the Genesis creation account.

The best place to begin our biblical discussion of the whole issue is at Genesis 1 to 11, followed by what the author of Hebrews says at the beginning of his book, chapter 1:2-3. Remember what the author said in 11:3 as well: "...the universe was formed at God's command." No details are given regarding the creation, either by way of when it began, or how long it took, or in what order events occurred. Those words eliminate the first position above.

The next clause under discussion, "what is seen was not made out of what was visible," agrees with what nuclear scientists say, that matter (which is seen) and energy (only the results of which can be seen) are interchangeable. People need to accept the fact that since God is power (Matt. 28:18-20) He transformed His power into matter, in order to create the universe.

The next thing to deal with is the matter of living things. If God is Life itself, then He was able to give life to the creatures He made. Although I began my studies and career in the field of engineering, I have not discovered any scientific basis for claiming that life could possibly begin spontaneously, or from some combination of chemistry and energy. That such a thing could happen is to me the wildest, most far-fetched theory that could possibly be invented by the mind of man. Effective evidence of such an impossibility is that although scores of scientists have been attempting to make life come into being, they have not done so, even with all their intelligence and scientific support behind their efforts. Nor has one scientist yet discovered one example of spontaneous life. I am convinced that no man will be able to create life in a test tube. Not even the second beast of Rev. 13 will be able to give life to the image of the first beast, even though verse 15 tells us, "He was given power to give breath to the image of the first beast, so that it could speak and cause all who refused to worship the image to be killed." That verse does not say that the beast will create life in the image, or even that there will be life in the image, but only "breath" whatever that means. Further, the verse says that the beast was "given power" to do whatever he was able to do; he did not do it by his own power. God allowed him to do it.

Regarding the controversy over evolution, I want to add my thoughts. First, if God simply by the power of His word (repeated eight times in the account of creation in Gen. 1:3-26) was able to create the whole universe, surely He could create each separate species, one at a time, from the dust of the ground and not from some earlier species. Does anyone think God is so stupid that He could not do so? There are two specific statements in Gen. 1 and 2 which forbid me to believe otherwise. The first is found in Gen. 1:11-12 when God created the flora; we read:

> Then God said, "Let the land produce vegetation: seed-bearing plants and trees on the land that bear fruit with seed in it, according to their various kinds." And it was so. The land produced vegetation: plants bearing seed according to their kinds and trees bearing fruit with seed in it according to their kinds. And God saw that it was good.

Each kind of plant produced seeds for its own kind of plant; no plant grew out of seed from some other kind of plant. It does no good to argue about things like hybridization; no change of species occurs there. Nor is there any basis for evolution in the matter of mutation; such a process always produces something defective rather than superior, and no change of species occurs. Beyond that, as long as scientists have been studying and observing the matter, not one case of evolution has been noted, and no evidence for it has been found in artifacts in the earth—they are still looking for even one "missing link."

My other biblical argument against evolution is found in the comments in Genesis 2:7 about the creation of man. It is impossible for a sensible person to misconstrue what Moses said there. He wrote, "And the LORD God formed man from the dust of the ground and breathed into his nostrils the breath of life, and man became a living being." Man's creation was accomplished in two steps: first, God shaped a physical being, using only mineral materials He had created earlier; no organic matter was used, either living or previously living. The second step was God's breathing His own breath (or wind, or Spirit) into the nostrils of the material form He had shaped; when that happened that material entity became a "living being," or as the KJV translates, a "living soul." The only way for a person to claim that man was derived from the upward evolution of any other living thing is for him to deny the truth of how the Bible says God did it. There is no "interpretation"of this verse that will allow someone to change its meaning to mean that some other living creature somehow became a more complex or "higher" creature by some natural process. It is worth noting that it is in the biblical description of the creation of man alone that we find that God "breathed" into him. By this I believe we may safely assume that no other living creature made by God has the capacity to commune with God.

Some people try to escape from the biblical record by claiming that

God could have taken a chimpanzee which, through multiple steps of evolution had come ultimately from the "dust of the ground," and by His act of breathing into him this particular creature became a man distinct from all other creatures. But although some people make a concession to the biblical record by acknowledging this act of God's breathing into the man as part of the "creation" of man, they still deny the physical part of the description. So that half-way attempt to cling to evolution still rejects the biblical report as to how it happened.

In order to form the universe, God did not take scraps of material from some other place and reshape that material to form our universe. The answer to the ninth question of our Westminster Shorter Catechism about the "work of creation" is, "The work of creation is, God's making all things of nothing, by the word of his power, in the space of six days, and all very good." This is in conformity with a better translation of Heb. 11:3 than we have in the NIV; the KJV says, "...the worlds were framed by the word of God," not simply "at God's command." Again I say, God spoke, and it happened. There is sufficient power in God's words that the universe was made to exist, and all things in it were created.

At the beginning of this great chapter on faith, the author of Hebrews chose to include us, his hearers, in that long train of believers. Are you, my reader, truly able to count yourself among those who believe all the Bible says about God and what He wants to do for you?

### Heb. 11:4.  By faith Abel offered God a better sacrifice than Cain did.

We now come to the main track of this chapter, the naming and description of a number of Old Testament people who trusted in God for all they needed, both in this life and in the next. We may wonder why the author did not begin with the first man, Adam, and his wife, Eve. It is not profitable to speculate, since we cannot know for sure. But one possibility is because their sin was so heinous and had such extensive repercussions, that the author decided their faith was not worth mentioning. Abel's faith, on the other hand, was described as very strong, especially by contrast to that of Cain.

We read of Abel's faith in Gen. 4:4: "Abel brought fat portions from some of the firstborn of his flock. The LORD looked with favor on Abel and his offering." God's reaction to Abel's offering was quite different from how He looked on Cain's (verse 5): "...but on Cain and his offering he did not look with favor."

There are different opinions as to why God favored one brother and not the other. One opinion is that Abel's offering was a blood sacrifice, while Cain's was not. After all, such people say, is this not the crux of the whole book of Hebrews, the Levitical sacrifices versus the superior sacrifice of Jesus, both of which were blood sacrifices?

One argument against such a thought is that the brothers were not at that point making sacrifices for sin, but were bringing offerings to God. The Hebrew word for sacrifice is not used at all in the Genesis passage, but the word for offering, מִנְחָה, is used throughout. Nearly always the Hebrew word stands for a grain offering, which often was offered with a sacrificial animal. Since this is the case, and sin is not mentioned as the reason the offerings of Cain and Abel were brought to God, there is no reason to suppose that God should have been offended if one of those offerings was not a sacrificed animal. Also, the verse in Hebrews does not say, or imply, that the absence of a sacrificial animal was what displeased God in respect of Cain's offering.

A second reason why we should not suppose God was offended because Cain failed to bring a sacrifice is that Abel alone was the shepherd, while Cain was what we might call a "truck gardener." I do not recall any place in scripture where God requires a person to give back to Him anything the giver does not possess. Too often we are reluctant to give what we do have; Cain may well have been reluctant to give even some of what he had. It might be argued that Cain could have traded some of his fruit and vegetables for some of Abel's sheep, but that still would not have been of the fruit of Cain's labors, but of Abel's.

A third argument against the idea that God disapproved of Cain's offering because it was merely a grain offering is the most telling argument. That is, that in both Genesis 4 and Hebrews 11 we read that God accepted Abel's offering because of his righteousness or faith, not because his offering was categorically different from his brother's. God was not looking so much at the nature of the gift as He was at the heart of the giver. This is supported by what John has to say about the brothers in I John 3:12, "Do not be like Cain, who belonged to the evil one and murdered his brother. And why did he murder him? Because his own actions were evil and his brother's were righteous." In this verse John gives us two reasons why God rejected Cain and his offering: first, Cain "belonged to the evil one," that is, to the devil. The second reason is because Cain's "actions were evil and his brother's were righteous." It is not an "evil act" in itself to make an offering to God, unless the offering was made insincerely.

**By faith he was commended as a righteous man, when God spoke well of his offerings.**

This is what we just concluded. God's word supports the idea of faith rather than the idea of the nature of the offering. Also, this whole chapter 11 of Hebrews is about faith, not so much about the object of faith.

Have you ever asked yourself, "How did the two sons of the same parents get to be so diverse?" Also we might ask, "Is the oldest child in a family often more rebellious than the rest of the children in the family?" We all have observed that children from the same parents can be radically diverse. There seems to be no way to predict how any one will develop into maturity. I have a private theory, that there may be a parallel between physical heredity and spiritual heredity. For instance, Mendel's Law says that if a red sweet pea is mated to a white sweet pea, some of their seed will bring forth red flowers and others white, while some of them are pink. The same will hold true for many generations. So also with the faith or spirituality of humans. This is not to say that Adam was pure spiritually and Eve wholly blemished, or vice versa; the fact is that after they both sinned, both received fallen natures, but after God clothed them with His garments made of the animal, they recovered at least a measure of their spiritual lives they had lost. Then it is possible to conceive that Cain inherited "spiritual genes" which were mainly sinful, while Abel inherited genes which leaned in the righteous direction, as evidenced by his faith and righteousness.

### And by faith he still speaks, even though he is dead.

We must be careful that the phrase "by faith" shall not become meaningless by overuse, or misuse. For one thing, is it by Abel's faith that we can hear him now, or is it by our faith that we receive his message today? We may say that faith is the instrument of communication here. So because Abel had faith, his life and attitudes are recorded for us. However, it is we who must be tuned to the Spirit of God, so that we will be able to pick up the message transmitted from Abel.

That Abel still speaks today is truly an amazing, challenging statement, but how far may we go in our interpretation of what it means for us? First, we ought to be sure that we are listening to his message, especially since God thinks it is sufficiently important to be broadcast no less than six millennia after Abel died. And secondly, if Abel is "able" to speak so long after his death, is it not possible that you and I will be able to speak long after we are dead? If that is so, what will your testimony be? Will it be a message of God's word and working in your life to demonstrate your faith to all who tune in to the memory of you?

### Heb. 11:5. By faith Enoch was taken from this life, so that he did not experience death....

The record of this is found in Gen. 5:24, after we read that he lived for 365 years: "Enoch walked with God; then he was no more, because God took him away." We think it must have been an exceptional blessing to Enoch that he did not have to experience physical death. We ought to remember that what is more blessed by far, but less exceptional, is that all people who have faith like Enoch, and who walk with God like Enoch, will not experience spiritual death.

We read in Heb. 9:27 that "man is destined to die once," but that does not mean that man must die even once. There have been two people in history who did not die physically; Enoch, and Elijah who according to II Kings 2:11-12 was taken up to heaven in a fiery chariot without having to endure the ordeal of physical death. Thus we read how Elijah was taken out of this world, but we are not told how Enoch was translated, nor do we need to know. Beyond those two men, everyone else died, even Jesus who, because He was sinless, did not need to die; yet He was willing to die for our sakes so that we might live forever by having faith in Him. Some time in the future, there will be many more people who will escape physical death; they are the people who are trusting in Jesus as their Savior and Lord when He returns to take all His own to heaven to be with Him forever.

Enoch must have been a very righteous man to have obtained this blessing from God, but otherwise we have no clue as to why God selected him. We do know that Enoch was a sinner, because every human except for Jesus has sinned. Despite that, God is able to do whatever He wants to do, consistent with His being, and in agreement with His written word, since He can never change, as He said in Mal. 3:6: "I the LORD do not change."

**...he could not be found, because God had taken him away.**

I do not know whether anyone looked carefully for the body of Enoch, like other people did later for the body of Elijah (II Kings 2:15-18), when Elisha ridiculed them for trying. The author of Hebrews implies that search was made for Enoch, because he said "he could not be found."

**For before he was taken, he was commended as one who pleased God.**

What a wonderful commendation that was! Enoch was "one who pleased God." Would you like to hear that about yourself? You may be acclaimed as a rock star by multitudes of adoring listeners; you may be a famous preacher with thousands in your congregation; you may be knighted by a king. But anything like that would pale into insignificance compared to God's commendation. Years ago Henrietta Mears, the great Christian Educator, used to say, "The only degree I'm really looking for is the A.U.G. degree: the 'Approved Unto God' [II Tim. 2:15, KJV] degree." You can be assured that you will some day hear a commendation similar to that. Jesus promised it through His parable of the talents (Matt. 25:21): "Well done, good and faithful servant! You have been faithful with a few things; I will put you in charge of many things. Come and share your master's happiness!"

**Heb. 11:6. And without faith it is impossible to please God....**

Here the author inserts a brief parenthesis related to faith, in that it tells how a person can receive benefits from faith, and expresses those benefits.

Does anyone of your acquaintance try to please God without having faith in Him? That may sound like a silly question, but surely you know many people who try to please God, or at least to receive benefits from Him, without being obedient to Him. James tells us repeatedly in his little book that we cannot claim to have faith in God if we are not demonstrating in our lives that we also are seeking to obey Him. Such people are called carnal Christians, because they live trying to please themselves rather than God.

You may try to please God with all your being, and with all the aid the Holy Spirit will give you, but you should not expect as a result that you will be excused from physical death like Enoch was. None of us is able to please God perfectly. But worthy or not, many people at some time in the future will escape death, when Jesus returns to earth. Perhaps at that time there will be a more clear-cut distinction between believers and non-believers than there is now. Certainly today it is difficult to judge whether some people have faith or not. How thankful we should be that we are not the final judges, although in this life we must give at least tentative judgment. The most important thing for each of us is that we are sure in our own hearts that we have faith in God. If we have such faith, one of the greatest blessings we receive is that we "please God."

**...because anyone who comes to him must believe that he exists, and that he rewards those who earnestly seek him.**

There is but one key by which we have access to God, and that is faith or trust. No one comes to Him by any other means. It is likely that we come to God for some reward or benefit. But that must never be the primary motive for approaching Him. If it is, then we will never be in His presence. The only way to get there is to earnestly seek Him by faith. If we approach in faith, we shall arrive; if we get there, we shall glorify Him; if we glorify Him, we shall receive a reward, or rewards. And the rewards are there for the taking. If our journey to God has been successful, we shall never try to grasp more than God is pleased to give us.

**Heb. 11:7. By faith Noah, when warned about things not yet seen, in holy fear built an ark to save his family.**

This story is in Gen. 6:13-22. One of the amazing things about Noah's faith was that a hundred years before he had "seen" anything, still he was willing to believe the God who told him to build an ark; he not only believed, but he acted on his faith. This kind of faith is similar to that of Abraham, who comes next in the list of people of faith. Oh, to have such faith as that, to believe utterly on what God has commanded without concern for the logic of the command, without doubting it was God who spoke, without being worried about the consequences of his obedience, and without caring what the neighbors or even the whole world thinks of you for it! What ridicule

Noah and his three sons must have endured! They were building an ark, a huge ship, scores if not hundreds of miles from the nearest ocean or body of water that could accommodate such a monster. They expended money, and energy, and one-sixth of Noah's life in building the ark. But they persisted and, as we know, prevailed.

The "holy fear" Noah had may have been in two dimensions. He may have been in fear of what God would do to him if he refused to obey; Jonah discovered the results of God's displeasure when he turned his back on Nineveh contrary to God's orders. We have observed in this study how it should be easy to both love and fear God at the same time. Also, surely Noah was fearful at God's threat to destroy the earth and all its inhabitants (verse 13): "I am going to put an end to all people, for the earth is filled with violence because of them. I am surely going to destroy both them and the earth." Such a threat should put fear into the heart of anyone who hears it.

### By faith he condemned the world....

The world ridiculed Noah for building the ark, but Noah, in the act of building it, "condemned" the world. He knew that he believed in God, and they knew that they refused to believe in God. But Noah did not waver from his work in order to avoid condemning the world. Far too many Christians hide their witness, both their words and their godly actions, for fear they might either condemn or offend their loved ones, their neighbors, strangers, or even people who adhere to a different religion. In holding back, they fail to realize that every Christian, by both act and word, whether intentional or not, does condemn the world, just as Noah did. But Christians by their reticence fail to realize that the offense is not the fault of the Christians. The unbeliever is free to listen and receive Christ as Savior and Lord; he also has complete freedom to reject the Savior; he may turn and walk away from the witness, but he cannot erase from his mind what was witnessed to him, since it is already engraved in his heart by God. Jesus told His disciples that He did not bring peace but a sword to the world (Matt. 10:34). Jesus follows those words with a quotation from Micah 7:6:

> For a son dishonors his father,
> a daughter rises up against her mother,
> a daughter-in-law against her mother-in-law—
> a man's enemies are the members of his own household.

So come on, Christians! Let us get with it! We are in the world to bear witness to the world of God's glory. The evangelistic organization called Jews For Jesus has this motto: "We exist to make the Messiahship of Jesus an unavoidable issue to our Jewish people worldwide."[1] You also must believe and live the Gospel regardless of the world's reaction to your witness.

---

[1] This motto is included in each monthly Jews For Jesus newsletter from the year 2002.

**...and became heir of the righteousness that comes by faith.**

Those words sound very Pauline. They echo what Paul said in Rom. 3:28: "We maintain that a man is justified by faith apart from observing the law." And in Rom. 8:15-17 Paul talks about an "heir:" "You did not receive a spirit that makes you a slave again to fear, but you received the Spirit of sonship [or, adoption]....Now if we are children, then we are heirs—heirs of God and co-heirs with Christ...." Remember we are told in 9:16 that we (along with Noah) are heirs of God through His will/covenant.

### Heb. 11:8. By faith Abraham....

In both testaments, we see Abraham set forth as probably the greatest example of faith of any human God made. He holds a large place in the Genesis record (from 11:26 to 25:11, with many notations sprinkled through the Old Testament). This eleventh chapter of Hebrews gives more space to the discussion of the faith of Abraham, and of his wife Sarah, than to any other person mentioned there. That discussion includes five verses here (verses 8 to 12), and continues in three additional verses (verses 17 to 19). We have discussed what Paul says about Abraham's faith in Rom. 4, and the relationship between Abraham and all believers through their mutual, identical faith. If we are saved by faith in Jesus Christ alone, and if our faith must be identical to that of Abraham, then Abraham had to have faith in Jesus Christ alone in order for him to go to heaven.

**...when called to go to a place he would later receive as his inheritance, obeyed and went, even though he did not know where he was going.**

Turn to Gen. 12:1-2 for the basis for this verse. In addition, mention of Abraham's inheritance occurs in Gen. 12:7; 13:14-15, 17; 15:7; and 17:8. You will recall that God made an additional huge promise to Abraham besides the inheritance of land; He promised him an heir who would be the forerunner of a great nation that would possess that land through all time.

It is easy for us to imagine what tremendous faith it took for Abraham to start out on a journey to a place not yet identified to him! Although the scriptures do not tell us whether Abraham had traveled extensively in his youth, it is likely that he had not gone westward as far as Canaan. Except for reports from traveling salesmen in caravans, he would not have known much about that part of the world, and what he might have been told could have been yarns spun thin apart from truth. Our son John was a submariner for twenty-three years. When he was the ship's captain, he received sealed orders to direct him on each trip, but he was forbidden to open the packet until he had left port and had submerged at sea. Even that was a small matter compared to Abraham's orders; John usually had a fairly good idea where he would be sent, and before he went, he knew he would be back in home port in less than six months. But Abraham's journey was a one-way ticket. How would you react if someone gave you legitimate orders to leave home and go to a far country that was left unnamed until after you got a third of the way there?

All I have been talking about can be called "temporal faith." John's oceanic voyages, Abraham's mission, and your theoretical journey, all have to do with a few years' life in this world at most. But there is an even greater kind of faith required of us, by which we begin to move out into eternity. Our years in this world are but steps toward the eternal habitation we shall achieve; the steps we take here and now determine our home forever. The course you take is mostly unseen; even the next step is often shrouded by a fog which even your faith cannot penetrate. The course you take is uncharted, except for the trip ticket you have in the word of God. But since that is all you have, you must make your choice of direction based solely on whether you believe God has spoken to you through the Bible, and whether you are willing to follow God in that direction.

### Heb. 11:9. By faith he made his home in the promised land like a stranger in a foreign country....

In Gen. 23:4, we read how Abraham considered himself "an alien and a stranger" in the land to which God had sent him, and in which he then had to bury his wife Sarah. Although he knew his time spent there was temporary, he clung to the promise of God that the land would become his home, and the home of his descendants. Furthermore, the people whom God counted as Abraham's sole descendants was strictly limited by God Himself. For emphasis, that designation is repeated in the early chapters of Genesis more than once. The first occurrence is in Gen. 17:19-21:

> Then God said, "Yes, but your wife Sarah will bear you a son, and you will call him Isaac. I will establish my covenant with him as an everlasting covenant for his descendants after him. And as for Ishmael, I have heard you: I will surely bless him; I will make him fruitful and will greatly increase his numbers. He will be the father of twelve rulers, and I will make him into a great nation. But my covenant I will establish with Isaac, whom Sarah will bear to you by this time next year."

These verses make explicit that although God would bless Ishmael, the son of Sarah's Egyptian servant Hagar and his descendants, still it was Isaac who was yet to be born of Sarah who would be the ancestor of the recipients of the Promised Land. That is to say, the whole of what was then Canaan was specifically appointed by God to be the inheritance of the Jewish nation; no part of it was to belong to the Arabs (who according to the Arabs themselves today are the descendants of Ishmael). The people of Ishmael were given land, but none of it was in any part of what is now known as Israel—including the West Bank and Gaza. You may feel sorry for the Palestinians, as I do, but they have no right to any of the land of Israel as their nation. It is God's decision. The Palestinians, being Arabic people, whether believers in Islam or in Christianity or in no religion, have a right to inheritance in any of the several lands occupied by Arabs today, as well as Egypt, since their mother was Hagar an Egyptian, and she chose an Egyptian maiden to be Ishmael's wife as well (see Gen. 21:21).

Another place where God repeated the uniqueness of Isaac as the heir is Gen. 21:11-13, although God repeated His promise to make a great nation of Ishmael (though outside the Promised Land):

> The matter distressed Abraham greatly because it concerned his son. But God said to him, "Do not be so distressed about the boy [Ishmael] and your maidservant [Hagar]. Listen to whatever Sarah tells you, because it is through Isaac that your offspring will be reckoned. I will make the son of the maidservant into a nation also, because he is your offspring."

A third place where God promised Abraham that the designated heir of His promises was limited to Isaac is found in the story of Abraham's willingness to sacrifice Isaac at God's command, in Gen. 22, where in verse 2 God tells Abraham, "Take your son, your only son Isaac, whom you love, and go to the region of Moriah. Sacrifice him there as a burnt offering on one of the mountains I will tell you about." God specifies here that the only descendant of Abraham that God would recognize as legitimate was Isaac, not Ishmael, nor any other of Abraham's children he sired after Sarah had died (see Gen. 25:1-6). Again it is indicated that Isaac must be counted as the only enfranchised descendant of Abraham. It is evident that Abraham accepted this limitation, as mentioned in Gen. 25, where in verses 5 and 6 we read that "Abraham left everything he owned to Isaac. But while he was still living, he gave gifts to the sons of his concubines and sent them away from his son Isaac to the land of the east."

## ...he lived in tents, as did Isaac and Jacob, who were heirs with him of the same promise.

We have just seen the several times God made promise to Abraham that he would have a son of Sarah, Isaac, who would be sole heir of all Abraham's possessions and the Promised Land. Those promises were repeated to Isaac in Gen. 26:2-6, which reads in part:

> ...Stay in this land for a while, and I will be with you and will bless you. For to you and your descendants I will give all these lands and will confirm the oath I swore to your father Abraham. I will make your descendants as numerous as the stars in the sky and will give them all these lands....

He gave these promises as well to Jacob in the dream at Bethel before he went east to find a bride, 28:13-15:

> I am the LORD, the God of your father Abraham and the God of Isaac. I will give you and your descendants the land on which you are lying. Your descendants will be like the dust of the earth, and you will spread out to the west and to the east, to the north and to the south. All peoples on earth will be blessed through you and your offspring....I will bring you back to this

land. I will not leave you until I have done what I have promised you.

None of the three patriarchs lived a settled life in the land, as the history recorded from Gen. 12 to Gen. 50 demonstrates. They were nomads, living in tents during those three generations.

**Heb. 11:10. For he was looking forward to the city with foundations, whose architect and builder is God.**

This verse gives us a very important transition, which sets the pace for much of what we find of the relationship between the two Testaments. In a sense, Abraham had one foot set on the world and its possessions, and the other foot set firmly on the promises of better things to come. Those better things are revealed in the Christ of the New Testament. The Old Testament records God's giving of temporal things, like the Promised Land, and descendants, to the generations that followed Abraham; the New Testament offers spiritual, heavenly blessings of which the things of the world were a prototype. I think Paul put this relationship well in I Cor. 10:6 and 11: "Now these things occurred as examples, to keep us from setting our hearts on evil things as they did....These things happened to them as examples and were written down as warnings for us, on whom the fulfillment of the ages has come." The author of Hebrews implies this idea by his use of the words "copy and shadow of what is in heaven" in 8:5; and in 9:1 and 9:11 he made a contrast between the "earthly sanctuary" and the "greater and more perfect tabernacle that is not man-made, that is to say, not a part of this creation."

I believe it is important to note that Abraham (as a representative of the Old Testament saints) not only received temporal blessings, but he foresaw eternal blessings for which he waited eagerly.

**Heb. 11:11. By faith Abraham....**

We have already noted that Abraham takes up a disproportionately large space in this chapter on faith (verses 8-19). After all, Abraham was considered to be a most important person in Old Testament times, and he deserves the honor since he was chosen by God to be the father of all Jews. For the same reason his fame continued into New Testament times, and remains today.

**...even though he was past age—and Sarah herself was barren—was enabled to become a father because he considered him faithful who had made the promise.**

The fulfillment of that promise is recorded in Gen. 21:2: "Sarah became pregnant and bore a son to Abraham in his old age, at the very time God had promised him." The statement of the author of Hebrews in our NIV has a note appended showing that it is uncertain whether the author was speaking of Abraham who had faith to become a father, or of Sarah who had faith to become a mother. In this case, the Greek original is no help, but it could be construed to mean either Abraham or Sarah who had sufficient faith. We ought not to argue the point, because we rightly gather that they both had faith enough to participate in the act of procreation. As a matter of fact, we have legitimate reason to question whether either Abraham or his wife truly had sufficient faith to believe God's promise to them, because Sarah stood in her tent door snooping at the conversation between God and her husband, and when she heard the promise she laughed at such a preposterous thought (Gen. 18:12), and when God told Abraham He knew Sarah had laughed, Sarah lied and denied that she had laughed (verse 15). Her ridicule of the promise is probably more famous than Abraham's, but he also laughed at the thought (Gen. 17:17). The son of this conception was named "Isaac," which in Hebrew means "he [or she] laughs," according to BDB. Ultimately, however, both Abraham and Sarah did trust in God's promise sufficiently to do their part in causing it to happen, as we see in Gen. 21:1-5. Then in verse 6 we see that Sarah laughed again, but this time by way of rejoicing that finally she had become a mother after so many childless years: "God has brought me laughter, and everyone who hears about this will laugh with me."

**Heb. 11:12. And so from this one man, and he as good as dead, came descendants as numerous as the stars in the sky and as countless as the sand on the seashore.**

Yes, God takes the things that are not, and makes of them things that are important. He did it then, and He does the same today. We read a general rule about this in I Pet. 2:10: "Once you were not a people, but now you are the people of God; once you had not received mercy, but now you have received mercy." An expanded version of the same thought is found in I Cor. 1:26-29, and it ends with the words, "Let him who boasts boast in the Lord."

There are several Old Testament references that support this verse from Hebrews. They are Gen. 15:5; 16:10; 17:2, 4, and 5; 22:17, and 32:12. They include not only the descendants of Isaac, but also of Ishmael. Beyond all those, there are other descendants of Abraham's six other children by Keturah named in Gen. 25:1-4; and in verse 6 we read that Abraham had additional children by concubines not named or numbered.

Try to count the descendants of Abraham who are alive today. Within the Jewish population alone we could not begin to number them. It is said that in Chicago alone there live more Jews than in Israel. That is not to mention Jewish populations in Los Angeles, San Francisco, New York City, Anchorage, and even Schuyler, Nebraska. The mission organization known as Jews For Jesus right now is in the middle of a several-year campaign to reach people in every city around the globe that has a Jewish population of more than 25,000. That is not to count the people of mixed ancestry who no longer consider themselves Jews. And then there are all the people in the world who have received Christ as Savior and Lord, who are called by Paul in Rom. 4 spiritual children of Abraham. From the Jews we turn to the Arabs of the world, and could say of them similar things about their several nations where they live in the Middle East, not to speak of those scattered throughout the world. Truly, although they may not be as numerous as the sand on the seashore or the stars in the heavens, yet their number is at least "like" them.

**Heb. 11:13. All these people [just named, and yet to list] were still living by faith when they died.**

It should give us comfort to note that even though all those people had faith, still all of them died. Their death did not deter them from continuing in faith in God their Savior. What gives us comfort is that their death was only a physical death, and they knew that was the only death they would be required to suffer. The real, troublesome, everlasting death is spiritual death. That is the death we should fear until we, along with the Old Testament saints, put our faith in Jesus Christ. Then we know, as they knew, that our abiding faith will shelter us effectively from the "second death."

**They did not receive the things promised; they only saw them....**

Their faith remained strong, even though they left this earth before having received all the things God had promised them. One factor, however, helped to sustain them in their faith, so that it was not a blind faith with no tangible evidence. Generally speaking, they did receive children; they received the Promised Land; they received flocks, fruits, fat from olive trees, and wine from their vineyards. It may not have been as abundant or as amazing as the bunches of grapes the spies brought back, of which we read in Num. 13:21-27. But God cared for them, often in miraculous ways.

The author of Hebrews is not talking about material gifts from God, but spiritual, heavenly, eternal things. But even at that, the author says the people *saw* those things God had promised. If this is so, we do an injustice to the word of God, and to God Himself, to claim that the people in Old Testament times did not know of the salvation of Jesus or of the way to heaven by Him. The author claims that they were aware of these things promised, through the prophets, through direct revelation, and through natural revelation.

**...and welcomed them from a distance.**

If the people saw the things promised, it was certain that they welcomed them. Both the KJV (which translates "distance" as "afar off") and the NIV here imply the people were distant spatially from the promises they saw. However, it is sensible to presume the author meant a "distant time" rather than a "distant place" when speaking of seeing the promises. The Greek word here is πόρρωθεν, which ordinarily means in a distant place, according to Thayer, but Louw and Nida[2] agree that although this is the basic meaning of

---

[2] GREEK-ENGLISH LEXICON, Vol. I, page 635.

the word, it also can mean "from a point of time considerably prior to another point of time — 'far ahead of time, long before.'" This is the more sensible interpretation, since Jesus had not yet been incarnated although He came to their own small country.

However, we remember that the promises they saw were not on the earth, but were in heaven. So in that sense they were far distant from them.

### And they admitted that they were aliens and strangers on earth.

Paul reminds us in Phil. 3:20 that "our citizenship is in heaven." These Old Testament people knew that as well. Why do Christians today seem not to realize that as seen from our actions and conversation? We have the Bible to read all about it, but we seem more illiterate than the ancient people who had no copy of the Bible except for the few in the priests' hands, and what they had was without the New Testament. Besides, most of them probably could not read. Abraham surely had not one word of the Bible to read; scholars say the first book of the Bible, Job, was written three hundred years after Abraham lived.

If we really believe that we are merely "aliens and strangers" here, we should be eager in our anticipation of getting to heaven where all those promises will be heaped upon us. It was Paul who reminded us in Phil. 1:21, "For to me, to live is Christ and to die is gain," and in verse 23, "I desire to depart and be with Christ, which is better by far." Yet for all his passion to arrive in heaven to gain his reward, he made no effort to hasten the transition. He knew he would stay here until his work for Christ was finished (verses 25-26): "I know that I will remain, and I will continue with all of you for your progress and joy in the faith, so that through my being with you again your joy in Christ Jesus will overflow on account of me." Later he was able to inform his young friend Timothy (II Tim. 4:6-8): "...the time has come for my departure. I have fought the good fight, I have finished the race, I have kept the faith. Now there is in store for me the crown of righteousness...."

### Heb. 11:14. People who say such things show that they are looking for a country of their own.

The "such things" they had said were that they were "aliens and strangers" in the world. Today many people are obsessed with the idea of "alien invaders" to our world. Astronomers and others spend much effort searching the skies for planets which might be able to support life. It is unlikely that they will be successful in their search, although life exists in many places within this universe and far beyond it. But they will be denied success because they seek only physical life, while the universe is teeming with spiritual life, not only the saints who have lived before us, but also angels, and

God Himself. And we who know our Savior have full assurance that we too can "look for a country" with great joy, because Jesus has already gone to prepare a place for us.

Those Old Testament saints know that what they are looking for will be a place "of their own." Because we are God's adopted children, we are "heirs of God and co-heirs with Christ" (Rom. 8:17), that is, owners of heaven and all that is in it.

**Heb. 11:15. If they had been thinking of the country they had left, they would have had opportunity to return.**

This statement sounds rather cryptic, unless the author is thinking specifically of Abraham and Sarah, in which case it makes the most sense. They had left a country, Ur of the Chaldees, where the people worshiped the Moongod. They left, because the true God had spoken directly to Abraham and told him to leave and go to a place yet to be revealed. In the Promised Land he was free to worship the God of creation, and to learn of all the promises to him yet to be fulfilled, promises not only of this world, but of heaven. If, however, he and Sarah had chosen to return to their ancestral home, no doubt they would have returned to the former pagan worship as well, and never would have received the promises God had in store for them.

If Abraham and Sarah joined the Promised Land and heaven in their thoughts, they would never wish to return to the former place, knowing they would lose not only the promises for this life, but for eternal life as well. The same is true for us today. If we fill our arms and hearts with the things of this world, we will have no room for the things of God. On the other hand, if we press on to spiritual things in this life, we will see the promises of eternity as clearly as did our spiritual ancestors, and we will never want to return to the old life, even if we could. It can be likened to a pilot flying across the Atlantic Ocean. Before he leaves the airport, he calculates where on his route is the "point of no return." That is the place on his flight at which, if he encounters trouble, he will not have sufficient fuel to return to his point of origin, but only enough to keep going toward his destination. We ought to be able to sense that point in our spiritual lives too; and not turn back to the things of the world.

**Heb. 11:16. Instead, they were longing for a better country—a heavenly one.**

This verse may contradict my theory about verse 15. Even when Abraham and Sarah arrived in the Promised Land which was much better than Ur from which they had come, they were aware of an even "better country" beyond that: their heavenly country. Not much is said in Genesis about their attitude toward heaven, but surely they were drawn to its promises by the God who had brought them thus far.

**Therefore God is not ashamed to be called their God, for he has prepared a city for them.**

What a gracious God we have! When we long to be in His presence, He sanctifies us and makes us more like Himself day by day as we walk more closely with Him. As we reflect His glory, He is willing to acknowledge that He is our God and continue to bless us as we draw ever nearer to Him.

One of the great truths of the Bible is that God has chosen us, His people, to belong to Him. We never can boast that we worked out the process for ourselves. When we were dead in Christ, we had no power to make ourselves alive in Him. Only He could have done it for us. Many quotations from both Old and New Testaments verify this great truth. As I quote a few here, search the scriptures to find others, some of which will become your favorites.

In the Old Testament we find such promises of God's choosing us as in Is. 41:8-9:

> But you, O Israel, my servant,
>> Jacob, whom I have chosen,
>> you descendants of Abraham my friend,
> I took you from the ends of the earth,
>> from its farthest corners I called you.
> I said, "You are my servant";
>> I have chosen you and have not rejected you.

The result of God's choosing is in verse 10:

> So do not fear, for I am with you;
>> do not be dismayed, for I am your God.
> I will strengthen you and help you;
>> I will uphold you with my righteous right hand.

Even more direct is this statement from Deut. 7:7-8:

> The LORD did not set his affection on you and choose you because you were more numerous than other peoples, for you were the fewest of all peoples. But it was because the LORD loved you and kept the oath he swore to your forefathers that he brought you out with a mighty hand and redeemed you from the land of slavery, from the power of Pharaoh king of Egypt.

One of my favorite verses from the New Testament to prove that God chose us and not we Him is in the words of Jesus in John 6:44: "No one can come to me unless the Father who sent me draws him, and I will raise him up at the last day." We also find Jesus' words in John 15:16: "You did not choose me, but I chose you to go and bear fruit—fruit that will last." John is not the only biblical author who says such things.

The author of Hebrews said that God had "prepared a city for them." Jesus had said in John 14:1-4 that there were "rooms" in God's house, and He was going to prepare "a place" for His disciples. After all, a "city" can be a very important place, as were the Greek city states with which the people in Jesus' day were acquainted. And today, we think of Singapore, which is both a city and a nation; it is probably more powerful than many other nations in the world. More importantly, we read in Rev. 21:1 that the place God will prepare for those Old Testament people and for us is a "new heaven and a new earth." Such a place is so vast our minds cannot comprehend it. If we think only of the New Jerusalem, its dimensions far exceed a place with elbow room to spare for all who will be there. Those dimensions are stated in Rev. 21:16, said there to be 12,000 stadia (or about 1,400 miles) on each side of a perfect cube. If the city contained but one floor-level of people and each person occupied one square mile of area, there would be room for 1,960,000 people. And if there was only one "floor" per mile high in the city, with only one person per square mile, there would be room for 2,744,000,000, which is roughly half the present world's population, or, according to some statistics, one-quarter of all people who have ever lived on earth. But if the population of heaven was that scattered, it would be more like a wilderness than a city. So if each person's "room" in the New Jerusalem was a whole block in size (counting twelve blocks per mile), but each floor was a mile from the next floor, the population would then be 282,240,000 per floor, or 395,136,000,000. Now, if the New Jerusalem was only one city in the new heaven and new earth, anyone could travel beyond the city if he felt crowded, so I think there will be room for everyone who arrives there. This is true, especially because Jesus, in his parable of the narrow and wide gates (Lu. 13:22-25) showed that few people will go to heaven compared with the many who will never get there.

### Heb. 11:17. By faith Abraham, when God tested him, offered Isaac as a sacrifice.

We return to the account of Abraham (we noted earlier that his story takes up verses 8-19 of chapter 11). This part of the life of Abraham is found in Gen. 22:1-19. To me, this story, along with that of the birth and childhood of Samuel in I Sam. 1:1 to 2:11, and 2:18-21, is the most poignant story in all scripture. Abraham, together with his young teen-aged son of promise walked to the top of Mount Moriah after having left the two servants at the bottom of the hill. Abraham was obeying God's orders to sacrifice Isaac there.

God was "testing" Abraham. The Greek word πειράζω, used as a participle here, can have any one of several distinct but related meanings. Thayer says its first basic meaning is "to try whether a thing can be done; to attempt, endeavor." In this sense, Paul "tried" to join the disciples in Jerusalem after his conversion (Acts 9:26), but they were afraid of him. The second meaning Thayer offers is divided into two parts: a "good" sense, and a "bad" sense. In its good sense the word can mean "to try, make trial of, test" someone "for the purpose of ascertaining his quality, or what he thinks, or how he will behave himself." This is what God was doing to Abraham in our present story. In its bad sense, the word means "to test one maliciously, craftily to put to the proof his feelings or judgment." The Gospel stories are sprinkled with the attempt of the Pharisees, scribes, and other enemies of Jesus to cause Him to stumble in the things He said, as in Matt. 16:1. The word also can mean "to try or test one's faith, virtue, character, by enticement to sin," that is, "to solicit to sin, to tempt," as Satan did to Jesus on the Mount of Temptation described in Matt. 4:1 and 3. Thayer adds that in the Old Testament sense, God occasionally causes or allows evil to come upon someone "to prove his character and the steadfastness of his faith," as He did with Job. In a similar sense, men sometimes try to "test God's justice and patience, and to challenge him, as it were, to give proof of his perfections." This is what God accused the people of doing in the wilderness, as noted in Heb. 3:9. Whenever this word is used in the Greek text, it is important to discern which sense in the English language is to be applied there. For instance, we could become confused or wander from the truth in trying to understand what James was saying in James 1:13-14:

> When tempted, no one should say, "God is tempting me." For God cannot
> be tempted by evil, nor does he tempt anyone; but each one is tempted
> when, by his own evil desire, he is dragged away and enticed.

The author of Hebrews says that Abraham "offered" Isaac, which implies that he actually went through with the slaying of his son. But we know from Gen. 22 it did not happen. The matter is resolved two verses later in Hebrews, when the author says that he acted "figuratively speaking."

We note also that the author was talking about offering Isaac as a "sacrifice." This was a ritual performed solely for the purpose of making atonement for sin, so in obeying God's command, Abraham was acknowledging that he had sinned, and needed to make a sacrifice. What Abraham's sin was, we are not told, and we do not need to know. Sin is sin, as James says, "whoever keeps the whole law and yet stumbles at just one point is guilty of breaking all of it" (James 2:10). Likewise, we all have sinned, and are in need of a sacrifice. Thank God that He Himself has been our Sacrifice, so by faith we, like Abraham, are free from guilt and punishment.


**He who had received the promises was about to sacrifice his one and only son....**

The "promises" Abraham had received included the promise of a legitimate son: not merely a slave born in his house, as was Eliezer of Damascus (Gen. 15:2); nor yet a bastard son of Abraham's wife's maidservant Hagar (Gen. 16:1-16); or even the several children born to Abraham of his second wife Keturah and other concubines after Sarah had died (Gen. 25:1-6). Another promise to Abraham was that that one son (the only one acknowledged by God) would be the ancestor of multitudes of people (Gen. 26:4).

Since Abraham knew that Isaac would be the father of an innumerable host of people, his thoughts and feelings must have been mixed. Think about how you would feel, if you had only one child whom God gave to you in a special way, and promised you many descendants through that child; and then God would speak to you and require you to kill him. It seems so contradictory, for God to promise one son, and then demand that you eliminate that only hope of further generations of children. Except for Abraham's faith, he would have had huge misgivings and refused to carry out God's orders.

How might Abraham have thought God could work through this dilemma? He might have believed that God could provide another son. He might have thought God would instantly heal the wound, just like Jesus restored Malchus' ear (John 18:10). But the author tells us in verse 19 that this was what Abraham thought: "Abraham reasoned that God could raise the dead." He believed that Isaac could really die, but that God would restore him to life and have children. So even Abraham believed in the resurrection, although he lived two thousand years before Christ was raised. He held that faith three hundred years before Job also believed it. See Job 19:25-27, where he says:

> I know that my Redeemer lives,
>> and that in the end he will stand upon the earth.
> And after my skin has been destroyed,
>> yet in my flesh I will see God;
> I myself will see him
>> with my own eyes—I, and not another.
> How my heart yearns within me!

Abraham believed this a thousand years before his great descendant King David said that he believed it (Ps. 16:9-10):

> Therefore my heart is glad and my tongue rejoices;
>> my body also will rest secure,
> because you will not abandon me to the grave,
>> nor will you let your Holy One see decay.

The author speaks here about Abraham's "one and only" son. We have already discussed this. Since the idea is emphasized many times in scripture, it must have been a very important idea to God, and we ought to acknowledge it. God did not count any other of Abraham's physical children as part of the seed of promise. The word the author uses for "one and only" is μονογενής, the same word used for God's "one and only" Son Jesus. Of course, God claims to have many children, but they are merely children by adoption (Rom. 8:15, where the footnote rightly uses the term "adoption"), therefore they are in a different category from the One and Only Son of God. So Isaac in the same way is the "one and only" son of Abraham. The rest may be blessed by God, but they are not counted as heirs.

### Heb. 11:18.  ...even though God had said to him, "It is through Isaac that your offspring will be reckoned."

This is a verbatim quotation from Gen. 21:12, in which God alleviates Abraham's qualms about abandoning his child born of Hagar. God promises Abraham that He will take care of Ishmael, and even see to it that he will be the ancestor of many great nations. We see the fulfillment of that promise, in the several Arab nations, along with the Palestinians who today are trying to preempt two large parts of the land which God had promised to Isaac alone.

### Heb. 11:19. Abraham reasoned that God could raise the dead....

We have covered our thoughts about this clause just above, in our discussion of verse 17, when we considered several ways Abraham might have thought God could see Isaac die and still keep His promise to Abraham of multitudes of people coming from Isaac.

### ...and figuratively speaking, he did receive Isaac back from the dead.

As I mentioned earlier, the term, "figuratively speaking" is the governing idea here. Even if Abraham had thought such a thought, it took immense fortitude to go through the motions of traveling to Moriah, carrying the wood for the sacrifice, the fire to kindle the wood, and the knife. Will you have sufficient faith in God's promises to you, when you are confronted with a decision God wants you to make which seems as ominous in its consequences as the death of Isaac must have been to Abraham? Let us pray for resolve from the Holy Spirit to follow through on God's directives to the very end, knowing the God of resurrection will make it right in His way and His time.

From Abraham and Sarah we turn to additional people of faith.

### Heb. 11:20. By faith Isaac blessed Jacob and Esau in regard to their future.

Turn to Gen. 27:27-29 and 39-40 to read the blessings Isaac gave his children. In that chapter you will read how Rebekah conspired to filch from Esau his rightful blessing as the elder son, and obtain it for Jacob her favorite, while Isaac loved Esau better. It is important to note that Jacob was God's favorite too, as He revealed His will to Rebekah before the twins were born (Gen. 25:23), that Esau would be a servant to Jacob. In addition, Isaac finally acquiesced in God's choice, after he discovered Rebekah and Jacob's deceit. He told his new decision to Esau, in Gen. 27:33: "I ate [Jacob's food] just before you came and I blessed him—and indeed he will be blessed!" This was the final indignity for Esau: Jacob had already torn from him his birthright, when he fed him a bowl of bean soup because Esau was very hungry after returning from the hunt (Gen. 25:27-34).

Poor Isaac! Although he lived 180 years (Gen 35:28), which was five years longer than his father Abraham had lived (Gen. 25:7), he seems to have lived a most colorless existence. His life was sandwiched between that of an ultra-famous father and an equally famous son. He gets short shrift in the Genesis record: his birth is mentioned in chapter 21; the story of his almost-sacrifice is in chapter 22; the process of finding a wife for him is in chapter 24; but all this is part of the life of Abraham principally, not of Isaac. The life of Isaac begins in 25:19 where we read, "This is the account of Abraham's son Isaac," but the story of Isaac's life is overshadowed almost immediately by the account of the strange circumstances surrounding the birth of Jacob (in 25:24-26). Chapter 26 tells more about Isaac than any other chapter, and little is told there. Chapter 27 is the account of Jacob's deceit and theft of Esau's blessing. After that, Isaac is hardly mentioned until the note of his death in 35:27-29. So Isaac's life is compacted into hardly more than two chapters in Genesis, while that of Abraham covers fourteen chapters; Jacob's covers twelve; and Joseph's is in fourteen chapters. Now, in Hebrews Isaac gets mentioned in one verse, and that is all.

Isaac's blessings upon Jacob and Esau were peculiar. The glowing blessing Isaac pronounced on Jacob was not intended for him, but for Esau, and Isaac's almost total blindness (Gen. 27:1) made Jacob's deceit possible. Isaac loved his son Esau, because he was his firstborn. Surely Isaac knew that God had favored Jacob; God's message to Rebekah that the elder would serve the younger twin (Gen. 25:22-23) would hardly have been concealed from Isaac. Surely that is the reason why Isaac, after he had already blessed Jacob, and Rebekah and Jacob's ruse was uncovered, the father told Esau (Gen. 27:33), "...I blessed him—and indeed he will be blessed!"

After Isaac had given Jacob the blessing he had intended for Esau, and had confirmed it, he then blessed Esau, but the blessing sounds more like a backward blessing at best, and a curse at worst. In Gen. 27:39-40 we read:

> Your dwelling will be
> away from the earth's richness,
> away from the dew of heaven above.
> You will live by the sword
> and you will serve your brother.
> But when you grow restless,
> you will throw his yoke
> from off your neck.

The first part of Isaac's blessing to Esau was a declaration that he would live in a place bereft of natural resources; the value of petroleum was not known in those days, and Esau's descendants have long since disappeared from the face of the earth. Isaac's second statement in Esau's "blessing" was that his dwelling would be a desert place, so precious few crops or animals could live there. The third thing Isaac said to Esau was that he would have to fight constantly for his existence. After that he gave the most galling prediction, that Esau and his descendants would be slaves of Jacob and his children. There was one final prediction: ultimately Esau's descendants would free themselves from the slavery imposed on them by Jacob's progeny. The relationship between the Edomites and Israelites was fractious at best throughout Old Testament history, and the Edomites were almost completely destroyed several times.[3]

---

[3] Davis-Gehman, WESTMINSTER DICTIONARY OF THE BIBLE, under the article on "Edomites," page 148.

But remnants survived, until in New Testament times they were incorporated into the fold of the people of Judah.

**Heb. 11:21. By faith Jacob, when he was dying, blessed each of Joseph's sons, and worshiped as he leaned on the top of his staff.**

The account of the blessing upon Joseph's sons is found in Gen. 48:12-20, with the words of blessing in verses 15-16 and 20. The reason the blessing is divided is because Jacob decided to bless Ephraim more favorably than Manasseh although Manasseh was the elder of the two (Gen. 41:51-52). Perhaps Jacob recalled that God and his father Isaac had blessed him above his elder brother as well.

The author of Hebrews thought it was important to mention specifically that Jacob "worshiped" God in the last days of his life. At the beginning of his journey to escape from Esau and to find a wife, he had made a bargain with God at Bethel, when God promised to bless him. Among the things Jacob promised God (Gen. 28:20-22) was, "If God will be with me and will watch over me...so that I return safely to my father's house, then the LORD will be my God." So Jacob fulfilled his part of the bargain, even though he was weak with age. We read in Gen. 47:31, "Israel worshiped as he leaned on the top of his staff."

I have a spiritual heritage similar to that of Jacob's children. When my father died, my mother was too sick and weak to fly with us from her home in Escondido, CA to our home in Anchorage. So we found a good nursing home for her. However, because of her many maladies, she could not survive; her husband had been literally her life support system. Less than three weeks after he died, she also succumbed. As a young girl she had signed a pledge at Christian Endeavor to read at least one chapter of the Bible every day of her life, and she had done so. My parents had kept a log of their readings: the date, the chapter read, and the one who had read it. For months the reader had been my father, because my mother's eyes were so weak she could not read the numbers on the telephone dial. After her death, we picked up her few remaining belongings from the nursing home, among which was the Bible. In it we found the log of readings. After my father's death, she kept the record of daily readings, one chapter each evening before she went to bed. But on the last day before she died, the last notation was a large scrawl which fell away off the line: "Read only six verses; too tired." I am thankful to God for the great spiritual heritage I received. Oh that each of us would be able to transmit such a spiritual heritage to our children!

**Heb. 11:22. By faith Joseph, when his end was near, spoke about the exodus of the Israelites from Egypt and gave instructions about his bones.**

The author of Hebrews distills but one detail from the astounding life of Joseph; he must have considered it a sort of summary of the life-long faith Joseph displayed. This detail is from the very end of his life, and is found in Gen. 50:24-25: "Then Joseph said to his brothers, 'I am about to die. But God will surely come to your aid and take you up out of this land to the land he promised...and then you must carry my bones up from this place.'" Joseph remembered the promises God had given to Abraham, Isaac and Jacob regarding a Promised Land which would be given in perpetuity to their descendants (except for brief hiatuses, including during and after the days of Joseph for over four hundred years; and for a time before 1948 in our day). We note that Joseph was confident both that the land would be theirs, and that they would be delivered back to it even though they were then in Egypt. Joseph wanted to make sure he would be a part of that land, so he instructed the people to save his bones and carry them with them when they returned to the land of Israel. This directive was carried out, as we read in Ex. 13:19, "Moses took the bones of Joseph with him because Joseph had made the sons of Israel swear an oath. He had said, 'God will surely come to your aid, and then you must carry my bones up with you from this place.'"

Someone has remarked that there is a world of difference between the beginning and the ending of the book of Genesis. It starts out, "In the beginning God..," and it ends, "...in a coffin in Egypt." What had intervened to make that vast difference was sin.

There is much controversy these days about the dating of the Exodus. Many liberal theologians set the date around the twelfth century BC, while a strict biblical dating would make it near 1450 BC. It seems to me that this question is part of another issue in Egyptian/Israelite history, the assumption that in the 1700s BC there were Hyksos who seemed to rule Egypt, but no one claims to know exactly who the Hyksos were, or from whence they came or where they went. Here are some of my thoughts on this double issue.

Early in my ministry I developed a chart of the chronology of the Old Testament times. I discovered that if you begin at the end of that chronology, with 586 as the date for the fall of Jerusalem (to which nearly everyone agrees), everything fits perfectly as you go all the way back to Abraham. If you start with Abraham at about 2000 BC, you find a biblical detail for every date needed to make an unbroken time-line from Abraham to the fall of Jerusalem. In that biblical time-line you find Moses started the Exodus in 1462 BC. If you date the Exodus from the 1200s, as some do, there is no room for all the Judges to lead Israel afterwards. From the biblical data, I see Saul beginning his reign at 1061 BC, and if he started any later, there would be no room for all the kings of Israel and Judah with their dates, even compacting the time-line with co-regencies you find occasionally.

My main thought on all this is the question of the so-called Hyksos who supposedly reigned in Egypt around the 1700s BC. No one who rejects the biblical timeline seems to know who they are. But the Jews' sojourn in Egypt lasted 430 years, according to Ex. 12:40, 41, and 51, beginning, according to my calculation, in 1893 BC. Joseph died in 1822, and that is when the period of slavery is supposed to have begun, because new Pharaohs arose who did not know him or his beneficence to the land.

During the time of Joseph's leadership in Egypt, it may be that foreign travelers might have thought that some foreigners (read "Hyksos" if you are liberal, "Israelites" if you believe the Bible) were rulers in Egypt. And except for Pharaoh, who was Number One, Joseph was at least Number Two, and as such held all the power except for Pharaoh's household. It then could be a natural mistake for outsiders to believe that Egypt had been invaded by barbarians who ruled the country until somehow the Egyptians were able to wrest the country back from the "enemy."

I have thought lately of one more detail. In this I am not trying to belittle the horrible servitude under which Israel bowed while they were building Raamses and other places, particularly in Goshen which was their part of the country of Egypt, but there are hints that despite their position as slaves, they held a certain amount of respect and even fear among the Egyptians. Occasionally they went on strike for more straw. They must have been fed well; the people yearned for the leeks and melons when they got into the wilderness. The midwives were not especially submissive; Moses was saved by their hesitations and Moses' mother's refusal to obey. And how did Aaron escape the threatened "late-term abortion"? Even at the end of their time as slaves in Egypt, the natives showered them with costly gifts. Surely their motive was partly to get the people out of their country to end the plagues. I believe other reasons were that they appreciated all the Israelites did for them, and may have feared them because of the great influence the Jews surely imposed on them during their stay in Egypt. The Israelites may have been slaves, but some of them must have held positions of power in the government, or else Pharaoh's daughter would not have been allowed to keep Moses when it became known that he was a Hebrew.

Another clue that it was the Israelites who were the rulers in Egypt is found in the story of Balaam and Balak in Num. 22-24. At the beginning of that story, we read what terror the very thought of the Israelites brought to Moab and the surrounding peoples (Num. 22:2-4):

> Now Balak son of Zippor saw all that Israel had done to the Amorites, and Moab was terrified because there were so many people. Indeed, Moab was filled with dread because of the Israelites. The Moabites said to the elders of Midian, "This horde is going to lick up everything around us, as an ox licks up the grass of the field."

It is hard to imagine that the Moabites and their neighbors were that frightened of the Israelites merely because of what they had done to the Amorites. Without doubt they knew the power they exerted in Egypt before they began their journey to the Promised Land. A further indication of the knowledge the people in and around Canaan had of the power of the Israelites in Egypt is found in what Rahab said to the spies at Jericho in Josh. 2:9-11. For our discussion of that, please read the comments you find on verse 31 of Heb. 11.

I believe the Israelites were the supposed "Hyksos" and that the Exodus was in the fifteenth century BC. That agrees with what the Bible says.

**Heb. 11:23. By faith Moses' parents hid him for three months after he was born, because they saw he was no ordinary child, and they were not afraid of the king's edict.**

Here is the beginning of the account of another great Old Testament person, one who was comparable to Abraham in the minds of all Jews. The author of Hebrews expends seven verses to tell about Moses, more than for any other person except Abraham. The basis for the first part of this verse is found in Ex. 2:2.

Actually, this verse is not about Moses' faith, but about his parents' faith, and specifically his mother's: "When she saw that he was a fine child, she hid him for three months." Because she exercised faith, the right thing got done, and Moses delivered the Children of Israel from bondage in Egypt.

How did Moses' brother, Aaron, escape? We remember the story. Pharaoh had ordered the Israelite midwives to kill all male children because the nation was becoming too populous and the Egyptians feared a takeover from their slaves. If such a thing happened (and, as we presume in the case of the Hyksos), it would not have been the only time in history. For instance, it is recorded[4] that one group of Athenians called Chians, who "are said to have been the first Grecian people who engaged in a regular slave-trade...themselves were compelled to drain the bitter cup of servitude. For, as we find recorded, they were subjugated by Mithridates, and were delivered up to their own slaves, to be carried away captive into Colchis."

The author of Hebrews says that Moses "was no ordinary child." This echoes the account in Exodus where Moses' mother "saw that he was a fine child." He was well-rounded, that is, spiritually, mentally, and physically. He was no spiritual babe as he grew, but an apex of his spiritual journey occurred when he saw the burning bush in the desert (Ex. 3:1-4:17), and from then he grew more dependent on God's guidance for his life. Also, he had to be a mental giant to be able to stand up to the Pharaohs, and then the would-be leaders of the Israelites. Finally, only a most rugged man could have lived as a shepherd in the desert of Midian from ages forty to eighty, and following that as a shepherd of people for the next forty years through the Sinai desert. God gave him everything he had, and he used it all for God's glory with few exceptions. It is no wonder that the People of God exalted Moses through the rest of their history.

The author says that Moses' parents "were not afraid of the king's

[4] W. O. Blake, compiler, THE HISTORY OF SLAVERY AND THE SLAVE TRADE, ANCIENT AND MODERN, pages 25 and 27.

edict." It took great courage to save the infant's life. It may have taken even greater boldness for them to expose the child when he was three months old, by letting him rest in a basket in the Nile River, so the daughter of Pharaoh could find him.

**Heb. 11:24. By faith Moses, when he had grown up, refused to be known as the son of Pharaoh's daughter.**

We read in Ex. 2:11 that "One day, after Moses had grown up, he went out to where his own people were and watched them at their hard labor." It is possible that this was not the first time Moses made his identity as a Jew generally known. The incidents that follow this statement in Exodus indicate that his own people knew who he was, since the Jewish worker who had attacked his co-laborer seemed to distinguish between the Egyptian Moses had killed the day before, and himself (Ex. 2:12-15). It may be that Pharaoh's daughter never tried to hide the real identity of Moses, even from the first, since she had servant girls with her who could have made the truth known. Adoptions are seldom secret affairs.

Moses could have stayed safely in Pharaoh's palace, whether or not he was known as a Hebrew. He might have become a ruler over Egypt, even as his uncle Joseph had been several hundred years earlier. He could have lived a life of ease offered to rulers in the land of plenty. Yet he deliberately counted himself as "one of them," the lowly Israelites. Was that an ungrateful act on Moses' part? Certainly it was, from a human standpoint. A better question is, Did Moses do the right thing? Apparently God thought so, because He chose Moses to be the deliverer of His people from their bondage in Egypt.

On what basis do you make your decisions? Do you consider only yourself and your benefits, or are you willing to defer to what you know is God's will for your life?

**Heb. 11:25. He chose to be mistreated along with the people of God rather than to enjoy the pleasures of sin for a short time.**

Was Moses mistreated? We usually think of Moses' time in Pharaoh's court as living in the lap of luxury, with servants to bring whatever he could want by way of food, clothing, cooling fans, enjoyment of all kinds. Principally that is how Moses lived, probably. But near the end of his life in the palace, he came under major distress. First of all, he went out and observed the merciless conditions under which his own people were enslaved. Moses tried to give aid to a fellow-countryman, and he killed the Egyptian tormentor. The next day, Moses saw two of his own people fighting with one another. When he tried to stop them, since they were fellow-Jews, the one most to blame threw Moses' murder in his face (Ex. 2:14): "Who made you ruler and judge over us? Are you thinking of killing me as you killed the Egyptian?"

(Could it be that this man was one who later in the desert tried to usurp leadership from Moses, as Korah and his followers did in Num. 16?) Because the man accused Moses, he realized his act was known, and it finally came to the ears of Pharaoh. For his murder, the ruler sought to punish Moses with death, so Moses had to flee from his posh life and finally came to Midian (Ex. 2:15), where he stayed forty years, feeding sheep in the Sinai desert. For his efforts, Moses was blackballed for the rest of his life by the Egyptians, so that when he returned to deliver his people from bondage, he was vilified.

The author of Hebrews tells us that Moses gave up the "pleasures of sin" in order to align himself with the People of God. Does this mean that in a king's palace there is no room for righteousness, but only sinful pleasures? It may not be impossible, but according to Jesus, it is highly unlikely. In the parable of the rich but foolish farmer (Lu. 12:16-21), Jesus said God would say to him, "You fool! This very night your life will be demanded from you. Then who will get what you have prepared for yourself?" In another lesson (Matt. 19:23-30) Jesus told His disciples, "...it is hard for a rich man to enter the kingdom of heaven...it is easier for a camel to go through the eye of a needle than for a rich man to enter the kingdom of God." And when the disciples asked whether anyone could be saved, Jesus replied, "With man this is impossible, but with God all things are possible." That possibility is exemplified in the life of Zacchaeus who, though he was very rich, was commended for his faith and righteousness with these words (Lu. 19:9): "Today salvation has come to this house, because this man, too, is a son of Abraham." But because Moses left Pharaoh's home, he must have known he could not live a righteous life there.

According to the author of Hebrews, Moses could have enjoyed the pleasures of sin only for a short time at best. We may think his forty years living as Pharaoh's daughter' son was a pretty long time; and if he had lived there his whole life of one hundred twenty years, that would have been unusually long. But when we compare the length of time on earth with an eternity in heaven, we who are sensible will choose the "eternal pleasures" King David was looking forward to (Ps. 16:11) over the sinful pleasures of this world that bring only eternal punishment.

### Heb. 11:26. He regarded disgrace for the sake of Christ....

The authors of Ps. 69:9 and Ps. 89:50-51 could have been speaking for Moses when they wrote:

> ...for zeal for your house consumes me,
>> and the insults of those who insult you fall on me....
> Remember, LORD, how your servant has been mocked,
>> how I bear in my heart the taunts of all the nations,
> the taunts with which your enemies have mocked, O LORD,
>> with which they have mocked...your anointed one.

Here, at any rate, is another instance where people in Old Testament times knew Christ, according to the scriptural testimony. Those people were saved by faith in Christ. Jesus Himself gives the proof that Moses knew Him, when He said in John 5:46 at the end of His series of witnesses to Himself as the Savior, "If you believed Moses, you would believe me, for he wrote about me." This statement of Jesus' also confirms that it was Moses who wrote the books of Moses, and not a conglomeration of authors and redactors as some scholars claim.

You may want a more precise thought than the word "disgrace" offers. The Greek word is ὀνειδισμός, and is translated as "reproach" in the KJV. Thayer simply calls it "reproach." Schneider[5] adds to that word the terms "insult," "abuse," and "affliction." There is the implication that Moses suffered in a manner similar to Christ's suffering, though not to the extent to which Christ had to suffer to pay for the sins of the world, but simply to lead the people out of bondage in Egypt.

### ...as of greater value than the treasures of Egypt....

The world would say to you if you determined to travel the same path Moses took you were a fool. I believe Jim Elliot revealed the truth clearly when he penned this credo in one of his college textbooks, "He is no fool who gives up what he cannot keep, to gain what he cannot lose." Which way will you choose to go? Perhaps you have already made your decision. Every one must make a decision some time in our lives. Even if you refuse to make a decision now, that in itself is a decision. Several years ago a Nun filled with aphorisms said, "Not to decide is to decide." You may think you have never been confronted with the necessity to make such a decision. But it is a bad excuse to refuse to see both morality and evil which surround us constantly.

Years ago, in the first little church I served in upstate New York, it was my habit on Friday evenings to meet with the youth of the church and take them to an old folks' home nearby. We went from room to room to sing a few hymns, then talk individually with each of the old people, conversing about their lives and about the Lord, and give them tracts. I was amazed that those young people were willing to give up their school activities like football and basketball games, and dances, in order to go to such an uninteresting place. One evening I noticed one bed where a sweet Dutch lady had been was empty, so I inquired of her neighbor where she was. The neighbor answered, "Oh, she died this week!" When we left the home that evening to go for our weekly hot fudge sundaes, I was able to tell the youth how just two weeks before, the Dutch lady had received Christ as her Savior because someone had given her a tract which she had read. Now, because of their efforts, and willingness to give up their pleasures of school activities, that lady was now with Jesus whom she had just received. All those young people were ob-

---

5 Article on ὀνειδισμός by J. Schneider in TDNT, Vol. V, page 241.

viously moved at the results of their sacrifices, and rejoiced with me at what they had accomplished. Surely they had suffered disgrace from classmates who thought they were silly to give up their school activities to go to an old folks' home every Friday evening.

### ...because he was looking ahead to his reward.

Whether or not it is a worthy motive, this is what keeps us going for God. If that were our only motive, then we would surely lose the reward. For our labor is not for the sake of reaping a benefit, but of bringing glory to our God and Savior Jesus Christ. Further, if we have received salvation through faith in Christ, we have already received a reward which is unattainable elsewhere. But what rewards they are that we find named in scripture! We read of talents, crowns, treasures, and mansions. The very picture of the New Jerusalem is almost beyond description in John's human words (Rev. 21:10-22:5). And John surely would agree that his words were totally inadequate to describe what he saw in his visions.

Do you ever think that what you receive from God is too little? If so, think rather of the eternal benefits waiting for you.

### Heb. 11:27.   By faith he left Egypt, not fearing the king's anger....

Come now, was Moses really not afraid? We already quoted the statement in Ex. 2:14, "Then Moses was afraid and thought, 'What I did must have become known.'" At least Moses did not fear the king's anger after he got to Midian. It would have been hard to track him down in such an inhospitable place as the Sinai desert. In addition to that, Moses most certainly stood up to the new Pharaoh after his forty years in the Midianite desert.

### ...he persevered because he saw him who is invisible.

God talked to Moses as to no other man, that is, face to face. In Ex. 33:11, in a description of what happened at the tent of meeting, we read, "The LORD would speak to Moses face to face, as a man speaks with his friend." And in Deut. 34:10, at the end of Moses' life, there is this testimony: "Since then no prophet has risen in Israel like Moses, whom the LORD knew face to face...." Such meetings with God surely would be a strong incentive to be obedient to God's every command. Moses was one who was not disobedient to the unique vision, but continued throughout his life to do God's will.

### Heb. 11:28.   By faith he kept the Passover and the sprinkling of blood, so that the destroyer of the firstborn would not touch the firstborn of Israel.

The record of the institution of the Passover feast is in Ex. 12 (please reread the whole chapter now). We see how God determined to send His angel to be the "destroyer" of the firstborn of all Egyptian households. But He chose to save the firstborn of all Jewish families that trusted God enough to observe the feast, including putting the blood of the lamb on the door sideposts and lintels (KJV) of their homes.

Moses not only "kept" the Passover, he inaugurated it, but the author of Hebrews may have meant that.

It took faith on the part of all the people of Israel to sprinkle the blood on their doors at Moses' command. Surely nearly all of them did so. But it is conceivable that some Jews sneered at the idea and refused to do what they were directed to do. If they did, then their firstborn perished with those of the Egyptians. Likewise, it is just as conceivable that many Egyptians and people of other nationalities heard about the ritual and followed it in faith, hoping that their firstborn sons would be spared. If they did it in faith in God's promises, surely He did honor their faith and spared their children. I base my idea on what we read in Ex. 12:48, "An alien living among you who wants to celebrate the LORD's Passover must have all the males in his household circumcised...." Even in the Old Testament God did not automatically exclude all Gentiles from His promises just because they were Gentiles.

**Heb. 11:29. By faith the people passed through the Red Sea as on dry land; but when the Egyptians tried to do so, they were drowned.**

Two verses tell the core of the story, but you are encouraged to read the whole episode for yourself in chapters 12 to 14 in Exodus. In Ex. 14:21-22 we find the statement of the Jews' preservation:

> Then Moses stretched out his hand over the sea, and all that night the LORD drove the sea back with a strong east wind and turned it into dry land. The waters were divided, and the Israelites went through the sea on dry ground, with a wall of water on their right and on their left.

Following that, we read what happened to the Egyptians in Ex. 14:27-28:

> Moses stretched out his hand over the sea, and at daybreak the sea went back to its place. The Egyptians were fleeing toward it, and the LORD swept them into the sea. The water flowed back and covered the chariots and horsemen—the entire army of Pharaoh that had followed the Israelites into the sea. Not one of them survived.

We are told in Ex. 14:6 that Pharaoh led his army into the Red Sea. Years ago I read an article in an archaeological journal, in which the author claimed the body of that Pharaoh had been discovered, and the discoverers were certain they had found the right body because of evidence that he had been drowned. I find it hard to believe that a mummy that had been eviscerated and embalmed before burial in a tomb could provide evidence of drowning 3,500 years after it had happened. Even though Pharaoh had been with his army and had drowned, it may be that his body was found after the disaster: in Ex. 14:30 we read that the Israelites saw the Egyptian dead bodies on the sea shore. Beyond that, there is a debate among scholars today as to who was the Pharaoh at the time the Exodus began.[6] But we ought to be less interested in Pharaoh than in Moses and the people whom God delivered from the Egyptians because of their belief.

It is in fact the faith of the Israelite people, not Moses, spoken of by the author of Hebrews in this verse. It took great faith on their part to step where the Red Sea had been but a few moments before, and trust the waters would stay away until they had crossed safely. What is the difference between the faith of the followers of Moses, and that of the followers of Jim Jones who perished with them in South America several years ago? Mainly, the difference is that Moses had shown miracles from God already in the presence of the people, and when he spoke, he spoke of righteousness from the great God of creation. On the other hand, Jim Jones performed no miracles, but rather he pilfered from his people all their riches; and when he spoke he spoke sinful things. What a great God we have, who does marvelous things for us when we are willing to believe and obey Him!

God's timing was impeccable, in that He caused the wind to drive the water away just when the Israelites needed to escape. He kept the wind going until every Jew had got safely across and every enemy was in the middle of the Red Sea. Paul tells us in I Cor. 10:2 that the Israelites "were all baptized into Moses in the cloud and in the sea," yet not a drop of water touched them; it was the Egyptians who were immersed, and perished.

It may be that Moses did not know by what means God would deliver Israel from the Egyptian army when they were caught between the army and the Red Sea. It is certain that Moses did believe God would rescue them in some way, so he expressed his confidence in God by telling the people (Ex. 14:13): "Stand firm and you will see the deliverance the LORD will bring you today." It is obvious to us that standing still was not going to do it. So God had to countermand Moses' order by telling him (verse 15), "Why are you crying out to me? Tell the Israelites to move on." I believe there is a lesson for us today. If we expect to do great things for God, we must arise from our rocking chairs and begin to move ahead; God will guide every step as we go but probably not before we begin to move.

### Heb. 11:30. By faith the walls of Jericho fell, after the people had marched around them for seven days.

We have finished our study of the two great men of early Old Testament history—Abraham and Moses. Now we think of several people, who

---

[6] An interesting discussion of this is found in the article by William Shea, "Amenhotep II as Pharaoh of the Exodus," in the quarterly BIBLE AND SPADE, Spring 2003, Vol. 16, No. 2, pages 41-51. Shea names several Pharaohs as possible candidates: Thutmose III, Amenhotep IIA and Amenhotep IIB. Other scholars who believe in a late Exodus think Rameses II was the Pharaoh who may have died in the Red Sea.

along with their followers had faith in God and were willing to do His bidding. For their faith and obedience they were blessed, with special favors in this life, and always with the promises of a better life to come. The first leader we encounter is Joshua, even though the author of Hebrews does not name him here. (Joshua was named but one other time, in Heb. 4:8, in connection with the rest God offers.) It was Joshua who was leading the people of Israel into the Promised Land after Moses had brought them through the wilderness.

Joshua is spoken of as a great man of God. At the beginning of his leadership, God had said to him (Josh. 1:5): "As I was with Moses, so I will be with you; I will never leave you nor forsake you." Again, in verse 9, God encouraged him: "Be strong and courageous. Do not be terrified; do not be discouraged, for the LORD your God will be with you wherever you go." Joshua was a faithful leader during the five years[7] it took for the Israelites to occupy as much of the Promised Land as they would conquer then.

The story of the fall of Jericho is found in Josh. 6. The part of the story which tells of the fall of the walls is in verses 15-20. What God invited the children of Israel to do surely seemed like a child's game to some of them. Yet they did it, willingly. Surely Joshua was a good and faithful leader to motivate the people in this task.

Archaeologists who have been digging around ancient Jericho have discovered that the walls fell outward. If an enemy army is besieging a city and tries to break down the walls to get in, the walls fall inward. But it was not Israel that caused the walls to tumble. God was inside and forced the walls outward. The people of God could not boast that by their strength or craft they had conquered the city.

**Heb. 11:31. By faith the prostitute Rahab, because she welcomed the spies, was not killed with those who were disobedient.**

This account is part of the story of the fall of Jericho you just read in Josh. 6. But the account of her faithfulness to the people of God begins in Josh. 2:1. She had faith not only in the Israelites, but also in God, as is evident in what she said to the spies in 2:9-11:

> I know that the LORD has given this land to you and that a great fear of you has fallen on us....We have heard how the LORD dried up the water of the Red Sea...and what you did to Sihon and Og...for the LORD your God is God in heaven above and on the earth below."

Rahab was a woman of faith. Where did she obtain that faith? Rahab was a Gentile, a Canaanite, one whose people worshiped Baal and other such false gods. Moreover, the Bible calls her a "prostitute," and there is no evidence that the Hebrew word זוֹנָה ever meant anything as innocuous as

---

[7] You may calculate that five years for yourself by comparing the age of Caleb when he was sent to spy out the land at the beginning of the Exodus in Josh. 14:7; and his age at the end of the wars of occupation he gives in verse 10.

"innkeeper," although Rahab may have been an innkeeper also. The closest thing to a meaning different from harlotry is the use in scripture of the idea of commerce between the Chosen People and other nations that were idolatrous. If God's people dealt with them, the pagan practices and worship might be embraced and the people would turn from the true God. In many places harlotry was a symbol of Israel's forsaking God as a wife's turning from her husband. Erlandsson says it this way:[8] "The verb...can also be used for commercial contacts with pagan peoples, for any association that is not right in the eyes of Yahweh can be called harlotry."

Some people may hope that they can whitewash Jesus' ancestry by changing the meaning of Rahab's identity. But that would be little help in light of other female ancestors of Jesus who are also named in Matt. 1 and Lu. 3. We remember Bath-sheba the adulteress and wife of the adulterer and murderer David (II Sam. 11:1-27). Those two had a son, Solomon (II Sam. 12:24), who had seven hundred wives and three hundred concubines (I Kings 11:3), a lifestyle not conducive to great spirituality, especially since the "wives led him astray." We remember Ruth, the great-grandmother of David. Ruth was a Moabitess; we are told in the Law that a descendant of Moab was not allowed to enter the house of God for ten generations (Deut. 23:3-6), because the Moabites had treated badly the Israelites as they attempted to travel to the Promised Land.

It was not merely female ancestors of Jesus whose lives were sullied by great sinfulness. Judah, the head of the tribe from which Jesus descended, fell in love with a Canaanite woman, Shua. God had commanded that all Canaanites be put to death as Israel occupied the land, so they would not impose their false religion on God's people. Not only did Judah marry a pagan woman, but later he lay with the young woman who had been the wife of his first two sons, thinking she was a harlot. That young woman, Tamar, bore Judah twin sons, one of which became an ancestor of Jesus. This story is found in Gen. 38:1-30. Yet God, in His infinite wisdom, chose all these and more to be the ancestors of Jesus. We might think that was a terrible group of people through which to bring about the physical life of our Savior; on the other hand, who else in the world was better qualified spiritually to be in that line? Each of us must ask himself, "Would I have been better qualified?"

Let us return to Rahab, the subject of our verse in Hebrews. We may question where she got her faith. The only plausible answer is, she got it from God Himself. Her people did not worship God, and they had only a hearsay knowledge of God from those who had been in contact with the Jews. But if we can believe what the Bible says about how He has revealed Himself to every person who has ever lived, it is easy to assure ourselves that God had revealed Himself to Rahab and caused her to put her trust in Him. The main passages I think of when I see God as revealing Himself to everyone are Ps.

---

[8]  S. Erlandsson, in his article on זָנָה in TDOT, Vol. IV, page 100.

19:1-4 and Rom. 1:18-23. Please study those two statements carefully.

Following these people just named and described in Heb. 11:3-31, we find a more brief kind of listing. The author mentions six more individuals by name, and then identifies groups of people by the ways they demonstrated their faith in Old Testament times. Through the remainder of the chapter, I will simply give their names and add the Old Testament passage where they are described, with a brief comment. You are encouraged to read those passages, to get the full impact of their faith.

**Heb. 11:32. And what more shall I say? I do not have time to tell about**

**Gideon.** He trusted in God, not in a few soldiers. Judges 6 to 8.

**Barak.** Deborah had more faith than he. Judges 4.

**Samson.** He was pretty sinful, but had great faith. Judges 13 to 16.

**Jephthah.** What a sad ending to a brilliant career! Judges 11 and 12.

**David.** I Samuel 16:1 to I Kings 2:12.

**Samuel.** I Samuel 1 to 25:1.

**the prophets.** Not just those who wrote Bible books. There are others scattered here and there, such as Huldah in II Kings 22:14-20.

**33. through faith conquered kingdoms.** David, many others.

**administered justice.** I Sam. 12:2-5.

**gained what was promised.** The Promised Land; children.

**shut the mouths of lions.** Daniel 6.

**34. quenched the fury of the flames.** Daniel 3, especially verse 17.

**escaped the edge of the sword.** Elijah: I Kings 17:7-14; 19:3, 10. Elisha: II Kings 6:13-23; 6:30-7:2.

**weakness was turned to strength.** Abraham: Rom. 4:18-21.

\* \* \*

became powerful in battle and routed foreign armies. Many stories throughout the Old Testament; see especially Ex. 17:8-14.

**35. Women received back their dead, raised to life again.** We may think of the widow of Zarephath's son: I Kings 17:7-24; Shunammite's son: II Kings 4:8-37.

**others were tortured and refused to be released, so that they might gain a better resurrection.** Eleazar the Scribe and seven sons of a woman: Old Testament Apocrypha II Maccabees 6:18-7:42. In this verse is an interesting contrast. Some people received back their dead by a kind of resurrection, while others refused to stay alive but chose to die for their faith, in order to receive a better resurrection.

**36. Some faced jeers and flogging, while still others were chained and put in prison.** Micaiah: I Kings 22:14, 26-27; Hanani the Seer: II Chron. 16:7-10, and II Chron. 36:16; Jeremiah: Jer. 20:2, 37:14-15, 38:6.

**37. They were stoned.** Zechariah: II Chron. 24:20-22.

**they were sawed in two.** II Kings 21:16 (the Palestinian Targum implies that this is how Isaiah died). See also II Sam. 12:31; I Chron. 20:3.

**they were put to death by the sword.** A group of people: I Kings 19:10; Uriah the Prophet: Jer. 26:23.

**They went about in sheepskins and goatskins, destitute, persecuted and mistreated....** Elijah: I Kings 19:13, 19.

**38. ...the world was not worthy of them. They wandered in deserts and mountains, and in caves and holes in the ground.** Read of the wanderings of Israel through the wilderness in Exodus, Leviticus, Numbers, and Deuteronomy; Elijah's flight from Jezebel: I Kings 19:1-14. There are many other stories in the Old Testament. The world was not worthy of them, nor is the world worthy of you today if you are willing to follow the Lord's drumbeat, which is different from the world's.

This ends the list of people of faith in Heb. 11.

**Heb. 11:39. These were all commended for their faith....** They were commended even in the Old Testament, at least by fellow believers. They were great examples of faith for us; let us ponder their lives, and seek to grow closer to the Lord, as they did.

**...yet none of them received what had been promised.**

What was in the minds of those Old Testament saints? Did they expect to receive "what had been promised" in this life? It is likely that they expected to receive at least some of those promises here. They also realized that they might not receive everything here, but that some would be reserved for them in eternity. Did they truly hear the promises of the new covenant? Surely they did; that is precisely what Hebrews is about.

**Heb. 11:40. God had planned something better for us....**
Here are some of the better things God had planned for us:

- A better Messenger than angels
- A better Intercessor than Moses
- A better High Priest than Aaron
- A better Tabernacle than the Tent
- A better Sacrifice than animals
- A better Covenant than the Law
- A better Promise than punishment
- A better Inheritance than the Promised Land

**...so that only together with us would they be made perfect.**

How is that so? Here is one way to see it. The Hebrew believers of the Old Testament who are the physical children of Abraham, and the Christians of the New Testament who are the spiritual children of Abraham, are all Children of Jesus and have been made One Chosen People. For evidence read Eph. 2:14-18:

> For [Christ] is our peace, who has made the two one and has destroyed the barrier, the dividing wall of hostility, by abolishing in his flesh the law with its commandments and regulations. His purpose was to create in himself one new man out of the two, thus making peace, and in this one body to reconcile both of them to God through the cross, by which he put to death their hostility. He came and preached peace to you who were far away and peace to those who were near. For through him we both have access to the Father by one Spirit.

Together we make up the whole number of God's elect. They could not be complete until we finally join them. We ought to be glad they were willing to wait, because conversely we could not be complete without them.

How does the theme of chapter 11 of Hebrews fit in with the rest of the book? That is, how does a list of faithful people of Old Testament times fill in a gap in the basic argument that Jesus and His ministry is better than the Old Testament ministry? I invite you to ponder that question and form an answer for yourself. My answer follows, but yours may be equally valid.

Faith is the element that links the ancient people of faith and us in a common bond of fellowship with God. No matter which covenant we lived under, it was one *faith* that saved us ("without faith it is impossible to please God," verse 6). So the faithful people of Old Testament times are an example and encouragement to us, to remain faithful through all persecutions, so that we, like them, will receive the eternal inheritance. In the next chapter of Hebrews, we shall see that they are watching us, and encouraging us.

# CHAPTER XII
## JESUS IS OUR BEST HOPE.  HEB. 12:1-29.

Many people have a fuzzy notion of what hope is, especially as distinguished from faith. Perhaps we ought not to make a large separation between the two. They both indicate one's expectation of what may come to pass.

To me there are four major components to hope. First, what is hoped for has the possibility of realization. In this matter we can see a difference between a dream and a hope. A dream is something we may wish for intensely, but we may realize there is no possibility for its fulfillment. But something we hope for must have something to give us a basis for expecting it to happen for us.

A second component of hope is that it is still in the future. If it were a present reality, it would be a sure thing, so there would be no need for hope.

Thirdly, we occasionally talk of some hope's being "dashed." In other words, what we had hoped for did not come to pass, nor will it happen. But when we have true hope, that hope is based on some tangible object, or the promise someone has made to us. Depending on our trust (or faith ) in the person or object, we expect to obtain that for which we hoped. Therefore, hope must have some basis; otherwise it is only a dream.

The final component of hope is that what is hoped for is something beneficial to the person who hopes. Surely you have heard someone say something like, "If I'm lying, I hope a lightning bolt will strike me dead on the spot." No person ever really "hopes" such a thing. If he is telling the truth, he does not need to say such a thing. If he is lying, he is sure it will not happen, or he would not want to think of it's happening. You may hope something ill will happen to someone else (but you should not); if you do, it still is a hope that the ill that happens to him will bring benefit to you.

It has been mentioned before that Hebrews 12 is called a chapter of hope, as part of the trilogy (faith, hope, and love) we find in 10:22-24 and expanded in chapters 11 to 13. Chapter 11 is well known as the great Faith Chapter of the Bible. The Love Chapter is I Cor. 13. I am not aware of any chapter known generally as the Hope Chapter. I would like to suggest some thoughts, and propose three candidates for the honor.

It may be that no chapter has been selected because the word "hope" is not emphasized in one place more than in others. Daniel J. Simundson[1] suggests that the Greek words for hope in the New Testament "are used widely in the epistles, rarely in the Gospels, and not at all in the book of Revelation. This shows clearly that hope may be expressed by a text (such as in the words of Jesus or in Revelation) even when the specific word for hope is not present." Only one chapter in the New Testament contains the Greek noun and verb for hope as many as six times; that is Romans 8.

[1]  In THE OXFORD COMPANION TO THE BIBLE, edited by Metzger and Coogan, page 289.

Here are the three chapters I nominate for consideration. The first is a pair of Psalms, the 42nd and 43rd, which together are meant to be one literary whole. The song expresses deep distress with a pitiable appeal to God for help, in three distinct stanzas. Each of the stanzas ends (42:5 and 11, and 43:5) with identical words:

Why are you downcast, O my soul?
Why so disturbed within me?
Put your hope in God,
for I will yet praise him,
my Savior and my God.

My second choice is Romans 8. The two first verses are a great declaration of hope in total forgiveness from God: "Therefore, there is now no condemnation for those who are in Christ Jesus, because through Christ Jesus the law of the Spirit of life set me free from the law of sin and death." Verse 11 assures us that we can hope in the resurrection of our bodies: "And if the Spirit of him who raised Jesus from the dead is living in you, he who raised Christ from the dead will also give life to your mortal bodies through his Spirit, who lives in you." Verse 18 expresses the hope that our suffering will one day be exchanged for glory: "I consider that our present sufferings are not worth comparing with the glory that will be revealed in us." Verses 20 and 21 contain the word "hope" in connection with our expectation that our moldering bodies will become free from corruption some day. Verse 24 contains the words for hope four times, after Paul has talked about our adoption as children of God and the redemption of our bodies. Verses 28 to 30 give a progression of things we may hope for: good things from God; our calling by Him; His foreknowledge of us, which leads to His predestinating us to become like the Son; from there God calls us, justifies us, and finally glorifies us. The last two verses, 38 and 39, provide a fitting climax to all the things for which we may hope:

For I am convinced that neither death nor life, neither angels nor demons,
neither the present nor the future, nor any powers, neither height nor depth,
nor anything else in all creation, will be able to separate us from the love of
God that is in Christ Jesus our Lord.

My final nomination for the position of the great Hope Chapter is Titus 2. Verses 13 and 14 are preceded by Paul's exhortation to live moral and godly lives, "while we wait for the blessed hope—the glorious appearing of our great God and Savior, Jesus Christ, who gave himself for us to redeem us from all wickedness and to purify for himself a people that are his very own, eager to do what is good." Many people speak of our hope of Christ's return as a great watershed of the whole message of the Bible. Truly, all we have to hope for hinges on whether He returns as expected; if He does not, all our hopes are dashed.

If I were to choose just one verse of hope from the New Testament, it would be the ending of Col. 1:27: "Christ in you, the hope of glory." For me that is an excellent summary of all we hope for as Christians.

I have no great preference for any of these passages; I hold them all as setting forth powerful hope for believers. If you may have a favorite chapter which verbalizes your hope for eternity, I would like to hear from you, with your reasons for it.

**Heb. 12:1. Therefore, since we are surrounded by such a great cloud of witnesses....**

Who are these witnesses? The author is beginning to paint a picture of an Olympic stadium. Surely the witnesses in the stands include all the people named or alluded to in chapter 11, the people of faith, while you and I who are yet alive in the world are the athletes participating in the games. In addition the cloud includes all the Old Testament saints the author of Hebrews did not mention. It is entirely possible the group includes all the saints who have lived since the time of Jesus as well, including all your loved ones who knew Christ as Savior and Lord and now are in His presence in heaven. It may give you joy to know that your mother or other loved one is aware of some great deed you have accomplished for God, and has seen it all happen. On the other hand, surely none of us is eager to think about the time we committed some vile sin that the same loved one has observed. Be sure that you cannot have it one way without the other. God does not draw the curtain on the observation tower when you do something you are ashamed of, and then reopen the curtain when you do something you know will please everyone.

If you recall you are being watched every moment—and you are—you will probably act differently. It is often said that your real character shows when you are alone. But if you should be aware every moment that the cloud of witnesses is watching, your actions and your thoughts probably would be quite different.

Be sure you realize that cloud of witnesses has earned the right to see us in all our activities. They were the faithful ones, who trusted in God when they dwelled on earth. Likewise, we have hope that one day we shall graduate from being athletes in the race to being witnesses of those who still run.

**...let us throw off everything that hinders and the sin that so easily entangles....**

Be sure to note there are two different things we are urged to discard: our "hindrances," and our "sin." Those two things are very different. It ought to be easy to see that we must shed our sin in order to be successful in our race. But why must we put from us the "hindrances"?

First, what are these hindrances? Let us be clear that he is not talking about sin, or he would not have mentioned them separately. Let us design an illustration. He is talking about a race in a stadium, as we see at the end of verse 1. We all know there is no rule against a participant's wearing a heavy overcoat and hip waders in a hundred yard dash. But it would be foolish to do so; a competitor could not hope to win. Almost nobody participates in a race without at least some hope of winning, or at least making a good show. Once a girl from South Africa ran in an Olympic race with no shoes on her feet to avoid such a slight "hindrance" of weight to her running.

If there are hindrances in an Olympic race, there are also hindrances in the spiritual race. Indulge me as I name a few hindrances, some of which may be burdening your life. You may think some things I mention are sins; if so, then to you they are sins (see James 4:17), and you should avoid them as sin. You may think that some of the things I will mention are so inconsequential that they cannot be considered "hindrances;" I urge you to review the possibility that they are keeping you from doing your best for the Lord. My short list includes these: smoking, drinking alcoholic beverages, watching TV, eating too much or too many non-nourishing foods, boasting of accomplishments you did not perform, attending too many Bible classes which keeps you from serving the Lord effectively. In I Cor. 7 Paul would add that getting married is a hindrance. You may want to add to or subtract from my list, but let me attempt a definition of hindrance. In the context we are talking about, hindrance is anything that prevents your full freedom to serve the Lord, even though it is not an actual sin.

Without question any sin hinders you from serving the Lord effectively. For a definition of sin, I appreciate this answer in the Westminster Shorter Catechism: "Sin is any transgression of, or want of conformity unto, the will of God." A very small beginning for a list of sins is the Ten Commandments. A little thought reminds you that all of those commandments are negative except one; they tell us things we are forbidden to do. The catechism definition contains two parts: sin is not only a "transgression of" the will of God, or doing things contrary to what God wants us to do; sin also is a failure to do anything God has commanded us to do. Our thoughts must delve even deeper. In the negative sense, if we think of the Ten Commandments in the manner we ordinarily do, we miss their more extensive implications. Recall how Jesus interpreted several of those commandments in His Sermon on the Mount, especially in Matt. 5:21-48. For instance, He said that if you call your brother a fool, you have committed a sin worse than murdering him. Likewise, if you so much as look on a woman to desire her sexually, you have already committed adultery with her and deserve punishment for that sin. We see the result of that sin, in James 1:15, "...after desire has conceived, it gives birth to sin; and sin, when it is full-grown, gives birth to death."

In the positive sense of God's will, He gives us directions in scripture for all we must do in a general way, but He also gives us specific directions as individuals regarding our career, our family, our lifestyle, our acts of evangelism and almsgiving.

At this point you may think it is an impossible task to remember all the commandments and prohibitions we find in scripture, not to mention all God's directives we receive through prayer and guidance of the Holy Spirit. But the task is really not so overwhelming when we remember the summary Jesus gave us in His conversation with the legalist Pharisee found in Matt. 22:34-40. There He told us we must love God with our whole beings, and love our neighbor at least as much as we love ourselves. We must be sure to remember that love is not just a statement, "I love you," but actions filled with love and motivated by love. Further, let us not fall into a common trap of our generation, in which some people claim Jesus was saying we must be sure to love ourselves and then we can love our neighbor. It is never necessary to worry about loving ourselves; Paul told us in Eph. 5:29, "...no one ever hated his own body, but he feeds and cares for it, just as Christ does the church...." Jesus completed his instruction to the Pharisee with the words, "All the Law and the Prophets hang on these two commandments," so you see that you do not need to memorize books filled with directions to lead a life pleasing to God; just love Him totally, and love your neighbor (even the "Samaritan" in your life, see Lu. 10:25-37) without worrying about whether you are loving yourself enough. Paul regarded the matter of loving one's neighbor so highly that he said the same thing in two of his letters: Rom. 13:8-10, and Gal. 5:13-15. John Stott, the great English theologian-Pastor, said, "The local church cannot evangelize, proclaiming the gospel of love, if it is not itself a community of love."[2]

The author said that sin "so easily entangles" us. You probably have writhed in anguish after committing a sin, as you remember the incidents that led you to the final act. As we review our lives, we recognize that a large sin begins as a very small, seemingly insignificant temptation; if we succumb to it, it grows in enormity until the situation is totally unmanageable—or so it seems. It is like the first taste of beer, wine, or champagne. When I was a small boy, my mother hesitated to let me lick the spoon from the lemon extract she had put into a cake for fear I would get the taste of alcohol and want more. She often told me, "Tommy, if you never take the first drink, you will never take the drink that makes you a drunkard." Recovering alcoholics never fully recover, but they always rue the day they took their first drink. And one drink while they are recovering usually sets them off on another binge that is harder to escape. We find this truth set forth in James 1:15, "Then, after desire has conceived, it gives birth to sin; and sin, when it is full-grown, gives birth to death."

**...and let us run with perseverance the race marked out for us.**

"Perseverance" is a little-used word today. According to Thayer, its Greek counterpart ὑπομονη, means steadfastness, constancy, endurance.

[2]    John Stott, in an interview by Gary Barnes in the article, "Why Don't They Listen?" in CHRISTIANITY TODAY, September 2003, page 52.

Hauck[3] indicates that one of its meanings in the Old Testament LXX is "hope," the subject of this chapter of Hebrews. He adds, "Job is an example of pious endurance." In the New Testament, Hauck says that in II Thess. 3:5 the word is "the expectation of the Christ who will come again in glory." And in this verse in Hebrews Hauck says the word "reminds us of the tense perseverance to victory which is necessary if the prize is to be won." You have probably heard of athletes who have retched just before beginning a race, because they are so intent on winning that their whole bodies are affected. Certainly we need not become physically ill in order to run our spiritual race, but we ought to consider that most of us, most of the time, are far too complaisant in our effort to please God continually. I suppose most athletes try to avoid thinking of the day they must retire; but we who have hope in Christ's return for us long for the day when we can graduate from this arena and join the cloud of witnesses in the heavens.

An ever-present problem during the running of our race is the sight of roadblocks we encounter on the racecourse. Such roadblocks may be set there by Satan to try to avert us from attaining the goal; or they may be tests by God to see whether we will persevere; or they may be signs to indicate to us that He wants us to do something different. How are we to discover the reason for those roadblocks, in order to deal with them? There are two things we must do: read the Bible more diligently to learn and apply God's general rules for our lives; and be more earnest in our prayers, so that the Holy Spirit can guide us in what He wants us to do. If you are willing to do those two things, you may be fully assured that God will make His will clear. Years ago, Donald Grey Barnhouse told of a young Christian lady, dressed in her wedding gown, riding in the back seat of the limousine to church to marry a man she knew she should not be linked to because he was not a Christian. On the way to the church, she prayed that the Lord would get her involved in an auto wreck so she could not marry the man if He did not want her to be married. Barnhouse bellowed, "*Of course* there was no auto wreck. The girl need not have prayed. God's word was utterly clear to her, and she remembered it, 'Be not unequally yoked with an unbeliever'" (II Cor. 6:14). That may not be sufficient evidence for some of you. You may ask, "What does that verse really mean?" When asked that question in a Bible class, Virgil McAnally, a Minister and fine Bible teacher, used to reply, "What are you *afraid* it means?"

Each of us must run the race "marked out for us." No two people have ever had identical races to run. In the arena, some people run the hundred yard dash, others run the mile, some do the broad jump and others the high jump or pole vault, some throw the javelin or do the hammer toss or throw the discus. God designs each race for your capabilities and for the particular goals He wants you to attain. No one else in the world can tell you what is God's will

---

[3] F. Hauck's article on ὑπομονη, in TDNT, Vol. IV, pages 583-588.

for your life; no one ought to try to force you to do exactly what he is doing. You cannot do it. You may ask assistance from a Christian in whom you have confidence to help you in guidance from the word of God, and to pray with you. But ultimately God alone should direct you in your racetrack. And while you are racing, seek not the fame or prizes of the world, but only the "Christian of a Lifetime" award from the Lord.

There are three stories in the Bible which make it clear that you ought not obey the directive of any other person, just because he claims to be a Christian and to have received a message from the Lord to give to you. The first story (I Kings 13) is of the young prophet who traveled from Judah to Bethel to speak against King Jeroboam. After giving his message, the young man started for home. An old man of God met him and invited him to come home with him to eat and rest. The young man demurred, saying God had clearly told him to go straight home without stopping for anything. The old prophet disagreed, saying that God had given him a message to tell the young man to come home with him, so the young fellow acquiesced. As he ate, the old man prophesied, saying that because he had disobeyed the direct order of God and had listened to the old man instead, he would die along the way. The young man was frightened and started home quickly. But it was too late. He had already disobeyed God, and God caused a lion to kill him.

The second story is of another prophet named Micaiah. It is found in I Kings 22. King Ahab of Israel and King Jehoshaphat of Judah sent for him to ask him whether they would win a battle the next day. The messengers told Micaiah that all four hundred of the prophets of Baal had with one accord predicted the kings would win, and that he would be wise to do the same. But Micaiah refused, saying, "As surely as the LORD lives, I can tell him only what the LORD tells me" (verse 14). So instead of agreeing with the false prophets, Micaiah predicted that King Ahab would die the next day in battle, and that is what happened.

The third instance indicating that no person should obey the directive of another even though he is an earnest Christian, is the story of Paul who met friends on the way to Jerusalem before his imprisonment and journey to Rome to be put to death there. We read about it in Acts 20 and 21. Paul tells some disciples of the message he had received directly from the Holy Spirit, in Acts 20:22-23: "And now, compelled by the Spirit, I am going to Jerusalem, not knowing what will happen to me there. I only know that in every city the Holy Spirit warns me that prison and hardships are facing me." But in Acts 21:4, we read of some disciples in Tyre who even "through the Spirit they urged Paul not to go on to Jerusalem." Later, in Caesarea, a prophet of God named Agabus bound his own hands and feet with Paul's belt and predicted, "The Holy Spirit says, 'In this way the Jews of Jerusalem will bind the owner of this belt and will hand him over to the Gentiles'" (21:11). The disciples in the group earnestly begged Paul not to go to Jerusalem, but Paul knew what the Holy Spirit had told him directly, and answered (verse 13), "Why are you weeping and breaking my heart? I am ready not only to be bound, but also to die in Jerusalem for the name of the Lord Jesus." In the next verse, we read that the disciples stopped pleading and said, "The Lord's will be done."

**Heb. 12:2. Let us fix our eyes on Jesus, the author and perfecter of our faith....**

> Turn your eyes upon Jesus,
> Look full in His wonderful face;
> And the things of earth will grow strangely dim
> In the light of His glory and grace.

So wrote the hymnwriter. Remember Peter, who began to sink in the water when he diverted his eyes from Jesus to the waves around him (Matt. 14:25-33). Jesus may have been "despised and rejected by men" because His "appearance was disfigured" and His "form was marred" (Is. 52:14 and 53:3); but according to another hymnwriter He was "sweeter than ten thousand." For an exquisite word-picture of Jesus as seen by the spiritual eyes of one who loves and adores Him above anyone or anything else in the universe, read the poem Solomon wrote about Him in Song of Solomon 5:10-16.

The author of Hebrews next describes Jesus as the "author and perfecter" of our faith. There are several parallel allusions to this description of Jesus in other parts of scripture. In order to identify and understand them we must refer to their Greek words and related Greek words, and related Hebrew words as well from the Old Testament. First, the Greek word for "Author" used here is ἀρχηγός, and the Greek for "Perfecter" is τελειωτής. Two similar Greek words are used in Rev. 21:6, where Jesus said to John, "It is done. I am the Alpha and the Omega, the Beginning and the End." You probably know that "Alpha" is the first letter of the Greek alphabet (that is why we call it the *al-pha*bet), and the last Greek letter is "omega." Those two Greek letters look like A and Ω. When Jesus said "I am the Alpha and the Omega," that statement looks like this in the Greek: ἐγώ [εἰμι] τὸ Ἄλφα καί τὸ Ὦ. Immediately after that Jesus said ἡ ἀρχὴ καὶ τὸ τέλος. Surely you can recognize the similarity between Ἄλφα, the first letter of the alphabet, and ἀρχὴ, the "Beginning", and ἀρχηγός, the "Author." Similarly, you can see the similarity between τέλος, the "End," and τελειωτής, the "Perfecter," although there is no similarity between the Greek τέλος, the "End," and Ω, the "Omega" or the last letter of the Greek alphabet.

There is one more connection between these sets of Greek words and a set of Hebrew words, which may be significant. In the wilderness, Moses was commanded to make the Tabernacle and all its accessories strictly according to the pattern God gave him from heaven. We read about this in Ex. 25-40. Among the accessories were the special articles of clothing for Aaron and his sons the priests. The description of these articles begins in Ex. 28. There we read of two special elements, the ephod and the breastpiece, which were to be tied together inseparably and worn by the priest as he ministered before God. On the ephod was a pair of precious stones, on which were written the names of the twelve tribes of Israel, as a remembrance before God. Likewise, on the breastpiece were two objects (never described in scripture, but possibly two other precious stones), also to be worn by the priest whenever he ministered before God. The two objects on the breastpiece were called the "Urim" and the "Thummim" (first mentioned in Ex. 28:30). What interests me about these two objects is that the Hebrew word for "Urim" is אוּרִים, whose first letter א is the first letter of the Hebrew alphabet, just like "alpha" is the first letter of the Greek alphabet. Urim is a noun derived from the Hebrew verb אוֹר, which means "to be or become light." The other object, "Thummim," is the Hebrew word תֻּמִּים, whose first letter ת (tau) is the last letter of the Hebrew alphabet, just like "omega" is the last letter of the Greek alphabet. Thummim is a noun from the Hebrew verb תָּמַם, which means "to be complete or finished."

My strong suggestion from all this is twofold. First, since Jesus is the Alpha and Omega (the first and last Greek letters) of the New Testament, and since the Urim and Thummim (beginning with the first and last Hebrew letters) of the Old Testament, then the high priest in Old Testament times wore on his breast the symbols which represent Jesus Christ in His fullness whenever the priest ministered for the people before God. Secondly, since the Urim means "light" and Thummim means "completeness" and "perfection," then Jesus was ever present with the ancient Hebrew people to enlighten their ways and doings, and to complete and perfect their lives, if they were willing to follow His leading. His presence was made known to them by means of the Urim and Thummim which the high priest always wore when he ministered on their behalf.

Jesus is called the Author and Perfecter of our faith. You may have thought you gendered faith in your heart and mind by your own volition. From your point of view that may be so, since it is likely that your faith was not forced upon you, like Paul's was on the road to Damascus. But in a greater reality, Jesus Himself, the Object of your faith, imparted your faith to you, since He is the "Author" of your faith. And because He is the "Perfecter" of your faith, He will "perfect" (in the KJV) it until the day of Christ Jesus.[4]

### ...who for the joy set before him endured the cross, scorning its shame....

What was it that brought Jesus joy? Was it His absolute knowledge that, although He faced the cross, He would rise from the dead? Surely that brought joy to Him, but that was only part of the reason He had joy. Did His joy emanate from His assurance that His death on the cross was providing salvation to us? Again, He must have been joyful over that accomplishment. I

---

[4] Phil. 1:6.

believe His greatest joy came from the thrust of His whole life. Recall that He said when He was born, "I have come to do your will, O God" (Heb. 10:7). His joy was not fully realized before He faced the cross, but he had sufficient joy to be able to "endure the cross."

Here is an additional indication in Heb. 12 that we might have hope. If Jesus had joy in His suffering for our sakes, then we may have joy in our sufferings resulting from our living for Him.

Jesus "scorned" the shame of the cross. The Greek word used for "scorned" can have meanings as strong as despising and disdaining or as weak as belittling or not to be afraid of. Two different English versions of Matt. 18:10 translate the Greek word in the two extremes. The KJV reads, "Take heed that ye despise not one of these little ones....." Our NIV says, "See that you do not look down on one of these little ones."

It was the "shame" of the cross that Jesus scorned, more perhaps than the physical pain the cross would bring. Was Jesus put to shame by the cross? First and foremost, each of us must remember that it is I, it is you, who have put Jesus to shame. Turn to Heb. 6:6, and our discussion there, in which the author says that whenever we fall away from righteousness (that is, whenever we commit even the smallest sin), we are "crucifying the Son of God all over again and subjecting him to public disgrace." That "public disgrace" is explained by Paul, when in Gal. 3:13 he quotes Deut. 21:23, "Cursed is everyone who is hung on a tree." (The cross if often referred to simply as a "tree.") And how could we forget the famous words in Is. 53:3?

> He was despised and rejected by men,
> a man of sorrows, and familiar with suffering.
> Like one from whom men hide their faces
> he was despised, and we esteemed him not.

### ...and sat down at the right hand of the throne of God.

This is the third time the author of Hebrews says this of Jesus. First is 1:3, "After he had provided purification for sins, he sat down at the right hand of the Majesty in heaven." Next is 10:12, contrasting the priests' daily sacrifices with the one sacrifice of Jesus: "But when this priest had offered for all time one sacrifice for sins, he sat down at the right hand of God." Finally, here in 12:2, the author speaks again of Jesus' single sacrifice: He "endured the cross, scorning its shame, and sat down at the right hand of the throne of God." Would that each of us would hope to hear something similar of us: "When he or she had run with patience the race, he or she entered God's *rest*."

### Heb. 12:3. Consider him who endured such opposition from sinful men....

The author says the "opposition from sinful men" is worth thinking about. Was there opposition to Jesus? Even if there was, has it not ended, so there is nothing for us to consider any more?

First, there is no doubt that Jesus suffered great opposition. You may turn to almost any page of the Gospels, and you will see "opposition" from the Pharisees, Sadducees, the Jews in general, the Gentiles, and even from His own disciples and apostles, among whom was Judas who betrayed Him. The opposition did not end at the end of biblical times, however. The Church, the body of Christ, has been persecuted in every generation since Jesus' death, before Paul's attempts to imprison or kill as many Christians as he could find in Jerusalem, Damascus, and wherever he could go, until Christ turned him around and made him one of the greatest spokesman for the Savior. Read about it in the book of Acts. Opposition to Jesus continues today; read your own diary for evidence.

If Jesus endured all that opposition, which is still not ended, the next important question is, will *you* be willing to endure similar opposition when you seek to stand up for Him in your daily life? The question has been asked, "If you were accused in court of being a Christian, would there be enough evidence to convict you?" Your willingness to endure opposition is really what the author of Hebrews is driving at. Evidence is found in the very next clause.

### ...so that you will not grow weary and lose heart.

Jesus is our Great Example. Evangelical Christians do not like to say that, or even hear it. Many people admit that Jesus is an example for us all, but they are unwilling to proceed beyond that to acknowledge that Jesus, more than merely an example, is the Remedy for our sinfulness and lost state. However, it is not wrong to say that Jesus is our Great Example, because Jesus said it of Himself (John 13:15), "I have set you an example...." Jesus was speaking specifically of washing one another's feet. But we should consider Him as our example of living by helping the poor, healing, teaching, doing miracles—yes even miracles, because He told us, "I tell you the truth, anyone who has faith in me will do what I have been doing. He will do even greater things than these, because I am going to the Father" (John 14:12).

There is just one thing we cannot do, no matter how hard we try to follow Jesus' example: we can never save another person from punishment for his sin; we can only die for our own sins, and we will unless we receive Christ as the One who died for us. The apostle Paul said that he would like to die for the sins of his people the Jews (Rom. 9:3), although he knew his desire was futile. Instead, Paul urged us not to lose heart, in Gal. 6:9: "Let us not become weary in doing good, for at the proper time we will reap a harvest if we do not give up." He said the same thing to the people in Thessalonica, in II Thess. 3:13: "As for you, brothers, never tire of doing what is right." It will be much easier for us to persevere in our lives for Christ if we remember what He has done already for us. If we do not flag in our enduring suffering for Christ's sake we can have hope to gain the reward.

\* \* \*

**Heb. 12:4. In your struggle against sin, you have not yet resisted to the point of shedding your blood.**

This statement follows the theme of verse 3, where we read that Jesus endured the ultimate pain for you and me—such pain cannot be described, or understood by our limited human minds. In this verse, the author points out that neither you nor I have come anywhere near the tribulation Jesus suffered for us. He gives us two ideas by which to contrast Jesus' suffering with ours. First, he willingly acknowledges that we have "struggled against sin;" he does not dispute that. But our struggle is infinitesimally small compared to that of our Savior. Secondly, the author shows that our struggle against sin categorically fails to match what Jesus endured. Jesus shed His blood, all of it, for us; we have yet to shed one drop to avoid our own sins.

This statement appears in the form of a question in a few ancient manuscripts of the Greek: "In your struggle...have you resisted...?" The question implies a negative answer, just as our text indicates.

If we have "not yet" resisted by shedding our blood, does this mean that there is a future, greater struggle we must face? Our answer to that question ought to be "no," because Jesus has already gone to the extreme for us. Struggle on, yes; but die for our sins, no. Thanks be to our Savior, that has been done for us!

**Heb. 12:5. And you have forgotten....**

This statement, like the one preceding, is also posed as a question in some manuscripts: "Have you forgotten...?" In the form of a question, the idea is set forth more gently than as a statement.

**...that word of encouragement that addresses you as sons....**

In reading what the author of Hebrews wrote here, try to remember that this is a word of *encouragement*. Often people take the words of another person the wrong way. To avoid this error, we ought to be sensitive to the speaker's or writer's orientation lest we misjudge our informant.

Here is an example of what I mean. One day in the church office a lady gave a sizable handout to a beggar who I knew had no need to beg, because he was receiving substantial aid from more than one source regularly. In order to compensate the lady, I asked the church secretary to send a check from the Pastor's Special Fund to the lady for the amount she gave. After she had received it, the lady told me in strong language, "You insulted me by giving back that money!" My response was, "It is clear that you are insulted by what I did, but I did not insult you. On the contrary, I was attempting to do for you what was, through my knowledge of the situation, correct and gracious."

What God does for us may upset us on occasion. But we should be encouraged by everything God does, because He does it for our ultimate good.

Proverbs 3:11-12 is quoted next in Hebrews to express God's lovingkindness:

**My son, do not despise the LORD's discipline
and do not resent his rebuke,
because the LORD disciplines those he loves,
as a father the son he delights in.**

Although the words in Hebrews 12:5-6 are slightly different, the sentiment is the same. Moses agreed in Deut. 8:5, "Know then in your heart that as a man disciplines his son, so the LORD your God disciplines you." Remember, the author is talking about your *not* having resisted sin sufficiently (proved by the fact that you have not resisted to blood as Jesus did). Our NIV translation of "despise" is "make light of," which is not as strong as the word used in Proverbs, but follows more closely the meaning of the Greek word, ὀλιγωρέω, a word used only here in the New Testament, and basically means "to care little for, regard lightly, make small account of."[5] In other words, we ought not to dismiss as meaningless what the Lord does to us by way of punishment when we sin against Him. It is bad enough that we really have not tried hard enough to resist our sin in the first place. But to discount in the slightest God's reaction to our sin is to multiply our sin manifold. When our son David was four years old, he did something that displeased his mother, so she spanked him until she got weary. When she let go his arm, he looked up at her without a tear in his eye, and said, "That didn't hurt!" and walked away. You can imagine how his mother felt, which is a small example of how God reacts to us when we "make light of" His punishments.

I think of three possible kinds of reaction to God's discipline. We might have hurt feelings that he spoiled our fun; we might lash out at Him in anger for interfering with us; or we might dismiss whatever He did with an "I don't care" attitude. There is a fourth possible reaction, which is expressed in the author's next clause:

**...and do not lose heart when he rebukes
you....**

That fourth reaction is "I give up. I can never please God." That kind of discouragement came to me when I was about fourteen. We were sitting at the lunch table at home, when without any introduction my mother changed the subject and said to me, "Tommy, your father and I have decided not to spank you any more." When I heard those words I was elated, thinking that I finally had become good enough that they believed I no longer needed to be punished. Immediately however, she burst my euphoric bubble by adding, "We think you are too old to spank any more, so we have decided that we will punish you in other ways when you do something wrong." Upon hearing those words I was devastated. I thought to myself, "I still have not become good enough for my parents to think I need no more punishment." Some time after that I became even more despondent as I thought to myself, "If my

---

[5] Thayer's definition.

parents, who themselves are imperfect, still think I am not good enough to avoid punishment, then what does God, who is utterly perfect, think of me when He sees me do wrong?" That despondency lasted for longer than I care to remember, until one day I thought of the fact that Jesus shed His blood to pay for my sins so that I can still go to heaven just by receiving Him as my Savior. In addition, whatever "punishment" I receive in this life is as nothing compared to what I justly deserve for my sins.

In considering the things for which we may hope as expressed in this chapter of Hebrews, we ought to be glad we can hope to receive great benefit from God's chastening.

### Heb. 12:6.
#### ...because the Lord disciplines those he loves....

If the Lord disciplines us even though He loves us—perhaps *because* He loves us—then we who are parents ought to be willing to discipline our children if we truly love them. Unfortunately, many parents today seem to think just the opposite: if they truly love their children they will never discipline them or let them think they have done anything amiss, lest the children think they are not loved. The trend away from discipline or even instruction in righteousness seems to grow more universal day by day. In Sweden, a parent can be put in prison for spanking his own child. The trend in America is at least as bad: teens no longer need to tell their parents if they get pregnant, or if they want an abortion. A high school girl once told me that the school nurse offered her condoms and said, "It's all right to have sex with boys, if you want to. It's no different from going skiing, or doing anything else you want to do." Ask James Dobson about the trend of teaching our youth are receiving from both schools and parents these days. He has written books on the subject, given lectures, and supported his radio and television ministry to try to stem the tide, but nothing seems to avail.

If you are unsure about this matter of discipline, you need not go to James Dobson or to me; go to God. He tells it like it is right here, and throughout His word. Read it; absorb it; heed it in all you do.

#### ...and he punishes everyone he accepts as a son.

If you are disciplined by God, and are reasonably sure it is He who is doing the punishing, then you can be certain that you are one of His children; otherwise, He would not care about you or try to bring you closer to Himself. It is likely that you never spanked a child who lives down the street from you, for two good reasons: first, he is not your responsibility; and secondly, you do not care as much about his welfare or future as you do about your own child's. I admit I spanked my own children; I did so because I loved them. When I was a child and my parents disciplined me, I wasn't always sure they

429

loved me. But now that I am a parent, all doubt of their love has evaporated from my mind. Now that my children are grown and parents themselves, I am sure they are aware that I always loved them, and punished them when I thought punishment was good for them and ultimately would make them happier people. Once I boasted in a sermon to a congregation when the Minister was away, that I did spank my children when they were young, and I thought they turned out pretty good for it. I further boasted that I would be glad to compare my children with those of any parents who never disciplined their children. To my dismay, that sermon was very poorly received by most of the congregation. On thinking about the matter, I thought that those parents were the ones who needed discipline, self-discipline, in order to be willing to discipline their children when they knew they needed it.

### Heb. 12:7. Endure hardship as discipline; God is treating you as sons.

Remember that the word "son" or "sons" stands for the generic "children." The author of Hebrews was not excluding daughters; nor did the translators. They were using the common grammar, which is still proper.

Discipline takes many forms. It is not always what we might call "punishment." Sometimes it is hard to remember that God's hand is in everything that happens to us. It may be in the form of a broken leg just before acting in the school play; the death of a husband in mid-career. Once my father (who never worked on Sundays except to do the absolutely necessary chores of feeding the animals and milking the cows) cut the wheat on Sunday to harvest it before the rain came. However, he was not able to shock the bundles before the rain did come, and the grain on the ground rotted. I believe that was not just a "hardship" on my father, but also God's "discipline" to remind him of the Sabbath law.

In all this, we must remember that God is treating us as "sons;" nor should we forget that this is the way we ought to treat our own children.

### For what son is not disciplined by his father?

This statement tells it "the way it ought to be," but these days we are finding it more difficult to observe it as fact. Since we are living in this generation, we may have trouble knowing for sure how preceding generations lived. It is likely that our ancestors looked around their communities and found parents who failed to discipline their children, and thought the world was coming to an end because of it.

Even lions cuff their whelps. It may be only humans who have abandoned the natural tendency to discipline our children. The Greek language has a word for this natural tendency. That Greek word is one of four which express different kinds of love. The greatest and strongest kind of love is ἀγάπη, which is the kind of love God had for the world in giving His Son to be our

Savior. It is a selfless, unconditional love, asking nothing in return for the expressions of love made. Another kind of love in Greek is φίλος (as in *Phil*-adelphia), which we might call friendship-love. That kind of love says, "I'll be your friend as long as you are my friend." What is probably the lowest order of love in Greek is ἔρος, or erotic love, which more often is a self-love, merely using other people for one's own gratification. But between erotic love and friendship-love is the fourth kind of love, στόργη, which is the kind a parent has for a child which is reciprocated by the child. It is something ingrained in a person, virtually unavoidable, abandoned only by the tiniest number of people. That Greek word is not used in the New Testament, but the related opposite word, ἄστοργος, is found in Rom. 1:31 and II Tim. 3:3. Our NIV translates the former as "heartless," and the latter as "without love." The KJV expresses the distinction of this kind of love better by using the term "without natural affection" in both places. So we who are children are disciplined by God because as our Father He loves us with a filial love whose expression is demanded by His familial relationship to us. This is not to say that the Father does not love us with the ἀγάπη kind of love; that Greek word is used in verse 6, in the quotation from Proverbs.

**Heb. 12:8. If you are not disciplined (and everyone undergoes discipline), then you are illegitimate children and not true sons.**

The Greek word for "illegitimate" is νόθος, which can be used of a child born illegally, as one born out of wedlock, or born of a concubine, or of a slave. The older English word, used in the KJV, is "bastard," which today is seldom used in polite company but is the technically correct term.

Much agony has come into the world from the acts of fathers who sire children who were conceived through disobedience to God's word and will. Perhaps the most egregious example of this is the case of Abraham's bringing forth a son of Sarah's Egyptian servant-girl. Even before her son Ishmael was born, Sarah drove Hagar away (Gen. 16:6). Also, after Sarah's son Isaac was born, she saw Ishmael mocking, so Sarah demanded that Abraham send him away with his mother (Gen. 21:8-14). So there was enmity between the mothers of Ishmael and Isaac to begin with, and the angel of the Lord predicted that their descendants would be in conflict throughout history (Gen. 16:12):

> [Ishmael] will be a wild donkey of a man;
> > his hand will be against everyone
> > and everyone's hand against him,
> and he will live in hostility
> > toward all his brothers.

We ought not to be surprised, then, when we hear continually of bitter conflict between the Israelis and the Palestinians today (the day I write this, the day you read it, and into the future as long as the world exists). God had foretold the unending conflict between Israelite and Arab, so no one will be able to stop it, although it is honorable to seek peace in the Mideast. Even the apostle Paul said it would be so. In his allegory of the children born of the bond woman and of the free woman in Gal. 4:21-31, he wrote in verse 29, "At that time the son born in the ordinary way persecuted the son born by the power of the Spirit. It is the same now."

The author adds, "everyone undergoes discipline." In one way or another, it happens in the world. If your parents do not fulfill their obligations of natural love, and fail to discipline you gently when you are a child, then society is bound to discipline you more harshly as an adult—with fines, jail sentences, and perhaps the electric chair. Be fairly warned therefore, parents; show true love to your children by imposing just and loving discipline, so that they may become happy adults.

A great hope is hinted at in these words. We hope to receive tangible evidence that we are children of God, even beyond the promises we read in scripture. Another hope hinges on that: the hope that we are heirs together with Christ of all things, as Paul related in Rom. 8:17: "Now if we are children, then we are heirs—heirs of God and co-heirs with Christ, if indeed we share in his sufferings in order that we may also share in his glory."

**Heb. 12:9.   Moreover, we have all had human fathers who disciplined us and we respected them for it.**

Parental discipline is true, at least in general, and comes about naturally. My parents disciplined me, and I respected them for it, for the most part. There were occasions when they punished me and I thought I did not deserve it; but there were many more occasions when I knew I should have been punished but escaped their notice. I trust you can see that it was easy for me both to love my parents for all they did for me, and respect them for seeking to train me through discipline. When I thought of their discipline as punishment, my emotions toward them ran deeper than mere respect; I feared them for what could happen to me for my disobedience. Even my fear could not squelch my love for them.

**How much more should we submit to the Father of our spirits, and live!**

Our earthly fathers gave us physical life (by God's grace), but it is God who gives us spiritual life through our trust in Jesus as our Savior. Keep that thought in mind as you consider how much more important it is for us to submit to God's discipline and respect Him for giving it than we did to our earthly fathers.

Here God is called the "Father of our spirits." The Greek word for "our" is not found in this sentence, but some scholars believe it is implied by the definite article which is included. Certainly God's parenthood is not limited to us alone; the creation is filled with spirits, beginning with the Third

Person of the Trinity, and including angels and other spirit beings, both those who have bodies like ourselves, and those who have no physical bodies like angels. God is the Father of all things, and deserves to be honored as such by what He has created.

**Heb. 12:10. Our fathers disciplined us for a little while as they thought best....**

Two new thoughts about discipline are added here. The first thought is that our earthly parents' discipline was truncated, limited ordinarily from our birth to age eighteen or so. Of course some parents try to keep their apron strings attached to their children for many more years, but in nearly every case it is a bad practice. It is natural for children to grow into independence from parental care, and if anything blocks that natural tendency, the children are at best emotionally ill. On the other hand, God's discipline continues without interruption throughout this life. I am not sure whether our relationship to God should be called that of discipline when we get to heaven. We still will be under God's absolute lordship. But since we will be perfectly obedient, what we call discipline may be no longer existent. One of my great hopes is that I will be so righteous in heaven that God will not need to discipline me.

The second thought in this clause is that our parents' discipline was imperfect; they disciplined us "as they thought best." Let us be sure to give them credit: in virtually every case our parents really wanted what was best for us, and made every effort to provide it. However, they were fallible humans, so on occasion they made mistakes when they disciplined us. They may have disciplined us too harshly, or too gently. They sometimes disciplined us for something they thought was wrong but was not. Other times they failed to discipline us for something that deserved punishment.

**...but God disciplines us for our good, that we may share in his holiness.**

I have already stated that God's discipline is not flawed like that of our earthly fathers. But the important matter in this verse is that God does not discipline us merely to punish us for disobedience. His purpose always is to bring us good. Probably one of the best-known verses in scripture to say that is Rom. 8:28: "We know that in all things God works for the good of those who love him, who have been called according to his purpose." This is true for you only under both of two conditions: first, you must love God with your whole being; and secondly, you must make every effort to obey Him so He can fulfill His purpose in you. In times of loss, pain, sorrow, are you able to accept this as factual? When a terrible disease comes upon you, can you agree that God brought it upon you in order to bless you? Many people try to excuse God's complicity in our tragedies by saying "God had nothing to do with it." But if God cannot control your setbacks, then why do you think

He is able to bring blessing to you when you seek it? The middle of the Lord's Prayer reminds us that both are true: "Give us this day our daily bread...deliver us from evil."

When God disciplines us, we hope to receive two kinds of blessings from Him. The first blessing is indicated by the Greek term συμφέρον, which means what is helpful, profitable, or expedient;[6] but basically it has to do with material gain or well-being. In other words, we can hope to receive tangible rewards as a result of God's discipline.

The second blessing noted here is ἁγιότης, a word used only once in the New Testament, and means sanctity or holiness.[7] This blessing is of a purely spiritual quality, as the first was solely material. This is spiritual and/or moral good or well-being. But it is more than that; it is *God's* holiness of which we partake. There can be none better than that. John said it well in I John 3:2-3, "We know that when [Jesus] appears, we shall be like him, for we shall see him as he is. Everyone who has this hope in him purifies himself, just as he is pure." In quoting this we must remind ourselves that it is not we who purify ourselves as it is that we allow God to purify us with His own purity or holiness.

### Heb. 12:11. No discipline seems pleasant at the time, but painful.

How true this is! None of us likes to be disciplined, for several reasons. For one, it shows that we did something wrong. For another, we never like to have our faults exposed to public view; it embarrasses us. And as the author implies, discipline is painful, often physically as well as emotionally. For these and other reasons we like to avoid discipline whenever possible. If we could live more in harmony with God's will for us, we could avoid much discipline.

### Later on, however, it produces a harvest of righteousness and peace for those who have been trained by it.

Too many people live too much in the present. We are like the monkey who sticks his hand in the small hole in the coconut-trap and will not let go of the fistful of raisins even though he probably knows he will get caught. So, too often we try to avoid discipline by telling a lie to escape from the punishment due a previous sin, only to discover too late that we will be punished for both the sin and the falsehood.

It may be that some people think the punishment's pain is a good trade for the pleasure derived from committing the sin—and surely that is true too often in our human relations. If we reason this way, we ought to ask ourselves whether the pain of God's punishment is worth the "fun" of our sin. When we realize, however, that the only punishment God has set for all sin is

[6] Thayer's definitions.
[7] *Loc. cit.*

spiritual, eternal death, then we ought to take a hard look at whatever sin we want to commit, to decide whether such punishment is worth the transitory pleasure derived from that small sin.

This, however, is not really what the author of Hebrews is saying. Rather, he is talking about sins we have already committed, for which God has already disciplined us—not with spiritual death but some temporal hurt to wake us up to our sinful state. What we must ask ourselves in that case is how we plan to react to that earthly discipline. Do we shake our fists at God for catching us as well as for imposing pain for our sin? The author says that should be far from our response to God's loving discipline. Instead, we should look gladly and eagerly for the "harvest of righteousness and peace" which follows the discipline. Then the question becomes, do we want to reap a dual harvest of righteousness and peace?

Many people really do not want to be known as righteous, "goodie-goodie," or "holier-than-thou." Such a person was the man with whom I was working in the General Electric aircraft jet engine accessory testing lab in Lynn, Massachusetts. He had taken two huge handsful of soap to wash his not very grimy hands after his work shift. The man in the tool cage who was responsible for dispensing the soap criticized him, and reminded him of other things he apparently had taken in days past. The man responded, "What are you, a *#%$&X@ GE cop?" When I heard his answer, I was too frightened to say out loud, "I'd rather be a GE cop than a GE robber!" Turning to your own reaction to discipline, do you really want a harvest of righteousness in your life? Or do you poke fun at the concept? Do you cut corners on your income tax report, sure you will get away with it? Do you cheat on your spouse? Do you eat a few grapes in the grocery store? Do you tell a white lie? Do you think you will be happier doing such things than being known by God as a righteous person? Or would you rather be like Samuel who told the people of Israel (in I Sam. 12:1-5) how righteous he had been in all his dealings with them before he gave the reins of government to Saul?

The second "crop" we may reap if we accept willingly God's discipline is peace. Let us consider whether that is a worthy harvest for enduring God's discipline. My wife Jeanne and I met Mrs. Adams, a Methodist Lay Preacher in London, during my year of theological study at the University of Edinburgh. Several years later, God tested (disciplined) her powerfully. Then she wrote to us, "God has placed me in a hospital bed for the past six months. I have lain on my back, unable to move. But throughout that time I have had great peace. All the while, God has put in my heart to pray for you, so day and night for these six months I have been praying for you. Now I would like to know from you whether there was something special in your lives that caused God to lead me to pray for you?" Our reply to Mrs. Adams was to this effect: "Our very dear friend, we most certainly do know why you have been praying for us for the past six months. During that time, the little church we were working to organize has been in the throes of splitting down the middle. It has been almost like losing our own baby. We have been exceedingly sad and despondent; we were virtually ready to give up the ministry. But now we know why we did not. Although at the time we did not know you were praying for us, it was surely your prayers that sustained us, and made us willing to continue to serve the Lord despite the tragedy that confronted us." We never learned, and it is possible Mrs. Adams did not know, why she had to endure such discipline in her life. But two things we did know; Mrs. Adams was filled with curiosity, but much more importantly, she was at total peace with God throughout her testing, because she willingly accepted God's discipline, and obeyed Him the whole time. The hymnwriter put it this way:

> When peace, like a river, attendeth my way,
> When sorrows, like sea-billows roll—
> Whatever my lot, Thou hast taught me to say,
> It is well, it is well with my soul.

Paul put it this way in Phil. 4:7: "And the peace of God, which transcends all understanding, will guard your hearts and your minds in Christ Jesus."

One more factor is involved in your obtaining peace from God. James wrote it in a rather cryptic statement in James 3:18: "Peacemakers who sow in peace raise a harvest of righteousness." If we are peacemakers, then we shall be immersed in peace ourselves. We remember that the author of Hebrews included righteousness in the harvest of peace, just as James does. We might think of righteousness and peace as Siamese twins, inseparable.

### Heb. 12:12. Therefore, strengthen your feeble arms and weak knees.

There is no footnote to these words in my edition of the NIV, but the thought is a duplication of what we read in Is. 35:3:

> Strengthen the feeble hands,
> steady the knees that give way.

In its context in Isaiah, surely he is making a plea to God to "strengthen the feeble hands" and "steady the knees that give way." We are certain that it is God alone who is able to do this for us, although the author of Hebrews implies that we ought to be diligent to do that for ourselves. But just as I John 3:1-3 says we cannot purify ourselves, so also we can never make ourselves strong. God does it for us. None of us wants, or likes, to be weak. Yet strangely not all of us are willing to pay the price to get strong, which is to allow God to discipline us and to be thankful for it.

### Heb. 12:13. "Make level paths for your feet"....

This is a quotation from Prov. 4:26; it is in a chapter where Solomon, the wisest man who ever lived, urges his son to get wisdom and hold to it. The author of Hebrews is exhorting us to "make level paths" for ourselves. Having just finished saying that we cannot "strengthen our feeble hands" or "steady the knees that give way," we now must say that we are responsible ourselves to make our paths level. How often it is in life that we seek consciously the rock-strewn path of sin, littered with clods of moral dirt and grime! But it is our choice, perhaps not to make a pavement, at least not without God's help, but to seek out and walk on the smooth though narrow road that leads to righteousness. Many people deliberately choose the rugged sinful way, and then try to escape responsibility for their choices in life. If you are one of those, do not blame God; do not blame parents, or poverty, or your society, or a lack of education. You alone can determine whether your path is level; you alone make your choice.

**...so that the lame may not be disabled, but rather healed.**

We cut down curbs, so the handicapped may ride from sidewalk to street in their wheelchairs. We put bells and Braille numbers on elevators for the blind. We have sound-enhanced telephones, and caption vision on television screens for those who cannot hear. All these aides are at great public and private expense.

If we care for people's physical problems, what about their spiritual well-being? Do we "shoot our own soldiers"? Do we build higher spiritual curbs for the spiritually handicapped? That is, do we blazon pornography on TV, in magazines, in newspapers, even in medical anatomy texts, for those whose greatest temptations are sexual? Do we place alcohol ads before alcoholics, or offer them cocktails for dinner? Paul said something about catering to the weak, not offending him or causing him to stumble (Rom. 14:1-13):

Accept him whose faith is weak, without passing judgment on disputable matters....The man who eats everything must not look down on him who does not, and the man who does not eat everything must not condemn the man who does, for God has accepted him....For none of us lives to himself alone and none of us dies to himself alone....You, then, why do you judge your brother? Or why do you look down on your brother? For we will all stand before God's judgment seat....Therefore let us stop passing judgment on one another. Instead, make up your mind not to put any stumbling block or obstacle in your brother's way.

Paul repeated these kinds of warnings to the people of Corinth, in I Cor. 10:24 and 32: "Nobody should seek his own good, but the good of others....Do not cause anyone to stumble, whether Jews, Greeks or the church of God." And Paul gives the reason why he attempts to live this way in verse 33: "For I am not seeking my own good but the good of many, so that they may be saved."

All this is written by the author of Hebrews because he has been talking about God's discipline and how we are to react to it. He wants to be sure that we do not add to God's discipline of others our own vindictive judgment. Instead, we ought to "make level paths" not only for our own feet, but also

437

for the feet of those we meet.

**Heb. 12:14. Make every effort to live in peace with all men and to be holy; without holiness no one will see the Lord.**

Here the author begins a new paragraph with a new subject, one that is related to what precedes it. He begins to talk about holy living, which is necessary for us to avoid discipline from God.

This is another exhortation. If we were not supposed to "make every effort" to live in holiness, God would not have bothered to urge us to do so. That is to say, if we think we have nothing to do with our lives or destination, we will blame God for what we do, and say, "I was predestined to do it." We must be assured that there are two sides to the coin: On the obverse we read that God has indeed decreed everything that happens; but the reverse says that we must accept full responsibility for all we do.

A caution is appropriate as we discuss holiness. We must discover the perfect balance between being holy and being self-righteous. Let us never boast that we are "holier than thou," but we ought to live in such a way that those who do not want to live in righteousness will call us "holier than thou." Certainly we must never retreat from living God's way to avoid having people think we are holier than they.

Another caution to heed is, we must recognize that success in living peaceably or holily is made possible only by God's dwelling in us by His Holy Spirit. We must be willing, yes, even eager, to accept His help in achieving peace and holiness.

A stern warning follows: "Without holiness no one will see the Lord." Some people who immerse themselves in Pauline theology shun the words of James. But the fact is that Paul said exactly the same thing, except with a different emphasis. Paul said of himself (I Cor. 9:26-27), "Therefore I do not run like a man running aimlessly; I do not fight like a man beating the air. No, I beat my body and make it my slave so that after I have preached to others, I myself will not be disqualified for the prize." Paul knew that merely mouthing the words "I have accepted Jesus Christ as my Savior" will get no one to heaven. It was Martin Luther who added in the margin of Rom. 1:17 ("The righteous will live by faith") the Latin word *sola!* (alone). It is the Paulinists who quote Eph. 2:8-9, "For it is by grace you have been saved, through faith—and this not from yourselves, it is the gift of God—not by works, so that no one can boast." But they cringe when you quote the next verse, without which Paul's message is lost, "For we are God's workmanship, created in Christ Jesus to do good works, which God prepared in advance for us to do." Paul put it together in Gal. 5:6, "The only thing that counts is faith expressing itself through love." However, lest anyone misinterpret this translation to mean merely as "faith lovingly talking about itself," the Greek

438

word for "expressing" is ἐνεργουμένη which in the middle voice (the middle voice is not found in the English language) means "to display one's activity, show one's self operative."[8] In other words, it is action, not mere talk. Both the KJV and RSV come closer to the original sense with their translations: "faith which worketh by love," and "faith working through love."

Here is an example of people who spurn the warning in Hebrews. They are the homosexuals, who claim that their actions are not contrary to God's will. In fact, through absurd theological gymnastics they try to aver that the Bible does not teach that their activities are sinful. Although they claim to be Christians, and demand equal status with "straights" in churches, the Bible states unequivocally that they are sinners wherever the subject is discussed. This is true to such an extent that Paul (in I Cor. 6:9-10) agrees with the author of Hebrews, where he spells out a list of people who commit various sins, who cannot "inherit the kingdom of God." Such people would be better off eternally to accept willingly God's discipline, acknowledge the sinfulness of their actions, repent, and ask God's forgiveness; rather than to try to excuse themselves by denying guilt, and ultimately find themselves excluded from heaven forever.

**Heb. 12:15. See to it that no one misses the grace of God and that no bitter root grows up to cause trouble and defile many.**

"No one" includes yourself, and anyone whose life you influence for good or ill. Our strongest warning comes from the lips of Jesus Himself, when He talks to His disciples about their relationships to little children (Matt. 18:6): "If anyone causes one of these little ones who believe in me to sin, it would be better for him to have a large millstone hung around his neck and to be drowned in the depths of the sea." In this context, it is not wrong to let Jesus' words apply to our relationship to youth and adults as well as children. All our labors ought to be in the direction of bringing people, including ourselves, closer in the circle of God's wondrous grace.

A "bitter root" can never support a tree that might otherwise bear sweet fruit. Jesus reminded us of this in His statement about good trees and bad fruit in His Sermon on the Mount, Matt. 7:15-20.

We can remember incidents in our lives, or the lives of others, which caused a "chain reaction" like the falling of a string of dominoes. Such was the case of a small-plane pilot who got involved in drug traffic. He did something to displease someone in the drug chain, so that person secretly damaged his plane; next time he flew the plane crashed. Unfortunately, that was the time the pilot was carrying a large number of parachutists, all of whom died in the crash. In thinking about this, we must remember that to cause the spiritual death of one or more people is infinitely more serious than to bring

---

[8] Thayer's definition.

439

physical harm to anyone.

## Heb. 12:16.   See that no one is sexually immoral,...

It is important for us to notice the comma at the end of this clause. The author makes a significant shift in what he says here and what comes next. It was not his intent to accuse Esau of sexual immorality. Esau had enough against him without heaping false charges against him.

The author of Hebrews is explicit here. There must have been much sexual immorality in his day. Such sinfulness is not new, although some people call it the "new morality" now. In those days there was virtually no news media, nor were there motion pictures, television, newspapers, magazines, or books to show the world the sinful lifestyle of those who think they are on the "cutting edge" of life. We are told that the "Victorian" era in England was at least as bad as ours. We know this for certain: our generation is so bad that every conceivable kind of sexual sin mentioned or alluded to in scripture is bandied about. We learn about premarital sex, adultery, incest, pornography, homosexuality, pedophilia, bisexuality, transgendering, bestiality, rape, and abortion. The Bible condemns every sexual activity except the marriage relationship between one man and one woman during the life of them both. We see that sole sexual practice permitted near the beginning of the next chapter of Hebrews. Sexual immorality is one of those "bitter roots" that poisons all that it touches. An example of this is that the life-span of people in America today hovers around seventy-five years, while according to statistics published by homosexuals in an OMEGA study,[9] their average life-span is but thirty-nine years, and even less for those who consider themselves committed to one partner (although the average age for homosexuals without AIDS is one or two years longer).

### ...or is godless like Esau....

I never really thought of Esau as "godless," but merely foolishly infantile. On the other hand, Esau is not spoken of as having a close relationship to God, if he had any. One indication of his godlessness is his marriage to two Hittite women, of whom it was said (Gen. 26:34-35), "They were a source of grief to Isaac and Rebekah." The cause of the parents' grief was that Hittites were one of the godless tribes in Canaan whom God ordered the Israelites to destroy because of their evil religions and lives. Later, because Esau realized that his marriages were displeasing to Isaac and Rebekah, he tried to make amends by marrying one of Ishmael's daughters, thinking that since Ishmael was a half-brother of Isaac, this would be pleasing to them. But since there was no love lost between Isaac and Ishmael, the move probably proved of no benefit to Esau.

As we think more carefully of Esau's life, we know he committed great

[9] Reported by Norman Geisler and Frank Turek in their book, LEGISLATING MORALITY, page 132.

440

folly by throwing away his inheritance when he traded it for a mere bowl of bean soup. That act was much more than just an abandonment of an inheritance; it was in effect a rejection of the Creator and Governor of the laws of inheritance, even God. In that sense, Esau really was godless. As we think carefully about Esau's life, we ought to think soberly about our own foolish acts, whether they might be considered sinful or not. Running to acts of folly easily leads to acts of godlessness, as did Esau's.

### ...who for a single meal sold his inheritance rights as the oldest son.

You may read the story in the passage surrounding Gen. 25:33-34. Esau even swore with an oath about his birthright. But Jesus warns us (Matt. 5:34), "Do not swear at all...." And we ought to remember poor Jephthah (Judges 11), who made a most unfortunate vow which put him in a huge dilemma. Realizing this, none of us ought to say, "Esau may have been so foolish, but I never would!" We must not be so sure of ourselves, because Paul warned us in I Cor. 10:12, "So, if you think you are standing firm, be careful that you don't fall!"

In verses 14-16, we read that our hope for God's blessings can be assured by two factors; but it can be dashed by replacing those two by three "lests." The two factors that support our hope are mentioned in verse 14: following peace, and following sanctification. Verses 15 and 16 says we can have such hope, "lest" we: fall short of the grace of God; let a root of bitterness grow to trouble us; and, commit fornication or act "profane" as Esau did in losing his birthright, even though he pled with tears to retrieve it.

### Heb. 12:17. Afterward, as you know....

If you need your knowledge about Esau refreshed, please read or review Gen. 27:32-38.

### ...when he wanted to inherit this blessing, he was rejected.

After all, God had informed Rebekah, and probably Isaac as well, that the elder twin would serve the younger (Gen. 25:22-23). It is doubtful that both parents could have kept such an amazing prediction a secret from either Esau or Jacob. If, then, Esau knew about God's plan for him, He should have been forewarned that he would not receive Isaac's inheritance. I am no psychologist, so why Isaac would obliterate, or merely forget, or perhaps dismiss as untrue, the news is beyond me. The fact is that Esau acted as if he had not heard God's decision. Isaac's answer to Esau seems to indicate that he knew what God had said about the two brothers, when after Esau pleaded for a blessing, Isaac said (Gen. 27:33), "...just before you came...I blessed him—and indeed he will be blessed!" Your own experience in life tells you that rejection always hurts everyone who is rejected, whether he is forewarned or not.

**He could bring about no change of mind, though he sought the blessing with tears.**

We read of Esau's tears in Gen. 27:38. But by the time he wept, it was far too late to cry. The time to make the right decision is at the time of decision, not at the time of discipline. Far too often I have heard my children and children's children blurt out, "What? I'm not doing anything," when a sharp word from a parent reminds them of some disobedience they are committing. They think that by stopping as soon as they are aware they are caught, no punishment ought to come to them. In my opinion, they ought to be disciplined twice, once for the disobedience, and again for the attempted deceit. Adults are often guilty, and in the same way. We try to hide our sin from God by stopping when we recall we are disobedient, then try to gloss over our iniquity with words of excuse.

Following the reminder about Esau, there comes an allegory, similar to what Paul tells in Gal. 4:21-31. Read the Galatians passage as an introduction to what the author says here. The allegory is of two mountains, and the contrast between them, as depicting the lost and the righteous.

**Heb. 12:18-20. You have not come to a mountain that can be touched and that is burning with fire; to darkness, gloom and storm; to a trumpet blast or to such a voice speaking words, so that those who heard it begged that no further word be spoken to them, because they could not bear what was commanded: "If even an animal touches the mountain, it must be stoned."**

The original story of this incident is found in Ex. 19:12-19; read it to obtain a full understanding of the background. In relating the story, the author of Hebrews is *not* saying to his hearers, "You cannot touch that mountain," but rather he gives this encouraging thought: "The mountain that you could touch and that is burning with fire is *not* the mountain where you have arrived." This sentence in Hebrews describes the experience of the children of Israel camped at the foot of Mount Sinai, three months to the day after they left Egypt (Ex. 19:1). It occurred immediately preceding Moses' trek up the mountain to receive the two tablets of the Law from God the first time. All this corresponds, in the allegory, to the old covenant, its priests and ministry, and contrasts it with the new covenant, Christ and His salvation. The author is giving, in effect, these encouraging words, "Your journey of faith has not brought you into the bondage of the law."

* * *

**Heb. 12:21. The sight was so terrifying that Moses said, "I am trembling with fear."**

Moses related his reaction to this experience in Deut. 9:19, "I feared the anger and wrath of the LORD, for he was angry enough with you to destroy you." The sight had to be awesome; even Moses trembled with fear. After all, he had seen the presence of God in a fire already, when God commissioned him to lead the children of Israel out of Egypt. Certainly Moses was filled with consternation when he saw the bush burning but was not consumed. When people ridicule the idea that wicked people will burn consciously forever in the lake of fire, as threatened in Rev. 20:10 and 14-15, they ought to recall that such a non-consuming fire has already existed in Moses' sight.

Moses should not have been fearful, because we read in I John 4:18, "There is no fear in love. But perfect love drives out fear, because fear has to do with punishment. The man who fears is not made perfect in love." When my daughter Cynthia was a young teen she reminded me of this verse when I was fearful of some event in my life. I took to heart her gentle rebuke, and realized I did not possess perfect love. Obviously Moses did not have perfect love either; but that dares not be an excuse for you or me.

Now we come to the contrasting part of the allegory:

**Heb. 12:22. But you have come to Mount Zion, to the heavenly Jerusalem, the city of the living God.**

The author is not talking about the earthly Mount Zion, often called the City of David, just south of the Temple Mount in Jerusalem. Instead, he calls it the "heavenly Jerusalem;" and instead of the City of David, he calls it the "City of the Living God."

Since this is the kind of mount the author is speaking of, we understand why he said earlier that this mount cannot be touched by us—at least not yet. But the City of God will be our eternal home some day.

The author says that we have already come to this heavenly city, but our approach is not physical, but spiritual, confirmed by our embracing the scripture, and by our hope which fills this chapter. Paul reminds us that just because we have received Christ as our Savior, we have not yet received all the blessings that accompany that momentous event (Rom. 8:23-24): "not only so, but we ourselves, who have the firstfruits of the Spirit, groan inwardly as we wait eagerly [and, in verse 25, patiently] for our adoption as sons, the redemption of our bodies. For in this hope we are saved."

**You have come to thousands upon thousands of angels in joyful assembly....**

How many angels are there? How many compared to the number of human beings? Is their number increasing, or perhaps decreasing? God created them; is He creating more of them? We know that they did not, and do

443

not, procreate like humans do. Jesus said as much in Mark 12:18-27, when the Sadducees, who did not believe in the resurrection, posed a question about seven brothers who one after another had the same wife because each died in order without children. They asked Jesus, "Whose wife will she be, since the seven were married to her?" Jesus chided them for being ignorant of what the scriptures told them, that in heaven humans "will neither marry nor be given in marriage; they will be like the angels in heaven." We do know that there must be millions of angels, not only because of what the author says here. When Jesus warned His hearers not to cause any child to miss going to heaven in Matt. 18:1-11, He said, "...their angels in heaven always see the face of my Father in heaven." So millions of children must have at least millions of angels watching over them. It is pure speculation to number them.

The angels in heaven exist in "joyful assembly," because they know what the alternative to heaven is. The Greek term used here for "joyful assembly," πανήγυρις, is used only here in the New Testament. It was used in those days for "a festal gathering of the whole people to celebrate public games or other solemnities." [10]   The KJV translates it as "general assembly;" the Presbyterian name for its highest governing body. Unfortunately, most of the time those General Assemblies are neither festal nor celebratory.

### Heb. 12:23.       ...to the church of the firstborn, whose names are written in heaven.

Although the term "firstborn" (Greek πρωτότοκος) is used almost exclusively as a title for Jesus in the New Testament, there are two places it is used for other people. One of them is here, and the other is in Heb. 11:28. There the author was reviewing the story (see Ex. 11:5) of all the firstborn sons of the Egyptians as well as all firstborn males of their animals, that would be killed by the angel of death. Everywhere else in the New Testament it is Jesus who is called the "Firstborn." In the story of the birth of Jesus, He is called the Firstborn in Lu. 2:7 and in some manuscripts of Matt. 1:25. In Rom. 8:29 Jesus is called the "firstborn among many brothers." Paul calls Him the "firstborn over all creation" in Col. 1:15, and three verses later the "firstborn from among the dead." In Heb. 1:6, we read of Jesus as God's Firstborn brought into the world. And finally, Jesus is called the Firstborn in Rev. 1:5, where once again He is called the "firstborn from the dead" as well as the "faithful witness" and the "ruler of the kings of the earth."

In this verse in Heb. 12 we must notice that the author does not call the "church of the firstborn" the "Church of Jesus Christ." The reason we can be sure is because the term "firstborn" here is in the plural form. Therefore, it must mean the Church of those who have been redeemed by Jesus Christ, the Firstborn of the Father. It may mean the "firstborn" as people like those in Heb. 11 who are already in heaven. Alternatively, it may mean all Christians

---

[10]  Thayer's definition.

including the original hearers of the author's message and us who read it now. We, then, are the "firstborn," but not those who refused our Savior Jesus Christ. Christians are those whose names are "found written in the book of life" (see Rev. 20:12 and 15).

Does it strike you as harsh to call all those who have not received Jesus Christ as Savior and Lord as people who "will never be allowed in heaven"? I pondered using that language, knowing some people may be offended. Finally I decided to say it nevertheless, in hopes that some who read this book will first of all be sure they are not among those excluded forever from heaven, but also all of us may reconsider the urgency of spreading the Gospel to our loved ones, friends, and the world, so that some who hear may be transferred from death to eternal life with God and Christ in heaven.

### You have come to God, the judge of all men....

The Thompson Chain Reference Bible lists under Chain Reference #1355 titled "Christ as Judge" these verses from the New Testament: Matt. 25:32; John 5:22; Acts 10:42; Acts 17:31; Rom. 2:16; Rom. 14:10; and II Tim. 4:1. In this study we have seen Him already as the One sitting on the Great White Throne in Rev. 20:11, along with others who also will be judges under God's authority, in Rev. 20:4.

### ...to the spirits of righteous men made perfect....

Only those people who are righteous are made perfect; and only those made righteous by God are righteous. This is what Paul says in Rom. 3:25-26: "God presented [Jesus] as a sacrifice of atonement...to demonstrate his justice at the present time, so as to be just and the one who justifies the man who has faith in Jesus." The author of Hebrews is saying that the people to whom he wrote had come already to those righteous spirits who had become perfect, that is, they were in their company, and one day would be inducted into their number.

### Heb. 12:24.    ...to Jesus the mediator of a new covenant....

Jesus is the only Mediator (I Tim. 2:5-6): "For there is one God and one mediator between God and men, the man Christ Jesus, who gave himself as a ransom for all men...." This is what it is all about. Our only hope lies in Jesus, who is better than anything offered in the Old Testament, and beyond whom there is none at all. To arrive in heaven, our hope must lie in Him alone, the sole Mediator, the Judge of all men.

### ...and to the sprinkled blood that speaks a better word than the blood of Abel.

The "sprinkled blood" is none other than the blood of Jesus, which He

445

poured out on the cross from the blows of the soldiers, the thorns of the crown forced upon His brow, the nailprints in His hands and feet, and the spear's wound in His side. Spiritually speaking, His blood is sprinkled on all who have confessed their sins and asked His forgiveness, and have been assured that their punishment has been paid by Him who poured out His blood for them.

Jesus' "sprinkled blood" speaks "a better word." Once again, this is what the whole book of Hebrews is about. Everything about Jesus is "better than" anything else that could be offered to us by anyone. Whatever our imaginations could devise, we are hemmed in by ever-diminishing circles until we stand alone within the circle occupied only by ourselves and the blood of Jesus. Nothing else will benefit us; nothing else will be accepted by God.

Jesus' blood is better than the "blood of Abel." We recall that the author spoke of the blood of Abel in Heb. 11:4. Abel's sacrifice was better than whatever offering Cain made. But Abel's blood sacrifice was puny indeed compared to that of God's Son Jesus.

There is another consideration with regard to Abel's blood. In Gen. 4:8 we read that "Cain attacked his brother Abel and killed him." Then God said to Cain in verse 10, "Your brother's blood cries out to me from the ground." It was not the blood of Abel's sacrifice, but the blood of Abel himself which was shed by his murderous brother. Jesus commented on this incident, recorded in Matt. 23:35, "And upon you will come all the righteous blood that has been shed on earth, from the blood of righteous Abel to the blood of Zechariah the son of Berakiah...." Jesus' blood was better than that of Abel, and Jesus Himself tells us that His is better than "all the righteous blood" of everyone who has died.

At this point, let us list the eight things the author of Hebrews wrote in verses 22-24 that the believers had "come to" because they had received Jesus as better than anything offered in the Old Testament:

1. Mount Zion
2. The heavenly Jerusalem, the city of the living God
3. Thousands (myriads) of angels
4. The Church of the firstborn
5. God, the Judge of all men
6. The spirits of righteous men made perfect
7. Jesus the Mediator of the new covenant
8. The better sprinkled blood

**Heb. 12:25. See to it that you do not refuse him who speaks.**

Here we recall what was written at the very beginning of Hebrews. The irreducible minimum of the first sentence is "God has spoken." The important thing which opens chapter 2 is "We have heard." And in 2:1-4 we learn the supreme thing which God spoke; it is "this salvation, which was first announced by the Lord." We are challenged with the rhetorical question in verse 3, "How shall we escape?" The rest of chapter 12 elaborates on this question.

**If they did not escape when they refused him who warned them on earth....**

We might add here, "And they did not escape." We discussed the fact that only Joshua and Caleb escaped, and those who were under twenty years of age when they left Egypt; the discussion accompanies Heb. 3:17, and, you will note again, is expressed in Num. 14:29.

Who "warned them on earth"? We may think it was God, and ultimately it was, of course. But the message was transmitted by Moses who was "trembling with fear." So they were dullards indeed because they failed to fear the wrath of God.

**...how much less will we, if we turn away from him who warns us from heaven?**

So as we just said, it was Moses who warned the people in the wilderness; but it is God Himself who has warned us. Moses spoke from earth, but God speaks from heaven. Since this is so, there is no hope for us if we spurn the message from God Almighty. Those who have rejected God's message altogether will be altogether condemned.

**Heb. 12:26. At that time his voice shook the earth....**

The bravest of us would have been frightened indeed if we had been at the foot of Sinai when this occurred (Ex. 19:18-19): "...the whole mountain trembled violently, and the sound of the trumpet grew louder and louder. Then Moses spoke and the voice of God answered him."

**...but now he has promised, "Once more I will shake not only the earth but also the heavens."**

This prophecy was written by Haggai under the inspiration of the Holy Spirit. Haggai's little prophecy is a call to the people of Jerusalem to rebuild the temple. But the people were too busy rebuilding their own homes. For encouragement, Haggai reports this prophecy about God's shaking earth and heaven (Hag. 2:6-9):

This is what the LORD Almighty says: "In a little while I will once more shake the heavens and the earth, the sea and the dry land. I will shake all nations, and the desired of all nations will come, and I will fill this house with glory," says the LORD Almighty. "The silver is mine and the gold is mine," declares the LORD Almighty. "The glory of this present house will be greater than the glory of the former house," says the LORD Almighty, "And in this place I will grant peace," declares the LORD Almighty.

447

This prophecy sounds to me like a prediction of things that will happen when the Messiah returns: there will be a division of nations; righteous people will flow to Jerusalem; there will be great glory in the Temple, and peace will come. These events have not yet all happened, but will be fulfilled one by one as time goes on.

Haggai mentions a second time the shaking of the earth, in 2:21, in connection with his prophecy to Governor Zerubbabel that his position will be secure. This sounds close to parallel with Malachi's prophecy in his chapter 4 about the coming of Elijah again to precede the coming of the Messiah. Although Zerubbabel may not have been an ancestor of Jesus, he was a type of the Great Ruler who was to come.

If the shaking of the earth in Moses' day was terrifying to him as well as to all the people, how much more petrifying will be the shaking of both the heavens as well as the earth! Unless our feet are planted firmly on the Rock Christ Jesus who cannot be shaken, we will not be able to stand.

**Heb. 12:27. The words "once more" indicate the removing of what can be shaken—that is, created things—so that what cannot be shaken may remain.**

The earth was shaken in Moses' day, to demonstrate God's power to the people, so that they would not only be terrified by the God who did it, but also be drawn to Him in trust that He would protect them by that same power. The shaking that will occur the second time will be more awesome in two ways. First, there will be a shaking of more than the earth; the heavens also will be shaken. Our modern laws of physics cannot show us how people will be able to observe such a shaking, especially of the heavens which scientists believe are more than twenty billion light years in diameter. By the same token, it is impossible for us to comprehend how God, who is more "immense" (that is a theological term for how big God is) than the universe, can cause one of His hands to know what His other hand is doing at one instant. But since God is God, and time means nothing to Him, He can do such things. The second thing will be not only the shaking, but the annihilation of both heaven and earth. They will cease to exist.

We might think that if the earth and all it contains, together with the bodies of heaven, cease to exist, then there must be nothing left. That, however, is the great error of people who cannot think beyond what to them is tangible. The adult Jews in the wilderness all died, but their souls were not destroyed; they still existed in spirit form someplace. Nor will their souls ever cease to exist, but will continue either in heaven or hell forevermore. And we ought to be aware that God who created all things out of nothing is able to cause them all to cease to exist while He Himself continues forever. The same God who created the original heavens and earth is fully capable of creating new heavens and a new earth in any fashion He desires to replace what has been "removed." Peter says all this in his second letter, in II Pet. 3:7-13.

**Heb. 12:28. Therefore, since we are receiving a kingdom that cannot be shaken, let us be thankful, and so worship God acceptably with reverence and awe....**

Once again (see 6:9 and 10:39) the author graciously switches from the second person plural to the first person plural, to indicate that his readers—at least those original readers—had in fact abandoned the Old Testament ministries as their means of salvation, and had come to adhere irreversibly to Jesus and to God's grace for their access to heaven.

That new kingdom had been planned by God from all eternity, and was even then in preparation for the arrival of those selected to enter it. All those saints listed and alluded to in chapter 11 were prepared to enter it, as soon as the "full number of the Gentiles" (Rom. 11:25) was fulfilled. Since that new heaven has been offered, then "we [also] are receiving" it, although we have not yet fully entered it. We are on track to receive it, and nothing can keep us from our destination. Because that new heaven is "unshakeable," we need not worry that it will disappear before we arrive, or after we get there.

The author reminds us, "let us be thankful." That is the only pay we can offer to God for His magnificent gift to us. But how often is it that our prayers consist exclusively of "give me this, and give me that," with no hint that we have already been given such abundance of gifts from God that we can neither count them nor be aware of most of them? How often grandparents stop giving birthday and Christmas gifts to their grandchildren who neglect to write thank-you notes. How tragic it would be if God ceased to give us what we need whenever we forget to thank Him!

If one obligation we have toward God is to give Him thanks for all He gives us, another obligation equally important is, "and so worship God." How many of us really know what worship is, or practice worship in a way acceptable to God? In my childhood and youth, worship was pure rote, something that as my mother told me once when I balked at "going to church:" "Why, Tommy, we never think about not going to church. We are Christians, and that's what we do on Sunday mornings." Unfortunately, that is all that "worship" meant to me. Several years ago, a fellow Minister said to a group of us going together to a meeting, "I have to get home right away after the meeting, because I want to prepare a fun worship experience for next Sunday morning." When I heard those words, I thought I had just heard the prime example of an oxymoron. If a Minister's main intent is to dream up something "fun" for the congregation, there is hardly room left for "worship." Not only that, but we ought not go to church for the purpose of "getting an experience," nor of giving God an "experience" from our attendance in that building at that hour.

The author of Hebrews gives us some guidelines to help us to define worship. First, he says we must worship God "acceptably." To do that, we must worship Him in our hearts and minds. Jesus said as much in John 4:23-24: "...the true worshipers will worship the Father in spirit and truth, for they are the kind of worshipers the Father seeks. God is spirit, and his worshipers must worship in spirit and in truth." It should be easy for us to contrast this kind of worship with what Isaiah describes in Is. 1:10-17; these parts strike me most powerfully: "The multitude of your sacrifices—what are they to me?...who asked this of you, this trampling of my courts?...When you spread out your hands in prayer, I will hide my eyes from you....Stop doing wrong, learn to do right!"

In addition to worshiping God "acceptably," we must worship Him with "reverence." The Greek word for reverence is εὐλάβεια, used here and only one other time in the New Testament, in Heb. 5:7, where we have already read of Jesus' "reverent submission" to the Father when He pleaded for the removal of the cup. If I read correctly what Thayer says about the different English words that could be used to translate this Greek word, the basic meaning here should be "reverence, veneration, piety." However, along with this basic meaning is a strong overtone of "fear, anxiety, dread." In other words, our worship of God must be accomplished with our hearts filled with a desire to be as close to God in our spiritual attitude as possible, while at the same time recognizing that in our sinful state we can never be like Him. Because of our shortcomings, we must be filled with godly fear, recognizing what punishment we deserve.

Finally, we see one other factor in our attitude of worship. We must worship God not only acceptably, and reverently, but also with "awe." The Greek word for "awe" is δέος, which is used only here in the New Testament. Its meaning is so closely allied to the Greek word for "fear," φόβος, that there is no separate article for it in TDNT; but one brief comment on it is found in the article for fear by Horst Balz.[11] Surely there is no need for us to discuss the meaning of "fear" at length, except to warn ourselves again that there is such a thing as godly fear which must not be diminished by anyone's desire to whitewash it with unmingled love. The reason for this is found in the next, and last, verse in this chapter.

### Heb. 12:29. ...for our God is a consuming fire.

At the beginning of our discussion of verse 28, we saw that the author gave his readers the benefit of the doubt, assuming they were true believers in Jesus Christ as their Savior and Lord, having abandoned any hope of salvation by means of Old Testament sacrifices. In case any of them (or any of us) might not have arrived at that state, he proffers this final warning, "our God is a consuming fire." We dare not turn away from a proper fear of God by claiming that He is a God of love, implying that He cannot be a God of wrath

---

[11] TDNT, Vol. IX, page 214.

as well. God has required Himself to punish sin, and has warned everyone of that fact, beginning with our first parents, Adam and Eve, by giving them His guidelines for life in the garden and threatening them with sore punishment for disobedience. We know all that from Genesis 3. We see the contrasting sides of God's relationship to people in Is. 1:19-20:

> If you are willing and obedient,
>> you will eat the best from the land;
> but if you resist and rebel,
>> you will be devoured by the sword.
>> For the mouth of the LORD has spoken.

### Heb. 13:1.  Keep on loving each other as brothers.

We come finally to the love chapter in Hebrews, which is the end of the trilogy we saw in Heb. 10:22-24, and read in I Cor. 13:13. Refresh your memories on the four kinds of love expressed in four different Greek words in our discussion of the second part of Heb. 12:7.

The kind of love the author of Hebrews discusses here is φίλος love, or φιλαδέλφια, philadelphia. This kind of love is not as strong as the love expressed by ἀγάπη love, but it is very important to cultivate this kind of love also. The author makes the statement as an exhortation, something he urges us to do. Christians ought to treat each other at least as kindly as they ought to treat their brothers and sisters. After all, we are spiritual brothers and sisters. I said we ought to do this as "we ought" to love our physical brothers and sisters, because often we fall short of dealing with our siblings as we should.

This Greek word φίλος is used several times in II Tim. 3:1-4 in combination words, as Paul writes of several particular sins of evil people: lovers of themselves, lovers of money, not lovers of the good, lovers of pleasure rather than lovers of God.

In this chapter, we can translate our relations to the people mentioned as loving them and doing whatever else the text encourages us to do.

### Heb. 13:2.  Do not forget to entertain strangers....

We might excuse our lack of hospitality by claiming that there are many hotels and motels today. When Joseph and Mary traveled to Bethlehem to be enrolled, they sought an inn for lodging. They were turned away, not because there were too few inns normally, but the whole inhabited world was required to travel in the space of a few days, so there was a glut of seekers of lodging, just as today when there is a large convention in a city, the hotels and motels are booked months ahead, and the ordinary traveler is left to fend for himself. Also, we recall that thirteen centuries before Jesus, there was an innkeeper named Rahab in Jericho, and it is not necessary to believe that she was the only one in town.

We should not end our thinking about hospitality in this way. There are transients, poor, or disabled people who need more than just a place to stay overnight. They may need specialized facilities, or may lack funds to pay for a commercial room. The Greek word used to describe what we ought to do is φιλοξενία (a companion to φιλαδέλφια, the first part of the two words is identical), and can be translated as "hospitality," or "love to strangers."

In my ministry I have had great difficulty distinguishing between people who were truly needy and those "parasites" whose career was begging. One time I was quite sure of my judgment. A man barged into my study, sat down and said, "I'm a born-again Christian and I go to church every Sunday and I want you to give me twenty dollars." It was obvious he had rehearsed his speech numerous times, and thought it would incite my sympathy. My response as I turned back to my desk was, "I'm not going to give you any money." He sat there dumbfounded for fully ten seconds, then blurted out, "You mean you're not going to give me any money?" Without looking up, I said, "Not one penny." Again, he sat silent for a while, then jumped from his seat and stomped out, slamming the door behind him. I was certain I did not need to try to get him "saved," because if he knew the lingo already, he was sufficiently familiar with the message to be able to accept it if he so chose. Another time, after an evening Worship Service, a woman came to the front of the sanctuary where I was standing and began to ask for a handout. She looked truly needy, and I was about to reach for my billfold when a member of the church came hastily forward and in very stern language told the woman to get out of the church or he would turn her in. After she left, I asked how he knew she should not receive money, and he told me he had been on the police force for many years and knew exactly what kinds of people were ripoffs. In another instance, when I was at home, a lady with two small children and seemed obviously pregnant came to the door and asked for food for her family. At the very beginning of our conversation, our cleaning lady came rushing to the door and told me I was needed on the phone right away. I was nonplused, because I had not heard the phone ring, but I followed her back into the house. She told me quickly that she knew the woman, she had a pillow under her dress, and she traveled around begging although she was supplied with everything she needed.

On the other hand, I am positive I have turned away many people who had legitimate needs. Often I am reminded of the tenor of a book by William Law called A SERIOUS CALL TO A DEVOUT AND HOLY LIFE; he showed how he judged whether to give money to one who was needy:[1]

> If we are angry at a poor man, and look upon him as a wretch, when he throws away that which should buy his own bread; how must we appear in the sight of God, if we make a wanton idle use of that which should buy bread and clothes for the hungry and naked brethren, who are as near and dear to God as we are, and fellow-heirs of the same state of future glory?

An even greater condemnation of my attitude toward hospitality is contained in words Mr. Law put into the mouth of Miranda, a poor yet devout woman:[2]

> Shall I withhold a little money, or food, from my fellow-creature, for fear he should not be good enough to receive it of me? Do I beg of God to deal with me, not according to my merit, but according to His own great goodness; and shall I be so absurd as to withhold my charity from a poor brother, because he may perhaps not deserve it? Shall I use a measure towards him, which I pray God never to use towards me?

* * *

---

[1] Pages 76-77.

[2] Page 82.

...for by so doing some people have entertained angels without knowing it.

Years ago Dale Evans Rogers wrote a book entitled ANGEL UN-AWARES, which uses the KJV word of this verse. It was about a little girl born to her, very handicapped from birth. Because Dale and her husband Roy were earnest Christians, they kept their daughter, cherished her, loved her all her life. The book is filled with the blessings that came to that family because they were willing to undergo the heartache, the agony, the extra labor involved in caring for their little angel.

About the same time Evans' book was written, another handicapped girl, named only "Baby Doe," was allowed to starve to death, because the parents did not want the burden of caring for her. Only when we do what is right, the seeming burden is converted into a blessing.

**Heb. 13:3. Remember those in prison as if you were their fellow prisoners....**

One thing that troubles me about this clause is that it omits any reference to whether the prisoners we are to "remember" (translate "love") are only those who are unjustly incarcerated, or whether we must also love those who have committed heinous crimes and remain unrepentant. Of course, you know I ought not to be troubled at the omission. When the Holy Spirit directed the author to pen these words, He intended to leave out any such reference, just for people like me, and perhaps like you also. Should I show love to Winona M. Fletcher, the fourteen-year-old girl who shot her man-friend's wife? Should the wife show kindness to her? It might be easy for me to love her—at a distance—because what she did caused me no harm. But what about the man who broke into our church one night, entered the sanctuary, and tore down the large cross in the center of the platform? Must I go to the prison and visit him, show him kindness, do what I can to help him? When you are the one who is harmed, can you be forgiving; more to the point, can you show forgiveness and love? If you have ever been in prison, rightly or wrongly, you know how desperately you needed love.

You have heard of the ministry Charles Colson established called "Prison Fellowship." After having committed a "white-collar" crime, he was kept in a "white-collar" prison for a few years. His experience was far more mild than that of most prisoners. Yet it was sufficiently painful that he recognized a great need to minister to those people, not only spiritually but also in material ways. Too, he became aware that it was necessary to minister to the needs of the family members of those put away. Besides the efforts of Colson and his organization, there have been prison Chaplains, and ministries of small groups from churches across the country, but they all touch the lives of only a small percentage of those in need of the touch of God's love from His people.

**...and those who are mistreated as if you yourselves were suffering.**

The author says we must "remember" them. But what does that mean? Often I hear Christians respond to a Christian worker's plea for help with the words, "I'll remember you in prayer." They may "remember" to pray once or twice, and then forget the matter. On the contrary, remembrance must include at least some of the following: take a casserole to the family; take a birthday cake to the prisoner; help the family with school clothes; provide a job for the prisoner when he is freed, or his wife before he is out; find means of rehabilitation for the prisoner so he will not return to prison. Would you dare take him into your own home to show Christ's love to him? God has given the marching orders; it is God who can protect you; it is God who can give you wisdom how or whether to do such a thing.

### Heb. 13:4. Marriage should be honored by all....

What does this say to the Women's Libber who says, "All men are rapists;" or to the man whose bumper sticker reads, "Stop rape; say yes"? The author does not say that all people must be married; Paul said he preferred that all Christians ought to remain unmarried as he was, if they could tolerate it (I Cor. 7:7). Life in the world today is filled with a perversion of God's view of marriage. Today's alternatives to marriage are myriad: premarital sex, extramarital sex, polygamy, polyandry, divorce and remarriage which some like to call "serial" polygamy; sodomy; the attempt to legitimize same-sex unions; cross-dressing; transgendering; bisexual relations; pedophilia; rape; prostitution; pornography. Our hearts are sick at a mere review of debauchery we know of today. God created mankind "male and female," and said, "A man will leave his father and mother and be united to his wife, and they will become one flesh" (Gen. 1:27 and 2:24, quoted by Jesus in Mark 10:6-9 with His additional comments). The best way for a man to love and honor all women is to be married to one and remain utterly faithful to her. In addition, the best way for a man to love and honor all men is to be united only to his own wife, a woman. Any other sexual relationship is at best "confusion," and at worst perversion, abomination, and detestation (see several translations of Lev. 18:22-23 and Lev. 20:12).

### ...and the marriage bed kept pure...

These first two phrases in verse 4 contain no verbs, so it is difficult to say whether they are merely declarations, or whether we should accept them as exhortations. The author probably intended them to be directives for the lives of the readers.

The Greek word translated here as "pure" is ἀμίαντος. We found it in 7:26, used there of Jesus as our High Priest, who needed no sacrifice for His own sins since He was sinless—pure in that sense. The best definition for the word seems to be "undefiled." In this verse we can be sure it means free from adultery on the part of either spouse. The Greek word is found also in I Pet. 1:4, where our inheritance in Jesus Christ is undefiled (according to the KJV), or it can never spoil (according to our NIV). The fourth place the Greek word is used in the New Testament is in James 1:27, where the only religion acceptable to God is called "pure and faultless" or "pure and undefiled." In this case the Greek word for "pure" is καθαρός, where Thayer says it could be translated as "genuine." Solomon wrote several times in his Proverbs on this subject: in 2:16-19; 5:1-20; 6:20-29; and 7:1-27, the best. Solomon should have followed his own admonitions, instead of accumulating seven hundred wives and three hundred concubines; they ultimately led him astray from God who had blessed him so mightily (I Kings 11:1-8). God had clearly set forth both His offer of blessing for Solomon's obedience, and His threat of abandonment for turning away from Himself. The history of Israel from that day to this day tells the story of God's fulfillment of His words.

Besides the common interpretation of this verse, there are two extreme and erroneous interpretations. One is to claim that the marriage bed cannot be defiled by any kind of sinful act on the part of either spouse; the other is that all sexual activity between the two married partners is wrong or defiled, and thus ought not to occur. People can dream of the most strange ideas, simply to satisfy their desires or agree with their skewed ideas.

### ...for God will judge the adulterer and all the sexually immoral.

We all know the seventh commandment. Again I say, people will go to extremes to avoid confrontation with the reality of their sins. Some would make excuses such as claiming that fornication is not as bad a sin as adultery, or not a sin at all. Both fornication and adultery are condemned in scripture; in God's sight there is no difference. If merely eating a piece of forbidden fruit could terminate the spiritual lives of Adam and Eve, then the punishment for fornication can be no less harsh than that for adultery. Scripture thoroughly condemns every form of sexual activity and even sexual thought imaginable, except for the one acceptable marriage relationship. Lest anyone think he can escape God's punishment, let us remind ourselves of what Paul says in I Cor. 6:9-10, that *no one* who practices any of these sins "will inherit the kingdom of God." The only escape from this condemnation is for those who have acknowledged the sinfulness of what they have done, turned in disgust from their sins, and received Jesus Christ as Savior and Lord, will be saved from the punishment due them, according to what Paul says in I Cor. 6:11, "And that is what some of you were. But you were washed, you were sanctified, you were justified in the name of the Lord Jesus Christ and by the Spirit of our God." God's forgiveness is available—for those who repent, not for those who reject the sinfulness of their sins.

**Heb. 13:5.  Keep your lives free from the love of money and be content with what you have....**

Several verses in this chapter contain words which begin with the Greek letters φιλ—. From our discussion of verse 1, you can see that φιλ: philadelphia, the love of the brothers in Christ, starts the parade. Here the word is φιλάργυρος, which is the love of money, a warning similar to Paul's in I Tim. 6:10, "The love of money is a root of all kinds of evil." Money of itself does not produce evil, but it is the love of money which nurtures evil. Zacchaeus (Lu. 19:1-10) was a rich man, but upon receiving Jesus he gave half his wealth to the poor, and he promised to restore fourfold any money he had fraudulently taken in his tax-gathering business. For his change of heart, Jesus said, "Today salvation has come to this house, because this man, too, is a son of Abraham. For the Son of Man came to seek and to save what was lost" (verses 9-10). The possession of money is not what is sinful. You and I have known beggars who love money; we also are acquainted with rich people who are as righteous as Zacchaeus.

**...because God has said,**
 **"Never will I leave you;**
  **never will I forsake you."**

God said this several times in the Old Testament: Deut. 31:6; 31:8; Josh. 1:5. The author of Hebrews is still thinking about our attitude toward money. God's promise is worth more than all the money in the world; it is absolute, not contingent. Paul expressed the same promise in Rom. 8:31: "If God is for us, who can be against us?"

**Heb. 13:6.  So we say with confidence,**
 **"The Lord is my helper; I will not be afraid.**
  **What can man do to me?"**

We are still thinking about money, and the reasons why we need not love money. Whether we are rich or poor, God takes care of all our needs if we trust Him. Whether we are rich or poor, God can cause us to starve if we reject Him.

Sometimes it is difficult for me to remember these words of confidence when opposition comes my way. When my wife Claire and I were confronted by a shotgun-toting robber in a dark parking lot in Los Angeles, I confess I was not thinking too much about God's protection. Even when we heard from the policemen who responded to the report of the attack, and learned from their radio that a man had been killed by a shotgun not two blocks from us, I must confess I was too excited and confused to think about the Lord's hedge about me. I believe that because my life has been immersed in God's assurances, He was gracious to us during our moments of fear.

The disruptions in our lives need not be so severe as the threat of a

457

shotgun blast. Several times in my ministry I have been confronted by church members who by some slip-up in their own schedules thought the whole church had to veer aside to make way for them to get back on track with no effort spent on their own part. The Lord helped me on those occasions. Usually after such bouts, my meditations led me to see the foolishness of my being upset at such minor disturbances.

I need to remember that "the Lord is my helper; I will not be afraid. What can man do to me?" Jesus said the same thing in His Sermon on the Mount. In Matt. 6:19-21, He reminded us that we need not store up treasures on earth; it would be infinitely better to store up our treasures in heaven, where they will endure forever. And in verses 25-34, He pointed to the birds and the flowers, neither of which stores nor spins, and God takes care of them. In God's sight, are you more important than birds and flowers? Act and think as though you know you are.

**Heb. 13:7. Remember your leaders, who spoke the word of God to you.**

Here is an invitation to show love and gratitude to those who helped lead you to Christ. What they did for you brought you eternal blessings beyond anything you can dream of. In doing this, be careful you do not err on the side of too much gratitude. You must not idolize your leaders, or allow the thought of them to displace your adoration of God who not only saved you but also sent them to you to turn you to Him.

**Consider the outcome of their way of life and imitate their faith.**

The author is saying we ought to observe how well the Lord took care of our spiritual leaders because of their faith in Him; then be sure He will do the same for us.

I am not sure the author meant to exclude the "way of life" of our leaders as we "imitate their faith." If he did, I think he was wise in his omission. Often we spiritual followers see the sins of our spiritual leaders and think that because they committed them we ought to have the right to do the same. That can be a fatal error. To make sure that does not happen, Paul added a demurer when he wrote in I Cor. 11:1, "Follow my example, *as I follow the example of Christ.*"

Spiritual leaders often have great difficulty keeping their egos in check. It is easy for leaders to stand in the way, so people no longer can see Christ. The reason I wore my clerical collar and robe in the pulpit was in hopes that people would not look at my flashy (or out-of-style) clothing and thus be distracted from the message I sought to proclaim. My objective was to make myself obscure so the congregation would see only Christ in His glory.

\* \* \*

**Heb. 13:8.    Jesus Christ is the same yesterday and today and forever.**

This verse seems to be a parenthesis. To make the connection with the context, I gather he was saying in verse 6 that people may try to harm us, but we should not fear because God will protect us. Then in verse 7 he informs us that our spiritual leaders try to lead us by their example of works and faith, although that is not fully reliable. He sums up those ideas by reminding us that Jesus Christ is our great and perfect Leader whom we can trust utterly; because He has been perfect from eternity, He is perfect now, and He will continue perfect forevermore. Our Savior is the only great "I Am" of John 8:58 as well as the one who promised us in Matt. 28:20, "Surely I will be with you always, to the very end of the age."

**Heb. 13:9.    Do not be carried away by all kinds of strange teachings.**

True faith in the God of the Bible is like the point at the center of a circle. No matter how small or large you draw the circle, there is an infinite number of points outside the center point, both in the area of the circle and on its edge. That is just like the myriad of aberrations surrounding the one true faith. Our Christian "teaching" began with God's self-revelation to Adam and Eve when He created them. Their faith was a single monotheistic faith in the God of creation, until Satan appeared to Eve and set himself up as a rival "teacher." Adam and Eve became confused, and we humans have been confused ever since.

We look around us, and we see today's three world religions: Judaism, Christianity, and Islam. Each of these is divided into sects: Judaism has its Orthodox, Conservative, and Reformed branches; Christianity has its Orthodox, Roman Catholic, and Protestant groups; and Islam has its Sunni, Shiite, and Wahabi religions. There are strange mixtures, as exemplified by the Bahai religion. We could think of less-than-world religions, like Hinduism, Buddhism, Taoism,Confucianism, Shintoism; some claim not to be religions but they are. Even in Christian Protestantism we see more than five hundred denominations in the United States alone; surely not all of them embrace the whole of Christian truth, not even the ones who claim to be "orthodox." Further afield are all the non-Christian cults, groups that claim to be Christian but are not because they deny the deity of Christ.

One of the most deadly assumptions a person can hold is that it really does not matter what a person believes, only how he lives. The reason such a thought is deadly is that theology determines lifestyle. It takes no special discernment to determine what a person believes simply by observing how he lives. For the most part, the person you observe need not verbalize what he believes for you to discover it. His actions speak louder than his words.

One example of how one's life reveals his doctrine may help you to understand how this can be so. In the past few years there has arisen a strong movement among liberals in Christian churches toward what is called "inclusiveness." That is, the liberals press for full acceptance from those who resist embracing them because they do not live as forgiven Christians and so probably are not. But those same people who fight so strongly for "inclusiveness" are the ones who make it obvious by their actions (as well as words) that they refuse to be inclusive, because they exclude everyone who stands in the way of including them in full participation in the Church.

Sometimes it is difficult for us to sift the "wheat" from the "tares" in our churches. But this is nothing new. The author of Hebrews warned against "all kinds of strange teachings." Some such teachings begin in so subtle a way that many people are led into the nefarious doctrines before they realize they have been duped. Then to avoid losing face for having been led astray they continue to turn aside as if what they now believe is the truth instead of what the Bible teaches.

Paul gives the same warning. In I Tim. 6:3-5 he warns his young friend to avoid "false doctrines" and other errors which corrupt peoples' minds in every way. In his second letter to Timothy, chapter 2, verses 14-19, he charges him to be "a workman who does not need to be ashamed and who correctly handles the word of truth;" and in verses 23-26 he urges Timothy to be careful to teach only what is God's revealed truth. To the people of the Galatian churches, Paul expresses astonishment that they had quickly turned away from the truth to what they thought was a "different gospel" but was "no gospel at all" (Gal. 1:6-9). In Gal. 3:1-5, Paul renews his consternation at the Galatians for turning away from the clear Gospel of grace he had preached to them in favor of an effort to gain salvation by works as in Old Testament times. This, you recall, is the basic theme of the whole of Hebrews.

**It is good for our hearts to be strengthened by grace, not by ceremonial foods, which are of no value to those who eat them.**

The author echoes what he said in 9:10, about the many celebratory meals described in the Old Testament. In those days, the people got so used to repeating their traditional feasts that they forgot the God who commanded them in the first place, and they became no longer religious rituals but excuses for revelry. We have already noted how God despised such observances that were totally void of any spiritual value (see for instance Is. 1:10-15). Even when the Israelites observed the holy days, it was not the food that brought spiritual benefit to them or led them closer to God, but it was His grace that ushered them into His presence.

The effort to enhance "ceremony" in occasions of worship tend to blur the real purpose for gathering together. The fine vestments of the clergy; the tapestries, stained glass windows, and filigreed decorations on the walls; the statues, icons, and other craftwork for decoration; the incense, tinkling bells, chants and mantras, colored lights, anointing oils and waters, the plush cushions that tweak the senses; and the elaborately planned liturgy: all these are designed to appeal to fleshly desires of people rather than to urge them to draw near to God in humility and worship the Almighty. Jesus told the woman at the well (John 4:24), "God is spirit, and his worshipers must worship in spirit and in truth."

**Heb. 13:10. We have an altar from which those who minister at the tabernacle have no right to eat.**

The author makes a stark contrast between the old and new covenants which seems more overpowering than any argument he has made before. He says that the two covenants are so mutually exclusive that even the Levitical priests ("those who minister at the tabernacle") were totally excluded from the benefits of the new covenant unless they forsook that outdated ministry. Of course the author unquestionably means that such a priest was excluded from the benefits of the Melchizedek priesthood only as long as he clung to the old agreement. If, however, he abandoned the old priesthood to embrace the benefits of Christ's priesthood, he would not only receive those benefits but also would become a part of the priesthood of all the saints described by Peter in I Pet. 2:5 and 9. The conversion of priests to the new faith in Jesus is affirmed in Acts 6:7: "The number of disciples in Jerusalem increased rapidly, and a large number of priests became obedient to the faith." In writing his words, the author of Hebrews leaves nothing to the imagination.

Just as in the previous verse, the author is emphasizing the fact that it is the spiritual realm and not the physical that is important for our association with God. Jesus put the same emphasis in His conversation with His followers in John 6. The crowd had been fed miraculously from the five loaves and two fish. Having a desire for more physical food, they ran around the Sea of Galilee to find Jesus the next day. He chided them for their effort to receive a free handout, and began telling them that there was something even better than the manna from heaven that blanketed the earth in old times. He offered in lieu of that His own body and blood for them to partake and find life. The Jews became offended, perhaps even nauseated, at what they thought was Jesus' allusion to cannibalism. We read their reaction in John 6:52, "How can this man give us his flesh to eat?" But Jesus cleared up the matter in His statement in verse 63, "The Spirit gives life; the flesh counts for nothing. The words I have spoken to you are spirit and they are life." He had already hinted at this in verses 47-51, "I tell you the truth, he who believes has everlasting life....If a man eats of this bread, he will live forever. This bread is my flesh, which I will give for the life of the world."

Even when we partake of the elements in Communion, what is important is not the bread or the grape juice or wine. Therefore, it is unnecessary for us to claim or believe that we actually eat the physical body of Jesus or drink His physical blood which would need to come down from heaven. Although the apostle Paul wrote in his rendition of the Lord's Supper in I Cor. 11:23-26, "This is my body....This cup is the new covenant in my blood..," he ends his statement by writing, "For whenever you eat *this bread* and drink *this cup*, you proclaim the Lord's death until he comes" (emphasis added).

**Heb. 13:11. The high priest carries the blood of animals into the Most Holy Place as a sin offering, but the bodies are burned outside the camp.**

This is a continuation of what we read in the previous verse. But the author adds a detail, so small it might seem insignificant and be overlooked unless he had noted it here. Although it is seemingly unimportant, it is just one more fine detail which shows how carefully the whole Bible was put together so that not one small point is out of place or contradicted by any other part of God's word. The reason it is so perfect is because it was God the Holy Spirit who caused it to be written. Many people chide us for thinking that, but even the critics know it is unique or they would not bother to study it so carefully.

This verse comes from Lev. 16:27, which reads, "The bull and the goat for the sin offerings, whose blood was brought into the Most Holy Place to make atonement, must be taken outside the camp; their hides, flesh and offal [that is, their bodies] are to be burned up."

You may be curious regarding the small detail, and why it relates to the author's purpose. We discover that in the next verse.

**Heb. 13:12. And so Jesus also suffered outside the city gate to make the people holy through his own blood.**

There are two elements to the detail: the blood and the body. Under the old plan, the high priest was required to take the blood of the sin offering and sprinkle it in the Most Holy Place. This was fulfilled in Jesus when He was examined by the high priest, because the soldiers had thrust the crown of thorns on His head, so as He stood before the high priest and the Sanhedrin, His blood was sprinkled there in the place of the high priest.

The second detail regards the body of the sacrifice. We read in the verse quoted from Leviticus that the body of the sacrificial animal was taken outside the city gate and disposed of there. So also, Jesus' body was removed to Golgotha for crucifixion, and placed in Gordon's Tomb for disposition. There is a great church within the Old City, which some people claim was built over the place where Jesus was buried. But that flies in the face of the scriptural statement that Jesus was killed and buried outside the city wall. Scholars who have visited both sites agree that the place Gordon discovered matches the biblical description in every detail.

462

More important than the places we discuss as the true whereabouts of the events is the result of what happened to Jesus, and why it happened. The author says Jesus did what He did to "make the people holy through his own blood." We rejoice constantly in the salvation Jesus wrought for us by His death on the cross, and we ought to be at least as glad that He has made us holy. Most of us do not think of that very often. Even if we do, sometimes the world tugs so strongly that we do not want to be holy. We tend to forget that it is not sinful pleasures that truly please us. David in Ps. 16:11 reminds us how we can be happy:

> ...you will fill me with joy in your presence,
> with eternal pleasures at your right hand.

### Heb. 13:13. Let us, then, go to him outside the camp, bearing the disgrace he bore.

There may be several ideas innate in this verse. To me, one of the important ideas stems from two common names given to the body of Christ in scripture. One name is the "Congregation," or "Assembly," which comes from the Greek συναγωγή, a gathering together. The other name is commonly translated as "Church," from the Greek ἐκκλησία, which means those called or scattered out. We, then, who are followers of Christ are obligated to do two opposite things in order to obey Him: we must meet together for fellowship, instruction, and encouragement, as the author of Hebrews reminded us in 10:25; and we must go away from our gathering into the world to proclaim the Gospel, as the Great Commission tells us at the end of each Gospel and in Acts where we read in 1:8: "...you will be my witnesses in Jerusalem, and in all Judea and Samaria, and to the ends of the earth." We must not neglect either one in favor of the other. We gain security in company with one another; we have greater security in going "to him outside the camp" where He is interceding for us continually ("surely I will be with you always," Matt. 28:20) and guiding us in our witness for Him.

Both Paul and Peter remind us that we must "bear the disgrace he bore." Paul says it in Phil. 3:10-11: "I want to know Christ and the power of his resurrection and the fellowship of sharing in his sufferings, becoming like him in his death, and so, somehow, to attain to the resurrection from the dead." Paul implies that if we are unwilling to share in Christ's suffering and disgrace, then we will likewise not share in His resurrection. That is a heavy thought to ponder. Then Peter wrote, with Paul's warning more hidden, in I Pet. 4:13, "...rejoice that you participate in the sufferings of Christ, so that you may be overjoyed when his glory is revealed."

### Heb. 13:14. For here we do not have an enduring city, but we are looking for the city that is to come.

Everything in this world is transitory. It had a beginning—when God created it; and it will have an end, when He decides He has had enough of man's rebellion. The author is not referring to the city in which any of us lives, like Philadelphia, or Miami, or San Diego, or Bettles, AK, when he speaks of a city that does not endure. Rather, he means the earthly spiritual city indicated by Paul in Gal. 4:24-25, and by the author here in 12:18-21; that is, Mount Sinai, from which Moses brought the law. When this world is dissolved, as we read in II Pet. 3:10, the law will disappear with it. There will be no need for the law, because all who arrive in heaven will be made perfect; will know God's will and be perfectly willing to follow it.

When we finally see what "we are looking for," the "enduring city," the law will be replaced by God's grace, by which we will exist forevermore. While we are waiting for that new Jerusalem, we should be encouraged that it comes apace. We now groan from our many afflictions. When you were a small child, your anticipations surely were like mine: all during each school year I thought it would never end, but finally it did. Looking back, those school days were a fleeting moment in the total of my lifetime. Also, the aggravations of adult life seem much heavier to us than the puny troubles of our school days, so we torment ourselves with the thought that heaven will never come. But it will come, and soon. God promises it.

Too many people cling to the things of this world, as if they could possess them forever and there is nothing else worthwhile to obtain. But that is just the opposite of the reality taught in the Bible. Jim Elliot, the martyred missionary to the Auca Indians, had the right idea, and put it well: "He is no fool who gives up what he cannot keep in order to obtain what he cannot lose."

**Heb. 13:15. Through Jesus, therefore, let us continually offer to God a sacrifice of praise—the fruit of lips that confess his name.**

Among these verses we see the beginning of the practical part of this letter of Hebrews. Before this, the author has been building up a theological base on which to set forth his exhortations. There have been exhortations scattered throughout the letter, but now there is a concentration of them, to focus what we believe on what we ought to do about that belief. Paul did the same thing in all his letters, with one difference. While most of Paul's practical parts occupied large parts of his letters, the author of Hebrews reserves a few meager verses at the very end of his message to urge his readers to live their lives for Christ.

Sacrifice is what both old and new covenants are all about. In both covenants the sacrifices are explicitly the slaying of living things for the forgiveness of people. To make atonement for sin, those living things had to be slain; specifically, their blood had to be shed in order for the atonement to be effective. Therefore, even Jesus in His sacrifice had to shed His blood for the remission of sins, as the author of Hebrews said in 9:22, "...without the shedding of blood there is no forgiveness."

As we just noted, both Old and New Testament sacrifices were for the forgiveness of sins. However, there is a different kind of sacrifice, mentioned here and in Rom. 12:1. Let us look at what Paul said in Romans: "...I urge you, brothers, in view of God's mercy, to offer your bodies as living sacrifices, holy and pleasing to God—which is your spiritual worship." While Paul urges his readers to sacrifice their bodies, he makes it clear that what he seeks to induce them to do is offer their whole lives in holy living, apart from sin and the frailties of the body; in other words, to make every moment an act of worship to God. The author of Hebrews narrows his admonition to the control of all our communication: a "sacrifice of praise;" "the fruit of lips;" and continually to "confess his name." In thinking of your conversations, how much time do you spend on "what you will eat or drink; or about your body, what you will wear" (Matt. 6:25); or on how much money you will make or lose; or on what your neighbor is doing to your property? Note carefully that your living sacrifice, that is, doing and saying good things, contributes not one iota to forgiving your sins; only a blood sacrifice does that. Your living sacrifice is the result of your having already been forgiven by the blood sacrifice of Christ on the cross, so that now you serve God joyfully because He has saved you from the punishment of sin.

**Heb. 13:16. And do not forget to do good and to share with others, for with such sacrifices God is pleased.**

The author continues the theme of sacrifice from verse 15, the different kind of sacrifice from the shedding of blood for the remission of sins. In that verse he spoke specifically of the sacrificial kind of conversation which pleases God. Now he turns to sacrificial activities which will make God happy. In this verse the author mentions two things we ought to do.

First, we are to "do good." The author uses the Greek word εὐποιΐα, which has nothing to do with being morally good or righteous, but rather with doing good things, especially doing good for others, or beneficence.[3] Paul says the same thing in several places, among which are Tit. 3:14, I Tim. 6:18, and an extended statement mostly urging the doing of good in I Thess. 5:15-23, whose beginning and ending are:

Make sure that nobody pays back wrong for wrong, but always try to be kind to each other and to everyone else....May God himself, the God of peace, sanctify you through and through. May your whole spirit, soul and body be kept blameless at the coming of our Lord Jesus Christ.

The second thing we must do is very much like the first, we must "share with others." The Greek word for this is κοινωνία, a "common" word in the New Testament which, with its related forms is found nearly fifty times. The word can have any of three general meanings:[4] fellowship, a

---

[3] Thayer.

[4] Louw and Nida.

share, or a willing contribution. It is the same thing that Paul urges the Romans to do in Rom. 15:26, and the Corinthians in II Cor. 8:4. We usually think of the word as meaning what Christians feel for one another because they are united in a "common" bond. I have placed "common" in quotation marks in this paragraph, because that may be considered the root meaning of the Greek word. Another related Greek word (not found in the New Testament) is κοινή, or "koine," indicating that the special Greek of the New Testament is the "common" language of the people, not the formal, even stilted, classical Greek used by Homer the historian, or Greek philosophers like Plato. We may summarize the meaning of the Greek word used here by saying that Christians ought to insure their identity in Christ by helping one another in their needs.

These two attributes which the author of Hebrews urges upon his hearers are the same attributes James identifies as the marks of true religion in James 1:27: "...to look after orphans and widows in their distress and to keep oneself from being polluted by the world."

The author of Hebrews concludes this exhortation with a very good reason why we ought to follow his advice; he says "with such sacrifices God is pleased." James echoes this sentiment in his prelude to the verse quoted above: "Religion that God our Father accepts as pure and faultless is this...."

### Heb. 13:17. Obey your leaders and submit to their authority.

We may question whether the author has in mind spiritual leaders, or civil rulers, or perhaps both. Since he does not specify which he means, I find no reason to eliminate either, especially since we find in the writings of both Paul and Peter their admonitions to submit to both. Without copying them here, I urge you to look up each reference in your Bible, to prove to yourself that you ought to obey, or submit to, both civil and spiritual rulers over you. These verses urge submission to spiritual authorities: I Cor. 16:16; Eph. 5:21; I Tim. 5:1, 17; and I Pet. 5:5. The following verses say we must follow civil rulers: Rom. 13:1-7; I Tim. 2:2; Tit. 3:1-2; and I Pet. 2:17. These are just a sampling of passages we could quote.

### They keep watch over you as men who must give an account.

This statement could apply to either spiritual or civil leaders. Nor does it matter whether or not they claim to know or obey God. The most vile civil master you can think of has an innate recognition of his necessary submission to God's authority. In the twentieth century we remember that Stalin studied for the priesthood before he grasped power in Russia and developed the Soviet Union. Even without such a background every civil leader has a knowledge of God and His will planted in his soul at birth. That is exactly what Paul says about such wicked rulers in Rom. 1:19-20: "...what may be known about God is plain to them, because God has made it plain to them," and continues that it is made plain in all God's creation. Paul even emphasizes that these things "have been clearly seen, being understood from what has been made, so that *men are without excuse*" (my emphasis). Such people do not need to attend seminary, or hear a preacher, or stand at a godly mother's knee to know all about God. God can reveal Himself to them in His own way. Note the example of Nebuchadnezzar, a godless Babylonian ruler reared in a godless empire; yet God gave him dreams, and sent his messenger Daniel to interpret them in Dan. 2:31-49, and Dan. 4:9-37.

**Obey them so that their work will be a joy, not a burden, for that would be of no advantage to you.**

Whether or not you have attended one of the Armed Forces academies in our country, it is likely you have heard of their Plebe system. Even now that old-fashioned hazing has been practically eliminated, still upperclassmen hold sway over large portions of Plebes' lives, and often make them miserable.

Before hazing was fully abolished, my son David told me how he conquered the system. He reported that he anticipated what an upper-classman might demand of him, but he would do it before he was asked to do so. In that way, he would escape punishment or recrimination, and had a much more pleasant Plebe year than most of his classmates.

This is exactly what Paul urges us to do in relation to our rulers in the world, found in Rom. 13:1-4:

The authorities that exist have been established by God. Consequently, he who rebels against the authority is rebelling against what God has instituted, and those who do so will bring judgment on themselves. For rulers hold no terror for those who do right, but for those who do wrong. Do you want to be free from fear of the one in authority? Then do what is right and he will commend you. For he is God's servant to do you good. But if you do wrong, be afraid, for he does not bear the sword for nothing. He is God's servant, an agent of wrath to bring punishment on the wrongdoer.

We may think it is too much to ask us to love our unreasonable boss or evil ruler. This last chapter of Hebrews is about love; and we recall that John has reminded us (in I John 4:18) that "perfect love drives out fear, because fear has to do with punishment." In addition, Jesus taught us that we must love even our enemies (Matt. 5:44); surely that applies to our superiors as well as to our equals or subordinates.

### Heb. 13:18.   Pray for us.

Here begins a new paragraph in this very brief practical portion of Hebrews. It matters not what other people may think of prayer, whether it is a futile waste of time; or a crutch because the petitioner is not strong enough to take care of himself; or whether God has no interest in you, or has too many prayers to answer at once, or is too busy with important things; or whether God does not hear your prayer because you are too sinful, or do not know how to pray. The Bible is filled with admonitions to talk to God about how great He is, what wonderful things He has done for you, to confess your sins and ask for forgiveness and cleansing and strength to overcome temptation, to ask for things for others and for yourself, and to offer yourself in service to God's will. Prayers ought to be made in one's closet (Matt. 6:6), with one or two friends who believe as you do (Matt. 18:20), or before a huge congregation (I Kings 8:22). The author of Hebrews asks his hearers to pray for him, and for unnamed companions. One of the greatest privileges a member of a congregation has is to pray for his spiritual leader. It was not only the author of Hebrews who asked for prayer; or if the author was Paul, he gave the same invitation to many other congregations: see Rom. 15:30; Eph. 6:19; I Thess. 5:25; and II Thess. 3:1.

**We are sure that we have a clear conscience and desire to live honorably in every way.**

In this verse, the author writes in the first person plural, indicating he is not alone in his mission but has at least one companion. The apostle Paul did the same thing. He writes of himself and one friend in his introductions of both his letters to Corinth—1:1 in both, and in his letters to Ephesus 1:1, Philippi 1:1, Colossae 1:1 and to Philemon verse 1. He names two assistants in both his letters to Thessalonica—1:1 in both. He writes alone to Timothy both times as well as to Titus; these are more personal, private letters, so it is a great privilege that we partake in their messages. Paul also wrote alone to the churches in Galatia. In addition we know that Paul had a group of companions in his missionary travels by Luke's use of the pronoun "we" a number of times in Acts, beginning at Acts 16:10, showing that at least Luke accompanied him.

Another similarity to Paul's writings occurs here, because both authors protest their upright lives among the people to whom they ministered. Paul hints at it in II Tim. 4:7, "I have fought the good fight, I have finished the race, I have kept the faith." In I Cor. 9, Paul elaborates on his relationships with the Corinthian people at least, pointing out in verses 3-6 that he and Barnabas had every right to earn a living from wages earned in their ministry and to have families like the rest of the apostles. He concludes in verse 12, "If others have this right of support from you, shouldn't we have it all the more? But we did not use this right. On the contrary, we put up with anything rather than hinder the gospel of Christ."

A more startling parallel to these thoughts is found in the Old Testament. Near the end of his life, the seer Samuel boasted that he had not done anything wrong to the people all his life. His words, and the people's response, are in I Sam. 12:3-4:

"Here I stand. Testify against me in the presence of the LORD and his anointed. Whose ox have I taken? Whose donkey have I taken? Whom have I cheated? Whom have I oppressed? From whose hand have I accepted a bribe to make me shut my eyes? If I have done any of these, I will make it right." "You have not cheated or oppressed us," they replied. "You have not taken anything from anyone's hand."

Oh that every Priest and Minister of the Gospel today could truthfully say the same! I know of a Minister who used church funds outside his adequate salary to pay for his lunches; or the Minister who refused to repay his church a $10,000.00 loan simply because the transaction was not on paper. You probably are aware of instances in your own church life. It is to be hoped that you have also known Ministers or Priests who have been utterly honorable and of a good conscience in their dealings with people in the world. After all, there is a rich reward for being such a person, as Paul said in the summary of his ministerial life-style (I Cor. 9:23): "I do all this for the sake of the gospel, that I may share in its blessings."

### Heb. 13:19.   I particularly urge you to pray so that I may be restored to you soon.

The author began this paragraph by asking his listeners to pray for him. Prayer was an important part of his life, and wanted it so in theirs.

If what we have in our Bibles was at first a preached sermon, as is implied in 5:11, the author wanted to return to his audience for fellowship. There is no indication why he absented himself after his message. He may have gone on a missionary journey; he may have been imprisoned for preaching; he may have lived elsewhere and wanted to go home for a while; we are not sure. But his plea for them to pray for his return indicates that he was not in full control of his traveling, so he asked them to pray for God's intervention in the case.

Paul likewise often said that he wanted to return to people he had seen earlier in his ministry. After his first missionary journey with Barnabas, and after the great Jerusalem Conference in about 49 AD, Paul invited Barnabas, "Let us go back and visit the brothers in all the towns where we preached the word of the Lord and see how they are doing" (Acts 15:36).

### Heb.   13:20-21.

In these verses we find one of the greatest doxologies or benedictions in the whole Bible. I consider this at least on a par with what is called the Apostolic Benediction written by Paul to Corinth (II Cor. 13:14). I believe the Hebrews benediction is highly appropriate as the conclusion of a Worship Service where the Lord's Supper is celebrated, and I have used it nearly every time I have conducted such a service. My other personal favorite benediction is in Eph. 3:20-21. Dr. Frank A. Hunger, the Senior Minister in Montclair, NJ, always quoted Jude verses 24-25 as his benediction. And the favorite of Dr. Donald Grey Barnhouse, the great Bible teacher from Tenth Presbyterian

Church in Philadelphia was Rev. 1:5b-6. You are invited to search these out in your Bible, meditate on them, and memorize them to give yourself a spiritual feast on great doxologies in the Bible.

Let me share with you why I like the benediction in Hebrews. I memorized it in the KJV, so please indulge me for quoting that version.

### Now the God of peace....

Because He is the God of peace, then I can have peace; I *do* have peace if I am in Him and He dwells in me by His Holy Spirit. Outside our God there is no peace in the world.

### ...that brought again from the dead....

Here is a reaffirmation of the resurrection, first of Christ, and then of those who are in Christ. This is the driving force behind the whole of the Gospel and behind everything that has to do with God.

### ...our Lord Jesus, that great shepherd of the sheep....

This is a beautiful figure of Jesus as our Shepherd. He is "our Shepherd" in Psalm 23; and claims to be our Good Shepherd in John 10:14.

### ...through the blood of the everlasting covenant....

Jesus is not only our Good and Great Shepherd; He also is the Sheep that was slain for us. The author reemphasizes the centrality of the blood of Jesus as the only effective agent of our salvation. Take comfort that it is an "everlasting" covenant. God will not change it, nor any of its terms. The requirements to participate in the covenant remain unchanged forever, and the benefits will never be diminished or depleted. Review the study of 9:15 about "eternal" or "everlasting."

### ...make you perfect in every good work to do his will....

We approach perfection as we work His will. Let us remind ourselves that it is not we who accomplish the perfection.

### ...working in you that which is wellpleasing in his sight....

No, it is not we, but God working in us that leads us closer to perfection. He deserves all the credit for all the good works you and I have done in our lives.

### ...through Jesus Christ; to whom be glory for ever and ever. Amen.

It is *all* done through our mighty Savior Jesus Christ. He is the sole Mediator (I Tim. 2:5) between God and us. For all that He has done for us,

470

He deserves all glory. And He shall be glorified, by all His creation, both in this world, and forever. He asked His Father to glorify Him (John 17:1, 5).

Amen!

**Heb. 13:22. Brothers, I urge you to bear with my word of exhortation, for I have written you only a short letter.**

Following his benediction, the author concludes with a few words of summary. He begins the conclusion with the word "brothers." By this word he indicates that he together with his hearers and readers (including us who accept his teachings) are on a par with one another. Although he is their teacher and preacher—he may have been even an Elder or ordained Minister—he does not consider himself superior to them. He is not their father, their tribal chief; he holds no power over them, and does not intend to govern them in any way. They are brothers, members of the same family, the family of God, where there is "neither Jew nor Greek, slave nor free, male nor female, circumcised or uncircumcised, barbarian, Scythian, for you are all one in Christ Jesus" (Gal. 3:28 and Col. 3:11 combined). Yet, for all that, in God's economy, the man must be the head of his household, just as Christ is head of the Church, for which see Eph. 5:23.

The author sees his letter as an exhortation, not as a narrative, not as preaching or teaching (though it is both), certainly not as an entertaining novel; but the whole letter is an exhortation. He wants his hearers and readers to do something about what they have learned. I trust you who read this devotional study of Hebrews will likewise recall what you have learned and make yourself willing to follow it.

The author comments not only on the style of his letter, but on its size, claiming brevity for it. As letters go in our day, it seems rather long. But in his day, there was no mass media to spread the news, or to preach to millions in a radio or television audience. Travel was slow and difficult, so when letters were written, it is natural to suppose they were extended. If we compare the size of Hebrews with other letters in the New Testament, we see it is about average. Paul wrote smaller letters and larger letters. Those of James, Peter, John and Jude were smaller; but if we think of the Gospels and Acts as letters, they are larger. The author of Hebrews says his reason for writing briefly was to make a greater impact on his readers, again because he wanted them to heed his exhortations.

**Heb. 13:23. I want you to know that our brother Timothy has been released.**

I have surveyed all references to Timothy in the New Testament, and find no indication that he had been imprisoned. Of the twenty-one verses where Timothy is mentioned, they talk about his background, his faith, his work with Paul, and his faithfulness. On the other hand, if Timothy had been imprisoned, it is not necessary to believe that Paul must have mentioned it. There is a slight possibility that Paul implies that Timothy was in prison, when he wrote to him in II Tim. 1:8: "So do not be ashamed to testify about our Lord, or ashamed of me his prisoner. But join with me in suffering for the gospel, by the power of God."

It is sufficient to know that the author of Hebrews says that Timothy had been in prison. The important thing to note is that both Paul and the author of Hebrews (if they are different people) as well as the congregation of Hebrews were acquainted with Timothy. Because the author mentions it, we are sure they all would rejoice at Timothy's release, especially because he was saintly in his life, and such a diligent worker for Christ along with all he met. Surely you would be gratified if you knew that your many friends would be delighted at any good news about your welfare, because you were devoted to the cause of Christ.

**If he arrives soon, I will come with him to see you.**

This is the second time the author has indicated he wanted to visit the people to whom he was writing. The first instance is in verse 19. He must have known them well, or he could not have written about their lazy hearts in 5:11 and 6:12. Yet it is obvious that despite their sluggishness in spiritual things, he loved them dearly, because he said in the earlier verse that his desire was to be *restored* to them *soon.*

At the outset of our study, we noted that the author did not address his hearers or readers; instead, he immediately launched into his message. The only other time he mentioned the recipients was when he called them "hearers" in 5:11. In fact, the book is known as "Hebrews" only because the content of the letter seems to imply that the recipients were well acquainted with the Old Testament and its rituals, especially those having to do with sin offerings. For this reason, some people believe this letter's message was intended for Jews alone. But God never limited His "clientele" to the Jews.

The author surely had a particular congregation in mind when he wrote this letter. Whether it was a Christian congregation in Jerusalem or elsewhere in the Diaspora, or to a group of Gentile Christians, we cannot be certain. If he intended to visit them, or return to them, they had to be a particular group.

As we near the end of this chapter on love, it is obvious that the author deeply loved the people to whom he was writing. He longed for personal fellowship with them.

It seems the author is saying that he needs Timothy's help in order to travel to see them. Further, that help needs to be soon. It may be that the author was feeling his age, or was burdened with a deadly illness, or was in some other kind of danger. We remember that Paul had said to Timothy in the same vein, "get here before winter" (II Tim. 4:21). Could it be that Paul was indeed the author of Hebrews? There are hints throughout such as these, but still we cannot know for certain.

### Heb. 13:24.   Greet all your leaders and all God's people.

You may be curious, as I am, why the church leaders would be absent when the people receive the letter. Perhaps persecution had forced them underground. The author may have known they were away on a mission trip. Or it could be that they were in prison, as he had intimated about Timothy. On the other hand, since the author asked the recipients to greet "all God's people," it may be that his letter was intended for several congregations in a particular area. This was the case when Paul wrote the letter we know as "Galatians," which was a cluster of churches in that geographical area, not just one church.

### Those from Italy send you their greetings.

From these words I presume that the author was writing from somewhere in Italy, perhaps even from Rome. Otherwise he would not be in touch with those Christians, to be able to transmit their greetings.

Paul, we know, had been in Rome, and he was always sending greetings in his letters. Peter and John sent greetings in their letters, although James and Jude did not. Surely there were other Christians, even church leaders, in Rome during those days. As we noted before, there was virtually no communication medium in those days except for travelers. Surely letters were scarce as well, since few people could read or write, and travel was more difficult and slow than the Pony Express.

### Heb. 13:25.   Grace be with you all.

Since this letter has been all about God's grace being better than the Levitical law, this is a fitting conclusion to the letter and to our study.

Grace be with you all.

# INDEX OF SCRIPTURE REFERENCES

475

490

# INDEX OF PEOPLE AND SUBJECTS

# BIBLIOGRAPHY

Aland, Kurt, Matthew Black, Bruce M. Metzger, Allen Wikgren, editors, THE GREEK NEW TESTAMENT. New York: United Bible Societies, 1966. Pp. lv, 920.

AMPLIFIED NEW TESTAMENT, THE. Grand Rapids: Zondervan Publishing House, 1958. Pp. 989, plus Title Page; Preface; Introduction; Explanation of arbitrary punctuation marks, etc.; Contents; Bibliography and Index of Authors and Books Quoted or Referred to in the Footnores; and Acknowledgments.

BIBLE, THE, Revised Standard Version. New York: American Bible Society, 1946, 1952. Pp. x, 1087.

BIBLE, THE HOLY, American Standard Edition. New York: Thomas Nelson & Sons, 1929; commonly known as the American Standard Version, or ASV. Pp. xv, 969 (Old Testament); xvi, 295 (New Testament); plus 12 maps.

BIBLE, THE HOLY, Scofield Reference Edition, King James Version. New York: Oxford, 1947. Pp. vi, 1362; Dictionary and Concordance from pp. 153-378 (following Bible page 1362); Indexed Atlas unpaged.

BIBLE, THE HOLY, New International Version. Grand Rapids: Zondervan Bible Publishers, 1978. Pp. x, 1156, plus maps.

BIBLE, NEW AMERICAN STANDARD: New Testament; Soul Winner's Edition, commonly known as the NASV. Longview, TX: Word for the World Publishers, Inc., 1972. Pp. xvii, 358.

BIBLE, THE NEW ENGLISH. Oxford University Press and Cambridge University Press, 1970. Pp. xxi, 1166 (Old Testament), and ix, 336 (New Testament).

Bittinger, Desmond W., WU FENG, COMPANION OF HEAD HUNTERS. Taichung, Taiwan: Tunghai University, 1963. Pp. 236.

Blake, W. O., compiler, THE HISTORY OF SLAVERY AND THE SLAVE TRADE, ANCIENT AND MODERN. Columbus, Ohio: J & H. Miller, 1857. Pp. xvi, 832 (which includes pp. i to xvi).

\* \* \*

Botterweck, G. Johannes, Helmer Ringgren, and Heinz Josef Fabry, editors; John T. Willis, Geoffrey W. Bromily, and David E. Green, translators, THEOLOGICAL DICTIONARY OF THE OLD TESTAMENT. Grand Rapids: William B. Eerdmans Publishing Company, 1974 to 2001. I have the first eleven volumes.

Brown, Francis, S. R. Driver, and Charles A. Briggs, editors, A HEBREW AND ENGLISH LEXICON OF THE OLD TESTAMENT, based on the lexicon of William Gesenius. Oxford: Oxford University Press, 1907, 1952. Pp. xix, 1126. Sometimes referred to as "Brown, Driver, and Briggs", or even simply "BDB."

Callihan, Wesley J., "Plundering the Egyptians." VERBUM, September 2000 newsletter of Veritas Academy, Lancaster, PA.

Calvin, John, CALVIN'S COMMENTARIES: 1 THE PENTATEUCH. Grand Rapids: Associated Publishers, no date, but c. 1972. Pp. xiii, 1228.

Chafer, Louis Sperry, DISPENSATIONALISM. Dallas: Dallas Seminary Press, 1936, 1951. Pp. 108.

CONSTITUTION OF THE PRESBYTERIAN CHURCH IN THE UNITED STATES OF AMERICA, THE. Philadelpha: The Board of Christian Education, 1955. Pp. ix, 455.

Davis, John D., editor; revised and rewritten by Henry Snyder Gehman, THE WESTMINSTER DICTIONARY OF THE BIBLE. Philadelphia: The Westminster Press, 1944. Pp. xii, 658, plus 16 maps.

Delitzsch, Franz; *see C. F. Keil.*

Driver, S. R., A. Plummer, and C. A. Briggs; THE INTERNATIONAL CRITICAL COMMENTARY ON THE HOLY SCRIPTURES OF THE OLD AND NEW TESTAMENTS. Edinburgh: T. & T. Clark, 1948. I have six volumes. *See Moffatt for Hebrews.*

Edersheim, Alfred, THE LIFE AND TIMES OF JESUS THE MESSIAH. Grand Rapids: Wm. B. Eerdmans Publishing Company, 1950. Vol. I: pp. xxxv, 695; Vol. II: pp. xii, 828.

Elwell, Walter A., editor, EVANGELICAL DICTIONARY OF THEOLOGY. Grand Rapids: Baker Book House, 1985. Pp. xxii, 1204.

Gehman, Henry S., *see John D. Davis.*

Geisler, Norman, and Frank Turek, LEGISLATING MORALITY. Minneapolis: Bethany House Publishers, 1998. Pp. 272.

Goodspeed, Edgar J., THE APOCRYPHA, AN AMERICAN TRANSLATION. Chicago: The University of Chicago Press, 1938. Pp. ix, 493.

Jennings, F. C., STUDIES IN ISAIAH. New York: Loizeaux Brothers, Inc., 1950. Pp. 784.

Jews For Jesus, Newsletters, published monthly.

Josephus, Flavius, translated by William Whiston, THE LIFE AND WORKS OF FLAVIUS JOSEPHUS. Philadelphia: The John C. Winston Company, no date, but probably c. 1945. Pp. xvi, 1055. Contents include a brief life of Josephus, his ANTIQUITIES OF THE JEWS, and his WARS OF THE JEWS.

Keil, C. F., and F. Delitzsch, authors; and James Martin, translator, BIBLICAL COMMENTARY ON THE OLD TESTAMENT. Grand Rapids: Wm. B. Eerdmans Publishing Company, 1951. I have eight volumes in the series.

Kittel, Gerhard, editor of Volumes I to V; Gerhard Friedrich, editor of Volumes VI to IX; Ronald E. Pitkin, compiler of Vol. X; and Geoffrey W. Bromiley, translator and editor of Volumes I to IX, THEOLOGICAL DICTIONARY OF THE NEW TESTAMENT. Grand Rapids: Wm B. Eerdmans Publishing Company, 1964 to 1976. Ten volumes.

Kittel, Rudolf, editor, BIBLIA HEBRAICA. Stuttgart: Privileg. Württ. Bibelänstalt, 1949. Pp. XL, 1434, plus 2 maps.

Knox, Ronald A., THE OLD TESTAMENT IN ENGLISH. London: Burns Oates and Washbourne Ltd., 1949. Vol. I, Genesis - Esther: pp. xi, 739. Vol. II, Job - Machabees *(sic)*: pp. 741 to 1604.

_____, THE NEW TESTAMENT IN ENGLISH. New York: Sheed & Ward, 1949. Pp. vi, 573.

KORAN, THE (QUR' ÂN). Translated by E. H. Palmer. London: Oxford University Press, 1949. Pp. xix, 551.

* * *

Law, Wiliam, A SERIOUS CALL TO A DEVOUT AND HOLY LIFE. Philadelphia: The Westminster Press, 1948. Pp. xxv, 353, plus notes. Law lived from 1686 to 1761.

Lenski, R. C. H., a series of volumes entitled THE INTERPRETATION OF..., followed by ST. MATTHEW'S GOSPEL; ST. MARK'S GOSPEL; ST. LUKE'S GOSPEL; ST. JOHN'S GOSPEL; THE ACTS OF THE APOSTLES; ROMANS; I AND II CORINTHIANS; GALATIANS, EPHESIANS, PHILIP-PIANS; COLOSSIANS, THESSSALONIANS, TIMOTHY, TITUS, PHILE-MON; HEBREWS, JAMES; PETER, JOHN, JUDE; ST. JOHN'S REVELA-TION. All published in Columbus, Ohio, by Wartburg Press, be-tween 1943 and 1946.

LIVING NEW TESTAMENT PARAPHRASED, THE. Wheaton, IL: Tyndale House, Publishers, 1967. Pp. v, 650. The whole Bible in this ver-sion is commonly called the LB.

Louw, Johannes P., and Eugene A. Nida, editors, GREEK-ENGLISH LEXICON OF THE NEW TESTAMENT, BASED ON SEMANTIC DOMAINS. New York: United Bible Societies, 1988. Vol. 1: pp. xxv, 843, plus end maps; Vol. 2: pp. iv, 375, plus end maps.

MacEwen, Alex. R., A HISTORY OF THE CHURCH IN SCOTLAND. London: Hodder and Stoughton. Vol. I, published in 1913; pp. xv, 487, plus 2 maps. Vol. II, published in 1918, pp. viii, 199.

Metzger, Bruce M., and Michael D. Coogan, editors, THE OXFORD COMPAN-ION TO THE BIBLE. New York and Oxford, Oxford University Press, 1993. Pp. xxi, 874, plus 14 Bible Maps with index to maps.

Moffatt, James, A CRITICAL AND EXEGETICAL COMMENTARY ON THE EPIS-TLE TO THE HEBREWS. Part of the INTERNATIONAL CRITICAL COMMENTARY series. Pp. lxxvi, 264. *See Driver, S. R. for infor-mation.*

NEW TESTAMENT, THE AMPLIFIED. *See AMPLIFIED NEW TESTAMENT.*

NEW WORLD TRANSLATION OF THE HOLY SCRIPTURES. New York: Watch-tower Bible and Tract Society of New York, Inc. [Commonly known as Jehovah's witnesses], 1961. Pp. 1460, plus 4 maps and 4 dia-grams.

Palmer, E. H., see KORAN.

Phillips, J. B., LETTERS TO YOUNG CHURCHES: A translation of the New Testament Epistles. New York: The Macmillan Company, 1948. Pp. xv, 224.

Rahlfs, Alfred, editor, SEPTUAGINTA: ID EST VETUS TESTAMENTUM GRAECE IUXTA LXX INTERPRETES. Stuttgart: Privilegierte Württembergische Bibelanstalt, 1950. Vol. I: LEGES ET HISTORIAE, pp. l, 1184. Vol. II: LIBRI POETICI ET PROPHETICI, pp. i, 941 plus two maps.

RANDOM HOUSE DICTIONARY, *see Stein, Jess, editor in chief.*

Robertson, A. T., A GRAMMAR OF THE GREEK NEW TESTAMENT IN THE LIGHT OF HISTORICAL RESEARCH. Nashville: Broadman Press, 1934. Pp. lxxxvi, 1454.

_____, WORD PICTURES IN THE NEW TESTAMENT, in six Volumes. New York: Harper & Brothers Publishers, 1930-1933.

SERVICE HYMNAL, THE. Chicago: Hope Publishing Company, 1949. Pp. 480.

Shea, William, "Amenhotep II as the Pharaoh of the Exodus," in BIBLE AND SPADE, Spring 2003, Vol. 16, No. 2, pp. 41-51.

Smith, George Adam, THE BOOK OF ISAIAH. London: Hodder and Stoughton, 1889-1890. Vol. I: ISAIAH I.-XXXIX. Pp. xvi, 456. Vol. II: ISAIAH XL.-LXVI. Pp. xvi, 474. Part of THE EXPOSITOR'S BIBLE, edited by W. Robertson Nicoll.

Soltau, Henry W., THE TABERNACLE THE PRIESTHOOD AND THE OFFERINGS. Grand Rapids: Kregel Publications, 1976. Pp. xii, 474.

Stein, Jess, Editor in Chirf, and Laurence Urdang, Managing Editor, THE RANDOM HOUSE DICTIONARY OF THE ENGLISH LANGUAGE. New York: Random House, 1966. Pp. xxxii, 2059, including 64 page atlas.

Stott, John R. W., "Why Don't They Listen?" Interview by Gary Barnes, CHRISTIANITY TODAY, September 2003, pp. 50-52.

Taylor, Ken, *see THE LIVING NEW TESTAMENT PARAPHRASED.*

Teply, Thomas R., THE SPIRIT OF SCRIPTURE. Gold Beach, Oregon: Tiger-Claw Enterprises, 1998. Pp. vi, 198. Available from the author, 94040 Doyle Point Road, Gold Beach, OR 97444-9533.

Thayer, Joseph Henry, A GREEK-ENGLISH LEXICON OF THE NEW TESTMANET. New York: American Book Company, 1889. Pp. xix, 727.

Thompson, Frank Charles, compiler and editor, THE NEW CHAIN-REFERENCE BIBLE. Indianapolis: B. B. Kirkbride Bible Co., Inc., 1934. Pp. VIII, 876 (Old Testament), 270 (New Testament), XXII (General Index), 293 (various helps),80 (Concordance), plus unnumbered pages of scripture atlas and maps.

Unger, Merrill F., UNGER'S BIBLE DICTIONARY. Chicago: Moody Press, 1957. Pp. viii, 1192.

Westminster Confession, *see CONSTITUTION.*

Williams, Charles B., THE NEW TESTAMENT: A TRANSLATION IN THE LANGUAGE OF THE PEOPLE. Chicago: Moody Press, 1950. Pp. 575.

# LIST OF ABBREVIATIONS

ASV: American Standard Version of the Bible, 1901.

BDB: *see Brown, Driver, and Briggs.*

Brown, Driver, and Briggs: A HEBREW AND ENGLISH LEXICON OF THE OLD TESTAMENT.

Calvin: CALVIN'S COMMENTARIES: I: THE PENTATEUCH.

KJV: King James Version of the Bible.

LB: The Living Bible.

LXX: Septuagint (Greek) translation of the Old Testament.

Louw and Nida: GREEK-ENGLISH LEXICON OF THE NEW TESTAMENT.

NASV: New American Standard Version of the Bible, 1972.

NEB: NEW ENGLISH BIBLE.

NIV: New International Version of the Bible.

Phillips: Translations of various books of the Bible, by J. B. Phillips.

Qumran: The Dead Sea Scrolls.

RSV: Revised Standard Version of the Bible, 1946, 1952.

Robertson, GRAMMAR: A GRAMMAR OF THE GREEK NEW TESTAMENT IN THE LIGHT OF HISTORICAL RESEARCH.

Robertson, WORD PICTURES: Robertson, A. T., WORD PICTURES IN THE NEW TESTAMENT.

TDNT: THEOLOGICAL DICTIONARY OF THE NEW TESTAMENT.

TDOT: THEOLOGICAL DICTIONARY OF THE OLD TESTAMENT.

Thayer: A GREEK-ENGLISH LEXICON OF THE NEW TESTAMNET.

Williams: Translation of the New Testament.